LEO TOLSTOY

The Kingdom of God is Within You and Other Religious Writings

Edited by ALFIE BINGHAM

Copyright © Alfie Bingham, 2024

All rights reserved.

ISBN: 9798879539004

CONTENTS

1	God Sees the Truth, But Waits	1
2	My Religion	10
3	What Men Live By	186
4	Where Love is, God is	209
5	The Kingdom of God is Within You	225
6	Father Sergius	549
7	Alyosha the Pot	597
8	There Are No Guilty People	603
9	Three Questions	615
10	The Coffee House of Surat	620

1. GOD SEES THE TRUTH, BUT WAITS

In the town of Vladimir lived a young merchant named Ivan Dmitrich Aksionov. He had two shops and a house of his own.

Aksionov was a handsome, fair-haired, curly-headed fellow, full of fun, and very fond of singing. When quite a young man he had been given to drink, and was riotous when he had had too much; but after he married he gave up drinking, except now and then.

One summer Aksionov was going to the Nizhny Fair, and as he bade good-bye to his family, his wife said to him, "Ivan Dmitrich, do not start to-day; I have had a bad dream about you."

Aksionov laughed, and said, "You are afraid that when I get to the fair I shall go on a spree."

His wife replied: "I do not know what I am afraid of; all I know is that I had a bad dream. I dreamt you returned from the town, and when you took off your cap I saw that your hair was quite grey."

Aksionov laughed. "That's a lucky sign," said he. "See if I don't sell out all my goods, and bring you some presents from the fair."

So he said good-bye to his family, and drove away.

When he had travelled half-way, he met a merchant whom he knew, and they put up at the same inn for the night. They had some tea together, and then went to bed in adjoining rooms.

It was not Aksionov's habit to sleep late, and, wishing to travel while it was still cool, he aroused his driver before dawn, and told him to put in the horses.

Then he made his way across to the landlord of the inn (who lived in a cottage at the back), paid his bill, and continued his journey.

When he had gone about twenty-five miles, he stopped for the horses to be fed. Aksionov rested awhile in the passage of the inn, then he stepped out into the porch, and, ordering a samovar to be heated, got out his guitar and began to play.

Suddenly a troika drove up with tinkling bells and an official alighted, followed by two soldiers. He came to Aksionov and began to question him, asking him who he was and whence he came. Aksionov answered him fully, and said, "Won't you have some tea with me?" But the official went on cross-questioning him and asking him. "Where did you spend last night? Were you alone, or with a fellow-merchant? Did you see the other merchant this morning? Why did you leave the inn before dawn?"

Aksionov wondered why he was asked all these questions, but he described all that had happened, and then added, "Why do you cross-question me as if I were a thief or a robber? I am travelling on business of my own, and there is no need to question me."

Then the official, calling the soldiers, said, "I am the police-officer of this district, and I question you because the merchant with whom you spent last night has been found with his throat cut. We must search your things."

They entered the house. The soldiers and the police-officer unstrapped Aksionov's luggage and searched it. Suddenly the officer drew a knife out of a bag, crying, "Whose knife is this?"

Aksionov looked, and seeing a blood-stained knife taken from his bag, he was frightened.

"How is it there is blood on this knife?"

Aksionov tried to answer, but could hardly utter a word, and only stammered: "I—don't know—not mine." Then the police-officer said: "This morning the merchant was found in bed with his throat cut. You are the only person who could have done it. The house was locked from inside, and no one else was there. Here is this blood-stained knife in your bag and your face and manner betray you! Tell me how you killed him, and how much money you stole?"

Aksionov swore he had not done it; that he had not seen the merchant after they had had tea together; that he had no money except eight thousand rubles of his own, and that the knife was not his. But his voice was broken, his face pale, and he trembled with fear as though he went guilty.

The police-officer ordered the soldiers to bind Aksionov and to put him in the cart. As they tied his feet together and flung him into the cart, Aksionov crossed himself and wept. His money and goods were taken from him, and he was sent to the nearest town and imprisoned there. Enquiries as to his character were made in Vladimir. The merchants and other inhabitants of that town said that in former days he used to drink and waste his time, but that he was a good man. Then the trial came on: he was charged with murdering a merchant from Ryazan, and robbing him of twenty thousand rubles.

His wife was in despair, and did not know what to believe. Her children were all quite small; one was a baby at her breast. Taking them all with her, she went to the town where her husband was in jail. At first she was not allowed to see him; but after much begging, she obtained permission from the officials, and was taken to him. When she saw her husband in prison-dress and in chains, shut up with thieves and criminals, she fell down, and did not come to her senses for a long time. Then she drew her children to her, and sat down near him. She told him of things at home, and asked about what had happened to him. He told her all, and she asked, "What can we do now?"

"We must petition the Czar not to let an innocent man perish."

His wife told him that she had sent a petition to the Czar, but it had not been accepted.

Aksionov did not reply, but only looked downcast.

Then his wife said, "It was not for nothing I dreamt your hair had turned grey. You remember? You should not have started that day." And passing her fingers through his hair, she said: "Vanya dearest, tell your wife the truth; was it not you who did it?"

"So you, too, suspect me!" said Aksionov, and, hiding his face in his hands, he began to weep. Then a soldier came to say that the wife and children must go away; and Aksionov said good-bye to his family for the last time.

When they were gone, Aksionov recalled what had been said, and when he remembered that his wife also had suspected him, he said to himself, "It seems that only God can know the truth; it is to Him alone we must appeal, and from Him alone expect mercy."

And Aksionov wrote no more petitions; gave up all hope, and only prayed to God.

Aksionov was condemned to be flogged and sent to the mines. So he was flogged with a knot, and when the wounds made by the knot were healed, he was driven to Siberia with other convicts.

For twenty-six years Aksionov lived as a convict in Siberia. His hair turned white as snow, and his beard grew long, thin, and grey. All his mirth went; he stooped; he walked slowly, spoke little, and never laughed, but he often prayed.

In prison Aksionov learnt to make boots, and earned a little money, with which he bought *The Lives of the Saints*. He read this book when there was light enough in the prison; and on Sundays in the prison-church he read the lessons and sang in the choir; for his voice was still good.

The prison authorities liked Aksionov for his meekness, and his fellow-prisoners respected him: they called him "Grandfather," and "The Saint." When they wanted to petition the prison authorities about anything, they always made Aksionov their spokesman, and when there were quarrels among the prisoners they came to him to put things right, and to judge the matter.

No news reached Aksionov from his home, and he did not even know if his wife and children were still alive.

One day a fresh gang of convicts came to the prison. In the evening the old prisoners collected round the new ones and asked them what towns or villages they came from, and what they were sentenced for. Among the rest Aksionov sat down near the newcomers, and listened with downcast air to what was said.

One of the new convicts, a tall, strong man of sixty, with a closely-cropped grey beard, was telling the others what he had been arrested for.

"Well, friends," he said, "I only took a horse that was tied to a sledge, and I was arrested and accused of stealing. I said I had only taken it to get home quicker, and had then let it go; besides, the driver was a personal friend of mine. So I said, 'It's all right.' 'No,' said they, 'you stole it.' But how or where I stole it they could not say. I once really did something wrong, and ought by rights to have come here long ago, but that time I was not found out. Now I have been sent here for nothing at all... Eh, but it's lies I'm telling you; I've been to Siberia before, but I did not stay long."

"Where are you from?" asked some one.

"From Vladimir. My family are of that town. My name is Makar, and they also call me Semyonich."

Aksionov raised his head and said: "Tell me, Semyonich, do you know anything of the merchants Aksionov of Vladimir? Are they still alive?"

"Know them? Of course I do. The Aksionovs are rich, though their father is in Siberia: a sinner like ourselves, it seems! As for you, Gran'dad, how did you come here?"

Aksionov did not like to speak of his misfortune. He only sighed, and said, "For my sins I have been in prison these twenty-six years."

"What sins?" asked Makar Semyonich.

But Aksionov only said, "Well, well—I must have deserved it!" He would have said no more, but his companions told the newcomers how Aksionov came to be in Siberia; how some one had killed a merchant, and had put the knife among Aksionov's things, and Aksionov had been unjustly condemned.

When Makar Semyonich heard this, he looked at Aksionov, slapped his *own* knee, and exclaimed, "Well, this is wonderful! Really wonderful! But how old you've grown, Gran'dad!"

The others asked him why he was so surprised, and where he had seen Aksionov before; but Makar Semyonich did not reply. He only said: "It's wonderful that we should meet here, lads!"

These words made Aksionov wonder whether this man knew who had killed the merchant; so he said, "Perhaps, Semyonich, you have heard of that affair, or maybe you've seen me before?"

"How could I help hearing? The world's full of rumours. But it's a long time ago, and I've forgotten what I heard."

"Perhaps you heard who killed the merchant?" asked Aksionov.

Makar Semyonich laughed, and replied: "It must have been him in whose bag the knife was found! If some one else hid the knife there, 'He's not a thief till he's caught,' as the saying is. How could any one put a knife into your bag while it was under your head? It would surely have woke you up."

When Aksionov heard these words, he felt sure this was the man who had killed the merchant. He rose and went away. All that night Aksionov lay awake. He felt terribly unhappy, and all sorts of images rose in his mind. There was the image of his wife as she was when he parted from her to go to the fair. He saw her as if she were present; her face and her eyes rose before him; he heard her speak and laugh. Then he saw his children, quite little, as they were at that time: one with a little cloak on, another at his mother's breast. And then he remembered himself as he used to be-young and merry. He remembered how he sat playing the guitar in the porch of the inn where he was arrested, and how free from care he had been. He saw, in his mind, the place where he was flogged, the executioner, and the people standing around; the chains, the convicts, all the twenty-six years of his prison life, and his premature old age. The thought of it all made him so wretched that he was ready to kill himself.

"And it's all that villain's doing!" thought Aksionov. And his anger was so great against Makar Semyonich that he longed for vengeance, even if he himself should perish for it. He kept repeating prayers all night, but could get no peace. During the day he did not go near Makar Semyonich, nor even look at him.

A fortnight passed in this way. Aksionov could not sleep at night, and was so miserable that he did not know what to do.

One night as he was walking about the prison he noticed some earth that came rolling out from under one of the shelves on which the prisoners slept. He stopped to see what it was. Suddenly Makar Semyonich crept out from under the shelf, and looked up at Aksionov with frightened face. Aksionov tried to pass without looking at him, but Makar seized his hand and told him that he had dug a hole under the wall, getting rid of the earth by putting it into his high-boots, and emptying it out every day on the road when the prisoners were driven to their work.

"Just you keep quiet, old man, and you shall get out too. If you blab, they'll flog the life out of me, but I will kill you first."

Aksionov trembled with anger as he looked at his enemy. He drew his hand away, saying, "I have no wish to escape, and you have no need to kill me; you killed me long ago! As to telling of you—I may do so or not, as God shall direct."

Next day, when the convicts were led out to work, the convoy soldiers noticed that one or other of the prisoners emptied some earth out of his boots. The prison was searched and the tunnel found. The Governor came and questioned all the prisoners to find out who had dug the hole. They all denied any knowledge of it. Those who knew would not betray Makar Semyonich, knowing he would be flogged almost to death. At last the Governor turned to Aksionov whom he knew to be a just man, and said:

"You are a truthful old man; tell me, before God, who dug the hole?"

Makar Semyonich stood as if he were quite unconcerned, looking at the Governor and not so much as glancing at Aksionov. Aksionov's lips and hands trembled, and for a long time he could not utter a word. He thought, "Why should I screen him who ruined my life? Let him pay for what I have suffered. But if I tell, they will probably flog the life out of him, and maybe I suspect him wrongly. And, after all, what good would it be to me?"

"Well, old man," repeated the Governor, "tell me the truth: who has been digging under the wall?"

Aksionov glanced at Makar Semyonich, and said, "I cannot say, your honour. It is not God's will that I should tell! Do what you like with me; I am in your hands."

However much the Governor tried, Aksionov would say no more, and so the matter had to be left.

That night, when Aksionov was lying on his bed and just beginning to doze, some one came quietly and sat down on his bed. He peered through the darkness and recognised Makar.

"What more do you want of me?" asked Aksionov. "Why have you come here?"

Makar Semyonich was silent. So Aksionov sat up and said, "What do you want? Go away, or I will call the guard!"

Makar Semyonich bent close over Aksionov, and whispered, "Ivan Dmitrich, forgive me!"

"What for?" asked Aksionov.

"It was I who killed the merchant and hid the knife among your things. I meant to kill you too, but I heard a noise outside, so I hid the knife in your bag and escaped out of the window."

Aksionov was silent, and did not know what to say. Makar Semyonich slid off the bed-shelf and knelt upon the ground. "Ivan Dmitrich," said he, "forgive me! For the love of God, forgive me! I will confess that it was I who killed the merchant, and you will be released and can go to your home."

"It is easy for you to talk," said Aksionov, "but I have suffered for you these twenty-six years. Where could I go to now?... My wife is dead, and my children have forgotten me. I have nowhere to go..."

Makar Semyonich did not rise, but beat his head on the floor. "Ivan Dmitrich, forgive me!" he cried. "When they flogged me with the knot it was not so hard to bear as it is to see you now ... yet you had pity on me, and did not tell. For Christ's sake forgive me, wretch that I am!" And he began to sob.

When Aksionov heard him sobbing he, too, began to weep. "God will forgive you!" said he. "Maybe I am a hundred times worse than you." And at these words his heart grew light, and the longing for home left him. He no longer had any desire to leave the prison, but only hoped for his last hour to come.

In spite of what Aksionov had said, Makar Semyonich confessed his guilt. But when the order for his release came, Aksionov was already dead.

2. MY RELIGION

INTRODUCTION.

I HAVE not always been possessed of the religious ideas set forth in this book. For thirty-five years of my life I was, in the proper acceptation of the word, a nihilist,—not a revolutionary socialist, but a man who believed in nothing. Five years ago faith came to me; I believed in the doctrine of Jesus, and my whole life underwent a sudden transformation. What I had once wished for I wished for no longer, and I began to desire what I had never desired before. What had once appeared to me right now became wrong, and the wrong of the past I beheld as right. My condition was like that of a man who goes forth upon some errand, and having traversed a portion of the road, decides that the matter is of no importance, and turns back. What was at first on his right hand is now on his left, and what was at his left hand is now on his right; instead of going away from his abode, he desires to get back to it as soon as possible. My life and my desires were completely changed; good and evil interchanged meanings. Why so? Because I understood the doctrine of Jesus in a different way from that in which I had understood it before.

It is not my purpose to expound the doctrine of Jesus; I wish only to tell how it was that I came to understand what there is in this doctrine that is simple, clear, evident, indisputable; how I understand that part of it which appeals to all men, and how this understanding refreshed my soul and gave me happiness and peace.

I do not intend to comment on the doctrine of Jesus; I desire only that all comment shall be forever done away with. The Christian sects have always maintained that all men, however unequal in education and intelligence, are equal before God; that divine truth is accessible to every one. Jesus has even declared it to be the will of God that what is concealed from the wise shall be revealed to the simple. Not every one is able to understand the mysteries of dogmatics, homiletics, liturgics, hermeneutics, apologetics; but every one is able and ought to understand what Jesus Christ said to the millions of simple and ignorant people who have lived, and who are living to-day. Now, the things that Jesus said to simple people who could not avail themselves of the comments of Paul, of Clement, of Chrysostom, and of others, are just what I did not understand, and which, now that I have come to understand them, I wish to make plain to all.

The thief on the cross believed in the Christ, and was saved. If the thief, instead of dying on the cross, had descended from it, and told all men of his belief in the Christ, would not the result have been of great good? Like the thief on the cross, I believe in the doctrine of Jesus, and this belief has made me whole. This is not a vain comparison, but a truthful expression of my spiritual condition; my soul, once filled with despair of life and fear of death, is now full of happiness and peace.

Like the thief, I knew that my past and present life was vile; I saw that the majority of men about me lived unworthy lives. I knew, like the thief, that I was wretched and suffering, that all those about me suffered and were wretched; and I saw before me nothing but death to save me from this condition. As the thief was nailed to his cross, so I was nailed to a life of suffering and evil by an incomprehensible power. And as the thief saw before him, after the sufferings of a foolish life, the horrible shadows of death, so I beheld the same vista opening before me.

In all this I felt that I was like the thief. There was, however, a difference in our conditions; he was about to die, and I—I still lived. The dying thief thought perhaps to find his salvation beyond the grave, while I had before me life and its mystery this side the grave. I understood nothing of this life; it seemed to me a frightful thing, and then—I understood the words of Jesus, and life and death ceased to be evil; instead of despair, I tasted joy and happiness that death could not take away.

Will any one, then, be offended if I tell the story of how all this came about?

CHAPTER I.

I SHALL explain elsewhere, in two voluminous treatises, why I did not understand the doctrine of Jesus, and how at length it became clear to me. These works are a criticism of dogmatic theology and a new translation of the four Gospels, followed by a concordance. In these writings I seek methodically to disentangle everything that tends to conceal the truth from men; I translate the four Gospels anew, verse by verse, and I bring them together in a new concordance. The work has lasted for six years. Each year, each month, I discover new meanings which corroborate the fundamental idea; I correct the errors which have crept in, and I put the last touches to what I have already written. My life, whose final term is not far distant, will doubtless end before I have finished my work; but I am convinced that the work will be of great service; so I shall do all that I can to bring it to completion.

I do not now concern myself with this outward work upon theology and the Gospels, but with an inner work of an entirely different nature. I have to do now with nothing systematic or methodical, only with that sudden light which showed me the Gospel doctrine in all its simple beauty.

The process was something similar to that experienced by one who, following an erroneous model, seeks to restore a statue from broken bits of marble, and who with one of the most refractory fragments in hand perceives the hopelessness of his ideal; then he begins anew, and instead of the former incongruities he finds, as he observes the outlines of each fragment, that all fit well together and form one consistent whole. That is exactly what happened to me, and is what I wish to relate. I wish to tell how I found the key to the true meaning of the doctrine of Jesus, and how by this meaning doubt was absolutely driven from my soul. The discovery came about in this way.

From my childhood, from the time I first began to read the New Testament, I was touched most of all by that portion of the doctrine of Jesus which inculcates love, humility, self-denial, and the duty of returning good for evil. This, to me, has always been the substance of Christianity; my heart recognized its truth in spite of scepticism and despair, and for this reason I submitted to a religion professed by a multitude of toilers, who find in it the solution of life,—the religion taught by the Orthodox Church. But in making my submission to the Church, I soon saw that I should not find in its creed the confirmation of the essence of Christianity; what was to me essential seemed to be in the dogma of the Church merely an accessory. What was to me the most important of the teachings of Jesus was not so regarded by the Church. No doubt (I thought) the Church sees in Christianity, aside from its inner meaning of love, humility, and self-denial, an outer, dogmatic meaning, which, however strange and even repulsive to me, is not in itself evil or pernicious. But the further I went on in submission to the doctrine of the Church, the more clearly I saw in this particular point something of greater importance than I had at first realized. What I found most repulsive in the doctrine of the Church was the strangeness of its dogmas and the approval, nay, the support, which it gave to persecutions, to the death penalty, to wars stirred up by the intolerance common to all sects; but my faith was chiefly shattered by the indifference of the Church to what seemed to me essential in the teachings of Jesus, and its partiality for what seemed to me of secondary importance. I felt that something was wrong; but I could not see where the fault lay, because the doctrine of the Church did not deny what seemed to me essential in the doctrine of Jesus; this essential was fully recognized, yet in such a way as not to give it the first place. I could not accuse the Church of denying the essence of the doctrine of Jesus, but it was recognized in a way which did not satisfy me. The Church did not give me what I expected from her. I had passed from nihilism to the Church simply because I felt it to be impossible to live without religion, that is, without a knowledge of good and evil aside from animal instincts. I hoped to find this knowledge in Christianity; but Christianity I then saw only as a vague spiritual tendency, from which it was impossible to deduce any clear and peremptory rules for the guidance of life. These I sought and these I demanded of the Church. The Church offered me rules wherein I not only sought in vain the practice of the Christian life so dear to me, but which drove me still further away. I could not become a disciple of the Church. An existence based upon Christian truth was to me indispensable, and the Church only offered me rules completely at variance with the truth that I loved. The rules of the Church touching articles of faith, dogmas, the observance of the sacrament, fasts, prayers, were not necessary to me, and did not seem to be based on Christian truth. Moreover, the rules of the Church weakened and sometimes destroyed the Christian disposition of soul which alone gave meaning to my life.

I was troubled most that the miseries of humanity, the habit of judging one another, of passing judgment upon nations and religions, and the wars and massacres which resulted in consequence, all went on with the approbation of the Church. The doctrine of Jesus,—judge not, be humble, forgive offences, deny self, love,—this doctrine was extolled by the Church in words, but at the same time the Church approved what was incompatible with the doctrine. Was it possible that the doctrine of Jesus admitted of such contradiction? I could not believe so.

Another astonishing thing about the Church was that the passages upon which it based affirmation of its dogmas were those which were most obscure. On the other hand, the passages from which came the moral laws were the most clear and precise. And yet the dogmas and the duties depending upon them were definitely formulated by the Church, while the recommendation to obey the moral law was put in the most vague and mystical terms. Was this the intention of Jesus? The Gospels alone could dissipate my doubts. I read them once and again.

Of all the other portions of the Gospels, the Sermon on the Mount always had for me an exceptional importance. I now read it more frequently than ever. Nowhere does Jesus speak with greater solemnity, nowhere does he propound moral rules more definitely and practically, nor do these rules in any other form awaken more readily an echo in the human heart; nowhere else does he address himself to a larger multitude of the common people. If there are any clear and precise Christian principles, one ought to find them here. I therefore sought the solution of my doubts in Matthew v., vi., and vii., comprising the Sermon on the Mount. These chapters I read very often, each time with the same emotional ardor, as I came to the verses which exhort the hearer to turn the other cheek, to give up his cloak, to be at peace with all the world, to love his enemies,—but each time with the same disappointment. The divine words were not clear. They exhorted to a renunciation so absolute as to entirely stifle life as I understood it; to renounce everything, therefore, could not, it seemed to me, be essential to salvation. And the moment this ceased to be an absolute condition, clearness and precision were at an end.

I read not only the Sermon on the Mount; I read all the Gospels and all the theological commentaries on the Gospels. I was not satisfied with the declarations of the theologians that the Sermon on the Mount was only an indication of the degree of perfection to which man should aspire; that man, weighed down by sin, could not reach such an ideal; and that the salvation of humanity was in faith and prayer and grace. I could not admit the truth of these propositions. It seemed to me a strange thing that Jesus should propound rules so clear and admirable, addressed to the understanding of every one, and still realize man's inability to carry his doctrine into practice.

Then as I read these maxims I was permeated with the joyous assurance that I might that very hour, that very moment, begin to practise them. The burning desire I felt led me to the attempt, but the doctrine of the Church rang in my ears,—*Man is weak, and to this he cannot attain*;—my strength soon failed. On every side I heard, "You must believe and pray"; but my wavering faith impeded prayer. Again I heard, "You must pray, and God will give you faith; this faith will inspire prayer, which in turn will invoke faith that will inspire more prayer, and so on, indefinitely." Reason and experience alike convinced me that such methods were useless. It seemed to me that the only true way was for me to try to follow the doctrine of Jesus.

And so, after all this fruitless search and careful meditation over all that had been written for and against the divinity of the doctrine of Jesus, after all this doubt and suffering, I came back face to face with the mysterious Gospel message. I could not find the meanings that others found, neither could I discover what I sought. It was only after I had rejected the interpretations of the wise critics and theologians, according to the words of Jesus, "*Except ye... become as little children, ye shall not enter into the kingdom of heaven*" (Matt. xviii. 3),—it was only then that I suddenly understood what had been so meaningless before. I understood, not through exegetical fantasies or profound and ingenious textual combinations; I understood everything, because I put all commentaries out of my mind. This was the passage that gave me the key to the whole:—

"*Ye have heard that it hath been said, An eye for an eye, and a tooth for a tooth: But I say unto you, That ye resist not evil.*" (Matt. v. 38, 39.)

One day the exact and simple meaning of these words came to me; I understood that Jesus meant neither more nor less than what he said. What I saw was nothing new; only the veil that had hidden the truth from me fell away, and the truth was revealed in all its grandeur.

"*Ye have heard that it hath been said, An eye for an eye, and a tooth for a tooth: But I say unto you, That ye resist not evil.*"

These words suddenly appeared to me as if I had never read them before. Always before, when I had read this passage, I had, singularly enough, allowed certain words to escape me, "*But I say unto you, that ye resist not evil.*" To me it had always been as if the words just quoted had never existed, or had never possessed a definite meaning. Later on, as I talked with many Christians familiar with the Gospel, I noticed frequently the same blindness with regard to these words. No one remembered them, and often in speaking of this passage, Christians took up the Gospel to see for themselves if the words were really there. Through a similar neglect of these words I had failed to understand the words that follow:—

"*But whosoever shall smite thee on thy right cheek, turn to him the other also,*" etc. (Matt. v. 39, *et seq.*)

Always these words had seemed to me to demand long-suffering and privation contrary to human nature. They touched me; I felt that it would be noble to follow them, but I also felt that I had not the strength to put them into practice. I said to myself, "If I turn the other cheek, I shall get another blow; if I give, all that I have will be taken away. Life would be an impossibility. Since life is given to me, why should I deprive myself of it? Jesus cannot demand as much as that." Thus I reasoned, persuaded that Jesus, in exalting long-suffering and privation, made use of exaggerated terms lacking in clearness and precision; but when I understood the words "*Resist not evil*," I saw that Jesus did not exaggerate, that he did not demand suffering for suffering, but that he had formulated with great clearness and precision exactly what he wished to say.

"*Resist not evil*," knowing that you will meet with those who, when they have struck you on one cheek and met with no resistance, will strike you on the other; who, having taken away your coat, will take away your cloak also; who, having profited by your labor, will force you to labor still more without reward. And yet, though all this should happen to you, "*Resist not evil*"; do good to them that injure you. When I understood these words as they are written, all that had been obscure became clear to me, and what had seemed exaggerated I saw to be perfectly reasonable. For the first time I grasped the pivotal idea in the words "*Resist not evil*"; I saw that what followed was only a development of this command; I saw that Jesus did not exhort us to turn the other cheek that we might endure suffering, but that his exhortation was, "*Resist not evil*," and that he afterward declared suffering to be the possible consequence of the practice of this maxim.

A father, when his son is about to set out on a far journey, commands him not to tarry by the way; he does not tell him to pass his nights without shelter, to deprive himself of food, to expose himself to rain and cold. He says, "Go thy way, and tarry not, though thou should'st be wet or cold." So Jesus does not say, "Turn the other cheek and suffer." He says, "*Resist not evil*"; no matter what happens, "*Resist not.*"

These words, "*Resist not evil,*" when I understood their significance, were to me the key that opened all the rest. Then I was astonished that I had failed to comprehend words so clear and precise.

"*Ye have heard that it hath been said, An eye for an eye, and a tooth for a tooth: But I say unto you, That ye resist not evil.*"

Whatever injury the evil-disposed may inflict upon you, bear it, give all that you have, but resist not. Could anything be more clear, more definite, more intelligible than that? I had only to grasp the simple and exact meaning of these words, just as they were spoken, when the whole doctrine of Jesus, not only as set forth in the Sermon on the Mount, but in the entire Gospels, became clear to me; what had seemed contradictory was now in harmony; above all, what had seemed superfluous was now indispensable. Each portion fell into harmonious unison and filled its proper part, like the fragments of a broken statue when adjusted in harmony with the sculptor's design. In the Sermon on the Mount, as well as throughout the whole Gospel, I found everywhere affirmation of the same doctrine, "*Resist not evil.*"

In the Sermon on the Mount, as well as in many other places, Jesus represents his disciples, those who observe the rule of non-resistance to evil, as turning the other cheek, giving up their cloaks, persecuted, used despitefully, and in want. Everywhere Jesus says that he who taketh not up his cross, he who does not renounce worldly advantage, he who is not ready to bear all the consequences of the commandment, "*Resist not evil*," cannot become his disciple.

To his disciples Jesus says, Choose to be poor; bear all things without resistance to evil, even though you thereby bring upon yourself persecution, suffering, and death.

Prepared to suffer death rather than resist evil, he reproved the resentment of Peter, and died exhorting his followers not to resist and to remain always faithful to his doctrine. The early disciples observed this rule, and passed their lives in misery and persecution, without rendering evil for evil.

It seems, then, that Jesus meant precisely what he said. We may declare the practice of such a rule to be very difficult; we may deny that he who follows it will find happiness; we may say with the unbelievers that Jesus was a dreamer, an idealist who propounded impracticable maxims; but it is impossible not to admit that he expressed in a manner at once clear and precise what he wished to say; that is, that according to his doctrine a man must not resist evil, and, consequently, that whoever adopts his doctrine will not resist evil. And yet neither believers nor unbelievers will admit this simple and clear interpretation of Jesus' words.

CHAPTER II.

WHEN I apprehended clearly the words "*Resist not evil*," my conception of the doctrine of Jesus was entirely changed; and I was astounded, not that I had failed to understand it before, but that I had misunderstood it so strangely. I knew, as we all know, that the true significance of the doctrine of Jesus was comprised in the injunction to love one's neighbor. When we say, "*Turn the other cheek*," "*Love your enemies*," we express the very essence of Christianity. I knew all that from my childhood; but why had

I failed to understand aright these simple words? Why had I always sought for some ulterior meaning? "*Resist not evil*" means, never resist, never oppose violence; or, in other words, never do anything contrary to the law of love. If any one takes advantage of this disposition and affronts you, bear the affront, and do not, above all, have recourse to violence. This Jesus said in words so clear and simple that it would be impossible to express the idea more clearly. How was it then, that believing or trying to believe these to be the words of God, I still maintained the impossibility of obeying them? If my master says to me, "Go; cut some wood," and I reply, "It is beyond my strength," I say one of two things: either I do not believe what my master says, or I do not wish to obey his commands. Should I then say of God's commandment that I could not obey it without the aid of a supernatural power? Should I say this without having made the slightest effort of my own to obey? We are told that God descended to earth to save mankind; that salvation was secured by the second person of the Trinity, who suffered for men, thereby redeeming them from sin, and gave them the Church as the shrine for the transmission of grace to all believers; but aside from this, the Saviour gave to men a doctrine and the example of his own life for their salvation. How, then, could I say that the rules of life which Jesus has formulated so clearly and simply for every one—how could I say that these rules were difficult to obey, that it was impossible to obey them without the assistance of a supernatural power? Jesus saw no such impossibility; he distinctly declared that those who did not obey could not enter into the kingdom of God. Nowhere did he say that obedience would be difficult; on the contrary, he said in so many words, "*My yoke is easy and my burden is light*" (Matt. xi. 30). And John, the evangelist, says, "*His commandments are not grievous*" (1 John v. 3). Since God declared the practice of his law to be easy, and himself practised it in human form, as did also his disciples, how dared I speak of the impossibility of obedience without the aid of a supernatural power?

If one bent all his energies to overthrow any law, what could he say of greater force than that the law was essentially impracticable, and that the maker of the law knew it to be impracticable and unattainable without the aid of a supernatural power? Yet that is exactly what I had been thinking of the command, "*Resist not evil.*" I endeavored to find out how it was that I got the idea that Jesus' law was divine, but that it could not be obeyed; and as I reviewed my past history, I perceived that the idea had not been communicated to me in all its crudeness (it would then have been revolting to me), but insensibly I had been imbued with it from childhood, and all my after life had only confirmed me in error.

From my childhood I had been taught that Jesus was God, and that his doctrine was divine, but at the same time I was taught to respect as sacred the institutions which protected me from violence and evil. I was taught to resist evil, that it was humiliating to submit to evil, and that resistance to it was praiseworthy. I was taught to judge, and to inflict punishment. Then I was taught the soldier's trade, that is, to resist evil by homicide; the army to which I belonged was called "The Christophile Army," and it was sent forth with a Christian benediction. From infancy to manhood I learned to venerate things that were in direct contradiction to the law of Jesus,—to meet an aggressor with his own weapons, to avenge myself by violence for all offences against my person, my family, or my race. Not only was I not blamed for this; I learned to regard it as not at all contrary to the law of Jesus. All that surrounded me, my personal security and that of my family and my property—depended then upon a law which Jesus reproved,—the law of "a tooth for a tooth." My spiritual instructors taught me that the law of Jesus was divine, but, because of human weakness, impossible of practice, and that the grace of Jesus Christ alone could aid us to follow its precepts. And this instruction agreed with what I received in secular institutions and from the social organization about me. I was so thoroughly possessed with this idea of the impracticability of the divine doctrine, and it harmonized so well with my desires, that not till the time of awakening did I realize its falsity. I did not see how impossible it was to confess Jesus and his doctrine, "*Resist not evil,*" and at the same time deliberately assist in the organization of property, of tribunals, of governments, of armies; to contribute to the establishment of a polity entirely contrary to the doctrine of Jesus, and at the same time pray to Jesus to help us to obey his commands, to forgive our sins, and to aid us that we resist not evil. I did not see, what is very clear to me now, how much more simple it would be to organize a method of living conformable to the law of Jesus, and then to pray for tribunals, and massacres, and wars, and all other things indispensable to our happiness.

Thus I came to understand the source of error into which I had fallen. I had confessed Jesus with my lips, but my heart was still far from him. The command, "*Resist not evil*," is the central point of Jesus' doctrine; it is not a mere verbal affirmation; it is a rule whose practice is obligatory. It is verily the key to the whole mystery; but the key must be thrust to the bottom of the lock. When we regard it as a command impossible of performance, the value of the entire doctrine is lost. Why should not a doctrine seem impracticable, when we have suppressed its fundamental proposition? It is not strange that unbelievers look upon it as totally absurd. When we declare that one may be a Christian without observing the commandment, "*Resist not evil*," we simply leave out the connecting link which transmits the force of the doctrine of Jesus into action.

Some time ago I was reading in Hebrew, the fifth chapter of Matthew with a Jewish rabbi. At nearly every verse the rabbi said, "This is in the Bible," or "This is in the Talmud," and he showed me in the Bible and in the Talmud sentences very like the declarations of the Sermon on the Mount. When we reached the words, "*Resist not evil*," the rabbi did not say, "This is in the Talmud," but he asked me, with a smile, "Do the Christians obey this command? Do they turn the other cheek?" I had nothing to say in reply, especially as at that particular time, Christians, far from turning the other cheek, were smiting the Jews upon both cheeks. I asked him if there were anything similar in the Bible or in the Talmud. "No," he replied, "there is nothing like it; but tell me, do the Christians obey this law?" It was only another way of saying that the presence in the Christian doctrine of a commandment which no one observed, and which Christians themselves regarded as impracticable, is simply an avowal of the foolishness and nullity of that law. I could say nothing in reply to the rabbi.

Now that I understand the exact meaning of the doctrine, I see clearly the strangely contradictory position in which I was placed. Having recognized the divinity of Jesus and of his doctrine, and having at the same time organized a life wholly contrary to that doctrine, what remained for me but to look upon the doctrine as impracticable? In words I had recognized the doctrine of Jesus as sacred; in actions, I had professed a doctrine not at all Christian, and I had recognized and reverenced the anti-Christian customs which hampered my life upon every side. The persistent message of the Old Testament is that misfortunes came upon the Hebrew people because they believed in false gods and denied Jehovah. Samuel (I. viii.-xii.) accuses the people of adding to their other apostasies the choice of a man, upon whom they depended for deliverance instead of upon Jehovah, who was their true King. "Turn not aside after *tohu*, after vain things," Samuel says to the people (I. xii. 21); "turn not aside after vain things, which cannot profit nor deliver; for they are *tohu*, are vain." "Fear Jehovah and serve him.... But if ye shall still do wickedly, ye shall be consumed, both ye and your king" (I. xii. 24, 25). And so with me, faith in *tohu*, in vain things, in empty idols, had concealed the truth from me. Across the path which led to the truth, *tohu*, the idol of vain things, rose before me, cutting off the light, and I had not the strength to beat it down.

On a certain day, at this time, I was walking in Moscow towards the Borovitzky Gate, where was stationed an old lame beggar, with a dirty cloth wrapped about his head. I took out my purse to bestow an alms; but at the same moment I saw a young soldier emerging from the Kremlin at a rapid pace, head well up, red of face, wearing the State insignia of military dignity. The beggar, on perceiving the soldier, arose in fear, and ran with all his might towards the Alexander Garden. The soldier, after a vain attempt to come up with the fugitive, stopped, shouting forth an imprecation upon the poor wretch who had established himself under the gateway contrary to regulations. I waited for the soldier. When he approached me, I asked him if he knew how to read.

"Yes; why do you ask?"

"Have you read the New Testament?"

"Yes."

"And do you remember the words, 'If thine enemy hunger, feed him...'?"

I repeated the passage. He remembered it, and heard me to the end. I saw that he was uneasy. Two passers-by stopped and listened. The soldier seemed to be troubled that he should be condemned for doing his duty in driving persons away from a place where they had been forbidden to linger. He thought himself at fault, and sought for an excuse. Suddenly his eye brightened; he looked at me over his shoulder, as if he were about to move away.

"And the military regulation, do you know anything about that?" he demanded.

"No," I said.

"In that case, you have nothing to say to me," he retorted, with a triumphant wag of the head, and elevating his plume once more, he marched away to his post. He was the only man that I ever met who had solved, with an inflexible logic, the question which eternally confronted me in social relations, and which rises continually before every man who calls himself a Christian.

CHAPTER III.

WE are wrong when we say that the Christian doctrine is concerned only with the salvation of the individual, and has nothing to do with questions of State. Such an assertion is simply a bold affirmation of an untruth, which, when we examine it seriously, falls of itself to the ground. It is well (so I said); I will resist not evil; I will turn the other cheek in private life; but hither comes the enemy, or here is an oppressed nation, and I am called upon to do my part in the struggle against evil, to go forth and kill. I must decide the question, to serve God or *tohu*, to go to war or not to go. Perhaps I am a peasant; I am appointed mayor of a village, a judge, a juryman; I am obliged to take the oath of office, to judge, to condemn. What ought I to do? Again I must choose between the divine law and the human law. Perhaps I am a monk living in a monastery; the neighboring peasants trespass upon our pasturage, and I am appointed to resist evil, to plead for justice against the wrong-doers. Again I must choose. It is a dilemma from which no man can escape.

I do not speak of those whose entire lives are passed in resisting evil, as military authorities, judges, or governors. No one is so obscure that he is not obliged to choose between the service of God and the service of *tohu*, in his relation to the State. My very existence, entangled with that of the State and the social existence organized by the State, exacts from me an anti-Christian activity directly contrary to the commandments of Jesus. In fact, with conscription and compulsory jury service, this pitiless dilemma arises before every one. Every one is forced to take up murderous weapons; and even if he does not get as far as murder, his weapons must be ready, his carbine loaded, and his sword keen of edge, that he may declare himself ready for murder. Every one is forced into the service of the courts to take part in meting out judgment and sentence; that is, to deny the commandment of Jesus, "*Resist not evil*," in acts as well as in words.

The soldier's problem, the Gospel or military regulations, divine law or human law, is before mankind to-day as it was in the time of Samuel. It was forced upon Jesus and upon his disciples; it is forced in these times upon all who would be Christians; and it was forced upon me.

The law of Jesus, with its doctrine of love, humility, and self-denial, touched my heart more deeply than ever before. But everywhere, in the annals of history, in the events that were going on about me, in my individual life, I saw the law opposed in a manner revolting to sentiment, conscience, and reason, and encouraging to brute instincts. I felt that if I adopted the law of Jesus, I should be alone; I should pass many unhappy hours; I should be persecuted and afflicted as Jesus had said. But if I adopted the human law, everybody would approve; I should be in peace and safety, with all the resources of civilization at my command to put my conscience at ease. As Jesus said, I should laugh and be glad. I felt all this, and so I did not analyze the meaning of the doctrine of Jesus, but sought to understand it in such a way that it might not interfere with my life as an animal. That is, I did not wish to understand it at all. This determination not to understand led me into delusions which now astound me. As an instance in point, let me explain my former understanding of these words:—

"*Judge not, that ye be not judged.*" (Matt. vii. 1.)

"*Judge not, and ye shall not be judged; condemn not, and ye shall not be condemned.*" (Luke vi. 37.)

The courts in which I served, and which insured the safety of my property and my person, seemed to be institutions so indubitably sacred and so entirely in accord with the divine law, it had never entered into my head that the words I have quoted could have any other meaning than an injunction not to speak ill of one's neighbor. It never occurred to me that Jesus spoke in these words of the courts of human law and justice. It was only when I understood the true meaning of the words, "*Resist not evil*," that the question arose as to Jesus' advice with regard to tribunals. When I understood that Jesus would denounce them, I asked myself, Is not this the real meaning: Not only do not judge your neighbor, do not speak ill of him, but do not judge him in the courts, do not judge him in any of the tribunals that you have instituted? Now in Luke (vi. 37-49) these words follow immediately the doctrine that exhorts us to resist not evil and to do good to our enemies. And after the injunction, "*Be ye therefore merciful, as your Father also is merciful*," Jesus says, "*Judge not, and ye shall not be judged; condemn not, and ye shall not be condemned.*" "*Judge not;*" does not this mean, Institute no tribunals for the judgment of your neighbor? I had only to bring this boldly before myself when heart and reason united in an affirmative reply.

To show how far I was before from the true interpretation, I shall confess a foolish pleasantry for which I still blush. When I was reading the New Testament as a divine book at the time that I had become a believer, I was in the habit of saying to my friends who were judges or attorneys, "And you still judge, although it is said, 'Judge not, and ye shall not be judged'?" I was so sure that these words could have no other meaning than a condemnation of evil-speaking that I did not comprehend the horrible blasphemy which I thus committed. I was so thoroughly convinced that these words did not mean what they did mean, that I quoted them in their true sense in the form of a pleasantry.

I shall relate in detail how it was that all doubt with regard to the true meaning of these words was effaced from my mind, and how I saw their purport to be that Jesus denounced the institution of all human tribunals, of whatever sort; that he meant to say so, and could not have expressed himself otherwise. When I understood the command, "*Resist not evil*," in its proper sense, the first thing that occurred to me was that tribunals, instead of conforming to this law, were directly opposed to it, and indeed to the entire doctrine; and therefore that if Jesus had thought of tribunals at all, he would have condemned them.

Jesus said, "*Resist not evil*"; the sole aim of tribunals is to resist evil. Jesus exhorted us to return good for evil; tribunals return evil for evil. Jesus said that we were to make no distinction between those who do good and those who do evil; tribunals do nothing else. Jesus said, Forgive, forgive not once or seven times, but without limit; love your enemies, do good to them that hate you—but tribunals do not forgive, they punish; they return not good but evil to those whom they regard as the enemies of society. It would seem, then, that Jesus denounced judicial institutions. Perhaps (I said) Jesus never had anything to do with courts of justice, and so did not think of them. But I saw that such a theory was not tenable. Jesus, from his childhood to his death, was concerned with the tribunals of Herod, of the Sanhedrim, and of the High Priests. I saw that Jesus must have regarded courts of justice as wrong. He told his disciples that they would be dragged before the judges, and gave them advice as to how they should comport themselves. He said of himself that he should be condemned by a tribunal, and he showed what the attitude toward judges ought to be. Jesus, then, must have thought of the judicial institutions which condemned him and his disciples; which have condemned and continue to condemn millions of men.

Jesus saw the wrong and faced it. When the sentence against the woman taken in adultery was about to be carried into execution, he absolutely denied the possibility of human justice, and demonstrated that man could not be the judge since man himself was guilty. And this idea he has propounded many times, as where it is declared that one with a beam in his eye cannot see the mote in another's eye, or that the blind cannot lead the blind. He even pointed out the consequences of such misconceptions,—the disciple would be above his Master.

Perhaps, however, after having denounced the incompetency of human justice as displayed in the case of the woman taken in adultery, or illustrated in the parable of the mote and the beam; perhaps, after all, Jesus would admit of an appeal to the justice of men where it was necessary for protection against evil; but I soon saw that this was inadmissible. In the Sermon on the Mount, he says, addressing the multitude,

"And if any man will sue thee at the law, and take away thy coat, let him have thy cloak also." (Matt. v. 40.)

Once more, perhaps Jesus spoke only of the personal bearing which a man should have when brought before judicial institutions, and did not condemn justice, but admitted the necessity in a Christian society of individuals who judge others in properly constituted forms. But I saw that this view was also inadmissible. When he prayed, Jesus besought all men, without exception, to forgive others, that their own trespasses might be forgiven. This thought he often expresses. He who brings his gift to the altar with prayer must first grant forgiveness. How, then, could a man judge and condemn when his religion commanded him to forgive all trespasses, without limit? So I saw that according to the doctrine of Jesus no Christian judge could pass sentence of condemnation.

But might not the relation between the words "*Judge not, and ye shall not be judged*" and the preceding or subsequent passages permit us to conclude that Jesus, in saying "*Judge not*," had no reference whatever to judicial institutions? No; this could not be so; on the contrary, it is clear from the relation of the phrases that in saying "*Judge not*," Jesus did actually speak of judicial institutions. According to Matthew and Luke, before saying "*Judge not, condemn not*," his command was to resist not evil. And prior to this, as Matthew tells us, he repeated the ancient criminal law of the Jews, "*An eye for an eye, and a tooth for a tooth*." Then, after this reference to the old criminal law, he added, "*But I say unto you, That ye resist not evil*"; and, after that, "*Judge not*." Jesus did, then, refer directly to human criminal law, and reproved it in the words, "*Judge not*." Moreover, according to Luke, he not only said, "*Judge not*," but also, "*Condemn not*." It was not without a purpose that he added this almost synonymous word; it shows clearly what meaning should be attributed to the other. If he had wished to say "Judge not your neighbor," he would have said "neighbor"; but he added the words which are translated "*Condemn not*," and then completed the sentence, "*And ye shall not be condemned: forgive, and ye shall be forgiven*." But some may still insist that Jesus, in expressing himself in this way, did not refer at all to the tribunals, and that I have read my own thoughts into his teachings. Let the apostles tell us what they thought of courts of justice, and if they recognized and approved of them. The apostle James says (iv. 11, 12):—

"*Speak not evil one of another, brethren. He that speaketh evil of his brother, and judgeth his brother, speaketh evil of the law, and judgeth the law: but if thou judge the law, thou art not a doer of the law, but a judge. There is one lawgiver, who is able to save and to destroy: who art thou that judgest another?*"

The word translated "speak evil" is the verb καταλαλέω, which means "to speak against, to accuse"; this is its true meaning, as any one may find out for himself by opening a dictionary. In the translation we read, "*He that speaketh evil of his brother, ... speaketh evil of the law.*" Why so? is the question that involuntarily arises. I may speak evil of my brother, but I do not thereby speak evil of the law. If, however, I *accuse* my brother, if I bring him to justice, it is plain that I thereby accuse the law of Jesus of insufficiency: I accuse and judge the law. It is clear, then, that I do not practise the law, but that I make myself a judge of the law. "*Not to judge, but to save*" is Jesus' declaration. How then shall I, who cannot save, become a judge and punish? The entire passage refers to human justice, and denies its authority. The whole epistle is permeated with the same idea. In the second chapter we read:—

"*For he shall have judgment without mercy, that hath shewed no mercy; and mercy is exalted above judgment.*" (Jas. ii. 13.)

(The last phrase has been translated in such a way as to declare that judgment is compatible with Christianity, but that it ought to be merciful.)

James exhorts his brethren to have no respect of persons. If you have respect of the condition of persons, you are guilty of sin; you are like the untrustworthy judges of the tribunals. You look upon the beggar as the refuse of society, while it is the rich man who ought to be so regarded. He it is who oppresses you and draws you before the judgment-seats. If you live according to the law of love for your neighbor, according to the law of mercy (which James calls "*the law of liberty*," to distinguish it from all others)—if you live according to this law, it is well. But if you have respect of persons, you transgress the law of mercy. Then (doubtless thinking of the case of the woman taken in adultery, who, when she was brought before Jesus, was about to be put to death according to the law), thinking, no doubt, of that case, James says that he who inflicts death upon the adulterous woman would himself be guilty of murder, and thereby transgress the eternal law; for the same law forbids both adultery and murder.

"So speak ye, and so do, as they that shall be judged by the law of liberty. For he shall have judgment without mercy, that hath shewed no mercy; and mercy is exalted above judgment." (Jas. ii. 12, 13.)

Could the idea be expressed in terms more clear and precise? Respect of persons is forbidden, as well as any judgment that shall classify persons as good or bad; human judgment is declared to be inevitably defective, and such judgment is denounced as criminal when it condemns for crime; judgment is blotted out by the eternal law, the law of mercy.

I open the epistles of Paul, who had been a victim of tribunals, and in the letter to the Romans I read the admonitions of the apostle for the vices and errors of those to whom his words are addressed; among other matters he speaks of courts of justice:—

"Who, knowing the judgment of God, that they which commit such things are worthy of death, not only do the same, but have pleasure in them that do them." (Rom. i. 32.)

"Therefore thou art inexcusable, O man, whosoever thou art that judgest: for wherein thou judgest another, thou condemnest thyself; for thou that judgest doest the same things." (Rom. ii. 1.)

"Or despisest thou the riches of his goodness and forbearance and long-suffering; not knowing that the goodness of God leadeth thee to repentance?" (Rom. ii. 4.)

Such was the opinion of the apostles with regard to tribunals, and we know that human justice was among the trials and sufferings that they endured with steadfastness and resignation to the will of God. When we think of the situation of the early Christians, surrounded by unbelievers, we can understand that a denial of the right to judge persecuted Christians before the tribunals was not considered. The apostles spoke of it only incidentally as an evil, and denied its authority on every occasion.

I examined the teachings of the early Fathers of the Church, and found them to agree in obliging no one to judge or to condemn, and in urging all to bear the inflictions of justice. The martyrs, by their acts, declared themselves to be of the same mind. I saw that Christianity before Constantine regarded tribunals only as an evil which was to be endured with patience; but it never could have occurred to any early Christian that he could take part in the administration of the courts of justice. It is plain, therefore, that Jesus' words, "*Judge not, condemn not*," were understood by his first disciples, as they ought to be understood now, in their direct and literal meaning: judge not in courts of justice; take no part in them.

All this seemed absolutely to corroborate my conviction that the words, "*Judge not, condemn not*," referred to the justice of tribunals. Yet the meaning, "Speak not evil of your neighbor," is so firmly established, and courts of justice flaunt their decrees with so much assurance and audacity in all Christian societies, with the support even of the Church, that for a long time still I doubted the wisdom of my interpretation. If men have understood the words in this way (I thought), and have instituted Christian tribunals, they must certainly have some reason for so doing; there must be a good reason for regarding these words as a denunciation of evil-speaking, and there is certainly a basis of some sort for the institution of Christian tribunals; perhaps, after all, I am in the wrong.

I turned to the Church commentaries. In all, from the fifth century onward, I found the invariable interpretation to be, "Accuse not your neighbor"; that is, avoid evil-speaking. As the words came to be understood exclusively in this sense, a difficulty arose,—How to refrain from judgment? It being impossible not to condemn evil, all the commentators discussed the question, What is blamable and what is not blamable? Some, such as Chrysostom and Theophylact, said that, as far as servants of the Church were concerned, the phrase could not be construed as a prohibition of censure, since the apostles themselves were censorious. Others said that Jesus doubtless referred to the Jews, who accused their neighbors of shortcomings, and were themselves guilty of great sins.

Nowhere a word about human institutions, about tribunals, to show how they were affected by the warning, "*Judge not.*" Did Jesus sanction courts of justice, or did he not? To this very natural question I found no reply—as if it was evident that from the moment a Christian took his seat on the judge's bench he might not only judge his neighbor, but condemn him to death.

I turned to other writers, Greek, Catholic, Protestant, to the Tübingen school, to the historical school. Everywhere, even by the most liberal commentators, the words in question were interpreted as an injunction against evil-speaking.

But why, contrary to the spirit of the whole doctrine of Jesus, are these words interpreted in so narrow a way as to exclude courts of justice from the injunction, "*Judge not*"? Why the supposition that Jesus in forbidding the comparatively light offence of speaking evil of one's neighbor did not forbid, did not even consider, the more deliberate judgment which results in punishment inflicted upon the condemned? To all this I got no response; not even an allusion to the least possibility that the words "to judge" could be used as referring to a court of justice, to the tribunals from whose punishments so many millions have suffered.

Moreover, when the words, "*Judge not, condemn not,*" are under discussion, the cruelty of judging in courts of justice is passed over in silence, or else commended. The commentators all declare that in Christian societies tribunals are necessary, and in no way contrary to the law of Jesus.

Realizing this, I began to doubt the sincerity of the commentators; and I did what I should have done in the first place; I turned to the textual translations of the words which we render "to judge" and "to condemn." In the original these words are κρίνω and καταδικάζω. The defective translation in James of καταλαλέω, which is rendered "to speak evil," strengthened my doubts as to the correct translation of the others. When I looked through different versions of the Gospels, I found καταδικάζω rendered in the Vulgate by *condemnare*, "to condemn"; in the Sclavonic text the rendering is equivalent to that of the Vulgate; Luther has *verdammen*, "to speak evil of." These divergent renderings increased my doubts, and I was obliged to ask again the meaning of κρίνω, as used by the two evangelists, and of καταδικάζω, as used by Luke who, scholars tell us, wrote very correct Greek.

How would these words be translated by a man who knew nothing of the evangelical creed, and who had before him only the phrases in which they are used?

Consulting the dictionary, I found that the word κρίνω had several different meanings, among the most used being "to condemn in a court of justice," and even "to condemn to death," but in no instance did it signify "to speak evil." I consulted a dictionary of New Testament Greek, and found that was often used in the sense "to condemn in a court of justice," sometimes in the sense "to choose," never as meaning "to speak evil." From which I inferred that the word κρίνω might be translated in different ways, but that the rendering "to speak evil" was the most forced and far-fetched.

I searched for the word καταδικάζω, which follows κρίνω, evidently to define more closely the sense in which the latter is to be understood. I looked for καταδικάζω in the dictionary, and found that it had no other signification than "to condemn in judgment," or "to judge worthy of death." I found that the word was used four times in the New Testament, each time in the sense "to condemn under sentence, to judge worthy of death." In James (v. 6) we read, "*Ye have condemned and killed the just.*" The word rendered "condemned" is this same καταδικάζω, and is used with reference to Jesus, who was condemned to death by a court of justice. The word is never used in any other sense, in the New Testament or in any other writing in the Greek language.

What, then, are we to say to all this? Is my conclusion a foolish one? Is not every one who considers the fate of humanity filled with horror at the sufferings inflicted upon mankind by the enforcement of criminal codes,—a scourge to those who condemn as well as to the condemned,—from the slaughters of Genghis Khan to those of the French Revolution and the executions of our own times? He would indeed be without compassion who could refrain from feeling horror and repulsion, not only at the sight of human beings thus treated by their kind, but at the simple recital of death inflicted by the knout, the guillotine, or the gibbet.

The Gospel, of which every word is sacred to you, declares distinctly and without equivocation: "You have from of old a criminal law, An eye for an eye, a tooth for a tooth; but a new law is given you, That you resist not evil. Obey this law; render not evil for evil, but do good to every one, forgive every one, under all circumstances." Further on comes the injunction, "*Judge not*," and that these words might not be misunderstood, Jesus added, "*Condemn not*; condemn not in justice the crimes of others."

"No more death-warrants," said an inner voice—"no more death-warrants," said the voice of science; "evil cannot suppress evil." The Word of God, in which I believed, told me the same thing. And when in reading the doctrine, I came to the words, "*Condemn not, and ye shall not be condemned: forgive, and ye shall be forgiven*," could I look upon them as meaning simply that I was not to indulge in gossip and evil-speaking, and should continue to regard tribunals as a Christian institution, and myself as a Christian judge?

I was overwhelmed with horror at the grossness of the error into which I had fallen.

CHAPTER IV.

I NOW understood the words of Jesus: "*Ye have heard that it hath been said, An eye for an eye, and a tooth for a tooth: but I say unto you, That ye resist not evil.*" Jesus' meaning is: "You have thought that you were acting in a reasonable manner in defending yourself by violence against evil, in tearing out an eye for an eye, by fighting against evil with criminal tribunals, guardians of the peace, armies; but I say unto you, Renounce violence; have nothing to do with violence; do harm to no one, not even to your enemy." I understood now that in saying "*Resist not evil*," Jesus not only told us what would result from the observance of this rule, but established a new basis for society conformable to his doctrine and opposed to the social basis established by the law of Moses, by Roman law, and by the different codes in force to-day. He formulated a new law whose effect would be to deliver humanity from its self-inflicted woes. His declaration was: "You believe that your laws reform criminals; as a matter of fact, they only make more criminals. There is only one way to suppress evil, and that is to return good for evil, without respect of persons. For thousands of years you have tried the other method; now try mine, try the reverse."

Strange to say, in these later days, I talked with different persons about this commandment of Jesus, "*Resist not evil*," and rarely found any one to coincide with my opinion! Two classes of men would never, even by implication, admit the literal interpretation of the law. These men were at the extreme poles of the social scale,—they were the conservative Christian patriots who maintained the infallibility of the Church, and the atheistic revolutionists. Neither of these two classes was willing to renounce the right to resist by violence what they regarded as evil. And the wisest and most intelligent among them would not acknowledge the simple and evident truth, that if we once admit the right of any man to resist by violence what he regards as evil, every other man has equally the right to resist by violence what he regards as evil.

Not long ago I had in my hands an interesting correspondence between an orthodox Slavophile and a Christian revolutionist. The one advocated violence as a partisan of a war for the relief of brother Slavs in bondage; the other, as a partisan of revolution, in the name of our brothers the oppressed Russian peasantry. Both invoked violence, and each based himself upon the doctrine of Jesus. The doctrine of Jesus is understood in a hundred different ways; but never, unhappily, in the simple and direct way which harmonizes with the inevitable meaning of Jesus' words.

Our entire social fabric is founded upon principles that Jesus reproved; we do not wish to understand his doctrine in its simple and direct acceptation, and yet we assure ourselves and others that we follow his doctrine, or else that his doctrine is not expedient for us. Believers profess that Christ as God, the second person of the Trinity, descended upon earth to teach men by his example how to live; they go through the most elaborate ceremonies for the consummation of the sacraments, the building of temples, the sending out of missionaries, the establishment of priesthoods, for parochial administration, for the performance of rituals; but they forget one little detail,—the practice of the commandments of Jesus. Unbelievers endeavor in every possible way to organize their existence independent of the doctrine of Jesus, they having decided *a priori* that this doctrine is of no account. But to endeavor to put his teachings in practice, this each refuses to do; and the worst of it is, that without any attempt to put them in practice, both believers and unbelievers decide *a priori* that it is impossible.

Jesus said, simply and clearly, that the law of resistance to evil by violence, which has been made the basis of society, is false, and contrary to man's nature; and he gave another basis, that of non-resistance to evil, a law which, according to his doctrine, would deliver man from wrong. "You believe" (he says in substance) "that your laws, which resort to violence, correct evil; not at all; they only augment it. For thousands of years you have tried to destroy evil by evil, and you have not destroyed it; you have only augmented it. Do as I command you, follow my example, and you will know that my doctrine is true." Not only in words, but by his acts, by his death, did Jesus propound his doctrine, "*Resist not evil.*"

Believers listen to all this. They hear it in their churches, persuaded that the words are divine; they worship Jesus as God, and then they say: "All this is admirable, but it is impossible; as society is now organized, it would derange our whole existence, and we should be obliged to give up the customs that are so dear to us. We believe it all, but only in this sense: That it is the ideal toward which humanity ought to move; the ideal which is to be attained by prayer, and by believing in the sacraments, in the redemption, and in the resurrection of the dead."

The others, the unbelievers, the free-thinkers who comment on the doctrine of Jesus, the historians of religions, the Strausses, the Renans,—completely imbued with the teachings of the Church, which says that the doctrine of Jesus accords with difficulty with our conceptions of life,—tell us very seriously that the doctrine of Jesus is the doctrine of a visionary, the consolation of feeble minds; that it was all very well preached in the fishermen's huts by Galilee; but that for us it is only the sweet dream of one whom Renan calls the "charmant docteur."

In their opinion, Jesus could not rise to the heights of wisdom and culture attained by our civilization. If he had been on an intellectual level with his modern critics, he never would have uttered his charming nonsense about the birds of the air, the turning of the other cheek, the taking no thought for the morrow. These historical critics judge of the value of Christianity by what they see of it as it now exists. The Christianity of our age and civilization approves of society as it now is, with its prison-cells, its factories, its houses of infamy, its parliaments; but as for the doctrine of Jesus, which is opposed to modern society, it is only empty words. The historical critics see this, and, unlike the so-called believers, having no motives for concealment, submit the doctrine to a careful analysis; they refute it systematically, and prove that Christianity is made up of nothing but chimerical ideas.

It would seem that before deciding upon the doctrine of Jesus, it would be necessary to understand of what it consisted; and to decide whether his doctrine is reasonable or not, it would be well first to realize that he said exactly what he did say. And this is precisely what we do not do, what the Church commentators do not do, what the free-thinkers do not do—and we know very well why. We know perfectly well that the doctrine of Jesus is directed at and denounces all human errors, all *tohu*, all the empty idols that we try to except from the category of errors, by dubbing them "Church," "State," "Culture," "Science," "Art," "Civilization." But Jesus spoke precisely of all these, of these and all other *tohu*. Not only Jesus, but all the Hebrew prophets, John the Baptist, all the true sages of the world denounced the Church and State and culture and civilization of their times as sources of man's perdition.

Imagine an architect who says to a house-owner, "Your house is good for nothing; you must rebuild it," and then describes how the supports are to be cut and fastened. The proprietor turns a deaf ear to the words, "Your house is good for nothing," and only listens respectfully when the architect begins to discuss the arrangement of the rooms. Evidently, in this case, all the subsequent advice of the architect will seem to be impracticable; less respectful proprietors would regard it as nonsensical. But it is precisely in this way that we treat the doctrine of Jesus. I give this illustration for want of a better. I remember now that Jesus in teaching his doctrine made use of the same comparison. "*Destroy this temple*," he said, "*and in three days I will raise it up.*" It was for this they put him on the cross, and for this they now crucify his doctrine.

The least that can be asked of those who pass judgment upon any doctrine is that they shall judge of it with the same understanding as that with which it was propounded. Jesus understood his doctrine, not as a vague and distant ideal impossible of attainment, not as a collection of fantastic and poetical reveries with which to charm the simple inhabitants on the shores of Galilee; to him his doctrine was a doctrine of action, of acts which should become the salvation of mankind. This he showed in his manner of applying his doctrine. The crucified one who cried out in agony of spirit and died for his doctrine was not a dreamer; he was a man of action. They are not dreamers who have died, and still die, for his doctrine. No; that doctrine is not a chimera!

All doctrine that reveals the truth is chimerical to the blind. We may say, as many people do say (I was of the number), that the doctrine of Jesus is chimerical because it is contrary to human nature. It is against nature, we say, to turn the other cheek when we have been struck, to give all that we possess, to toil not for ourselves but for others. It is natural, we say, for a man to defend his person, his family, his property; that is to say, it is the nature of man to struggle for existence. A learned person has proved scientifically that the most sacred duty of man is to defend his rights, that is, to fight.

But the moment we detach ourselves from the idea that the existing organization established by man is the best, is sacred, the moment we do this, the objection that the doctrine of Jesus is contrary to human nature turns immediately upon him who makes it. No one will deny that not only to kill or torture a man, but to torture a dog, to kill a fowl or a calf, is to inflict suffering reproved by human nature. (I have known of farmers who had ceased to eat meat solely because it had fallen to their lot to slaughter animals.) And yet our existence is so organized that every personal enjoyment is purchased at the price of human suffering contrary to human nature.

We have only to examine closely the complicated mechanism of our institutions that are based upon coercion to realize that coercion and violence are contrary to human nature. The judge who has condemned according to the code, is not willing to hang the criminal with his own hands; no clerk would tear a villager from his weeping family and cast him into prison; the general or the soldier, unless he be hardened by discipline and service, will not undertake to slay a hundred Turks or Germans or destroy a village, would not, if he could help it, kill a single man. Yet all these things are done, thanks to the administrative machinery which divides responsibility for misdeeds in such a way that no one feels them to be contrary to nature.

Some make the laws, others execute them; some train men by discipline to automatic obedience; and these last, in their turn, become the instruments of coercion, and slay their kind without knowing why or to what end. But let a man disentangle himself for a moment from this complicated network, and he will readily see that coercion is contrary to his nature. Let us abstain from affirming that organized violence, of which we make use to our own profit, is a divine, immutable law, and we shall see clearly which is most in harmony with human nature,—the doctrine of violence or the doctrine of Jesus.

What is the law of nature? Is it to know that my security and that of my family, all my amusements and pleasures, are purchased at the expense of misery, deprivation, and suffering to thousands of human beings—by the terror of the gallows; by the misfortune of thousands stifling within prison walls; by the fear inspired by millions of soldiers and guardians of civilization, torn from their homes and besotted by discipline, to protect our pleasures with loaded revolvers against the possible interference of the famishing? Is it to purchase every fragment of bread that I put in my mouth and the mouths of my children by the numberless privations that are necessary to procure my abundance? Or is it to be certain that my piece of bread only belongs to me when I know that every one else has a share, and that no one starves while I eat?

It is only necessary to understand that, thanks to our social organization, each one of our pleasures, every minute of our cherished tranquility, is obtained by the sufferings and privations of thousands of our fellows—it is only necessary to understand this, to know what is conformable to human nature; not to our animal nature alone, but the animal and spiritual nature which constitutes man. When we once understand the doctrine of Jesus in all its bearings, with all its consequences, we shall be convinced that his doctrine is not contrary to human nature; but that its sole object is to supplant the chimerical law of the struggle against evil by violence—itself the law contrary to human nature and productive of so many evils.

Do you say that the doctrine of Jesus, "*Resist not evil*," is vain? What, then, are we to think of the lives of those who are not filled with love and compassion for their kind,—of those who make ready for their fellow-men punishment at the stake, by the knout, the wheel, the rack, chains, compulsory labor, the gibbet, dungeons, prisons for women and children, the hecatombs of war, or bring about periodical revolutions; of those who carry these horrors into execution; of those who benefit by these calamities or prepare reprisals,—are not such lives vain?

We need only understand the doctrine of Jesus, to be convinced that existence,—not the reasonable existence which gives happiness to humanity, but the existence men have organized to their own hurt,—that such an existence is a vanity, the most savage and horrible of vanities, a veritable delirium of folly, to which, once reclaimed, we do not again return.

God descended to earth, became incarnate to redeem Adam's sin, and (so we were taught to believe) said many mysterious and mystical things which are difficult to understand, which it is not possible to understand except by the aid of faith and grace—and suddenly the words of God are found to be simple, clear, and reasonable! God said, Do no evil, and evil will cease to exist. Was the revelation from God really so simple—nothing but that? It would seem that every one might understand it, it is so simple!

The prophet Elijah, a fugitive from men, took refuge in a cave, and was told that God would appear to him. There came a great wind that devastated the forest; Elijah thought that the Lord had come, but the Lord was not in the wind. After the wind came the thunder and the lightning, but God was not there. Then came the earthquake: the earth belched forth fire, the rocks were shattered, the mountain was rent to its foundations; Elijah looked for the Lord, but the Lord was not in the earthquake. Then, in the calm that followed, a gentle breeze came to the prophet, bearing the freshness of the fields; and Elijah knew that God was there. It is a magnificent illustration of the words, "*Resist not evil*."

They are very simple, these words; but they are, nevertheless, the expression of a law divine and human. If there has been in history a progressive movement for the suppression of evil, it is due to the men who understood the doctrine of Jesus—who endured evil, and resisted not evil by violence. The advance of humanity towards righteousness is due, not to the tyrants, but to the martyrs. As fire cannot extinguish fire, so evil cannot suppress evil. Good alone, confronting evil and resisting its contagion, can overcome evil. And in the inner world of the human soul, the law is as absolute as it was for the hearers by Galilee, more absolute, more clear, more immutable. Men may turn aside from it, they may hide its truth from others; but the progress of humanity towards righteousness can only be attained in this way. Every step must be guided by the command, "*Resist not evil.*" A disciple of Jesus may say now, with greater assurance than they of Galilee, in spite of misfortunes and threats: "And yet it is not violence, but good, that overcomes evil." If the progress is slow, it is because the doctrine of Jesus (which, through its clearness, simplicity, and wisdom, appeals so inevitably to human nature), because the doctrine of Jesus has been cunningly concealed from the majority of mankind under an entirely different doctrine falsely called by his name.

CHAPTER V.

THE true meaning of the doctrine of Jesus was revealed to me; everything confirmed its truth. But for a long time I could not accustom myself to the strange fact, that after the eighteen centuries during which the law of Jesus had been professed by millions of human beings, after the eighteen centuries during which thousands of men had consecrated their lives to the study of this law, I had discovered it for myself anew. But strange as it seemed, so it was. Jesus' law, "*Resist not evil*," was to me wholly new, something of which I had never had any conception before. I asked myself how this could be; I must certainly have had a false idea of the doctrine of Jesus to cause such a misunderstanding. And a false idea of it I unquestionably had. When I began to read the Gospel, I was not in the condition of one who, having heard nothing of the doctrine of Jesus, becomes acquainted with it for the first time; on the contrary, I had a preconceived theory as to the manner in which I ought to understand it. Jesus did not appeal to me as a prophet revealing the divine law, but as one who continued and amplified the absolute divine law which I already knew; for I had very definite and complex notions about God, the creator of the world and of man, and about the commandments of God given to men through the instrumentality of Moses.

When I came to the words, "*Ye have heard that it hath been said, An eye for an eye, and a tooth for a tooth: But I say unto you, That ye resist not evil*,"—the words, "*An eye for an eye, and a tooth for a tooth*," expressed the law given by God to Moses; the words, "*But I say unto you, That ye resist not evil*," expressed the new law, which was a negation of the first. If I had seen Jesus' words, simply, in their true sense, and not as a part of the theological theory that I had imbibed at my mother's breast, I should have understood immediately that Jesus abrogated the old law, and substituted for it a new law. But I had been taught that Jesus did not abrogate the law of Moses, that, on the contrary, he confirmed it to the slightest iota, and that he made it more complete. Verses 17-20 of the fifth chapter of Matthew always impressed me, when I read the Gospel, by their obscurity, and they plunged me into doubt. I knew the Old Testament, particularly the last books of Moses, very thoroughly, and recalling certain passages in which minute doctrines, often absurd and even cruel in their purport, are preceded by the words, "And the Lord said unto Moses," it seemed to me very singular that Jesus should confirm all these injunctions; I could not understand why he did so. But I allowed the question to pass without solution, and accepted with confidence the explanations inculcated in my infancy,—that the two laws were equally inspired by the Holy Spirit, that they were in perfect accord, and that Jesus confirmed the law of Moses while completing and amplifying it. I did not concern myself with accounting for the process of this amplification, with the solution of the contradictions apparent throughout the whole Gospel, in verses 17-20 of the fifth chapter, in the words, "*But I say unto you.*"

Now that I understood the clear and simple meaning of the doctrine of Jesus, I saw clearly that the two laws are directly opposed to one another; that they can never be harmonized; that, instead of supplementing one by the other, we must inevitably choose between the two; and that the received explanation of the verses, Matthew v. 17-20, which had impressed me by their obscurity, must be incorrect.

When I now came to read once more the verses that had before impressed me as obscure, I was astonished at the clear and simple meaning which was suddenly revealed to me. This meaning was revealed, not by any combination and transposition, but solely by rejecting the factitious explanations with which the words had been encumbered. According to Matthew, Jesus said (v. 17-18):—

"*Think not that I am come to destroy the law, or the prophets* (the doctrine of the prophets): *I am not come to destroy, but to fulfil. For verily I say unto you, Till heaven and earth pass, one jot or one tittle shall in no wise pass from the law, till all be fulfilled.*"

And in verse 20 he added:—

"*For I say unto you, That except your righteousness shall exceed the righteousness of the scribes and Pharisees, ye shall in no case enter into the kingdom of heaven.*"

I am not come (Jesus said) to destroy the eternal law of whose fulfilment your books of prophecy foretell. I am come to teach you the fulfilment of the eternal law; not of the law that your scribes and pharisees call the divine law, but of that eternal law which is more immutable than the earth and the heavens.

I have expressed the idea in other words in order to detach the thoughts of my readers from the traditional false interpretation. If this false interpretation had never existed, the idea expressed in the verses could not be rendered in a better or more definite manner.

The view that Jesus did not abrogate the old law arises from the arbitrary conclusion that "law" in this passage signifies the written law instead of the law eternal, the reference to the iota—jot and tittle—perhaps furnishing the grounds for such an opinion. But if Jesus had been speaking of the written law, he would have used the expression "the law and the prophets," which he always employed in speaking of the written law; here, however, he uses a different expression,—"the law *or* the prophets." If Jesus had meant the written law, he would have used the expression, "the law and the prophets," in the verses that follow and that continue the thought; but he says, briefly, "the law." Moreover, according to Luke, Jesus made use of the same phraseology, and the context renders the meaning inevitable. According to Luke, Jesus said to the Pharisees, who assumed the justice of their written law:—

"*Ye are they which justify yourselves before men; but God knoweth your hearts: for that which is highly esteemed among men is abomination in the sight of God. The law and the prophets were until John: since that time the kingdom of God is preached, and every man presseth into it. And it is easier for heaven and earth to pass, than one tittle of the law to fail.*" (Luke xvi. 15-17.)

In the words, "*The law and the prophets were until John*," Jesus abrogated the written law; in the words, "*And it is easier for heaven and earth to pass, than one tittle of the law to fail*," Jesus confirmed the law eternal. In the first passage cited he said, "the law *and* the prophets," that is, the written law; in the second he said "the law" simply, therefore the law eternal. It is clear, then, that the eternal law is opposed to the written law, exactly as in the context of Matthew where the eternal law is defined by the phrase, "the law *or* the prophets."

The history of the variants of the text of these verses is quite worthy of notice. The majority of texts have simply "the law," without the addition, "and the prophets," thus avoiding a false interpretation in the sense of the written law. In other texts, notably that of Tischendorf, and in the canonical versions, we find the word "prophets" used, not with the conjunction "and," but with the conjunction "or,"—"the law *or* the prophets,"—which also excludes any question of the written law, and indicates, as the proper signification, the law eternal. In several other versions, not countenanced by the Church, we find the word "prophets" used with the conjunction "and," not with "or"; and in these versions every repetition of the words "the law" is followed by the phrase, "and the prophets," which would indicate that Jesus spoke only of the written law.

The history of the commentaries on the passage in question coincides with that of the variants. The only clear meaning is that authorized by Luke,—that Jesus spoke of the eternal law. But among the copyists of the Gospel were some who desired that the written law of Moses should continue to be regarded as obligatory. They therefore added to the words "the law" the phrase "and the prophets," and thereby changed the interpretation of the text.

Other Christians, not recognizing to the same degree the authority of the books of Moses, suppressed the added phrase, and replaced the particle καί, "and," with ἤ, "or"; and with this substitution the passage was admitted to the canon. Nevertheless, in spite of the unequivocal clearness of the text as thus written, the commentators perpetuated the interpretation supported by the phrase which had been rejected in the canon. The passage evoked innumerable comments, which stray from the true signification in proportion to the lack, on the part of the commentators, of fidelity to the simple and obvious meaning of Jesus' doctrine. Most of them recognize the reading rejected by the canonical text.

To be absolutely convinced that Jesus spoke only of the eternal law, we need only examine the true meaning of the word which has given rise to so many false interpretations. The word "law" (in Greek νόμος, in Hebrew תּוֹרָה, *torah*) has in all languages two principal meanings: one, law in the abstract sense, independent of formulæ; the other, the written statutes which men generally recognize as law. In the Greek of Paul's Epistles the distinction is indicated by the use of the article. Without the article Paul uses νόμος the most frequently in the sense of the divine eternal law. By the ancient Hebrews, as in books of Isaiah and the other prophets, תּוֹרָה, *torah*, is always used in the sense of an eternal revelation, a divine intuition. It was not till the time of Esdras, and later in the Talmud, that "Torah" was used in the same sense in which we use the word "Bible"—with this difference, that while we have words to distinguish between the Bible and the divine law, the Jews employed the same word to express both meanings.

And so Jesus sometimes speaks of law as the divine law (of Isaiah and the other prophets), in which case he confirms it; and sometimes in the sense of the written law of the Pentateuch, in which case he rejects it. To distinguish the difference, he always, in speaking of the written law, adds, "and the prophets," or prefixes the word "your,"—"your law."

When he says: "*Therefore all things whatsoever ye would that men should do to you, do ye even so to them: for this is the law and the prophets*" (Matt. vii. 12), he speaks of the written law. The entire written law, he says, may be reduced to this expression of the eternal law, and by these words he abrogated the eternal law. When he says, "*The law and the prophets were until John*" (Luke xvi. 16), he speaks of the written law, and abrogates it. When he says, "*Did not Moses give you the law, and yet none of you keepeth the law*" (John vii. 19), "*It is also written in your law*" (John viii. 17), "*that the word might be fulfilled that is written in their law*" (John xv. 25), he speaks of the written law, the law whose authority he denied, the law that condemned him to death: "*The Jews answered him, We have a law, and by our law he ought to die*" (John xix. 7). It is plain that this Jewish law, which authorized condemnation to death, was not the law of Jesus. But when Jesus says, "I am not come to destroy the law, but to teach you the fulfilment of the law; for nothing of this law shall be changed, but all shall be fulfilled," then he speaks, not of the written law, but of the divine and eternal law.

Admit that all this is merely formal proof; admit that I have carefully combined contexts and variants, and excluded everything contrary to my theory; admit that the commentators of the Church are clear and convincing, that, in fact, Jesus did not abrogate the law of Moses, but upheld it—admit this: then the question is, what were the teachings of Jesus?

According to the Church, he taught that he was the second person of the Trinity, the Son of God, and that he came into the world to atone by his death for Adam's sin. Those, however, who have read the Gospels know that Jesus taught nothing of the sort, or at least spoke but very vaguely on these topics. The passages in which Jesus affirms that he is the second person of the Trinity, and that he was to atone for the sins of humanity, form a very inconsiderable and very obscure portion of the Gospels. In what, then, does the rest of Jesus' doctrine consist? It is impossible to deny, for all Christians have recognized the fact, that the doctrine of Jesus aims summarily to regulate the lives of men, to teach them how they ought to live with regard to one another. But to realize that Jesus taught men a new way of life, we must have some idea of the condition of the people to whom his teachings were addressed.

When we examine into the social development of the Russians, the English, the Chinese, the Indians, or even the races of insular savages, we find that each people invariably has certain practical rules or laws which govern its existence; consequently, if any one would inculcate a new law, he must at the same time abolish the old; in any race or nation this would be inevitable. Laws that we are accustomed to regard as almost sacred would assuredly be abrogated; with us, perhaps, it might happen that a reformer who taught a new law would abolish only our civil laws, the official code, our administrative customs, without touching what we consider as our divine laws, although it is difficult to believe that such could be the case. But with the Jewish people, who had but one law, and that recognized as divine,—a law which enveloped life to its minutest details,—what could a reformer accomplish if he declared in advance that the existing law was inviolable?

Admit that this argument is not conclusive, and try to interpret the words of Jesus as an affirmation of the entire Mosaic law; in that case, who were the Pharisees, the scribes, the doctors of the law, denounced by Jesus during the whole of his ministry? Who were they that rejected the doctrine of Jesus and, their High Priests at their head, crucified him? If Jesus approved the law of Moses, where were the faithful followers of that law, who practised it sincerely, and must thereby have obtained Jesus' approval? Is it possible that there was not one such? The Pharisees, we are told, constituted a sect; where, then, were the righteous?

In the Gospel of John the enemies of Jesus are spoken of directly as "the Jews." They are opposed to the doctrine of Jesus; they are hostile because they are Jews. But it is not only the Pharisees and the Sadducees who figure in the Gospels as the enemies of Jesus: we also find mention of the doctors of the law, the guardians of the law of Moses, the scribes, the interpreters of the law, the ancients, those who are always considered as representatives of the people's wisdom. Jesus said, "*I am not come to call the righteous, but sinners to repentance*," to change their way of life (μετάνοια). But where were the righteous? Was Nicodemus the only one? He is represented as a good, but misguided man.

We are so habituated to the singular opinion that Jesus was crucified by the Pharisees and a number of Jewish shopkeepers, that we never think to ask, Where were the true Jews, the good Jews, the Jews that practised the law? When we have once propounded this query, everything becomes perfectly clear. Jesus, whether he was God or man, brought his doctrine to a people possessing rules, called the divine law, governing their whole existence. How could Jesus avoid denouncing that law?

Every prophet, every founder of a religion, inevitably meets, in revealing the divine law to men, with institutions which are regarded as upheld by the laws of God. He cannot, therefore, avoid a double use of the word "law," which expresses what his hearers wrongfully consider the law of God ("your law"), and the law he has come to proclaim, the true law, the divine and eternal law. A reformer not only cannot avoid the use of the word in this manner; often he does not wish to avoid it, but purposely confounds the two ideas, thus indicating that, in the law confessed by those whom he would convert, there are still some eternal truths. Every reformer takes these truths, so well known to his hearers, as the basis of his teaching. This is precisely what Jesus did in addressing the Jews, by whom the two laws were vaguely grouped together as "Torah." Jesus recognized that the Mosaic law, and still more the prophetical books, especially the writings of Isaiah, whose words he constantly quotes,—Jesus recognized that these contained divine and eternal truths in harmony with the eternal law, and these he takes as the basis of his own doctrine. This method was many times referred to by Jesus; thus he said, "*What is written in the law? how readest thou?*" (Luke x. 26). That is, one may find eternal truth in the law, if one reads it aright. And more than once he affirms that the commandments of the Mosaic law, to love the Lord and one's neighbor, are also commandments of the eternal law. At the conclusion of the parables by which Jesus explained the meaning of his doctrine to his disciples, he pronounced words that have a bearing upon all that precedes:—

"*Therefore every scribe which is instructed unto the kingdom of heaven* (the truth) *is like unto a man that is a householder, which bringeth forth out of his treasure* (without distinction) *things new and old.*" (Matt. xiii. 52.)

The Church understands these words, as they were understood by Irenæus; but at the same time, in defiance of the true signification, it arbitrarily attributes to them the meaning that everything old is sacred. The manifest meaning is this: He who seeks for the good, takes not only the new, but also the old; and because a thing is old, he does not therefore reject it. By these words Jesus meant that he did not deny what was eternal in the old law. But when they spoke to him of the whole law, or of the formalities exacted by the old law, his reply was that new wine should not be put into old bottles. Jesus could not affirm the whole law; neither could he deny the entire teachings of the law and the prophets,—the law which says, "*love thy neighbor as thyself*," the prophets whose words often served to express his own thoughts. And yet, in place of this clear and simple explanation of Jesus' words, we are offered a vague interpretation which introduces needless contradictions, which reduces the doctrine of Jesus to nothingness, and which re-establishes the doctrine of Moses in all its savage cruelty.

Commentators of the Church, particularly those who have written since the fifth century, tell us that Jesus did not abolish the written law; that, on the contrary, he affirmed it. But in what way? How is it possible that the law of Jesus should harmonize with the law of Moses? To these inquiries we get no response. The commentators all make use of a verbal juggle to the effect that Jesus fulfilled the law of Moses, and that the sayings of the prophets were fulfilled in his person; that Jesus fulfilled the law as our mediator by our faith in him. And the essential question for every believer—How to harmonize two conflicting laws, each designed to regulate the lives of men?—is left without the slightest attempt at explanation. Thus the contradiction between the verse where it is said that Jesus did not come to destroy the law, but to fulfil the law, and Jesus' saying, "*Ye have heard that it hath been said, An eye for an eye... But I say unto you*,"—the contradiction between the doctrine of Jesus and the very spirit of the Mosaic doctrine,—is left without any mitigation.

Let those who are interested in the question look through the Church commentaries touching this passage from the time of Chrysostom to our day. After a perusal of the voluminous explanations offered, they will be convinced not only of the complete absence of any solution for the contradiction, but of the presence of a new, factitious contradiction arising in its place. Let us see what Chrysostom says in reply to those who reject the law of Moses:—

"He made this law, not that we might strike out one another's eyes, but that fear of suffering by others might restrain us from doing any such thing to them. As therefore He threatened the Ninevites with overthrow, not that He might destroy them (for had that been His will, He ought to have been silent), but that He might by fear make them better, and so quiet His wrath: so also hath He appointed a punishment for those who wantonly assail the eyes of others, that if good principle dispose them not to refrain from such cruelty, fear may restrain them from injuring their neighbors' sight.

"And if this be cruelty, it is cruelty also for the murderer to be restrained, and the adulterer checked. But these are the sayings of senseless men, and of those that are mad to the extreme of madness. For I, so far from saying that this comes of cruelty, should say that the contrary to this would be unlawful, according to men's reckoning. And whereas thou sayest, 'Because He commanded to pluck out *an eye for an eye*, therefore He is cruel'; I say that if He had not given this commandment, then He would have seemed, in the judgment of most men, to be that which thou sayest He is."

Chrysostom clearly recognized the law. *An eye for an eye*, as divine, and the contrary of that law, that is, the doctrine of Jesus, *Resist not evil*, as an iniquity. "For let us suppose," says Chrysostom further:—

"For let us suppose that this law had been altogether done away, and that no one feared the punishment ensuing thereupon, but that license had been given to all the wicked to follow their own dispositions in all security to adulterers, and to murderers, to perjured persons, and to parricides; would not all things have been turned upside down? would not cities, market-places and houses, sea and land, and the whole world have been filled with unnumbered pollutions and murders? Every one sees it. For if, when there are laws, and fear, and threatening, our evil dispositions are hardly checked; were even this security taken away, what is there to prevent men's choosing vice? and what degree of mischief would not then come revelling upon the whole of human life?

"The rather, since cruelty lies not only in allowing the bad to do what they will, but in another thing too quite as much,—to overlook, and leave uncared for, him who hath done no wrong, but who is without cause or reason suffering ill. For tell me; were any one to gather together wicked men from all quarters, and arm them with swords, and bid them go about the whole city, and massacre all that came in their way, could there be anything more like a wild beast than he? And what if some others should bind, and confine with the utmost strictness, those whom that man had armed, and should snatch from those lawless hands them who were on the point of being butchered; could anything be greater humanity than this?"

Chrysostom does not say what would be the estimate of these others in the opinion of the wicked. And what if these others were themselves wicked and cast the innocent into prison? Chrysostom continues:—

"Now then, I bid thee transfer these examples to the Law likewise; for He that commands to pluck out *an eye for an eye* hath laid the fear as a kind of strong chain upon the souls of the bad, and so resembles him who detains those assassins in prison; whereas he who appoints no punishment for them, doth all but arm them by such security, and acts the part of that other, who was putting the swords in their hands, and letting them loose over the whole city." ("Homilies on the Gospel of St. Matthew," xvi.)

If Chrysostom had understood the law of Jesus, he would have said, Who is it that strikes out another's eyes? who is it that casts men into prison? If God, who made the law, does this, then there is no contradiction; but it is men who carry out the decrees, and the Son of God has said to men that they must abstain from violence. God commanded to strike out, and the Son of God commanded not to strike out. We must accept one commandment or the other; and Chrysostom, like all the rest of the Church, accepted the commandment of Moses and denied that of the Christ, whose doctrine he nevertheless claims to believe.

Jesus abolished the Mosaic law, and gave his own law in its place. To one who really believes in Jesus there is not the slightest contradiction; such an one will pay no attention to the law of Moses, but will practise the law of Jesus, which he believes. To one who believes in the law of Moses there is no contradiction. The Jews looked upon the words of Jesus as foolishness, and believed in the law of Moses. The contradiction is only for those who would follow the law of Moses under the cover of the law of Jesus—for those whom Jesus denounced as hypocrites, as a generation of vipers.

Instead of recognizing as divine truth the one or the other of the two laws, the law of Moses or that of Jesus, we recognize the divine quality of both. But when the question comes with regard to the acts of every-day life, we reject the law of Jesus and follow that of Moses. And this false interpretation, when we realize its importance, reveals the source of that terrible drama which records the struggle between evil and good, between darkness and light.

To the Jewish people, trained to the innumerable formal regulations instituted by the Levites in the rubric of divine laws, each preceded by the words, "And the Lord said unto Moses"—to the Jewish people Jesus appeared. He found everything, to the minutest detail, prescribed by rule; not only the relation of man with God, but his sacrifices, his feasts, his fasts, his social, civil, and family duties, the details of personal habits, circumcision, the purification of the body, of domestic utensils, of clothing—all these regulated by laws recognized as commandments of God, and therefore as divine.

Excluding the question of Jesus' divine mission, what could any prophet or reformer do who wished to establish his own doctrines among a people so enveloped in formalism—what but abolish the law by which all these details were regulated? Jesus selected from what men considered as the law of God the portions which were really divine; he took what served his purpose, rejected the rest, and upon this foundation established the eternal law. It was not necessary to abolish all, but inevitable to abrogate much that was looked upon as obligatory. This Jesus did, and was accused of destroying the divine law; for this he was condemned and put to death. But his doctrine was cherished by his disciples, traversed the centuries, and is transmitted to other peoples. Under these conditions it is again hidden beneath heterogeneous dogmas, obscure comments, and factitious explanations. Pitiable human sophisms replace the divine revelation. For the formula, "And the Lord said unto Moses," we substitute "Thus saith the Holy Spirit." And again formalism hides the truth. Most astounding of all, the doctrine of Jesus is amalgamated with the written law, whose authority he was forced to deny. This *Torah*, this written law, is declared to have been inspired by the Holy Spirit, the spirit of truth; and thus Jesus is taken in the snare of his own revelation—his doctrine is reduced to nothingness.

This is why, after eighteen hundred years, it so singularly happened that I discovered the meaning of the doctrine of Jesus as some new thing. But no; I did not discover it; I did simply what all must do who seek after God and His law; I sought for the eternal law amid the incongruous elements that men call by that name.

CHAPTER VI.

WHEN I understood the law of Jesus as the law of Jesus, and not as the law of Jesus and of Moses, when I understood the commandment of this law which absolutely abrogated the law of Moses, then the Gospels, before to me so obscure, diffuse, and contradictory, blended into a harmonious whole, the substance of whose doctrine, until then incomprehensible, I found to be formulated in terms simple, clear, and accessible to every searcher after truth.

Throughout the Gospels we are called upon to consider the commandments of Jesus and the necessity of practising them. All the theologians discuss the commandments of Jesus; but what are these commandments? I did not know before. I thought that the commandment of Jesus was to love God, and one's neighbor as one's self. I did not see that this could not be a new commandment of Jesus, since it was given by them of old in Deuteronomy and Leviticus. The words:—

"*Whosoever therefore shall break one of these least commandments, and shall teach men so, he shall be called the least in the kingdom of heaven: but whosoever shall do and teach them, the same shall be called great in the kingdom of heaven,*" (Matt. v. 19.)—these words I believed to relate to the Mosaic law. But it never had occurred to me that Jesus had propounded, clearly and precisely, new laws. I did not see that in the passage where Jesus declares, "*Ye have heard that it was said.... But I say unto you,*" he formulated a series of very definite commandments—five entirely new, counting as one the two references to the ancient law against adultery. I had heard of the beatitudes of Jesus and of their number; their explanation and enumeration had formed a part of my religious instruction; but the commandments of Jesus—I had never heard them spoken of. To my great astonishment, I now discovered them for myself. In the fifth chapter of Matthew I found these verses:—

"*Ye have heard that it was said by them of old time, Thou shalt not kill; and whosoever shall kill shall be in danger of the judgment: But I say unto you, That whosoever is angry with his brother without a cause shall be in danger of the judgment: and whosoever shall say to his brother, Raca, shall be in danger of the council: but whosoever shall say, Thou fool, shall be in danger of the Gehenna of fire. Therefore if thou bring thy gift to the altar, and there rememberest that thy brother hath aught against thee; Leave there thy gift before the altar, and go thy way; first be reconciled to thy brother, and then come and offer thy gift. Agree with thine adversary quickly, while thou art in the way with him; lest at any time the adversary deliver thee to the judge, and the judge deliver thee to the officer, and thou be cast into prison. Verily I say unto thee, Thou shalt by no means come out thence, till thou hast paid the uttermost farthing.*" (Matt. v. 21-26.)

When I understood the commandment, "*Resist not evil,*" it seemed to me that these verses must have a meaning as clear and intelligible as has the commandment just cited. The meaning I had formerly given to the passage was, that every one ought to avoid angry feelings against others, ought never to utter abusive

LEO TOLSTOY

language, and ought to live in peace with all men, without exception. But there was in the text a phrase which excluded this meaning, "Whosoever shall be angry with his brother *without a cause*"—the words could not then be an exhortation to absolute peace. I was greatly perplexed, and I turned to the commentators, the theologians, for the removal of my doubts. To my surprise I found that the commentators were chiefly occupied with the endeavor to define under what conditions anger was permissible. All the commentators of the Church dwelt upon the qualifying phrase "*without a cause*," and explained the meaning to be that one must not be offended without a reason, that one must not be abusive, but that anger is not always unjust; and, to confirm their view, they quoted instances of anger on the part of saints and apostles. I saw plainly that the commentators who authorized anger "for the glory of God" as not reprehensible, although entirely contrary to the spirit of the Gospel, based their argument on the phrase "without a cause," in the twenty-second verse. These words change entirely the meaning of the passage.

Be not angry without cause? Jesus exhorts us to pardon every one, to pardon without restriction or limit. He pardoned all who did him wrong, and chided Peter for being angry with Malchus when the former sought to defend his Master at the time of the betrayal, when, if at any time, it would seem that anger might have been justifiable. And yet did this same Jesus formally teach men not to be angry "without a cause," and thereby sanction anger for a cause? Did Jesus enjoin peace upon all men, and then, in the phrase "without a cause," interpolate the reservation that this rule did not apply to all cases; that there were circumstances under which one might be angry with a brother, and so give the commentators the right to say that anger is sometimes expedient?

But who is to decide when anger is expedient and when it is not expedient? I never yet encountered an angry person who did not believe his wrath to be justifiable. Every one who is angry thinks anger legitimate and serviceable. Evidently the qualifying phrase "without a cause" destroys the entire force of the verse. And yet there were the words in the sacred text, and I could not efface them. The effect was the same as if the word "good" had been added to the phrase. "Love thy neighbor"—love thy good neighbor, the neighbor that agrees with thee!

The entire signification of the passage was changed by this phrase, "without a cause." Verses 23 and 24, which exhort us to be reconciled with all men before appealing for divine aid, also lost their direct and imperative meaning and acquired a conditional import through the influence of the foregoing qualification. It had seemed to me, however, that Jesus forbade all anger, all evil sentiment, and, that it might not continue in our hearts, exhorted us before entering into communion with God to ask ourselves if there were any person who might be angry with us. If such were the case, whether this anger were with cause or without cause, he commanded us to be reconciled. In this manner I had interpreted the passage; but it now seemed, according to the commentators, that the injunction must be taken as a conditional affirmation. The commentators all explained that we ought to try to be at peace with everybody; but, they added, if this is impossible, if, actuated by evil instincts, any one is at enmity with you, try to be reconciled with him in spirit, in idea, and then the enmity of others will be no obstacle to divine communion.

Nor was this all. The words, "Whosoever shall say to his brother, Raca, shall be in danger of the council," always seemed to me strange and absurd. If we are forbidden to be abusive, why this example with its ordinary and harmless epithet; why this terrible threat against those that utter abuse so feeble as that implied in the word *raca*, which means a good-for-nothing? All this was obscure to me.

I was convinced that I had before me a problem similar to that which had confronted me in the words, "*Judge not*." I felt that here again the simple, grand, precise, and practical meaning of Jesus had been hidden, and that the commentators were groping in gloom. It seemed to me that Jesus, in saying, "*be reconciled to thy brother*," could not have meant, "be reconciled in idea,"— an explanation not at all clear, supposing it were true. I understood what Jesus meant when, using the words of the prophet, he said, "*I will have mercy, and not sacrifice;*" that is, I will that men shall love one another. If you would have your acts acceptable to God, then, before offering prayer, interrogate your conscience; and if you find that any one is angry with you, go and make your peace with him, and then pray as you desire. After this clear interpretation, what was I to understand by the comment, "be reconciled in idea"?

I saw that what seemed to me the only clear and direct meaning of the verse was destroyed by the phrase, "without a cause." If I could eliminate that, there would be no difficulty in the way of a lucid interpretation. But all the commentators were united against any such course; and the canonical text authorized the rendering to which I objected. I could not drop these words arbitrarily, and yet, if they were excluded, everything would become clear. I therefore sought for some interpretation which would not conflict with the sense of the entire passage.

I consulted the dictionary. In ordinary Greek, the word εἰκῆ means "heedlessly, inconsiderately." I tried to find some term that would not destroy the sense; but the words, "without a cause," plainly had the meaning attributed to them. In New Testament Greek the signification of εἰκῆ is exactly the same. I consulted the concordances. The word occurs but once in the Gospels, namely, in this passage. In the first epistle to the Corinthians, xv. 2, it occurs in exactly the same sense. It is impossible to interpret it otherwise, and if we accept it, we must conclude that Jesus uttered in vague words a commandment easily so construed as to be of no effect. To admit this seemed to me equivalent to rejecting the entire Gospel. There remained one more resource—was the word to be found in all the manuscripts? I consulted Griesbach, who records all recognized variants, and discovered to my joy that the passage in question was not invariable, and that the variation depended upon the word εἰκῆ. In most of the Gospel texts and the citations of the Fathers, this word does not occur. I consulted Tischendorf for the most ancient reading: the word εἰκῆ did not appear.

This word, so destructive to the meaning of the doctrine of Jesus, is then an interpolation which had not crept into the best copies of the Gospel as late as the fifth century. Some copyist added the word; others approved it and undertook its explanation. Jesus did not utter, could not have uttered, this terrible word; and the primary meaning of the passage, its simple, direct, impressive meaning, is the true interpretation.

Now that I understood Jesus to forbid anger, whatever the cause, and without distinction of persons, the warning against the use of the words "raca" and "fool" had a purport quite distinct from any prohibition with regard to the utterance of abusive epithets. The strange Hebrew word, *raca*, which is not translated in the Greek text, serves to reveal the meaning. *Raca* means, literally, "vain, empty, that which does not exist." It was much used by the Hebrews to express exclusion. It is employed in the plural form in Judges ix. 4, in the sense, "empty and vain." This word Jesus forbids us to apply to any one, as he forbids us to use the word "fool," which, like "raca," relieves us of all the obligations of humanity. We get angry, we do evil to men, and then to excuse ourselves we say that the object of our anger is an empty person, the refuse of a man, a fool. It is precisely such words as these that Jesus forbids us to apply to men. He exhorts us not to be angry with any one, and not to excuse our anger with the plea that we have to do with a vain person, a person bereft of reason.

And so in place of insignificant, vague, and uncertain phrases subject to arbitrary interpretation, I found in Matthew v. 21-26 the first commandment of Jesus: Live in peace with all men. Do not regard anger as justifiable under any circumstances. Never look upon a human being as worthless or as a fool. Not only refrain from anger yourself, but do not regard the anger of others toward you as vain. If any one is angry with you, even without reason, be reconciled to him, that all hostile feelings may be effaced. Agree quickly with those that have a grievance against you, lest animosity prevail to your loss.

The first commandment of Jesus being thus freed from obscurity, I was able to understand the second, which also begins with a reference to the ancient law:—

"*Ye have heard that it was said by them of old time, Thou shalt not commit adultery: But I say unto you, That whosoever looketh on a woman to lust after her hath committed adultery with her already in his heart. And if thy right eye offend thee, pluck it out, and cast it from thee: for it is profitable for thee that one of thy members should perish, and not that thy whole body should be cast into hell. And if thy right hand offend thee, cut it off, and cast it from thee: for it is profitable for thee that one of thy members should perish, and not that thy whole body should be cast into hell. It hath been said, Whosoever shall put away his wife, saving for the cause of fornication, causeth her to commit adultery: and whosoever shall marry her that is divorced committeth adultery.* (Matt. v. 27-32.)

By these words I understood that a man ought not, even in imagination, to admit that he could approach any woman save her to whom he had once been united, and her he might never abandon to take another, although permitted to do so by the Mosaic law.

In the first commandment, Jesus counselled us to extinguish the germ of anger, and illustrated his meaning by the fate of the man who is delivered to the judges; in the second commandment, Jesus declares that debauchery arises from the disposition of men and women to regard one another as instruments of voluptuousness, and, this being so, we ought to guard against every idea that excites to sensual desire, and, once united to a woman, never to abandon her on any pretext, for women thus abandoned are sought by other men, and so debauchery is introduced into the world.

The wisdom of this commandment impressed me profoundly. It would suppress all the evils in the world that result from the sexual relations. Convinced that license in the sexual relations leads to contention, men, in obedience to this injunction, would avoid every cause for voluptuousness, and, knowing that the law of humanity is to live in couples, would so unite themselves, and never destroy the bond of union. All the evils arising from dissensions caused by sexual attraction would be suppressed, since there would be neither men nor women deprived of the sexual relation.

But I was much more impressed, as I read the Sermon on the Mount, with the words, "Saving for the cause of fornication," which permitted a man to repudiate his wife in case of infidelity. The very form in which the idea was expressed seemed to me unworthy of the dignity of the occasion, for here, side by side with the profound truths of the Sermon on the Mount, occurred, like a note in a criminal code, this strange exception to the general rule; but I shall not dwell upon the question of form; I shall speak only of the exception itself, so entirely in contradiction with the fundamental idea.

I consulted the commentators; all, Chrysostom and the others, even authorities on exegesis like Reuss, all recognized the meaning of the words to be that Jesus permitted divorce in case of infidelity on the part of the woman, and that, in the exhortation against divorce in the nineteenth chapter of Matthew, the same words had the same signification. I read the thirty-second verse of the fifth chapter again and again, and reason refused to accept the interpretation. To verify my doubts I consulted the other portions of the New Testament texts, and I found in Matthew (xix.), Mark (x.), Luke (xvi.), and in the first epistle of Paul to the Corinthians, affirmation of the doctrine of the indissolubility of marriage. In Luke (xvi. 18) it is said:—

"*Whosoever putteth away his wife, and marrieth another, committeth adultery: and whosoever marrieth her that is put away from her husband committeth adultery.*"

In Mark (x. 5-12) the doctrine is also proclaimed without any exception whatever:—

"*For the hardness of your heart he* [Moses] *wrote you this precept. But from the beginning of the creation God made them male and female. For this cause shall a man leave his father and mother, and cleave to his wife; And they twain shall be one flesh: so then they are no more twain, but one flesh. What therefore God hath joined together, let not man put asunder. And in the house his disciples asked him again of the same matter. And he said unto them, Whosoever shall put away his wife, and marry another, committeth adultery against her. And if a woman shall put away her husband, and be married to another, she committeth adultery."*

The same idea is expressed in Matt. xix. 4-9. Paul, in the first epistle to the Corinthians (vii. 1-11), develops systematically the idea that the only way of preventing debauchery is that every man have his own wife, and every woman have her own husband, and that they mutually satisfy the sexual instinct; then he says, without equivocation, "*Let not the wife depart from her husband: But and if she depart, let her remain unmarried, or be reconciled to her husband: and let not the husband put away his wife.*"

According to Mark, and Luke, and Paul, divorce is forbidden. It is forbidden by the assertion repeated in two of the Gospels, that husband and wife are one flesh whom God hath joined together. It is forbidden by the doctrine of Jesus, who exhorts us to pardon every one, without excepting the adulterous woman. It is forbidden by the general sense of the whole passage, which explains that divorce is provocative of debauchery, and for this reason that divorce with an adulterous woman is prohibited.

Upon what, then, is based the opinion that divorce is permissible in case of infidelity on the part of the woman? Upon the words which had so impressed me in Matt. v. 32; the words every one takes to mean that Jesus permits divorce in case of adultery by the woman; the words, repeated in Matt. xix. 9, in a number of copies of the Gospel text, and by many Fathers of the Church,— the words, "unless for the cause of adultery." I studied these words carefully anew. For a long time I could not understand them. It seemed to me that there must be a defect in the translation, and an erroneous exegesis; but where was the source of the error? I could not find it; and yet the error itself was very plain.

In opposition to the Mosaic law, which declares that if a man take an aversion to his wife he may write her a bill of divorcement and send her out of his house—in opposition to this law Jesus is made to declare, "*But I say unto you, That whosoever shall put away his wife, saving for the cause of fornication, causeth her to commit adultery.*" I saw nothing in these words to allow us to affirm that divorce was either permitted or forbidden. It is said that whoever shall put away his wife causes her to commit adultery, and then an exception is made with regard to a woman guilty of adultery. This exception, which throws the guilt of marital infidelity entirely upon the *woman* is, in general, strange and unexpected; but here, in relation to the context, it is simply absurd, for even the very doubtful meaning which might otherwise be attributed to it is wholly destroyed. Whoever puts away his wife exposes her to the crime of adultery, and yet a man is permitted to put away a wife guilty of adultery, as if a woman guilty of adultery would no more commit adultery after she were put away.

But this is not all; when I had examined this passage attentively, I found it also to be lacking in grammatical meaning. The words are, "Whoever shall put away his wife, except for the fault of adultery, exposes her to the commission of adultery,"—and the proposition is complete. It is a question of the husband, of him who in putting away his wife exposes her to the commission of the crime of adultery; what, then, is the purport of the qualifying phrase, "except for the fault of adultery"? If the proposition were in this form: Whoever shall put away his wife is guilty of adultery, unless the wife herself has been unfaithful—it would be grammatically correct. But as the passage now stands, the subject "whoever" has no other predicate than the word "exposes," with which the phrase "except for the fault of adultery" cannot be connected. What, then, is the purport of this phrase? It is plain that whether for or without the fault of adultery on the part of the woman, the husband who puts away his wife exposes her to the commission of adultery.

The proposition is analogous to the following sentence: Whoever refuses food to his son, besides the fault of spitefulness, exposes him to the possibility of being cruel. This sentence evidently cannot mean that a father may refuse food to his son if the latter is spiteful. It can only mean that a father who refuses food to his son, besides being spiteful towards his son, exposes his son to the possibility of becoming cruel. And in the same way, the

Gospel proposition would have a meaning if we could replace the words, "the fault of adultery," by libertinism, debauchery, or some similar phrase, expressing not an act but a quality.

And so I asked myself if the meaning here was not simply that whoever puts away his wife, besides being himself guilty of libertinism (since no one puts away his wife except to take another), exposes his wife to the commission of adultery? If, in the original text, the word translated "adultery" or "fornication" had the meaning of libertinism, the meaning of the passage would be clear. And then I met with the same experience that had happened to me before in similar instances. The text confirmed my suppositions and entirely effaced my doubts.

The first thing that occurred to me in reading the text was that the word πορνεία, translated in common with μοιχᾶσθαι, "adultery" or "fornication," is an entirely different word from the latter. But perhaps these two words are used as synonyms in the Gospels? I consulted the dictionary, and found that the word πορνεία, corresponding in Hebrew to *zanah*, in Latin to *fornicatio*, in German to *hurerei*, in French to *libertinage*, has a very precise meaning, and that it never has signified, and never can signify, the act of adultery, *ehebruch*, as Luther and the Germans after him have rendered the word. It signifies a state of depravity,—a quality, and not an act,—and never can be properly translated by "adultery" or "fornication." I found, moreover, that "adultery" is expressed throughout the Gospel, as well as in the passage under consideration, by the word μοιχεύω. I had only to correct the false translation, which had evidently been made intentionally, to render absolutely inadmissible the meaning attributed by commentators to the text, and to show the proper grammatical relation of πορνεία to the subject of the sentence.

A person acquainted with Greek would construe as follows: παρεκτὸς, "except, outside," λόγου, "the matter, the cause," πορνείας, "of libertinism," ποιεῖ, "obliges," αὐτὴν, "her," μοιχᾶσθαι, "to be an adulteress"—which rendering gives, word for word, Whoever puts away his wife, besides the fault of libertinism, obliges her to be an adulteress.

We obtain the same meaning from Matt. xix. 9. When we correct the unauthorized translation of πορνεία, by substituting "libertinism" for "fornication," we see at once that the phrase εἰ μὴ ἐπὶ πορνείᾳ cannot apply to "wife." And as the words παρεκτὸς λόγου πορνείας could signify nothing else than the fault of libertinism on the part of the husband, so the words εἰ μὴ ἐπὶ πορνείᾳ, in the nineteenth chapter, can have no other than the same meaning. The phrase εἰ μὴ ἐπὶ πορνείᾳ is, word for word, "if this is not through libertinism" (to give one's self up to libertinism). The meaning then becomes clear. Jesus replies to the theory of the Pharisees, that a man who abandons his wife to marry another without the intention of giving himself up to libertinism does not commit adultery—Jesus replies to this theory that the abandonment of a wife, that is, the cessation of sexual relations, even if not for the purpose of libertinism, but to marry another, is none the less adultery. Thus we come at the simple meaning of this commandment—a meaning which accords with the whole doctrine, with the words of which it is the complement, with grammar, and with logic. This simple and clear interpretation, harmonizing so naturally with the doctrine and the words from which it was derived, I discovered after the most careful and prolonged research. Upon a premeditated alteration of the text had been based an exegesis which destroyed the moral, religious, logical, and grammatical meaning of Jesus' words.

And thus once more I found a confirmation of the terrible fact that the meaning of the doctrine of Jesus is simple and clear, that its affirmations are emphatic and precise, but that commentaries upon the doctrine, inspired by a desire to sanction existing evil, have so obscured it that determined effort is demanded of him who would know the truth. If the Gospels had come down to us in a fragmentary condition, it would have been easier (so it seemed to me) to restore the true meaning of the text than to find that meaning now, beneath the accumulations of fallacious comments which have apparently no purpose save to conceal the doctrine they are supposed to expound. With regard to the passage under consideration, it is plain that to justify the divorce of some Byzantine emperor this ingenious pretext was employed to obscure the doctrine regulating the relations between the sexes. When we have rejected the suggestions of the commentators, we escape from the mist of uncertainty, and the second commandment of Jesus becomes precise and clear. "Guard against libertinism. Let every man justified in entering into the sexual relation have one wife, and every wife one husband, and under no pretext whatever let this union be violated by either."

Immediately after the second commandment is another reference to the ancient law, followed by the third commandment:—

"*Again, ye have heard that it hath been said by them of old time, Thou shalt not forswear thyself, but shalt perform unto the Lord thine oaths: But I say unto you, Swear not at all; neither by heaven; for it is God's throne: Nor by the earth; for it is his footstool: neither by Jerusalem; for it is the city of the great king. Neither shalt thou swear by thy head, because thou canst not make one hair white or black. But let your communications be, Yea, yea; Nay, nay: for whatsoever is more than these cometh of evil.*" (Matt. v. 33-37.)

This passage always troubled me when I read it. It did not trouble me by its obscurity, like the passage about divorce; or by conflicting with other passages, like the authorization of anger for cause; or by the difficulty in the way of obedience, as in the case of the command to turn the other cheek;—it troubled me rather by its very clearness, simplicity, and practicality. Side by side with rules whose magnitude and importance I felt profoundly, was this saying, which seemed to me superfluous, frivolous, weak, and without consequence to me or to others. I naturally did not swear, either by Jerusalem, or by heaven, or by anything else, and it cost me not the least effort to refrain from doing so; on the other hand, it seemed to me that whether I swore or did not swear could not be of the slightest importance to any one. And desiring to find an explanation of this rule, which troubled me through its very simplicity, I consulted the commentators. They were in this case of great assistance to me.

The commentators all found in these words a confirmation of the third commandment of Moses,—not to swear by the name of the Lord; but, in addition to this, they explained that this commandment of Jesus against an oath was not always obligatory, and had no reference whatever to the oath which citizens are obliged to take before the authorities. And they brought together Scripture citations, not to support the direct meaning of Jesus' commandment, but to prove when it ought and ought not to be obeyed. They claimed that Jesus had himself [88]sanctioned the oath in courts of justice by his reply, "*Thou hast said*," to the words of the High Priest, "*I adjure thee by the living God*;" that the apostle Paul invoked God to witness the truth of his words, which invocation was evidently equivalent to an oath; that the law of Moses proscribing the oath was not abrogated by Jesus; and that Jesus forbade only false oaths, the oaths of Pharisees and hypocrites. When I had read these comments, I understood that unless I excepted from the oaths forbidden by Jesus the oath of fidelity to the State, the commandment was as insignificant as superficial, and as easy to practise as I had supposed.

And I asked myself the question, Does this passage contain an exhortation to abstain from an oath that the commentators of the Church are so zealous to justify? Does it not forbid us to take the oath indispensable to the assembling of men into political groups and the formation of a military caste? The soldier, that special instrument of violence, goes in Russia by the nickname of *prissaiaga* (sworn in). If I had asked the soldier at the Borovitzky Gate how he solved the contradiction between the Gospels and military regulations, he would have replied that he had taken the oath, that is, that he had sworn by the Gospels. This is the reply that soldiers always make. The oath is so indispensable to the horrors of war and armed coercion that in France, where Christianity is out of favor, the oath remains in full force. If Jesus did not say in so many words, "Do not take an oath," the prohibition ought to be a consequence of his teaching. He came to suppress evil, and, if he did not condemn the oath, he left a terrible evil untouched. It may be said, perhaps, that at the time at which Jesus lived this evil passed unperceived; but this is not true. Epictetus and Seneca declare against the taking of oaths. A similar rule is inscribed in the laws of Mani. The Jews of the time of Jesus made proselytes, and obliged them to take the oath. How could it be said that Jesus did not perceive this evil when he forbade it in clear, direct, and circumstantial terms? He said, "*Swear not at all.*" This expression is as simple, clear, and absolute as the expression, "*Judge not, condemn not*," and is as little subject to explanation; moreover, he added to this, "*Let your communication be, Yea, yea; Nay, nay: for whatsoever is more than these cometh of evil.*"

If obedience to the doctrine of Jesus consists in perpetual observance of the will of God, how can a man swear to observe the will of another man or other men? The will of God cannot coincide with the will of man. And this is precisely what Jesus said in Matt. v. 36:—

"*Neither shalt thou swear by thy head, because thou canst not make one hair white or black.*"

And the apostle James says in his epistle, v. 12:—

"*But above all things, my brethren, swear not, neither by heaven, neither by earth, neither by any other oath: but let your yea be yea; and your nay, nay; lest ye fall into condemnation.*"

The apostle tells us clearly why we must not swear: the oath in itself may be unimportant, but by it men are condemned, and so we ought not to swear at all. How could we express more clearly the saying of Jesus and his apostle?

My ideas had become so confused that for a long time I had kept before me the question, Do the words and the meaning of this passage agree?—it does not seem possible. But, after having read the commentaries attentively, I saw that the impossible had become a fact. The explanations of the commentators were in harmony with those they had offered concerning the other commandments of Jesus: judge not, be not angry, do not violate the marital bonds.

We have organized a social order which we cherish and look upon as sacred. Jesus, whom we recognize as God, comes and tells us that our social organization is wrong. We recognize him as God, but we are not willing to renounce our social institutions. What, then, are we to do? Add, if we can, the words "without a cause" to render void the command against anger; mutilate the sense of another law, as audacious prevaricators have done by substituting for the command absolutely forbidding divorce, phraseology which permits divorce; and if there is no possible way of deriving an equivocal meaning, as in the case of the commands, "*Judge not, condemn not*," and "*Swear not at all*," then with the utmost effrontery openly violate the rule while affirming that we obey it.

In fact, the principal obstacle to a comprehension of the truth that the Gospel forbids all manner of oaths exists in the fact that our pseudo-Christian commentators themselves, with unexampled audacity, take oath upon the Gospel itself. They make men swear by the Gospel, that is to say, they do just the contrary of what the Gospel commands. Why does it never occur to the man who is made to take an oath upon the cross and the Gospel that the cross was made sacred only by the death of one who forbade all oaths, and that in kissing the sacred book he perhaps is pressing his lips upon the very page where is recorded the clear and direct commandment, "*Swear not at all*"?

But I was troubled no more with regard to the meaning of the passage comprised in Matt. v. 33-37 when I found the plain declaration of the third commandment, that we should take no oath, since all oaths are imposed for an evil purpose.

After the third commandment comes the fourth reference to the ancient law and the enunciation of the fourth commandment:—

"*Ye have heard that it hath been said, An eye for an eye, and a tooth for a tooth: But I say unto you, That ye resist not evil: but whosoever shall smite thee on thy right cheek, turn to him the other also. And if any man will sue thee at the law, and take away thy coat, let him have thy cloak also. And whosoever shall compel thee to go a mile, go with him twain. Give to him that asketh thee, and from him that would borrow of thee turn not thou away."* (Matt. V. 38-42.)

I have already spoken of the direct and precise meaning of these words; I have already said that we have no reason whatever for basing upon them an allegorical explanation. The comments that have been made upon them, from the time of Chrysostom to our day, are really surprising. The words are pleasing to every one, and they inspire all manner of profound reflections save one,— that these words express exactly what Jesus meant to say. The Church commentators, not at all awed by the authority of one whom they recognize as God, boldly distort the meaning of his words. They tell us, of course, that these commandments to bear offences and to refrain from reprisals are directed against the vindictive character of the Jews; they not only do not exclude all general measures for the repression of evil and the punishment of evil-doers, but they exhort every one to individual and personal effort to sustain justice, to apprehend aggressors, and to prevent the wicked from inflicting evil upon others,—for, otherwise (they tell us) these spiritual commandments of the Saviour would become, as they became among the Jews, a dead letter, and would serve only to propagate evil and to suppress virtue. The love of the Christian should be patterned after the love of God; but divine love circumscribes and reproves evil only as may be required for the glory of God and the safety of his servants. If evil is propagated, we must set bounds to evil and punish it,—now this is the duty of authorities.

Christian scholars and free-thinkers are not embarrassed by the meaning of these words of Jesus, and do not hesitate to correct them. The sentiments here expressed, they tell us, are very noble, but are completely inapplicable to life; for if we practised to the letter the commandment, "*Resist not evil*," our entire social fabric would be destroyed. This is what Renan, Strauss, and all the liberal commentators tell us. If, however, we take the words of Jesus as we would take the words of any one who speaks to us, and admit that he says exactly what he does say, all these profound circumlocutions vanish away. Jesus says, "Your social system is absurd and wrong. I propose to you another." And then he utters the teachings reported by Matthew (v. 38-42). It would seem that before correcting them one ought to understand them; now this is exactly what no one wishes to do. We decide in advance that the social order which controls our existence, and which is abolished by these words, is the superior law of humanity.

For my part, I consider our social order to be neither wise nor sacred; and that is why I have understood this commandment when others have not. And when I had understood these words just as they are written, I was struck with their truth, their lucidity, and their precision. Jesus said, "You wish to suppress evil by evil; this is not reasonable. To abolish evil, avoid the commission of evil." And then he enumerates instances where we are in the habit of returning evil for evil, and says that in these cases we ought not so to do.

This fourth commandment was the one that I first understood; and it revealed to me the meaning of all the others. This simple, clear, and practical fourth commandment says: "Never resist evil by force, never return violence for violence: if any one beat you, bear it; if one would deprive you of anything, yield to his wishes; if any one would force you to labor, labor; if any one would take away your property, abandon it at his demand."

After the fourth commandment we find a fifth reference to the ancient law, followed by the fifth commandment:—

"*Ye have heard that it hath been said, Thou shall love thy neighbor and hate thine enemy. But I say unto you, Love your enemies, bless them that curse you, do good to them that hate you, and pray for them which despitefully use you, and persecute you; That ye may be the children of your Father which is in heaven: for he maketh his sun to rise on the evil and on the good, and sendeth rain on the just and on the unjust. For if ye love them which love you, what reward have ye? do not even the publicans the same? And if ye salute your brethren only, what do ye more than others? do not even the publicans so? Be ye therefore perfect, even as your Father which is in heaven is perfect.*" (Matt. v. 43-48.)

These verses I had formerly regarded as a continuation, an exposition, an enforcement, I might almost say an exaggeration, of the words, "*Resist not evil.*" But as I had found a simple, precise, and practical meaning in each of the passages beginning with a reference to the ancient law, I anticipated a similar experience here. After each reference of this sort had thus far come a commandment, and each commandment had been important and distinct in meaning; it ought to be so now. The closing words of the passage, repeated by Luke, which are to the effect that God makes no distinction of persons, but lavishes his gifts upon all, and that we, following his precepts, ought to regard all men as equally worthy, and to do good to all,—these words were clear; they seemed to me to be a confirmation and exposition of some definite law—but what was this law? For a long time I could not understand it.

To love one's enemies?—this was impossible. It was one of those sublime thoughts that we must look upon only as an indication of a moral ideal impossible of attainment. It demanded all or nothing. We might, perhaps, refrain from doing injury to our enemies—but to love them!—no; Jesus did not command the impossible. And besides, in the words referring to the ancient law, "*Ye have heard that it hath been said, Thou shalt ... hate thine enemy,*" there was cause for doubt. In other references Jesus cited textually the terms of the Mosaic law; but here he apparently cites words that have no such authority; he seems to calumniate the law of Moses.

As with regard to my former doubts, so now the commentators gave me no explanation of the difficulty. They all agreed that the words "*hate thine enemy*" were not in the Mosaic law, but they offered no suggestion as to the meaning of the unauthorized phrase. They spoke of the difficulty of loving one's enemies, that is, wicked men (thus they emended Jesus' words); and they said that while it is impossible to love our enemies, we may refrain from wishing them harm and from inflicting injury upon them. Moreover, they insinuated that we might and should "convince" our enemies, that is, resist them; they spoke of the different degrees of love for our enemies which we might attain—from all of which the final conclusion was that Jesus, for some inexplicable reason, quoted as from the law of Moses words not to be found therein, and then uttered a number of sublime phrases which at bottom are impracticable and empty of meaning.

I could not agree with this conclusion. In this passage, as in the passages containing the first four commandments, there must be some clear and precise meaning. To find this meaning, I set myself first of all to discover the purport of the words containing the inexact reference to the ancient law, "*Ye have heard that it hath been said, Thou shalt... hate thine enemy.*" Jesus had some reason for placing at the head of each of his commandments certain portions of the ancient law to serve as the antitheses of his own doctrine. If we do not understand what is meant by the citations from the ancient law, we cannot understand what Jesus proscribed. The commentators say frankly (it is impossible not to say so) that Jesus in this instance made use of words not to be found in the Mosaic law, but they do not tell us why he did so or what meaning we are to attach to the words thus used.

It seemed to me above all necessary to know what Jesus had in view when he cited these words which are not to be found in the law. I asked myself what these words could mean. In all other references of the sort, Jesus quotes a single rule from the ancient law: "Thou shalt not kill"—"Thou shalt not commit adultery"—"Thou shalt not forswear thyself"—"An eye for an eye, a tooth for a tooth"—and with regard to each rule he propounds his own doctrine. In the instance under consideration, he cites two contrasting rules: "*Ye have heard that it hath been said, Thou shalt love thy neighbor and hate thine enemy*,"—from which it would appear that the contrast between these two rules of the ancient law, relative to one's neighbor and one's enemy, should be the basis of the new law. To understand clearly what this contrast was, I sought for the meanings of the words "neighbor" and "enemy," as used in the Gospel text. After consulting dictionaries and Biblical texts, I was convinced that "neighbor" in the Hebrew language meant, invariably and exclusively, a Hebrew. We find the same meaning expressed in the Gospel parable of the Samaritan. From the inquiry of the Jewish scribe

(Luke x. 29), "*And who is my neighbor?*" it is plain that he did not regard the Samaritan as such. The word "neighbor" is used with the same meaning in Acts vii. 27. "Neighbor," in Gospel language, means a compatriot, a person belonging to the same nationality. And so the antithesis used by Jesus in the citation, "*love thy neighbor, hate thine enemy*," must be in the distinction between the words "compatriot" and "foreigner." I then sought for the Jewish understanding of "enemy," and I found my supposition confirmed. The word "enemy" is nearly always employed in the Gospels in the sense, not of a personal enemy, but, in general, of a "hostile people" (Luke i. 71, 74; Matt. xxii. 44; Mark xii. 36; Luke xx. 43, etc.). The use of the word "enemy" in the singular form, in the phrase "*hate thine enemy*," convinced me that the meaning is a "hostile people." In the Old Testament, the conception "hostile people" is nearly always expressed in the singular form.

When I understood this, I understood why Jesus, who had before quoted the authentic words of the law, had here cited the words "*hate thine enemy*." When we understand the word "enemy" in the sense of "hostile people," and "neighbor" in the sense of "compatriot," the difficulty is completely solved. Jesus spoke of the manner in which Moses directed the Hebrews to act toward "hostile peoples." The various passages scattered through the different books of the Old Testament, prescribing the oppression, slaughter, and extermination of other peoples, Jesus summed up in one word, "hate,"—make war upon the enemy. He said, in substance: "You have heard that you must love those of your own race, and hate foreigners; but I say unto you, love every one without distinction of nationality." When I had understood these words in this way, I saw immediately the force of the phrase, "*Love your enemies*." It is impossible to love one's personal enemies; but it is perfectly possible to love the citizens of a foreign nation equally with one's compatriots. And I saw clearly that in saying, "*Ye have heard that it hath been said, Thou shalt love thy neighbor, and hate thine enemy. But I say unto you, Love your enemies*," Jesus meant to say that men are in the habit of looking upon compatriots as neighbors, and foreigners as enemies; and this he reproved. His meaning was that the law of

Moses established a difference between the Hebrew and the foreigner—the hostile peoples; but he forbade any such difference. And then, according to Matthew and Luke, after giving this commandment, he said that with God all men are equal, all are warmed by the same sun, all profit by the same rain. God makes no distinction among peoples, and lavishes his gifts upon all men; men ought to act exactly in the same way toward one another, without distinction of nationality, and not like the heathen, who divide themselves into distinct nationalities.

Thus once more I found confirmed on all sides the simple, clear, important, and practical meaning of the words of Jesus. Once more, in place of an obscure sentence, I had found a clear, precise, important, and practical rule: To make no distinction between compatriots and foreigners, and to abstain from all the results of such distinction,—from hostility towards foreigners, from wars, from all participation in war, from all preparations for war; to establish with all men, of whatever nationality, the same relations granted to compatriots. All this was so simple and so clear, that I was astonished that I had not perceived it from the first.

The cause of my error was the same as that which had perplexed me with regard to the passages relating to judgments and the taking of oaths. It is very difficult to believe that tribunals upheld by professed Christians, blest by those who consider themselves the guardians of the law of Jesus, could be incompatible with the Christian religion; could be, in fact, diametrically opposed to it. It is still more difficult to believe that the oath which we are obliged to take by the guardians of the law of Jesus, is directly reproved by this law. To admit that everything in life that is considered essential and natural, as well as what is considered the most noble and grand,—love of country, its defence, its glory, battle with its enemies,—to admit that all this is not only an infraction of the law of Jesus, but is directly denounced by Jesus,—this, I say, is difficult.

Our existence is now so entirely in contradiction with the doctrine of Jesus, that only with the greatest difficulty can we understand its meaning. We have been so deaf to the rules of life that he has given us, to his explanations,—not only when he commands us not to kill, but when he warns us against anger, when he commands us not to resist evil, to turn the other cheek, to love our enemies; we are so accustomed to speak of a body of men especially organized for murder, as a Christian army, we are so accustomed to prayers addressed to the Christ for the assurance of victory, we who have made the sword, that symbol of murder, an almost sacred object (so that a man deprived of this symbol, of his sword, is a dishonored man); we are so accustomed, I say, to this, that the words of Jesus seem to us compatible with war. We say, "If he had forbidden it, he would have said so plainly." We forget that Jesus did not foresee that men having faith in his doctrine of humility, love, and fraternity, could ever, with calmness and premeditation, organize themselves for the murder of their brethren.

Jesus did not foresee this, and so he did not forbid a Christian to participate in war. A father who exhorts his son to live honestly, never to wrong any person, and to give all that he has to others, would not forbid his son to kill people upon the highway. None of the apostles, no disciple of Jesus during the first centuries of Christianity, realized the necessity of forbidding a Christian that form of murder which we call war.

Here, for example, is what Origen says in his reply to Celsus:—

"In the next place, Celsus urges us 'to help the king with all our might, and to labor with him in the maintenance of justice, to fight for him; and, if he requires it, to fight under him, or lead an army along with him.' To this, our answer is that we do, when occasion requires, give help to kings, and that, so to say, a divine help, 'putting on the whole armour of God.' And this we do in obedience to the injunction of the apostle, 'I exhort, therefore, that first of all, supplications, prayers, intercessions, and giving of thanks, be made for all men, for kings, and for all that are in authority'; and the more any one excels in piety, the more effective help does he render to kings, even more than is given by soldiers, who go forth to fight and slay as many of the enemy as they can. And to those enemies of our faith who require us to bear arms for the commonwealth, and to slay men, we can reply:

'Do not those who are priests at certain shrines, and those who attend on certain gods, as you account them, keep their hands free from blood, that they may with hands unstained and free from human blood, offer the appointed sacrifices to your gods? and even when war is upon you, you never enlist the priests in the army. If that, then, is a laudable custom, how much more so, that while others are engaged in battle, these too should engage as the priests and ministers of God, keeping their hands pure, and wrestling in prayers to God on behalf of those who are fighting in a righteous cause, and for the king who reigns righteously, that whatever is opposed to those who act righteously may be destroyed!'"

And at the close of the chapter, in explaining that Christians, through their peaceful lives, are much more helpful to kings than soldiers are, Origen says:—

"And none fight better for the king than we do. We do not, indeed, fight under him, although he require it; but we fight on his behalf, forming a special army,—an army of piety,—by offering our prayers to God."

This is the way in which the Christians of the first centuries regarded war, and such was the language that their leaders addressed to the rulers of the earth at a period when martyrs perished by hundreds and by thousands for having confessed the religion of Jesus, the Christ.

And now is not the question settled as to whether a Christian may or may not go to war? All young men brought up according to the doctrine of the Church called Christian, are obliged at a specified date during every autumn, to report at the bureaus of conscription and, under the guidance of their spiritual directors, deliberately to renounce the religion of Jesus. Not long ago, there was a peasant who refused military service on the plea that it was contrary to the Gospel. The doctors of the Church explained to the peasant his error; but, as the peasant had faith, not in their words, but in those of Jesus, he was thrown into prison, where he remained until he was ready to renounce the law of Christ. And all this happened after Christians had heard for eighteen hundred years the clear, precise, and practical commandment of their Master, which teaches not to consider men of different nationality as enemies, but to consider all men as brethren, and to maintain with them the same relations existing among compatriots; to refrain not only from killing those who are called enemies, but to love them and to minister to their needs.

When I had understood these simple and precise commandments of Jesus, these commandments so ill adapted to the ingenious distortions of commentators,—I asked myself what would be the result if the whole Christian world believed in them, believed not only in reading and chanting them for the glory of God, but also in obeying them for the good of humanity? What would be the result if men believed in the observance of these commandments at least as seriously as they believe in daily devotions, in attendance on Sunday worship, in weekly fasts, in the holy sacrament? What would be the result if the faith of men in these commandments were as strong as their faith in the requirements of the Church? And then I saw in imagination a Christian society living according to these commandments and educating the younger generation to follow their precepts. I tried to picture the results if we taught our children from infancy, not what we teach them now—to maintain personal dignity, to uphold personal privileges against the encroachments of others (which we can never do without humiliating or offending others)—but to teach them that no man has a right to privileges, and can neither be above or below any one else; that he alone debases and demeans himself who tries to domineer over others; that a man can be in a no more contemptible condition than when he is angry with another; that what may seem to be foolish and despicable in another is no excuse for wrath or enmity. I sought to imagine the results if, instead of extolling our social organization as it now is, with its theatres, its romances, its sumptuous methods for stimulating sensuous desires—if, instead of this, we taught our children by precept and by example, that the reading of lascivious romances and attendance at theatres and balls are the most vulgar of all distractions, and that there is nothing more grotesque and humiliating than to pass one's time in the collection and arrangement of personal finery to make of one's body an object of show. I endeavored to imagine a state of society where, instead of permitting and approving libertinism in young men before marriage, instead of regarding the separation of husband and wife as natural and desirable, instead of giving to women the legal right to practise the trade of prostitution, instead of countenancing and sanctioning divorce—if, instead of this, we taught by words and actions that the state of celibacy, the solitary existence of a man properly endowed for, and who has not renounced the sexual relation, is a monstrous and opprobrious wrong; and that the abandonment of wife by husband or of husband by wife for the sake of another, is an act against nature, an act bestial and inhuman.

Instead of regarding it as natural that our entire existence should be controlled by coercion; that every one of our amusements should be provided and maintained by force; that each of us from childhood to old age should be by turns victim and executioner—instead of this I tried to picture the results if, by precept and example, we endeavored to inspire the world with the conviction that vengeance is a sentiment unworthy of humanity; that violence is not only debasing, but that it deprives us of all capacity for happiness; that the true pleasures of life are not those maintained by force; and that our greatest consideration ought to be bestowed, not upon those who accumulate riches to the injury of others, but upon those who best serve others and give what they have to lessen the woes of their kind. If instead of regarding the taking of an oath and the placing of ourselves and our lives at the disposition of another as a rightful and praiseworthy act,—I tried to imagine what would be the result if we taught that the enlightened will of man is alone sacred; and that if a man place himself at the disposition of any one, and promise by oath anything whatever, he renounces his rational manhood and outrages his most sacred right. I tried to imagine the results, if, instead of the national hatred with which we are inspired under the name of "patriotism"; if, in place of the glory associated with that form of murder which we call war,—if, in place of this, we were taught, on the contrary, horror and contempt for all the means—military, diplomatic, and political—which serve to divide men; if we were educated to look upon the division of men into political States, and a diversity of codes and frontiers, as an indication of barbarism; and that to massacre others is a most horrible forfeit, which can only be exacted of a depraved and misguided man, who has fallen to the lowest level of the brute. I imagined that all men had arrived at these convictions, and I considered what I thought would be the result.

Up to this time (I said), what have been the practical results of the doctrine of Jesus as I understand it? and the involuntary reply was, Nothing. We continue to pray, to partake of the sacraments, to believe in the redemption, and in our personal salvation as well as that of the world by Jesus the Christ,—and yet that this salvation will never come by our efforts, but will come because the period set for the end of the world will have arrived when the Christ will appear in his glory to judge the quick and the dead, and the kingdom of heaven will be established.

Now the doctrine of Jesus, as I understood it, had an entirely different meaning. The establishment of the kingdom of God depended upon our personal efforts in the practice of Jesus' doctrine as propounded in the five commandments, which instituted the kingdom of God upon earth. The kingdom of God upon earth consists in this, that all men should be at peace with one another. It was thus that the Hebrew prophets conceived of the rule of God. Peace among men is the greatest blessing that can exist upon this earth, and it is within reach of all men. This ideal is in every human heart. The prophets all brought to men the promise of peace. The whole doctrine of Jesus has but one object, to establish peace—the kingdom of God—among men.

In the Sermon on the Mount, in the interview with Nicodemus, in the instructions given to his disciples, in all his teachings, Jesus spoke only of this, of the things that divided men, that kept them from peace, that prevented them from entering into the kingdom of heaven. The parables make clear to us what the kingdom of heaven is, and show us the only way of entering therein, which is to love our brethren, and to be at peace with all. John the Baptist, the forerunner of Jesus, proclaimed the approach of the kingdom of God, and declared that Jesus was to bring it upon earth. Jesus himself said that his mission was to bring peace:—

"*Peace I leave with you, my peace I give unto you: not as the world giveth, give I unto you. Let not your heart be troubled, neither let it be afraid*" (John xiv. 27).

And the observance of his five commandments will bring peace upon the earth. They all have but one object,—the establishment of peace among men. If men will only believe in the doctrine of Jesus and practise it, the reign of peace will come upon earth,— not that peace which is the work of man, partial, precarious, and at the mercy of chance; but the peace that is all-pervading, inviolable, and eternal.

The first commandment tells us to be at peace with every one and to consider none as foolish or unworthy. If peace is violated, we are to seek to re-establish it. The true religion is in the extinction of enmity among men. We are to be reconciled without delay, that we may not lose that inner peace which is the true life (Matt. v. 22-24). Everything is comprised in this commandment; but Jesus knew the worldly temptations that prevent peace among men. The first temptation perilous to peace is that of the sexual relation. We are not to consider the body as an instrument of lust; each man is to have one wife, and each woman one husband, and one is never to forsake the other under any pretext (Matt. v. 28-32). The second temptation is that of the oath, which draws men into sin; this is wrong, and we are not to be bound by any such promise (Matt. v. 34-37). The third temptation is that of vengeance, which we call human justice; this we are not to resort to under any pretext; we are to endure offences and never to return evil for evil (Matt. v. 38-42). The fourth temptation is that arising from difference in nationalities, from hostility between peoples and States; but we are to remember that all men are brothers, and children of the same Father, and thus take care that difference in nationality leads not to the destruction of peace (Matt. v. 43-48).

If men abstain from practising any one of these commandments, peace will be violated. Let men practise all these commandments, which exclude evil from the lives of men, and peace will be established upon earth. The practice of these five commandments would realize the ideal of human life existing in every human heart. All men would be brothers, each would be at peace with others, enjoying all the blessings of earth to the limit of years accorded by the Creator. Men would beat their swords into ploughshares, and their spears into pruning-hooks, and then would come the kingdom of God,—that reign of peace foretold by all the prophets, which was foretold by John the Baptist as near at hand, and which Jesus proclaimed in the words of Isaiah:—

"*The Spirit of the Lord is upon me, because he hath anointed me to preach the gospel to the poor; he hath sent me to heal the broken hearted, to preach deliverance to the captives, and recovering of sight to the blind, to set at liberty them that are bruised, to preach the acceptable year of the Lord.'... And he began to say unto them, To-day hath this Scripture been fulfilled in your ears*" (Luke iv. 18, 19, 21).

The commandments for peace given by Jesus,—those simple and clear commandments, foreseeing all possibilities of discussion, and anticipating all objections,—these commandments proclaimed the kingdom of God upon earth. Jesus, then, was, in truth, the Messiah. He fulfilled what had been promised. But we have not fulfilled the commands we must fulfil if the kingdom of God is to be established upon earth,—that kingdom which men in all ages have earnestly desired, and have sought for continually, all their days.

CHAPTER VII.

WHY is it that men have not done as Jesus commanded them, and thus secured the greatest happiness within their reach, the happiness they have always longed for and still desire? The reply to this inquiry is always the same, although expressed in different ways. The doctrine of Jesus (we are told) is admirable, and it is true that if we practised it, we should see the kingdom of God established upon earth; but to practise it is difficult, and consequently this doctrine is impracticable. The doctrine of Jesus, which teaches men how they should live, is admirable, is divine; it brings true happiness, but it is difficult to practise. We repeat this, and hear it repeated so many, many times, that we do not observe the contradiction contained in these words.

It is natural to each human being to do what seems to him best. Any doctrine teaching men how they should live instructs them only as to what is best for each. If we show men what they have to do to attain what is best for each, how can they say that they would like to do it, but that it is impossible of attainment? According to the law of their nature they cannot do what is worse for each, and yet they declare that they cannot do what is best.

The reasonable activity of man, from his earliest existence, has been applied to the search for what is best among the contradictions that envelop human life. Men struggled for the soil, for objects which are necessary to them; then they arrived at the division of goods, and called this property; finding that this arrangement, although difficult to establish, was best, they maintained ownership. Men fought with one another for the possession of women, they abandoned their children; then they found it was best that each should have his own family; and although it was difficult to sustain a family, they maintained the family, as they did ownership and many other things. As soon as they discover that a thing is best, however difficult of attainment, men do it. What, then, is the meaning of the saying that the doctrine of Jesus is admirable, that a life according to the doctrine of Jesus would be better than the life which men now lead, but that men cannot lead this better life because it is difficult?

If the word "difficult," used in this way, is to be understood in the sense that it is difficult to renounce the fleeting satisfaction of sensual desires that we may obtain a greater good, why do we not say that it is difficult to labor for bread, difficult to plant a tree that we may enjoy the fruit? Every being endowed with even the most rudimentary reason knows that he must endure difficulties to procure any good, superior to that which he has enjoyed before. And yet we say that the doctrine of Jesus is admirable, but impossible of practice, because it is difficult! Now it is difficult, because in following it we are obliged to deprive ourselves of many things that we have hitherto enjoyed. Have we never heard that it is far more to our advantage to endure difficulties and privations than to satisfy all our desires? Man may fall to the level of the beasts, but he ought not to make use of his reason to devise an apology for his bestiality. From the moment that he begins to reason, he is conscious of being endowed with reason, and this consciousness stimulates him to distinguish between the reasonable and the unreasonable. Reason does not proscribe; it enlightens.

Suppose that I am shut into a dark room, and in searching for the door I continually bruise myself against the walls. Some one brings me a light, and I see the door. I ought no longer to bruise myself when I see the door; much less ought I to affirm that, although it is best to go out through the door, it is difficult to do so, and that, consequently, I prefer to bruise myself against the walls.

In this marvellous argument that the doctrine of Jesus is admirable, and that its practice would give the world true happiness, but that men are weak and sinful, that they would do the best and do the worst, and so cannot do the best,—in this strange plea there is an evident misapprehension; there is something else besides defective reasoning; there is also a chimerical idea. Only a chimerical idea, mistaking reality for what does not exist, and taking the non-existent for reality, could lead men to deny the possibility of practising that which by their own avowal would be for their true welfare.

The chimerical idea which has reduced men to this condition is that of the dogmatic Christian religion, as it is taught through the various catechisms, to all who profess the Christianity of the Church. This religion, according to the definition of it given by its followers, consists in accepting as real that which does not exist—these are Paul's words, and they are repeated in all the theologies and catechisms as the best definition of faith. It is this faith in the reality of what does not exist that leads men to make the strange affirmation that the doctrine of Jesus is excellent for all men, but is worth nothing as a guide to their way of living. Here is an exact summary of what this religion teaches:—

A personal God, who is from all eternity—one of three persons—decided to create a world of spirits. This God of goodness created the world of spirits for their own happiness, but it so happened that one of the spirits became spontaneously wicked. Time passed, and God created a material world, created man for man's own happiness, created man happy, immortal, and without sin. The felicity of man consisted in the enjoyment of life without toil; his immortality was due to the promise that this life should last forever; his innocence was due to the fact that he had no conception of evil.

Man was beguiled in paradise by one of the spirits of the first creation, who had become spontaneously wicked. From this dates the fall of man, who engendered other men fallen like himself, and from this time men have endured toil, sickness, suffering, death, the physical and moral struggle for existence; that is to say, the fantastic being preceding the fall became real, as we know him to be, as we have no right or reason to imagine him not to be. The state of man who toils, who suffers, who chooses what is for his own welfare and rejects what would be injurious to him, who dies,—this state, which is the real and only conceivable state, is not, according to the doctrine of this religion, the normal state of man, but a state which is unnatural and temporary.

Although this state, according to the doctrine, has lasted for all humanity since the expulsion of Adam from paradise, that is, from the commencement of the world until the birth of Jesus, and has continued since the birth of Jesus under exactly the same conditions, the faithful are asked to believe that this is an abnormal and temporary state. According to this doctrine, the Son of God, the second person of the Trinity, who was himself God, was sent by God into the world in the garb of humanity to rescue men from this temporary and abnormal state; to deliver them from the pains with which they had been stricken by this same God because of Adam's sin; and to restore them to their former normal state of felicity,—that is to immortality, innocence, and idleness. The second person of the Trinity (according to this doctrine), by suffering death at the hands of man, atoned for Adam's sin, and put an end to that abnormal state which had lasted from the commencement of the world. And from that time onward, the men who have had faith in Jesus have returned to the state of the first man in paradise; that is, have become immortal, innocent, and idle.

The doctrine does not concern itself too closely with the practical result of the redemption, in virtue of which the earth after Jesus' coming ought to have become once more, at least for believers, everywhere fertile, without need of human toil; sickness ought to have ceased, and mothers have borne children without pain;— since it is difficult to assure even believers who are worn by excessive labor and broken down by suffering, that toil is light, and suffering easy to endure.

But that portion of the doctrine which proclaims the abrogation of death and of sin, is affirmed with redoubled emphasis. It is asserted that the dead continue to live. And as the dead cannot bear witness that they are dead or prove that they are living (just as a stone is unable to affirm either that it can or cannot speak), this absence of denial is admitted as proof, and it is affirmed that dead men are not dead. It is affirmed with still more solemnity and assurance that, since the coming of Jesus, the man who has faith in him is free from sin; that is, that since the coming of Jesus, it is no longer necessary that man should guide his life by reason, and choose what is best for himself. He has only to believe that Jesus has redeemed his sins and he then becomes infallible, that is, perfect. According to this doctrine, men ought to believe that reason is powerless, and that for this cause they are without sin, that is, cannot err. A faithful believer ought to be convinced that since the coming of Jesus, the earth brings forth without labor, that childbirth no longer entails suffering, that diseases no longer exist, and that death and sin, that is, error, are destroyed; in a word, that what is, is not, and what is not, is.

Such is the rigorously logical theory of Christian theology. This doctrine, by itself, seems to be innocent. But deviations from truth are never inoffensive, and the significance of their consequences is in proportion to the importance of the subject to which these errors are applied. And here the subject at issue is the whole life of man. What this doctrine calls the true life, is a life of personal happiness, without sin, and eternal; that is, a life that no one has ever known, and which does not exist. But the life that is, the only life that we know, the life that we live and that all humanity lives and has lived, is, according to this doctrine, a degraded and evil existence, a mere phantasmagoria of the happy life which is our due.

Of the struggle between animal instincts and reason, which is the essence of human life, this doctrine takes no account. The struggle that Adam underwent in paradise, in deciding whether to eat or not to eat the fruit of the tree of knowledge, is, according to this doctrine, no longer within the range of human experience. The question was decided, once for all, by Adam in paradise. Adam sinned for all; in other words, he did wrong, and all men are irretrievably degraded; and all our efforts to live by reason are vain and even impious. This I ought to know, for I am irreparably bad. My salvation does not depend upon living by the light of reason, and, after distinguishing between good and evil, choosing the good; no, Adam, once for all, sinned for me, and Jesus, once for all, has atoned for the wrong committed by Adam; and so I ought, as a looker-on, to mourn over the fall of Adam and rejoice at the redemption through Jesus.

All the love for truth and goodness in the heart of man, all his efforts to illuminate his spiritual life by the light of reason, are not only of slight importance, according to this doctrine; they are a temptation, an incitement to pride. Life as it is upon this earth, with all its joys and its splendors, its struggles of reason with darkness,—the life of all men that have lived before me, my own life with its inner struggles and triumphs,—all this is not the true life; it is the fallen life, a life irretrievably bad. The true life, the life without sin, is only in faith, that is, in imagination, that is, in lunacy.

Let any one break the habit contracted from infancy of believing in all this; let him look boldly at this doctrine as it is; let him endeavor to put himself in the position of a man without prejudice, educated independently of this doctrine—and then let him ask himself if this doctrine would not appear to such a man as a product of absolute insanity.

However strange and shocking all this might appear to me, I was obliged to examine into it, for here alone I found the explanation of the objection, so devoid of logic and common-sense, that I heard everywhere with regard to the impossibility of practising the doctrine of Jesus: It is admirable, and would give true happiness to men, but men are not able to obey it.

Only a conviction that reality does not exist, and that the nonexistent is real, could lead men to this surprising contradiction. And this false conviction I found in the pseudo-Christian religion which men had been teaching for fifteen hundred years.

The objection that the doctrine of Jesus is excellent but impracticable, comes not only from believers, but from sceptics, from those who do not believe, or think that they do not believe, in the dogmas of the fall of man and the redemption; from men of science and philosophers who consider themselves free from all prejudice. They believe, or imagine that they believe, in nothing, and so consider themselves as above such a superstition as the dogma of the fall and the redemption. At first it seemed to me that all such persons had serious motives for denying the possibility of practising the doctrine of Jesus. But when I came to look into the source of their negation, I was convinced that the sceptics, in common with the believers, have a false conception of life; to them life is not what it is, but what they imagine it ought to be,—and this conception rests upon the same foundation as does that of the believers. It is true that the sceptics, who pretend to believe in nothing, believe not in God, or in Jesus, or in Adam; but they believe in a fundamental idea which is at the basis of their misconception,—in the rights of man to a life of happiness,—much more firmly than do the theologians.

In vain do science and philosophy pose as the arbiters of the human mind, of which they are in fact only the servants. Religion has provided a conception of life, and science travels in the beaten path. Religion reveals the meaning of life, and science only applies this meaning to the course of circumstances. And so, if religion falsifies the meaning of human life, science, which builds upon the same foundation, can only make manifest the same fantastic ideas.

According to the doctrine of the Church, men have a right to happiness, and this happiness is not the result of their own efforts, but of external causes. This conception has become the base of science and philosophy. Religion, science, and public opinion all unite in telling us that the life we now live is bad, and at the same time they affirm that the doctrine which teaches us how we can succeed in ameliorating life by becoming better, is an impracticable doctrine. Religion says that the doctrine of Jesus, which provides a reasonable method for the improvement of life by our own efforts, is impracticable because Adam fell and the world was plunged into sin. Philosophy says that the doctrine of Jesus is impracticable because human life is developed according to laws that are independent of the human will. In other words, the conclusions of science and philosophy are exactly the same as the conclusion reached by religion in the dogmas of original sin and the redemption.

There are two leading theses at the basis of the doctrine of the redemption: (1) the normal life of man is a life of happiness, but our life on earth is one of misery, and it can never be bettered by our own efforts; (2) our salvation is in faith, which enables us to escape from this life of misery. These two theses are the source of the religious conceptions of the believers and sceptics who make up our pseudo-Christian societies. The second thesis gave birth to the Church and its organization; from the first is derived the received tenets of public opinion and our political and philosophical theories. The germ of all political and philosophical theories that seek to justify the existing order of things—such as Hegelianism and its offshoots—is in this second thesis. Pessimism, which demands of life what it cannot give and then denies its value, has also its origin in the same dogmatic proposition. Materialism, with its strange and enthusiastic affirmation that man is the product of natural forces and nothing more, is the legitimate result of the doctrine that teaches that life on earth is a degraded existence. Spiritism, with its learned adherents, is the best proof we have that the conclusions of philosophy and science are based upon the religious doctrine of that eternal happiness which should be the natural heritage of man.

This false conception of life has had a deplorable influence upon all reasonable human activity. The dogma of the fall and the redemption has debarred man from the most important and legitimate field for the exercise of his powers, and has deprived him entirely of the idea that he can of himself do anything to make his life happier or better. Science and philosophy, proudly believing themselves hostile to pseudo-Christianity, only carry out its decrees. Science and philosophy concern themselves with everything except the theory that man can do anything to make himself better or happier. Ethical and moral instruction have disappeared from our pseudo-Christian society without leaving a trace.

Believers and sceptics who concern themselves so little with the problem how to live, how to make use of the reason with which we are endowed, ask why our earthly life is not what they imagine it ought to be, and when it will become what they wish. This singular phenomenon is due to the false doctrine which has penetrated into the very marrow of humanity. The effects of the knowledge of good and evil, which man so unhappily acquired in paradise, do not seem to have been very lasting; for, neglecting the truth that life is only a solution of the contradictions between animal instincts and reason, he stolidly refrains from applying his reason to the discovery of the historical laws that govern his animal nature.

Excepting the philosophical doctrines of the pseudo-Christian world, all the philosophical and religious doctrines of which we have knowledge—Judaism, the doctrine of Confucius, Buddhism, Brahmanism, the wisdom of the Greeks—all aim to regulate human life, and to enlighten men with regard to what they must do to improve their condition. The doctrine of Confucius teaches the perfecting of the individual; Judaism, personal fidelity to an alliance with God; Buddhism, how to escape from a life governed by animal instincts; Socrates taught the perfecting of the individual through reason; the Stoics recognized the independence of reason as the sole basis of the true life.

The reasonable activity of man has always been—it could not be otherwise—to light by the torch of reason his progress toward beatitude. Philosophy tells us that free-will is an illusion, and then boasts of the boldness of such a declaration. Free-will is not only an illusion; it is an empty word invented by theologians and experts in criminal law; to refute it would be to undertake a battle with a wind-mill. But reason, which illuminates our life and impels us to modify our actions, is not an illusion, and its authority can never be denied. To obey reason in the pursuit of good is the substance of the teachings of all the masters of humanity, and it is the substance of the doctrine of Jesus; it is reason itself, and we cannot deny reason by the use of reason.

Making use of the phrase "son of man," Jesus teaches that all men have a common impulse toward good and toward reason, which leads to good. It is superfluous to attempt to prove that "son of man" means "Son of God." To understand by the words "son of man" anything different from what they signify is to assume that Jesus, to say what he wished to say, intentionally made use of words which have an entirely different meaning. But even if, as the Church says, "son of man" means "Son of God," the phrase "son of man" applies none the less to man, for Jesus himself called all men "the sons of God."

The doctrine of the "son of man" finds its most complete expression in the interview with Nicodemus. Every man, Jesus says, aside from his consciousness of his material, individual life and of his birth in the flesh, has also a consciousness of a spiritual birth (John iii. 5, 6, 7), of an inner liberty, of something within;

this comes from on high, from the infinite that we call God (John iii. 14-17); now it is this inner consciousness born of God, the son of God in man, that we must possess and nourish if we would possess true life. The son of man is homogeneous (of the same race) with God.

Whoever lifts up within himself this son of God, whoever identifies his life with the spiritual life, will not deviate from the true way. Men wander from the way because they do not believe in this light which is within them, the light of which John speaks when he says, "*In him was life; and the life was the light of men.*" Jesus tells us to lift up the son of man, who is the son of God, for a light to all men. When we have lifted up the son of man, we shall then know that we can do nothing without his guidance (John viii. 28). Asked, "Who is this son of man?" Jesus answers:—

"*Yet a little while is the light in you. Walk while ye have the light, lest darkness come upon you: for he that walketh in darkness knoweth not whither he goeth.*" (John xii. 35.)

The son of man is the light in every man that ought to illuminate his life. "*Take heed therefore, that the light which is in thee be not darkness,*" is Jesus' warning to the multitude (Luke xi. 35).

In all the different ages of humanity we find the same thought, that man is the receptacle of the divine light descended from heaven, and that this light is reason, which alone should be the object of our worship, since it alone can show the way to true well-being. This has been said by the Brahmins, by the Hebrew prophets, by Confucius, by Socrates, by Marcus Aurelius, by Epictetus, and by all the true sages,—not by compilers of philosophical theories, but by men who sought goodness for themselves and for others. And yet we declare, in accordance with the dogma of the redemption, that it is entirely superfluous to think of the light that is in us, and that we ought not to speak of it at all!

We must, say the believers, study the three persons of the Trinity; we must know the nature of each of these persons, and what sacraments we ought or ought not to perform, for our salvation depends, not on our own efforts, but on the Trinity and the regular performance of the sacraments. We must, say the sceptics, know the laws by which this infinitesimal particle of matter was evolved in infinite space and infinite time; but it is absurd to believe that by reason alone we can secure true wellbeing, because the amelioration of man's condition does not depend upon man himself, but upon the laws that we are trying to discover.

I firmly believe that, a few centuries hence, the history of what we call the scientific activity of this age will be a prolific subject for the hilarity and pity of future generations. For a number of centuries, they will say, the scholars of the western portion of a great continent were the victims of epidemic insanity; they imagined themselves to be the possessors of a life of eternal beatitude, and they busied themselves with divers lucubrations in which they sought to determine in what way this life could be realized, without doing anything themselves, or even concerning themselves with what they ought to do to ameliorate the life which they already had. And what to the future historian will seem much more melancholy, it will be found that this group of men had once had a master who had taught them a number of simple and clear rules, pointing out what they must do to render their lives happy,—and that the words of this master had been construed by some to mean that he would come on a cloud to reorganize human society, and by others as admirable doctrine, but impracticable, since human life was not what they conceived it to be, and consequently was not worthy of consideration; as to human reason, it must concern itself with the study of the laws of an imaginary existence, without concerning itself about the welfare of the individual man.

The Church says that the doctrine of Jesus cannot be literally practised here on earth, because this earthly life is naturally evil, since it is only a shadow of the true life. The best way of living is to scorn this earthly existence, to be guided by faith (that is, by imagination) in a happy and eternal life to come, and to continue to live a bad life here and to pray to the good God.

Philosophy, science, and public opinion all say that the doctrine of Jesus is not applicable to human life as it now is, because the life of man does not depend upon the light of reason, but upon general laws; hence it is useless to try to live absolutely conformable to reason; we must live as we can with the firm conviction that according to the laws of historical and sociological progress, after having lived very imperfectly for a very long time, we shall suddenly find that our lives have become very good.

People come to a farm; they find there all that is necessary to sustain life,—a house well furnished, barns filled with grain, cellars and store-rooms well stocked with provisions, implements of husbandry, horses and cattle,—in a word, all that is needed for a life of comfort and ease. Each wishes to profit by this abundance, but each for himself, without thinking of others, or of those who may come after him. Each wants the whole for himself, and begins to seize upon all that he can possibly grasp. Then begins a veritable pillage; they fight for the possession of the spoils; oxen and sheep are slaughtered; wagons and other implements are broken up into firewood; they fight for the milk and grain; they grasp more than they can consume. No one is able to sit down to the tranquil enjoyment of what he has, lest another take away the spoils already secured, to surrender them in turn to some one stronger. All these people leave the farm, bruised and famished. Thereupon the Master puts everything to rights, and arranges matters so that one may live there in peace. The farm is again a treasury of abundance. Then comes another group of seekers, and the same struggle and tumult is repeated, till these in their turn go away bruised and angry, cursing the Master for providing so little and so ill. The good Master is not discouraged; he again provides for all that is needed to sustain life,—and the same incidents are repeated over and over again.

Finally, among those who come to the farm, is one who says to his companions: "Comrades, how foolish we are! see how abundantly everything is supplied, how well everything is arranged! There is enough here for us and for those who will come after us; let us act in a reasonable manner. Instead of robbing each other, let us help one another. Let us work, plant, care for the dumb animals, and every one will be satisfied." Some of the company understand what this wise person says; they cease from fighting and from robbing one another, and begin to work. But others, who have not heard the words of the wise man, or who distrust him, continue their former pillage of the Master's goods. This condition of things lasts for a long time. Those who have followed the counsels of the wise man say to those about them: "Cease from fighting, cease from wasting the Master's goods; you will be better off for doing so; follow the wise man's advice." Nevertheless, a great many do not hear and will not believe, and matters go on very much as they did before.

All this is natural, and will continue as long as people do not believe the wise man's words. But, we are told, a time will come when every one on the farm will listen to and understand the words of the wise man, and will realize that God spoke through his lips, and that the wise man was himself none other than God in person; and all will have faith in his words. Meanwhile, instead of living according to the advice of the wise man, each struggles for his own, and they slay each other without pity, saying, "The struggle for existence is inevitable; we cannot do otherwise."

What does it all mean? Even the beasts graze in the fields without interfering with each other's needs, and men, after having learned the conditions of the true life, and after being convinced that God himself has shown them how to live the true life, follow still their evil ways, saying that it is impossible to live otherwise. What should we think of the people at the farm if, after having heard the words of the wise man, they had continued to live as before, snatching the bread from each other's mouths, fighting, and trying to grasp everything, to their own loss? We should say that they had misunderstood the wise man's words, and imagined things to be different from what they really were. The wise man said to them, "Your life here is bad; amend your ways, and it will become good." And they imagined that the wise man had condemned their life on the farm, and had promised them another and a better life somewhere else. They decided that the farm was only a temporary dwelling-place, and that it was not worth while to try to live well there; the important thing was not to be cheated out of the other life promised them elsewhere. This is the only way in which we can explain the strange conduct of the people on the farm, of whom some believed that the wise man was God, and others that he was a man of wisdom, but all continued to live as before in defiance of the wise man's words. They understood everything but the one significant truth in the wise man's teachings,—that they must work out for themselves their own peace and happiness there on the farm, which they took for a temporary abode thinking all the time of the better life they were to possess elsewhere.

Here is the origin of the strange declaration that the precepts of the wise man were admirable, even divine, but that they were difficult to practise.

Oh, if men would only cease from evil ways while waiting for the Christ to come in his chariot of fire to their aid; if they would only cease to invoke the law of the differentiation or integration of forces, or any historical law whatever! None will come to their aid if they do not aid themselves. And to aid ourselves to a better life, we need expect nothing from heaven or from earth; we need only to cease from ways that result in our own loss.

CHAPTER VIII.

IF it be admitted that the doctrine of Jesus is perfectly reasonable, and that it alone can give to men true happiness, what would be the condition of a single follower of that doctrine in the midst of a world that did not practise it at all? If all men would decide at the same time to obey, its practice would then be possible. But one man alone cannot act in defiance of the whole world; and so we hear continually this plea: "If, among men who do not practise the doctrine of Jesus, I alone obey it; if I give away all that I possess; if I turn the other cheek; if I refuse to take an oath or to go to war, I should find myself in profound isolation; if I did not die of hunger, I should be beaten; if I survived that, I should be cast into prison; I should be shot, and all the happiness of my life—my life itself—would be sacrificed in vain."

This plea is founded upon the doctrine of *quid pro quo*, which is the basis of all arguments against the possibility of practising the doctrine of Jesus. It is the current objection, and I sympathized with it in common with all the rest of the world, until I finally broke entirely away from the dogmas of the Church which prevented me from understanding the true significance of the doctrine of Jesus. Jesus prepared his doctrine as a means of salvation from the life of perdition organized by men contrary to his precepts; and I declared that I should be very glad to follow this doctrine if it were not for fear of this very perdition. Jesus offered me the true remedy against a life of perdition, and I clung to the life of perdition! from which it was plain that I did not consider this life as a life of perdition, but as something good, something real. The conviction that my personal, worldly life was something real and good constituted the misunderstanding, the obstacle, that prevented me from comprehending Jesus' doctrine. Jesus knew the disposition of men to regard their personal, worldly life as real and good, and so, in a series of apothegms and parables, he taught them that they had no right to life, and that they were given life only that they might assure themselves of the true life by renouncing their worldly and fantastic organization of existence.

To understand what is meant by "saving" one's life, according to the doctrine of Jesus, we must first understand what the prophets, what Solomon, what Buddha, what all the wise men of the world have said about the personal life of man. But, as Pascal says, we cannot endure to think upon this theme, and so we carry always before us a screen to conceal the abyss of death, toward which we are constantly moving. It suffices to reflect on the isolation of the personal life of man, to be convinced that this life, in so far as it is personal, is not only of no account to each separately, but that it is a cruel jest to heart and reason. To understand the doctrine of Jesus, we must, before all, return to ourselves, reflect soberly, undergo the μετάνοια of which John the Baptist, the precursor of Jesus, speaks, when addressing himself to men of clouded judgment. "Repent" (such was his preaching); "repent, have another mind, or you shall all perish. The axe is laid unto the root of the trees. Death and perdition await each one of you. Be warned, turn back, repent." And Jesus declared, "*Except ye repent, ye shall all likewise perish.*" When Jesus was told of the death of the Galileans massacred by Pilate, he said:—

"*Suppose ye that these Galileans were sinners above all the Galileans, because they suffered such things? I tell you, Nay: but, except ye repent, ye shall all likewise perish. Or those eighteen upon whom the tower in Siloam fell, and slew them, think ye that they were sinners above all men that dwelt in Jerusalem? I tell you. Nay: but, except ye repent, ye shall all likewise perish.*" (Luke xiii. 1-5.)

If he had lived in our day, in Russia, he would have said: "Think you that those who perished in the circus at Berditchef or on the slopes of Koukouyef were sinners above all others? I tell you, No; but you, if you do not repent, if you do not arouse yourselves, if you do not find in your life that which is imperishable, you also shall perish. You are horrified by the death of those crushed by the tower, burned in the circus; but your death, equally as frightful and as inevitable, is here, before you. You are wrong to conceal it or to forget it; unlocked for, it is only more hideous."

To the people of his own time he said:—

"*When ye see a cloud rise out of the west, straightway ye say, There cometh a shower; and so it is. And when ye see the south wind blow, ye say, There will be heat; and it cometh to pass. Ye hypocrites, ye can discern the face of the sky and of the earth; but how is it that ye do not discern this time? Yea, and why even of yourselves judge ye not what is right?*" (Luke xii. 54-57.)

We know how to interpret the signs of the weather; why, then, do we not see what is before us? It is in vain that we fly from danger, and guard our material life by all imaginable means; in spite of all, death is before us, if not in one way, then in another; if not by massacre, or the falling of a tower, then in our beds, amidst much greater suffering.

Make a simple calculation, as those do who undertake any worldly project, any enterprise whatever, such as the construction of a house, or the purchase of an estate, such as those make who labor with the hope of seeing their calculations realized.

"*For which of you intending to build a tower, sitteth not down first, and counteth the cost whether he have sufficient to finish it? Lest haply, after he hath laid the foundation, and is not able to finish it, all that behold it begin to mock him, saying, This man began to build, and was not able to finish. Or what king, going to make war against another king, sitteth not down first and consulteth whether he be able with ten thousand to meet him that cometh against him with twenty thousand?*" (Luke xiv. 28-31.)

Is it not the act of a madman to labor at what, under any circumstances, one can never finish? Death will always come before the edifice of worldly prosperity can be completed. And if we knew beforehand that, however we may struggle with death, it is not we, but death, that will triumph; is it not an indication that we ought not to struggle with death, or to set our hearts upon that which will surely perish, but to seek to perform the task whose results cannot be destroyed by our inevitable departure?

"*And he said unto his disciples, Therefore I say unto you, Take no thought for your life what ye shall eat; neither for the body, what ye shall put on. The life is more than meat and the body is more than raiment. Consider the ravens: for they neither sow nor reap; which neither have storehouse nor barn; and God feedeth them: How much more are ye better than the fowls? And which of you with taking thought can add to his stature one cubit? If ye then be not able to do that thing which is least, why take ye thought for the rest? Consider the lilies how they grow: they toil not, they spin not; and yet I say unto you that Solomon in all his glory was not arrayed like one of these.*" (Luke xii. 22-27.)

Whatever pains we may take for our nourishment, for the care of the body, we cannot prolong life by a single hour. Is it not folly to trouble ourselves about a thing that we cannot possibly accomplish? We know perfectly well that our material life will end with death, and we give ourselves up to evil to procure riches. Life cannot be measured by what we possess; if we think so, we only delude ourselves. Jesus tells us that the meaning of life does not lie in what we possess or in what we can accumulate, but in something entirely different. He says:—

"The ground of a certain rich man brought forth plentifully: And he thought within himself, saying, What shall I do, because I have no room where to bestow my fruits? And he said, This will I do: I will pull down my barns, and build greater; and there will I bestow all my fruits and my goods. And I will say to my soul, Soul, thou hast much goods lead up for many years; take thine ease, eat, drink, and be merry. But God said unto him, Thou fool, this night thy soul shall be required of thee: then whose shall those things be, which thou hast provided? So is he that layeth up treasure for himself, and is not rich toward God." (Luke xii. 16-21.)

Death threatens us every moment; Jesus says:—

"Let your loins be girded about, and your lights burning; and ye yourselves like unto men that wait for their lord, when he will return from the wedding; that, when he cometh and knocketh, they may open unto him immediately. Blessed are those servants, whom the lord when he cometh shall find watching; ...And if he shall come in the second watch, or come in the third watch, and find them so, blessed are those servants. And this know, that if the goodman of the house had known what hour the thief would come, he would have watched, and not have suffered his house to be broken through. Be ye therefore ready also: for the son of man cometh at an hour when ye think not." (Luke xii. 35-40.)

The parable of the virgins waiting for the bridegroom, that of the consummation of the age and the last judgment, as the commentators all agree, are designed to teach that death awaits us at every moment. Death awaits us at every moment. Life is passed in sight of death. If we labor for ourselves alone, for our personal future, we know that what awaits us in the future is death. And death will destroy all the fruits of our labor. Consequently, a life for self can have no meaning. The reasonable life is different; it has another aim than the poor desires of a single individual. The reasonable life consists in living in such a way that life cannot be destroyed by death. We are troubled about many things, but only one thing is necessary.

From the moment of his birth, man is menaced by an inevitable peril, that is, by a life deprived of meaning, and a wretched death, if he does not discover the thing essential to the true life. Now it is precisely this one thing which insures the true life that Jesus reveals to men. He invents nothing, he promises nothing through divine power; side by side with this personal life, which is a delusion, he simply reveals to men the truth.

In the parable of the husbandmen (Matt. xxi. 33-42), Jesus explains the cause of that blindness in men which conceals the truth from them, and which impels them to take the apparent for the real, their personal life for the true life. Certain men, having leased a vineyard, imagined that they were its masters. And this delusion leads them into a series of foolish and cruel actions, which ends in their exile. So each one of us imagines that life is his personal property, and that he has a right to enjoy it in such a way as may seem to him good, without recognizing any obligation to others. And the inevitable consequence of this delusion is a series of foolish and cruel actions followed by exclusion from life. And as the husbandmen killed the servants and at last the son of the householder, thinking that the more cruel they were, the better able they would be to gain their ends, so we imagine that we shall obtain the greatest security by means of violence.

Expulsion, the inevitable sentence visited upon the husbandmen for having taken to themselves the fruits of the vineyard, awaits also all men who imagine that the personal life is the true life. Death expels them from life; they are replaced by others, as a consequence of the error which led them to misconceive the meaning of life. As the husbandmen forgot, or did not wish to remember, that they had received a vineyard already hedged about and provided with winepress and tower, that some one had labored for them and expected them to labor in their turn for others;—so the men who would live for themselves forget, or do not wish to remember, all that has been done for them during their life; they forget that they are under an obligation to labor in their turn, and that all the blessings of life which they enjoy are fruits that they ought to divide with others.

This new manner of looking at life, this μετάνοια, or repentance, is the corner-stone of the doctrine of Jesus. According to this doctrine, men ought to understand and feel that they are insolvent, as the husbandmen should have understood and felt that they were insolvent to the householder, unable to pay the debt contracted by generations past, present, and to come, with the overruling power. They ought to feel that every hour of their existence is only a mortgage upon this debt, and that every man who, by a selfish life, rejects this obligation, separates himself from the principle of life, and so forfeits life. Each one should remember that in striving to save his own life, his personal life, he loses the true life, as Jesus so many times said. The true life is the life which adds something to the store of happiness accumulated by past generations, which increases this heritage in the present, and hands it down to the future. To take part in this true life, man should renounce his personal will for the will of the Father, who gives this life to man. In John viii. 35, we read:—

"*And the servant abideth not in the house forever: but the son abideth forever.*"

That is, only the son who observes the will of the father shall have eternal life. Now, the will of the Father of Life is not the personal, selfish life, but the filial life of the son of man; and so a man saves his life when he considers it as a pledge, as something confided to him by the Father for the profit of all, as something with which to live the life of the son of man.

A man, about to travel into a far country, called his servants together and divided among them his goods. Although receiving no precise instructions as to the manner in which they were to use these goods, some of the servants understood that the goods still belonged to the master, and that they ought to employ them for the master's gain. And the servants who had labored for the good of the master were rewarded, while the others, who had not so labored, were despoiled even of what they had received. (Matt. xxv. 14-46.)

The life of the son of man has been given to all men, and they know not why. Some of them understand that life is not for their personal use, but that they must use it for the good of the son of man; others, feigning not to understand the true object of life, refuse to labor for the son of man; and those that labor for the true life will be united with the source of life; those that do not so labor, will lose the life they already have. Jesus tells us in what the service of the son of man consists and what will be the recompense of that service. The son of man, endowed with kingly authority, will call upon the faithful to inherit the true life; they have fed the hungry, given drink to the thirsty, clothed and consoled the wretched, and in so doing they have ministered to the son of man, who is the same in all men; they have not lived the personal life, but the life of the son of man, and they are given the life eternal.

According to all the Gospels, the object of Jesus' teaching was the life eternal. And, strange as it may seem, Jesus, who is supposed to have been raised in person, and to have promised a general resurrection,—Jesus not only said nothing in affirmation of individual resurrection and individual immortality beyond the grave, but on the contrary, every time that he met with this superstition (introduced at this period into the Talmud, and of which there is not a trace in the records of the Hebrew prophets), he did not fail to deny its truth. The Pharisees and the Sadducees were constantly discussing the subject of the resurrection of the dead. The Pharisees believed in the resurrection of the dead, in angels, and in spirits (Acts xxiii. 8), but the Sadducees did not believe in resurrection, or angel, or spirit. We do not know the source of the difference in belief, but it is certain that it was one of the polemical subjects among the secondary questions of the

Hebraic doctrine that were constantly under discussion in the Synagogues. And Jesus not only did not recognize the resurrection, but denied it every time he met with the idea. When the Sadducees demanded of Jesus, supposing that he believed with the Pharisees in the resurrection, to which of the seven brethren the woman should belong, he refuted with clearness and precision the idea of individual resurrection, saying that on this subject they erred, knowing neither the Scriptures nor the power of God. Those who are worthy of resurrection, he said, will remain like the angels of heaven (Mark xii. 21-24); and with regard to the dead:—

"*Have ye not read in the book of Moses, how in the bush God spake unto him, saying, I am the God of Abraham, and the God of Isaac, and the God of Jacob? He is not the God of the dead, but the God of the living: ye, therefore, do greatly err.*" (Mark xii. 26, 27.)

Jesus' meaning was that the dead are living in God. God said to Moses, "I am the God of Abraham, and of Isaac, and of Jacob." To God, all those who have lived the life of the son of man, are living. Jesus affirmed only this, that whoever lives in God, will be united to God; and he admitted no other idea of the resurrection. As to personal resurrection, strange as it may appear to those who have never carefully studied the Gospels for themselves, Jesus said nothing about it whatever.

If, as the theologians teach, the foundation of the Christian faith is the resurrection of Jesus, is it not strange that Jesus, knowing of his own resurrection, knowing that in this consisted the principal dogma of faith in him—is it not strange that Jesus did not speak of the matter at least once, in clear and precise terms? Now, according to the canonical Gospels, he not only did not speak of it in clear and precise terms; he did not speak of it at all, not once, not a single word.

The doctrine of Jesus consisted in the elevation of the son of man, that is, in the recognition on the part of man, that he, man, was the son of God. In his own individuality Jesus personified the man who has recognized the filial relation with God. He asked his disciples whom men said that he was—the son of man? His disciples replied that some took him for John the Baptist, and some for Elijah. Then came the question, "*But whom say ye that I am?*" And Peter answered, "*Thou art the Messiah, the son of the living God.*" Jesus responded, "*Flesh and blood hath not revealed it unto thee, but my Father which is in heaven;*" meaning that Peter understood, not through faith in human explanations, but because, feeling himself to be the son of God, he understood that Jesus was also the son of God. And after having explained to Peter that the true faith is founded upon the perception of the filial relation to God, Jesus charged his other disciples that they should tell no man that he was the Messiah. After this, Jesus told them that although he might suffer many things and be put to death, he, that is his doctrine, would be triumphantly re-established. And these words are interpreted as a prophecy of the resurrection (Matt. xvi. 13-21).

Of the thirteen passages which are interpreted as prophecies of Jesus in regard to his own resurrection, two refer to Jonah in the whale's belly, another to the rebuilding of the temple. The others affirm that the son of man shall not be destroyed; but there is not a word about the resurrection of Jesus. In none of these passages is the word "resurrection" found in the original text. Ask any one who is ignorant of theological interpretations, but who knows Greek, to translate them, and he will never agree with the received versions. In the original we find two different words, ἀνίστημι and ἐγείρω, which are rendered in the sense of resurrection; one of these words means to "re-establish"; the other means "to awaken, to rise up, to arouse one's self." But neither the one nor the other can ever, in any case, mean to "resuscitate"—to raise from the dead. With regard to these Greek words and the corresponding Hebrew word, *qum*, we have only to examine the scriptural passages where these words are employed, as they are very frequently, to see that in no case is the meaning "to resuscitate" admissible. The word *voskresnovit*, *auferstehn*, *resusciter*—"to resuscitate"— did not exist in the Greek or Hebrew tongues, for the reason that the conception corresponding to this word did not exist. To express the idea of resurrection in Greek or in Hebrew, it is necessary to employ a periphrasis, meaning, "is arisen, has awakened among the dead." Thus, in the Gospel of Matthew (xiv. 2) where reference is made to Herod's belief that John the Baptist had been resuscitated, we read, αὐτὸς ἠγέρθη ἀπὸ τῶν νεκρῶν, "has awakened among the dead." In the same manner, in Luke (xvi. 31), at the close of the parable of Lazarus, where it said that if men believe not the prophets, they would not believe even though one be resuscitated, we find the periphrasis, ἐάν τις ἐκ νεκρῶν ἀναστῇ, "if one arose among the dead." But, if in these passages the words "among the dead" were not added to the words "arose or awakened," the last two could never signify resuscitation. When Jesus spoke of himself, he did not once use the words "among the dead" in any of the passages quoted in support of the affirmation that Jesus foretold his own resurrection.

Our conception of the resurrection is so entirely foreign to any idea that the Hebrews possessed with regard to life, that we cannot even imagine how Jesus would have been able to talk to them of the resurrection, and of an eternal, individual life, which should be the lot of every man. The idea of a future eternal life comes neither from Jewish doctrine nor from the doctrine of Jesus, but from an entirely different source. We are obliged to believe that belief in a future life is a primitive and crude conception based upon a confused idea of the resemblance between death and sleep,—an idea common to all savage races.

The Hebraic doctrine (and much more the Christian doctrine) was far above this conception. But we are so convinced of the elevated character of this superstition, that we use it as a proof of the superiority of our doctrine to that of the Chinese or the Hindus, who do not believe in it at all. Not the theologians only, but the free-thinkers, the learned historians of religions, such as Tiele, and Max Müller, make use of the same argument. In their classification of religions, they give the first place to those which recognize the superstition of the resurrection, and declare them to be far superior to those not professing that belief. Schopenhauer boldly denounced the Hebraic religion as the most despicable of all religions because it contains not a trace of this belief. Not only the idea itself, but all means of expressing it, were wanting to the Hebraic religion. Eternal life is in Hebrew *hayail eolam*. By *olam* is meant the infinite, that which is permanent in the limits of time; *olam* also means "world" or "cosmos." Universal life, and much more *hayai leolam*, "eternal life," is, according to the Jewish doctrine, the attribute of God alone. God is the God of life, the living God. Man, according to the Hebraic idea, is always mortal. God alone is always living. In the Pentateuch, the expression "eternal life" is twice met with; once in Deuteronomy and once in Genesis. God is represented as saying:—

> "*See now that I, even I, am he,*
> *And there is no god with me:*
> *I kill, and I make alive;*
> *I have wounded, and I heal:*
> *And there is none that can deliver out of my hand.*
> *For I lift up my hand to heaven,*
> *And say, As I live forever.*"
> (Deut. xxxii. 39, 40.)

"*And Jehovah said, Behold, the man is become as one of us, to know good and evil; and now, lest he put forth his hand, and take also the tree of life, and live forever.*" (Gen. iii. 22.)

These two sole instances of the use of the expression "eternal life" in the Old Testament (with the exception of another instance in the apocryphal book of Daniel) determine clearly the Hebraic conception of the life of man and the life eternal. Life itself, according to the Hebrews, is eternal, is in God; but man is always mortal: it is his nature to be so. According to the Jewish doctrine, man as man, is mortal. He has life only as it passes from one generation to another, and is so perpetuated in a race. According to the Jewish doctrine, the faculty of life exists in the *people*. When God said, "Ye may live, and not die," he addressed these words to the people. The life that God breathed into man is mortal for each separate human being; this life is perpetuated from generation to generation, if men fulfil the union with God, that is, obey the conditions imposed by God. After having propounded the Law, and having told them that this Law was to be found not in heaven, but in their own hearts, Moses said to the people:—

"*See, I have set before thee this day life and good, and death and evil; in that I command thee this day to love the Eternal, to walk in his ways, and to keep his commandments, that thou mayest live.... I call heaven and earth to witness against you this day, that I have set before thee life and death, the blessing and the curse: therefore choose life, that thou mayest live, thou and thy seed: to love the Eternal, to obey his voice, and to cleave unto him: for he is thy life, and the length of thy days.*" (Deut. xxx. 15-19.)

The principal difference between our conception of human life and that possessed by the Jews is, that while we believe that our mortal life, transmitted from generation to generation, is not the true life, but a fallen life, a life temporarily depraved,—the Jews, on the contrary, believed this life to be the true and supreme good, given to man on condition that he obey the will of God. From our point of view, the transmission of the fallen life from generation to generation is the transmission of a curse; from the Jewish point of view, it is the supreme good to which man can attain, on condition that he accomplish the will of God. It is precisely upon the Hebraic conception of life that Jesus founded his doctrine of the true or eternal life, which he contrasted with the personal and mortal life. Jesus said to the Jews:—

"*Search the Scriptures; for in them ye think ye have eternal life: and they are they which testify of me.*" (John v. 39.)

To the young man who asked what he must do to have eternal life, Jesus said in reply, "*If thou wilt enter into life, keep the commandments.*" He did not say "the eternal life," but simply "the life" (Matt. xix. 17). To the same question propounded by the scribe, the answer was, "*This do, and thou shalt live*" (Luke x. 28), once more promising life, but saying nothing of eternal life. From these two instances, we know what Jesus meant by eternal life; whenever he made use of the phrase in speaking to the Jews, he employed it in exactly the same sense in which it was expressed in their own law,—the accomplishment of the will of God. In contrast with the life that is temporary, isolated, and personal, Jesus taught of the eternal life promised by God to Israel—with this difference, that while the Jews believed the eternal life was to be perpetuated solely by their chosen people, and that whoever wished to possess this life must follow the exceptional laws given by God to Israel,—the doctrine of Jesus holds that the eternal life is perpetuated in the son of man, and that to obtain it we must practise the commandments of Jesus, who summed up the will of God for all humanity.

As opposed to the personal life, Jesus taught us, not of a life beyond the grave, but of that universal life which comprises within itself the life of humanity, past, present, and to come. According to the Jewish doctrine, the personal life could be saved from death only by accomplishing the will of God as propounded in the Mosaic law. On this condition only the life of the Jewish race would not perish, but would pass from generation to generation of the chosen people of God. According to the doctrine of Jesus, the personal life is saved from death by the accomplishment of the will of God as propounded in the commandments of Jesus. On this condition alone the personal life does not perish, but becomes eternal and immutable, in union with the son of man. The difference is, that while the religion given by Moses was that of a people for a national God, the religion of Jesus is the expression of the aspirations of all humanity. The perpetuity of life in the posterity of a people is doubtful, because the people itself may disappear, and perpetuity depends upon a posterity in the flesh. Perpetuity of life, according to the doctrine of Jesus, is indubitable, because life, according to his doctrine, is an attribute of all humanity in the son of man who lives in harmony with the will of God.

If we believe that Jesus' words concerning the last judgment and the consummation of the age, and other words reported in the Gospel of John, are a promise of a life beyond the grave for the souls of men,—if we believe this, it is none the less true that his teachings in regard to the light of life and the kingdom of God have the same meaning for us that they had for his hearers eighteen centuries ago; that is, that the only real life is the life of the son of man conformable to the will of the Giver of Life. It is easier to admit this than to admit that the doctrine of the true life, conformable to the will of the Giver of Life, contains the promise of the immortality of life beyond the grave.

Perhaps it is right to think that man, after this terrestrial life passed in the satisfaction of personal desires, will enter upon the possession of an eternal personal life in paradise, there to taste all imaginable enjoyments; but to believe that this is so, to endeavor to persuade ourselves that for our good actions we shall be recompensed with eternal felicity, and for our bad actions punished with eternal torments,—to believe this, does not aid us in understanding the doctrine of Jesus, but, on the contrary, takes away the principal foundation of that doctrine. The entire doctrine of Jesus inculcates renunciation of the personal, imaginary life, and a merging of this personal life in the universal life of humanity, in the life of the son of man. Now the doctrine of the individual immortality of the soul does not impel us to renounce the personal life; on the contrary, it affirms the continuance of individuality forever.

The Jews, the Chinese, the Hindus, all men who do not believe in the dogma of the fall and the redemption, conceive of life as it is. A man lives, is united with a woman, engenders children, cares for them, grows old, and dies. His life continues in his children, and so passes on from one generation to another, like everything else in the world,—stones, metals, earth, plants, animals, stars. Life is life, and we must make the best of it.

To live for self alone, for the animal life, is not reasonable. And so men, from their earliest existence, have sought for some reason for living aside from the gratification of their own desires; they live for their children, for their families, for their nation, for humanity, for all that does not die with the personal life.

But according to the doctrine of the Church, human life, the supreme good that we possess, is but a very small portion of another life of which we are deprived for a season. Our life is not the life that God intended to give us or such as is our due. Our life is degenerate and fallen, a mere fragment, a mockery, compared with the real life to which we think ourselves entitled. The principal object of life is not to try to live this mortal life conformably to the will of the Giver of Life; or to render it eternal in the generations, as the Hebrews believed; or to identify ourselves with the will of God, as Jesus taught; no, it is to believe that after this unreal life the true life will begin.

Jesus did not speak of the imaginary life that we believe to be our due, and that God did not give to us for some unexplained reason. The theory of the fall of Adam, of eternal life in paradise, of an immortal soul breathed by God into Adam, was unknown to Jesus; he never spoke of it, never made the slightest allusion to its existence. Jesus spoke of life as it is, as it must be for all men; we speak of an imaginary life that has never existed. How, then, can we understand the doctrine of Jesus?

Jesus did not anticipate such a singular change of view in his disciples. He supposed that all men understood that the destruction of the personal life is inevitable, and he revealed to them an imperishable life. He offers true peace to them that suffer; but to those who believe that they are certain to possess more than Jesus gives, his doctrine can be of no value. How shall I persuade a man to toil in return for food and clothing if this man is persuaded that he already possesses great riches? Evidently he will pay no attention to my exhortations. So it is with regard to the doctrine of Jesus. Why should I toil for bread when I can be rich without labor? Why should I trouble myself to live this life according to the will of God when I am sure of a personal life for all eternity?

That Jesus Christ, as the second person of the Trinity, as God made manifest in the flesh, was the salvation of men; that he took upon himself the penalty for the sin of Adam and the sins of all men; that he atoned to the first person of the Trinity for the sins of humanity; that he instituted the Church and the sacraments for our salvation—believing this, we are saved, and shall enter into the possession of personal, eternal life beyond the grave. But meanwhile we cannot deny that he has saved and still saves men by revealing to them their inevitable loss, showing them that he is the way, the truth, and the life, the true way to life instead of the false way to the personal life that men had heretofore followed.

If there are any who doubt the life beyond the grave and salvation based upon redemption, no one can doubt the salvation of all men, and of each individual man, if they will accept the evidence of the destruction of the personal life, and follow the true way to safety by bringing their personal wills into harmony with the will of God. Let each man endowed with reason ask himself, What is life? and What is death? and let him try to give to life and death any other meaning than that revealed by Jesus, and he will find that any attempt to find in life a meaning not based upon the renunciation of self, the service of humanity, of the son of man, is utterly futile. It cannot be doubted that the personal life is condemned to destruction, and that a life conformable to the will of God alone gives the possibility of salvation. It is not much in comparison with the sublime belief in the future life! It is not much, but it is sure.

I am lost with my companions in a snow-storm. One of them assures me with the utmost sincerity that he sees a light in the distance, but it is only a mirage which deceives us both; we strive to reach this light, but we never can find it. Another resolutely brushes away the snow; he seeks and finds the road, and he cries to us, "Go not that way, the light you see is false, you will wander to destruction; here is the road, I feel it beneath my feet; we are saved." It is very little, we say. We had faith in that light that gleamed in our deluded eyes, that told us of a refuge, a warm shelter, rest, deliverance,—and now in exchange for it we have nothing but the road. Ah, but if we continue to travel toward the imaginary light, we shall perish; if we follow the road, we shall surely arrive at a haven of safety.

What, then, must I do if I alone understand the doctrine of Jesus, and I alone have trust in it among a people who neither understand it nor obey it? What ought I to do, to live like the rest of the world, or to live according to the doctrine of Jesus? I understood the doctrine of Jesus as expressed in his commandments, and I believed that the practice of these commandments would bring happiness to me and to all men. I understood that the fulfilment of these commandments is the will of God, the source of life. More than this, I saw that I should die like a brute after a farcical existence if I did not fulfil the will of God, and that the only chance of salvation lay in the fulfilment of His will. In following the example of the world about me, I should unquestionably act contrary to the welfare of all men, and, above all, contrary to the will of the Giver of Life; I should surely forfeit the sole possibility of bettering my desperate condition. In following the doctrine of Jesus, I should continue the work common to all men who had lived before me; I should contribute to the welfare of my fellows, and of those who were to live after me; I should obey the command of the Giver of Life; I should seize upon the only hope of salvation.

The circus at Berditchef is in flames. A crowd of people are struggling before the only place of exit,—a door that opens inward. Suddenly, in the midst of the crowd, a voice rings out: "Back, stand back from the door; the closer you press against it, the less the chance of escape; stand back; that is your only chance of safety!" Whether I am alone in understanding this command, or whether others with me also hear and understand, I have but one duty, and that is, from the moment I have heard and understood, to fall back from the door and to call upon every one to obey the voice of the saviour. I may be suffocated, I may be crushed beneath the feet of the multitude, I may perish; my sole chance of safety is to do the one thing necessary to gain an exit. And I can do nothing else. A saviour should be a saviour, that is, one who saves. And the salvation of Jesus is the true salvation. He came, he preached his doctrine, and humanity is saved.

The circus may burn in an hour, and those penned up in it may have no time to escape. But the world has been burning for eighteen hundred years; it has burned ever since Jesus said, "*I am come to send fire on the earth*;" and I suffer as it burns, and it will continue to burn until humanity is saved. Was not this fire kindled that men might have the felicity of salvation? Understanding this, I understood and believed that Jesus is not only the Messiah, that is, the Anointed One, the Christ, but that he is in truth the Saviour of the world. I know that he is the only way, that there is no other way for me or for those who are tormented with me in this life. I know, that for me as for all, there is no other safety than the fulfilment of the commandments of Jesus, who gave to all humanity the greatest conceivable sum of benefits.

Would there be great trials to endure? Should I die in following the doctrine of Jesus? This question did not alarm me. It might seem frightful to any one who does not realize the nothingness and absurdity of an isolated personal life, and who believes that he will never die. But I know that my life, considered in relation to my individual happiness, is, taken by itself, a stupendous farce, and that this meaningless existence will end in a stupid death. Knowing this, I have nothing to fear. I shall die as others die who do not observe the doctrine of Jesus; but my life and my death will have a meaning for myself and for others. My life and my death will have added something to the life and salvation of others, and this will be in accordance with the doctrine of Jesus.

CHAPTER IX.

LET all the world practise the doctrine of Jesus, and the reign of God will come upon earth; if I alone practise it, I shall do what I can to better my own condition and the condition of those about me. There is no salvation aside from the fulfilment of the doctrine of Jesus. But who will give me the strength to practise it, to follow it without ceasing, and never to fail? "*Lord, I believe; help thou mine unbelief.*" The disciples called upon Jesus to strengthen their faith. "*When I would do good*," says the apostle Paul, "*evil is present with me.*" It is hard to work out one's salvation.

A drowning man calls for aid. A rope is thrown to him, and he says: "Strengthen my belief that this rope will save me. I believe that the rope will save me; but help my unbelief." What is the meaning of this? If a man will not seize upon his only means of safety, it is plain that he does not understand his condition.

How can a Christian who professes to believe in the divinity of Jesus and of his doctrine, whatever may be the meaning that he attaches thereto, say that he wishes to believe, and that he cannot believe? God comes upon earth, and says, "Fire, torments, eternal darkness await you; and here is your salvation—fulfil my doctrine." It is not possible that a believing Christian should not believe and profit by the salvation thus offered to him; it is not possible that he should say, "Help my unbelief." If a man says this, he not only does not believe in his perdition, but he must be certain that he shall not perish.

A number of children have fallen from a boat into the water. For an instant their clothes and their feeble struggles keep them on the surface of the stream, and they do not realize their danger. Those in the boat throw out a rope. They warn the children against their peril, and urge them to grasp the rope (the parables of the woman and the piece of silver, the shepherd and the lost sheep, the marriage feast, the prodigal son, all have this meaning), but the children do not believe; they refuse to believe, not in the rope, but that they are in danger of drowning. Children as frivolous as themselves have assured them that they can continue to float gaily along even when the boat is far away. The children do not believe; but when their clothes are saturated, the strength of their little arms exhausted, they will sink and perish. This they do not believe, and so they do not believe in the rope of safety.

Just as the children in the water will not grasp the rope that is thrown to them, persuaded that they will not perish, so men who believe in the resurrection of the soul, convinced that there is no danger, do not practise the commandments of Jesus. They do not believe in what is certain, simply because they do believe in what is uncertain. It is for this cause they cry, "Lord, strengthen our faith, lest we perish." But this is impossible. To have the faith that will save them from perishing, they must cease to do what will lead them to perdition, and they must begin to do something for their own safety; they must grasp the rope of safety. Now this is exactly what they do not wish to do; they wish to persuade themselves that they will not perish, although they see their comrades perishing one after another before their very eyes. They wish to persuade themselves of the truth of what does not exist, and so they ask to be strengthened in faith. It is plain that they have not enough faith, and they wish for more.

When I understood the doctrine of Jesus, I saw that what these men call faith is the faith denounced by the apostle James:—

"What doth it profit, my brethren, if a man believe he hath faith, but hath not works? can that faith save him? If a brother or sister be naked and in lack of daily food, and one of you say unto them, Go in peace, be ye warmed and filled; and yet ye give them not the things needful to the body; what doth it profit? Even so faith, if it have not works, is dead in itself. But some one will say, Thou hast faith, and I have works: Shew me thy faith which is without works, and I, by my works, will show thee my faith. Thou believest there is one God; thou doest well: the demons also believe, and tremble. But wilt thou know, O vain man, that faith without works is dead? Was not Abraham our father justified by works when he offered up Isaac his son upon the altar? Thou seest that faith wrought with his works, and by works was faith made perfect.... Ye see that by works a man is justified, and not only by faith.... For as the body without the spirit is dead, so faith is dead without works." (James ii. 14-26.)

James says that the indication of faith is the acts that it inspires, and consequently that a faith which does not result in acts is of words merely, with which one cannot feed the hungry, or justify belief, or obtain salvation. A faith without acts is not faith. It is only a disposition to believe in something, a vain affirmation of belief in something in which one does not really believe. Faith, as the apostle James defines it, is the motive power of actions, and actions are a manifestation of faith.

The Jews said to Jesus: *"What signs shewest thou then, that we may see, and believe thee? what dost thou work?"* (John vi. 30. See also Mark xv. 32; Matt. xxvii. 42). Jesus told them that their desire was vain, and that they could not be made to believe what they did not believe. "*If I tell you,*" he said, "*ye will not believe*" (Luke xxii. 67); "*I told you, and ye believed not.... But ye believe not because ye are not of my sheep*" (John x. 25, 26).

The Jews asked exactly what is asked by Christians brought up in the Church; they asked for some outward sign which should make them believe in the doctrine of Jesus. Jesus explained that this was impossible, and he told them why it was impossible. He told them that they could not believe because they were not of his sheep; that is, they did not follow the road he had pointed out. He explained why some believed, and why others did not believe, and he told them what faith really was. He said: "*How can ye believe which receive your doctrine* (δόξα) *one of another, and seek not the doctrine that cometh only from God?*" (John v. 44).

To believe, Jesus says, we must seek for the doctrine that comes from God alone.

"*He that speaketh of himself seeketh* (to extend) *his own doctrine, δόξαν τὴν ἰδίαν, but he that seeketh* (to extend) *the doctrine of him that sent him, the same is true, and no untruth is in him.*" (John vii. 18.)

The doctrine of life, δόξα, is the foundation of faith, and actions result spontaneously from faith. But there are two doctrines of life: Jesus denies the one and affirms the other. One of these doctrines, a source of all error, consists of the idea that the personal life is one of the essential and real attributes of man. This doctrine has been followed, and is still followed, by the majority of men; it is the source of divergent beliefs and acts. The other doctrine, taught by Jesus and by all the prophets, affirms that our personal life has no meaning save through fulfilment of the will of God. If a man confess a doctrine that emphasizes his own personal life, he will consider that his personal welfare is the most important thing in the world, and he will consider riches, honors, glory, pleasure, as true sources of happiness; he will have a faith in accordance with his inclination, and his acts will always be in harmony with his faith. If a man confess a different doctrine, if he find the essence of life in fulfilment of the will of God in accordance with the example of Abraham and the teaching and example of Jesus, his faith will accord with his principles, and his acts will be conformable to his faith. And so those who believe that true happiness is to be found in the personal life can never have faith in the doctrine of Jesus. All their efforts to fix their faith upon it will be always vain. To believe in the doctrine of Jesus, they must look at life in an entirely different way. Their actions will coincide always with their faith and not with their intentions and their words.

In men who demand of Jesus that he shall work miracles we may recognize a desire to believe in his doctrine; but this desire never can be realized in life, however arduous the efforts to obtain it. In vain they pray, and observe the sacraments, and give in charity, and build churches, and convert others; they cannot follow the example of Jesus because their acts are inspired by a faith based upon an entirely different doctrine from that which they confess. They could not sacrifice an only son as Abraham was ready to do, although Abraham had no hesitation whatever as to what he should do, just as Jesus and his disciples were moved to give their lives for others, because such action alone constituted for them the true meaning of life. This incapacity to understand the substance of faith explains the strange moral state of men, who, acknowledging that they ought to live in accordance with the doctrine of Jesus, endeavor to live in opposition to this doctrine, conformably to their belief that the personal life is a sovereign good.

The basis of faith is the meaning that we derive from life, the meaning that determines whether we look upon life as important and good, or trivial and corrupt. Faith is the appreciation of good and of evil. Men with a faith based upon their own doctrines do not succeed at all in harmonizing this faith with the faith inspired by the doctrine of Jesus; and so it was with the early disciples. This misapprehension is frequently referred to in the Gospels in clear and decisive terms. Several times the disciples asked Jesus to strengthen their faith in his words (Matt. xx. 20-28; Mark x. 35-48). After the message, so terrible to every man who believes in the personal life and who seeks his happiness in the riches of this world, after the words, "*How hardly shall they that have riches enter into the kingdom of God*," and after words still more terrible for men who believe only in the personal life, "*Sell whatsoever thou hast and give to the poor*;" after these warning words Peter asked, "*Behold, we have forsaken all and followed thee; what shall we have therefore?*" Then James and John and, according to the Gospel of Matthew, their mother, asked him that they might be allowed to sit with him in glory. They asked Jesus to strengthen their faith with a promise of future recompense. To Peter's question Jesus replied with a parable (Matt. xx. 1-16); to James he replied that they did not know what they asked; that they asked what was impossible; that they did not understand the doctrine, which meant a renunciation of the personal life, while they demanded personal glory, a personal recompense; that they should drink the cup he drank of (that is, live as he lived), but to sit upon his right hand and upon his left was not his to give. And Jesus added that the great of this world had their profit and enjoyment of glory and personal power only in the worldly life; but that his disciples ought to know that the true meaning of human life is not in personal happiness, but in ministering to others; "*the son of man came not to be ministered unto, but to minister, and to give his life a ransom for many.*" In reply to the unreasonable demands which revealed their slowness to understand his doctrine, Jesus did not command his disciples to have faith in his doctrine, that is, to modify the ideas inspired by their own doctrine (he knew that to be impossible), but he explained to them the meaning of that life which is the basis of true faith, that is, taught them how to discern good from evil, the important from the secondary.

To Peter's question, "*What shall we receive?*" Jesus replies with the parable of the laborers in the vineyard (Matt. xx. 1-16), beginning with the words "*For the kingdom of heaven is like unto a man that is a householder*," and by this means Jesus explains to Peter that failure to understand the doctrine is the cause of lack of faith; and that remuneration in proportion to the amount of work done is important only from the point of view of the personal life.

This faith is based upon the presumption of certain imaginary rights; but a man has a right to nothing; he is under obligations for the good he has received, and so he can exact nothing. Even if he were to give up his whole life to the service of others, he could not pay the debt he has incurred, and so he cannot complain of injustice. If a man sets a value upon his rights to life, if he keeps a reckoning with the Overruling Power from whom he has received life, he proves simply that he does not understand the meaning of life. Men who have received a benefit act far otherwise. The laborers employed in the vineyard were found by the householder idle and unhappy; they did not possess life in the proper meaning of the term. And then the householder gave them the supreme welfare of life,—work. They accepted the benefits offered, and were discontented because their remuneration was not graduated according to their imaginary deserts. They did the work, believing in their false doctrine of life and work as a right, and consequently with an idea of the remuneration to which they were entitled. They did not understand that work is the supreme good, and that they should be thankful for the opportunity to work, instead of exacting payment. And so all men who look upon life as these laborers looked upon it, never can possess true faith. This parable of the laborers, related by Jesus in response to the request by his disciples that he strengthen their faith, shows more clearly than ever the basis of the faith that Jesus taught.

When Jesus told his disciples that they must forgive a brother who trespassed against them not only once, but seventy times seven times, the disciples were overwhelmed at the difficulty of observing this injunction, and said, "*Increase our faith*," just as a little while before they had asked, "*What shall we receive?*" Now they uttered the language of would-be Christians: "We wish to believe, but cannot; strengthen our faith that we may be saved; make us believe" (as the Jews said to Jesus when they demanded miracles); "either by miracles or promises of recompense, make us to have faith in our salvation."

The disciples said what we all say: "How pleasant it would be if we could live our selfish life, and at the same time believe that it is far better to practise the doctrine of God by living for others."

This disposition of mind is common to us all; it is contrary to the meaning of the doctrine of Jesus, and yet we are astonished at our lack of faith. Jesus disposed of this misapprehension by means of a parable illustrating true faith. Faith cannot come of confidence in his words; faith can come only of a consciousness of our condition; faith is based only upon the dictates of reason as to what is best to do in a given situation. He showed that this faith cannot be awakened in others by promises of recompense or threats of punishment, which can only arouse a feeble confidence that will fail at the first trial; but that the faith which removes mountains, the faith that nothing can shatter, is inspired by the consciousness of our inevitable loss if we do not profit by the salvation that is offered.

To have faith, we must not count on any promise of recompense; we must understand that the only way of escape from a ruined life is a life conformable to the will of the Master. He who understands this will not ask to be strengthened in his faith, but will work out his salvation without the need of any exhortation. The householder, when he comes from the fields with his workman, does not ask the latter to sit down at once to dinner, but directs him to attend first to other duties and to wait upon him, the master, and then to take his place at the table and dine. This the workman does without any sense of being wronged; he does not boast of his labor nor does he demand recognition or recompense, for he knows that labor is the inevitable condition of his existence and the true welfare of his life. So Jesus says that when we have done all that we are commanded to do, we have only fulfilled our duty. He who understands his relations to his master will understand that he has life only as he obeys the master's will; he will know in what his welfare consists, and he will have a faith that does not demand the impossible. This is the faith taught by Jesus, which has for its foundation a thorough perception of the true meaning of life. The source of faith is light:—

"*That was the true light which lighteth every man that cometh into the world. He was in the world, and the world was made by him, and the world knew him not. He came unto his own, and his own received him not. But as many as received him, to them gave he the right to become the children of God, even to them that believe on his name."* (John i. 9-12.)

"And this is the condemnation, that light is come into the world, and men loved darkness rather than light, because their deeds were evil. For every one that doeth ill hateth the light, and cometh not to the light, lest his works should be reproved. But he that doeth the truth cometh to the light, that his works may be made manifest, because they have been wrought in God." (John iii. 19-21.)

He who understands the doctrine of Jesus will not ask to be strengthened in his faith. The doctrine of Jesus teaches that faith is inspired by the light of truth. Jesus never asked men to have faith in his person; he called upon them to have faith in truth. To the Jews he said:—

"Ye seek to kill me, a man that hath told you the truth which I have heard of God." (John viii. 40.)

"Which of you convicteth me of sin? If I say truth, why do ye not believe me?" (John viii. 46.)

"To this end have I been born, and to this end am I come into the world, that I should bear witness unto the truth. Every one that is of the truth heareth my voice." (John xviii. 37.)

To his disciples he said:—

"I am the way, and the truth, and the life." (John xiv. 6.)

"The Father ... shall give you another Comforter, that he may be with you forever, even the Spirit of truth: whom the world cannot receive; for it beholdeth him not, neither knoweth him: ye know him; for he abideth with you, and shall be in you." (John xiv. 16, 17.)

Jesus' doctrine, then, is truth, and he himself is truth. The doctrine of Jesus is the doctrine of truth. Faith in Jesus is not belief in a system based upon his personality, but a consciousness of truth. No one can be persuaded to believe in the doctrine of Jesus, nor can any one be stimulated by any promised reward to practise it. He who understands the doctrine of Jesus will have faith in him, because this doctrine is true. He who knows the truth indispensable to his happiness must believe in it, just as a man who knows that he is drowning grasps the rope of safety. Thus, the question, What must I do to believe? is an indication that he who asks it does not understand the doctrine of Jesus.

CHAPTER X.

WE say, It is difficult to live according to the doctrine of Jesus! And why should it not be difficult, when by our organization of life we carefully hide from ourselves our true situation; when we endeavor to persuade ourselves that our situation is not at all what it is, but that it is something else? We call this faith, and regarding it as sacred, we endeavor by all possible means, by threats, by flattery, by falsehood, by stimulating the emotions, to attract men to its support. In this mad determination to believe what is contrary to sense and reason, we reach such a degree of aberration that we are ready to take as an indication of truth the very absurdity of the object in whose behalf we solicit the confidence of men. Are there not Christians who are ready to declare with enthusiasm "Credo quia absurdum," supposing that the absurd is the best medium for teaching men the truth? Not long ago a man of intelligence and great learning said to me that the Christian doctrine had no importance as a moral rule of life. Morality, he said, must be sought in the teachings of the Stoics and the Brahmins, and in the Talmud. The essence of the Christian doctrine is not in morality, he said, but in the theosophical doctrine propounded in its dogmas. According to this I ought to prize in the Christian doctrine not what it contains of eternal good to humanity, not its teachings indispensable to a reasonable life; I ought to regard as the most important element of Christianity that portion of it which it is impossible to understand, and therefore useless,—and this in the name of thousands of men who have perished for their faith.

We have a false conception of life, a conception based upon wrong doing and inspired by selfish passions, and we consider our faith in this false conception (which we have in some way attached to the doctrine of Jesus), as the most important and necessary thing with which we are concerned. If men had not for centuries maintained faith in what is untrue, this false conception of life, as well as the truth of the doctrine of Jesus, would long ago have been revealed.

It is a terrible thing to say, but it seems to me that if the doctrine of Jesus, and that of the Church which has been foisted upon it, had never existed, those who to-day call themselves Christians would be much nearer than they are to the truth of the doctrine of Jesus; that is, to the reasonable doctrine which teaches the true meaning of life. The moral doctrines of all the prophets of the world would not then be closed to them. They would have their little ideas of truth, and would regard them with confidence. Now, all truth is revealed, and this truth has so horrified those whose manner of life it condemned, that they have disguised it in falsehood, and men have lost confidence in the truth.

In our European society, the words of Jesus, "*To this end I am come into the world, that I shall bear witness unto the truth. Every one that is of the truth heareth my voice*,"—have been for a long time supplanted by Pilate's question, "*What is truth?*" This question, quoted as a bitter and profound irony against a Roman, we have taken as of serious purport, and have made of it an article of faith.

With us, all men live not only without truth, not only without the least desire to know truth, but with the firm conviction that, among all useless occupations, the most useless is the endeavor to find the truth that governs human life. The rule of life, the doctrine that all peoples, excepting our European societies, have always considered as the most important thing, the rule of which Jesus spoke as the one thing needful, is an object of universal disdain. An institution called the Church, in which no one, not even if he belong to it, really believes, has for a long time usurped the place of this rule.

The only source of light for those who think and suffer is hidden. For a solution of the questions, What am I? what ought I to do? I am not allowed to depend upon the doctrine of him who came to save; I am told to obey the authorities, and believe in the Church. But why is life so full of evil? Why so much wrongdoing? May I not abstain from taking part therein? Is it impossible to lighten this heavy load that weighs me down? The reply is that this is impossible, that the desire to live well and to help others to live well is only a temptation of pride; that one thing is possible,—to save one's soul for the future life. He who is not willing to take part in this miserable life may keep aloof from it; this way is open to all; but, says the doctrine of the Church, he who chooses this way can take no part in the life of the world; he ceases to live. Our masters tell us that there are only two ways,—to believe in and obey the powers that be, to participate in the organized evil about us, or to forsake the world and take refuge in convent or monastery; to take part in the offices of the Church, doing nothing for men, and declaring the doctrine of Jesus impossible to practise, accepting the iniquity of life sanctioned by the Church, or to renounce life for what is equivalent to slow suicide.

However surprising the belief that the doctrine of Jesus is excellent, but impossible of practice, there is a still more surprising tradition that he who wishes to practise this doctrine, not in word, but in deed, must retire from the world. This erroneous belief that it is better for a man to retire from the world than to expose himself to temptations, existed amongst the Hebrews of old, but is entirely foreign, not only to the spirit of Christianity, but to that of the Jewish religion. The charming and significant story of the prophet Jonah, which Jesus so loved to quote, was written in regard to this very error. The prophet Jonah, wishing to remain upright and virtuous, retires from the perverse companionship of men. But God shows him that as a prophet he ought to communicate to misguided men a knowledge of the truth, and so ought not to fly from men, but ought rather to live in communion with them. Jonah, disgusted with the depravity of the inhabitants of Nineveh, flies from the city; but he cannot escape his vocation. He is brought back, and the will of God is accomplished; the Ninevites receive the words of Jonah and are saved. Instead of rejoicing that he has been made the instrument of God's will, Jonah is angry, and condemns God for the mercy shown the Ninevites, arrogating to himself alone the exercise of reason and goodness. He goes out into the desert and makes him a shelter, whence he addresses his reproaches to God. Then a gourd comes up over Jonah and protects him from the sun, but the next day it withers. Jonah, smitten by the heat, reproaches God anew for allowing the gourd to wither. Then God says to him:—

"Thou hast had pity on the gourd, for the which thou hast not labored, neither madest it grow; which came up in a night, and perished in a night: and should I not have pity on Nineveh, that great city; wherein are more than six score thousand persons that cannot discern between their right hand and their left hand?"

Jesus knew this story, and often referred to it. In the Gospels we find it related how Jesus, after the interview with John, who had retired into the desert, was himself subjected to the same temptation before beginning his mission. He was led by the Spirit into the wilderness, and there tempted by the Devil (error), over which he triumphed and returned to Galilee. Thereafter he mingled with the most depraved men, and passed his life among publicans, Pharisees, and fishermen, teaching them the truth.

Even according to the doctrine of the Church, Jesus, as God in man, has given us the example of his life. All of his life that is known to us was passed in the company of publicans, of the downfallen, and of Pharisees. The principal commandments of Jesus are that his followers shall love others and spread his doctrine. Both exact constant communion with the world. And yet the deduction is made that the doctrine of Jesus permits retirement from the world. That is, to imitate Jesus we may do exactly contrary to what he taught and did himself.

As the Church explains it, the doctrine of Jesus offers itself to men of the world and to dwellers in monasteries, not as a rule of life for bettering one's own condition and the condition of others, but as a doctrine which teaches the man of the world how to live an evil life and at the same time gain for himself another life, and the monk how to render existence still more difficult than it naturally is. But Jesus did not teach this. Jesus taught the truth, and if metaphysical truth is the truth, it will remain such in practice. If life in God is the only true life, and is in itself profitable, then it is so here in this world in spite of all that may happen. If in this world a life in accordance with the doctrine of Jesus is not profitable, his doctrine cannot be true.

Jesus did not ask us to pass from better to worse, but, on the contrary, from worse to better. He had pity upon men, who to him were like sheep without a shepherd. He said that his disciples would be persecuted for his doctrine, and that they must bear the persecutions of the world with resolution. But he did not say that those who followed his doctrine would suffer more than those who followed the world's doctrine; on the contrary, he said that those who followed the world's doctrine would be wretched, and that those who followed his doctrine would have joy and peace. Jesus did not teach salvation by faith in asceticism or voluntary torture, but he taught us a way of life which, while saving us from the emptiness of the personal life, would give us less of suffering and more of joy. Jesus told men that in practising his doctrine among unbelievers they would be, not more unhappy, but, on the contrary, much more happy, than those who did not practise it. There was, he said, one infallible rule, and that was to have no care about the worldly life. When Peter said to Jesus, "*We have forsaken all, and followed thee; what then shall we have?*" Jesus replied:—

"*There is no man that hath left house, or brethren, or sisters, or mother, or father, or children, or lands, for my sake, and for the gospel's sake, but he shall receive a hundred fold more in this time, houses, and brethren, and sisters, and mothers, and children, and lands, with persecutions; and in the age to come eternal life.*" (Mark x. 28-30.)

Jesus declared, it is true, that those who follow his doctrine must expect to be persecuted by those who do not follow it, but he did not say that his disciples will be the worse off for that reason; on the contrary, he said that his disciples would have, here, in this world, more benefits than those who did not follow him. That Jesus said and thought this is beyond a doubt, as the clearness of his words on this subject, the meaning of his entire doctrine, his life and the life of his disciples, plainly show. But was his teaching in this respect true?

When we examine the question as to which of the two conditions would be the better, that of the disciples of Jesus or that of the disciples of the world, we are obliged to conclude that the condition of the disciples of Jesus ought to be the most desirable, since the disciples of Jesus, in doing good to every one, would not arouse the hatred of men. The disciples of Jesus, doing evil to no one, would be persecuted only by the wicked. The disciples of the world, on the contrary, are likely to be persecuted by every one, since the law of the disciples of the world is the law of each for himself, the law of struggle; that is, of mutual persecution. Moreover, the disciples of Jesus would be prepared for suffering, while the disciples of the world use all possible means to avoid suffering; the disciples of Jesus would feel that their sufferings were useful to the world; but the disciples of the world do not know why they suffer. On abstract grounds, then, the condition of the disciples of Jesus would be more advantageous than that of the disciples of the world. But is it so in reality? To answer this, let each one call to mind all the painful moments of his life, all the physical and moral sufferings that he has endured, and let him ask himself if he has suffered these calamities in behalf of the doctrine of the world or in behalf of the doctrine of Jesus. Every sincere man will find in recalling his past life that he has never once suffered for practising the doctrine of Jesus. He will find that the greater part of the misfortunes of his life have resulted from following the doctrines of the world. In my own life (an exceptionally happy one from a worldly point of view) I can reckon up as much suffering caused by following the doctrine of the world as many a martyr has endured for the doctrine of Jesus. All the most painful moments of my life,—

the orgies and duels in which I took part as a student, the wars in which I have participated, the diseases that I have endured, and the abnormal and insupportable conditions under which I now live,—all these are only so much martyrdom exacted by fidelity to the doctrine of the world. But I speak of a life exceptionally happy from a worldly point of view. How many martyrs have suffered for the doctrine of the world torments that I should find difficulty in enumerating!

We do not realize the difficulties and dangers entailed by the practice of the doctrine of the world, simply because we are persuaded that we could not do otherwise than follow that doctrine. We are persuaded that all the calamities that we inflict upon ourselves are the result of the inevitable conditions of life, and we cannot understand that the doctrine of Jesus teaches us how we may rid ourselves of these calamities and render our lives happy. To be able to reply to the question, Which of these two conditions is the happier? we must, at least for the time being, put aside our prejudices and take a careful survey of our surroundings.

Go through our great cities and observe the emaciated, sickly, and distorted specimens of humanity to be found therein; recall your own existence and that of all the people with whose lives you are familiar; recall the instances of violent deaths and suicides of which you have heard,—and then ask yourself for what cause all this suffering and death, this despair that leads to suicide, has been endured. You will find, perhaps to your surprise, that nine-tenths of all human suffering endured by men is useless, and ought not to exist, that, in fact, the majority of men are martyrs to the doctrine of the world.

One rainy autumn day I rode on the tramway by the Sukhareff Tower in Moscow. For the distance of half a verst the vehicle forced its way through a compact crowd which quickly reformed its ranks. From morning till night these thousands of men, the greater portion of them starving and in rags, tramped angrily through the mud, venting their hatred in abusive epithets and acts of violence. The same sight may be seen in all the market-places of Moscow. At sunset these people go to the taverns and gaming-houses; their nights are passed in filth and wretchedness. Think of the lives of these people, of what they abandon through choice for their present condition; think of the heavy burden of labor without reward which weighs upon these men and women, and you will see that they are true martyrs. All these people have forsaken houses, lands, parents, wives, and children; they have renounced all the comforts of life, and they have come to the cities to acquire that which according to the gospel of the world is indispensable to every one. And all these tens of thousands of unhappy people sleep in hovels, and subsist upon strong drink and wretched food. But aside from this class, all, from factory workman, cab-driver, sewing girl, and lorette, to merchant and government official, all endure the most painful and abnormal conditions without being able to acquire what, according to the doctrine of the world, is indispensable to each.

Seek among all these men, from beggar to millionaire, one who is contented with his lot, and you will not find one such in a thousand. Each one spends his strength in pursuit of what is exacted by the doctrine of the world, and of what he is unhappy not to possess, and scarcely has he obtained one object of his desires when he strives for another, and still another, in that infinite labor of Sisyphus which destroys the lives of men. Run over the scale of individual fortunes, ranging from a yearly income of three hundred roubles to fifty thousand roubles, and you will rarely find a person who is not striving to gain four hundred roubles if he have three hundred, five hundred if he have four hundred, and so on to the top of the ladder. Among them all you will scarcely find one who, with five hundred roubles, is willing to adopt the mode of life of him who has only four hundred. When such an instance does occur, it is not inspired by a desire to make life more simple, but to amass money and make it more sure. Each strives continually to make the heavy burden of existence still more heavy, by giving himself up body and soul to the practice of the doctrine of the world. To-day we must buy an overcoat and galoches, to-morrow, a watch and chain; the next day we must install ourselves in an apartment with a sofa and a bronze lamp; then we must have carpets and velvet gowns; then a house, horses and carriages, paintings and decorations, and then—then we fall ill of overwork and die. Another continues the same task, sacrifices his life to this same Moloch, and then dies also, without realizing for what he has lived.

But possibly this existence is in itself attractive? Compare it with what men have always called happiness, and you will see that it is hideous. For what, according to the general estimate, are the principal conditions of earthly happiness? One of the first conditions of happiness is that the link between man and nature shall not be severed, that is, that he shall be able to see the sky above him, and that he shall be able to enjoy the sunshine, the pure air, the fields with their verdure, their multitudinous life. Men have always regarded it as a great unhappiness to be deprived of all these things. But what is the condition of those men who live according to the doctrine of the world? The greater their success in practising the doctrine of the world, the more they are deprived of these conditions of happiness. The greater their worldly success, the less they are able to enjoy the light of the sun, the freshness of the fields and woods, and all the delights of country life. Many of them—including nearly all the women—arrive at old age without having seen the sun rise or the beauties of the early morning, without having seen a forest except from a seat in a carriage, without ever having planted a field or a garden, and without having the least idea as to the ways and habits of dumb animals.

These people, surrounded by artificial light instead of sunshine, look only upon fabrics of tapestry and stone and wood fashioned by the hand of man; the roar of machinery, the roll of vehicles, the thunder of cannon, the sound of musical instruments, are always in their ears; they breathe an atmosphere heavy with distilled perfumes and tobacco smoke; because of the weakness of their stomachs and their depraved tastes they eat rich and highly spiced food. When they move about from place to place, they travel in closed carriages. When they go into the country, they have the same fabrics beneath their feet; the same draperies shut out the sunshine; and the same array of servants cut off all communication with the men, the earth, the vegetation, and the animals about them. Wherever they go, they are like so many captives shut out from the conditions of happiness. As prisoners sometimes console themselves with a blade of grass that forces its way through the pavement of their prison yard, or make pets of a spider or a mouse, so these people sometimes amuse themselves with sickly plants, a parrot, a poodle, or a monkey, to whose needs however they do not themselves administer.

Another inevitable condition of happiness is work: first, the intellectual labor that one is free to choose and loves; secondly, the exercise of physical power that brings a good appetite and tranquil and profound sleep. Here, again, the greater the imagined prosperity that falls to the lot of men according to the doctrine of the world, the more such men are deprived of this condition of happiness. All the prosperous people of the world, the men of dignity and wealth, are as completely deprived of the advantages of work as if they were shut up in solitary confinement. They struggle unsuccessfully with the diseases caused by the need of physical exercise, and with the ennui which pursues them—unsuccessfully, because labor is a pleasure only when it is necessary, and they have need of nothing; or they undertake work that is odious to them, like the bankers, solicitors, administrators, and government officials, and their wives, who plan receptions and routs and devise toilettes for themselves and their children. (I say odious, because I never yet met any person of this class who was contented with his work or took as much satisfaction in it as the porter feels in shovelling away the snow from before their doorsteps.) All these favorites of fortune are either deprived of work or are obliged to work at what they do not like, after the manner of criminals condemned to hard labor.

The third undoubted condition of happiness is the family. But the more men are enslaved by worldly success, the more certainly are they cut off from domestic pleasures. The majority of them are libertines, who deliberately renounce the joys of family life and retain only its cares. If they are not libertines, their children, instead of being a source of pleasure, are a burden, and all possible means are employed to render marriage unfruitful. If they have children, they make no effort to cultivate the pleasures of companionship with them. They leave their children almost continually to the care of strangers, confiding them first to the instruction of persons who are usually foreigners, and then sending them to public educational institutions, so that of family life they have only the sorrows, and the children from infancy are as unhappy as their parents and wish their parents dead that they may become the heirs. These people are not confined in prisons, but the consequences of their way of living with regard to the family are more melancholy than the deprivation from the domestic relations inflicted upon those who are kept in confinement under sentence of the law.

The fourth condition of happiness is sympathetic and unrestricted intercourse with all classes of men. And the higher a man is placed in the social scale, the more certainly is he deprived of this essential condition of happiness. The higher he goes, the narrower becomes his circle of associates; the lower sinks the moral and intellectual level of those to whose companionship he is restrained.

The peasant and his wife are free to enter into friendly relations with every one, and if a million men will have nothing to do with them, there remain eighty millions of people with whom they may fraternize, from Archangel to Astrakhan, without waiting for a ceremonious visit or an introduction. A clerk and his wife will find hundreds of people who are their equals; but the clerks of a higher rank will not admit them to a footing of social equality, and they, in their turn, are excluded by others. The wealthy man of the world reckons by dozens the families with whom he is willing to maintain social ties—all the rest of the world are strangers. For the cabinet minister and the millionaire there are only a dozen people as rich and as important as themselves. For kings and emperors, the circle is still more narrow. Is not the whole system like a great prison where each inmate is restricted to association with a few fellow-convicts?

Finally, the fifth condition of happiness is bodily health. And once more we find that as we ascend the social scale this condition of happiness is less and less within the reach of the followers of the doctrine of the world. Compare a family of medium social status with a family of peasants. The latter toil unremittingly and are robust of body; the former is made up of men and women more or less subject to disease. Recall to mind the rich men and women whom you have known; are not most of them invalids? A person of that class whose physical disabilities do not oblige him to take a periodical course of hygienic and medical treatment is as rare as is an invalid among the laboring classes. All these favorites of fortune are the victims and practitioners of sexual vices that have become a second nature, and they are toothless, gray, and bald at an age when a workingman is in the prime of manhood. Nearly all are afflicted with nervous or other diseases arising from excesses in eating, drunkenness, luxury, and perpetual medication. Those who do not die young, pass half of their lives under the influence of morphine or other drugs, as melancholy wrecks of humanity incapable of self-attention, leading a parasitic existence like that of a certain species of ants which are nourished by their slaves. Here is the death list. One has blown out his brains, another has rotted away from the effects of syphilitic poison; this old man succumbed to sexual excesses, this young man to a wild outburst of sensuality; one died of drunkenness, another of gluttony, another from the abuse of morphine, another from an induced abortion. One after another they perished, victims of the doctrine of the world. And a multitude presses on behind them, like an army of martyrs, to undergo the same sufferings, the same perdition.

To follow the doctrine of Jesus is difficult! Jesus said that they who would forsake houses, and lands, and brethren, and follow his doctrine should receive a hundred-fold in houses, and lands, and brethren, and besides all this, eternal life. And no one is willing even to make the experiment. The doctrine of the world commands its followers to leave houses, and lands, and brethren; to forsake the country for the filth of the city, there to toil as a bath-keeper soaping the backs of others; as an apprentice in a little underground shop passing life in counting kopecks; as a prosecuting attorney to serve in bringing unhappy wretches under condemnation of the law; as a cabinet minister, perpetually signing documents of no importance; as the head of an army, killing men.—"Forsake all and live this hideous life ending in a cruel death, and you shall receive nothing in this world or the other," is the command, and every one listens and obeys. Jesus tells us to take up the cross and follow him, to bear submissively the lot apportioned out to us. No one hears his words or follows his command. But let a man in a uniform decked out with gold lace, a man whose speciality is to kill his fellows, say, "Take, not your cross, but your knapsack and carbine, and march to suffering and certain death,"—and a mighty host is ready to receive his orders. Leaving parents, wives, and children, clad in grotesque costumes, subject to the will of the first comer of a higher rank, famished, benumbed, and exhausted by forced marches, they go, like a herd of cattle to the slaughter-house, not knowing where,—and yet these are not cattle, they are men.

With despair in their hearts they move on, to die of hunger, or cold, or disease, or, if they survive, to be brought within range of a storm of bullets and commanded to kill. They kill and are killed, none of them knows why or to what end. An ambitious stripling has only to brandish his sword and shout a few magniloquent words to induce them to rush to certain death. And yet no one finds this to be difficult. Neither the victims, nor those whom they have forsaken, find anything difficult in such sacrifices, in which parents encourage their children to take part. It seems to them not only that such things should be, but that they could not be otherwise, and that they are altogether admirable and moral.

If the practice of the doctrine of the world were easy, agreeable, and without danger, we might perhaps believe that the practice of the doctrine of Jesus is difficult, frightful, and cruel. But the doctrine of the world is much more difficult, more dangerous, and more cruel, than is the doctrine of Jesus. Formerly, we are told, there were martyrs for the cause of Jesus; but they were exceptional. We cannot count up more than about three hundred and eighty thousand of them, voluntary and involuntary, in the whole course of eighteen hundred years; but who shall count the martyrs to the doctrine of the world? For each Christian martyr there have been a thousand martyrs to the doctrine of the world, and the sufferings of each one of them have been a hundred times more cruel than those endured by the others. The number of the victims of wars in our century alone amounts to thirty millions of men. These are the martyrs to the doctrine of the world, who would have escaped suffering and death even if they had refused to follow the doctrine of the world, to say nothing of following the doctrine of Jesus.

If a man will cease to have faith in the doctrine of the world and not think it indispensable to wear varnished boots and a gold chain, to maintain a useless salon, or to do the various other foolish things the doctrine of the world demands, he will never know the effects of brutalizing occupations, of unlimited suffering, of the anxieties of a perpetual struggle; he will remain in communion with nature; he will be deprived neither of the work he loves, or of his family, or of his health, and he will not perish by a cruel and brutish death.

The doctrine of Jesus does not exact martyrdom similar to that of the doctrine of the world; it teaches us rather how to put an end to the sufferings that men endure in the name of the false doctrine of the world. The doctrine of Jesus has a profound metaphysical meaning; it has a meaning as an expression of the aspirations of humanity; but it has also for each individual a very simple, very clear, and very practical meaning with regard to the conduct of his own life. In fact, we might say that Jesus taught men not to do foolish things. The meaning of the doctrine of Jesus is simple and accessible to all.

Jesus said that we were not to be angry, and not to consider ourselves as better than others; if we were angry and offended others, so much the worse for us. Again, he said that we were to avoid libertinism, and to that end choose one woman, to whom we should remain faithful. Once more, he said that we were not to bind ourselves by promises or oaths to the service of those who may constrain us to commit acts of folly and wickedness. Then he said that we were not to return evil for evil, lest the evil rebound upon ourselves with redoubled force. And, finally, he says that we are not to consider men as foreigners because they dwell in another country and speak a language different from our own. And the conclusion is, that if we avoid doing any of these foolish things, we shall be happy.

This is all very well (we say), but the world is so organized that, if we place ourselves in opposition to it, our condition will be much more calamitous than if we live in accordance with its doctrine. If a man refuses to perform military service, he will be shut up in a fortress, and possibly will be shot. If a man will not do what is necessary for the support of himself and his family, he and his family will starve. Thus argue the people who feel themselves obliged to defend the existing social organization; but they do not believe in the truth of their own words. They only say this because they cannot deny the truth of the doctrine of Jesus which they profess, and because they must justify themselves in some way for their failure to practise it. They not only do not believe in what they say; they have never given any serious consideration to the subject. They have faith in the doctrine of the world, and they only make use of the plea they have learned from the Church,—that much suffering is inevitable for those who would practise the doctrine of Jesus; and so they have never tried to practise the doctrine of Jesus at all.

We see enough of the frightful suffering endured by men in following the doctrine of the world, but in these times we hear nothing of suffering in behalf of the doctrine of Jesus. Thirty millions of men have perished in wars, fought in behalf of the doctrine of the world; thousands of millions of beings have perished, crushed by a social system organized on the principle of the doctrine of the world; but where, in our day, shall we find a million, a thousand, a dozen, or a single one, who has died a cruel death, or has even suffered from hunger and cold, in behalf of the doctrine of Jesus? This fear of suffering is only a puerile excuse that proves how little we really know of Jesus' doctrine. We not only do not follow it; we do not even take it seriously. The Church has explained it in such a way that it seems to be, not the doctrine of a happy life, but a bugbear, a source of terror.

Jesus calls men to drink of a well of living water, which is free to all. Men are parched with thirst, they have eaten of filth and drunk blood, but they have been told that they will perish if they drink of this water that is offered them by Jesus, and men believe in the warnings of superstition. They die in torment, with the water that they dare not touch within their reach. If they would only have faith in Jesus' words, and go to this well of living water and quench their thirst, they would realize how cunning has been the imposture practised upon them by the Church, and how needlessly their sufferings have been prolonged. If they would only accept the doctrine of Jesus, frankly and simply, they would see at once the horrible error of which we are each and all the victims.

One generation after another strives to find the security of its existence in violence, and by violence to protect its privileges. We believe that the happiness of our life is in power, and domination, and abundance of worldly goods. We are so habituated to this idea that we are alarmed at the sacrifices exacted by the doctrine of Jesus, which teaches that man's happiness does not depend upon fortune and power, and that the rich cannot enter into the kingdom of God. But this is a false idea of the doctrine of Jesus, which teaches us, not to do what is the worst, but to do what is the best for ourselves here in this present life. Inspired by his love for men, Jesus taught them not to depend upon security based upon violence, and not to seek after riches, just as we teach the common people to abstain, for their own interest, from quarrels and intemperance. He said that if men lived without defending themselves against violence, and without possessing riches, they would be more happy; and he confirms his words by the example of his life. He said that a man who lives according to his doctrine must be ready at any moment to endure violence from others, and, possibly, to die of hunger and cold. But this warning, which seems to exact such great and unbearable sacrifices, is simply a statement of the conditions under which men always have existed, and always will continue to exist.

A disciple of Jesus should be prepared for everything, and especially for suffering and death. But is the disciple of the world in a more desirable situation? We are so accustomed to believe in all we do for the so-called security of life (the organization of armies, the building of fortresses, the provisioning of troops), that our wardrobes, our systems of medical treatment, our furniture, and our money, all seem like real and stable pledges of our existence. We forget the fate of him who resolved to build greater storehouses to provide an abundance for many years: he died in a night. Everything that we do to make our existence secure is like the act of the ostrich, when she hides her head in the sand, and does not see that her destruction is near. But we are even more foolish than the ostrich. To establish the doubtful security of an uncertain life in an uncertain future, we sacrifice a life of certainty in a present that we might really possess.

The illusion is in the firm conviction that our existence can be made secure by a struggle with others. We are so accustomed to this illusory so-called security of our existence and our property, that we do not realize what we lose by striving after it. We lose everything,—we lose life itself. Our whole life is taken up with anxiety for personal security, with preparations for living, so that we really never live at all.

If we take a general survey of our lives, we shall see that all our efforts in behalf of the so-called security of existence are not made at all for the assurance of security, but simply to help us to forget that existence never has been, and never can be, secure. But it is not enough to say that we are the dupes of our own illusions, and that we forfeit the true life for an imaginary life; our efforts for security often result in the destruction of what we most wish to preserve. The French took up arms in 1870 to make their national existence secure, and the attempt resulted in the destruction of hundreds of thousands of Frenchmen. All people who take up arms undergo the same experience. The rich man believes that his existence is secure because he possesses money, and his money attracts a thief who kills him. The invalid thinks to make his life secure by the use of medicines, and the medicines slowly poison him; if they do not bring about his death, they at least deprive him of life, till he is like the impotent man who waited thirty-five years at the pool for an angel to come down and trouble the waters. The doctrine of Jesus, which teaches us that we cannot possibly make life secure, but that we must be ready to die at any moment, is unquestionably preferable to the doctrine of the world, which obliges us to struggle for the security of existence. It is preferable because the impossibility of escaping death, and the impossibility of making life secure, is the same for the disciples of Jesus as it is for the disciples of the world; but, according to the doctrine of Jesus, life itself is not absorbed in the idle attempt to make existence secure. To the follower of Jesus life is free, and can be devoted to the end for which it is worthy,—its own welfare and the welfare of others. The disciple of Jesus will be poor, but that is only saying that he will always enjoy the gifts that God has lavished upon men. He will not ruin his own existence. We make the word poverty a synonym for calamity, but it is in truth a source of happiness, and however much we may regard it as a calamity, it remains a source of happiness still. To be poor means not to live in cities, but in the country, not to be shut up in close rooms, but to labor out of doors, in the woods and fields, to have the delights of sunshine, of the open heavens, of the earth, of observing the habits of dumb animals; not to rack our brains with inventing dishes to stimulate an appetite, and not to endure the pangs of indigestion. To be poor is to be hungry three times a day, to sleep without passing hours tossing upon the pillow a victim of insomnia, to have children, and have them always with us, to do nothing that we do not wish to do (this is essential), and to have no fear for anything that may happen. The poor person will be ill and will suffer; he will die like the rest of the world; but his sufferings and his death will probably be less painful than those of the rich; and he will certainly live more happily. Poverty is one of the conditions of following the doctrine of Jesus, a condition indispensable to those who would enter into the kingdom of God and be happy.

The objection to this is, that no one will care for us, and that we shall be left to die of hunger. To this objection we may reply in the words of Jesus, (words that have been interpreted to justify the idleness of the clergy):—

"*Get you no gold, nor silver, nor brass in your purses; no wallet for your journey, neither two coats, nor shoes, nor staff: for the laborer is worthy of his food*" (Matt. x. 10).

"*And into whatsoever house ye shall enter, ... in that same house remain, eating and drinking such things as they give: for the laborer is worthy of his hire*" (Luke x. 5, 7).

The laborer is worthy of (ἄξιος ἐστί means, word for word, can and ought to have) his food. It is a very short sentence, but he who understands it as Jesus understood it, will no longer have any fear of dying of hunger. To understand the true meaning of these words we must get rid of that traditional idea which we have developed from the doctrine of the redemption that man's felicity consists in idleness. We must get back to that point of view natural to all men who are not fallen, that work, and not idleness, is the indispensable condition of happiness for every human being; that man cannot, in fact, refrain from work. We must rid ourselves of the savage prejudice which leads us to think that a man who has an income from a place under the government, from landed property, or from stocks and bonds, is in a natural and happy position because he is relieved from the necessity of work. We must get back into the human brain the idea of work possessed by undegenerate men, the idea that Jesus has, when he says that the laborer is worthy of his food. Jesus did not imagine that men would regard work as a curse, and consequently he did not have in mind a man who would not work, or desired not to work. He supposed that all his disciples would work, and so he said that if a man would work, his work would bring him food. He who makes use of the labor of another will provide food for him who labors, simply because he profits by that labor. And so he who works will always have food; he may not have property, but as to food, there need be no uncertainty whatever.

With regard to work there is a difference between the doctrine of Jesus and the doctrine of the world. According to the doctrine of the world, it is very meritorious in a man to be willing to work; he is thereby enabled to enter into competition with others, and to demand wages proportionate to his qualifications. According to the doctrine of Jesus, labor is the inevitable condition of human life, and food is the inevitable consequence of labor. Labor produces food, and food produces labor. However cruel and grasping the employer may be, he will always feed his workman, as he will always feed his horse; he feeds him that he may get all the work possible, and in this way he contributes to the welfare of the workman.

"*For verily the Son of man came not to be ministered unto, but to minister and to give his life a ransom for many.*"

According to the doctrine of Jesus, every individual will be the happier the more clearly he understands that his vocation consists, not in exacting service from others, but in ministering to others, in giving his life for the ransom of many. A man who does this will be worthy of his food and will not fail to have it. By the words, "*came not to be ministered unto but to minister*," Jesus established a method which would insure the material existence of man; and by the words, "*the laborer is worthy of his food*," he answered once for all the objection that a man who should practise the doctrine of Jesus in the midst of those who do not practise it would be in danger of perishing from hunger and cold. Jesus practised his own doctrine amid great opposition, and he did not perish from hunger and cold. He showed that a man does not insure his own subsistence by amassing worldly goods at the expense of others, but by rendering himself useful and indispensable to others. The more necessary he is to others, the more will his existence be made secure.

There are in the world as it is now organized millions of men who possess no property and do not practise the doctrine of Jesus by ministering unto others, but they do not die of hunger. How, then, can we object to the doctrine of Jesus, that those who practise it by working for others will perish for want of food? Men cannot die of hunger while the rich have bread. In Russia there are millions of men who possess nothing and subsist entirely by their own toil. The existence of a Christian would be as secure among pagans as it would be among those of his own faith. He would labor for others; he would be necessary to them, and therefore he would be fed. Even a dog, if he be useful, is fed and cared for; and shall not a man be fed and cared for whose service is necessary to the whole world?

But those who seek by all possible means to justify the personal life have another objection. They say that if a man be sick, even if he have a wife, parents, and children dependent upon him,—if this man cannot work, he will not be fed. They say so, and they will continue to say so; but their own actions prove that they do not believe what they say. These same people who will not admit that the doctrine of Jesus is practicable, practise it to a certain extent themselves. They do not cease to care for a sick sheep, a sick ox, or a sick dog. They do not kill an old horse, but they give him work in proportion to his strength. They care for all sorts of animals without expecting any benefit in return; and can it be that they will not care for a useful man who has fallen sick, that they will not find work suited to the strength of the old man and the child, that they will not care for the very babes who later on will be able to work for them in return? As a matter of fact they do all this. Nine-tenths of men are cared for by the other tenth, like so many cattle. And however great the darkness in which this one-tenth live, however mistaken their views in regard to the other nine-tenths of humanity, the tenth, even if they had the power, would not deprive the other nine-tenths of food. The rich will not deprive the poor of what is necessary, because they wish them to multiply and work, and so in these days the little minority of rich people provide directly or indirectly for the nourishment of the majority, that the latter may furnish the maximum of work, and multiply, and bring up a new supply of workers. Ants care for the increase and welfare of their slaves. Shall not men care for those whose labor they find necessary? Laborers are necessary. And those who profit by labor will always be careful to provide the means of labor for those who are willing to work.

The objection concerning the possibility of practising the doctrine of Jesus, that if men do not acquire something for themselves and have wealth in reserve no one will take care of their families, is true, but it is true only in regard to idle and useless and obnoxious people such as make up the majority of our opulent classes. No one (with the exception of foolish parents) takes the trouble to care for lazy people, because lazy people are of no use to any one, not even to themselves; as for the workers, the most selfish and cruel of men will contribute to their welfare. People breed and train and care for oxen, and a man, as a beast of burden, is much more useful than an ox, as the tariff of the slave-mart shows. This is why children will never be left without support.

Man is not in the world to work for himself; he is in the world to work for others, and the laborer is worthy of his hire. These truths are justified by universal experience; now, always, and everywhere, the man who labors receives the means of bodily subsistence. This subsistence is assured to him who works against his will; for such a workman desires only to relieve himself of the necessity of work, and acquires all that he possibly can in order that he may take the yoke from his own neck and place it upon the neck of another. A workman like this—envious, grasping, toiling against his will—will never lack for food and will be happier than one, who without labor, lives upon the labor of others. How much more happy, then, will that laborer be who labors in obedience to the doctrine of Jesus with the object of accomplishing all the work of which he is capable and wishing for it the least possible return? How much more desirable will his condition be, as, little by little, he sees his example followed by others. For services rendered he will then be the recipient of equal services in return.

The doctrine of Jesus with regard to labor and the fruits of labor is expressed in the story of the loaves and fishes, wherein it was shown that man enjoys the greatest sum of the benefits accessible to humanity, not by appropriating all that he can possibly grasp and using what he has for his personal pleasure, but by administering to the needs of others, as Jesus did by the borders of Galilee.

There were several thousand men and women to be fed. One of the disciples told Jesus that there was a lad who had five loaves and two fishes. Jesus understood that some of the people coming from a distance had brought provisions with them and that some had not, for after all were filled, the disciples gathered up twelve basketsful of fragments. (If no one but the boy had brought anything, how could so much have been left after so many were fed?) If Jesus had not set them an example, the people would have acted as people of the world act now. Some of those who had food would have eaten all that they had through gluttony or avidity, and some, after eating what they could eat, would have taken the rest to their homes. Those who had nothing would have been famished, and would have regarded their more fortunate companions with envy and hatred; some of them would perhaps have tried to take food by force from them who had it, and so hunger and anger and quarrels would have been the result. That is, the multitude would have acted just as people act nowadays.

But Jesus knew exactly what to do. He asked that all be made to sit down, and then commanded his disciples to give of what they had to those who had nothing, and to request others to do the same. The result was that those who had food followed the example of Jesus and his disciples, and offered what they had to others. Every one ate and was satisfied, and with the broken pieces that remained the disciples filled twelve baskets.

Jesus teaches every man to govern his life by the law of reason and conscience, for the law of reason is as applicable to the individual as it is to humanity at large. Work is the inevitable condition of human life, the true source of human welfare. For this reason a refusal to divide the fruits of one's labor with others is a refusal to accept the conditions of true happiness. To give of the fruits of one's labor to others is to contribute to the welfare of all men. The retort is made that if men did not wrest food from others, they would die of hunger. To me it seems more reasonable to say, that if men do wrest their food from one another, some of them will die of hunger, and experience confirms this view.

Every man, whether he lives according to the doctrine of Jesus or according to the doctrine of the world, lives only by the sufferance and care of others. From his birth, man is cared for and nourished by others. According to the doctrine of the world, man has a right to demand that others should continue to nourish and care for him and for his family, but, according to the doctrine of Jesus, he is only entitled to care and nourishment on the condition that he do all he can for the service of others, and so render himself useful and indispensable to mankind. Men who live according to the doctrine of the world are usually anxious to rid themselves of any one who is useless and whom they are obliged to feed; at the first possible opportunity they cease to feed such a one, and leave him to die, because of his uselessness; but him who lives for others according to the doctrine of Jesus, all men, however wicked they may be, will always nourish and care for, that he may continue to labor in their behalf.

Which, then, is the more reasonable; which offers the more joy and the greater security, a life according to the doctrine of the world, or a life according to the doctrine of Jesus?

CHAPTER XI.

THE doctrine of Jesus is to bring the kingdom of God upon earth. The practice of this doctrine is not difficult; and not only so, its practice is a natural expression of the belief of all who recognize its truth. The doctrine of Jesus offers the only possible chance of salvation for those who would escape the perdition that threatens the personal life. The fulfilment of this doctrine not only will deliver men from the privations and sufferings of this life, but will put an end to nine-tenths of the suffering endured in behalf of the doctrine of the world.

When I understood this I asked myself why I had never practised a doctrine which would give me so much happiness and peace and joy; why, on the other hand, I always had practised an entirely different doctrine, and thereby made myself wretched? Why? The reply was a simple one. Because I never had known the truth. The truth had been concealed from me.

When the doctrine of Jesus was first revealed to me, I did not believe that the discovery would lead me to reject the doctrine of the Church.[22] I dreaded this separation, and in the course of my studies I did not attempt to search out the errors in the doctrine of the Church. I sought, rather, to close my eyes to propositions that seemed to be obscure and strange, provided they were not in evident contradiction with what I regarded as the substance of the Christian doctrine.

But the further I advanced in the study of the Gospels, and the more clearly the doctrine of Jesus was revealed to me, the more inevitable the choice became. I must either accept the doctrine of Jesus, a reasonable and simple doctrine in accordance with my conscience and my hope of salvation; or I must accept an entirely different doctrine, a doctrine in opposition to reason and conscience and that offered me nothing except the certainty of my own perdition and that of others. I was therefore forced to reject, one after another, the dogmas of the Church. This I did against my will, struggling with the desire to mitigate as much as possible my disagreement with the Church, that I might not be obliged to separate from the Church, and thereby deprive myself of communion with fellow-believers, the greatest happiness that religion can bestow. But when I had completed my task, I saw that in spite of all my efforts to maintain a connecting-link with the Church, the separation was complete. I knew before that the bond of union, if it existed at all, must be a very slight one, but I was soon convinced that it did not exist at all.

My son came to me one day, after I had completed my examination of the Gospels, and told me of a discussion that was going on between two domestics (uneducated persons who scarcely knew how to read) concerning a passage in some religious book which maintained that it was not a sin to put criminals to death, or to kill enemies in war. I could not believe that an assertion of this sort could be printed in any book, and I asked to see it. The volume bore the title of "*A Book of Selected Prayers*; third edition; eighth ten thousand; Moscow: 1879." On page 163 of this book I read:—

"What is the sixth commandment of God?

"Thou shalt not kill.

"What does God forbid by this commandment?

"He forbids us to kill, to take the life of any man.

"Is it a sin to punish a criminal with death according to the law, or to kill an enemy in war?

"No; that is not a sin. We take the life of the criminal to put an end to the wrong that he commits; we slay an enemy in war, because in war we fight for our sovereign and our native land."

And in this manner was enjoined the abrogation of the law of God! I could scarcely believe that I had read aright.

My opinion was asked with regard to the subject at issue. To the one who maintained that the instruction given by the book was true, I said that the explanation was not correct.

"Why, then, do they print untrue explanations contrary to the law?" was his question, to which I could say nothing in reply.

I kept the volume and looked over its contents. The book contained thirty-one prayers with instructions concerning genuflexions and the joining of the fingers; an explanation of the *Credo*; a citation from the fifth chapter of Matthew without any explanation whatever, but headed, "Commands for those who would possess the Beatitudes"; the ten commandments accompanied by comments that rendered most of them void; and hymns for every saint's day.

As I have said, I not only had sought to avoid censure of the religion of the Church; I had done my best to see only its most favorable side; and knowing its academic literature from beginning to end, I had paid no attention whatever to its popular literature. This book of devotion, spread broadcast in an enormous number of copies, awakening doubts in the minds of the most unlearned people, set me to thinking. The contents of the book seemed to me so entirely pagan, so wholly out of accord with Christianity, that I could not believe it to be the deliberate

LEO TOLSTOY

purpose of the Church to propagate such a doctrine. To verify my belief, I bought and read all the books published by the synod with its "benediction" (*blagoslovnia*), containing brief expositions of the religion of the Church for the use of children and the common people.

Their contents were to me almost entirely new, for at the time when I received my early religious instruction, they had not yet appeared. As far as I could remember there were no commandments with regard to the beatitudes, and there was no doctrine which taught that it was not a sin to kill. No such teachings appeared in the old catechisms; they were not to be found in the catechism of Peter Mogilas, or in that of Beliokof, or the abridged Catholic catechisms. The innovation was introduced by the metropolitan Philaret, who prepared a catechism with proper regard for the susceptibilities of the military class, and from this catechism the *Book of Selected Prayers* was compiled. Philaret's work is entitled, *The Christian Catechism of the Orthodox Church, for the Use of all Orthodox Christians*, and is published, "by order of his Imperial Majesty."[23]

The book is divided into three parts, "Concerning Faith," "Concerning Hope," and "Concerning Love." The first part contains the analysis of the symbol of faith as given by the Council of Nice. The second part is made up of an exposition of the *Pater Noster*, and the first eight verses of the fifth chapter of Matthew, which serve as an introduction to the Sermon on the Mount, and are called (I know not why) "Commands for those who would possess the Beatitudes." These first two parts treat of the dogmas of the Church, prayers, and the sacraments, but they contain no rules with regard to the conduct of life. The third part, "Concerning Love," contains an exposition of Christian duties, based not on the commandments of Jesus, but upon the ten commandments of Moses. This exposition of the commandments of Moses seems to have been made for the especial purpose of teaching men not to obey them. Each commandment is followed by a reservation which completely destroys its force. With regard to the first commandment, which enjoins the worship of God alone, the catechism inculcates the worship of saints and angels, to say nothing of the Mother of God and the three persons of the Trinity ("Special Catechism," pp. 107, 108) . With regard to the second commandment, against the worship of idols, the catechism enjoins the worship of images (p. 108). With regard to the third commandment, the catechism enjoins the taking of oaths as the principal token of legitimate authority (p. 111). With regard to the fourth commandment, concerning the observance of the Sabbath, the catechism inculcates the observance of Sunday, of the thirteen principal feasts, of a number of feasts of less importance, the observance of Lent, and of fasts on Wednesdays and Fridays (pp. 112-115). With regard to the fifth commandment, "*Honor thy father and thy mother*," the catechism prescribes honor to the sovereign, the country, spiritual fathers, all persons in authority, and of these last gives an enumeration in three pages, including college authorities, civil, judicial, and military authorities, and owners of serfs, with instructions as to the manner of honoring each of these classes (pp. 116-119). My citations are taken from the sixty-fourth edition of the catechism, dated 1880. Twenty years have passed since the abolition of serfdom, and no one has taken the trouble to strike out the phrase which, in connection with the commandment of God to honor parents, was introduced into the catechism to sustain and justify slavery.

With regard to the sixth commandment, "*Thou shalt not kill*," the instructions of the catechism are from the first in favor of murder.

"*Question.*—What does the sixth commandment forbid?

"*Answer.*—It forbids manslaughter, to take the life of one's neighbor in any manner whatever.

"*Question.*—Is all manslaughter a transgression of the law?

"*Answer.*—Manslaughter is not a transgression of the law when life is taken in pursuance of its mandate. For example:

"1st. When a criminal condemned in justice is punished by death.

"2d. When we kill *in war* for the sovereign and our country."

The italics are in the original. Further on we read:—

"*Question.*—With regard to manslaughter, when is the law transgressed?

"*Answer.*—When any one conceals a murderer or sets him at liberty" (*sic*).

All this is printed in hundreds of thousands of copies, and under the name of Christian doctrine is taught by compulsion to every Russian, who is obliged to receive it under penalty of castigation. This is taught to all the Russian people. It is taught to the innocent children,—to the children whom Jesus commanded to be brought to him as belonging to the kingdom of God; to the children whom we must resemble, in ignorance of false doctrines, to enter into the kingdom of God; to the children whom Jesus tried to protect in proclaiming woe on him who should cause one of the little ones to stumble! And the little children are obliged to learn all this, and are told that it is the only and sacred law of God. These are not proclamations sent out clandestinely, whose authors are punished with penal servitude; they are proclamations which inflict the punishment of penal servitude upon all those who do not agree with the doctrines they inculcate.

As I write these lines, I experience a feeling of insecurity, simply because I have allowed myself to say that men cannot render void the fundamental law of God inscribed in all the codes and in all hearts, by such words as these:—

"Manslaughter is not a transgression of the law when life is taken in pursuance of its mandate... when we kill in war for our sovereign and our country."

I tremble because I have allowed myself to say that such things should not be taught to children.

It was against such teachings as these that Jesus warned men when he said:—

"*Look, therefore, whether the light that is in thee be not darkness.*" (Luke xi. 35.)

The light that is in us has become darkness; and the darkness of our lives is full of terror.

"*Woe unto you, scribes and Pharisees, hypocrites! because ye shut the kingdom of heaven against men: for ye enter not in yourselves, neither suffer ye them that are entering in to enter. Woe unto you, scribes and Pharisees, hypocrites! for ye devour widows' houses, even while for a pretense ye make long prayers: therefore ye shall receive greater condemnation. Woe unto you, scribes and Pharisees, hypocrites! for ye compass sea and land to make one proselyte; and when he is become so, ye make him twofold more a son of hell than yourselves. Woe unto you, ye blind guides....*

"*Woe unto you, scribes and Pharisees, hypocrites! for ye build the sepulchres of the prophets, and garnish the tombs of the righteous, and say, If we had been in the days of our fathers, ice should not have been partakers with them in the blood of the prophets. Wherefore ye witness to yourselves, that ye are sons of them that slew the prophets. Fill ye up, then, the measure of your fathers.... I send unto you prophets, and wise men, and scribes: some of them shall ye kill and crucify; and some of them shall ye scourge in your synagogues, and persecute from city to city: that upon you may come all the righteous blood shed on the earth, from the blood of Abel....*

"*Every sin and blasphemy shall be forgiven unto men; but the blasphemy against the Spirit shall not be forgiven.*"

Of a truth we might say that all this was written but yesterday, not against men who no longer compass sea and land to blaspheme against the Spirit, or to convert men to a religion that renders its proselytes worse than they were before, but against men who deliberately force people to embrace their religion, and persecute and bring to death all the prophets and the righteous who seek to reveal their falsehoods to mankind. I became convinced that the doctrine of the Church, although bearing the name of "Christian," is one with the darkness against which Jesus struggled, and against which he commanded his disciples to strive.

The doctrine of Jesus, like all religious doctrines, is regarded in two ways,—first, as a moral and ethical system which teaches men how they should live as individuals, and in relation to each other; second, as a metaphysical theory which explains why men should live in a given manner and not otherwise. One necessitates the other. Man should live in this manner because such is his destiny; or, man's destiny is this way, and consequently he should follow it. These two methods of doctrinal expression are common to all the religions of the world, to the religion of the Brahmins, to that of Confucius, to that of Buddha, to that of Moses, and to that of the Christ. But, with regard to the doctrine of Jesus, as with regard to all other doctrines, men wander from its precepts, and they always find some one to justify their deviations. Those who, as Jesus said, sit in Moses' seat, explain the metaphysical theory in such a way that the ethical prescriptions of the doctrine cease to be regarded as obligatory, and are replaced by external forms of worship, by ceremonial. This is a condition common to all religions, but, to me, it seems that it never has been manifested with so much pomp as in connection with Christianity,—and for two reasons: first, because the doctrine of Jesus is the most elevated of all doctrines (the most elevated because the metaphysical and ethical portions are so closely united that one cannot be separated from the other without destroying the vitality of the whole); second, because the doctrine of Jesus is in itself a protest against all forms, a negation not only of Jewish ceremonial, but of all exterior rites of worship. Therefore, the arbitrary separation of the metaphysical and ethical aspects of Christianity entirely disfigures the doctrine, and deprives it of every sort of meaning. The separation began with the preaching of Paul, who knew but imperfectly the ethical doctrine set forth in the Gospel of Matthew, and who preached a metaphysico-cabalistic theory entirely foreign to the doctrine of Jesus; and this theory was perfected under Constantine, when the existing pagan social organization was proclaimed Christian simply by covering it with the mantle of Christianity. After Constantine, that arch-pagan, whom the Church in spite of all his crimes and vices admits to the category of the saints, after Constantine began the domination of the councils, and the centre of gravity of Christianity was permanently displaced till only the metaphysical portion was left in view. And this metaphysical theory with its accompanying ceremonial deviated more and more from its true and primitive meaning, until it has reached its present stage of development, as a doctrine which explains the mysteries of a celestial life beyond the comprehension of human reason, and, with all its complicated formulas, gives no religious guidance whatever with regard to the regulation of this earthly life.

All religions, with the exception of the religion of the Christian Church, demand from their adherents aside from forms and ceremonies, the practice of certain actions called good, and abstinence from certain actions that are called bad. The Jewish religion prescribed circumcision, the observance of the Sabbath, the giving of alms, the feast of the Passover. Mohammedanism prescribes circumcision, prayer five times a day, the giving of tithes to the poor, pilgrimage to the tomb of the Prophet, and many other things. It is the same with all other religions. Whether these prescriptions are good or bad, they are prescriptions which exact the performance of certain actions. Pseudo-Christianity alone prescribes nothing. There is nothing that a Christian is obliged to observe except fasts and prayers, which the Church itself does not recognize as obligatory. All that is necessary to the pseudo-Christian is the sacrament. But the sacrament is not fulfilled by the believer; it is administered to him by others. The pseudo-Christian is obliged to do nothing or to abstain from nothing for his own salvation, since the Church administers to him everything of which he has need. The Church baptizes him, anoints him, gives him the eucharist, confesses him, even after he has lost consciousness, administers extreme unction to him, and prays for him,—and he is saved. From the time of Constantine the Christian Church has prescribed no religious duties to its adherents. It has never required that they should abstain from anything. The Christian Church has recognized and sanctioned divorce, slavery, tribunals, all earthly powers, the death penalty, and war; it has exacted nothing except a renunciation of a purpose to do evil on the occasion of baptism, and this only in its early days: later on, when infant baptism was introduced, even this requirement was no longer observed.

The Church confesses the doctrine of Jesus in theory, but denies it in practice. Instead of guiding the life of the world, the Church, through affection for the world, expounds the metaphysical doctrine of Jesus in such a way as not to derive from it any obligation as to the conduct of life, any necessity for men to live differently from the way in which they have been living. The Church has surrendered to the world, and simply follows in the train of its victor. The world does as it pleases, and leaves to the Church the task of justifying its actions with explanations as to the meaning of life. The world organizes an existence in absolute opposition to the doctrine of Jesus, and the Church endeavors to demonstrate that men who live contrary to the doctrine of Jesus really live in accordance with that doctrine. The final result is that the world lives a worse than pagan existence, and the Church not only approves, but maintains that this existence is in exact conformity to the doctrine of Jesus.

But a time comes when the light of the true doctrine of Jesus shines forth from the Gospels, notwithstanding the guilty efforts of the Church to conceal it from men's eyes, as, for instance, in prohibiting the translation of the Bible; there comes a time when the light reaches the people, even through the medium of sectarians and free-thinkers, and the falsity of the doctrine of the Church is shown so clearly that men begin to transform the method of living that the Church has justified.

Thus men of their own accord, and in opposition to the sanction of the Church, have abolished slavery, abolished the divine right of emperors and popes, and are now proceeding to abolish property and the State. And the Church cannot forbid such action because the abolition of these iniquities is in conformity to the Christian doctrine, that the Church preaches after having falsified.

And in this way the conduct of human life is freed from the control of the Church, and subjected to an entirely different authority. The Church retains its dogmas, but what are its dogmas worth? A metaphysical explanation can be of use only when there is a doctrine of life which it serves to make manifest. But the Church possesses only the explanation of an organization which it once sanctioned, and which no longer exists. The Church has nothing left but temples and shrines and canonicals and vestments and words.

For eighteen centuries the Church has hidden the light of Christianity behind its forms and ceremonials, and by this same light it is put to shame. The world, with an organization sanctioned by the Church, has rejected the Church in the name of the very principles of Christianity that the Church has professed. The separation between the two is complete and cannot be concealed. Everything that truly lives in the world of Europe to-day (everything not cold and dumb in hateful isolation),—everything that is living, is detached from the Church, from all churches, and has an existence independent of the Church. Let it not be said that this is true only of the decayed civilizations of Western Europe. Russia, with its millions of civilized and uncivilized Christian rationalists, who have rejected the doctrine of the Church, proves incontestably that as regards emancipation from the yoke of the Church, she is, thanks be to God, in a worse condition of decay than the rest of Europe.

All that lives is independent of the Church. The power of the State is based upon tradition, upon science, upon popular suffrage, upon brute force, upon everything except upon the Church. Wars, the relation of State with State, are governed by principles of nationality, of the balance of power, but not by the Church. The institutions established by the State frankly ignore the Church. The idea that the Church can, in these times, serve as a basis for justice or the conservation of property, is simply absurd. Science not only does not sustain the doctrine of the Church, but is, in its development, entirely hostile to the Church. Art, formerly entirely devoted to the service of the Church, has wholly forsaken the Church. It is little to say that human life is now entirely emancipated from the Church; it has now, with regard to the Church, only contempt when the Church does not interfere with human affairs, and hatred when the Church seeks to re-assert its ancient privileges. The Church is still permitted a formal existence simply because men dread to shatter the chalice that once contained the water of life. In this way only can we account, in our age, for the existence of Catholicism, of Orthodoxy, and of the different Protestant churches.

All these churches—Catholic, Orthodox, Protestant—are like so many sentinels still keeping careful watch before the prison doors, although the prisoners have long been at liberty before their eyes, and even threaten their existence. All that actually constitutes life, that is, the activity of humanity towards progress and its own welfare, socialism, communism, the new politico-economical theories, utilitarianism, the liberty and equality of all social classes, and of men and women, all the moral principles of humanity, the sanctity of work, reason, science, art,—all these that lend an impulse to the world's progress in hostility to the Church are only fragments of the doctrine which the Church has professed, and so carefully endeavored to conceal. In these times, the life of the world is entirely independent of the doctrine of the Church. The Church is left so far behind, that men no longer hear the voices of those who preach its doctrines. This is easily to be understood because the Church still clings to an organization of the world's life, which has been forsaken, and is rapidly falling to destruction.

Imagine a number of men rowing a boat, a pilot steering. The men rely upon the pilot, and the pilot steers well; but after a time the good pilot is replaced by another, who does not steer at all. The boat moves along rapidly and easily. At first the men do not notice the negligence of the new pilot; they are only pleased to find that the boat goes along so easily. Then they discover that the new pilot is utterly useless, and they mock at him, and drive him from his place.

The matter would not be so serious if the men, in thrusting aside the unskilful pilot, did not forget that without a pilot they are likely to take a wrong course. But so it is with our Christian society. The Church has lost its control; we move smoothly onward, and we are a long way from our point of departure. Science, that especial pride of this nineteenth century, is sometimes alarmed; but that is because of the absence of a pilot. We are moving onward, but to what goal? We organize our life without in the least knowing why, or to what end. But we can no longer be contented to live without knowing why, any more than we can navigate a boat without knowing the course that we are following.

If men could do nothing of themselves, if they were not responsible for their condition, they might very reasonably reply to the question, "Why are you in this situation?"—"We do not know; but here we are, and submit." But men are the builders of their own destiny, and more especially of the destiny of their children; and so when we ask, "Why do you bring together millions of troops, and why do you make soldiers of yourselves, and mangle and murder one another? Why have you expended, and why do you still expend, an enormous sum of human energy in the construction of useless and unhealthful cities? Why do you organize ridiculous tribunals, and send people whom you consider as criminals from France to Cayenne, from Russia to Siberia, from England to Australia, when you know the hopeless folly of it? Why do you abandon agriculture, which you love, for work in factories and mills, which you despise? Why do you bring up your children in a way that will force them to lead an existence which you find worthless? Why do you do this?" To all these questions men feel obliged to make some reply.

If this existence were an agreeable one, and men took pleasure in it, even then men would try to explain why they continued to live under such conditions. But all these things are terribly difficult; they are endured with murmuring and painful struggles, and men cannot refrain from reflecting upon the motive which impels them to such a course. They must cease to maintain the accepted organization of existence, or they must explain why they give it their support. And so men never have allowed this question to pass unanswered. We find in all ages some attempt at a response. The Jew lived as he lived, that is, made war, put criminals to death, built the Temple, organized his entire existence in one way and not another, because, as he was convinced, he thereby followed the laws which God himself had promulgated. We may say the same of the Hindu, the Chinaman, the Roman, and the Mohammedan. A similar response was given by the Christian a century ago, and is given by the great mass of Christians now.

A century ago, and among the ignorant now, the nominal Christian makes this reply: "Compulsory military service, wars, tribunals, and the death penalty, all exist in obedience to the law of God transmitted to us by the Church. This is a fallen world. All the evil that exists, exists by God's will, as a punishment for the sins of men. For this reason we can do nothing to palliate evil. We can only save our own souls by faith, by the sacraments, by prayers, and by submission to the will of God as transmitted by the Church. The Church teaches us that all Christians should unhesitatingly obey their rulers, who are the Lord's anointed, and obey also persons placed in authority by rulers; that they ought to defend their property and that of others by force, wage war, inflict the death penalty, and in all things submit to the authorities, who command by the will of God."

Whatever we may think of the reasonableness of these explanations, they once sufficed for a believing Christian, as similar explanations satisfied a Jew or a Mohammedan, and men were not obliged to renounce all reason for living according to a law which they recognized as divine. But in this time only the most ignorant people have faith in any such explanations, and the number of these diminishes every day and every hour. It is impossible to check this tendency. Men irresistibly follow those who lead the way, and sooner or later must pass over the same ground as the advance guard. The advance guard is now in a critical position; those who compose it organize life to suit themselves, prepare the same conditions for those who are to follow, and absolutely have not the slightest idea of why they do so. No civilized man in the vanguard of progress is able to give any reply now to the direct questions, "Why do you lead the life that you do lead? Why do you establish the conditions that you do establish?" I have propounded these questions to hundreds of people, and never have got from them a direct reply. Instead of a direct reply to the direct question, I have received in return a response to a question that I had not asked.

When we ask a Catholic, or Protestant, or Orthodox believer why he leads an existence contrary to the doctrine of Jesus, instead of making a direct response he begins to speak of the melancholy state of scepticism characteristic of this generation, of evil-minded persons who spread doubt broadcast among the masses, of the importance of the future of the existing Church. But he will not tell you why he does not act in conformity to the commands of the religion that he professes. Instead of speaking of his own condition, he will talk to you about the condition of humanity in general, and of that of the Church, as if his own life were not of the slightest significance, and his sole preoccupations were the salvation of humanity, and of what he calls the Church.

A philosopher of whatever school he may be, whether an idealist or a spiritualist, a pessimist or a positivist, if we ask of him why he lives as he lives, that is to say, in disaccord with his philosophical doctrine, will begin at once to talk about the progress of humanity and about the historical law of this progress which he has discovered, and in virtue of which humanity gravitates toward righteousness. But he never will make any direct reply to the question why he himself, on his own account, does not live in harmony with what he recognizes as the dictates of reason. It would seem as if the philosopher were as preoccupied as the believer, not with his personal life, but with observing the effect of general laws upon the development of humanity.

The "average" man (that is, one of the immense majority of civilized people who are half sceptics and half believers, and who all, without exception, deplore existence, condemn its organization, and predict universal destruction),—the average man, when we ask him why he continues to lead a life that he condemns, without making any effort towards its amelioration, makes no direct reply, but begins at once to talk about things in general, about justice, about the State, about commerce, about civilization. If he be a member of the police or a prosecuting attorney, he asks, "And what would become of the State, if I, to ameliorate my existence, were to cease to serve it?" "What would become of commerce?" is his demand if he be a merchant; "What of civilization, if I cease to work for it, and seek only to better my own condition?" will be the objection of another. His response always will be in this form, as if the duty of his life were not to seek the good conformable to his nature, but to serve the State, or commerce, or civilization.

The average man replies in just the same manner as does the believer or the philosopher. Instead of making the question a personal one, he glides at once to generalities. This subterfuge is employed simply because the believer and the philosopher, and the average man have no positive doctrine concerning existence, and cannot, therefore, reply to the personal question, "What of your own life?" They are disgusted and humiliated at not possessing the slightest trace of a doctrine with regard to life, for no one can live in peace without some understanding of what life really means. But nowadays only Christians cling to a fantastic and worn-out creed as an explanation of why life is as it is, and is not otherwise. Only Christians give the name of religion to a system which is not of the least use to any one. Only among Christians is life separated from any or all doctrine, and left without any definition whatever. Moreover, science, like tradition, has formulated from the fortuitous and abnormal condition of humanity a general law. Learned men, such as Tiele and Spencer, treat religion as a serious matter, understanding by religion the metaphysical doctrine of the universal principle, without suspecting that they have lost sight of religion as a whole by confining their attention entirely to one of its phases.

From all this we get very extraordinary results. We see learned and intelligent men artlessly believing that they are emancipated from all religion simply because they reject the metaphysical explanation of the universal principle which satisfied a former generation. It does not occur to them that men cannot live without some theory of existence; that every human being lives according to some principle, and that this principle by which he governs his life is his religion. The people of whom we have been speaking are persuaded that they have reasonable convictions, but that they have no religion. Nevertheless, however serious their asseverations, they have a religion from the moment that they undertake to govern their actions by reason, for a reasonable act is determined by some sort of faith. Now their faith is in what they are told to do. The faith of those who deny religion is in a religion of obedience to the will of the ruling majority; in a word, submission to established authority.

We may live a purely animal life according to the doctrine of the world, without recognizing any controlling motive more binding than the rules of established authority. But he who lives this way cannot affirm that he lives a reasonable life. Before affirming that we live a reasonable life, we must determine what is the doctrine of the life which we regard as reasonable. Alas! wretched men that we are, we possess not the semblance of any such doctrine, and more than that, we have lost all perception of the necessity for a reasonable doctrine of life.

Ask the believers or sceptics of this age, what doctrine of life they follow. They will be obliged to confess that they follow but one doctrine, the doctrine based upon laws formulated by the judiciary or by legislative assemblies, and enforced by the police—the favorite doctrine of most Europeans. They know that this doctrine does not come from on high, or from prophets, or from sages; they are continually finding fault with the laws drawn up by the judiciary or formulated by legislative assemblies, but nevertheless they submit to the police charged with their enforcement. They submit without murmuring to the most terrible exactions. The clerks employed by the judiciary or the legislative assemblies decree by statute that every young man must be ready to take up arms, to kill others, and to die himself, and that all parents who have adult sons must favor obedience to this law which was drawn up yesterday by a mercenary official, and may be revoked to-morrow.

We have lost sight of the idea that a law may be in itself reasonable, and binding upon every one in spirit as well as in letter. The Hebrews possessed a law which regulated life, not by forced obedience to its requirements, but by appealing to the conscience of each individual; and the existence of this law is considered as an exceptional attribute of the Hebrew people. That the Hebrews should have been willing to obey only what they recognized by spiritual perception as the incontestable truth direct from God is considered a remarkable national trait. But it appears that the natural and normal state of civilized men is to obey what to their own knowledge is decreed by despicable officials and enforced by the co-operation of armed police.

The distinctive trait of civilized man is to obey what the majority of men regard as iniquitous, contrary to conscience. I seek in vain in civilized society as it exists to-day for any clearly formulated moral bases of life. There are none. No perception of their necessity exists. On the contrary, we find the extraordinary conviction that they are superfluous; that religion is nothing more than a few words about God and a future life, and a few ceremonies very useful for the salvation of the soul according to some, and good for nothing according to others; but that life happens of itself and has no need of any fundamental rule, and that we have only to do what we are told to do.

The two substantial sources of faith, the doctrine that governs life, and the explanation of the meaning of life, are regarded as of very unequal value. The first is considered as of very little importance, and as having no relation to faith whatever; the second, as the explanation of a bygone state of existence, or as made up of speculations concerning the historical development of life, is considered as of great significance. As to all that constitutes the life of man expressed in action, the members of our modern society depend willingly for guidance upon people who, like themselves, know not why they direct their fellows to live in one way and not in another. This disposition holds good whether the question at issue is to decide whether to kill or not to kill, to judge or not to judge, to bring up children in this way or in that. And men look upon an existence like this as reasonable, and have no feeling of shame!

The explanations of the Church which pass for faith, and the true faith of our generation, which is in obedience to social laws and the laws of the State, have reached a stage of sharp antagonism. The majority of civilized people have nothing to regulate life but faith in the police. This condition would be unbearable if it were universal. Fortunately there is a remnant, made up of the noblest minds of the age, who are not contented with this religion, but have an entirely different faith with regard to what the life of man ought to be. These men are looked upon as the most malevolent, the most dangerous, and generally as the most unbelieving of all human beings, and yet they are the only men of our time believing in the Gospel doctrine, if not as a whole, at least in part. These people, as a general thing, know little of the doctrine of Jesus; they do not understand it, and, like their adversaries, they refuse to accept the leading principle of the religion of Jesus, which is to resist not evil; often they have nothing but a hatred for the name of Jesus; but their whole faith with regard to what life ought to be is unconsciously based upon the humane and eternal truths comprised in the Christian doctrine. This remnant, in spite of calumny and persecution, are the only ones who do not tamely submit to the orders of the first comer. Consequently they are the only ones in these days who live a reasonable and not an animal life, the only ones who have faith.

The connecting link between the world and the Church, although carefully cherished by the Church, becomes more and more attenuated. To-day it is little more than a hindrance. The union between the Church and the world has no longer any justification. The mysterious process of maturation is going on before our eyes. The connecting bond will soon be severed, and the vital social organism will begin to exercise its functions as a wholly independent existence. The doctrine of the Church, with its dogmas, its councils, and its hierarchy, is manifestly united to the doctrine of Jesus. The connecting link is as perceptible as the cord which binds the newly-born child to its mother; but as the umbilical cord and the placenta become after parturition useless pieces of flesh, which are carefully buried out of regard for what they once nourished, so the Church has become a useless organism, to be preserved, if at all, in some museum of curiosities out of regard for what it has once been. As soon as respiration and circulation are established, the former source of nutrition becomes a hindrance to life. Vain and foolish would it be to attempt to retain the bond, and to force the child that has come into the light of day to receive its nourishment by a pre-natal process. But the deliverance of the child from the maternal tie does not ensure life. The life of the newly born depends upon another bond of union which is established between it and its mother that its nourishment may be maintained.

And so it must be with our Christian world of to-day. The doctrine of Jesus has brought the world into the light. The Church, one of the organs of the doctrine of Jesus, has fulfilled its mission and is now useless. The world cannot be bound to the Church; but the deliverance of the world from the Church will not ensure life. Life will begin when the world perceives its own weakness and the necessity for a different source of strength. The Christian world feels this necessity: it proclaims its helplessness, it feels the impossibility of depending upon its former means of nourishment, the inadequacy of any other form of nourishment except that of the doctrine by which it was brought forth. This modern European world of ours, apparently so sure of itself, so bold, so decided, and within so preyed upon by terror and despair, is exactly in the situation of a newly born animal: it writhes, it cries aloud, it is perplexed, it knows not what to do; it feels that its former source of nourishment is withdrawn, but it knows not where to seek for another. A newly born lamb shakes its head, opens its eyes and looks about, and leaps, and bounds, and would make us think by its apparently intelligent movements that it already has mastered the secret of living; but of this the poor little creature knows nothing. The impetuosity and energy it displays were drawn from its mother through a medium of transmission that has just been broken, nevermore to be renewed. The situation of the new comer is one of delight, and at the same time is full of peril. It is animated by youth and strength, but it is lost if it cannot avail itself of the nourishment only to be had from its mother.

And so it is with our European world. What complex activities, what energy, what intelligence, does it apparently possess! It would seem as if all its deeds were governed by reason. With what enthusiasm, what vigor, what youthfulness do the denizens of this modern world manifest their abounding vitality! The arts and sciences, the various industries, political and administrative details, all are full of life. But this life is due to inspiration received through the connecting link that binds it to its source. The Church, by transmitting the truth of the doctrine of Jesus, has communicated life to the world. Upon this nourishment the world has grown and developed. But the Church has had its day and is now superfluous.

The world is possessed of a living organism; the means by which it formerly received its nourishment has withered away, and it has not yet found another; and it seeks everywhere, everywhere but at the true source of life. It still possesses the animation derived from nourishment already received, and it does not yet understand that its future nourishment is only to be had from one source, and by its own efforts. The world must now understand that the period of gestation is ended, and that a new process of conscious nutrition must henceforth maintain its life. The truth of the doctrine of Jesus, once unconsciously absorbed by humanity through the organism of the Church, must now be consciously recognized; for in the truth of this doctrine humanity has always obtained its vital force. Men must lift up the torch of truth, which has so long remained concealed, and carry it before them, guiding their actions by its light.

The doctrine of Jesus, as a religion that governs the actions of men and explains to them the meaning of life, is now before the world just as it was eighteen hundred years ago. Formerly the world had the explanations of the Church which, in concealing the doctrine, seemed in itself to offer a satisfactory interpretation of life; but now the time is come when the Church has lost its usefulness, and the world, having no other means for sustaining its true existence, can only feel its helplessness and go for aid directly to the doctrine of Jesus.

Now, Jesus first taught men to believe in the light, and that the light is within themselves. Jesus taught men to lift on high the light of reason. He taught them to live, guiding their actions by this light, and to do nothing contrary to reason. It is unreasonable, it is foolish, to go out to kill Turks or Germans; it is unreasonable to make use of the labor of others that you and yours may be clothed in the height of fashion and maintain that mortal source of ennui, a salon; it is unreasonable to take people already corrupted by idleness and depravity and shut them up within prison walls, and thereby devote them to an existence of absolute idleness and deprivation; it is unreasonable to live in the pestilential air of cities when a purer atmosphere is within your reach; it is unreasonable to base the education of your children on the grammatical laws of dead languages;—all this is unreasonable, and yet it is to-day the life of the European world, which lives a life of no meaning; which acts, but acts without a purpose, having no confidence in reason, and existing in opposition to its decrees.

The doctrine of Jesus is the light. The light shines forth, and the darkness cannot conceal it. Men cannot deny it, men cannot refuse to accept its guidance. They must depend on the doctrine of Jesus, which penetrates among all the errors with which the life of men is surrounded. Like the insensible ether filling universal space, enveloping all created things, so the doctrine of Jesus is inevitable for every man in whatever situation he may be found. Men cannot refuse to recognize the doctrine of Jesus; they may deny the metaphysical explanation of life which it gives (we may deny everything), but the doctrine of Jesus alone offers rules for the conduct of life without which humanity has never lived, and never will be able to live; without which no human being has lived or can live, if he would live as man should live,—a reasonable life. The power of the doctrine of Jesus is not in its explanation of the meaning of life, but in the rules that it gives for the conduct of life. The metaphysical doctrine of Jesus is not new; it is that eternal doctrine of humanity inscribed in all the hearts of men, and preached by all the prophets of all the ages. The power of the doctrine of Jesus is in the application of this metaphysical doctrine to life.

The metaphysical basis of the ancient doctrine of the Hebrews, which enjoined love to God and men, is identical with the metaphysical basis of the doctrine of Jesus. But the application of this doctrine to life, as expounded by Moses, was very different from the teachings of Jesus. The Hebrews, in applying the Mosaic law to life, were obliged to fulfil six hundred and thirteen commandments, many of which were absurd and cruel, and yet all were based upon the authority of the Scriptures. The doctrine of life, as given by Jesus upon the same metaphysical basis, is expressed in five reasonable and beneficent commandments, having an obvious and justifiable meaning, and embracing within their restrictions the whole of human life. A Jew, a disciple of Confucius, a Buddhist, or a Mohammedan, who sincerely doubts the truth of his own religion, cannot refuse to accept the doctrine of Jesus; much less, then, can this doctrine be rejected by the Christian world of to-day, which is now living without any moral law. The doctrine of Jesus cannot interfere in any way with the manner in which men of to-day regard the world; it is, to begin with, in harmony with their metaphysics, but it gives them what they have not now, what is indispensable to their existence, and what they all seek,—it offers them a way of life; not an unknown way, but a way already explored and familiar to all.

Let us suppose that you are a sincere Christian, it matters not of what confession. You believe in the creation of the world, in the Trinity, in the fall and redemption of man, in the sacraments, in prayer, in the Church. The doctrine of Jesus is not opposed to your dogmatic belief, and is absolutely in harmony with your theory of the origin of the universe; and it offers you something that you do not possess. While you retain your present religion you feel that your own life and the life of the world is full of evil that you know not how to remedy. The doctrine of Jesus (which should be binding upon you since it is the doctrine of your own God) offers you simple and practical rules which will surely deliver you, you and your fellows, from the evils with which you are tormented.

Believe, if you will, in paradise, in hell, in the pope, in the Church, in the sacraments, in the redemption; pray according to the dictates of your faith, attend upon your devotions, sing your hymns,—but all this will not prevent you from practising the five commandments given by Jesus for your welfare: Be not angry; Do not commit adultery; Take no oaths; Resist not evil; Do not make war. It may happen that you will break one of these rules; you will perhaps yield to temptation, and violate one of them, just as you violate the rules of your present religion, or the articles of the civil code, or the laws of custom. In the same way you may, perhaps, in moments of temptation, fail of observing all the commandments of Jesus. But, in that case, do not calmly sit down as you do now, and so organize your existence as to render it a task of extreme difficulty not to be angry, not to commit adultery, not to take oaths, not to resist evil, not to make war; organize rather an existence which shall render the doing of all these things as difficult as the non-performance of them is now laborious. You cannot refuse to recognize the validity of these rules, for they are the commandments of the God whom you pretend to worship.

Let us suppose that you are an unbeliever, a philosopher, it matters not of what special school. You affirm that the progress of the world is in accordance with a law that you have discovered. The doctrine of Jesus does not oppose your views; it is in harmony with the law that you have discovered. But, aside from this law, in pursuance of which the world will in the course of a thousand years reach a state of felicity, there is still your own personal life to be considered. This life you can use by living in conformity to reason, or you can waste it by living in opposition to reason, and you have now for its guidance no rule whatever, except the decrees drawn up by men whom you do not esteem, and enforced by the police. The doctrine of Jesus offers you rules which are assuredly in accord with your law of "altruism," which is nothing but a feeble paraphrase of this same doctrine of Jesus.

Let us suppose that you are an average man, half sceptic, half believer, one who has no time to analyze the meaning of human life, and one therefore who has no determinate theory of existence. You live as lives the rest of the world about you. The doctrine of Jesus is not at all contrary to your condition. You are incapable of reason, of verifying the truths of the doctrines that are taught you; it is easier for you to do as others do. But however modest may be your estimate of your powers of reason, you know that you have within you a judge that sometimes approves your acts and sometimes condemns them. However modest your social position, there are occasions when you are bound to reflect and ask yourself, "Shall I follow the example of the rest of the world, or shall I act in accordance with my own judgment?" It is precisely on these occasions when you are called upon to solve some problem with regard to the conduct of life, that the commandments of Jesus appeal to you in all their efficiency. The commandments of Jesus will surely respond to your inquiry, because they apply to your whole existence. The response will be in accord with your reason and your conscience. If you are nearer to faith than to unbelief, you will, in following these commandments, act in harmony with the will of God. If you are nearer to scepticism than to belief, you will, in following the doctrine of Jesus, govern your actions by the laws of reason, for the commandments of Jesus make manifest their own meaning, and their own justification.

"*Now is the judgment of this world: now shall the prince of this world be cast out.*" (John xii. 31.)

"*These things have I spoken unto you, that in me ye may have peace. In the world ye have tribulation: but be of good cheer; I have overcome the world.*" (John xvi. 33.)

The world, that is, the evil in the world, is overcome. If evil still exists in the world, it exists only through the influence of inertia; it no longer contains the principle of vitality. For those who have faith in the commandments of Jesus, it does not exist at all. It is vanquished by an awakened conscience, by the elevation of the son of man. A train that has been put in motion continues to move in the direction in which it was started; but the time comes when the intelligent effort of a controlling hand is made manifest, and the movement is reversed.

LEO TOLSTOY

"*Ye are of God, and have overcome them because greater is he that is within you than he that is in the world.*" (1 John v. 4.)

The faith that triumphs over the doctrines of the world is faith in the doctrine of Jesus.

CHAPTER XII.

I BELIEVE in the doctrine of Jesus, and this is my religion:—

I believe that nothing but the fulfilment of the doctrine of Jesus can give true happiness to men. I believe that the fulfilment of this doctrine is possible, easy, and pleasant. I believe that although none other follows this doctrine, and I alone am left to practise it, I cannot refuse to obey it, if I would save my life from the certainty of eternal loss; just as a man in a burning house if he find a door of safety, must go out, so I must avail myself of the way to salvation. I believe that my life according to the doctrine of the world has been a torment, and that a life according to the doctrine of Jesus can alone give me in this world the happiness for which I was destined by the Father of Life. I believe that this doctrine is essential to the welfare of humanity, will save me from the certainty of eternal loss, and will give me in this world the greatest possible sum of happiness. Believing thus, I am obliged to practise its commandments.

"*The law was given by Moses; grace and truth came by Jesus Christ.*" (John i. 17.)

The doctrine of Jesus is a doctrine of grace and truth. Once I knew not grace and knew not truth. Mistaking evil for good, I fell into evil, and I doubted the righteousness of my tendency toward good. I understand and believe now that the good toward which I was attracted is the will of the Father, the essence of life.

Jesus has told us to live in pursuit of the good, and to beware of snares and temptations (σκάνδαλον) which, by enticing us with the semblance of good, draw us away from true goodness, and lead us into evil. He has taught us that our welfare is to be sought in fellowship with all men; that evil is a violation of fellowship with the son of man, and that we must not deprive ourselves of the welfare to be had by obedience to his doctrine.

Jesus has demonstrated that fellowship with the son of man, the love of men for one another, is not merely an ideal after which men are to strive; he has shown us that this love and this fellowship are natural attributes of men in their normal condition, the condition into which children are born, the condition in which all men would live if they were not drawn aside by error, illusions, and temptations.

In his commandments, Jesus has enumerated clearly and unmistakably the temptations that interfere with this natural condition of love and fellowship and render it a prey to evil. The commandments of Jesus offer the remedies by which I must save myself from the temptations that have deprived me of happiness; and so I am forced to believe that these commandments are true. Happiness was within my grasp and I destroyed it. In his commandments Jesus has shown me the temptations that lead to the destruction of happiness. I can no longer work for the destruction of my happiness, and in this determination, and in this alone, is the substance of my religion.

Jesus has shown me that the first temptation destructive of happiness is enmity toward men, anger against them. I cannot refuse to believe this, and so I cannot willingly remain at enmity with others. I cannot, as I could once, foster anger, be proud of it, fan into a flame, justify it, regarding myself as an intelligent and superior man and others as useless and foolish people. Now, when I give up to anger, I can only realize that I alone am guilty, and seek to make peace with those who have aught against me.

But this is not all. While I now see that anger is an abnormal, pernicious, and morbid state, I also perceive the temptation that led me into it. The temptation was in separating myself from my fellows, recognizing only a few of them as my equals, and regarding all the others as persons of no account (*rekim*) or as uncultivated animals (*fools*). I see now that this wilful separation from other men, this judgment of *raca* or *fool* passed upon others, was the principal source of my disagreements. In looking over my past life I saw that I had rarely permitted my anger to rise against those whom I considered as my equals, whom I seldom abused. But the least disagreeable action on the part of one whom I considered an inferior inflamed my anger and led me to abusive words or actions, and the more superior I felt myself to be, the less careful I was of my temper; sometimes the mere supposition that a man was of a lower social position than myself was enough to provoke me to an outrageous manner.

I understand now that he alone is above others who is humble with others and makes himself the servant of all. I understand now why those that are great in the sight of men are an abomination to God, who has declared woe upon the rich and mighty and invoked blessedness upon the poor and humble. Now I understand this truth, I have faith in it, and this faith has transformed my perception of what is right and important, and what is wrong and despicable. Everything that once seemed to me right and important, such as honors, glory, civilization, wealth, the complications and refinements of existence, luxury, rich food, fine clothing, etiquette, have become for me wrong and despicable. Everything that formerly seemed to me wrong and despicable, such as rusticity, obscurity, poverty, austerity, simplicity of surroundings, of food, of clothing, of manners, all have now become right and important to me. And so although I may at times give myself up to anger and abuse another, I cannot deliberately yield to wrath and so deprive myself of the true source of happiness,—fellowship and love; for it is possible that a man should lay a snare for his own feet and so be lost. Now, I can no longer give my support to anything that lifts me above or separates me from others. I cannot, as I once did, recognize in myself or others titles or ranks or qualities aside from the title and quality of manhood. I can no longer seek for fame and glory; I can no longer cultivate a system of instruction which separates me from men. I cannot in my surroundings, my food, my clothing, my manners, strive for what not only separates me from others but renders me a reproach to the majority of mankind.

Jesus showed me another temptation destructive of happiness, that is, debauchery, the desire to possess another woman than her to whom I am united. I can no longer, as I did once, consider my sensuality as a sublime trait of human nature. I can no longer justify it by my love for the beautiful, or my amorousness, or the faults of my companion. At the first inclination toward debauchery I cannot fail to recognize that I am in a morbid and abnormal state, and to seek to rid myself of the besetting sin.

Knowing that debauchery is an evil, I also know its cause, and can thus evade it. I know now that the principal cause of this temptation is not the necessity for the sexual relation, but the abandonment of wives by their husbands, and of husbands by their wives. I know now that a man who forsakes a woman, or a woman who forsakes a man, when the two have once been united, is guilty of the divorce which Jesus forbade, because men and women abandoned by their first companions are the original cause of all the debauchery in the world.

In seeking to discover the influences that led to debauchery, I found one to be a barbarous physical and intellectual education that developed the erotic passion which the world endeavors to justify by the most subtle arguments. But the principal influence I found to be the abandonment of the woman to whom I had first been united, and the situation of the abandoned women around me. The principal source of temptation was not in carnal desires, but in the fact that those desires were not satisfied in the men and women by whom I was surrounded. I now understand the words of Jesus when he says:—

"*He which made them from the beginning, made them male and female.... So that they are no more twain, but one flesh. What, therefore, God hath joined together, let not man put asunder.*" (Matt. xix. 4-6.)

I understand now that monogamy is the natural law of humanity, which cannot with impunity be violated. I now understand perfectly the words declaring that the man or woman who separates from a companion to seek another, forces the forsaken one to resort to debauchery, and thus introduces into the world an evil that returns upon those who cause it.

This I believe; and the faith I now have has transformed my opinions with regard to the right and important, and the wrong and despicable, things of life. What once seemed to me the most delightful existence in the world, an existence made up of dainty, æsthetic pleasures and passions, is now revolting to me. And a life of simplicity and indigence, which moderates the sexual desires, now seems to me good. The human institution of marriage, which gives a nominal sanction to the union of man and woman, I regard as of less grave importance than that the union, when accomplished, should be regarded as the will of God, and never be broken.

Now, when in moments of weakness I yield to the promptings of desire, I know the snare that would deliver me into evil, and so I cannot deliberately plan my method of existence as formerly I was accustomed to do. I no longer habitually cherish physical sloth and luxury, which excite to excessive sensuality. I can no longer pursue amusements which are oil to the fire of amorous sensuality,—the reading of romances and the most of poetry, listening to music, attendance at theatres and balls,— amusements that once seemed to me elevated and refining, but which I now see to be injurious. I can no longer abandon the woman with whom I have been united, for I know that by forsaking her, I set a snare for myself, for her, and for others. I can no longer encourage the gross and idle existence of others. I can no longer encourage or take part in licentious pastimes, romantic literature, plays, operas, balls, which are so many snares for myself and for others. I cannot favor the celibacy of persons fitted for the marriage relation. I cannot encourage the separation of wives from their husbands. I cannot make any distinction between unions that are called by the name of marriage, and those that are denied this name. I am obliged to consider as sacred and absolute the sole and unique union by which man is once for all indissolubly bound to the first woman with whom he has been united.

Jesus has shown me that the third temptation destructive to true happiness is the oath. I am obliged to believe his words; consequently, I cannot, as I once did, bind myself by oath to serve any one for any purpose, and I can no longer, as I did formerly, justify myself for having taken an oath because "it would harm no one," because everybody did the same, because it is necessary for the State, because the consequences might be bad for me or for some one else if I refuse to submit to this exaction. I know now that it is an evil for myself and for others, and I cannot conform to it.

Nor is this all. I now know the snare that led me into evil, and I can no longer act as an accomplice. I know that the snare is in the use of God's name to sanction an imposture, and that the imposture consists in promising in advance to obey the commands of one man, or of many men, while I ought to obey the commands of God alone. I know now that evils the most terrible of all in their result—war, imprisonments, capital punishment—exist only because of the oath, in virtue of which men make themselves instruments of evil, and believe that they free themselves from all responsibility. As I think now of the many evils that have impelled me to hostility and hatred, I see that they all originated with the the oath, the engagement to submit to the will of others. I understand now the meaning of the words:—

"*But let your speech be, Yea, yea; nay, nay; and whatsoever is more than these is of evil.*" (Matt. v. 37.)

Understanding this, I am convinced that the oath is destructive of my true welfare and of that of others, and this belief changes my estimate of right and wrong, of the important and despicable. What once seemed to me right and important,—the promise of fidelity to the government supported by the oath, the exacting of oaths from others, and all acts contrary to conscience, done because of the oath, now seem to me wrong and despicable. Therefore I can no longer evade the commandment of Jesus forbidding the oath, I can no longer bind myself by oath to any one, I cannot exact an oath from another, I cannot encourage men to take an oath, or to cause others to take an oath; nor can I regard the oath as necessary, important, or even inoffensive.

Jesus has shown me that the fourth temptation destructive to my happiness is the resort to violence for the resistance of evil. I am obliged to believe that this is an evil for myself and for others; consequently, I cannot, as I did once, deliberately resort to violence, and seek to justify my action with the pretext that it is indispensable for the defence of my person and property, or of the persons and property of others. I can no longer yield to the first impulse to resort to violence; I am obliged to renounce it, and to abstain from it altogether.

But this is not all. I understand now the snare that caused me to fall into this evil. I know now that the snare consisted in the erroneous belief that my life could be made secure by violence, by the defence of my person and property against the encroachments of others. I know now that a great portion of the evils that afflict mankind are due to this,—that men, instead of giving their work for others, deprive themselves completely of the privilege of work, and forcibly appropriate the labor of their fellows. Every one regards a resort to violence as the best possible security for life and for property, and I now see that a great portion of the evil that I did myself, and saw others do, resulted from this practice. I understood now the meaning of the words:—

"*Not to be ministered unto, but to minister.*" "*The laborer is worthy of his food.*"

I believe now that my true welfare, and that of others, is possible only when I labor not for myself, but for another, and that I must not refuse to labor for another, but to give with joy that of which he has need. This faith has changed my estimate of what is right and important, and wrong and despicable. What once seemed to me right and important—riches, proprietary rights, the point of honor, the maintenance of personal dignity and personal privileges—have now become to me wrong and despicable.

Labor for others, poverty, humility, the renunciation of property and of personal privileges, have become in my eyes right and important.

When, now, in a moment of forgetfulness, I yield to the impulse to resort to violence, for the defence of my person or property, or of the persons or property of others, I can no longer deliberately make use of this snare for my own destruction and the destruction of others. I can no longer acquire property. I can no longer resort to force in any form for my own defence or the defence of another. I can no longer co-operate with any power whose object is the defence of men and their property by violence. I can no longer act in a judicial capacity, or clothe myself with any authority, or take part in the exercise of any jurisdiction whatever. I can no longer encourage others in the support of tribunals, or in the exercise of authoritative administration.

Jesus has shown me that the fifth temptation that deprives me of well-being, is the distinction that we make between compatriots and foreigners. I must believe this; consequently, if, in a moment of forgetfulness, I have a feeling of hostility toward a man of another nationality, I am obliged, in moments of reflection, to regard this feeling as wrong. I can no longer, as I did formerly, justify my hostility by the superiority of my own people over others, or by the ignorance, the cruelty, or the barbarism of another race. I can no longer refrain from striving to be even more friendly with a foreigner than with one of my own countrymen.

I know now that the distinction I once made between my own people and those of other countries is destructive of my welfare; but, more than this, I now know the snare that led me into this evil, and I can no longer, as I did once, walk deliberately and calmly into this snare. I know now that this snare consists in the erroneous belief that my welfare is dependent only upon the welfare of my countrymen, and not upon the welfare of all mankind. I know now that my fellowship with others cannot be shut off by a frontier, or by a government decree which decides that I belong to some particular political organization. I know

now that all men are everywhere brothers and equals. When I think now of all the evil that I have done, that I have endured, and that I have seen about me, arising from national enmities, I see clearly that it is all due to that gross imposture called patriotism,—love for one's native land. When I think now of my education, I see how these hateful feelings were grafted into my mind. I understand now the meaning of the words:—

"*Love your enemies, and pray for them that persecute you; that ye may be sons of your Father that is in heaven: for he maketh his sun to rise on the evil and the good, and sendeth rain on the just and the unjust.*"

I understand now that true welfare is possible for me only on condition that I recognize my fellowship with the whole world. I believe this, and the belief has changed my estimate of what is right and wrong, important and despicable. What once seemed to me right and important—love of country, love for those of my own race, for the organization called the State, services rendered at the expense of the welfare of other men, military exploits—now seem to me detestable and pitiable. What once seemed to me shameful and wrong—renunciation of nationality, and the cultivation of cosmopolitanism—now seem to me right and important. When, now, in a moment of forgetfulness, I sustain a Russian in preference to a foreigner, and desire the success of Russia or of the Russian people, I can no longer in lucid moments allow myself to be controlled by illusions so destructive to my welfare and the welfare of others. I can no longer recognize states or peoples; I can no longer take part in any difference between peoples or states, or any discussion between them either verbal or written, much less in any service in behalf of any particular state. I can no longer co-operate with measures maintained by divisions between states,—the collection of custom duties, taxes, the manufacture of arms and projectiles, or any act favoring armaments, military service, and, for a stronger reason, wars,—neither can I encourage others to take any part in them.

I understand in what my true welfare consists, I have faith in that, and consequently I cannot do what would inevitably be destructive of that welfare. I not only have faith that I ought to live thus, but I have faith that if I live thus, and only thus, my life will attain its only possible meaning, and be reasonable, pleasant, and indestructible by death. I believe that my reasonable life, the light I bear with me, was given to me only that it might shine before men, not in words only, but in good deeds, that men may thereby glorify the Father. I believe that my life and my consciousness of truth is the talent confided to me for a good purpose, and that this talent fulfils its mission only when it is of use to others. I believe that I am a Ninevite with regard to other Jonahs from whom I have learned and shall learn of the truth; but that I am a Jonah in regard to other Ninevites to whom I am bound to transmit the truth. I believe that the only meaning of my life is to be attained by living in accordance with the light that is within me, and that I must allow this light to shine forth to be seen of all men. This faith gives me renewed strength to fulfil the doctrine of Jesus, and to overcome the obstacles which still arise in my pathway. All that once caused me to doubt the possibility of practising the doctrine of Jesus, everything that once turned me aside, the possibility of privations, and of suffering, and death, inflicted by those who know not the doctrine of Jesus, now confirm its truth and draw me into its service. Jesus said, "*When you have lifted up the son of man, then shall you know that I am he*,"—then shall you be drawn into my service,—and I feel that I am irresistibly drawn to him by the influence of his doctrine. "*The truth*," he says again, "*The truth shall make you free*," and I know that I am in perfect liberty.

I once thought that if a foreign invasion occurred, or even if evil-minded persons attacked me, and I did not defend myself, I should be robbed and beaten and tortured and killed with those whom I felt bound to protect, and this possibility troubled me. But this that once troubled me now seems desirable and in conformity with the truth. I know now that the foreign enemy and the malefactors or brigands are all men like myself; that, like myself, they love good and hate evil; that they live as I live, on the borders of death; and that, with me, they seek for salvation, and will find it in the doctrine of Jesus. The evil that they do to me will be evil to them, and so can be nothing but good for me.

But if truth is unknown to them, and they do evil thinking that they do good, I, who know the truth, am bound to reveal it to them, and this I can do only by refusing to participate in evil, and thereby confessing the truth by my example.

"But hither come the enemy,—Germans, Turks, savages; if you do not make war on them, they will exterminate you!" They will do nothing of the sort. If there were a society of Christian men that did evil to none and gave of their labor for the good of others, such a society would have no enemies to kill or to torture them. The foreigners would take only what the members of this society voluntarily gave, making no distinction between Russians, or Turks, or Germans. But when Christians live in the midst of a non-Christian society which defends itself by force of arm, and calls upon the Christians to join in waging war, then the Christians have an opportunity for revealing the truth to them who know it not. A Christian knowing the truth bears witness of the truth before others, and this testimony can be made manifest only by example. He must renounce war and do good to all men, whether they are foreigners or compatriots.

"But there are wicked men among compatriots; they will attack a Christian, and if the latter do not defend himself, will pillage and massacre him and his family." No; they will not do so. If all the members of this family are Christians, and consequently hold their lives only for the service of others, no man will be found insane enough to deprive such people of the necessaries of life or to kill them. The famous Maclay lived among the most bloodthirsty of savages; they did not kill him, they reverenced him and followed his teachings, simply because he did not fear them, exacted nothing from them, and treated them always with kindness.

"But what if a Christian lives in a non-Christian family, accustomed to defend itself and its property by a resort to violence, and is called upon to take part in measures of defence?" This solicitation is simply an appeal to the Christian to fulfil the decrees of truth. A Christian knows the truth only that he may show it to others, more especially to his neighbors and to those who are bound to him by ties of blood and friendship, and a

Christian can show the truth only by refusing to join in the errors of others, by taking part neither with aggressors or defenders, but by abandoning all that he has to those who will take it from him, thus showing by his acts that he has need of nothing save the fulfilment of the will of God, and that he fears nothing except disobedience to that will.

"But how, if the government will not permit a member of the society over which it has sway, to refuse to recognize the fundamental principles of governmental order or to decline to fulfil the duties of a citizen? The government exacts from a Christian the oath, jury service, military service, and his refusal to conform to these demands may be punished by exile, imprisonment, and even by death." Then, once more, the exactions of those in authority are only an appeal to the Christian to manifest the truth that is in him. The exactions of those in authority are to a Christian the exactions of those who do not know the truth. Consequently, a Christian who knows the truth must bear witness of the truth to those who know it not. Exile and imprisonment and death afford to the Christian the possibility of bearing witness of the truth, not in words, but in acts. Violence, war, brigandage, executions, are not accomplished through the forces of unconscious nature; they are accomplished by men who are blinded, and do not know the truth. Consequently, the more evil these men do to Christians, the further they are from the truth, the more unhappy they are, and the more necessary it is that they should have knowledge of the truth. Now a Christian cannot make known his knowledge of truth except by abstaining from the errors that lead men into evil; he must render good for evil. This is the life-work of a Christian, and if it is accomplished, death cannot harm him, for the meaning of his life can never be destroyed.

Men are united by error into a compact mass. The prevailing power of evil is the cohesive force that binds them together. The reasonable activity of humanity is to destroy the cohesive power of evil. Revolutions are attempts to shatter the power of evil by violence. Men think that by hammering upon the mass they will be able to break it in fragments, but they only make it more dense and impermeable than it was before. External violence is of no avail. The disruptive movement must come from within when molecule releases its hold upon molecule and the whole mass falls into disintegration. Error is the force that binds men together; truth alone can set them free. Now truth is truth only when it is in action, and then only can it be transmitted from man to man. Only truth in action, by introducing light into the conscience of each individual, can dissolve the homogeneity of error, and detach men one by one from its bonds.

This work has been going on for eighteen hundred years. It began when the commandments of Jesus were first given to humanity, and it will not cease till, as Jesus said, "*all things be accomplished*" (Matt. v. 18). The Church that sought to detach men from error and to weld them together again by the solemn affirmation that it alone was the truth, has long since fallen to decay. But the Church composed of men united, not by promises or sacraments, but by deeds of truth and love, has always lived and will live forever. Now, as eighteen hundred years ago, this Church is made up not of those who say "*Lord, Lord,*" and bring forth iniquity, but of those who hear the words of truth and reveal them in their lives. The members of this Church know that life is to them a blessing as long as they maintain fraternity with others and dwell in the fellowship of the son of man; and that the blessing will be lost only to those who do not obey the commandments of Jesus. And so the members of this Church practise the commandments of Jesus and thereby teach them to others. Whether this Church be in numbers little or great, it is, nevertheless, the Church that shall never perish, the Church that shall finally unite within its bonds the hearts of all mankind.

"*Fear not, little flock; for it is your Father's good purpose to give you the kingdom.*"

3. WHAT MEN LIVE BY

CHAPTER I.

A shoemaker named Simon, who had neither house nor land of his own, lived with his wife and children in a peasant's hut, and earned his living by his work. Work was cheap, but bread was dear, and what he earned he spent for food. The man and his wife had but one sheepskin coat between them for winter wear, and even that was torn to tatters, and this was the second year he had been wanting to buy sheep-skins for a new coat. Before winter Simon saved up a little money: a three-rouble note lay hidden in his wife's box, and five roubles and twenty kopeks were owed him by customers in the village.

So one morning he prepared to go to the village to buy the sheep-skins. He put on over his shirt his wife's wadded nankeen jacket, and over that he put his own cloth coat. He took the three-rouble note in his pocket, cut himself a stick to serve as a staff, and started off after breakfast. "I'll collect the five roubles that are due to me," thought he, "add the three I have got, and that will be enough to buy sheep-skins for the winter coat."

He came to the village and called at a peasant's hut, but the man was not at home. The peasant's wife promised that the money should be paid next week, but she would not pay it herself. Then Simon called on another peasant, but this one swore he had no money, and would only pay twenty kopeks which he owed for a pair of boots Simon had mended. Simon then tried to buy the sheep-skins on credit, but the dealer would not trust him.

"Bring your money," said he, "then you may have your pick of the skins. We know what debt-collecting is like." So all the business the shoemaker did was to get the twenty kopeks for boots he had mended, and to take a pair of felt boots a peasant gave him to sole with leather.

Simon felt downhearted. He spent the twenty kopeks on vodka, and started homewards without having bought any skins. In the morning he had felt the frost; but now, after drinking the vodka, he felt warm, even without a sheep-skin coat. He trudged along, striking his stick on the frozen earth with one hand, swinging the felt boots with the other, and talking to himself.

CHAPTER II.

"I'm quite warm," said he, "though I have no sheep-skin coat. I've had a drop, and it runs through all my veins. I need no sheep-skins. I go along and don't worry about anything. That's the sort of man I am! What do I care? I can live without sheep-skins. I don't need them. My wife will fret, to be sure. And, true enough, it is a shame; one works all day long, and then does not get paid. Stop a bit! If you don't bring that money along, sure enough I'll skin you, blessed if I don't. How's that? He pays twenty kopeks at a time! What can I do with twenty kopeks? Drink it-that's all one can do! Hard up, he says he is! So he may be—but what about me? You have a house, and cattle, and everything; I've only what I stand up in! You have corn of your own growing; I have to buy every grain. Do what I will, I must spend three roubles every week for bread alone. I come home and find the bread all used up, and I have to fork out another rouble and a half. So just pay up what you owe, and no nonsense about it!"

By this time he had nearly reached the shrine at the bend of the road. Looking up, he saw something whitish behind the shrine. The daylight was fading, and the shoemaker peered at the thing without being able to make out what it was. "There was no white stone here before. Can it be an ox? It's not like an ox. It has a head like a man, but it's too white; and what could a man be doing there?"

He came closer, so that it was clearly visible. To his surprise it really was a man, alive or dead, sitting naked, leaning motionless against the shrine. Terror seized the shoemaker, and he thought, "Some one has killed him, stripped him, and left him there. If I meddle I shall surely get into trouble."

So the shoemaker went on. He passed in front of the shrine so that he could not see the man. When he had gone some way, he looked back, and saw that the man was no longer leaning against the shrine, but was moving as if looking towards him. The shoemaker felt more frightened than before, and thought, "Shall I go back to him, or shall I go on? If I go near him something dreadful may happen. Who knows who the fellow is? He has not come here for any good. If I go near him he may jump up and throttle me, and there will be no getting away. Or if not, he'd still be a burden on one's hands. What could I do with a naked man? I couldn't give him my last clothes. Heaven only help me to get away!"

So the shoemaker hurried on, leaving the shrine behind him—when suddenly his conscience smote him, and he stopped in the road.

"What are you doing, Simon?" said he to himself. "The man may be dying of want, and you slip past afraid. Have you grown so rich as to be afraid of robbers? Ah, Simon, shame on you!"

So he turned back and went up to the man.

CHAPTER III.

Simon approached the stranger, looked at him, and saw that he was a young man, fit, with no bruises on his body, only evidently freezing and frightened, and he sat there leaning back without looking up at Simon, as if too faint to lift his eyes. Simon went close to him, and then the man seemed to wake up. Turning his head, he opened his eyes and looked into Simon's face. That one look was enough to make Simon fond of the man. He threw the felt boots on the ground, undid his sash, laid it on the boots, and took off his cloth coat.

"It's not a time for talking," said he. "Come, put this coat on at once!" And Simon took the man by the elbows and helped him to rise. As he stood there, Simon saw that his body was clean and in good condition, his hands and feet shapely, and his face good and kind. He threw his coat over the man's shoulders, but the latter could not find the sleeves. Simon guided his arms into them, and drawing the coat well on, wrapped it closely about him, tying the sash round the man's waist.

Simon even took off his torn cap to put it on the man's head, but then his own head felt cold, and he thought: "I'm quite bald, while he has long curly hair." So he put his cap on his own head again. "It will be better to give him something for his feet," thought he; and he made the man sit down, and helped him to put on the felt boots, saying, "There, friend, now move about and warm yourself. Other matters can be settled later on. Can you walk?"

The man stood up and looked kindly at Simon, but could not say a word.

"Why don't you speak?" said Simon. "It's too cold to stay here, we must be getting home. There now, take my stick, and if you're feeling weak, lean on that. Now step out!"

The man started walking, and moved easily, not lagging behind.

As they went along, Simon asked him, "And where do you belong to?" "I'm not from these parts."

"I thought as much. I know the folks hereabouts. But, how did you come to be there by the shrine?"

"I cannot tell."

"Has some one been ill-treating you?"

"No one has ill-treated me. God has punished me."

"Of course God rules all. Still, you'll have to find food and shelter somewhere. Where do you want to go to?"

"It is all the same to me."

Simon was amazed. The man did not look like a rogue, and he spoke gently, but yet he gave no account of himself. Still Simon thought, "Who knows what may have happened?" And he said to the stranger: "Well then, come home with me, and at least warm yourself awhile."

So Simon walked towards his home, and the stranger kept up with him, walking at his side. The wind had risen and Simon felt it cold under his shirt. He was getting over his tipsiness by now, and began to feel the frost. He went along sniffling and wrapping his wife's coat round him, and he thought to himself: "There now—talk about sheep-skins! I went out for sheep-skins and come home without even a coat to my back, and what is more, I'm bringing a naked man along with me. Matryona won't be pleased!" And when he thought of his wife he felt sad; but when he looked at the stranger and remembered how he had looked up at him at the shrine, his heart was glad.

CHAPTER IV.

Simon's wife had everything ready early that day. She had cut wood, brought water, fed the children, eaten her own meal, and now she sat thinking. She wondered when she ought to make bread: now or tomorrow? There was still a large piece left.

"If Simon has had some dinner in town," thought she, "and does not eat much for supper, the bread will last out another day."

She weighed the piece of bread in her hand again and again, and thought: "I won't make any more today. We have only enough flour left to bake one batch; We can manage to make this last out till Friday."

So Matryona put away the bread, and sat down at the table to patch her husband's shirt. While she worked she thought how her husband was buying skins for a winter coat.

"If only the dealer does not cheat him. My good man is much too simple; he cheats nobody, but any child can take him in. Eight roubles is a lot of money—he should get a good coat at that price. Not tanned skins, but still a proper winter coat. How difficult it was last winter to get on without a warm coat. I could neither get down to the river, nor go out anywhere. When he went out he put on all we had, and there was nothing left for me. He did not start very early today, but still it's time he was back. I only hope he has not gone on the spree!"

Hardly had Matryona thought this, when steps were heard on the threshold, and some one entered. Matryona stuck her needle into her work and went out into the passage. There she saw two men: Simon, and with him a man without a hat, and wearing felt boots.

Matryona noticed at once that her husband smelt of spirits. "There now, he has been drinking," thought she. And when she saw that he was coatless, had only her jacket on, brought no parcel, stood there silent, and seemed ashamed, her heart was ready to break with disappointment. "He has drunk the money," thought she, "and has been on the spree with some good-for-nothing fellow whom he has brought home with him."

Matryona let them pass into the hut, followed them in, and saw that the stranger was a young, slight man, wearing her husband's coat. There was no shirt to be seen under it, and he had no hat. Having entered, he stood, neither moving, nor raising his eyes, and Matryona thought: "He must be a bad man—he's afraid."

Matryona frowned, and stood beside the oven looking to see what they would do.

Simon took off his cap and sat down on the bench as if things were all right.

"Come, Matryona; if supper is ready, let us have some."

Matryona muttered something to herself and did not move, but stayed where she was, by the oven. She looked first at the one and then at the other of them, and only shook her head. Simon saw that his wife was annoyed, but tried to pass it off. Pretending not to notice anything, he took the stranger by the arm.

"Sit down, friend," said he, "and let us have some supper."

The stranger sat down on the bench.

"Haven't you cooked anything for us?" said Simon.

Matryona's anger boiled over. "I've cooked, but not for you. It seems to me you have drunk your wits away. You went to buy a sheep-skin coat, but come home without so much as the coat you had on, and bring a naked vagabond home with you. I have no supper for drunkards like you."

"That's enough, Matryona. Don't wag your tongue without reason. You had better ask what sort of man—"

"And you tell me what you've done with the money?"

Simon found the pocket of the jacket, drew out the three-rouble note, and unfolded it.

"Here is the money. Trifonof did not pay, but promises to pay soon."

Matryona got still more angry; he had bought no sheep-skins, but had put his only coat on some naked fellow and had even brought him to their house.

She snatched up the note from the table, took it to put away in safety, and said: "I have no supper for you. We can't feed all the naked drunkards in the world."

"There now, Matryona, hold your tongue a bit. First hear what a man has to say-"

"Much wisdom I shall hear from a drunken fool. I was right in not wanting to marry you-a drunkard. The linen my mother gave me you drank; and now you've been to buy a coat-and have drunk it, too!"

Simon tried to explain to his wife that he had only spent twenty kopeks; tried to tell how he had found the man—but Matryona would not let him get a word in. She talked nineteen to the dozen, and dragged in things that had happened ten years before.

Matryona talked and talked, and at last she flew at Simon and seized him by the sleeve.

"Give me my jacket. It is the only one I have, and you must needs take it from me and wear it yourself. Give it here, you mangy dog, and may the devil take you."

Simon began to pull off the jacket, and turned a sleeve of it inside out; Matryona seized the jacket and it burst its seams, She snatched it up, threw it over her head and went to the door. She meant to go out, but stopped undecided—she wanted to work off her anger, but she also wanted to learn what sort of a man the stranger was.

CHAPTER V.

Matryona stopped and said: "If he were a good man he would not be naked. Why, he hasn't even a shirt on him. If he were all right, you would say where you came across the fellow."

"That's just what I am trying to tell you," said Simon. "As I came to the shrine I saw him sitting all naked and frozen. It isn't quite the weather to sit about naked! God sent me to him, or he would have perished. What was I to do? How do we know what may have happened to him? So I took him, clothed him, and brought him along. Don't be so angry, Matryona. It is a sin. Remember, we all must die one day."

Angry words rose to Matryona's lips, but she looked at the stranger and was silent. He sat on the edge of the bench, motionless, his hands folded on his knees, his head drooping on his breast, his eyes closed, and his brows knit as if in pain. Matryona was silent: and Simon said: "Matryona, have you no love of God?"

Matryona heard these words, and as she looked at the stranger, suddenly her heart softened towards him. She came back from the door, and going to the oven she got out the supper. Setting a cup on the table, she poured out some kvas. Then she brought out the last piece of bread, and set out a knife and spoons.

"Eat, if you want to," said she.

Simon drew the stranger to the table.

"Take your place, young man," said he.

Simon cut the bread, crumbled it into the broth, and they began to eat. Matryona sat at the corner of the table resting her head on her hand and looking at the stranger.

And Matryona was touched with pity for the stranger, and began to feel fond of him. And at once the stranger's face lit up;

his brows were no longer bent, he raised his eyes and smiled at Matryona.

When they had finished supper, the woman cleared away the things and began questioning the stranger. "Where are you from?" said she.

"I am not from these parts."

"But how did you come to be on the road?"

"I may not tell."

"Did some one rob you?"

"God punished me."

"And you were lying there naked?"

"Yes, naked and freezing. Simon saw me and had pity on me. He took off his coat, put it on me and brought me here. And you have fed me, given me drink, and shown pity on me. God will reward you!"

Matryona rose, took from the window Simon's old shirt she had been patching, and gave it to the stranger. She also brought out a pair of trousers for him.

"There," said she, "I see you have no shirt. Put this on, and lie down where you please, in the loft or on the oven."

The stranger took off the coat, put on the shirt, and lay down in the loft. Matryona put out the candle, took the coat, and climbed to where her husband lay.

Matryona drew the skirts of the coat over her and lay down, but could not sleep; she could not get the stranger out of her mind.

When she remembered that he had eaten their last piece of bread and that there was none for tomorrow, and thought of the shirt and trousers she had given away, she felt grieved; but when she remembered how he had smiled, her heart was glad.

Long did Matryona lie awake, and she noticed that Simon also was awake—he drew the coat towards him.

"Simon!"

"Well?"

"You have had the last of the bread, and I have not put any to rise. I don't know what we shall do tomorrow. Perhaps I can borrow some of neighbor Martha."

"If we're alive we shall find something to eat."

The woman lay still awhile, and then said, "He seems a good man, but why does he not tell us who he is?"

"I suppose he has his reasons."

"Simon!"

"Well?"

"We give; but why does nobody give us anything?"

Simon did not know what to say; so he only said, "Let us stop talking," and turned over and went to sleep.

CHAPTER VI.

In the morning Simon awoke. The children were still asleep; his wife had gone to the neighbor's to borrow some bread. The stranger alone was sitting on the bench, dressed in the old shirt and trousers, and looking upwards. His face was brighter than it had been the day before.

Simon said to him, "Well, friend; the belly wants bread, and the naked body clothes. One has to work for a living What work do you know?"

"I do not know any."

This surprised Simon, but he said, "Men who want to learn can learn anything."

"Men work, and I will work also."

"What is your name?"

"Michael."

"Well, Michael, if you don't wish to talk about yourself, that is your own affair; but you'll have to earn a living for yourself. If you will work as I tell you, I will give you food and shelter."

"May God reward you! I will learn. Show me what to do."

Simon took yarn, put it round his thumb and began to twist it.

"It is easy enough—see!"

Michael watched him, put some yarn round his own thumb in the same way, caught the knack, and twisted the yarn also.

Then Simon showed him how to wax the thread. This also Michael mastered. Next Simon showed him how to twist the bristle in, and how to sew, and this, too, Michael learned at once.

Whatever Simon showed him he understood at once, and after three days he worked as if he had sewn boots all his life. He worked without stopping, and ate little. When work was over he sat silently, looking upwards. He hardly went into the street, spoke only when necessary, and neither joked nor laughed. They never saw him smile, except that first evening when Matryona gave them supper.

CHAPTER VII.

Day by day and week by week the year went round. Michael lived and worked with Simon. His fame spread till people said that no one sewed boots so neatly and strongly as Simon's workman, Michael; and from all the district round people came to Simon for their boots, and he began to be well off.

One winter day, as Simon and Michael sat working, a carriage on sledge-runners, with three horses and with bells, drove up to the hut. They looked out of the window; the carriage stopped at their door, a fine servant jumped down from the box and opened the door. A gentleman in a fur coat got out and walked up to Simon's hut. Up jumped Matryona and opened the door wide. The gentleman stooped to enter the hut, and when he drew himself up again his head nearly reached the ceiling, and he seemed quite to fill his end of the room.

Simon rose, bowed, and looked at the gentleman with astonishment. He had never seen any one like him. Simon himself was lean, Michael was thin, and Matryona was dry as a bone, but this man was like some one from another world: red-faced, burly, with a neck like a bull's, and looking altogether as if he were cast in iron.

The gentleman puffed, threw off his fur coat, sat down on the bench, and said, "Which of you is the master bootmaker?"

"I am, your Excellency," said Simon, coming forward.

Then the gentleman shouted to his lad, "Hey, Fedka, bring the leather!"

The servant ran in, bringing a parcel. The gentleman took the parcel and put it on the table.

"Untie it," said he. The lad untied it.

The gentleman pointed to the leather.

"Look here, shoemaker," said he, "do you see this leather?"

"Yes, your honor."

"But do you know what sort of leather it is?"

Simon felt the leather and said, "It is good leather."

"Good, indeed! Why, you fool, you never saw such leather before in your life. It's German, and cost twenty roubles."

Simon was frightened, and said, "Where should I ever see leather like that?"

"Just so! Now, can you make it into boots for me?"

"Yes, your Excellency, I can."

Then the gentleman shouted at him: "You can, can you? Well, remember whom you are to make them for, and what the leather is. You must make me boots that will wear for a year, neither losing shape nor coming unsown. If you can do it, take the leather and cut it up; but if you can't, say so. I warn you now if your boots become unsewn or lose shape within a year, I will have you put in prison. If they don't burst or lose shape for a year I will pay you ten roubles for your work."

Simon was frightened, and did not know what to say. He glanced at Michael and nudging him with his elbow, whispered: "Shall I take the work?"

Michael nodded his head as if to say, "Yes, take it."

Simon did as Michael advised, and undertook to make boots that would not lose shape or split for a whole year.

Calling his servant, the gentleman told him to pull the boot off his left leg, which he stretched out.

"Take my measure!" said he.

Simon stitched a paper measure seventeen inches long, smoothed it out, knelt down, wiped his hand well on his apron so as not to soil the gentleman's sock, and began to measure. He measured the sole, and round the instep, and began to measure the calf of the leg, but the paper was too short. The calf of the leg was as thick as a beam.

"Mind you don't make it too tight in the leg."

Simon stitched on another strip of paper. The gentleman twitched his toes about in his sock, looking round at those in the hut, and as he did so he noticed Michael.

"Whom have you there?" asked he.

"That is my workman. He will sew the boots."

"Mind," said the gentleman to Michael, "remember to make them so that they will last me a year."

Simon also looked at Michael, and saw that Michael was not looking at the gentleman, but was gazing into the corner behind the gentleman, as if he saw some one there. Michael looked and looked, and suddenly he smiled, and his face became brighter.

"What are you grinning at, you fool?" thundered the gentleman. "You had better look to it that the boots are ready in time."

"They shall be ready in good time," said Michael.

"Mind it is so," said the gentleman, and he put on his boots and his fur coat, wrapped the latter round him, and went to the door. But he forgot to stoop, and struck his head against the lintel.

He swore and rubbed his head. Then he took his seat in the carriage and drove away.

When he had gone, Simon said: "There's a figure of a man for you! You could not kill him with a mallet. He almost knocked out the lintel, but little harm it did him."

And Matryona said: "Living as he does, how should he not grow strong? Death itself can't touch such a rock as that."

CHAPTER VIII.

Then Simon said to Michael: "Well, we have taken the work, but we must see we don't get into trouble over it. The leather is dear, and the gentleman hot-tempered. We must make no mistakes. Come, your eye is truer and your hands have become nimbler than mine, so you take this measure and cut out the boots. I will finish off the sewing of the vamps."

Michael did as he was told. He took the leather, spread it out on the table, folded it in two, took a knife and began to cut out.

Matryona came and watched him cutting, and was surprised to see how he was doing it. Matryona was accustomed to seeing boots made, and she looked and saw that Michael was not cutting the leather for boots, but was cutting it round.

She wished to say something, but she thought to herself: "Perhaps I do not understand how gentleman's boots should be made. I suppose Michael knows more about it—and I won't interfere."

When Michael had cut up the leather, he took a thread and began to sew not with two ends, as boots are sewn, but with a single end, as for soft slippers.

Again Matryona wondered, but again she did not interfere. Michael sewed on steadily till noon. Then Simon rose for dinner, looked around, and saw that Michael had made slippers out of the gentleman's leather.

"Ah," groaned Simon, and he thought, "How is it that Michael, who has been with me a whole year and never made a mistake before, should do such a dreadful thing? The gentleman ordered high boots, welted, with whole fronts, and Michael has made soft slippers with single soles, and has wasted the leather.

What am I to say to the gentleman? I can never replace leather such as this."

And he said to Michael, "What are you doing, friend? You have ruined me! You know the gentleman ordered high boots, but see what you have made!"

Hardly had he begun to rebuke Michael, when "rat-tat" went the iron ring that hung at the door. Some one was knocking. They looked out of the window; a man had come on horseback, and was fastening his horse. They opened the door, and the servant who had been with the gentleman came in.

"Good day," said he.

"Good day," replied Simon. "What can we do for you?"

"My mistress has sent me about the boots."

"What about the boots?"

"Why, my master no longer needs them. He is dead."

"Is it possible?"

"He did not live to get home after leaving you, but died in the carriage. When we reached home and the servants came to help him alight, he rolled over like a sack. He was dead already, and so stiff that he could hardly be got out of the carriage. My mistress sent me here, saying: 'Tell the bootmaker that the gentleman who ordered boots of him and left the leather for them no longer needs the boots, but that he must quickly make soft slippers for the corpse. Wait till they are ready, and bring them back with you.' That is why I have come."

Michael gathered up the remnants of the leather; rolled them up, took the soft slippers he had made, slapped them together, wiped them down with his apron, and handed them and the roll of leather to the servant, who took them and said: "Good-bye, masters, and good day to you!"

CHAPTER IX.

Another year passed, and another, and Michael was now living his sixth year with Simon. He lived as before. He went nowhere, only spoke when necessary, and had only smiled twice in all those years—once when Matryona gave him food, and a second time when the gentleman was in their hut. Simon was more than pleased with his workman. He never now asked him where he came from, and only feared lest Michael should go away.

They were all at home one day. Matryona was putting iron pots in the oven; the children were running along the benches and looking out of the window; Simon was sewing at one window, and Michael was fastening on a heel at the other.

One of the boys ran along the bench to Michael, leant on his shoulder, and looked out of the window.

"Look, Uncle Michael! There is a lady with little girls! She seems to be coming here. And one of the girls is lame."

When the boy said that, Michael dropped his work, turned to the window, and looked out into the street.

Simon was surprised. Michael never used to look out into the street, but now he pressed against the window, staring at something. Simon also looked out, and saw that a well-dressed woman was really coming to his hut, leading by the hand two little girls in fur coats and woolen shawls. The girls could hardly be told one from the other, except that one of them was crippled in her left leg and walked with a limp.

The woman stepped into the porch and entered the passage. Feeling about for the entrance she found the latch, which she lifted, and opened the door. She let the two girls go in first, and followed them into the hut.

"Good day, good folk!"

"Pray come in," said Simon. "What can we do for you?"

The woman sat down by the table. The two little girls pressed close to her knees, afraid of the people in the hut.

"I want leather shoes made for these two little girls for spring."

"We can do that. We never have made such small shoes, but we can make them; either welted or turnover shoes, linen lined. My man, Michael, is a master at the work."

Simon glanced at Michael and saw that he had left his work and was sitting with his eyes fixed on the little girls. Simon was surprised. It was true the girls were pretty, with black eyes, plump, and rosy-cheeked, and they wore nice kerchiefs and fur coats, but still Simon could not understand why Michael should look at them like that—just as if he had known them before. He was puzzled, but went on talking with the woman, and arranging the price. Having fixed it, he prepared the measure. The woman lifted the lame girl on to her lap and said: "Take two measures from this little girl. Make one shoe for the lame foot and three for the sound one. They both have the same size feet. They are twins."

Simon took the measure and, speaking of the lame girl, said: "How did it happen to her? She is such a pretty girl. Was she born so?"

"No, her mother crushed her leg."

Then Matryona joined in. She wondered who this woman was, and whose the children were, so she said: "Are not you their mother then?"

"No, my good woman; I am neither their mother nor any relation to them. They were quite strangers to me, but I adopted them."

"They are not your children and yet you are so fond of them?"

"How can I help being fond of them? I fed them both at my own breasts. I had a child of my own, but God took him. I was not so fond of him as I now am of them."

"Then whose children are they?"

CHAPTER X.

The woman, having begun talking, told them the whole story. "It is about six years since their parents died, both in one week: their father was buried on the Tuesday, and their mother died on the Friday. These orphans were born three days after their father's death, and their mother did not live another day. My husband and I were then living as peasants in the village. We were neighbors of theirs, our yard being next to theirs. Their father was a lonely man; a wood-cutter in the forest. When felling trees one day, they let one fall on him. It fell across his body and crushed his bowels out. They hardly got him home before his soul went to God; and that same week his wife gave birth to twins—these little girls. She was poor and alone; she had no one, young or old, with her. Alone she gave them birth, and alone she met her death."

"The next morning I went to see her, but when I entered the hut, she, poor thing, was already stark and cold. In dying she had rolled on to this child and crushed her leg. The village folk came to the hut, washed the body, laid her out, made a coffin, and buried her. They were good folk. The babies were left alone. What was to be done with them? I was the only woman there who had a baby at the time. I was nursing my first-born—eight weeks old. So I took them for a time. The peasants came together, and thought and thought what to do with them; and at last they said to me: 'For the present, Mary, you had better keep the girls, and later on we will arrange what to do for them.' So I nursed the sound one at my breast, but at first I did not feed this crippled one. I did not suppose she would live. But then I thought to myself, why should the poor innocent suffer? I pitied her, and began to feed her. And so I fed my own boy and these two—the three of them—at my own breast. I was young and strong, and had good food, and God gave me so much milk that at times it even overflowed. I used sometimes to feed two at a time, while the third was waiting. When one had enough I nursed the third. And God so ordered it that these grew up, while my own was buried before he was two years old. And I had no more children, though we prospered. Now my husband is working for the corn merchant at the mill. The pay is good, and we are well off. But I have no children of my own, and how lonely I should be without these little girls! How can I help loving them! They are the joy of my life!"

She pressed the lame little girl to her with one hand, while with the other she wiped the tears from her cheeks.

And Matryona sighed, and said: "The proverb is true that says, 'One may live without father or mother, but one cannot live without God.'"

So they talked together, when suddenly the whole hut was lighted up as though by summer lightning from the corner where Michael sat. They all looked towards him and saw him sitting, his hands folded on his knees, gazing upwards and smiling.

CHAPTER XI.

The woman went away with the girls. Michael rose from the bench, put down his work, and took off his apron. Then, bowing low to Simon and his wife, he said: "Farewell, masters. God has forgiven me. I ask your forgiveness, too, for anything done amiss."

And they saw that a light shone from Michael. And Simon rose, bowed down to Michael, and said: "I see, Michael, that you are no common man, and I can neither keep you nor question you. Only tell me this: how is it that when I found you and brought you home, you were gloomy, and when my wife gave you food you smiled at her and became brighter? Then when the gentleman came to order the boots, you smiled again and became brighter still? And now, when this woman brought the little girls, you smiled a third time, and have become as bright as day? Tell me, Michael, why does your face shine so, and why did you smile those three times?"

And Michael answered: "Light shines from me because I have been punished, but now God has pardoned me. And I smiled three times, because God sent me to learn three truths, and I have learnt them. One I learnt when your wife pitied me, and that is why I smiled the first time. The second I learnt when the rich man ordered the boots, and then I smiled again. And now, when I saw those little girls, I learn the third and last truth, and I smiled the third time."

And Simon said, "Tell me, Michael, what did God punish you for? and what were the three truths? that I, too, may know them."

And Michael answered: "God punished me for disobeying Him. I was an angel in heaven and disobeyed God. God sent me to fetch a woman's soul. I flew to earth, and saw a sick woman lying alone, who had just given birth to twin girls. They moved feebly at their mother's side, but she could not lift them to her breast. When she saw me, she understood that God had sent me for her soul, and she wept and said: 'Angel of God! My husband has just been buried, killed by a falling tree. I have neither sister, nor aunt, nor mother: no one to care for my orphans. Do not take my soul! Let me nurse my babes, feed them, and set them on their feet before I die. Children cannot live without father or mother.' And I hearkened to her. I placed one child at her breast and gave the other into her arms, and returned to the Lord in heaven. I flew to the Lord, and said: 'I could not take the soul of the mother. Her husband was killed by a tree; the woman has twins, and prays that her soul may not be taken. She says: "Let me nurse and feed my children, and set them on their feet. Children cannot live without father or mother." I have not taken her soul.' And God said: 'Go-take the mother's soul, and learn three truths: Learn What dwells in man, What is not given to man, and What men live by. When thou has learnt these things, thou shalt return to heaven.' So I flew again to earth and took the mother's soul. The babes dropped from her breasts. Her body rolled over on the bed and crushed one babe, twisting its leg. I rose above the village, wishing to take her soul to God; but a wind seized me, and my wings drooped and dropped off. Her soul rose alone to God, while I fell to earth by the roadside."

CHAPTER XII.

And Simon and Matryona understood who it was that had lived with them, and whom they had clothed and fed. And they wept with awe and with joy. And the angel said: "I was alone in the field, naked. I had never known human needs, cold and hunger, till I became a man. I was famished, frozen, and did not know what to do. I saw, near the field I was in, a shrine built for God, and I went to it hoping to find shelter. But the shrine was locked, and I could not enter. So I sat down behind the shrine to shelter myself at least from the wind. Evening drew on. I was hungry, frozen, and in pain. Suddenly I heard a man coming along the road. He carried a pair of boots, and was talking to himself. For the first time since I became a man I saw the mortal face of a man, and his face seemed terrible to me and I turned from it. And I heard the man talking to himself of how to cover his body from the cold in winter, and how to feed wife and children. And I thought: 'I am perishing of cold and hunger, and here is a man thinking only of how to clothe himself and his wife, and how to get bread for themselves. He cannot help me.' When the man saw me he frowned and became still more terrible, and passed me by on the other side. I despaired; but suddenly I heard him coming back. I looked up, and did not recognize the same man; before, I had seen death in his face; but now he was alive, and I recognized in him the presence of God. He came up to me, clothed me, took me with him, and brought me to his home. I entered the house; a woman came to meet us and began to speak. The woman was still more terrible than the man had been; the spirit of death came from her mouth; I could not breathe for the stench of death that spread around her. She wished to drive me out into the cold, and I knew that if she did so she would die. Suddenly her husband spoke to her of God, and the woman changed at once. And when she brought me food and looked at me, I glanced at her and saw that death no longer dwelt in her; she had become alive, and in her, too, I saw God.

"Then I remembered the first lesson God had set me: 'Learn what dwells in man.' And I understood that in man dwells Love! I was glad that God had already begun to show me what He had promised, and I smiled for the first time. But I had not yet learnt all. I did not yet know What is not given to man, and What men live by.

"I lived with you, and a year passed. A man came to order boots that should wear for a year without losing shape or cracking. I looked at him, and suddenly, behind his shoulder, I saw my comrade—the angel of death. None but me saw that angel; but I knew him, and knew that before the sun set he would take that rich man's soul. And I thought to myself, 'The man is making preparations for a year, and does not know that he will die before evening.' And I remembered God's second saying, 'Learn what is not given to man.'

"What dwells in man I already knew. Now I learnt what is not given him. It is not given to man to know his own needs. And I smiled for the second time. I was glad to have seen my comrade angel—glad also that God had revealed to me the second saying.

"But I still did not know all. I did not know What men live by. And I lived on, waiting till God should reveal to me the last lesson. In the sixth year came the girl-twins with the woman; and I recognized the girls, and heard how they had been kept alive. Having heard the story, I thought, 'Their mother besought me for the children's sake, and I believed her when she said that children cannot live without father or mother; but a stranger has nursed them, and has brought them up.' And when the woman showed her love for the children that were not her own, and wept over them, I saw in her the living God and understood What men live by. And I knew that God had revealed to me the last lesson, and had forgiven my sin. And then I smiled for the third time."

CHAPTER XIII.

And the angel's body was bared, and he was clothed in light so that eye could not look on him; and his voice grew louder, as though it came not from him but from heaven above. And the angel said:

"I have learnt that all men live not by care for themselves but by love.

"It was not given to the mother to know what her children needed for their life. Nor was it given to the rich man to know what he himself needed. Nor is it given to any man to know whether, when evening comes, he will need boots for his body or slippers for his corpse.

"I remained alive when I was a man, not by care of myself, but because love was present in a passer-by, and because he and his wife pitied and loved me. The orphans remained alive not because of their mother's care, but because there was love in the heart of a woman, a stranger to them, who pitied and loved them. And all men live not by the thought they spend on their own welfare, but because love exists in man.

"I knew before that God gave life to men and desires that they should live; now I understood more than that.

"I understood that God does not wish men to live apart, and therefore he does not reveal to them what each one needs for himself; but he wishes them to live united, and therefore reveals to each of them what is necessary for all.

"I have now understood that though it seems to men that they live by care for themselves, in truth it is love alone by which they live. He who has love, is in God, and God is in him, for God is love."

And the angel sang praise to God, so that the hut trembled at his voice. The roof opened, and a column of fire rose from earth to heaven. Simon and his wife and children fell to the ground. Wings appeared upon the angel's shoulders, and he rose into the heavens.

And when Simon came to himself the hut stood as before, and there was no one in it but his own family.

4. WHERE LOVE IS, GOD IS

In the city lived the shoemaker, Martuin Avdyeitch. He lived in a basement, in a little room with one window. The window looked out on the street. Through the window he used to watch the people passing by; although only their feet could be seen, yet by the boots, Martuin Avdyeitch recognized the people. Martuin Avdyeitch had lived long in one place, and had many acquaintances. Few pairs of boots in his district had not been in his hands once and again. Some he would half-sole, some he would patch, some he would stitch around, and occasionally he would also put on new uppers. And through the window he often recognized his work.

Avdyeitch had plenty to do, because he was a faithful workman, used good material, did not make exorbitant charges, and kept his word. If it was possible for him to finish an order by a certain time, he would accept it; otherwise, he would not deceive you,—he would tell you so beforehand. And all knew Avdyeitch, and he was never out of work.

Avdyeitch had always been a good man; but as he grew old, he began to think more about his soul, and get nearer to God. Martuin's wife had died when he was still living with his master. His wife left him a boy three years old. None of their other children had lived. All the eldest had died in childhood. Martuin at first intended to send his little son to his sister in the village, but afterward he felt sorry for him; he thought to himself:—

"It will be hard for my Kapitoshka to live in a strange family. I shall keep him with me."

And Avdyeitch left his master, and went into lodgings with his little son. But God gave Avdyeitch no luck with his children. As Kapitoshka grew older, he began to help his father, and would have been a delight to him, but a sickness fell on him, he went to bed, suffered a week, and died. Martuin buried his son, and fell into despair. So deep was this despair that he began to complain of God. Martuin fell into such a melancholy state, that more than once he prayed to God for death, and reproached God because He had not taken him who was an old man, instead of his beloved only son. Avdyeitch also ceased to go to church.

And once a little old man from the same district came from Troïtsa to see Avdyeitch; for seven years he had been wandering about. Avdyeitch talked with him, and began to complain about his sorrows.

"I have no desire to live any longer," he said, "I only wish I was dead. That is all I pray God for. I am a man without anything to hope for now."

And the little old man said to him:—

"You don't talk right, Martuin, we must not judge God's doings. The world moves, not by our skill, but by God's will. God decreed for your son to die,—for you—to live. So it is for the best. And you are in despair, because you wish to live for your own happiness."

"But what shall one live for?" asked Martuin.

And the little old man said:—

"We must live for God, Martuin. He gives you life, and for His sake you must live. When you begin to live for Him, you will not grieve over anything, and all will seem easy to you."

Martuin kept silent for a moment, and then said, "But how can one live for God?"

And the little old man said:—

"Christ has taught us how to live for God. You know how to read? Buy a Testament, and read it; there you will learn how to live for God. Everything is explained there."

And these words kindled a fire in Avdyeitch's heart. And he went that very same day, bought a New Testament in large print, and began to read.

At first Avdyeitch intended to read only on holidays; but as he began to read, it so cheered his soul that he used to read every day. At times he would become so absorbed in reading, that all the kerosene in the lamp would burn out, and still he could not tear himself away. And so Avdyeitch used to read every evening.

And the more he read, the clearer he understood what God wanted of him, and how one should live for God; and his heart kept growing easier and easier. Formerly, when he lay down to sleep, he used to sigh and groan, and always thought of his Kapitoshka; and now his only exclamation was:—

"Glory to Thee! glory to Thee, Lord! Thy will be done."

And from that time Avdyeitch's whole life was changed. In other days he, too, used to drop into a public-house as a holiday amusement, to drink a cup of tea; and he was not averse to a little brandy, either. He would take a drink with some acquaintance, and leave the saloon, not intoxicated, exactly, yet in a happy frame of mind, and inclined to talk nonsense, and shout, and use abusive language at a person. Now he left off that sort of thing. His life became quiet and joyful. In the morning he would sit down to work, finish his allotted task, then take the little lamp from the hook, put it on the table, get his book from the shelf, open it, and sit down to read. And the more he read, the more he understood, and the brighter and happier it grew in his heart.

Once it happened that Martuin read till late into the night. He was reading the Gospel of Luke. He was reading over the sixth chapter; and he was reading the verses:—

"*And unto him that smiteth thee on the one cheek offer also the other; and him that taketh away thy cloak forbid not to take thy coat also. Give to every man that asketh of thee; and of him that taketh away thy goods ask them not again. And as ye would that men should do to you, do ye also to them likewise.*"

He read farther also those verses, where God speaks:

"*And why call ye me, Lord, Lord, and do not the things which I say? Whosoever cometh to me, and heareth my sayings, and doeth them, I will shew you to whom he is like: he is like a man which built an house, and digged deep, and laid the foundation on a rock: and when the flood arose, the stream beat vehemently upon that house, and could not shake it; for it was founded upon a rock. But he that heareth, and doeth not, is like a man that without a foundation built an house upon the earth; against which the stream did beat vehemently, and immediately it fell; and the ruin of that house was great.*"

Avdyeitch read these words, and joy filled his soul. He took off his spectacles, put them down on the book, leaned his elbows on the table, and became lost in thought. And he began to measure his life by these words. And he thought to himself:—

"Is my house built on the rock, or on the sand? 'Tis well if on the rock. It is so easy when you are alone by yourself; it seems as if you had done everything as God commands; but when you forget yourself, you sin again. Yet I shall still struggle on. It is very good. Help me, Lord!"

Thus ran his thoughts; he wanted to go to bed, but he felt loath to tear himself away from the book. And he began to read farther in the seventh chapter. He read about the centurion, he read about the widow's son, he read about the answer given to John's disciples, and finally he came to that place where the rich Pharisee desired the Lord to sit at meat with him; and he read how the woman that was a sinner anointed His feet, and washed them with her tears, and how He forgave her. He reached the forty-fourth verse, and began to read:—

"*And he turned to the woman, and said unto Simon, Seest thou this woman? I entered into thine house, thou gavest me no water for my feet: but she hath washed my feet with tears, and wiped them with the hairs of her head. Thou gavest me no kiss: but this woman since the time I came in hath not ceased to kiss*" *my feet. My head with oil thou didst not anoint: but this woman hath anointed my feet with ointment."*

He finished reading these verses, and thought to himself:—

"Thou gavest me no water for my feet, thou gavest me no kiss. My head with oil thou didst not anoint."

And again Avdyeitch took off his spectacles, put them down on the book, and again he became lost in thought.

"It seems that Pharisee must have been such a man as I am. I, too, apparently have thought only of myself,—how I might have my tea, be warm and comfortable, but never to think about my guest. He thought about himself, but there was not the least care taken of the guest. And who was his guest? The Lord Himself. If He had come to me, should I have done the same way?"

Avdyeitch rested his head upon both his arms, and did not notice that he fell asleep.

"Martuin!" suddenly seemed to sound in his ears.

Martuin started from his sleep:—

"Who is here?"

He turned around, glanced toward the door—no one.

Again he fell into a doze. Suddenly, he plainly heard:—

"Martuin! Ah, Martuin! look to-morrow on the street. I am coming."

Martuin awoke, rose from the chair, began to rub his eyes. He himself could not tell whether he heard those words in his dream, or in reality. He turned down his lamp, and went to bed.

At daybreak next morning, Avdyeitch rose, made his prayer to God, lighted the stove, put on the shchi and the kasha, put the water in the samovar, put on his apron, and sat down by the window to work.

And while he was working, he kept thinking about all that had happened the day before. It seemed to him at one moment that it was a dream, and now he had really heard a voice.

"Well," he said to himself, "such things have been."

Martuin was sitting by the window, and looking out more than he was working. When anyone passed by in boots which he did not know, he would bend down, look out of the window, in order to see, not only the feet, but also the face.

The dvornik passed by in new felt boots, the water-carrier passed by; then there came up to the window an old soldier of Nicholas's time, in an old pair of laced felt boots, with a shovel in his hands. Avdyeitch recognized him by his felt boots. The old man's name was Stepanuitch; and a neighboring merchant, out of charity, gave him a home with him. He was required to assist the dvornik. Stepanuitch began to shovel away the snow from in front of Avdyeitch's window. Avdyeitch glanced at him, and took up his work again.

"Pshaw! I must be getting crazy in my old age," said Avdyeitch, and laughed at himself. "Stepanuitch is clearing away the snow, and I imagine that Christ is coming to see me. I was entirely out of my mind, old dotard that I am!"

Avdyeitch sewed about a dozen stitches, and then felt impelled to look through the window again. He looked out again through the window, and saw that Stepanuitch had leaned his shovel against the wall, and was warming himself, and resting. He was an old, broken-down man; evidently he had not strength enough even to shovel the snow. Avdyeitch said to himself:—

"I will give him some tea; by the way, the samovar has only just gone out." Avdyeitch laid down his awl, rose from his seat, put the samovar on the table, poured out the tea, and tapped with his finger at the glass. Stepanuitch turned around, and came to the window. Avdyeitch beckoned to him, and went to open the door.

"Come in, warm yourself a little," he said. "You must be cold."

"May Christ reward you for this! my bones ache," said Stepanuitch.

Stepanuitch came in, and shook off the snow, tried to wipe his feet, so as not to soil the floor, but staggered.

"Don't trouble to wipe your feet. I will clean it up myself; we are used to such things. Come in and sit down," said Avdyeitch. "Here, drink a cup of tea."

And Avdyeitch lifted two glasses, and handed one to his guest; while he himself poured his tea into a saucer, and began to blow it.

Stepanuitch finished drinking his glass of tea, turned the glass upside down, put the half-eaten lump of sugar on it, and began to express his thanks. But it was evident he wanted some more.

"Have some more," said Avdyeitch, filling both his own glass and his guest's. Avdyeitch drank his tea, but from time to time glanced out into the street.

"Are you expecting anyone?" asked his guest.

"Am I expecting anyone? I am ashamed even to tell whom I expect. I am, and I am not, expecting someone; but one word has kindled a fire in my heart. Whether it is a dream, or something else, I do not know. Don't you see, brother, I was reading yesterday the Gospel about Christ the Batyushka; how He suffered, how He walked on the earth. I suppose you have heard about it?"

"Indeed I have," replied Stepanuitch; "but we are people in darkness, we can't read."

"Well, now, I was reading about that very thing,—how He walked on the earth; I read, you know, how He came to the Pharisee, and the Pharisee did not treat Him hospitably. Well, and so, my brother, I was reading yesterday, about this very thing, and was thinking to myself how he did not receive Christ, the Batyushka, with honor. Suppose, for example, He should come to me, or anyone else, I said to myself, I should not even know how to receive Him. And he gave Him no reception at all. Well! while I was thus thinking, I fell asleep, brother, and I heard someone call me by name. I got up; the voice, just as if someone whispered, said, 'Be on the watch; I shall come to-morrow.' And this happened twice. Well! would you believe it, it got into my head? I scolded myself—and yet I am expecting Him, the Batyushka."

Stepanuitch shook his head, and said nothing; he finished drinking his glass of tea, and put it on the side; but Avdyeitch picked up the glass again, and filled it once more.

"Drink some more for your good health. You see, I have an idea that, when the Batyushka went about on this earth, He disdained no one, and had more to do with the simple people. He always went to see the simple people. He picked out His disciples more from among folk like such sinners as we are, from the working class. Said He, whoever exalts himself, shall be humbled, and he who is humbled shall become exalted. Said He, you call me Lord, and, said He, I wash your feet. Whoever wishes, said He, to be the first, the same shall be a servant to all. Because, said He, blessed are the poor, the humble, the kind, the generous."

And Stepanuitch forgot about his tea; he was an old man, and easily moved to tears. He was listening, and the tears rolled down his face.

"Come, now, have some more tea," said Avdyeitch; but Stepanuitch made the sign of the cross, thanked him, turned down his glass, and arose.

"Thanks to you," he says, "Martuin Avdyeitch, for treating me kindly, and satisfying me, soul and body."

"You are welcome; come in again; always glad to see a friend," said Avdyeitch.

Stepanuitch departed; and Martuin poured out the rest of the tea, drank it up, put away the dishes, and sat down again by the window to work, to stitch on a patch. He kept stitching away, and at the same time looking through the window. He was expecting Christ, and was all the while thinking of Him and His deeds, and his head was filled with the different speeches of Christ.

Two soldiers passed by: one wore boots furnished by the crown, and the other one, boots that he had made; then the master of the next house passed by in shining galoshes; then a baker with a basket passed by. All passed by; and now there came also by the window a woman in woolen stockings and rustic bashmaks on her feet. She passed by the window, and stood still near the window-case.

Avdyeitch looked up at her from the window, and saw it was a stranger, a woman poorly clad, and with a child; she was standing by the wall with her back to the wind, trying to wrap up the child, and she had nothing to wrap it up in. The woman was dressed in shabby summer clothes; and from behind the frame, Avdyeitch could hear the child crying, and the woman trying to pacify it; but she was not able to pacify it.

Avdyeitch got up, went to the door, ascended the steps, and cried:—

"My good woman. Hey! my good woman!"

The woman heard him and turned around.

"Why are you standing in the cold with the child? Come into my room, where it is warm; you can manage it better. Here, this way!"

The woman was astonished. She saw an old, old man in an apron, with spectacles on his nose, calling her to him. She followed him. They descended the steps and entered the room; the old man led the woman to his bed.

"There," says he, "sit down, my good woman, nearer to the stove; you can get warm, and nurse the little one."

"I have no milk for him. I myself have not eaten anything since morning," said the woman; but, nevertheless, she took the baby to her breast.

Avdyeitch shook his head, went to the table, brought out the bread and a dish, opened the oven door, poured into the dish some cabbage soup, took out the pot with the gruel, but it was not cooked as yet; so he filled the dish with shchi only, and put it on the table. He got the bread, took the towel down from the hook, and spread it upon the table.

"Sit down," he says, "and eat, my good woman; and I will mind the little one. You see, I once had children of my own; I know how to handle them."

The woman crossed herself, sat down at the table, and began to eat; while Avdyeitch took a seat on the bed near the infant. Avdyeitch kept smacking and smacking to it with his lips; but it was a poor kind of smacking, for he had no teeth. The little one kept on crying. And it occured to Avdyeitch to threaten the little one with his finger; he waved, waved his finger right before the child's mouth, and hastily withdrew it. He did not put it to its mouth, because his finger was black, and soiled with wax. And the little one looked at his finger, and became quiet; then it began to smile, and Avdyeitch also was glad. While the woman was eating, she told who she was, and whither she was going.

Said she:—

"I am a soldier's wife. It is now seven months since they sent my husband away off, and no tidings. I lived out as cook; the baby was born; no one cared to keep me with a child. This is the third month that I have been struggling along without a place. I ate up all I had. I wanted to engage as a wet-nurse—no one would take me—I am too thin, they say. I have just been to the merchant's wife, where lives a young woman I know, and so they promised to take us in. I thought that was the end of it. But she told me to come next week. And she lives a long way off. I got tired out; and it tired him, too, my heart's darling. Fortunately, our landlady takes pity on us for the sake of Christ, and gives us a room, else I don't know how I should manage to get along."

Avdyeitch sighed, and said:

"Haven't you any warm clothes?"

"Now is the time, friend, to wear warm clothes; but yesterday I pawned my last shawl for a twenty-kopek piece."

The woman came to the bed, and took the child; and Avdyeitch rose, went to the partition, rummaged round, and succeeded in finding an old coat.

"Na!" says he; "It is a poor thing, yet you may turn it to some use."

The woman looked at the coat and looked at the old man; she took the coat, and burst into tears; and Avdyeitch turned away his head; crawling under the bed, he pushed out a little trunk, rummaged in it, and sat down again opposite the woman.

And the woman said:—

"May Christ bless you, little grandfather! He must have sent me to your window. My little baby would have frozen to death. When I started out it was warm, but now it has grown cold. And He, the Batyushka, led you to look through the window and take pity on me, an unfortunate."

Avdyeitch smiled, and said:—

"Indeed, He did that! I have been looking through the window, my good woman, for some wise reason."

And Martuin told the soldier's wife his dream, and how he heard the voice,—how the Lord promised to come and see him that day.

"All things are possible," said the woman. She rose, put on the coat, wrapped up her little child in it; and, as she started to take leave, she thanked Avdyeitch again.

"Take this, for Christ's sake," said Avdyeitch, giving her a twenty-kopek piece; "redeem your shawl."

She made the sign of the cross, and Avdyeitch made the sign of the cross and went with her to the door.

The woman went away. Avdyeitch ate some shchi, washed the dishes, and sat down again to work. While he was working he still remembered the window; when the window grew darker he immediately looked out to see who was passing by. Acquaintances passed by and strangers passed by, and there was nothing out of the ordinary.

But here Avdyeitch saw that an old apple woman had stopped in front of his window. She carried a basket with apples. Only a few were left, as she had evidently sold them nearly all out; and over her shoulder she had a bag full of chips. She must have gathered them up in some new building, and was on her way home. One could see that the bag was heavy on her shoulder; she tried to shift it to the other shoulder. So she lowered the bag on the sidewalk, stood the basket with the apples on a little post, and began to shake down the splinters in the bag. And while she was shaking her bag, a little boy in a torn cap came along, picked up an apple from the basket, and was about to make his escape; but the old woman noticed it, turned around, and caught the youngster by his sleeve. The little boy began to struggle, tried to tear himself away; but the old woman grasped him with both hands, knocked off his cap, and caught him by the hair.

The little boy was screaming, the old woman was scolding. Avdyeitch lost no time in putting away his awl; he threw it upon the floor, sprang to the door,—he even stumbled on the stairs, and dropped his spectacles,—and rushed out into the street.

The old woman was pulling the youngster by his hair, and was scolding and threatening to take him to the policeman; the youngster was defending himself, and denying the charge.

"I did not take it," he said; "What are you licking me for? Let me go!"

Avdyeitch tried to separate them. He took the boy by his arm, and said:—

"Let him go, babushka; forgive him, for Christ's sake."

"I will forgive him so that he won't forget it till the new broom grows. I am going to take the little villain to the police."

Avdyeitch began to entreat the old woman:—

"Let him go, babushka," he said, "he will never do it again. Let him go, for Christ's sake."

The old woman let him loose; the boy started to run, but Avdyeitch kept him back.

"Ask the babushka's forgiveness," he said, "and don't you ever do it again; I saw you take the apple."

The boy burst into tears, and began to ask forgiveness.

"There now! that's right; and here's an apple for you."

And Avdyeitch took an apple from the basket, and gave it to the boy.

"I will pay you for it, babushka," he said to the old woman.

"You ruin them that way, the good-for-nothings," said the old woman. "He ought to be treated so that he would remember it for a whole week."

"Eh, babushka, babushka," said Avdyeitch, "that is right according to our judgment, but not according to God's. If he is to be whipped for an apple, then what ought to be done to us for our sins?"

The old woman was silent.

And Avdyeitch told her the parable of the master who forgave a debtor all that he owed him, and how the debtor went and began to choke one who owed him.

The old woman listened, and the boy stood listening.

"God has commanded us to forgive," said Avdyeitch, "else we, too, may not be forgiven. All should be forgiven, and the thoughtless especially."

The old woman shook her head, and sighed.

"That's so," said she; "but the trouble is that they are very much spoiled."

"Then we who are older must teach them," said Avdyeitch.

"That's just what I say," remarked the old woman. "I myself have had seven of them,—only one daughter is left."

And the old woman began to relate where and how she lived with her daughter, and how many grandchildren she had. "Here," she says, "my strength is only so-so, and yet I have to work. I pity the youngsters—my grandchildren—but what nice children they are! No one gives me such a welcome as they do. Aksintka won't go to anyone but me. 'Babushka, dear babushka, lovliest.'"

And the old woman grew quite sentimental.

"Of course, it is a childish trick. God be with him," said she, pointing to the boy.

The woman was just about to lift the bag up on her shoulder, when the boy ran up, and said:—

"Let me carry it, babushka; it is on my way."

The old woman nodded her head, and put the bag on the boy's back.

And side by side they passed along the street.

And the old woman even forgot to ask Avdyeitch to pay for the apple. Avdyeitch stood motionless, and kept gazing after them; and he heard them talking all the time as they walked away. After Avdyeitch saw them disappear, he returned to his room; he found his eye-glasses on the stairs,—they were not broken; he picked up his awl, and sat down to work again.

After working a little while, it grew darker, so that he could not see to sew; he saw the lamplighter passing by to light the street-lamps.

"It must be time to make a light," he said to himself; so he got his little lamp ready, hung it up, and he took himself again to his work. He had one boot already finished; he turned it around, looked at it: "Well done." He put away his tools, swept off the cuttings, cleared off the bristles and ends, took the lamp, set it on the table, and took down the Gospels from the shelf. He intended to open the book at the very place where he had yesterday put a piece of leather as a mark, but it happened to open at another place; and the moment Avdyeitch opened the Testament, he recollected his last night's dream. And as soon as he remembered it, it seemed as if he heard someone stepping about behind him. Avdyeitch looked around, and saw—there, in the dark corner, it seemed as if people were standing; he was at a loss to know who they were. And a voice whispered in his ear:—

"Martuin—ah, Martuin! did you not recognize me?"

"Who?" exclaimed Avdyeitch.

"Me," repeated the voice. "It was I;" and Stepanuitch stepped forth from the dark corner; he smiled, and like a little cloud faded away, and soon vanished.

"And it was I," said the voice.

From the dark corner stepped forth the woman with her child; the woman smiled, the child laughed, and they also vanished,

"And it was I," continued the voice; both the old woman and the boy with the apple stepped forward; both smiled and vanished.

Avdyeitch's soul rejoiced; he crossed himself, put on his spectacles, and began to read the Evangelists where it happened to open. On the upper part of the page he read:—

"For I was an hungered, and ye gave me meat; I was thirsty, and ye gave me drink; I was a stranger, and ye took me in."

And on the lower part of the page he read this:—

"Inasmuch as ye have done it unto one of the least of these my brethren, ye have done it unto me."—St. Matthew, Chap. xxv.

And Avdyeitch understood that his dream had not deceived him; that the Saviour really called on him that day, and that he really received Him.

5. THE KINGDOM OF GOD IS WITHIN YOU

PREFACE

In the year 1884 I wrote a book under the title "What I Believe," in which I did in fact make a sincere statement of my beliefs.

In affirming my belief in Christ's teaching, I could not help explaining why I do not believe, and consider as mistaken, the Church's doctrine, which is usually called Christianity.

Among the many points in which this doctrine falls short of the doctrine of Christ I pointed out as the principal one the absence of any commandment of non-resistance to evil by force. The perversion of Christ's teaching by the teaching of the Church is more clearly apparent in this than in any other point of difference.

I know—as we all do—very little of the practice and the spoken and written doctrine of former times on the subject of non-resistance to evil. I knew what had been said on the subject by the fathers of the Church—Origen, Tertullian, and others—I knew too of the existence of some so-called sects of Mennonites, Herrnhuters, and Quakers, who do not allow a Christian the use of weapons, and do not enter military service; but I knew little of what had been done by these so-called sects toward expounding the question.

My book was, as I had anticipated, suppressed by the Russian censorship; but partly owing to my literary reputation, partly because the book had excited people's curiosity, it circulated in manuscript and in lithographed copies in Russia and through translations abroad, and it evoked, on one side, from those who shared my convictions, a series of essays with a great deal of information on the subject, on the other side a series of criticisms on the principles laid down in my book.

LEO TOLSTOY

A great deal was made clear to me by both hostile and sympathetic criticism, and also by the historical events of late years; and I was led to fresh results and conclusions, which I wish now to expound.

First I will speak of the information I received on the history of the question of non-resistance to evil; then of the views of this question maintained by spiritual critics, that is, by professed believers in the Christian religion, and also by temporal ones, that is, those who do not profess the Christian religion; and lastly I will speak of the conclusions to which I have been brought by all this in the light of the historical events of late years.

CHAPTER I: THE DOCTRINE OF NON-RESISTANCE TO EVIL BY FORCE HAS BEEN PROFESSED BY A MINORITY OF MEN FROM THE VERY FOUNDATION OF CHRISTIANITY

Of the Book "What I Believe"—The Correspondence Evoked by it—Letters from Quakers—Garrison's Declaration—Adin Ballou, his Works, his Catechism—Helchitsky's "Net of Faith"—The Attitude of the World to Works Elucidating Christ's Teaching—Dymond's Book "On War"—Musser's "Non-resistance Asserted"—Attitude of the Government in 1818 to Men who Refused to Serve in the Army—Hostile Attitude of Governments Generally and of Liberals to Those who Refuse to Assist in Acts of State Violence, and their Conscious Efforts to Silence and Suppress these Manifestations of Christian Non-resistance.

Among the first responses called forth by my book were some letters from American Quakers. In these letters, expressing their sympathy with my views on the unlawfulness for a Christian of war and the use of force of any kind, the Quakers gave me details of their own so-called sect, which for more than two hundred years has actually professed the teaching of Christ on non-resistance to evil by force, and does not make use of weapons in self-defense. The Quakers sent me also their pamphlets, journals, and books, from which I learnt how they had, years ago, established beyond doubt the duty for a Christian of fulfilling the command of non-resistance to evil by force, and had exposed the error of the Church's teaching in allowing war and capital punishment.

In a whole series of arguments and texts showing that war—that is, the wounding and killing of men—is inconsistent with a religion founded on peace and good will toward men, the Quakers maintain and prove that nothing has contributed so much to the obscuring of Christian truth in the eyes of the heathen, and has hindered so much the diffusion of Christianity through the world, as the disregard of this command by men calling themselves Christians, and the permission of war and violence to Christians.

"Christ's teaching, which came to be known to men, not by means of violence and the sword," they say, "but by means of non-resistance to evil, gentleness, meekness, and peaceableness, can only be diffused through the world by the example of peace, harmony, and love among its followers."

"A Christian, according to the teaching of God himself, can act only peaceably toward all men, and therefore there can be no authority able to force the Christian to act in opposition to the teaching of God and to the principal virtue of the Christian in his relation with his neighbors."

"The law of state necessity," they say, "can force only those to change the law of God who, for the sake of earthly gains, try to reconcile the irreconcilable; but for a Christian who sincerely believes that following Christ's teaching will give him salvation, such considerations of state can have no force."

Further acquaintance with the labors of the Quakers and their works—with Fox, Penn, and especially the work of Dymond (published in 1827)—showed me not only that the impossibility of reconciling Christianity with force and war had been recognized long, long ago, but that this irreconcilability had been long ago proved so clearly and so indubitably that one could only wonder how this impossible reconciliation of Christian teaching with the use of force, which has been, and is still, preached in the churches, could have been maintained in spite of it.

In addition to what I learned from the Quakers I received about the same time, also from America, some information on the subject from a source perfectly distinct and previously unknown to me.

The son of William Lloyd Garrison, the famous champion of the emancipation of the negroes, wrote to me that he had read my book, in which he found ideas similar to those expressed by his father in the year 1838, and that, thinking it would be interesting to me to know this, he sent me a declaration or proclamation of "non-resistance" drawn up by his father nearly fifty years ago.

This declaration came about under the following circumstances: William Lloyd Garrison took part in a discussion on the means of suppressing war in the Society for the Establishment of Peace among Men, which existed in 1838 in America. He came to the conclusion that the establishment of universal peace can only be founded on the open profession of the doctrine of non-resistance to evil by violence (Matt. v. 39), in its full significance, as understood by the Quakers, with whom Garrison happened to be on friendly relations. Having come to this conclusion, Garrison thereupon composed and laid before the society a declaration, which was signed at the time—in 1838—by many members.

"DECLARATION OF SENTIMENTS ADOPTED BY THE PEACE CONVENTION.

"BOSTON, 1838.

"We, the undersigned, regard it as due to ourselves, to the cause which we love, to the country in which we live, to publish a declaration expressive of the purposes we aim to accomplish and the measures we shall adopt to carry forward the work of peaceful universal reformation.

"We do not acknowledge allegiance to any human government. We recognize but one King and Lawgiver, one Judge and Ruler of mankind. Our country is the world, our countrymen are all mankind. We love the land of our nativity only as we love all other lands. The interests and rights of American citizens are not dearer to us than those of the whole human race. Hence we can allow no appeal to patriotism to revenge any national insult or injury....

"We conceive that a nation has no right to defend itself against foreign enemies or to punish its invaders, and no individual possesses that right in his own case, and the unit cannot be of greater importance than the aggregate. If soldiers thronging from abroad with intent to commit rapine and destroy life may not be resisted by the people or the magistracy, then ought no resistance to be offered to domestic troublers of the public peace or of private security.

"The dogma that all the governments of the world are approvingly ordained of God, and that the powers that be in the United States, in Russia, in Turkey, are in accordance with his will, is no less absurd than impious. It makes the impartial Author of our existence unequal and tyrannical. It cannot be affirmed that the powers that be in any nation are actuated by the spirit or guided by the example of Christ in the treatment of enemies; therefore they cannot be agreeable to the will of God, and therefore their overthrow by a spiritual regeneration of their subjects is inevitable.

"We regard as unchristian and unlawful not only all wars, whether offensive or defensive, but all preparations for war; every naval ship, every arsenal, every fortification, we regard as unchristian and unlawful; the existence of any kind of standing army, all military chieftains, all monuments commemorative of victory over a fallen foe, all trophies won in battle, all celebrations in honor of military exploits, all appropriations for defense by arms; we regard as unchristian and unlawful every edict of government requiring of its subjects military service.

"Hence we deem it unlawful to bear arms, and we cannot hold any office which imposes on its incumbent the obligation to compel men to do right on pain of imprisonment or death. We therefore voluntarily exclude ourselves from every legislative and judicial body, and repudiate all human politics, worldly honors, and stations of authority. If we cannot occupy a seat in the legislature or on the bench, neither can we elect others to act as our substitutes in any such capacity. It follows that we cannot sue any man at law to force him to return anything he may have wrongly taken from us; if he has seized our coat, we shall surrender him our cloak also rather than subject him to punishment.

"We believe that the penal code of the old covenant—an eye for an eye, and a tooth for a tooth—has been abrogated by Jesus Christ, and that under the new covenant the forgiveness instead of the punishment of enemies has been enjoined on all his disciples in all cases whatsoever. To extort money from enemies, cast them into prison, exile or execute them, is obviously not to forgive but to take retribution.

"The history of mankind is crowded with evidences proving that physical coercion is not adapted to moral regeneration, and that the sinful dispositions of men can be subdued only by love; that evil can be exterminated only by good; that it is not safe to rely upon the strength of an arm to preserve us from harm; that there is great security in being gentle, long-suffering, and abundant in mercy; that it is only the meek who shall inherit the earth; for those who take up the sword shall perish by the sword.

"Hence as a measure of sound policy—of safety to property, life, and liberty—of public quietude and private enjoyment—as well as on the ground of allegiance to Him who is King of kings and Lord of lords, we cordially adopt the non-resistance principle, being confident that it provides for all possible consequences, is armed with omnipotent power, and must ultimately triumph over every assailing force.

"We advocate no Jacobinical doctrines. The spirit of Jacobinism is the spirit of retaliation, violence, and murder. It neither fears God nor regards man. We would be filled with the spirit of Christ. If we abide by our fundamental principle of not opposing evil by evil we cannot participate in sedition, treason, or violence. We shall submit to every ordinance and every requirement of government, except such as are contrary to the commands of the Gospel, and in no case resist the operation of law, except by meekly submitting to the penalty of disobedience.

"But while we shall adhere to the doctrine of non-resistance and passive submission to enemies, we purpose, in a moral and spiritual sense, to assail iniquity in high places and in low places, to apply our principles to all existing evil, political, legal, and ecclesiastical institutions, and to hasten the time when the kingdoms of this world will have become the kingdom of our Lord Jesus Christ. It appears to us a self-evident truth that whatever the Gospel is designed to destroy at any period of the world, being contrary to it, ought now to be abandoned. If, then, the time is predicted when swords shall be beaten into plowshares and spears into pruning hooks, and men shall not learn the art of war any more, it follows that all who manufacture, sell, or wield these deadly weapons do thus array themselves against the peaceful dominion of the Son of God on earth.

"Having thus stated our principles, we proceed to specify the measures we propose to adopt in carrying our object into effect.

"We expect to prevail through the Foolishness of Preaching. We shall endeavor to promulgate our views among all persons, to whatever nation, sect, or grade of society they may belong. Hence we shall organize public lectures, circulate tracts and publications, form societies, and petition every governing body. It will be our leading object to devise ways and means for effecting a radical change in the views, feelings, and practices of society respecting the sinfulness of war and the treatment of enemies.

"In entering upon the great work before us, we are not unmindful that in its prosecution we may be called to test our sincerity even as in a fiery ordeal. It may subject us to insult, outrage, suffering, yea, even death itself. We anticipate no small amount of misconception, misrepresentation, and calumny. Tumults may arise against us. The proud and pharisaical, the ambitious and tyrannical, principalities and powers, may combine to crush us. So they treated the Messiah whose example we are humbly striving to imitate. We shall not be afraid of their terror. Our confidence is in the Lord Almighty and not in man. Having withdrawn from human protection, what can sustain us but that faith which overcomes the world? We shall not think it strange concerning the fiery trial which is to try us, but rejoice inasmuch as we are partakers of Christ's sufferings.

"Wherefore we commit the keeping of our souls to God. For every one that forsakes houses, or brethren, or sisters, or father, or mother, or wife, or children, or lands for Christ's sake, shall receive a hundredfold, and shall inherit everlasting life.

"Firmly relying upon the certain and universal triumph of the sentiments contained in this declaration, however formidable may be the opposition arrayed against them, we hereby affix our signatures to it; commending it to the reason and conscience of mankind, and resolving, in the strength of the Lord God, to calmly and meekly abide the issue."

Immediately after this declaration a Society for Non-resistance was founded by Garrison, and a journal called the *Non-resistant*, in which the doctrine of non-resistance was advocated in its full significance and in all its consequences, as it had been expounded in the declaration. Further information as to the ultimate destiny of the society and the journal I gained from the excellent biography of W. L. Garrison, the work of his son.

The society and the journal did not exist for long. The greater number of Garrison's fellow-workers in the movement for the liberation of the slaves, fearing that the too radical programme of the journal, the *Non-resistant*, might keep people away from the practical work of negro-emancipation, gave up the profession of the principle of non-resistance as it had been expressed in the declaration, and both society and journal ceased to exist.

This declaration of Garrison's gave so powerful and eloquent an expression of a confession of faith of such importance to men, that one would have thought it must have produced a strong impression on people, and have become known throughout the world and the subject of discussion on every side. But nothing of the kind occurred. Not only was it unknown in Europe, even the Americans, who have such a high opinion of Garrison, hardly knew of the declaration.

Another champion of non-resistance has been overlooked in the same way—the American Adin Ballou, who lately died, after spending fifty years in preaching this doctrine. How great the ignorance is of everything relating to the question of non-resistance may be seen from the fact that Garrison the son, who has written an excellent biography of his father in four great volumes, in answer to my inquiry whether there are existing now societies for non-resistance, and adherents of the doctrine, told me that as far as he knew that society had broken up, and that there were no adherents of that doctrine, while at the very time when he was writing to me there was living, at Hopedale in Massachusetts, Adin Ballou, who had taken part in the labors of Garrison the father, and had devoted fifty years of his life to advocating, both orally and in print, the doctrine of non-resistance. Later on I received a letter from Wilson, a pupil and colleague of Ballou's, and entered into correspondence with Ballou himself. I wrote to Ballou, and he answered me and sent me his works. Here is the summary of some extracts from them:

"Jesus Christ is my Lord and teacher," says Ballou in one of his essays exposing the inconsistency of Christians who allowed a right of self-defense and of warfare. "I have promised, leaving all else, to follow him, through good and through evil, to death itself. But I am a citizen of the democratic republic of the United States; and in allegiance to it I have sworn to defend the Constitution of my country, if need be, with my life. Christ requires of me to do unto others as I would they should do unto me. The Constitution of the United States requires of me to do unto two millions of slaves [at that time there were slaves; now one might venture to substitute the word 'laborers'] the very opposite of what I would they should do unto me—that is, to help to keep them in their present condition of slavery. And, in spite of this, I continue to elect or be elected, I propose to vote, I am even ready to be appointed to any office under government. That will not hinder me from being a Christian. I shall still profess Christianity, and shall find no difficulty in carrying out my covenant with Christ and with the government.

"Jesus Christ forbids me to resist evil doers, and to take from them an eye for an eye, a tooth for a tooth, bloodshed for bloodshed, and life for life.

"My government demands from me quite the opposite, and bases a system of self-defense on gallows, musket, and sword, to be used against its foreign and domestic foes. And the land is filled accordingly with gibbets, prisons, arsenals, ships of war, and soldiers.

"In the maintenance and use of these expensive appliances for murder, we can very suitably exercise to the full the virtues of forgiveness to those who injure us, love toward our enemies, blessings to those who curse us, and doing good to those who hate us.

"For this we have a succession of Christian priests to pray for us and beseech the blessing of Heaven on the holy work of slaughter.

"I see all this (*i. e.*, the contradiction between profession and practice), and I continue to profess religion and take part in government, and pride myself on being at the same time a devout Christian and a devoted servant of the government. I do not want to agree with these senseless notions of non-resistance. I cannot renounce my authority and leave only immoral men in control of the government. The Constitution says the government has the right to declare war, and I assent to this and support it, and swear that I will support it. And I do not for that cease to be a Christian. War, too, is a Christian duty. Is it not a Christian duty to kill hundreds of thousands of one's fellow-men, to outrage women, to raze and burn towns, and to practice every possible cruelty? It is time to dismiss all these false sentimentalities. It is the truest means of forgiving injuries and loving enemies. If we only do it in the spirit of love, nothing can be more Christian than such murder."

In another pamphlet, entitled "How many Men are Necessary to Change a Crime into a Virtue?" he says: "One man may not kill. If he kills a fellow-creature, he is a murderer. If two, ten, a hundred men do so, they, too, are murderers. But a government or a nation may kill as many men as it chooses, and that will not be murder, but a great and noble action. Only gather the people together on a large scale, and a battle of ten thousand men becomes an innocent action. But precisely how many people must there be to make it so?—that is the question. One man cannot plunder and pillage, but a whole nation can. But precisely how many are needed to make it permissible? Why is it that one man, ten, a hundred, may not break the law of God, but a great number may?"

And here is a version of Ballou's catechism composed for his flock:

CATECHISM OF NON-RESISTANCE.

Q. Whence is the word "non-resistance" derived?

A. From the command, "Resist not evil." (M. v. 39.)

Q. What does this word express?

A. It expresses a lofty Christian virtue enjoined on us by Christ.

Q. Ought the word "non-resistance" to be taken in its widest sense—that is to say, as intending that we should not offer any resistance of any kind to evil?

A. No; it ought to be taken in the exact sense of our Saviour's teaching—that is, not repaying evil for evil. We ought to oppose evil by every righteous means in our power, but not by evil.

Q. What is there to show that Christ enjoined non-resistance in that sense?

A. It is shown by the words he uttered at the same time. He said: "Ye have heard, it was said of old, An eye for an eye, and a tooth for a tooth. But I say unto you Resist not evil. But if one smites thee on the right cheek, turn him the other also; and if one will go to law with thee to take thy coat from thee, give him thy cloak also."

Q. Of whom was he speaking in the words, "Ye have heard it was said of old"?

A. Of the patriarchs and the prophets, contained in the Old Testament, which the Hebrews ordinarily call the Law and the Prophets.

Q. What utterances did Christ refer to in the words, "It was said of old"?

A. The utterances of Noah, Moses, and the other prophets, in which they admit the right of doing bodily harm to those who inflict harm, so as to punish and prevent evil deeds.

Q. Quote such utterances.

A. "Whoso sheddeth man's blood, by man shall his blood be shed."—GEN. ix. 6.

"He that smiteth a man, so that he die, shall be surely put to death.... And if any mischief follow, then thou shalt give life for life, eye for eye, tooth for tooth, hand for hand, foot for foot, burning for burning, wound for wound, stripe for stripe."—EX. xxi. 12 and 23-25.

"He that killeth any man shall surely be put to death. And if a man cause a blemish in his neighbor, as he hath done, so shall it be done unto him: breach for breach, eye for eye, tooth for tooth."—LEV. xxiv. 17, 19, 20.

"Then the judges shall make diligent inquisition; and behold, if the witness be a false witness, and hath testified falsely against his brother, then shall ye do unto him as he had thought to have done unto his brother.... And thine eye shall not pity; but life shall go for life, eye for eye, tooth for tooth, hand for hand, foot for foot."—DEUT. xix. 18, 21.

Noah, Moses, and the Prophets taught that he who kills, maims, or injures his neighbors does evil. To resist such evil, and to prevent it, the evil doer must be punished with death, or maiming, or some physical injury. Wrong must be opposed by wrong, murder by murder, injury by injury, evil by evil. Thus taught Noah, Moses, and the Prophets. But Christ rejects all this.

"I say unto you," is written in the Gospel, "resist not evil," do not oppose injury with injury, but rather bear repeated injury from the evil doer. What was permitted is forbidden. When we understand what kind of resistance they taught, we know exactly what resistance Christ forbade.

Q. Then the ancients allowed the resistance of injury by injury?

A. Yes. But Jesus forbids it. The Christian has in no case the right to put to death his neighbor who has done him evil, or to do him injury in return.

Q. May he kill or maim him in self-defense?

A. No.

Q. May he go with a complaint to the judge that he who has wronged him may be punished?

A. No. What he does through others, he is in reality doing himself.

Q. Can he fight in conflict with foreign enemies or disturbers of the peace?

A. Certainly not. He cannot take any part in war or in preparations for war. He cannot make use of a deadly weapon. He cannot oppose injury to injury, whether he is alone or with others, either in person or through other people.

Q. Can he voluntarily vote or furnish soldiers for the government?

A. He can do nothing of that kind if he wishes to be faithful to Christ's law.

Q. Can he voluntarily give money to aid a government resting on military force, capital punishment, and violence in general?

A. No, unless the money is destined for some special object, right in itself, and good both in aim and means.

Q. Can he pay taxes to such a government?

A. No; he ought not voluntarily to pay taxes, but he ought not to resist the collecting of taxes. A tax is levied by the government, and is exacted independently of the will of the subject. It is impossible to resist it without having recourse to violence of some kind. Since the Christian cannot employ violence, he is obliged to offer his property at once to the loss by violence inflicted on it by the authorities.

Q. Can a Christian give a vote at elections, or take part in government or law business?

A. No; participation in election, government, or law business is participation in government by force.

Q. Wherein lies the chief significance of the doctrine of non-resistance?

A. In the fact that it alone allows of the possibility of eradicating evil from one's own heart, and also from one's neighbor's. This doctrine forbids doing that whereby evil has endured for ages and multiplied in the world. He who attacks another and injures him, kindles in the other a feeling of hatred, the root of every evil. To injure another because he has injured us, even with the aim of overcoming evil, is doubling the harm for him and for oneself; it is begetting, or at least setting free and inciting, that evil spirit which we should wish to drive out. Satan can never be driven out by Satan. Error can never be corrected by error, and evil cannot be vanquished by evil.

True non-resistance is the only real resistance to evil. It is crushing the serpent's head. It destroys and in the end extirpates the evil feeling.

Q. But if that is the true meaning of the rule of non-resistance, can it always be put into practice?

A. It can be put into practice like every virtue enjoined by the law of God. A virtue cannot be practiced in all circumstances without self-sacrifice, privation, suffering, and in extreme cases loss of life itself. But he who esteems life more than fulfilling the will of God is already dead to the only true life. Trying to save his life he loses it. Besides, generally speaking, where non-resistance costs the sacrifice of a single life or of some material welfare, resistance costs a thousand such sacrifices.

Non-resistance is Salvation; Resistance is Ruin.

It is incomparably less dangerous to act justly than unjustly, to submit to injuries than to resist them with violence, less dangerous even in one's relations to the present life. If all men refused to resist evil by evil our world would be happy.

Q. But so long as only a few act thus, what will happen to them?

A. If only one man acted thus, and all the rest agreed to crucify him, would it not be nobler for him to die in the glory of non-resisting love, praying for his enemies, than to live to wear the crown of Cæsar stained with the blood of the slain? However, one man, or a thousand men, firmly resolved not to oppose evil by evil are far more free from danger by violence than those who resort to violence, whether among civilized or savage neighbors. The robber, the murderer, and the cheat will leave them in peace, sooner than those who oppose them with arms, and those who take up the sword shall perish by the sword, but those who seek after peace, and behave kindly and harmlessly, forgiving and forgetting injuries, for the most part enjoy peace, or, if they die, they die blessed. In this way, if all kept the ordinance of non-resistance, there would obviously be no evil nor crime. If the majority acted thus they would establish the rule of love and good will even over evil doers, never opposing evil with evil, and never resorting to force. If there were a moderately large minority of such men, they would exercise such a salutary moral influence on society that every cruel punishment would be abolished, and violence and feud would be replaced by peace and love. Even if there were only a small minority of them, they would rarely experience anything worse than the world's contempt, and meantime the world, though unconscious of it, and not grateful for it, would be continually becoming wiser and better for their unseen action on it. And if in the worst case some members of the minority were persecuted to death, in dying for the truth they would have left behind them their doctrine, sanctified by the blood of their martyrdom. Peace, then, to all who seek peace, and may overruling love be the imperishable heritage of every soul who obeys willingly Christ's word, "Resist not evil."

ADIN BALLOU.

For fifty years Ballou wrote and published books dealing principally with the question of non-resistance to evil by force. In these works, which are distinguished by the clearness of their thought and eloquence of exposition, the question is looked at from every possible side, and the binding nature of this command on every Christian who acknowledges the Bible as the revelation of God is firmly established. All the ordinary objections to the doctrine of non-resistance from the Old and New Testaments are brought forward, such as the expulsion of the money-changers from the Temple, and so on, and arguments follow in disproof of them all. The practical reasonableness of this rule of conduct is shown independently of Scripture, and all the objections ordinarily made against its practicability are stated and refuted. Thus one chapter in a book of his treats of non-resistance in exceptional cases, and he owns in this connection that if there were cases in which the rule of non-resistance were impossible of application, it would prove that the law was not universally authoritative. Quoting these cases, he shows that it is precisely in them that the application of the rule is both necessary and reasonable. There is no aspect of the question, either on his side or on his opponents', which he has not followed up in his writings. I mention all this to show the unmistakable interest which such works ought to have for men who make a profession of Christianity, and because one would have thought Ballou's work would have been well known, and the ideas expressed by him would have been either accepted or refuted; but such has not been the case.

The work of Garrison, the father, in his foundation of the Society of Non-resistants and his Declaration, even more than my correspondence with the Quakers, convinced me of the fact that the departure of the ruling form of Christianity from the law of Christ on non-resistance by force is an error that has long been observed and pointed out, and that men have labored, and are still laboring, to correct. Ballou's work confirmed me still more in this view. But the fate of Garrison, still more that of Ballou, in being completely unrecognized in spite of fifty years of obstinate and persistent work in the same direction, confirmed me in the idea that there exists a kind of tacit but steadfast conspiracy of silence about all such efforts.

Ballou died in August, 1890, and there was an obituary notice of him in an American journal of Christian views (*Religiophilosophical Journal*, August 23). In this laudatory notice it is recorded that Ballou was the spiritual director of a parish, that he delivered from eight to nine thousand sermons, married one thousand couples, and wrote about five hundred articles; but there is not a single word said of the object to which he devoted his life; even the word "non-resistance" is not mentioned. Precisely as it was with all the preaching of the Quakers for two hundred years, and, too, with the efforts of Garrison the father, the foundation of his society and journal, and his Declaration, so it is with the life-work of Ballou. It seems just as though it did not exist and never had existed.

We have an astounding example of the obscurity of works which aim at expounding the doctrine of non-resistance to evil by force, and at confuting those who do not recognize this commandment, in the book of the Tsech Helchitsky, which has only lately been noticed and has not hitherto been printed.

Soon after the appearance of my book in German, I received a letter from Prague, from a professor of the university there, informing me of the existence of a work, never yet printed, by Helchitsky, a Tsech of the fifteenth century, entitled "The Net of Faith." In this work, the professor told me, Helchitsky expressed precisely the same view as to true and false Christianity as I had expressed in my book "What I Believe." The professor wrote to me that Helchitsky's work was to be published for the first time in the Tsech language in the *Journal of The Petersburg Academy of Science*. Since I could not obtain the book itself, I tried to make myself acquainted with what was known of Helchitsky, and I gained the following information from a German book sent me by the Prague professor and from Pypin's history of Tsech literature. This was Pypin's account:

"'The Net of Faith' is Christ's teaching, which ought to draw man up out of the dark depths of the sea of worldliness and his own iniquity. True faith consists in believing God's Word; but now a time has come when men mistake the true faith for heresy, and therefore it is for the reason to point out what the true faith consists in, if anyone does not know this. It is hidden in darkness from men, and they do not recognize the true law of Christ.

"To make this law plain, Helchitsky points to the primitive organization of Christian society—the organization which, he says, is now regarded in the Roman Church as an abominable heresy. This primitive Church was his special ideal of social organization, founded on equality, liberty, and fraternity. Christianity, in Helchitsky's view, still preserves these elements, and it is only necessary for society to return to its pure doctrine to render unnecessary every other form of social order in which kings and popes are essential; the law of love would alone be sufficient in every case.

"Historically, Helchitsky attributes the degeneration of Christianity to the times of Constantine the Great, whom the Pope Sylvester admitted into the Christian Church with all his heathen morals and life. Constantine, in his turn, endowed the Pope with worldly riches and power. From that time forward these two ruling powers were constantly aiding one another to strive for nothing but outward glory. Divines and ecclesiastical dignitaries began to concern themselves only about subduing the whole world to their authority, incited men against one another to murder and plunder, and in creed and life reduced Christianity to a nullity. Helchitsky denies completely the right to make war and to inflict the punishment of death; every soldier, even the 'knight,' is only a violent evil doer—a murderer."

The same account is given by the German book, with the addition of a few biographical details and some extracts from Helchitsky's writings.

Having learnt the drift of Helchitsky's teaching in this way, I awaited all the more impatiently the appearance of "The Net of Faith" in the journal of the Academy. But one year passed, then two and three, and still the book did not appear. It was only in 1888 that I learned that the printing of the book, which had been begun, was stopped. I obtained the proofs of what had been printed and read them through. It is a marvelous book from every point of view.

Its general tenor is given with perfect accuracy by Pypin. Helchitsky's fundamental idea is that Christianity, by allying itself with temporal power in the days of Constantine, and by continuing to develop in such conditions, has become completely distorted, and has ceased to be Christian altogether. Helchitsky gave the title "The Net of Faith" to his book, taking as his motto the verse of the Gospel about the calling of the disciples to be fishers of men; and, developing this metaphor, he says: "Christ, by means of his disciples, would have caught all the world in his net of faith, but the greater fishes broke the net and escaped out of it, and all the rest have slipped through the holes made by the greater fishes, so that the net has remained quite empty. The greater fishes who broke the net are the rulers, emperors, popes, kings, who have not renounced power, and instead of true Christianity have put on what is simply a mask of it." Helchitsky teaches precisely what has been and is taught in these days by the non-resistant Mennonites and Quakers, and in former times by the Bogomilites, Paulicians, and many others. He teaches that Christianity, expecting from its adherents gentleness, meekness, peaceableness, forgiveness of injuries, turning the other cheek when one is struck, and love for enemies, is inconsistent with the use of force, which is an indispensable condition of authority.

The Christian, according to Helchitsky's reasoning, not only cannot be a ruler or a soldier; he cannot take any part in government nor in trade, or even be a landowner; he can only be an artisan or a husbandman.

This book is one of the few works attacking official Christianity which has escaped being burned. All such so-called heretical works were burned at the stake, together with their authors, so that there are few ancient works exposing the errors of official Christianity. The book has a special interest for this reason alone. But apart from its interest from every point of view, it is one of the most remarkable products of thought for its depth of aim, for the astounding strength and beauty of the national language in which it is written, and for its antiquity. And yet for more than four centuries it has remained unprinted, and is still unknown, except to a few learned specialists.

One would have thought that all such works, whether of the Quakers, of Garrison, of Ballou, or of Helchitsky, asserting and proving as they do, on the principles of the Gospel, that our modern world takes a false view of Christ's teaching, would have awakened interest, excitement, talk, and discussion among spiritual teachers and their flocks alike.

Works of this kind, dealing with the very essence of Christian doctrine, ought, one would have thought, to have been examined and accepted as true, or refuted and rejected. But nothing of the kind has occurred, and the same fate has been repeated with all those works. Men of the most diverse views, believers, and, what is surprising, unbelieving liberals also, as though by agreement, all preserve the same persistent silence about them, and all that has been done by people to explain the true meaning of Christ's doctrine remains either ignored or forgotten.

But it is still more astonishing that two other books, of which I heard on the appearance of my book, should be so little known. I mean Dymond's book "On War," published for the first time in London in 1824, and Daniel Musser's book on "Non-resistance," written in 1864. It is particularly astonishing that these books should be unknown, because, apart from their intrinsic merits, both books treat not so much of the theory as of the practical application of the theory to life, of the attitude of Christianity to military service, which is especially important and interesting now in these days of universal conscription.

People will ask, perhaps: How ought a subject to behave who believes that war is inconsistent with his religion while the government demands from him that he should enter military service?

This question is, I think, a most vital one, and the answer to it is specially important in these days of universal conscription. All—or at least the great majority of the people—are Christians, and all men are called upon for military service. How ought a man, as a Christian, to meet this demand? This is the gist of Dymond's answer:

"His duty is humbly but steadfastly to refuse to serve."

There are some people, who, without any definite reasoning about it, conclude straightway that the responsibility of government measures rests entirely on those who resolve on them, or that the governments and sovereigns decide the question of what is good or bad for their subjects, and the duty of the subjects is merely to obey. I think that arguments of this kind only obscure men's conscience. I cannot take part in the councils of government, and therefore I am not responsible for its misdeeds. Indeed, but we are responsible for our own misdeeds. And the misdeeds of our rulers become our own, if we, knowing that they are misdeeds, assist in carrying them out. Those who suppose that they are bound to obey the government, and that the responsibility for the misdeeds they commit is transferred from them to their rulers, deceive themselves. They say: "We give our acts up to the will of others, and our acts cannot be good or bad; there is no merit in what is good nor responsibility for what is evil in our actions, since they are not done of our own will."

It is remarkable that the very same thing is said in the instructions to soldiers which they make them learn—that is, that the officer is alone responsible for the consequences of his command. But this is not right. A man cannot get rid of the responsibility for his own actions. And that is clear from the following example. If your officer commands you to kill your neighbor's child, to kill your father or your mother, would you obey? If you would not obey, the whole argument falls to the ground, for if you can disobey the governors in one case, where do you draw the line up to which you can obey them? There is no line other than that laid down by Christianity, and that line is both reasonable and practicable.

And therefore we consider it the duty of every man who thinks war inconsistent with Christianity, meekly but firmly to refuse to serve in the army. And let those whose lot it is to act thus, remember that the fulfillment of a great duty rests with them. The destiny of humanity in the world depends, so far as it depends on men at all, on their fidelity to their religion. Let them confess their conviction, and stand up for it, and not in words alone, but in sufferings too, if need be. If you believe that Christ forbade murder, pay no heed to the arguments nor to the commands of those who call on you to bear a hand in it. By such a steadfast refusal to make use of force, you call down on yourselves the blessing promised to those "who hear these sayings and do them," and the time will come when the world will recognize you as having aided in the reformation of mankind.

Musser's book is called "Non-resistance Asserted," or "Kingdom of Christ and Kingdoms of this World Separated." This book is devoted to the same question, and was written when the American Government was exacting military service from its citizens at the time of the Civil War. And it has, too, a value for all time, dealing with the question how, in such circumstances, people should and can refuse to enter military service. Here is the tenor of the author's introductory remarks: "It is well known that there are many persons in the United States who refuse to fight on grounds of conscience. They are called the 'defenseless,' or 'non-resistant' Christians. These Christians refuse to defend their country, to bear arms, or at the call of government to make war on its enemies. Till lately this religious scruple seemed a valid excuse to the government, and those who urged it were let off service. But at the beginning of our Civil War public opinion was agitated on this subject. It was natural that persons who considered it their duty to bear all the hardships and dangers of war in defense of their country should feel resentment against those persons who had for long shared with them the advantages of the protection of the government, and who now in time of need and danger would not share in bearing the labors and dangers of its defense. It was even natural that they should declare the attitude of such men monstrous, irrational, and suspicious."

A host of orators and writers, our author tells us, arose to oppose this attitude, and tried to prove the sinfulness of non-resistance, both from Scripture and on common-sense grounds. And this was perfectly natural, and in many cases the authors were right— right, that is, in regard to persons who did not renounce the benefits they received from the government and tried to avoid the hardships of military service, but not right in regard to the principle of non-resistance itself. Above all, our author proves the binding nature of the rule of non-resistance for a Christian, pointing out that this command is perfectly clear, and is enjoined upon every Christian by Christ without possibility of misinterpretation. "Bethink yourselves whether it is righteous to obey man more than God," said Peter and John. And this is precisely what ought to be the attitude of every man who wishes to be Christian to the claim on him for military service, when Christ has said, "Resist not evil by force." As for the question of the principle itself, the author regards that as decided. As to the second question, whether people have the right to refuse to serve in the army who have not refused the benefits conferred by a government resting on force, the author considers it in detail, and arrives at the conclusion that a Christian following the law of Christ, since he does not go to war, ought not either to take advantage of any of the institutions of government, courts of law, or elections, and that in his private concerns he must not have recourse to the authorities, the police, or the law. Further on in the book he treats of the relation of the Old Testament to the New, the value of government for those who are Christians, and makes some observations on the doctrine of non-resistance and the attacks made on it. The author concludes his book by saying: "Christians do not need government, and therefore they cannot either obey it in what is contrary to Christ's teaching nor, still less, take part in it." Christ took his disciples out of the world, he says. They do not expect worldly blessings and worldly happiness, but they expect eternal life. The Spirit in whom they live makes them contented and happy in every position. If the world tolerates them, they are always happy. If the world will not leave them in peace, they will go elsewhere, since they are pilgrims on the earth and they have no fixed place of habitation. They believe that "the dead may bury their dead." One thing only is needful for them, "to follow their Master."

Even putting aside the question as to the principle laid down in these two books as to the Christian's duty in his attitude to war, one cannot help perceiving the practical importance and the urgent need of deciding the question.

There are people, hundreds of thousands of Quakers, Mennonites, all our Douhobortsi, Molokani, and others who do not belong to any definite sect, who consider that the use of force—and, consequently, military service—is inconsistent with Christianity. Consequently there are every year among us in Russia some men called upon for military service who refuse to serve on the ground of their religious convictions. Does the government let them off then? No. Does it compel them to go, and in case of disobedience punish them? No. This was how the government treated them in 1818. Here is an extract from the diary of Nicholas Myravyov of Kars, which was not passed by the censor, and is not known in Russia:

"TIFLIS, October 2, 1818.

"In the morning the commandant told me that five peasants belonging to a landowner in the Tamboff government had lately been sent to Georgia. These men had been sent for soldiers, but they would not serve; they had been several times flogged and made to run the gauntlet, but they would submit readily to the cruelest tortures, and even to death, rather than serve. 'Let us go,' they said, 'and leave us alone; we will not hurt anyone; all men are equal, and the Tzar is a man like us; why should we pay him tribute; why should I expose my life to danger to kill in battle some man who has done me no harm? You can cut us to pieces and we will not be soldiers. He who has compassion on us will give us charity, but as for the government rations, we have not had them and we do not want to have them.' These were the words of those peasants, who declare that there are numbers like them in Russia. They brought them four times before the Committee of Ministers, and at last decided to lay the matter before the Tzar, who gave orders that they should be taken to Georgia for correction, and commanded the commander-in-chief to send him a report every month of their gradual success in bringing these peasants to a better mind."

How the correction ended is not known, as the whole episode indeed was unknown, having been kept in profound secrecy.

This was how the government behaved seventy-five years ago— this is how it has behaved in a great number of cases, studiously concealed from the people. And this is how the government behaves now, except in the case of the German Mennonites, living in the province of Kherson, whose plea against military service is considered well grounded. They are made to work off their term of service in labor in the forests.

But in the recent cases of refusal on the part of Mennonites to serve in the army on religious grounds, the government authorities have acted in the following manner:

To begin with, they have recourse to every means of coercion used in our times to "correct" the culprit and bring him to "a better mind," and these measures are carried out with the greatest secrecy. I know that in the case of one man who declined to serve in 1884 in Moscow, the official correspondence on the subject had two months after his refusal accumulated into a big folio, and was kept absolutely secret among the Ministry.

They usually begin by sending the culprit to the priests, and the latter, to their shame be it said, always exhort him to obedience. But since the exhortation in Christ's name to forswear Christ is for the most part unsuccessful, after he has received the admonitions of the spiritual authorities, they send him to the gendarmes, and the latter, finding, as a rule, no political cause for offense in him, dispatch him back again, and then he is sent to the learned men, to the doctors, and to the madhouse. During all these vicissitudes he is deprived of liberty and has to endure every kind of humiliation and suffering as a convicted criminal. (All this has been repeated in four cases.) The doctors let him out of the madhouse, and then every kind of secret shift is employed to prevent him from going free—whereby others would be encouraged to refuse to serve as he has done—and at the same time to avoid leaving him among the soldiers, for fear they too should learn from him that military service is not at all their duty by the law of God, as they are assured, but quite contrary to it.

The most convenient thing for the government would be to kill the non-resistant by flogging him to death or some other means, as was done in former days. But to put a man openly to death because he believes in the creed we all confess is impossible. To let a man alone who has refused obedience is also impossible. And so the government tries either to compel the man by ill-treatment to renounce Christ, or in some way or other to get rid of him unobserved, without openly putting him to death, and to hide somehow both the action and the man himself from other people. And so all kinds of shifts and wiles and cruelties are set on foot against him. They either send him to the frontier or provoke him to insubordination, and then try him for breach of discipline and shut him up in the prison of the disciplinary battalion, where they can ill treat him freely unseen by anyone, or they declare him mad, and lock him up in a lunatic asylum. They sent one man in this way to Tashkend—that is, they pretended to transfer him to the Tashkend army; another to Omsk; a third they convicted of insubordination and shut up in prison; a fourth they sent to a lunatic asylum.

Everywhere the same story is repeated. Not only the government, but the great majority of liberal, advanced people, as they are called, studiously turn away from everything that has been said, written, or done, or is being done by men to prove the incompatibility of force in its most awful, gross, and glaring form—in the form, that is, of an army of soldiers prepared to murder anyone, whoever it may be—with the teachings of Christianity, or even of the humanity which society professes as its creed.

So that the information I have gained of the attitude of the higher ruling classes, not only in Russia but in Europe and America, toward the elucidation of this question has convinced me that there exists in these ruling classes a consciously hostile attitude to true Christianity, which is shown pre-eminently in their reticence in regard to all manifestations of it.

CHAPTER II: CRITICISMS OF THE DOCTRINE OF NON-RESISTANCE TO EVIL BY FORCE ON THE PART OF BELIEVERS AND OF UNBELIEVERS

Fate of the Book "What I Believe"—Evasive Character of Religious Criticisms of Principles of my Book—1st Reply: Use of Force not Opposed to Christianity—2d Reply: Use of Force Necessary to Restrain Evil Doers—3d Reply: Duty of Using Force in Defense of One's Neighbor—4th Reply: The Breach of the Command of Non-resistance to be Regarded Simply as a Weakness—5th Reply: Reply Evaded by Making Believe that the Question has long been Decided—To Devise such Subterfuges and to take Refuge Behind the Authority of the Church, of Antiquity, and of Religion is all that Ecclesiastical Critics can do to get out of the Contradiction between Use of Force and Christianity in Theory and in Practice—General Attitude of the Ecclesiastical World and of the Authorities to Profession of True Christianity—General Character of Russian Freethinking Critics—Foreign Freethinking Critics—Mistaken Arguments of these Critics the Result of Misunderstanding the True Meaning of Christ's Teaching.

The impression I gained of a desire to conceal, to hush up, what I had tried to express in my book, led me to judge the book itself afresh.

On its appearance it had, as I had anticipated, been forbidden, and ought therefore by law to have been burnt. But, at the same time, it was discussed among officials, and circulated in a great number of manuscript and lithograph copies, and in translations printed abroad.

And very quickly after the book, criticisms, both religious and secular in character, made their appearance, and these the government tolerated, and even encouraged. So that the refutation of a book which no one was supposed to know anything about was even chosen as the subject for theological dissertations in the academies.

The criticisms of my book, Russian and foreign alike, fall under two general divisions—the religious criticisms of men who regard themselves as believers, and secular criticisms, that is, those of freethinkers.

I will begin with the first class. In my book I made it an accusation against the teachers of the Church that their teaching is opposed to Christ's commands clearly and definitely expressed in the Sermon on the Mount, and opposed in especial to his command in regard to resistance to evil, and that in this way they deprive Christ's teaching of all value. The Church authorities accept the teaching of the Sermon on the Mount on non-resistance to evil by force as divine revelation; and therefore one would have thought that if they felt called upon to write about my book at all, they would have found it inevitable before everything else to reply to the principal point of my charge against them, and to say plainly, do they or do they not admit the teaching of the Sermon on the Mount and the commandment of non-resistance to evil as binding on a Christian. And they were bound to answer this question, not after the usual fashion (*i. e.,* "that although on the one side one cannot absolutely deny, yet on the other side one cannot again fully assent, all the more seeing that," etc., etc.). No; they should have answered the question as plainly as it was put in my book—Did Christ really demand from his disciples that they should carry out what he taught them in the Sermon on the Mount? And can a Christian, then, or can he not, always remaining a Christian, go to law or make any use of the law, or seek his own protection in the law? And can the Christian, or can he not, remaining a Christian, take part in the administration of government, using compulsion against his neighbors? And—the most important question hanging over the heads of all of us in these days of universal military service—can the Christian, or can he not, remaining a Christian, against

Christ's direct prohibition, promise obedience in future actions directly opposed to his teaching? And can he, by taking his share of service in the army, prepare himself to murder men, and even actually murder them?

These questions were put plainly and directly, and seemed to require a plain and direct answer; but in all the criticisms of my book there was no such plain and direct answer. No; my book received precisely the same treatment as all the attacks upon the teachers of the Church for their defection from the Law of Christ of which history from the days of Constantine is full.

A very great deal was said in connection with my book of my having incorrectly interpreted this and other passages of the Gospel, of my being in error in not recognizing the Trinity, the redemption, and the immortality of the soul. A very great deal was said, but not a word about the one thing which for every Christian is the most essential question in life—how to reconcile the duty of forgiveness, meekness, patience, and love for all, neighbors and enemies alike, which is so clearly expressed in the words of our teacher, and in the heart of each of us—how to reconcile this duty with the obligation of using force in war upon men of our own or a foreign people.

All that are worth calling answers to this question can be brought under the following five heads. I have tried to bring together in this connection all I could, not only from the criticisms on my book, but from what has been written in past times on this theme.

The first and crudest form of reply consists in the bold assertion that the use of force is not opposed by the teaching of Christ; that it is permitted, and even enjoined, on the Christian by the Old and New Testaments.

Assertions of this kind proceed, for the most part, from men who have attained the highest ranks in the governing or ecclesiastical hierarchy, and who are consequently perfectly assured that no one will dare to contradict their assertion, and that if anyone does contradict it they will hear nothing of the contradiction. These men have, for the most part, through the intoxication of power, so lost the right idea of what that Christianity is in the name of which they hold their position that what is Christian in Christianity presents itself to them as heresy, while everything in the Old and New Testaments which can be distorted into an antichristian and heathen meaning they regard as the foundation of Christianity. In support of their assertion that Christianity is not opposed to the use of force, these men usually, with the greatest audacity, bring together all the most obscure passages from the Old and New Testaments, interpreting them in the most unchristian way—the punishment of Ananias and Sapphira, of Simon the Sorcerer, etc. They quote all those sayings of Christ's which can possibly be interpreted as justification of cruelty: the expulsion from the Temple; "It shall be more tolerable for the land of Sodom than for this city," etc., etc. According to these people's notions, a Christian government is not in the least bound to be guided by the spirit of peace, forgiveness of injuries, and love for enemies.

To refute such an assertion is useless, because the very people who make this assertion refute themselves, or, rather, renounce Christ, inventing a Christianity and a Christ of their own in the place of him in whose name the Church itself exists, as well as their office in it. If all men were to learn that the Church professes to believe in a Christ of punishment and warfare, not of forgiveness, no one would believe in the Church and it could not prove to anyone what it is trying to prove.

The second, somewhat less gross, form of argument consists in declaring that, though Christ did indeed preach that we should turn the left cheek, and give the cloak also, and this is the highest moral duty, yet that there are wicked men in the world, and if these wicked men were not restrained by force, the whole world and all good men would come to ruin through them. This argument I found for the first time in John Chrysostom, and I show how he is mistaken in my book "What I Believe."

This argument is ill grounded, because if we allow ourselves to regard any men as intrinsically wicked men, then in the first place we annul, by so doing, the whole idea of the Christian teaching, according to which we are all equals and brothers, as sons of one Father in heaven. Secondly, it is ill founded, because even if to use force against wicked men had been permitted by God, since it is impossible to find a perfect and unfailing distinction by which one could positively know the wicked from the good, so it would come to all individual men and societies of men mutually regarding each other as wicked men, as is the case now. Thirdly, even if it were possible to distinguish the wicked from the good unfailingly, even then it would be impossible to kill or injure or shut up in prison these wicked men, because there would be no one in a Christian society to carry out such punishment, since every Christian, as a Christian, has been commanded to use no force against the wicked.

The third kind of answer, still more subtle than the preceding, consists in asserting that though the command of non-resistance to evil by force is binding on the Christian when the evil is directed against himself personally, it ceases to be binding when the evil is directed against his neighbors, and that then the Christian is not only not bound to fulfill the commandment, but is even bound to act in opposition to it in defense of his neighbors, and to use force against transgressors by force. This assertion is an absolute assumption, and one cannot find in all Christ's teaching any confirmation of such an argument. Such an argument is not only a limitation, but a direct contradiction and negation of the commandment. If every man has the right to have recourse to force in face of a danger threatening another, the question of the use of force is reduced to a question of the definition of danger for another. If my private judgment is to decide the question of what is danger for another, there is no occasion for the use of force which could not be justified on the ground of danger threatening some other man. They killed and burnt witches, they killed aristocrats and girondists, they killed their enemies, because those who were in authority regarded them as dangerous for the people.

If this important limitation, which fundamentally undermines the whole value of the commandment, had entered into Christ's meaning, there must have been mention of it somewhere. This restriction is made nowhere in our Saviour's life or preaching. On the contrary, warning is given precisely against this treacherous and scandalous restriction which nullifies the commandment. The error and impossibility of such a limitation is shown in the Gospel with special clearness in the account of the judgment of Caiaphas, who makes precisely this distinction. He acknowledged that it was wrong to punish the innocent Jesus, but he saw in him a source of danger not for himself, but for the whole people, and therefore he said: It is better for one man to die, that the whole people perish not. And the erroneousness of such a limitation is still more clearly expressed in the words spoken to Peter when he tried to resist by force evil directed against Jesus (Matt. xxvi. 52). Peter was not defending himself, but his beloved and heavenly Master. And Christ at once reproved him for this, saying, that he who takes up the sword shall perish by the sword.

Besides, apologies for violence used against one's neighbor in defense of another neighbor from greater violence are always untrustworthy, because when force is used against one who has not yet carried out his evil intent, I can never know which would be greater—the evil of my act of violence or of the act I want to prevent. We kill the criminal that society may be rid of him, and we never know whether the criminal of to-day would not have been a changed man to-morrow, and whether our punishment of him is not useless cruelty. We shut up the dangerous—as we think—member of society, but the next day this man might cease to be dangerous and his imprisonment might be for nothing. I see that a man I know to be a ruffian is pursuing a young girl. I have a gun in my hand—I kill the ruffian and save the girl. But the death or the wounding of the ruffian has positively taken place, while what would have happened if this had not been I cannot know. And what an immense mass of evil must result, and indeed does result, from allowing men to assume the right of anticipating what may happen. Ninety-nine per cent. of the evil of the world is founded on this reasoning—from the Inquisition to dynamite bombs, and the executions or punishments of tens of thousands of political criminals.

A fourth, still more refined, reply to the question, What ought to be the Christian's attitude to Christ's command of non-resistance to evil by force? consists in declaring that they do not deny the command of non-resistance to evil, but recognize it; but they only do not ascribe to this command the special exclusive value attached to it by sectarians. To regard this command as the indispensable condition of Christian life, as Garrison, Ballou, Dymond, the Quakers, the Mennonites, and the Shakers do now, and as the Moravian brothers, the Waldenses, the Albigenses, the Bogomilites, and the Paulicians did in the past, is a one-sided heresy. This command has neither more nor less value than all the other commands, and the man who through weakness transgresses any command whatever, the command of non-resistance included, does not cease to be a Christian if he hold the true faith. This is a very skillful device, and many people who wish to be deceived are easily deceived by it. The device consists in reducing a direct conscious denial of a command to a casual breach of it. But one need only compare the attitude of the teachers of the Church to this and to other commands which they really do recognize, to be convinced that their attitude to this is completely different from their attitude to other duties.

The command against fornication they do really recognize, and consequently they do not admit that in any case fornication can cease to be wrong. The Church preachers never point out cases in which the command against fornication can be broken, and always teach that we must avoid seductions which lead to temptation to fornication. But not so with the command of non-resistance. All church preachers recognize cases in which that command can be broken, and teach the people accordingly. And they not only do not teach that we should avoid temptations to break it, chief of which is the military oath, but they themselves administer it. The preachers of the Church never in any other case advocate the breaking of any other commandment. But in connection with the commandment of non-resistance they openly teach that we must not understand it too literally, but that there are conditions and circumstances in which we must do the direct opposite, that is, go to law, fight, punish. So that occasions for fulfilling the commandment of non-resistance to evil by force are taught for the most part as occasions for not fulfilling it. The fulfillment of this command, they say, is very difficult and pertains only to perfection. And how can it not be difficult, when the breach of it is not only not forbidden, but law courts, prisons, cannons, guns, armies, and wars are under the immediate sanction of the Church? It cannot be true, then, that this command is recognized by the preachers of the Church as on a level with other commands.

The preachers of the Church clearly do not recognize it; only not daring to acknowledge this, they try to conceal their not recognizing it.

So much for the fourth reply.

The fifth kind of answer, which is the subtlest, the most often used, and the most effective, consists in avoiding answering, in making believe that this question is one which has long ago been decided perfectly clearly and satisfactorily, and that it is not worth while to talk about it. This method of reply is employed by all the more or less cultivated religious writers, that is to say, those who feel the laws of Christ binding for themselves. Knowing that the contradiction existing between the teaching of Christ which we profess with our lips and the whole order of our lives cannot be removed by words, and that touching upon it can only make it more obvious, they, with more or less ingenuity, evade it, pretending that the question of reconciling Christianity with the use of force has been decided already, or does not exist at all.

The majority of religious critics of my book use this fifth method of replying to it. I could quote dozens of such critics, in all of whom, without exception, we find the same thing repeated: everything is discussed except what constitutes the principal subject of the book. As a characteristic example of such criticisms, I will quote the article of a well-known and ingenious English writer and preacher—Farrar—who, like many learned theologians, is a great master of the art of circuitously evading a question. The article was published in an American journal, the *Forum*, in October, 1888.

After conscientiously explaining in brief the contents of my book, Farrar says: "Tolstoy came to the conclusion that a coarse deceit had been palmed upon the world when these words, 'Resist not evil,' were held by civil society to be compatible with war, courts of justice, capital punishment, divorce, oaths, national prejudice, and, indeed, with most of the institutions of civil and social life. He now believes that the kingdom of God would come if all men kept these five commandments of Christ, viz.: 1. Live in peace with all men. 2. Be pure. 3. Take no oaths. 4. Resist not evil. 5. Renounce national distinctions.

"Tolstoy," he says, "rejects the inspiration of the Old Testament; hence he rejects the chief doctrines of the Church—that of the Atonement by blood, the Trinity, the descent of the Holy Ghost on the Apostles, and his transmission through the priesthood." And he recognizes only the words and commands of Christ. "But is this interpretation of Christ a true one?" he says. "Are all men bound to act as Tolstoy teaches—*i. e.*, to carry out these five commandments of Christ?" You expect, then, that in answer to this essential question, which is the only one that could induce a man to write an article about the book, he will say either that this interpretation of Christ's teaching is true and we ought to follow it, or he will say that such an interpretation is untrue, will show why, and will give some other correct interpretation of those words which I interpret incorrectly. But nothing of the kind is done. Farrar only expresses his "belief" that, "though actuated by the noblest sincerity, Count Tolstoy has been misled by partial and one-sided interpretations of the meaning of the Gospel and the mind and will of Christ." What this error consists in is not made clear; it is only said: "To enter into the proof of this is impossible in this article, for I have already exceeded the space at my command."

And he concludes, in a tranquil spirit:

"Meanwhile, the reader who feels troubled lest it should be his duty also to forsake all the conditions of his life and to take up the position and work of a common laborer, may rest for the present on the principle, *securus judicat orbis terrarum*. With few and rare exceptions," he continues, "the whole of Christendom, from the days of the Apostles down to our own, has come to the firm conclusion that it was the object of Christ to lay down great eternal principles, but not to disturb the bases and revolutionize the institutions of all human society, which themselves rest on divine sanctions as well as on inevitable conditions. Were it my object to prove how untenable is the doctrine of communism, based by Count Tolstoy upon the divine paradoxes [*sic*], which can be interpreted only on historical principles in accordance with the whole method of the teaching of Jesus, it would require an ampler canvas than I have here at my disposal." What a pity he has not "an ampler canvas at his disposal"! And what a strange thing it is that for all these last fifteen centuries no one has had "a canvas ample enough" to prove that Christ, whom we profess to believe in, says something utterly unlike what he does say! Still, they could prove it if they wanted to. But it is not worth while to prove what everyone knows; it is enough to say, "*securus judicat orbis terrarum.*"

And of this kind, without exception, are all the criticisms of educated believers, who must, as such, understand the danger of their position. The sole escape from it for them lies in their hope that they may be able, by using the authority of the Church, of antiquity, and of their sacred office, to overawe the reader and draw him away from the idea of reading the Gospel for himself and thinking out the question in his own mind for himself. And in this they are successful; for, indeed, how could the notion occur to anyone that all that has been repeated from century to century with such earnestness and solemnity by all those archdeacons, bishops, archbishops, holy synods, and popes, is all of it a base lie and a calumny foisted upon Christ by them for the sake of keeping safe the money they must have to live luxuriously on the necks of other men? And it is a lie and a calumny so transparent that the only way of keeping it up consists in overawing people by their earnestness, their conscientiousness. It is just what has taken place of late years at recruiting sessions; at a table before the zertzal—the symbol of the Tzar's authority—in the seat of honor under the life-size portrait of the Tzar, sit dignified old officials, wearing decorations, conversing freely and easily, writing notes, summoning men before them, and giving orders. Here, wearing a cross on his breast, near them, is a prosperous-looking old priest in a silken cassock, with long gray hair flowing on to his cope, before a lectern who wears the golden cross and has a Gospel bound in gold.

They summon Ivan Petroff. A young man comes in, wretchedly, shabbily dressed, and in terror, the muscles of his face working, his eyes bright and restless; and in a broken voice, hardly above a whisper, he says: "I—by Christ's law—as a Christian—I cannot." "What is he muttering?" asks the president, frowning impatiently and raising his eyes from his book to listen. "Speak louder," the colonel with shining epaulets shouts to him. "I—I as a Christian——" And at last it appears that the young man refuses to serve in the army because he is a Christian. "Don't talk nonsense. Stand to be measured. Doctor, may I trouble you to measure him. He is all right?" "Yes." "Reverend father, administer the oath to him."

No one is the least disturbed by what the poor scared young man is muttering. They do not even pay attention to it. "They all mutter something, but we've no time to listen to it, we have to enroll so many."

The recruit tries to say something still. "It's opposed to the law of Christ." "Go along, go along; we know without your help what is opposed to the law and what's not; and you soothe his mind, reverend father, soothe him. Next: Vassily Nikitin." And they lead the trembling youth away. And it does not strike anyone— the guards, or Vassily Nikitin, whom they are bringing in, or any of the spectators of this scene—that these inarticulate words of the young man, at once suppressed by the authorities, contain the truth, and that the loud, solemnly uttered sentences of the calm, self-confident official and the priest are a lie and a deception.

Such is the impression produced not only by Farrar's article, but by all those solemn sermons, articles, and books which make their appearance from all sides directly there is anywhere a glimpse of truth exposing a predominant falsehood. At once begins the series of long, clever, ingenious, and solemn speeches and writings, which deal with questions nearly related to the subject, but skillfully avoid touching the subject itself.

That is the essence of the fifth and most effective means of getting out of the contradictions in which Church Christianity has placed itself, by professing its faith in Christ's teaching in words, while it denies it in its life, and teaches people to do the same.

Those who justify themselves by the first method, directly, crudely asserting that Christ sanctioned violence, wars, and murder, repudiate Christ's doctrine directly; those who find their defense in the second, the third, or the fourth method are confused and can easily be convicted of error; but this last class, who do not argue, who do not condescend to argue about it, but take shelter behind their own grandeur, and make a show of all this having been decided by them or at least by someone long ago, and no longer offering a possibility of doubt to anyone—they seem safe from attack, and will be beyond attack till men come to realize that they are under the narcotic influence exerted on them by governments and churches, and are no longer affected by it.

Such was the attitude of the spiritual critics—*i. e.*, those professing faith in Christ—to my book. And their attitude could not have been different. They are bound to take up this attitude by the contradictory position in which they find themselves between belief in the divinity of their Master and disbelief in his clearest utterances, and they want to escape from this contradiction. So that one cannot expect from them free discussion of the very essence of the question—that is, of the change in men's life which must result from applying Christ's teaching to the existing order of the world. Such free discussion I only expected from worldly, freethinking critics who are not bound to Christ's teaching in any way, and can therefore take an independent view of it. I had anticipated that freethinking writers would look at Christ, not merely, like the Churchmen, as the founder of a religion of personal salvation, but, to express it in their language, as a reformer who laid down new principles of life and destroyed the old, and whose reforms are not yet complete, but are still in progress even now.

Such a view of Christ and his teaching follows from my book. But to my astonishment, out of the great number of critics of my book there was not one, either Russian or foreign, who treated the subject from the side from which it was approached in the book—that is, who criticised Christ's doctrines as philosophical, moral, and social principles, to use their scientific expressions. This was not done in a single criticism. The freethinking Russian critics taking my book as though its whole contents could be reduced to non-resistance to evil, and understanding the doctrine of non-resistance to evil itself (no doubt for greater convenience in refuting it) as though it would prohibit every kind of conflict with evil, fell vehemently upon this doctrine, and for some years past have been very successfully proving that Christ's teaching is mistaken in so far as it forbids resistance to evil. Their refutations of this hypothetical doctrine of Christ were all the more successful since they knew beforehand that their arguments could not be contested or corrected, for the censorship, not having passed the book, did not pass articles in its defense.

It is a remarkable thing that among us, where one cannot say a word about the Holy Scriptures without the prohibition of the censorship, for some years past there have been in all the journals constant attacks and criticisms on the command of Christ simply and directly stated in Matt. v. 39. The Russian advanced critics, obviously unaware of all that has been done to elucidate the question of non-resistance, and sometimes even imagining apparently that the rule of non-resistance to evil had been invented by me personally, fell foul of the very idea of it. They opposed it and attacked it, and advancing with great heat arguments which had long ago been analyzed and refuted from every point of view, they demonstrated that a man ought invariably to defend (with violence) all the injured and oppressed, and that thus the doctrine of non-resistance to evil is an immoral doctrine.

To all Russian critics the whole import of Christ's command seemed reducible to the fact that it would hinder them from the active opposition to evil to which they are accustomed. So that the principle of non-resistance to evil by force has been attacked by two opposing camps: the conservatives, because this principle would hinder their activity in resistance to evil as applied to the revolutionists, in persecution and punishment of them; the revolutionists, too, because this principle would hinder their resistance to evil as applied to the conservatives and the overthrowing of them. The conservatives were indignant at the doctrine of non-resistance to evil by force hindering the energetic destruction of the revolutionary elements, which may ruin the national prosperity; the revolutionists were indignant at the doctrine of non-resistance to evil by force hindering the overthrow of the conservatives, who are ruining the national prosperity. It is worthy of remark in this connection that the revolutionists have attacked the principle of non-resistance to evil by force, in spite of the fact that it is the greatest terror and danger for every despotism. For ever since the beginning of the world, the use of violence of every kind, from the Inquisition to the Schlüsselburg fortress, has rested and still rests on the opposite principle of the necessity of resisting evil by force.

Besides this, the Russian critics have pointed out the fact that the application of the command of non-resistance to practical life would turn mankind aside out of the path of civilization along which it is moving. The path of civilization on which mankind in Europe is moving is in their opinion the one along which all mankind ought always to move.

So much for the general character of the Russian critics.

Foreign critics started from the same premises, but their discussions of my book were somewhat different from those of Russian critics, not only in being less bitter, and in showing more culture, but even in the subject-matter.

In discussing my book and the Gospel teaching generally, as it is expressed in the Sermon on the Mount, the foreign critics maintained that such doctrine is not peculiarly Christian (Christian doctrine is either Catholicism or Protestantism according to their views)—the teaching of the Sermon on the Mount is only a string of very pretty impracticable dreams *du charmant docteur*, as Renan says, fit for the simple and half-savage inhabitants of Galilee who lived eighteen hundred years ago, and for the half-savage Russian peasants—Sutaev and

Bondarev—and the Russian mystic Tolstoy, but not at all consistent with a high degree of European culture.

The foreign freethinking critics have tried in a delicate manner, without being offensive to me, to give the impression that my conviction that mankind could be guided by such a naïve doctrine as that of the Sermon on the Mount proceeds from two causes: that such a conviction is partly due to my want of knowledge, my ignorance of history, my ignorance of all the vain attempts to apply the principles of the Sermon on the Mount to life, which have been made in history and have led to nothing; and partly it is due to my failing to appreciate the full value of the lofty civilization to which mankind has attained at present, with its Krupp cannons, smokeless powder, colonization of Africa, Irish Coercion Bill, parliamentary government, journalism, strikes, and the Eiffel Tower.

So wrote de Vogüé and Leroy Beaulieu and Matthew Arnold; so wrote the American author Savage, and Ingersoll, the popular freethinking American preacher, and many others.

"Christ's teaching is no use, because it is inconsistent with our industrial age," says Ingersoll naïvely, expressing in this utterance, with perfect directness and simplicity, the exact notion of Christ's teaching held by persons of refinement and culture of our times. The teaching is no use for our industrial age, precisely as though the existence of this industrial age were a sacred fact which ought not to and could not be changed. It is just as though drunkards when advised how they could be brought to habits of sobriety should answer that the advice is incompatible with their habit of taking alcohol.

The arguments of all the freethinking critics, Russian and foreign alike, different as they may be in tone and manner of presentation, all amount essentially to the same strange misapprehension—namely, that Christ's teaching, one of the consequences of which is non-resistance to evil, is of no use to us because it requires a change of our life.

Christ's teaching is useless because, if it were carried into practice, life could not go on as at present; we must add: if we have begun by living sinfully, as we do live and are accustomed to live. Not only is the question of non-resistance to evil not discussed; the very mention of the fact that the duty of non-resistance enters into Christ's teaching is regarded as satisfactory proof of the impracticability of the whole teaching.

Meanwhile one would have thought it was necessary to point out at least some kind of solution of the following question, since it is at the root of almost everything that interests us.

The question amounts to this: In what way are we to decide men's disputes, when some men consider evil what others consider good, and *vice versa*? And to reply that that is evil which I think evil, in spite of the fact that my opponent thinks it good, is not a solution of the difficulty. There can only be two solutions: either to find a real unquestionable criterion of what is evil or not to resist evil by force.

The first course has been tried ever since the beginning of historical times, and, as we all know, it has not hitherto led to any successful results.

The second solution—not forcibly to resist what we consider evil until we have found a universal criterion—that is the solution given by Christ.

We may consider the answer given by Christ unsatisfactory; we may replace it by another and better, by finding a criterion by which evil could be defined for all men unanimously and simultaneously; we may simply, like savage nations, not recognize the existence of the question. But we cannot treat the question as the learned critics of Christianity do. They pretend either that no such question exists at all or that the question is solved by granting to certain persons or assemblies of persons the right to define evil and to resist it by force. But we know all the while that granting such a right to certain persons does not decide the question (still less so when we are ourselves the certain persons), since there are always people who do not recognize this right in the authorized persons or assemblies.

But this assumption, that what seems evil to us is really evil, shows a complete misunderstanding of the question, and lies at the root of the argument of freethinking critics about the Christian religion. In this way, then, the discussions of my book on the part of Churchmen and freethinking critics alike showed me that the majority of men simply do not understand either Christ's teaching or the questions which Christ's teaching solves.

CHAPTER III: CHRISTIANITY MISUNDERSTOOD BY BELIEVERS

Meaning of Christian Doctrine, Understood by a Minority, has Become Completely Incomprehensible for the Majority of Men—Reason of this to be Found in Misinterpretation of Christianity and Mistaken Conviction of Believers and Unbelievers Alike that they Understand it—The Meaning of Christianity Obscured for Believers by the Church—The First Appearance of Christ's Teaching—Its Essence and Difference from Heathen Religions—Christianity not Fully Comprehended at the Beginning, Became More and More Clear to those who Accepted it from its Correspondence with Truth—Simultaneously with this Arose the Claim to Possession of the Authentic Meaning of the Doctrine Based on the Miraculous Nature of its Transmission—Assembly of Disciples as Described in the Acts—The Authoritative Claim to the Sole Possession of the True Meaning of Christ's Teaching Supported by Miraculous Evidence has Led by Logical Development to the Creeds of the Churches—A Church Could Not be Founded by Christ—Definitions of a Church According to the Catechisms—The Churches have Always been Several in Number and Hostile to One Another—What is Heresy—The Work of G. Arnold on Heresies—Heresies the Manifestations of Progress in the Churches—Churches Cause Dissension among Men, and are Always Hostile to Christianity—Account of the Work Done by the Russian Church—Matt. xxiii. 23—The Sermon on the Mount or the Creed—The Orthodox Church Conceals from the People the True Meaning of Christianity—The Same Thing is Done by the Other Churches—All the External Conditions of Modern Life are such as to Destroy the Doctrine of the Church, and therefore the Churches use Every Effort to Support their Doctrines.

Thus the information I received, after my book came out, went to show that the Christian doctrine, in its direct and simple sense, was understood, and had always been understood, by a minority of men, while the critics, ecclesiastical and freethinking alike, denied the possibility of taking Christ's teaching in its direct sense. All this convinced me that while on one hand the true understanding of this doctrine had never been lost to a minority, but had been established more and more clearly, on the other hand the meaning of it had been more and more obscured for the majority. So that at last such a depth of obscurity has been reached that men do not take in their direct sense even the simplest precepts, expressed in the simplest words, in the Gospel.

Christ's teaching is not generally understood in its true, simple, and direct sense even in these days, when the light of the Gospel has penetrated even to the darkest recesses of human consciousness; when, in the words of Christ, that which was spoken in the ear is proclaimed from the housetops; and when the Gospel is influencing every side of human life—domestic, economic, civic, legislative, and international. This lack of true understanding of Christ's words at such a time would be inexplicable, if there were not causes to account for it.

One of these causes is the fact that believers and unbelievers alike are firmly persuaded that they have understood Christ's teaching a long time, and that they understand it so fully, indubitably, and conclusively that it can have no other significance than the one they attribute to it. And the reason of this conviction is that the false interpretation and consequent misapprehension of the Gospel is an error of such long standing. Even the strongest current of water cannot add a drop to a cup which is already full.

The most difficult subjects can be explained to the most slow-witted man if he has not formed any idea of them already; but the simplest thing cannot be made clear to the most intelligent man if he is firmly persuaded that he knows already, without a shadow of doubt, what is laid before him.

The Christian doctrine is presented to the men of our world today as a doctrine which everyone has known so long and accepted so unhesitatingly in all its minutest details that it cannot be understood in any other way than it is understood now.

Christianity is understood now by all who profess the doctrines of the Church as a supernatural miraculous revelation of everything which is repeated in the Creed. By unbelievers it is regarded as an illustration of man's craving for a belief in the supernatural, which mankind has now outgrown, as an historical phenomenon which has received full expression in Catholicism, Greek Orthodoxy, and Protestantism, and has no longer any living significance for us. The significance of the Gospel is hidden from believers by the Church, from unbelievers by Science.

I will speak first of the former. Eighteen hundred years ago there appeared in the midst of the heathen Roman world a strange new doctrine, unlike any of the old religions, and attributed to a man, Christ.

This new doctrine was in both form and content absolutely new to the Jewish world in which it originated, and still more to the Roman world in which it was preached and diffused.

In the midst of the elaborate religious observances of Judaism, in which, in the words of Isaiah, law was laid upon law, and in the midst of the Roman legal system worked out to the highest point of perfection, a new doctrine appeared, which denied not only every deity, and all fear and worship of them, but even all human institutions and all necessity for them. In place of all the rules of the old religions, this doctrine sets up only a type of inward perfection, truth, and love in the person of Christ, and—as a result of this inward perfection being attained by men—also the outward perfection foretold by the Prophets—the kingdom of God, when all men will cease to learn to make war, when all shall be taught of God and united in love, and the lion will lie down with the lamb. Instead of the threats of punishment which all the old laws of religions and governments alike laid down for non-fulfillment of their rules, instead of promises of rewards for fulfillment of them, this doctrine called men to it only because it was the truth. John vii. 17: "If any man will do His will, he shall know of the doctrine whether it be of God." John viii. 46: "If I say the truth, why do ye not believe me? But ye seek to kill me, a man that hath told you the truth. Ye shall know the truth, and the truth shall make you free. God is a spirit, and they that worship him must worship him in spirit and in truth. Keep my sayings, and ye shall know of my sayings whether they be true." No proofs of this doctrine were offered except its truth, the correspondence of the doctrine with the truth. The whole teaching consisted in the recognition of truth and following it, in a greater and greater attainment of truth, and a closer and closer following of it in the acts of life. There are no acts in this doctrine which could justify a man and make him saved. There is only the image of truth to guide him, for inward perfection in the person of Christ, and for outward perfection in the establishment of the kingdom of God. The fulfillment of this teaching consists only in walking in the chosen way, in getting nearer to inward perfection in the imitation of Christ, and outward perfection in the establishment of the kingdom of God. The greater or less blessedness of a man depends, according to this doctrine, not on the degree of perfection to which he has attained, but on the greater or less swiftness with which he is pursuing it.

The progress toward perfection of the publican Zaccheus, of the woman that was a sinner, of the robber on the cross, is a greater state of blessedness, according to this doctrine, than the stationary righteousness of the Pharisee. The lost sheep is dearer than ninety-nine that were not lost. The prodigal son, the piece of money that was lost and found again, are dearer, more precious to God than those which have not been lost.

Every condition, according to this doctrine, is only a particular step in the attainment of inward and outward perfection, and therefore has no significance of itself. Blessedness consists in progress toward perfection; to stand still in any condition whatever means the cessation of this blessedness.

"Let not thy left hand know what thy right hand doeth." "No man having put his hand to the plow and looking back is fit for the kingdom of God." "Rejoice not that the spirits are subject to you, but seek rather that your names be written in heaven." "Be ye perfect, even as your Father in heaven is perfect." "Seek ye first the kingdom of heaven and its righteousness."

The fulfillment of this precept is only to be found in uninterrupted progress toward the attainment of ever higher truth, toward establishing more and more firmly an ever greater love within oneself, and establishing more and more widely the kingdom of God outside oneself.

It is obvious that, appearing as it did in the midst of the Jewish and heathen world, such teaching could not be accepted by the majority of men, who were living a life absolutely different from what was required by it. It is obvious, too, that even for those by whom it was accepted, it was so absolutely opposed to all their old views that it could not be comprehensible in its full significance.

It has been only by a succession of misunderstandings, errors, partial explanations, and the corrections and additions of generations that the meaning of the Christian doctrine has grown continually more and more clear to men. The Christian view of life has exerted an influence on the Jewish and heathen, and the heathen and Jewish view of life has, too, exerted an influence on the Christian. And Christianity, as the living force, has gained more and more upon the extinct Judaism and heathenism, and has grown continually clearer and clearer, as it freed itself from the admixture of falsehood which had overlaid it. Men went further and further in the attainment of the meaning of Christianity, and realized it more and more in life.

The longer mankind lived, the clearer and clearer became the meaning of Christianity, as must always be the case with every theory of life.

Succeeding generations corrected the errors of their predecessors, and grew ever nearer and nearer to a comprehension of the true meaning. It was thus from the very earliest times of Christianity. And so, too, from the earliest times of Christianity there were men who began to assert on their own authority that the meaning they attribute to the doctrine is the only true one, and as proof bring forward supernatural occurrences in support of the correctness of their interpretation.

This was the principal cause at first of the misunderstanding of the doctrine, and afterward of the complete distortion of it.

It was supposed that Christ's teaching was transmitted to men not like every other truth, but in a special miraculous way. Thus the truth of the teaching was not proved by its correspondence with the needs of the mind and the whole nature of man, but by the miraculous manner of its transmission, which was advanced as an irrefutable proof of the truth of the interpretation put on it. This hypothesis originated from misunderstanding of the teaching, and its result was to make it impossible to understand it rightly.

And this happened first in the earliest times, when the doctrine was still not so fully understood and often interpreted wrongly, as we see by the Gospels and the Acts. The less the doctrine was understood, the more obscure it appeared and the more necessary were external proofs of its truth. The proposition that we ought not to do unto others as we would not they should do unto us, did not need to be proved by miracles and needed no exercise of faith, because this proposition is in itself convincing and in harmony with man's mind and nature; but the proposition that Christ was God had to be proved by miracles completely beyond our comprehension.

The more the understanding of Christ's teaching was obscured, the more the miraculous was introduced into it; and the more the miraculous was introduced into it, the more the doctrine was strained from its meaning and the more obscure it became; and the more it was strained from its meaning and the more obscure it became, the more strongly its infallibility had to be asserted, and the less comprehensible the doctrine became.

One can see by the Gospels, the Acts, and the Epistles how from the earliest times the non-comprehension of the doctrine called forth the need for proofs through the miraculous and incomprehensible.

The first example in the book of Acts is the assembly which gathered together in Jerusalem to decide the question which had arisen, whether to baptize or not the uncircumcised and those who had eaten of food sacrificed to idols.

The very fact of this question being raised showed that those who discussed it did not understand the teaching of Christ, who rejected all outward observances—ablutions, purifications, fasts, and sabbaths. It was plainly said, "Not that which goeth into a man's mouth, but that which cometh out of a man's mouth, defileth him," and therefore the question of baptizing the uncircumcised could only have arisen among men who, though they loved their Master and dimly felt the grandeur of his teaching, still did not understand the teaching itself very clearly. And this was the fact.

Just in proportion to the failure of the members of the assembly to understand the doctrine was their need of external confirmation of their incomplete interpretation of it. And then to settle this question, the very asking of which proved their misunderstanding of the doctrine, there was uttered in this assembly, as is described in the Acts, that strange phrase, which was for the first time found necessary to give external confirmation to certain assertions, and which has been productive of so much evil.

That is, it was asserted that the correctness of what they had decided was guaranteed by the miraculous participation of the Holy Ghost, that is, of God, in their decision. But the assertion that the Holy Ghost, that is, God, spoke through the Apostles, in its turn wanted proof. And thus it was necessary, to confirm this, that the Holy Ghost should descend at Pentecost in tongues of fire upon those who made this assertion. (In the account of it, the descent of the Holy Ghost precedes the assembly, but the book of Acts was written much later than both events.) But the descent of the Holy Ghost too had to be proved for those who had not seen the tongues of fire (though it is not easy to understand why a tongue of fire burning above a man's head should prove that what that man is going to say will be infallibly the truth). And so arose the necessity for still more miracles and changes, raisings of the dead to life, and strikings of the living dead, and all those marvels which have been a stumbling-block to men, of which the Acts is full, and which, far from ever convincing one of the truth of the Christian doctrine, can only repel men from it. The result of such a means of confirming the truth was that the more these confirmations of truth by tales of miracles were heaped up one after another, the more the doctrine was distorted from its original meaning, and the more incomprehensible it became.

Thus it was from the earliest times, and so it went on, constantly increasing, till it reached in our day the logical climax of the dogmas of transubstantiation and the infallibility of the Pope, or of the bishops, or of Scripture, and of requiring a blind faith rendered incomprehensible and utterly meaningless, not in God, but in Christ, not in a doctrine, but in a person, as in Catholicism, or in persons, as in Greek Orthodoxy, or in a book, as in Protestantism. The more widely Christianity was diffused, and the greater the number of people unprepared for it who were brought under its sway, the less it was understood, the more absolutely was its infallibility insisted on, and the less possible it became to understand the true meaning of the doctrine. In the times of Constantine the whole interpretation of the doctrine had been already reduced to a *résumé*—supported by the temporal authority—of the disputes that had taken place in the Council—to a creed which reckoned off—I believe in so and so, and so and so, and so and so to the end—to one holy, Apostolic Church, which means the infallibility of those persons who call themselves the Church. So that it all amounts to a man no longer believing in God nor Christ, as they are revealed to him, but believing in what the Church orders him to believe in.

But the Church is holy; the Church was founded by Christ. God could not leave men to interpret his teaching at random—therefore he founded the Church. All those statements are so utterly untrue and unfounded that one is ashamed to refute them. Nowhere nor in anything, except in the assertion of the Church, can we find that God or Christ founded anything like what Churchmen understand by the Church. In the Gospels there is a warning against the Church, as it is an external authority, a warning most clear and obvious in the passage where it is said that Christ's followers should "call no man master." But nowhere is anything said of the foundation of what Churchmen call the Church.

The word church is used twice in the Gospels—once in the sense of an assembly of men to decide a dispute, the other time in connection with the obscure utterance about a stone—Peter, and the gates of hell. From these two passages in which the word church is used, in the signification merely of an assembly, has been deduced all that we now understand by the Church.

But Christ could not have founded the Church, that is, what we now understand by that word. For nothing like the idea of the Church as we know it now, with its sacraments, miracles, and above all its claim to infallibility, is to be found either in Christ's words or in the ideas of the men of that time.

The fact that men called what was formed afterward by the same word as Christ used for something totally different, does not give them the right to assert that Christ founded the one, true Church.

Besides, if Christ had really founded such an institution as the Church for the foundation of all his teaching and the whole faith, he would certainly have described this institution clearly and definitely, and would have given the only true Church, besides tales of miracles, which are used to support every kind of superstition, some tokens so unmistakable that no doubt of its genuineness could ever have arisen. But nothing of the sort was done by him. And there have been and still are different institutions, each calling itself the true Church.

The Catholic catechism says: "L'Église est la société des fidéles établie par notre Seigneur Jésus Christ, répandue sur toute la terre et soumise à l'authorité des pasteurs légitimes, principalement notre Saint Père le Pape," understanding by the words "pasteurs légitimes" an association of men having the Pope at its head, and consisting of certain individuals bound together by a certain organization.

The Greek Orthodox catechism says: "The Church is a society founded upon earth by Jesus Christ, which is united into one whole, by one divine doctrine and by sacraments, under the rule and guidance of a priesthood appointed by God," meaning by the "priesthood appointed by God" the Greek Orthodox priesthood, consisting of certain individuals who happen to be in such or such positions.

The Lutheran catechism says: "The Church is holy Christianity, or the collection of all believers under Christ, their head, to whom the Holy Ghost through the Gospels and sacraments promises, communicates, and administers heavenly salvation," meaning that the Catholic Church is lost in error, and that the true means of salvation is in Lutheranism.

For Catholics the Church of God coincides with the Roman priesthood and the Pope. For the Greek Orthodox believer the Church of God coincides with the establishment and priesthood of Russia.

For Lutherans the Church of God coincides with a body of men who recognize the authority of the Bible and Luther's catechism.

Ordinarily, when speaking of the rise of Christianity, men belonging to one of the existing churches use the word church in the singular, as though there were and had been only one church. But this is absolutely incorrect. The Church, as an institution which asserted that it possessed infallible truth, did not make its appearance singly; there were at least two churches directly this claim was made.

While believers were agreed among themselves and the body was one, it had no need to declare itself as a church. It was only when believers were split up into opposing parties, renouncing one another, that it seemed necessary to each party to confirm their own truth by ascribing to themselves infallibility. The conception of one church only arose when there were two sides divided and disputing, who each called the other side heresy, and recognized their own side only as the infallible church.

If we knew that there was a church which decided in the year 51 to receive the uncircumcised, it is only so because there was another church—of the Judaists—who decided to keep the uncircumcised out.

If there is a Catholic Church now which asserts its own infallibility, that is only because there are churches—Greco-Russian, Old Orthodox, and Lutheran—each asserting its own infallibility and denying that of all other churches. So that the one Church is only a fantastic imagination which has not the least trace of reality about it.

As a real historical fact there has existed, and still exist, several bodies of men, each asserting that it is the one Church, founded by Christ, and that all the others who call themselves churches are only sects and heresies.

The catechisms of the churches of the most world-wide influence—the Catholic, the Old Orthodox, and the Lutheran—openly assert this.

In the Catholic catechism it is said: "Quels sont ceux qui sont hors de l'église? Les infidèles, les hérétiques, les schismatiques." The so-called Greek Orthodox are regarded as schismatics, the Lutherans as heretics; so that according to the Catholic catechism the only people in the Church are Catholics.

In the so-called Orthodox catechism it is said: By the one Christian Church is understood the Orthodox, which remains fully in accord with the Universal Church. As for the Roman Church and other sects (the Lutherans and the rest they do not even dignify by the name of church), they cannot be included in the one true Church, since they have themselves separated from it.

According to this definition the Catholics and Lutherans are outside the Church, and there are only Orthodox in the Church.

The Lutheran catechism says: "Die wahre Kirche wird darein erkannt, dass in ihr das Wort Gottes lauter und rein ohne Menschenzusätze gelehrt und die Sacramente treu nach Christi Einsetzung gewahret werden."

According to this definition all those who have added anything to the teaching of Christ and the apostles, as the Catholic and

Greek churches have done, are outside the Church. And in the Church there are only Protestants.

The Catholics assert that the Holy Ghost has been transmitted without a break in their priesthood. The Orthodox assert that the same Holy Ghost has been transmitted without a break in their priesthood. The Arians asserted that the Holy Ghost was transmitted in their priesthood (they asserted this with just as much right as the churches in authority now). The Protestants of every kind—Lutherans, Reformed Church, Presbyterians, Methodists, Swedenborgians, Mormons—assert that the Holy Ghost is only present in their communities. If the Catholics assert that the Holy Ghost, at the time of the division of the Church into Arian and Greek, left the Church that fell away and remained in the one true Church, with precisely the same right the Protestants of every denomination can assert that at the time of the separation of their Church from the Catholic the Holy Ghost left the Catholic and passed into the Church they professed. And this is just what they do.

Every church traces its creed through an uninterrupted transmission from Christ and the Apostles. And truly every Christian creed that has been derived from Christ must have come down to the present generation through a certain transmission. But that does not prove that it alone of all that has been transmitted, excluding all the rest, can be the sole truth, admitting of no doubt.

Every branch in a tree comes from the root in unbroken connection; but the fact that each branch comes from the one root, does not prove at all that each branch was the only one. It is precisely the same with the Church. Every church presents exactly the same proofs of the succession, and even the same miracles, in support of its authenticity, as every other. So that there is but one strict and exact definition of what is a church (not of something fantastic which we would wish it to be, but of what it is and has been in reality)—a church is a body of men who claim for themselves that they are in complete and sole possession of the truth. And these bodies, having in course of time, aided by the support of the temporal authorities, developed into powerful institutions, have been the principal obstacles to the diffusion of a true comprehension of the teaching of Christ.

It could not be otherwise. The chief peculiarity which distinguished Christ's teaching from previous religions consisted in the fact that those who accepted it strove ever more and more to comprehend and realize its teaching. But the Church doctrine asserted its own complete and final comprehension and realization of it.

Strange though it may seem to us who have been brought up in the erroneous view of the Church as a Christian institution, and in contempt for heresy, yet the fact is that only in what was called heresy was there any true movement, that is, true Christianity, and that it only ceased to be so when those heresies stopped short in their movement and also petrified into the fixed forms of a church.

And, indeed, what is a heresy? Read all the theological works one after another. In all of them heresy is the subject which first presents itself for definition; since every theological work deals with the true doctrine of Christ as distinguished from the erroneous doctrines which surround it, that is, heresies. Yet you will not find anywhere anything like a definition of heresy.

The treatment of this subject by the learned historian of Christianity, E. de Pressensé, in his "Histoire du Dogme" (Paris, 1869), under the heading "Ubi Christus, ibi Ecclesia," may serve as an illustration of the complete absence of anything like a definition of what is understood by the word heresy. Here is what he says in his introduction (p. 3): "Je sais que l'on nous conteste le droit de qualifier ainsi [that is, to call heresies] les tendances qui furent si vivement combattues par les premiers Pères. La désignation même d'hérésie semble une atteinte portée à la liberté de conscience et de pensée. Nous ne pouvons partager ce scrupule, car il n'irait à rien moins qu'à enlever au Christianisme tout caractère distinctif."

And though he tells us that after Constantine's time the Church did actually abuse its power by designating those who dissented from it as heretics and persecuting them, yet he says, when speaking of early times: "L'église est une libre association; il y a tout profit à se séparer d'elle. La polémique contre l'erreur n'a d'autres ressources que la pensée et le sentiment. Un type doctrinal uniforme n'a pas encore été élaboré; les divergences secondaires se produisent en Orient et en Occident avec une entière liberté; la théologie n'est point liée à d'invariables formules. Si au sein de cette diversité apparait un fonds commun de croyances, n'est-on pas en droit d'y voir non pas un système formulé et composé par les représentants d'une autorité d'école, mais la foi elle-même dans son instinct le plus sûr et sa manifestation la plus spontanée? Si cette même unanimité qui se révèle dans les croyances essentielles, se retrouve pour repousser telles ou telles tendances, ne serons-nous pas en droit de conclure que ces tendances étaient en désaccord flagrant avec les principes fondamentaux du christianisme? Cette présomption ne se transformera-t-elle pas en certitude si nous reconnaissons dans la doctrine universellement repoussée par l'Eglise les traits caractéristiques[64] de l'une des religions du passé? Pour dire que le gnosticisme ou l'ébionitisme sont les formes légitimes de la pensée chrétienne il faut dire hardiment qu'il n'y a pas de pensée chrétienne, ni de caractère spécifique qui la fasse reconnaître. Sous prétexte de l'élargir, on la dissout. Personne au temps de Platon n'eût osé couvrir de son nom une doctrine qui n'eut pas fait place à la théorie des idées; et l'on eût excité les justes moqueries de la Grèce, en voulant faire d'Epicure ou de Zénon un disciple de l'Académie. Reconnaissons donc que s'il existe une religion ou une doctrine qui s'appelle christianisme, elle peut avoir ses hérésies."

The author's whole argument amounts to this: that every opinion which differs from the code of dogmas we believe in at a given time, is heresy. But of course at any given time and place men always believe in something or other; and this belief in something, indefinite at any place, at some time, cannot be a criterion of truth.

It all amounts to this: since ubi Christus ibi Ecclesia, then Christus is where we are.

Every so-called heresy, regarding, as it does, its own creed as the truth, can just as easily find in Church history a series of illustrations of its own creed, can use all Pressensé's arguments on its own behalf, and can call its own creed the one truly Christian creed. And that is just what all heresies do and have always done.

The only definition of heresy (the word αἵρεσις, means a part) is this: the name given by a body of men to any opinion which rejects a part of the Creed professed by that body. The more frequent meaning, more often ascribed to the word heresy, is— that of an opinion which rejects the Church doctrine founded and supported by the temporal authorities.

There is a remarkable and voluminous work, very little known, "Unpartheyische Kirchen- und Ketzer-Historie," 1729, by Gottfried Arnold, which deals with precisely this subject, and points out all the unlawfulness, the arbitrariness, the senselessness, and the cruelty of using the word heretic in the sense of reprobate. This book is an attempt to write the history of Christianity in the form of a history of heresy.

In the introduction the author propounds a series of questions: (1) Of those who make heretics; (2) Of those whom they made heretics; (3) Of heretical subjects themselves; (4) Of the method of making heretics; and (5) Of the object and result of making heretics.

On each of these points he propounds ten more questions, the answers to which he gives later on from the works of well-known theologians. But he leaves the reader to draw for himself the principal conclusion from the expositions in the whole book. As examples of these questions, in which the answers are to some extent included also, I will quote the following. Under the 4th head, of the manner in which heretics are made, he says, in one of the questions (in the 7th):

"Does not all history show that the greatest makers of heretics and masters of that craft were just these wise men, from whom the Father hid his secrets, that is, the hypocrites, the Pharisees, and lawyers, men utterly godless and perverted (Question 20-

21)? And in the corrupt times of Christianity were not these very men cast out, denounced by the hypocrites and envious, who were endowed by God with great gifts and who would in the days of pure Christianity have been held in high honor? And, on the other hand, would not the men who, in the decline of Christianity raised themselves above all, and regarded themselves as the teachers of the purest Christianity, would not these very men, in the times of the apostles and disciples of Christ, have been regarded as the most shameless heretics and anti-Christians?"

He expounds, among other things in these questions, the theory that any verbal expression of faith, such as was demanded by the Church, and the departure from which was reckoned as heresy, could never fully cover the exact religious ideas of a believer, and that therefore the demand for an expression of faith in certain words was ever productive of heresy, and he says, in Question 21:

"And if heavenly things and thoughts present themselves to a man's mind as so great and so profound that he does not find corresponding words to express them, ought one to call him a heretic, because he cannot express his idea with perfect exactness?" And in Question 33:

"And is not the fact that there was no heresy in the earliest days due to the fact that the Christians did not judge one another by verbal expressions, but by deed and by heart, since they had perfect liberty to express their ideas without the dread of being called heretics; was it not the easiest and most ordinary ecclesiastical proceeding, if the clergy wanted to get rid of or to ruin anyone, for them to cast suspicion on the person's belief, and to throw a cloak of heresy upon him, and by this means to procure his condemnation and removal?

"True though it may be that there were sins and errors among the so-called heretics, it is no less true and evident," he says farther on, "from the innumerable examples quoted here (*i. e.*, in the history of the Church and of heresy), that there was not a single sincere and conscientious man of any importance whom the Churchmen would not from envy or other causes have ruined."

Thus, almost two hundred years ago, the real meaning of heresy was understood. And notwithstanding that, the same conception of it has gone on existing up to now. And it cannot fail to exist so long as the conception of a church exists. Heresy is the obverse side of the Church. Wherever there is a church, there must be the conception of heresy. A church is a body of men who assert that they are in possession of infallible truth. Heresy is the opinion of the men who do not admit the infallibility of the Church's truth.

Heresy makes its appearance in the Church. It is the effort to break through the petrified authority of the Church. All effort after a living comprehension of the doctrine has been made by heretics. Tertullian, Origen, Augustine, Luther, Huss, Savonarola, Helchitsky, and the rest were heretics. It could not be otherwise.

The follower of Christ, whose service means an ever-growing understanding of his teaching, and an ever-closer fulfillment of it, in progress toward perfection, cannot, just because he is a follower of Christ, claim for himself or any other that he understands Christ's teaching fully and fulfills it. Still less can he claim this for any body of men.

To whatever degree of understanding and perfection the follower of Christ may have attained, he always feels the insufficiency of his understanding and fulfillment of it, and is always striving toward a fuller understanding and fulfillment. And therefore, to assert of one's self or of any body of men, that one is or they are in possession of perfect understanding and fulfillment of Christ's word, is to renounce the very spirit of Christ's teaching.

Strange as it may seem, the churches as churches have always been, and cannot but be, institutions not only alien in spirit to Christ's teaching, but even directly antagonistic to it. With good reason Voltaire calls the Church *l'infâme*; with good reason have all or almost all so-called sects of Christians recognized the Church as the scarlet woman foretold in the Apocalypse; with good reason is the history of the Church the history of the greatest cruelties and horrors.

The churches as churches are not, as many people suppose, institutions which have Christian principles for their basis, even though they may have strayed a little away from the straight path. The churches as churches, as bodies which assert their own infallibility, are institutions opposed to Christianity. There is not only nothing in common between the churches as such and Christianity, except the name, but they represent two principles fundamentally opposed and antagonistic to one another. One represents pride, violence, self-assertion, stagnation, and death; the other, meekness, penitence, humility, progress, and life.

We cannot serve these two masters; we have to choose between them.

The servants of the churches of all denominations, especially of later times, try to show themselves champions of progress in Christianity. They make concessions, wish to correct the abuses that have slipped into the Church, and maintain that one cannot, on account of these abuses, deny the principle itself of a Christian church, which alone can bind all men together in unity and be a mediator between men and God. But this is all a mistake. Not only have the churches never bound men together in unity; they have always been one of the principal causes of division between men, of their hatred of one another, of wars, battles, inquisitions, massacres of St. Bartholomew, and so on. And the churches have never served as mediators between men and God. Such mediation is not wanted, and was directly forbidden by Christ, who has revealed his teaching directly and immediately to each man. But the churches set up dead forms in the place of God, and far from revealing God, they obscure him from men's sight. The churches, which originated from misunderstanding of Christ's teaching and have maintained this misunderstanding by their immovability, cannot but persecute and refuse to recognize all true understanding of Christ's words. They try to conceal this, but in vain; for every step forward along the path pointed out for us by Christ is a step toward their destruction.

To hear and to read the sermons and articles in which Church writers of later times of all denominations speak of Christian truths and virtues; to hear or read these skillful arguments that have been elaborated during centuries, and exhortations and professions, which sometimes seem like sincere professions, one is ready to doubt whether the churches can be antagonistic to Christianity. "It cannot be," one says, "that these people who can point to such men as Chrysostom, Fénelon, Butler, and others professing the Christian faith, were antagonistic to Christianity." One is tempted to say, "The churches may have strayed away from Christianity, they may be in error, but they cannot be hostile to it." But we must look to the fruit to judge the tree, as Christ taught us. And if we see that their fruits were evil, that the results of their activity were antagonistic to Christianity, we cannot but admit that however good the men were—the work of the Church in which these men took part was not Christian. The goodness and worth of these men who served the churches was the goodness and worth of the men, and not of the institution they served. All the good men, such as Francis of Assisi, and Francis of Sales, our Tihon Zadonsky, Thomas à Kempis, and others, were good men in spite of their serving an institution hostile to Christianity, and they would have been still better if they had not been under the influence of the error which they were serving.

But why should we speak of the past and judge from the past, which may have been misrepresented and misunderstood by us? The churches, with their principles and their practice, are not a thing of the past. The churches are before us to-day, and we can judge of them to some purpose by their practical activity, their influence on men.

What is the practical work of the churches to-day? What is their influence upon men? What is done by the churches among us, among the Catholics and the Protestants of all denominations—what is their practical work? and what are the results of their practical work?

The practice of our Russian so-called Orthodox Church is plain to all. It is an enormous fact which there is no possibility of hiding and about which there can be no disputing.

What constitutes the practical work of this Russian Church, this immense, intensely active institution, which consists of a regiment of half a million men and costs the people tens of millions of rubles?

The practical business of the Church consists in instilling by every conceivable means into the mass of one hundred millions of the Russian people those extinct relics of beliefs for which there is nowadays no kind of justification, "in which scarcely anyone now believes, and often not even those whose duty it is to diffuse these false beliefs." To instill into the people the formulas of Byzantine theology, of the Trinity, of the Mother of God, of Sacraments, of Grace, and so on, extinct conceptions, foreign to us, and having no kind of meaning for men of our times, forms only one part of the work of the Russian Church. Another part of its practice consists in the maintenance of idol-worship in the most literal meaning of the word; in the veneration of holy relics, and of ikons, the offering of sacrifices to them, and the expectation of their answers to prayer. I am not going to speak of what is preached and what is written by clergy of scientific or liberal tendencies in the theological journals. I am going to speak of what is actually done by the clergy through the wide expanse of the Russian land among a people of one hundred millions. What do they, diligently, assiduously, everywhere alike, without intermission, teach the people? What do they demand from the people in virtue of their (so-called) Christian faith?

I will begin from the beginning with the birth of a child. At the birth of a child they teach them that they must recite a prayer over the child and mother to purify them, as though without this prayer the mother of a newborn child were unclean. To do this the priest holds the child in his arms before the images of the saints (called by the people plainly gods) and reads words of exorcizing power, and this purifies the mother. Then it is suggested to the parents, and even exacted of them, under fear of punishment for non-fulfillment, that the child must be baptized; that is, be dipped by the priest three times into the water, while certain words, understood by no one, are read aloud, and certain actions, still less understood, are performed; various parts of the body are rubbed with oil, and the hair is cut, while the sponsors blow and spit at an imaginary devil. All this is necessary to purify the child and to make him a Christian. Then it is instilled into the parents that they ought to administer the sacrament to the child, that is, give him, in the guise of bread and wine, a portion of Christ's body to eat, as a result of which the child receives the grace of God within it, and so on. Then it is suggested that the child as it grows up must be taught to pray. To pray means to place himself directly before the wooden boards on which are painted the faces of Christ, the Mother of God, and the saints, to bow his head and his whole body, and to touch his forehead, his shoulders and his stomach with his right hand, holding his fingers in a certain position, and to utter some words of Slavonic, the most usual of which as taught to all children are: Mother of God, virgin, rejoice thee, etc., etc.

Then it is instilled into the child as it is brought up that at the sight of any church or ikon he must repeat the same action—*i. e.*, cross himself. Then it is instilled into him that on holidays (holidays are the days on which Christ was born, though no one knows when that was, on which he was circumcised, on which the Mother of God died, on which the cross was carried in procession, on which ikons have been set up, on which a lunatic saw a vision, and so on)—on holidays he must dress himself in his best clothes and go to church, and must buy candles and place them there before the images of the saints. Then he must give offerings and prayers for the dead, and little loaves to be cut up into three-cornered pieces, and must pray many times for the health and prosperity of the Tzar and the bishops, and for himself and his own affairs, and then kiss the cross and the hand of the priest.

Besides these observances, it is instilled into him that at least once a year he must confess. To confess means to go to the church and to tell the priest his sins, on the theory that this informing a stranger of his sins completely purifies him from them. And after that he must eat with a little spoon a morsel of bread with wine, which will purify him still more. Next it is instilled into him that if a man and woman want their physical union to be sanctified they must go to church, put on metal crowns, drink certain potions, walk three times round a table to the sound of singing, and that then the physical union of a man and woman becomes sacred and altogether different from all other such unions.

Further it is instilled into him in his life that he must observe the following rules: not to eat butter or milk on certain days, and on certain other days to sing Te Deums and requiems for the dead, on holidays to entertain the priest and give him money, and several times in the year to bring the ikons from the church, and to carry them slung on his shoulders through the fields and houses. It is instilled into him that on his death-bed a man must not fail to eat bread and wine with a spoon, and that it will be still better if he has time to be rubbed with sacred oil. This will guarantee his welfare in the future life. After his death it is instilled into his relatives that it is a good thing for the salvation of the dead man to place a printed paper of prayers in his hands; it is a good thing further to read aloud a certain book over the dead body, and to pronounce the dead man's name in church at a certain time. All this is regarded as faith obligatory on everyone.

But if anyone wants to take particular care of his soul, then according to this faith he is instructed that the greatest security of the salvation of the soul in the world is attained by offering money to the churches and monasteries, and engaging the holy men by this means to pray for him. Entering monasteries too, and kissing relics and miraculous ikons, are further means of salvation for the soul.

According to this faith ikons and relics communicate a special sanctity, power, and grace, and even proximity to these objects, touching them, kissing them, putting candles before them, crawling under them while they are being carried along, are all efficacious for salvation, as well as Te Deums repeated before these holy things.

So this, and nothing else, is the faith called Orthodox, that is the actual faith which, under the guise of Christianity, has been with all the forces of the Church, and is now with especial zeal, instilled into the people.

And let no one say that the Orthodox teachers place the essential part of their teaching in something else, and that all these are only ancient forms, which it is not thought necessary to do away with. That is false. This, and nothing but this, is the faith taught through the whole of Russia by the whole of the Russian clergy, and of late years with especial zeal. There is nothing else taught. Something different may be talked of and written of in the capitals; but among the hundred millions of the people this is what is done, this is what is taught, and nothing more. Churchmen may talk of something else, but this is what they teach by every means in their power.

All this, and the worship of relics and of ikons, has been introduced into works of theology and into the catechisms. Thus they teach it to the people in theory and in practice, using every resource of authority, solemnity, pomp, and violence to impress them. They compel the people, by overawing them, to believe in this, and jealously guard this faith from any attempt to free the people from these barbarous superstitions.

As I said when I published my book, Christ's teaching and his very words about non-resistance to evil were for many years a subject for ridicule and low jesting in my eyes, and Churchmen, far from opposing it, even encouraged this scoffing at sacred things. But try the experiment of saying a disrespectful word about a hideous idol which is carried sacrilegiously about Moscow by drunken men under the name of the ikon of the Iversky virgin, and you will raise a groan of indignation from these same Churchmen. All that they preach is an external observance of the rites of idolatry. And let it not be said that the one does not hinder the other, that "These ought ye to have done, and not to leave the other undone." "All, therefore, whatsoever they bid you observe, that observe and do; but do not ye after their works: for they say, and do not" (Matt. xxiii. 23, 3).

This was spoken of the Pharisees, who fulfilled all the external observances prescribed by the law, and therefore the words "whatsoever they bid you observe, that observe and do," refer to works of mercy and goodness, and the words "do not ye after their works, for they say and do not," refer to their observance of ceremonies and their neglect of good works, and have exactly the opposite meaning to that which the Churchmen try to give to the passage, interpreting it as an injunction to observe ceremonies. External observances and the service of truth and goodness are for the most part difficult to combine; the one excludes the other. So it was with the Pharisees, so it is now with Church Christians.

If a man can be saved by the redemption, by sacraments, and by prayer, then he does not need good works.

The Sermon on the Mount, or the Creed. One cannot believe in both. And Churchmen have chosen the latter. The Creed is taught and is read as a prayer in the churches, but the Sermon on the Mount is excluded even from the Gospel passages read in the churches, so that the congregation never hears it in church, except on those days when the whole of the Gospel is read. Indeed, it could not be otherwise. People who believe in a wicked and senseless God—who has cursed the human race and devoted his own Son to sacrifice, and a part of mankind to eternal torment—cannot believe in the God of love. The man who believes in a God, in a Christ coming again in glory to judge and to punish the quick and the dead, cannot believe in the Christ who bade us turn the left cheek, judge not, forgive those that wrong us, and love our enemies. The man who believes in the inspiration of the Old Testament and the sacred character of David, who commanded on his deathbed the murder of an old man who had cursed him, and whom he could not kill himself because he was bound by an oath to him, and the similar atrocities of which the Old Testament is full, cannot believe in the holy love of Christ. The man who believes in the Church's doctrine of the compatibility of warfare and capital punishment with Christianity cannot believe in the brotherhood of all men.

And what is most important of all—the man who believes in salvation through faith in the redemption or the sacraments, cannot devote all his powers to realizing Christ's moral teaching in his life.

The man who has been instructed by the Church in the profane doctrine that a man cannot be saved by his own powers, but that there is another means of salvation, will infallibly rely upon this means and not on his own powers, which, they assure him, it is sinful to trust in.

The teaching of every Church, with its redemption and sacraments, excludes the teaching of Christ; most of all the teaching of the Orthodox Church with its idolatrous observances.

"But the people have always believed of their own accord as they believe now," will be said in answer to this. "The whole history of the Russian people proves it. One cannot deprive the people of their traditions." This statement, too, is misleading. The people did certainly at one time believe in something like what the Church believes in now, though it was far from being the same thing. In spite of their superstitious regard for ikons, house-spirits, relics, and festivals with wreaths of birch leaves, there has still always been in the people a profound moral and living understanding of Christianity, which there has never been in the Church as a whole, and which is only met with in its best representatives. But the people, notwithstanding all the prejudices instilled into them by the government and the Church, have in their best representatives long outgrown that crude stage of understanding, a fact which is proved by the springing up everywhere of the rationalist sects with which Russia is swarming to-day, and on which Churchmen are now carrying on an ineffectual warfare. The people are advancing to a consciousness of the moral, living side of Christianity. And then the Church comes forward, not borrowing from the people, but zealously instilling into them the petrified formalities of an extinct paganism, and striving to thrust them back again into the darkness from which they are emerging with such effort.

"We teach the people nothing new, nothing but what they believe, only in a more perfect form," say the Churchmen. This is just what the man did who tied up the full-grown chicken and thrust it back into the shell it had come out of.

I have often been irritated, though it would be comic if the consequences were not so awful, by observing how men shut one another in a delusion and cannot get out of this magic circle.

The first question, the first doubt of a Russian who is beginning to think, is a question about the ikons, and still more the miraculous relics: Is it true that they are genuine, and that miracles are worked through them? Hundreds of thousands of men put this question to themselves, and their principal difficulty in answering it is the fact that bishops, metropolitans, and all men in positions of authority kiss the relics and wonder-working ikons. Ask the bishops and men in positions of authority why they do so, and they will say they do it for the sake of the people, while the people kiss them because the bishops and men in authority do so.

In spite of all the external varnish of modernity, learning, and spirituality which the members of the Church begin nowadays to assume in their works, their articles, their theological journals, and their sermons, the practical work of the Russian Church consists of nothing more than keeping the people in their present condition of coarse and savage idolatry, and worse still, strengthening and diffusing superstition and religious ignorance, and suppressing that living understanding of Christianity which exists in the people side by side with idolatry.

I remember once being present in the monks' bookshop of the Optchy Hermitage while an old peasant was choosing books for his grandson, who could read. A monk pressed on him accounts of relics, holidays, miraculous ikons, a psalter, etc. I asked the old man, "Has he the Gospel?" "No." "Give him the Gospel in Russian," I said to the monk. "That will not do for him," answered the monk. There you have an epitome of the work of our Church.

But this is only in barbarous Russia, the European and American reader will observe. And such an observation is just, but only so far as it refers to the government, which aids the Church in its task of stultification and corruption in Russia.

It is true that there is nowhere in Europe a government so despotic and so closely allied with the ruling Church. And therefore the share of the temporal power in the corruption of the people is greatest in Russia. But it is untrue that the Russian

Church in its influence on the people is in any respect different from any other church.

The churches are everywhere the same, and if the Catholic, the Anglican, or the Lutheran Church has not at hand a government as compliant as the Russian, it is not due to any indisposition to profit by such a government.

The Church as a church, whatever it may be—Catholic, Anglican, Lutheran, Presbyterian—every church, in so far as it is a church, cannot but strive for the same object as the Russian Church. That object is to conceal the real meaning of Christ's teaching and to replace it by their own, which lays no obligation on them, excludes the possibility of understanding the true teaching of Christ, and what is the chief consideration, justifies the existence of priests supported at the people's expense.

What else has Catholicism done, what else is it doing in its prohibition of reading the Gospel, and in its demand for unreasoning submission to Church authorities and to an infallible Pope? Is the religion of Catholicism any other than that of the Russian Church? There is the same external ritual, the same relics, miracles, and wonder-working images of Notre Dame, and the same processions; the same loftily vague discussions of Christianity in books and sermons, and when it comes to practice, the same supporting of the present idolatry. And is not the same thing done in Anglicanism, Lutheranism, and every denomination of Protestantism which has been formed into a church? There is the same duty laid on their congregations to believe in the dogmas expressed in the fourth century, which have lost all meaning for men of our times, and the same duty of idolatrous worship, if not of relics and ikons, then of the Sabbath Day and the letter of the Bible. There is always the same activity directed to concealing the real duties of Christianity, and to putting in their place an external respectability and cant, as it is so well described by the English, who are peculiarly oppressed by it. In Protestantism this tendency is specially remarkable because it has not the excuse of antiquity. And does not exactly the same thing show itself even in contemporary revivalism—the revived Calvinism and Evangelicalism, to which the Salvation Army owes its origin?

Uniform is the attitude of all the churches to the teaching of Christ, whose name they assume for their own advantage.

The inconsistency of all church forms of religion with the teaching of Christ is, of course, the reason why special efforts are necessary to conceal this inconsistency from people. Truly, we need only imagine ourselves in the position of any grown-up man, not necessarily educated, even the simplest man of the present day, who has picked up the ideas that are everywhere in the air nowadays of geology, physics, chemistry, cosmography, or history, when he, for the first time, consciously compares them with the articles of belief instilled into him in childhood, and maintained by the churches—that God created the world in six days, and light before the sun; that Noah shut up all the animals in his ark, and so on; that Jesus is also God the Son, who created all before time was; that this God came down upon earth to atone for Adam's sin; that he rose again, ascended into heaven, and sitteth on the right hand of the Father, and will come in the clouds to judge the world, and so on. All these propositions, elaborated by men of the fourth century, had a certain meaning for men of that time, but for men of to-day they have no meaning whatever. Men of the present day can repeat these words with their lips, but believe them they cannot. For such sentences as that God lives in heaven, that the heavens opened and a voice from somewhere said something, that Christ rose again, and ascended somewhere in heaven, and again will come from somewhere on the clouds, and so on, have no meaning for us.

A man who regarded the heavens as a solid, finite vault could believe or disbelieve that God created the heavens, that the heavens opened, that Christ ascended into heaven, but for us all these phrases have no sense whatever. Men of the present can only believe, as indeed they do, that they ought to believe in this; but believe it they cannot, because it has no meaning for them.

Even if all these phrases ought to be interpreted in a figurative sense and are allegories, we know that in the first place all Churchmen are not agreed about it, but, on the contrary, the majority stick to understanding the Holy Scripture in its literal sense; and secondly, that these allegorical interpretations are very varied and are not supported by any evidence.

But even if a man wants to force himself to believe in the doctrines of the Church just as they are taught to him, the universal diffusion of education and of the Gospel and of communication between people of different forms of religion presents a still more insurmountable obstacle to his doing so.

A man of the present day need only buy a Gospel for three copecks and read through the plain words, admitting of no misinterpretation, that Christ said to the Samaritan woman "that the Father seeketh not worshipers at Jerusalem, nor in this mountain nor in that, but worshipers in spirit and in truth," or the saying that "the Christian must not pray like the heathen, nor for show, but secretly, that is, in his closet," or that Christ's follower must call no man master or father—he need only read these words to be thoroughly convinced that the Church pastors, who call themselves teachers in opposition to Christ's precept, and dispute among themselves, constitute no kind of authority, and that what the Churchmen teach us is not Christianity. Less even than that is necessary. Even if a man nowadays did continue to believe in miracles and did not read the Gospel, mere association with people of different forms of religion and faith, which happens so easily in these days, compels him to doubt of the truth of his own faith. It was all very well when a man did not see men of any other form of religion than his own; he believed that his form of religion was the one true one. But a thinking man has only to come into contact—as constantly happens in these days—with people, equally good and bad, of different denominations, who condemn each other's beliefs, to doubt of the truth of the belief he professes himself. In these days only a man who is absolutely ignorant or absolutely indifferent to the vital questions with which religion deals, can remain in the faith of the Church.

What deceptions and what strenuous efforts the churches must employ to continue, in spite of all these tendencies subversive of the faith, to build churches, to perform masses, to preach, to teach, to convert, and, most of all, to receive for it all immense emoluments, as do all these priests, pastors, incumbents, superintendents, abbots, archdeacons, bishops, and archbishops. They need special supernatural efforts. And the churches do, with ever-increasing intensity and zeal, make such efforts. With us in Russia, besides other means, they employ simple brute force, as there the temporal power is willing to obey the Church. Men who refuse an external assent to the faith, and say so openly, are either directly punished or deprived of their rights; men who strictly keep the external forms of religion are rewarded and given privileges.

That is how the Orthodox clergy proceed; but indeed all churches without exception avail themselves of every means for the purpose—one of the most important of which is what is now called hypnotism.

Every art, from architecture to poetry, is brought into requisition to work its effect on men's souls and to reduce them to a state of stupefaction, and this effect is constantly produced. This use of hypnotizing influence on men to bring them to a state of stupefaction is especially apparent in the proceedings of the Salvation Army, who employ new practices to which we are unaccustomed: trumpets, drums, songs, flags, costumes, marching, dancing, tears, and dramatic performances.

But this only displeases us because these are new practices. Were not the old practices in churches essentially the same, with their special lighting, gold, splendor, candles, choirs, organ, bells, vestments, intoning, etc.?

But however powerful this hypnotic influence may be, it is not the chief nor the most pernicious activity of the Church. The chief and most pernicious work of the Church is that which is directed to the deception of children—these very children of whom Christ said: "Woe to him that offendeth one of these little ones." From the very first awakening of the consciousness of the child they begin to deceive him, to instill into him with the utmost solemnity what they do not themselves believe in, and they continue to instill it into him till the deception has by habit grown into the child's nature. They studiously deceive the child on the most important subject in life, and when the deception has so grown into his life that it would be difficult to uproot it, then they reveal to him the whole world of science and reality, which cannot by any means be reconciled with the beliefs that have been instilled into him, leaving it to him to find his way as best he can out of these contradictions.

If one set oneself the task of trying to confuse a man so that he could not think clearly nor free himself from the perplexity of two opposing theories of life which had been instilled into him from childhood, one could not invent any means more effectual than the treatment of every young man educated in our so-called Christian society.

It is terrible to think what the churches do to men. But if one imagines oneself in the position of the men who constitute the Church, we see they could not act differently. The churches are placed in a dilemma: the Sermon on the Mount or the Nicene Creed—the one excludes the other. If a man sincerely believes in the Sermon on the Mount, the Nicene Creed must inevitably lose all meaning and significance for him, and the Church and its representatives together with it. If a man believes in the Nicene Creed, that is, in the Church, that is, in those who call themselves its representatives, the Sermon on the Mount becomes superfluous for him. And therefore the churches cannot but make every possible effort to obscure the meaning of the Sermon on the Mount, and to attract men to themselves. It is only due to the intense zeal of the churches in this direction that the influence of the churches has lasted hitherto.

Let the Church stop its work of hypnotizing the masses, and deceiving children even for the briefest interval of time, and men would begin to understand Christ's teaching. But this understanding will be the end of the churches and all their influence. And therefore the churches will not for an instant relax their zeal in the business of hypnotizing grown-up people and deceiving children. This, then, is the work of the churches: to instill a false interpretation of Christ's teaching into men, and to prevent a true interpretation of it for the majority of so-called believers.

CHAPTER IV: CHRISTIANITY MISUNDERSTOOD BY MEN OF SCIENCE

Attitude of Men of Science to Religions in General—What Religion is, and What is its Significance for the Life of Humanity—Three Conceptions of Life—Christian Religion the Expression of the Divine Conception of Life—Misinterpretation of Christianity by Men of Science, who Study it in its External Manifestations Due to their Criticising it from Standpoint of Social Conception of Life—Opinion, Resulting from this Misinterpretation, that Christ's Moral Teaching is Exaggerated and Cannot be put into Practice—Expression of Divine Conception of Life in the Gospel—False Ideas of Men of Science on Christianity Proceed from their Conviction that they have an Infallible Method of Criticism—From which come Two Misconceptions in Regard to Christian Doctrine—First Misconception, that the Teaching Cannot be put into Practice, Due to the Christian Religion Directing Life in a Way Different from that of the Social Theory of Life—Christianity holds up Ideal, does not lay down Rules—To the Animal Force of Man Christ Adds the Consciousness of a Divine Force—Christianity Seems to Destroy Possibility of Life only when the Ideal held up is Mistaken for Rule—Ideal Must Not be Lowered—Life, According to Christ's Teaching, is Movement—The Ideal and the Precepts—Second Misconception Shown in Replacing Love and Service of God by Love and Service of Humanity—Men of Science Imagine their Doctrine of Service of Humanity and Christianity are Identical—Doctrine of Service of Humanity Based on Social Conception of Life—Love for Humanity, Logically Deduced from Love of Self, has No Meaning because Humanity is a Fiction—Christian Love Deduced from Love of God, Finds its Object in the whole World, not in Humanity Alone—Christianity Teaches Man to Live in Accordance with his Divine Nature—It Shows that the Essence of the Soul of Man is Love, and that his Happiness Ensues from Love of God, whom he Recognizes as Love within himself.

Now I will speak of the other view of Christianity which hinders the true understanding of it—the scientific view.

Churchmen substitute for Christianity the version they have framed of it for themselves, and this view of Christianity they regard as the one infallibly true one.

Men of science regard as Christianity only the tenets held by the different churches in the past and present; and finding that these tenets have lost all the significance of Christianity, they accept it as a religion which has outlived its age.

To see clearly how impossible it is to understand the Christian teaching from such a point of view, one must form for oneself an idea of the place actually held by religions in general, by the Christian religion in particular, in the life of mankind, and of the significance attributed to them by science.

Just as the individual man cannot live without having some theory of the meaning of his life, and is always, though often unconsciously, framing his conduct in accordance with the meaning he attributes to his life, so too associations of men living in similar conditions—nations—cannot but have theories of the meaning of their associated life and conduct ensuing from those theories. And as the individual man, when he attains a fresh stage of growth, inevitably changes his philosophy of life, and the grown-up man sees a different meaning in it from the child, so too associations of men—nations—are bound to change their philosophy of life and the conduct ensuing from their philosophy, to correspond with their development.

The difference, as regards this, between the individual man and humanity as a whole, lies in the fact that the individual, in forming the view of life proper to the new period of life on which he is entering and the conduct resulting from it, benefits by the experience of men who have lived before him, who have already passed through the stage of growth upon which he is entering. But humanity cannot have this aid, because it is always moving along a hitherto untrodden track, and has no one to ask how to understand life, and to act in the conditions on which it is entering and through which no one has ever passed before.

Nevertheless, just as a man with wife and children cannot continue to look at life as he looked at it when he was a child, so too in the face of the various changes that are taking place, the greater density of population, the establishment of communication between different peoples, the improvements of the methods of the struggle with nature, and the accumulation of knowledge, humanity cannot continue to look at life as of old, and it must frame a new theory of life, from which conduct may follow adapted to the new conditions on which it has entered and is entering.

To meet this need humanity has the special power of producing men who give a new meaning to the whole of human life—a theory of life from which follow new forms of activity quite different from all preceding them. The formation of this philosophy of life appropriate to humanity in the new conditions on which it is entering, and of the practice resulting from it, is what is called religion.

And therefore, in the first place, religion is not, as science imagines, a manifestation which at one time corresponded with the development of humanity, but is afterward outgrown by it. It is a manifestation always inherent in the life of humanity, and is as indispensable, as inherent in humanity at the present time as at any other. Secondly, religion is always the theory of the practice of the future and not of the past, and therefore it is clear that investigation of past manifestations cannot in any case grasp the essence of religion.

The essence of every religious teaching lies not in the desire for a symbolic expression of the forces of nature, nor in the dread of these forces, nor in the craving for the marvelous, nor in the external forms in which it is manifested, as men of science imagine; the essence of religion lies in the faculty of men of foreseeing and pointing out the path of life along which humanity must move in the discovery of a new theory of life, as a result of which the whole future conduct of humanity is changed and different from all that has been before.

This faculty of foreseeing the path along which humanity must move, is common in a greater or less degree to all men. But in all times there have been men in whom this faculty was especially strong, and these men have given clear and definite expression to what all men felt vaguely, and formed a new philosophy of life from which new lines of action followed for hundreds and thousands of years.

Of such philosophies of life we know three; two have already been passed through by humanity, and the third is that we are passing through now in Christianity. These philosophies of life are three in number, and only three, not because we have arbitrarily brought the various theories of life together under these three heads, but because all men's actions are always based on one of these three views of life—because we cannot view life otherwise than in these three ways.

These three views of life are as follows: First, embracing the individual, or the animal view of life; second, embracing the society, or the pagan view of life; third, embracing the whole world, or the divine view of life.

In the first theory of life a man's life is limited to his one individuality; the aim of life is the satisfaction of the will of this individuality. In the second theory of life a man's life is limited not to his own individuality, but to certain societies and classes of individuals: to the tribe, the family, the clan, the nation; the aim of life is limited to the satisfaction of the will of those associations of individuals. In the third theory of life a man's life is limited not to societies and classes of individuals, but extends to the principle and source of life—to God.

These three conceptions of life form the foundation of all the religions that exist or have existed.

The savage recognizes life only in himself and his personal desires. His interest in life is concentrated on himself alone. The highest happiness for him is the fullest satisfaction of his desires. The motive power of his life is personal enjoyment. His religion consists in propitiating his deity and in worshiping his gods, whom he imagines as persons living only for their personal aims.

The civilized pagan recognizes life not in himself alone, but in societies of men—in the tribe, the clan, the family, the kingdom—and sacrifices his personal good for these societies. The motive power of his life is glory. His religion consists in the exaltation of the glory of those who are allied to him—the founders of his family, his ancestors, his rulers—and in worshiping gods who are exclusively protectors of his clan, his family, his nation, his government.

The man who holds the divine theory of life recognizes life not in his own individuality, and not in societies of individualities (in the family, the clan, the nation, the tribe, or the government), but in the eternal undying source of life—in God; and to fulfill the will of God he is ready to sacrifice his individual and family and social welfare. The motor power of his life is love. And his religion is the worship in deed and in truth of the principle of the whole—God.

The whole historic existence of mankind is nothing else than the gradual transition from the personal, animal conception of life to the social conception of life, and from the social conception of life to the divine conception of life. The whole history of the ancient peoples, lasting through thousands of years and ending with the history of Rome, is the history of the transition from the animal, personal view of life to the social view of life. The whole of history from the time of the Roman Empire and the appearance of Christianity is the history of the transition, through which we are still passing now, from the social view of life to the divine view of life.

This view of life is the last, and founded upon it is the Christian teaching, which is a guide for the whole of our life and lies at the root of all our activity, practical and theoretic. Yet men of what is falsely called science, pseudo-scientific men, looking at it only in its externals, regard it as something outgrown and having no value for us.

Reducing it to its dogmatic side only—to the doctrines of the Trinity, the redemption, the miracles, the Church, the sacraments, and so on—men of science regard it as only one of an immense number of religions which have arisen among mankind, and now, they say, having played out its part in history, it is outliving its own age and fading away before the light of science and of true enlightenment.

We come here upon what, in a large proportion of cases, forms the source of the grossest errors of mankind. Men on a lower level of understanding, when brought into contact with phenomena of a higher order, instead of making efforts to understand them, to raise themselves up to the point of view from which they must look at the subject, judge it from their lower standpoint, and the less they understand what they are talking about, the more confidently and unhesitatingly they pass judgment on it.

To the majority of learned men, looking at the living, moral teaching of Christ from the lower standpoint of the state conception of life, this doctrine appears as nothing but a very indefinite and incongruous combination of Indian asceticism, Stoic and Neoplatonic philosophy, and insubstantial anti-social visions, which have no serious significance for our times. Its whole meaning is concentrated for them in its external manifestations—in Catholicism, Protestantism, in certain dogmas, or in the conflict with the temporal power. Estimating the value of Christianity by these phenomena is like a deaf man's judging of the character and quality of music by seeing the movements of the musicians.

The result of this is that all these scientific men, from Kant, Strauss, Spencer, and Renan down, do not understand the meaning of Christ's sayings, do not understand the significance, the object, or the reason of their utterance, do not understand even the question to which they form the answer. Yet, without even taking the pains to enter into their meaning, they refuse, if unfavorably disposed, to recognize any reasonableness in his doctrines; or if they want to treat them indulgently, they condescend, from the height of their superiority, to correct them, on the supposition that Christ meant to express precisely their own ideas, but did not succeed in doing so. They behave to his teaching much as self-assertive people talk to those whom they consider beneath them, often supplying their companions' words:

"Yes, you mean to say this and that." This correction is always with the aim of reducing the teaching of the higher, divine conception of life to the level of the lower, state conception of life.

They usually say that the moral teaching of Christianity is very fine, but overexaggerated; that to make it quite right we must reject all in it that is superfluous and unnecessary to our manner of life. "And the doctrine that asks too much, and requires what cannot be performed, is worse than that which requires of men what is possible and consistent with their powers," these learned interpreters of Christianity maintain, repeating what was long ago asserted, and could not but be asserted, by those who crucified the Teacher because they did not understand him—the Jews.

It seems that in the judgment of the learned men of our time the Hebrew law—a tooth for a tooth, and an eye for an eye—is a law of just retaliation, known to mankind five thousand years before the law of holiness which Christ taught in its place.

It seems that all that has been done by those men who understood Christ's teaching literally and lived in accordance with such an understanding of it, all that has been said and done by all true Christians, by all the Christian saints, all that is now reforming the world in the shape of socialism and communism—is simply exaggeration, not worth talking about.

After eighteen hundred years of education in Christianity the civilized world, as represented by its most advanced thinkers, holds the conviction that the Christian religion is a religion of dogmas; that its teaching in relation to life is unreasonable, and is an exaggeration, subversive of the real lawful obligations of morality consistent with the nature of man; and that very doctrine of retribution which Christ rejected, and in place of which he put his teaching, is more practically useful for us.

To learned men the doctrine of non-resistance to evil by force is exaggerated and even irrational. Christianity is much better without it, they think, not observing closely what Christianity, as represented by them, amounts to.

They do not see that to say that the doctrine of non-resistance to evil is an exaggeration in Christ's teaching is just like saying that the statement of the equality of the radii of a circle is an exaggeration in the definition of a circle. And those who speak thus are acting precisely like a man who, having no idea of what a circle is, should declare that this requirement, that every point of the circumference should be an equal distance from the center, is exaggerated. To advocate the rejection of Christ's command of non-resistance to evil, or its adaptation to the needs of life, implies a misunderstanding of the teaching of Christ.

And those who do so certainly do not understand it. They do not understand that this teaching is the institution of a new theory of life, corresponding to the new conditions on which men have entered now for eighteen hundred years, and also the definition of the new conduct of life which results from it. They do not believe that Christ meant to say what he said; or he seems to them to have said what he said in the Sermon on the Mount and in other places accidentally, or through his lack of intelligence or of cultivation.

Matt. vi. 25-34: "Therefore I say unto you, Take no thought for your life, what ye shall eat, or what ye shall drink; nor yet for your body, what ye shall put on. Is not the life more than meat, and the body than raiment? Behold the fowls of the air; for they sow not, neither do they reap, nor gather into barns; yet your heavenly Father feedeth them. Are ye not much better than they? Which of you by taking thought can add one cubit unto his stature? And why take ye thought for raiment? Consider the lilies of the field how they grow; they toil not, neither do they spin; and yet I say unto you, That even Solomon in all his glory was not arrayed like one of these. Wherefore, if God so clothe the grass of the field, which to-day is, and to-morrow is cast into the oven, shall he not much more clothe you, O ye of little faith? Therefore take no thought, saying, What shall we eat? or, What shall we drink? or, Where-withal shall we be clothed? (For after all these things do the Gentiles seek), for your heavenly Father knoweth that ye have need of all these things. But seek ye first the kingdom of God, and his righteousness, and all these things shall be added unto you. Take therefore no thought for the morrow; for the morrow shall take thought for the things of itself. Sufficient unto the day is the evil thereof." Luke xii. 33-34: "Sell that ye have, and give alms; provide yourselves bags which wax not old, a treasure in the heavens that faileth not, where no thief approacheth, neither moth corrupteth. For where your treasure is, there will your heart be also." Sell all thou hast and follow me; and he who will not leave father, or mother, or children, or brothers, or fields, or house, he cannot be my disciple. Deny thyself, take up thy cross each day and follow me. My meat is to do the will of him that sent me, and to perform his works. Not my will, but thine be done; not what I will, but as thou wilt. Life is to do not one's will, but the will of God.

All these principles appear to men who regard them from the standpoint of a lower conception of life as the expression of an impulsive enthusiasm, having no direct application to life. These principles, however, follow from the Christian theory of life, just as logically as the principles of paying a part of one's private gains to the commonwealth and of sacrificing one's life in defense of one's country follow from the state theory of life.

As the man of the state conception of life said to the savage: Reflect, bethink yourself! The life of your individuality cannot be true life, because that life is pitiful and passing. But the life of a society and succession of individuals, family, clan, tribe, or state, goes on living, and therefore a man must sacrifice his own individuality for the life of the family or the state. In exactly the same way the Christian doctrine says to the man of the social, state conception of life, Repent ye—μετανοσετε—*i. e.*, bethink yourself, or you will be ruined. Understand that this casual, personal life which now comes into being and to-morrow is no more can have no permanence, that no external means, no construction of it can give it consecutiveness and permanence. Take thought and understand that the life you are living is not real life—the life of the family, of society, of the state will not save you from annihilation. The true, the rational life is only possible for man according to the measure in which he can participate, not in the family or the state, but in the source of life—the Father; according to the measure in which he can merge his life in the life of the Father. Such is undoubtedly the Christian conception of life, visible in every utterance of the Gospel.

One may not share this view of life, one may reject it, one may show its inaccuracy and its erroneousness, but we cannot judge of the Christian teaching without mastering this view of life. Still less can one criticise a subject on a higher plane from a lower point of view. From the basement one cannot judge of the effect of the spire. But this is just what the learned critics of the day try to do. For they share the erroneous idea of the orthodox believers that they are in possession of certain infallible means for investigating a subject. They fancy if they apply their so-called scientific methods of criticism, there can be no doubt of their conclusion being correct.

This testing the subject by the fancied infallible method of science is the principal obstacle to understanding the Christian religion for unbelievers, for so-called educated people. From this follow all the mistakes made by scientific men about the Christian religion, and especially two strange misconceptions which, more than everything else, hinder them from a correct understanding of it. One of these misconceptions is that the Christian moral teaching cannot be carried out, and that therefore it has either no force at all—that is, it should not be accepted as the rule of conduct—or it must be transformed, adapted to the limits within which its fulfillment is possible in our society. Another misconception is that the Christian doctrine of love of God, and therefore of his service, is an obscure, mystic principle, which gives no definite object for love, and should therefore be replaced by the more exact and comprehensible principles of love for men and the service of humanity.

The first misconception in regard to the impossibility of following the principle is the result of men of the state conception of life unconsciously taking that conception as the standard by which the Christian religion directs men, and taking the Christian principle of perfection as the rule by which that life is to be ordered; they think and say that to follow Christ's teaching is impossible, because the complete fulfilment of all that is required by this teaching would put an end to life. "If a man were to carry out all that Christ teaches, he would destroy his own life; and if all men carried it out, then the human race would come to an end," they say.

"If we take no thought for the morrow, what we shall eat and what we shall drink, and wherewithal we shall be clothed, do not defend our life, nor resist evil by force, lay down our life for others, and observe perfect chastity, the human race cannot exist," they say.

And they are perfectly right if they take the principle of perfection given by Christ's teaching as a rule which everyone is bound to fulfill, just as in the state principles of life everyone is bound to carry out the rule of paying taxes, supporting the law, and so on.

The misconception is based precisely on the fact that the teaching of Christ guides men differently from the way in which the precepts founded on the lower conception of life guide men. The precepts of the state conception of life only guide men by requiring of them an exact fulfillment of rules or laws. Christ's teaching guides men by pointing them to the infinite perfection of their heavenly Father, to which every man independently and voluntarily struggles, whatever the degree of his imperfection in the present.

The misunderstanding of men who judge of the Christian principle from the point of view of the state principle, consists in the fact that on the supposition that the perfection which Christ points to, can be fully attained, they ask themselves (just as they ask the same question on the supposition that state laws will be carried out) what will be the result of all this being carried out? This supposition cannot be made, because the perfection held up to Christians is infinite and can never be attained; and Christ lays down his principle, having in view the fact that absolute perfection can never be attained, but that striving toward absolute, infinite perfection will continually increase the blessedness of men, and that this blessedness may be increased to infinity thereby.

Christ is teaching not angels, but men, living and moving in the animal life. And so to this animal force of movement Christ, as it were, applies the new force—the recognition of Divine perfection—and thereby directs the movement by the resultant of these two forces.

To suppose that human life is going in the direction to which Christ pointed it, is just like supposing that a little boat afloat on a rapid river, and directing its course almost exactly against the current, will progress in that direction.

Christ recognizes the existence of both sides of the parallelogram, of both eternal indestructible forces of which the life of man is compounded: the force of his animal nature and the force of the consciousness of kinship to God. Saying nothing of the animal force which asserts itself, remains always the same, and is therefore independent of human will, Christ speaks only of the Divine force, calling upon a man to know it more closely, to set it more free from all that retards it, and to carry it to a higher degree of intensity.

In the process of liberating, of strengthening this force, the true life of man, according to Christ's teaching, consists. The true life, according to preceding religions, consists in carrying out rules, the law; according to Christ's teaching it consists in an ever closer approximation to the divine perfection held up before every man, and recognized within himself by every man, in an ever closer and closer approach to the perfect fusion of his will in the will of God, that fusion toward which man strives, and the attainment of which would be the destruction of the life we know.

The divine perfection is the asymptote of human life to which it is always striving, and always approaching, though it can only be reached in infinity.

The Christian religion seems to exclude the possibility of life only when men mistake the pointing to an ideal as the laying down of a rule. It is only then that the principles presented in Christ's teaching appear to be destructive of life. These principles, on the contrary, are the only ones that make true life possible. Without these principles true life could not be possible.

"One ought not to expect so much," is what people usually say in discussing the requirements of the Christian religion. "One cannot expect to take absolutely no thought for the morrow, as is said in the Gospel, but only not to take too much thought for it; one cannot give away all to the poor, but one must give away a certain definite part; one need not aim at virginity, but one must avoid debauchery; one need not forsake wife and children, but one must not give too great a place to them in one's heart," and so on.

But to speak like this is just like telling a man who is struggling on a swift river and is directing his course against the current, that it is impossible to cross the river rowing against the current, and that to cross it he must float in the direction of the point he wants to reach.

In reality, in order to reach the place to which he wants to go, he must row with all his strength toward a point much higher up.

To let go the requirements of the ideal means not only to diminish the possibility of perfection, but to make an end of the ideal itself. The ideal that has power over men is not an ideal invented by someone, but the ideal that every man carries within his soul. Only this ideal of complete infinite perfection has power over men, and stimulates them to action. A moderate perfection loses its power of influencing men's hearts.

Christ's teaching only has power when it demands absolute perfection—that is, the fusion of the divine nature which exists in every man's soul with the will of God—the union of the Son with the Father. Life according to Christ's teaching consists of nothing but this setting free of the Son of God, existing in every man, from the animal, and in bringing him closer to the Father.

The animal existence of a man does not constitute human life alone. Life, according to the will of God only, is also not human life. Human life is a combination of the animal life and the divine life. And the more this combination approaches to the divine life, the more life there is in it.

Life, according to the Christian religion, is a progress toward the divine perfection. No one condition, according to this doctrine, can be higher or lower than another. Every condition, according to this doctrine, is only a particular stage, of no consequence in itself, on the way toward unattainable perfection, and therefore in itself it does not imply a greater or lesser degree of life. Increase of life, according to this, consists in nothing but the quickening of the progress toward perfection. And therefore the progress toward perfection of the publican Zaccheus, of the woman that was a sinner, and of the robber on the cross, implies a higher degree of life than the stagnant righteousness of the Pharisee. And therefore for this religion there cannot be rules which it is obligatory to obey. The man who is at a lower level but is moving onward toward perfection is living a more moral, a better life, is more fully carrying out Christ's teaching, than the man on a much higher level of morality who is not moving onward toward perfection.

It is in this sense that the lost sheep is dearer to the Father than those that were not lost. The prodigal son, the piece of money lost and found again, were more precious than those that were not lost.

The fulfillment of Christ's teaching consists in moving away from self toward God. It is obvious that there cannot be definite laws and rules for this fulfillment of the teaching. Every degree of perfection and every degree of imperfection are equal in it; no obedience to laws constitutes a fulfillment of this doctrine, and therefore for it there can be no binding rules and laws.

From this fundamental distinction between the religion of Christ and all preceding religions based on the state conception of life, follows a corresponding difference in the special precepts of the state theory and the Christian precepts. The precepts of the state theory of life insist for the most part on certain practical prescribed acts, by which men are justified and secure of being right. The Christian precepts (the commandment of love is not a precept in the strict sense of the word, but the expression of the very essence of the religion) are the five commandments of the Sermon on the Mount—all negative in character. They show only what at a certain stage of development of humanity men may not do.

These commandments are, as it were, signposts on the endless road to perfection, toward which humanity is moving, showing the point of perfection which is possible at a certain period in the development of humanity.

Christ has given expression in the Sermon on the Mount to the eternal ideal toward which men are spontaneously struggling, and also the degree of attainment of it to which men may reach in our times.

The ideal is not to desire to do ill to anyone, not to provoke ill will, to love all men. The precept, showing the level below which we cannot fall in the attainment of this ideal, is the prohibition of evil speaking. And that is the first command.

The ideal is perfect chastity, even in thought. The precept, showing the level below which we cannot fall in the attainment of this ideal, is that of purity of married life, avoidance of debauchery. That is the second command.

The ideal is to take no thought for the future, to live in the present moment. The precept, showing the level below which we cannot fall, is the prohibition of swearing, of promising anything in the future. And that is the third command.

The ideal is never for any purpose to use force. The precept, showing the level below which we cannot fall is that of returning good for evil, being patient under wrong, giving the cloak also. That is the fourth command.

The ideal is to love the enemies who hate us. The precept, showing the level below which we cannot fall, is not to do evil to our enemies, to speak well of them, and to make no difference between them and our neighbors.

All these precepts are indications of what, on our journey to perfection, we are already fully able to avoid, and what we must labor to attain now, and what we ought by degrees to translate into instinctive and unconscious habits. But these precepts, far from constituting the whole of Christ's teaching and exhausting it, are simply stages on the way to perfection. These precepts must and will be followed by higher and higher precepts on the way to the perfection held up by the religion.

And therefore it is essentially a part of the Christian religion to make demands higher than those expressed in its precepts; and by no means to diminish the demands either of the ideal itself, or of the precepts, as people imagine who judge it from the standpoint of the social conception of life.

So much for one misunderstanding of the scientific men, in relation to the import and aim of Christ's teaching. Another misunderstanding arising from the same source consists in substituting love for men, the service of humanity, for the Christian principles of love for God and his service.

The Christian doctrine to love God and serve him, and only as a result of that love to love and serve one's neighbor, seems to scientific men obscure, mystic, and arbitrary. And they would absolutely exclude the obligation of love and service of God, holding that the doctrine of love for men, for humanity alone, is far more clear, tangible, and reasonable.

Scientific men teach in theory that the only good and rational life is that which is devoted to the service of the whole of humanity. That is for them the import of the Christian doctrine, and to that they reduce Christ's teaching. They seek confirmation of their own doctrine in the Gospel, on the supposition that the two doctrines are really the same.

This idea is an absolutely mistaken one. The Christian doctrine has nothing in common with the doctrine of the Positivists, Communists, and all the apostles of the universal brotherhood of mankind, based on the general advantage of such a brotherhood. They differ from one another especially in Christianity's having a firm and clear basis in the human soul, while love for humanity is only a theoretical deduction from analogy.

The doctrine of love for humanity alone is based on the social conception of life.

The essence of the social conception of life consists in the transference of the aim of the individual life to the life of societies of individuals: family, clan, tribe, or state. This transference is accomplished easily and naturally in its earliest forms, in the transference of the aim of life from the individual to the family and the clan. The transference to the tribe or the nation is more difficult and requires special training. And the transference of the sentiment to the state is the furthest limit which the process can reach.

To love one's self is natural to everyone, and no one needs any encouragement to do so. To love one's clan who support and protect one, to love one's wife, the joy and help of one's existence, one's children, the hope and consolation of one's life, and one's parents, who have given one life and education, is natural. And such love, though far from being so strong as love of self, is met with pretty often.

To love—for one's own sake, through personal pride—one's tribe, one's nation, though not so natural, is nevertheless common. Love of one's own people who are of the same blood, the same tongue, and the same religion as one's self is possible, though far from being so strong as love of self, or even love of family or clan. But love for a state, such as Turkey, Germany, England, Austria, or Russia is a thing almost impossible. And though it is zealously inculcated, it is only an imagined sentiment; it has no existence in reality. And at that limit man's power of transferring his interest ceases, and he cannot feel any direct sentiment for that fictitious entity. The Positivists, however, and all the apostles of fraternity on scientific principles, without taking into consideration the weakening of sentiment in proportion to the extension of its object, draw further deductions in theory in the same direction. "Since," they say, "it was for the advantage of the individual to extend his personal interest to the family, the tribe, and subsequently to the nation and the state, it would be still more advantageous to extend his interest in societies of men to the whole of mankind, and so all to live for humanity just as men live for the family or the state."

Theoretically it follows, indeed, having extended the love and interest for the personality to the family, the tribe, and thence to the nation and the state, it would be perfectly logical for men to save themselves the strife and calamities which result from the division of mankind into nations and states by extending their love to the whole of humanity. This would be most logical, and theoretically nothing would appear more natural to its advocates, who do not observe that love is a sentiment which may or may not be felt, but which it is useless to advocate; and moreover, that love must have an object, and that humanity is not an object. It is nothing but a fiction.

The family, the tribe, even the state were not invented by men, but formed themselves spontaneously, like ant-hills or swarms of bees, and have a real existence. The man who, for the sake of his own animal personality, loves his family, knows whom he loves: Anna, Dolly, John, Peter, and so on. The man who loves his tribe and takes pride in it, knows that he loves all the Guelphs or all the Ghibellines; the man who loves the state knows that he loves France bounded by the Rhine, and the Pyrenees, and its principal city Paris, and its history and so on. But the man who loves humanity—what does he love? There is such a thing as a state, as a nation; there is the abstract conception of man; but humanity as a concrete idea does not, and cannot exist.

Humanity! Where is the definition of humanity? Where does it end and where does it begin? Does humanity end with the savage, the idiot, the dipsomaniac, or the madman? If we draw a line excluding from humanity its lowest representatives, where are we to draw the line? Shall we exclude the negroes like the Americans, or the Hindoos like some Englishmen, or the Jews like some others? If we include all men without exception, why should we not include also the higher animals, many of whom are superior to the lowest specimens of the human race.

We know nothing of humanity as an eternal object, and we know nothing of its limits. Humanity is a fiction, and it is impossible to love it. It would, doubtless, be very advantageous if men could love humanity just as they love their family. It would be very advantageous, as Communists advocate, to replace the competitive, individualistic organization of men's activity by a social universal organisation, so that each would be for all and all for each. Only there are no motives to lead men to do this. The Positivists, the Communists, and all the apostles of fraternity on scientific principles advocate the extension to the whole of humanity of the love men feel for themselves, their families, and the state. They forget that the love which they are discussing is a personal love, which might expand in a rarefied form to embrace a man's native country, but which disappears before it can embrace an artificial state such as Austria, England, or Turkey, and which we cannot even conceive of in relation to all humanity, an absolutely mystic conception.

"A man loves himself (his animal personality), he loves his family, he even loves his native country. Why should he not love humanity? That would be such an excellent thing. And by the way, it is precisely what is taught by Christianity." So think the advocates of Positivist, Communistic, or Socialistic fraternity.

It would indeed be an excellent thing. But it can never be, for the love that is based on a personal or social conception of life can never rise beyond love for the state.

The fallacy of the argument lies in the fact that the social conception of life, on which love for family and nation is founded, rests itself on love of self, and that love grows weaker and weaker as it is extended from self to family, tribe, nationality, and state; and in the state we reach the furthest limit beyond which it cannot go.

The necessity of extending the sphere of love is beyond dispute. But in reality the possibility of this love is destroyed by the necessity of extending its object indefinitely. And thus the insufficiency of personal human love is made manifest.

And here the advocates of Positivist, Communistic, Socialistic fraternity propose to draw upon Christian love to make up the default of this bankrupt human love; but Christian love only in its results, not in its foundations, They propose love for humanity alone, apart from love for God.

But such a love cannot exist. There is no motive to produce it. Christian love is the result only of the Christian conception of life, in which the aim of life is to love and serve God.

The social conception of life has led men, by a natural transition from love of self and then of family, tribe, nation, and state, to a consciousness of the necessity of love for humanity, a conception which has no definite limits and extends to all living things. And this necessity for love of what awakens no kind of sentiment in a man is a contradiction which cannot be solved by the social theory of life.

The Christian doctrine in its full significance can alone solve it, by giving a new meaning to life. Christianity recognizes love of self, of family, of nation, and of humanity, and not only of humanity, but of everything living, everything existing; it recognizes the necessity of an infinite extension of the sphere of love. But the object of this love is not found outside self in societies of individuals, nor in the external world, but within self, in the divine self whose essence is that very love, which the animal self is brought to feel the need of through its consciousness of its own perishable nature.

The difference between the Christian doctrine and those which preceded it is that the social doctrine said: "Live in opposition to your nature [understanding by this only the animal nature], make it subject to the external law of family, society, and state." Christianity says: "Live according to your nature [understanding by this the divine nature]; do not make it subject to anything— neither you (an animal self) nor that of others—and you will attain the very aim to which you are striving when you subject your external self."

The Christian doctrine brings a man to the elementary consciousness of self, only not of the animal self, but of the divine self, the divine spark, the self as the Son of God, as much God as the Father himself, though confined in an animal husk. The consciousness of being the Son of God, whose chief characteristic is love, satisfies the need for the extension of the sphere of love to which the man of the social conception of life had been brought. For the latter, the welfare of the personality demanded an ever-widening extension of the sphere of love; love was a necessity and was confined to certain objects—self, family, society. With the Christian conception of life, love is not a necessity and is confined to no object; it is the essential faculty of the human soul. Man loves not because it is his interest to love this or that, but because love is the essence of his soul, because he cannot but love.

The Christian doctrine shows man that the essence of his soul is love—that his happiness depends not on loving this or that object, but on loving the principle of the whole—God, whom he recognizes within himself as love, and therefore he loves all things and all men.

In this is the fundamental difference between the Christian doctrine and the doctrine of the Positivists, and all the theorizers about universal brotherhood on non-christian principles.

Such are the two principal misunderstandings relating to the Christian religion, from which the greater number of false reasonings about it proceed. The first consists in the belief that Christ's teaching instructs men, like all previous religions, by rules, which they are bound to follow, and that these rules cannot be fulfilled. The second is the idea that the whole purport of Christianity is to teach men to live advantageously together, as one family, and that to attain this we need only follow the rule of love to humanity, dismissing all thought of love of God altogether.

The mistaken notion of scientific men that the essence of Christianity consists in the supernatural, and that its moral teaching is impracticable, constitutes another reason of the failure of men of the present day to understand Christianity.

CHAPTER V: CONTRADICTION BETWEEN OUR LIFE AND OUR CHRISTIAN CONSCIENCE

Men Think they can Accept Christianity without Altering their Life—Pagan Conception of Life does not Correspond with Present Stage of Development of Humanity, and Christian Conception Alone Can Accord with it—Christian Conception of Life not yet Understood by Men, but the Progress of Life itself will Lead them Inevitably to Adopt it—The Requirements of a New Theory of Life Always Seem Incomprehensible, Mystic, and Supernatural—So Seem the Requirements of the Christian Theory of Life to the Majority of Men—The Absorption of the Christian Conception of Life will Inevitably be Brought About as the Result of Material and Spiritual Causes—The Fact of Men Knowing the Requirements of the Higher View of Life, and yet Continuing to Preserve Inferior Organizations of Life, Leads to Contradictions and Sufferings which Embitter Existence and Must Result in its Transformation—The Contradictions of our Life—The Economic Contradiction and the Suffering Induced by it for Rich and Poor Alike—The Political Contradiction and the Sufferings Induced by Obedience to the Laws of the State—The International Contradiction and the Recognition of it by Contemporaries: Komarovsky, Ferri, Booth, Passy, Lawson, Wilson, Bartlett, Defourney, Moneta—The Striking Character of the Military Contradiction.

There are many reasons why Christ's teaching is not understood. One reason is that people suppose they have understood it when they have decided, as the Churchmen do, that it was revealed by supernatural means, or when they have studied, as the scientific men do, the external forms in which it has been manifested. Another reason is the mistaken notion that it is impracticable, and ought to be replaced by the doctrine of love for humanity. But the principal reason, which is the source of all the other mistaken ideas about it, is the notion that Christianity is a doctrine which can be accepted or rejected without any change of life.

Men who are used to the existing order of things, who like it and dread its being changed, try to take the doctrine as a collection of revelations and rules which one can accept without their modifying one's life. While Christ's teaching is not only a doctrine which gives rules which a man must follow, it unfolds a new meaning in life, and defines a whole world of human activity quite different from all that has preceded it and appropriate to the period on which man is entering.

The life of humanity changes and advances, like the life of the individual, by stages, and every stage has a theory of life appropriate to it, which is inevitably absorbed by men. Those who do not absorb it consciously, absorb it unconsciously. It is the same with the changes in the beliefs of peoples and of all humanity as it is with the changes of belief of individuals. If the father of a family continues to be guided in his conduct by his childish conceptions of life, life becomes so difficult for him that he involuntarily seeks another philosophy and readily absorbs that which is appropriate to his age.

That is just what is happening now to humanity at this time of transition through which we are passing, from the pagan conception of life to the Christian. The socialized man of the present day is brought by experience of life itself to the necessity of abandoning the pagan conception of life, which is inappropriate to the present stage of humanity, and of submitting to the obligation of the Christian doctrines, the truths of which, however corrupt and misinterpreted, are still known to him, and alone offer him a solution of the contradictions surrounding him.

If the requirements of the Christian doctrine seem strange and even alarming to the man of the social theory of life, no less strange, incomprehensible, and alarming to the savage of ancient times seemed the requirements of the social doctrine when it was not fully understood and could not be foreseen in its results.

"It is unreasonable," said the savage, "to sacrifice my peace of mind or my life in defense of something incomprehensible, impalpable, and conventional—family, tribe, or nation; and above all it is unsafe to put oneself at the disposal of the power of others."

But the time came when the savage, on one hand, felt, though vaguely, the value of the social conception of life, and of its chief motor power, social censure, or social approbation—glory, and when, on the other hand, the difficulties of his personal life became so great that he could not continue to believe in the value of his old theory of life. Then he accepted the social, state theory of life and submitted to it.

That is just what the man of the social theory of life is passing through now.

"It is unreasonable," says the socialized man, "to sacrifice my welfare and that of my family and my country in order to fulfill some higher law, which requires me to renounce my most natural and virtuous feelings of love of self, of family, of kindred, and of country; and above all, it is unsafe to part with the security of life afforded by the organization of government."

But the time is coming when, on one hand, the vague consciousness in his soul of the higher law, of love to God and his neighbor, and, on the other hand, the suffering, resulting from the contradictions of life, will force the man to reject the social theory and to assimilate the new one prepared ready for him, which solves all the contradictions and removes all his sufferings—the Christian theory of life. And this time has now come.

We, who thousands of years ago passed through the transition, from the personal, animal view of life to the socialized view, imagine that that transition was an inevitable and natural one; but this transition through which we have been passing for the last eighteen hundred years seems arbitrary, unnatural, and alarming. But we only fancy this because that first transition has been so fully completed that the practice attained by it has become unconscious and instinctive in us, while the present transition is not yet over and we have to complete it consciously.

It took ages, thousands of years, for the social conception of life to permeate men's consciousness. It went through various forms and has now passed into the region of the instinctive through inheritance, education, and habit. And therefore it seems natural to us. But five thousand years ago it seemed as unnatural and alarming to men as the Christian doctrine in its true sense seems to-day.

We think to-day that the requirements of the Christian doctrine—of universal brotherhood, suppression of national distinctions, abolition of private property, and the strange injunction of non-resistance to evil by force—demand what is impossible. But it was just the same thousands of years ago, with every social or even family duty, such as the duty of parents to support their children, of the young to maintain the old, of fidelity in marriage. Still more strange, and even unreasonable, seemed the state duties of submitting to the appointed authority, and paying taxes, and fighting in defense of the country, and so on. All such requirements seem simple, comprehensible, and natural to us to-day, and we see nothing mysterious or alarming in them. But three or five thousand years ago they seemed to require what was impossible.

The social conception of life served as the basis of religion because at the time when it was first presented to men it seemed to them absolutely incomprehensible, mystic, and supernatural. Now that we have outlived that phase of the life of humanity, we understand the rational grounds for uniting men in families, communities, and states. But in antiquity the duties involved by such association were presented under cover of the supernatural and were confirmed by it.

The patriarchal religions exalted the family, the tribe, the nation. State religions deified emperors and states. Even now most ignorant people—like our peasants, who call the Tzar an earthly god—obey state laws, not through any rational recognition of their necessity, nor because they have any conception of the meaning of state, but through a religious sentiment.

In precisely the same way the Christian doctrine is presented to men of the social or heathen theory of life to-day, in the guise of a supernatural religion, though there is in reality nothing mysterious, mystic, or supernatural about it. It is simply the theory of life which is appropriate to the present degree of material development, the present stage of growth of humanity, and which must therefore inevitably be accepted.

The time will come—it is already coming—when the Christian principles of equality and fraternity, community of property, non-resistance of evil by force, will appear just as natural and simple as the principles of family or social life seem to us now.

Humanity can no more go backward in its development than the individual man. Men have outlived the social, family, and state conceptions of life. Now they must go forward and assimilate the next and higher conception of life, which is what is now taking place. This change is brought about in two ways: consciously through spiritual causes, and unconsciously through material causes.

Just as the individual man very rarely changes his way of life at the dictates of his reason alone, but generally continues to live as before, in spite of the new interests and aims revealed to him by his reason, and only alters his way of living when it has become absolutely opposed to his conscience, and consequently intolerable to him; so, too, humanity, long after it has learnt through its religions the new interests and aims of life, toward which it must strive, continues in the majority of its representatives to live as before, and is only brought to accept the new conception by finding it impossible to go on living its old life as before.

Though the need of a change of life is preached by the religious leaders and recognized and realized by the most intelligent men, the majority, in spite of their reverential attitude to their leaders, that is, their faith in their teaching, continue to be guided by the old theory of life in their present complex existence. As though the father of a family, knowing how he ought to behave at his age, should yet continue through habit and thoughtlessness to live in the same childish way as he did in boyhood.

That is just what is happening in the transition of humanity from one stage to another, through which we are passing now. Humanity has outgrown its social stage and has entered upon a new period. It recognizes the doctrine which ought to be made the basis of life in this new period. But through inertia it continues to keep up the old forms of life. From this inconsistency between the new conception of life and practical life follows a whole succession of contradictions and sufferings which embitter our life and necessitate its alteration.

One need only compare the practice of life with the theory of it, to be dismayed at the glaring antagonism between our conditions of life and our conscience.

Our whole life is in flat contradiction with all we know, and with all we regard as necessary and right. This contradiction runs through everything, in economic life, in political life, and in international life. As though we had forgotten what we knew and put away for a time the principles we believe in (we cannot help still believing in them because they are the only foundation we have to base our life on) we do the very opposite of all that our conscience and our common sense require of us.

We are guided in economical, political, and international questions by the principles which were appropriate to men of three or five thousand years ago, though they are directly opposed to our conscience and the conditions of life in which we are placed to-day.

It was very well for the man of ancient times to live in a society based on the division of mankind into masters and slaves, because he believed that such a distinction was decreed by God and must always exist. But is such a belief possible in these days?

The man of antiquity could believe he had the right to enjoy the good things of this world at the expense of other men, and to keep them in misery for generations, since he believed that men came from different origins, were base or noble in blood, children of Ham or of Japhet. The greatest sages of the world, the teachers of humanity, Plato and Aristotle, justified the existence of slaves and demonstrated the lawfulness of slavery; and even three centuries ago, the men who described an imaginary society of the future, Utopia, could not conceive of it without slaves.

Men of ancient and mediæval times believed, firmly believed, that men are not equal, that the only true men are Persians, or Greeks, or Romans, or Franks. But we cannot believe that now. And people who sacrifice themselves for the principles of aristocracy and of patriotism to-day, don't believe and can't believe what they assert.

We all know and cannot help knowing—even though we may never have heard the idea clearly expressed, may never have read of it, and may never have put it into words, still through unconsciously imbibing the Christian sentiments that are in the air—with our whole heart we know and cannot escape knowing the fundamental truth of the Christian doctrine, that we are all sons of one Father, wherever we may live and whatever language we may speak; we are all brothers and are subject to the same law of love implanted by our common Father in our hearts.

Whatever the opinions and degree of education of a man of to-day, whatever his shade of liberalism, whatever his school of philosophy, or of science, or of economics, however ignorant or superstitious he may be, every man of the present day knows that all men have an equal right to life and the good things of life, and that one set of people are no better nor worse than another, that all are equal. Everyone knows this, beyond doubt; everyone feels it in his whole being. Yet at the same time everyone sees all round him the division of men into two castes—the one, laboring, oppressed, poor, and suffering, the other idle, oppressing, luxurious, and profligate. And everyone not only sees this, but voluntarily or involuntarily, in one way or another, he takes part in maintaining this distinction which his conscience condemns. And he cannot help suffering from the consciousness of this contradiction and his share in it.

Whether he be master or slave, the man of to-day cannot help constantly feeling the painful opposition between his conscience and actual life, and the miseries resulting from it.

The toiling masses, the immense majority of mankind who are suffering under the incessant, meaningless, and hopeless toil and privation in which their whole life is swallowed up, still find their keenest suffering in the glaring contrast between what is and what ought to be, according to all the beliefs held by themselves, and those who have brought them to that condition and keep them in it.

They know that they are in slavery and condemned to privation and darkness to minister to the lusts of the minority who keep them down. They know it, and they say so plainly. And this knowledge increases their sufferings and constitutes its bitterest sting.

The slave of antiquity knew that he was a slave by nature, but our laborer, while he feels he is a slave, knows that he ought not to be, and so he tastes the agony of Tantalus, forever desiring and never gaining what might and ought to be his.

The sufferings of the working classes, springing from the contradiction between what is and what ought to be, are increased tenfold by the envy and hatred engendered by their consciousness of it.

The laborer of the present day would not cease to suffer even if his toil were much lighter than that of the slave of ancient times, even if he gained an eight-hour working day and a wage of three dollars a day. For he is working at the manufacture of things which he will not enjoy, working not by his own will for his own benefit, but through necessity, to satisfy the desires of luxurious and idle people in general, and for the profit of a single rich man, the owner of a factory or workshop in particular. And he knows that all this is going on in a world in which it is a recognized scientific principle that labor alone creates wealth, and that to profit by the labor of others is immoral, dishonest, and punishable by law; in a world, moreover, which professes to believe Christ's doctrine that we are all brothers, and that true merit and dignity is to be found in serving one's neighbor, not in exploiting him. All this he knows, and he cannot but suffer keenly from the sharp contrast between what is and what ought to be.

"According to all principles, according to all I know, and what everyone professes," the workman says to himself. "I ought to be free, equal to everyone else, and loved; and I am—a slave, humiliated and hated." And he too is filled with hatred and tries to find means to escape from his position, to shake off the enemy who is over-riding him, and to oppress him in turn. People say, "Workmen have no business to try to become capitalists, the poor to try to put themselves in the place of the rich." That is a mistake. The workingmen and the poor would be wrong if they tried to do so in a world in which slaves and masters were regarded as different species created by God; but they are living in a world which professes the faith of the Gospel, that all are alike sons of God, and so brothers and equal. And however men may try to conceal it, one of the first conditions of Christian life is love, not in words but in deeds.

The man of the so-called educated classes lives in still more glaring inconsistency and suffering. Every educated man, if he believes in anything, believes in the brotherhood of all men, or at least he has a sentiment of humanity, or else of justice, or else he believes in science. And all the while he knows that his whole life is framed on principles in direct opposition to it all, to all the principles of Christianity, humanity, justice, and science.

He knows that all the habits in which he has been brought up, and which he could not give up without suffering, can only be satisfied through the exhausting, often fatal, toil of oppressed laborers, that is, through the most obvious and brutal violation of the principles of Christianity, humanity, and justice, and even of science (that is, economic science). He advocates the principles of fraternity, humanity, justice, and science, and yet he lives so that he is dependent on the oppression of the working classes, which he denounces, and his whole life is based on the advantages gained by their oppression. Moreover he is directing every effort to maintaining this state of things so flatly opposed to all his beliefs.

We are all brothers—and yet every morning a brother or a sister must empty the bedroom slops for me. We are all brothers, but every morning I must have a cigar, a sweetmeat, an ice, and such things, which my brothers and sisters have been wasting their health in manufacturing, and I enjoy these things and demand them. We are all brothers, yet I live by working in a bank, or mercantile house, or shop at making all goods dearer for my brothers. We are all brothers, but I live on a salary paid me for prosecuting, judging, and condemning the thief or the prostitute whose existence the whole tenor of my life tends to bring about, and who I know ought not to be punished but reformed. We are all brothers, but I live on the salary I gain by collecting taxes from needy laborers to be spent on the luxuries of the rich and idle. We are all brothers, but I take a stipend for preaching a false Christian religion, which I do not myself believe in, and which only serves to hinder men from understanding true Christianity. I take a stipend as priest or bishop for deceiving men in the matter of the greatest importance to them. We are all brothers, but I will not give the poor the benefit of my educational, medical, or literary labors except for money. We are all brothers, yet I take a salary for being ready to commit murder, for teaching men to murder, or making firearms, gunpowder, or fortifications.

The whole life of the upper classes is a constant inconsistency. The more delicate a man's conscience is, the more painful this contradiction is to him.

A man of sensitive conscience cannot but suffer if he lives such a life. The only means by which he can escape from this suffering is by blunting his conscience, but even if some men succeed in dulling their conscience they cannot dull their fears.

The men of the higher dominating classes whose conscience is naturally not sensitive or has become blunted, if they don't suffer through conscience, suffer from fear and hatred. They are bound to suffer. They know all the hatred of them existing, and inevitably existing in the working classes. They are aware that the working classes know that they are deceived and exploited, and that they are beginning to organize themselves to shake off oppression and revenge themselves on their oppressors. The higher classes see the unions, the strikes, the May Day Celebrations, and feel the calamity that is threatening them, and their terror passes into an instinct of self-defense and hatred. They know that if for one instant they are worsted in the struggle with their oppressed slaves, they will perish, because the slaves are exasperated and their exasperation is growing more intense with every day of oppression. The oppressors, even if they wished to do so, could not make an end to oppression. They know that they themselves will perish directly they even relax the harshness of their oppression. And they do not relax it, in spite of all their pretended care for the welfare of the working classes, for the eight-hour day, for regulation of the labor of minors and of women, for savings banks and pensions. All that is humbug, or else simply anxiety to keep the slave fit to do his work. But the slave is still a slave, and the master who cannot live without a slave is less disposed to set him free than ever.

The attitude of the ruling classes to the laborers is that of a man who has felled his adversary to the earth and holds him down, not so much because he wants to hold him down, as because he knows that if he let him go, even for a second, he would himself be stabbed, for his adversary is infuriated and has a knife in his hand. And therefore, whether their conscience is tender or the reverse, our rich men cannot enjoy the wealth they have filched from the poor as the ancients did who believed in their right to it. Their whole life and all their enjoyments are embittered either by the stings of conscience or by terror.

So much for the economic contradiction. The political contradiction is even more striking.

All men are brought up to the habit of obeying the laws of the state before everything. The whole existence of modern times is defined by laws. A man marries and is divorced, educates his children, and even (in many countries) professes his religious faith in accordance with the law. What about the law then which defines our whole existence? Do men believe in it? Do they regard it as good? Not at all. In the majority of cases people of the present time do not believe in the justice of the law, they despise it, but still they obey it. It was very well for the men of the ancient world to observe their laws. They firmly believed that their law (it was generally of a religious character) was the only just law, which everyone ought to obey. But is it so with us? we know and cannot help knowing that the law of our country is not the one eternal law; that it is only one of the many laws of different countries, which are equally imperfect, often obviously wrong and unjust, and are criticised from every point of view in the newspapers. The Jew might well obey his laws, since he had not the slightest doubt that God had written them with his finger; the Roman too might well obey the laws which he thought had been dictated by the nymph Egeria. Men might well observe the laws if they believed the Tzars who made them were God's anointed, or even if they thought they were the work of assemblies of lawgivers who had the power and the desire to make them as good as possible. But we all know how our laws are made. We have all been behind the scenes, we know that they are the product of covetousness, trickery, and party struggles; that there is not and cannot be any real justice in them. And so modern men cannot believe that obedience to civic or political laws can satisfy the demands of the reason or of human nature. Men have long ago recognized that it is irrational to obey a law the justice of which is very doubtful, and so they cannot but suffer in obeying a law which they do not accept as judicious and binding.

A man cannot but suffer when his whole life is defined beforehand for him by laws, which he must obey under threat of punishment, though he does not believe in their wisdom or justice, and often clearly perceives their injustice, cruelty, and artificiality.

We recognize the uselessness of customs and import duties, and are obliged to pay them. We recognize the uselessness of the expenditure on the maintenance of the Court and other members of Government, and we regard the teaching of the Church as injurious, but we are obliged to bear our share of the expenses of these institutions. We regard the punishments inflicted by law as cruel and shameless, but we must assist in supporting them. We regard as unjust and pernicious the distribution of landed property, but we are obliged to submit to it. We see no necessity for wars and armies, but we must bear terribly heavy burdens in support of troops and war expenses.

But this contradiction is nothing in comparison with the contradiction which confronts us when we turn to international questions, and which demands a solution under pain of the loss of the sanity and even the existence of the human race. That is the contradiction between the Christian conscience and war.

We are all Christian nations living the same spiritual life, so that every noble and pregnant thought, springing up at one end of the world, is at once communicated to the whole of Christian humanity and evokes everywhere the same emotion of pride and rejoicing without distinction of nationalities. We who love thinkers, philanthropists, poets, and scientific men of foreign origin, and are as proud of the exploits of Father Damien as if he were one of ourselves, we, who have a simple love for men of foreign nationalities, Frenchmen, Germans, Americans, and Englishmen, who respect their qualities, are glad to meet them and make them so warmly welcome, cannot regard war with them as anything heroic. We cannot even imagine without horror the possibility of a disagreement between these people and ourselves which would call for reciprocal murder. Yet we are all bound to take a hand in this slaughter which is bound to come to pass to-morrow—if not to-day.

It was very well for the Jew, the Greek, and the Roman to defend the independence of his nation by murder. For he piously believed that his people was the only true, fine, and good people dear to God, and all the rest were Philistines, barbarians. Men of mediæval times—even up to the end of the last and beginning of this century—might continue to hold this belief. But however much we work upon ourselves we cannot believe it. And this contradiction for men of the present day has become so full of horror that without its solution life is no longer possible.

"We live in a time which is full of inconsistencies," writes Count Komarovsky, the professor of international law, in his learned treatise. "The press of all countries is continually expressing the universal desire for peace, and the general sense of its necessity for all nations.

"Representatives of governments, private persons, and official organs say the same thing; it is repeated in parliamentary debates, diplomatic correspondence, and even in state treaties. At the same time governments are increasing the strength of their armies every year, levying fresh taxes, raising loans, and leaving as a bequest to future generations the duty of repairing the blunders of the senseless policy of the present. What a striking contrast between words and deeds! Of course governments will plead in justification of these measures that all their expenditure and armament are exclusively for purposes of defense. But it remains a mystery to every disinterested man whence they can expect attacks if all the great powers are single-hearted in their policy, in pursuing nothing but self-defense. In reality it looks as if each of the great powers were every instant anticipating an attack on the part of the others. And this results in a general feeling of insecurity and superhuman efforts on the part of each government to increase their forces beyond those of the other powers. Such a competition of itself increases the danger of war. Nations cannot endure the constant increase of armies for long, and sooner or later they will prefer war to all the disadvantages of their present position and the constant menace of war. Then the most trifling pretext will be sufficient to throw the whole of Europe into the fire of universal war. And it is a mistaken idea that such a crisis might deliver us from the political and economical troubles that are crushing us. The experience of the wars of latter years teaches us that every war has only intensified national hatreds, made military burdens more crushing and insupportable, and rendered the political and economical position of Europe more grievous and insoluble."

"Modern Europe keeps under arms an active army of nine millions of men," writes Enrico Ferri, "besides fifteen millions of reserve, with an outlay of four hundred millions of francs per annum. By continual increase of the armed force, the sources of social and individual prosperity are paralyzed, and the state of the modern world may be compared to that of a man who condemns himself to wasting from lack of nutrition in order to provide himself with arms, losing thereby the strength to use the arms he provides, under the weight of which he will at last succumb."

Charles Booth, in his paper read in London before the Association for the Reform and Codification of the Law of Nations, June 26, 1887, says the same thing. After referring to the same number, nine millions of the active army and fifteen millions of reserve, and the enormous expenditure of governments on the support and arming of these forces, he says: "These figures represent only a small part of the real cost, because besides the recognized expenditure of the war budget of the various nations, we ought also to take into account the enormous loss to society involved in withdrawing from it such an immense number of its most vigorous men, who are taken from industrial pursuits and every kind of labor, as well as the enormous interest on the sums expended on military preparations without any return. The inevitable result of this expenditure on war and preparations for war is a continually growing national debt. The greater number of loans raised by the governments of Europe were with a view to war. Their total sum amounts to four hundred millions sterling, and these debts are increasing every year."

The same Professor Komarovsky says in another place: "We live in troubled times. Everywhere we hear complaints of the depression of trade and manufactures, and the wretchedness of the economic position generally, the miserable conditions of existence of the working classes, and the universal impoverishment of the masses. But in spite of this, governments in their efforts to maintain their independence rush to the greatest extremes of senselessness. New taxes and duties are being devised everywhere, and the financial oppression of the nations knows no limits. If we glance at the budgets of the states of Europe for the last hundred years, what strikes us most of all is their rapid and continually growing increase.

"How can we explain this extraordinary phenomenon, which sooner or later threatens us all with inevitable bankruptcy?

"It is caused beyond dispute by the expenditure for the maintenance of armaments which swallows up a third and even a half of all the expenditure of European states. And the most melancholy thing is that one can foresee no limit to this augmentation of the budget and impoverishment of the masses. What is socialism but a protest against this abnormal position in which the greater proportion of the population of our world is placed?"

"We are ruining ourselves," says Frederick Passy in a letter read before the last Congress of Universal Peace (in 1890) in London, "we are ruining ourselves in order to be able to take part in the senseless wars of the future or to pay the interest on debts we have incurred by the senseless and criminal wars of the past. We are dying of hunger so as to secure the means of killing each other."

Speaking later on of the way the subject is looked at in France, he says: "We believe that, a hundred years after the Declaration of the Rights of Man and of the citizen, the time has come to recognize the rights of nations and to renounce at once and forever all those undertakings based on fraud and force, which, under the name of conquests, are veritable crimes against humanity, and which, whatever the vanity of monarchs and the pride of nations may think of them, only weaken even those who are triumphant over them."

"I am surprised at the way religion is carried on in this country," said Sir Wilfrid Lawson at the same congress. "You send a boy to Sunday school, and you tell him: 'Dear boy, you must love your enemies. If another boy strikes you, you mustn't hit him back, but try to reform him by loving him.' Well. The boy stays in the Sunday school till he is fourteen or fifteen, and then his friends send him into the army. What has he to do in the army? He certainly won't love his enemy; quite the contrary, if he can only get at him, he will run him through with his bayonet. That is the nature of all religious teaching in this country. I do not think that that is a very good way of carrying out the precepts of religion. I think if it is a good thing for a boy to love his enemy, it is good for a grown-up man."

"There are in Europe twenty-eight millions of men under arms," says Wilson, "to decide disputes, not by discussion, but by murdering one another. That is the accepted method for deciding disputes among Christian nations. This method is, at the same time, very expensive, for, according to the statistics I have read, the nations of Europe spent in the year 1872 a hundred and fifty millions sterling on preparations for deciding disputes by means of murder. It seems to me, therefore, that in such a state of things one of two alternatives must be admitted: either Christianity is a failure, or those who have undertaken to expound it have failed in doing so. Until our warriors are disarmed and our armies disbanded, we have not the right to call ourselves a Christian nation."

In a conference on the subject of the duty of Christian ministers to preach against war, G. D. Bartlett said among other things: "If I understand the Scriptures, I say that men are only playing with Christianity so long as they ignore the question of war. I have lived a longish life and have heard our ministers preach on universal peace hardly half a dozen times. Twenty years ago, in a drawing room, I dared in the presence of forty persons to moot the proposition that war was incompatible with Christianity; I was regarded as an arrant fanatic. The idea that we could get on without war was regarded as unmitigated weakness and folly."

The Catholic priest Defourney has expressed himself in the same spirit. "One of the first precepts of the eternal law inscribed in the consciences of all men," says the Abbé Defourney, "is the prohibition of taking the life or shedding the blood of a fellow-creature without sufficient cause, without being forced into the necessity of it. This is one of the commandments which is most deeply stamped in the heart of man. But so soon as it is a question of war, that is, of shedding blood in torrents, men of the present day do not trouble themselves about a sufficient cause. Those who take part in wars do not even think of asking themselves whether there is any justification for these innumerable murders, whether they are justifiable or unjustifiable, lawful or unlawful, innocent or criminal; whether they are breaking that fundamental commandment that forbids killing without lawful cause. But their conscience is mute. War has ceased to be something dependent on moral considerations. In warfare men have in all the toil and dangers they endure no other pleasure than that of being conquerors, no sorrow other than that of being conquered. Don't tell me that they are serving their country. A great genius answered that long ago in the words that have become a proverb: 'Without justice, what is an empire but a great band of brigands?' And is not every band of brigands a little empire? They too have their laws; and they too make war to gain booty, and even for honor.

"The aim of the proposed institution [the institution of an international board of arbitration] is that the nations of Europe may cease to be nations of robbers, and their armies, bands of brigands. And one must add, not only brigands, but slaves. For our armies are simply gangs of slaves at the disposal of one or two commanders or ministers, who exercise a despotic control over them without any real responsibility, as we very well know.

"The peculiarity of a slave is that he is a mere tool in the hands of his master, a thing, not a man. That is just what soldiers, officers, and generals are, going to murder and be murdered at the will of a ruler or rulers. Military slavery is an actual fact, and it is the worst form of slavery, especially now when by means of compulsory service it lays its fetters on the necks of all the strong and capable men of a nation, to make them instruments of murder, butchers of human flesh, for that is all they are taken and trained to do.

"The rulers, two or three in number, meet together in cabinets, secretly deliberate without registers, without publicity, and consequently without responsibility, and send men to be murdered."

"Protests against armaments, burdensome to the people, have not originated in our times," says Signor E. G. Moneta. "Hear what Montesquieu wrote in his day. 'France [and one might say, Europe] will be ruined by soldiers. A new plague is spreading throughout Europe. It attacks sovereigns and forces them to maintain an incredible number of armed men. This plague is infectious and spreads, because directly one government increases its armament, all the others do likewise. So that nothing is gained by it but general ruin.

"'Every government maintains as great an army as it possibly could maintain if its people were threatened with extermination, and people call peace this state of tension of all against all. And therefore Europe is so ruined that if private persons were in the position of the governments of our continent, the richest of them would not have enough to live on. We are poor though we have the wealth and trade of the whole world.'

"That was written almost 150 years ago. The picture seems drawn from the world of to-day. One thing only has changed—the form of government. In Montesquieu's time it was said that the cause of the maintenance of great armaments was the despotic power of kings, who made war in the hope of augmenting by conquest their personal revenues and gaining glory. People used to say then: 'Ah, if only people could elect those who would have the right to refuse governments the soldiers and the money—then there would be an end to military politics.' Now there are representative governments in almost the whole of Europe, and in spite of that, war expenditures and the preparations for war have increased to alarming proportions.

"It is evident that the insanity of sovereigns has gained possession of the ruling classes. War is not made now because one king has been wanting in civility to the mistress of another king, as it was in Louis XIV.'s time. But the natural and honorable sentiments of national honor and patriotism are so exaggerated, and the public opinion of one nation so excited against another, that it is enough for a statement to be made (even though it may be a false report) that the ambassador of one state was not received by the principal personage of another state to cause the outbreak of the most awful and destructive war there has ever been seen. Europe keeps more soldiers under arms today than in the time of the great Napoleonic wars. All citizens with few exceptions are forced to spend some years in barracks. Fortresses, arsenals, and ships are built, new weapons are constantly being invented, to be replaced in a short time by fresh ones, for, sad to say, science, which ought always to be aiming at the good of humanity, assists in the work of destruction, and is constantly inventing new means for killing the greatest number of men in the shortest time. And to maintain so great a multitude of soldiers and to make such vast preparations for murder, hundreds of millions are spent annually, sums which would be sufficient for the education of the people and for immense works of public utility, and which would make it possible to find a peaceful solution of the social question.

"Europe, then, is, in this respect, in spite of all the conquests of science, in the same position as in the darkest and most barbarous days of the Middle Ages. All deplore this state of things—neither peace nor war—and all would be glad to escape from it. The heads of governments all declare that they all wish for peace, and vie with one another in the most solemn protestations of peaceful intentions. But the same day or the next they will lay a scheme for the increase of the armament before their legislative assembly, saying that these are the preventive measures they take for the very purpose of securing peace.

"But this is not the kind of peace we want. And the nations are not deceived by it. True peace is based on mutual confidence, while these huge armaments show open and utter lack of confidence, if not concealed hostility, between states. What should we say of a man who, wanting to show his friendly feelings for his neighbor, should invite him to discuss their differences with a loaded revolver in his hand?

"It is just this flagrant contradiction between the peaceful professions and the warlike policy of governments which all good citizens desire to put an end to, at any cost."

People are astonished that every year there are sixty thousand cases of suicide in Europe, and those only the recognized and recorded cases—and excluding Russia and Turkey; but one ought rather to be surprised that there are so few. Every man of the present day, if we go deep enough into the contradiction between his conscience and his life, is in a state of despair.

Not to speak of all the other contradictions between modern life and the conscience, the permanently armed condition of Europe together with its profession of Christianity is alone enough to drive any man to despair, to doubt of the sanity of mankind, and to terminate an existence in this senseless and brutal world. This contradiction, which is a quintessence of all the other contradictions, is so terrible that to live and to take part in it is only possible if one does not think of it—if one is able to forget it.

What! all of us, Christians, not only profess to love one another, but do actually live one common life; we whose social existence beats with one common pulse—we aid one another, learn from one another, draw ever closer to one another to our mutual happiness, and find in this closeness the whole meaning of life!—and to-morrow some crazy ruler will say some stupidity, and another will answer in the same spirit, and then I must go expose myself to being murdered, and murder men—who have done me no harm—and more than that, whom I love. And this is not a remote contingency, but the very thing we are all preparing for, which is not only probable, but an inevitable certainty.

To recognize this clearly is enough to drive a man out of his senses or to make him shoot himself. And this is just what does happen, and especially often among military men. A man need only come to himself for an instant to be impelled inevitably to such an end.

And this is the only explanation of the dreadful intensity with which men of modern times strive to stupefy themselves, with spirits, tobacco, opium, cards, reading newspapers, traveling, and all kinds of spectacles and amusements. These pursuits are followed up as an important, serious business. And indeed they are a serious business. If there were no external means of dulling their sensibilities, half of mankind would shoot themselves without delay, for to live in opposition to one's reason is the most intolerable condition. And that is the condition of all men of the present day. All men of the modern world exist in a state of continual and flagrant antagonism between their conscience and their way of life. This antagonism is apparent in economic as well as political life. But most striking of all is the contradiction between the Christian law of the brotherhood of men existing in the conscience and the necessity under which all men are placed by compulsory military service of being prepared for hatred and murder—of being at the same time a Christian and a gladiator.

CHAPTER VI: ATTITUDE OF MEN OF THE PRESENT DAY TO WAR

People do not Try to Remove the Contradiction between Life and Conscience by a Change of Life, but their Cultivated Leaders Exert Every Effort to Obscure the Demands of Conscience, and Justify their Life; in this Way they Degrade Society below Paganism to a State of Primeval Barbarism—Undefined Attitude of Modern Leaders of Thought to War, to Universal Militarism, and to Compulsory Service in Army—One Section Regards War as an Accidental Political Phenomenon, to be Avoided by External Measures only—Peace Congress—The Article in the *Revue des Revues*—Proposition of Maxime du Camp—Value of Boards of Arbitration and Suppression of Armies—Attitude of Governments to Men of this Opinion and What they Do—Another Section Regards War as Cruel, but Inevitable—Maupassant—Rod—A Third Section Regard War as Necessary, and not without its Advantages—Doucet—Claretie—Zola—Vogüé.

The antagonism between life and the conscience may be removed in two ways: by a change of life or by a change of conscience. And there would seem there can be no doubt as to these alternatives.

A man may cease to do what he regards as wrong, but he cannot cease to consider wrong what is wrong. Just in the same way all humanity may cease to do what it regards as wrong, but far from being able to change, it cannot even retard for a time the continual growth of a clearer recognition of what is wrong and therefore ought not to be. And therefore it would seem inevitable for Christian men to abandon the pagan forms of society which they condemn, and to reconstruct their social existence on the Christian principles they profess.

So it would be were it not for the law of inertia, as immutable a force in men and nations as in inanimate bodies. In men it takes the form of the psychological principle, so truly expressed in the words of the Gospel, "They have loved darkness better than light because their deeds were evil." This principle shows itself in men not trying to recognize the truth, but to persuade themselves that the life they are leading, which is what they like and are used to, is a life perfectly consistent with truth.

Slavery was opposed to all the moral principles advocated by Plato and Aristotle, yet neither of them saw that, because to renounce slavery would have meant the break up of the life they were living. We see the same thing in our modern world.

The division of men into two castes, as well as the use of force in government and war, are opposed to every moral principle professed by our modern society. Yet the cultivated and advanced men of the day seem not to see it.

The majority, if not all, of the cultivated men of our day try unconsciously to maintain the old social conception of life, which justifies their position, and to hide from themselves and others its insufficiency, and above all the necessity of adopting the Christian conception of life, which will mean the break up of the whole existing social order. They struggle to keep up the organization based on the social conception of life, but do not believe in it themselves, because it is extinct and it is impossible to believe in it.

All modern literature—philosophical, political, and artistic—is striking in this respect. What wealth of idea, of form, of color, what erudition, what art, but what a lack of serious matter, what dread of any exactitude of thought or expression! Subtleties, allegories, humorous fancies, the widest generalizations, but nothing simple and clear, nothing going straight to the point, that is, to the problem of life.

But that is not all; besides these graceful frivolities, our literature is full of simple nastiness and brutality, of arguments which would lead men back in the most refined way to primeval barbarism, to the principles not only of the pagan, but even of the animal life, which we have left behind us five thousand years ago.

And it could not be otherwise. In their dread of the Christian conception of life which will destroy the social order, which some cling to only from habit, others also from interest, men cannot but be thrown back upon the pagan conception of life and the principles based on it. Nowadays we see advocated not only patriotism and aristocratic principles just as they were advocated two thousand years ago, but even the coarsest epicureanism and animalism, only with this difference, that the men who then professed those views believed in them, while nowadays even the advocates of such views do not believe in them, for they have no meaning for the present day. No one can stand still when the earth is shaking under his feet. If we do not go forward we must go back. And strange and terrible to say, the cultivated men of our day, the leaders of thought, are in reality with their subtle reasoning drawing society back, not to paganism even, but to a state of primitive barbarism.

This tendency on the part of the leading thinkers of the day is nowhere more apparent than in their attitude to the phenomenon in which all the insufficiency of the social conception of life is presented in the most concentrated form—in their attitude, that is, to war, to the general arming of nations, and to universal compulsory service.

The undefined, if not disingenuous, attitude of modern thinkers to this phenomenon is striking. It takes three forms in cultivated society. One section look at it as an incidental phenomenon, arising out of the special political situation of Europe, and consider that this state of things can be reformed without a revolution in the whole internal social order of nations, by external measures of international diplomacy. Another section regard it as something cruel and hideous, but at the same time fated and inevitable, like disease and death. A third party with cool indifference consider war as an inevitable phenomenon, beneficial in its effects and therefore desirable.

Men look at the subject from different points of view, but all alike talk of war as though it were something absolutely independent of the will of those who take part in it. And consequently they do not even admit the natural question which presents itself to every simple man: "How about me—ought I to take any part in it?" In their view no question of this kind even exists, and every man, however he may regard war from a personal standpoint, must slavishly submit to the requirements of the authorities on the subject.

The attitude of the first section of thinkers, those who see a way out of war in international diplomatic measures, is well expressed in the report of the last Peace Congress in London, and the articles and letters upon war that appeared in No. 8 of the *Revue des Revues*, 1891. The congress after gathering together from various quarters the verbal and written opinion of learned men opened the proceedings by a religious service, and after listening to addresses for five whole days, concluded them by a public dinner and speeches. They adopted the following resolutions:

"1. The congress affirms its belief that the brotherhood of man involves as a necessary consequence a brotherhood of nations.

"2. The congress recognizes the important influence that Christianity exercises on the moral and political progress of mankind, and earnestly urges upon ministers of the Gospel and other religious teachers the duty of setting forth the principles of peace and good will toward men. *And it recommends that the third Sunday in December be set apart for that purpose.*

"3. The congress expresses the opinion that all teachers of history should call the attention of the young to the grave evils inflicted on mankind in all ages by war, and to the fact that such war has been waged for most inadequate causes.

"4. The congress protests against the use of military drill in schools by way of physical exercise, and suggests the formation of brigades for saving life rather than of a quasi-military character; and urges the desirability of impressing on the Board of Examiners who formulate the questions for examination the propriety of guiding the minds of children in the principles of peace.

"5. The congress holds that the doctrine of the Rights of Man requires that the aboriginal and weaker races, their territories and liberties, shall be guarded from injustice and fraud, and that these races shall be shielded against the vices so prevalent among the so-called advanced races of men. It further expresses its conviction that there should be concert of action among the nations for the accomplishment of these ends. The congress expresses its hearty appreciation of the resolutions of the Anti-slavery Conference held recently at Brussels for the amelioration of the condition of the peoples of Africa.

"6. The congress believes that the warlike prejudices and traditions which are still fostered in the various nationalities, and the misrepresentations by leaders of public opinion in legislative assemblies or through the press, are often indirect causes of war, and that these evils should be counteracted by the publication of accurate information tending to the removal of misunderstanding between nations, and recommends the importance of considering the question of commencing an international newspaper with such a purpose.

"7. The congress proposes to the Inter-parliamentary Conference that the utmost support should be given to every project for unification of weights and measures, coinage, tariff, postage, and telegraphic arrangements, etc., which would assist in constituting a commercial, industrial, and scientific union of the peoples.

"8. The congress, in view of the vast social and moral influence of woman, urges upon every woman to sustain the things that make for peace, as otherwise she incurs grave responsibility for the continuance of the systems of militarism.

"9. The congress expresses the hope that the Financial Reform Association and other similar societies in Europe and America should unite in considering means for establishing equitable commercial relations between states, by the reduction of import duties. The congress feels that it can affirm that the whole of Europe desires peace, and awaits with impatience the suppression of armaments, which, under the plea of defense, become in their turn a danger by keeping alive mutual distrust, and are, at the same time, the cause of that general economic disturbance which stands in the way of settling in a satisfactory manner the problems of labor and poverty, which ought to take precedence of all others.

"10. The congress, recognizing that a general disarmament would be the best guarantee of peace and would lead to the solution of the questions which now most divide states, expresses the wish that a congress of representatives of all the states of Europe may be assembled as soon as possible to consider the means of effecting a gradual general disarmament.

"11. The congress, in consideration of the fact that the timidity of a single power might delay the convocation of the above-mentioned congress, is of opinion that the government which should first dismiss any considerable number of soldiers would confer a signal benefit on Europe and mankind, because it would, by public opinion, oblige other governments to follow its example, and by the moral force of this accomplished fact would have increased rather than diminished the conditions of its national defense.

"12. The congress, considering the question of disarmament, as of peace in general, depends on public opinion, recommends the peace societies, as well as all friends of peace, to be active in its propaganda, especially at the time of parliamentary elections, in order that the electors should give their votes to candidates who are pledged to support Peace, Disarmament, and Arbitration.

"13. The congress congratulates the friends of peace on the resolution adopted by the International American Conference, held at Washington in April last, by which it was recommended that arbitration should be obligatory in all controversies, whatever their origin, except only those which may imperil the independence of one of the nations involved.

"14. The congress recommends this resolution to the attention of European statesmen, and expresses the ardent desire that similar treaties may speedily be entered into between the other nations of the world.

"15. The congress expresses its satisfaction at the adoption by the Spanish Senate on June 16 last of a project of law authorizing the government to negotiate general or special treaties of arbitration for the settlement of all disputes except those relating to the independence or internal government of the states affected;

also at the adoption of resolutions to a like effect by the Norwegian Storthing and by the Italian Chamber.

"16. The congress resolves that a committee be appointed to address communications to the principal political, religious, commercial, and labor and peace organizations, requesting them to send petitions to the governmental authorities praying that measures be taken for the formation of suitable tribunals for the adjudicature of international questions so as to avoid the resort to war.

"17. Seeing (1) that the object pursued by all peace societies is the establishment of judicial order between nations, and (2) that neutralization by international treaties constitutes a step toward this judicial state and lessens the number of districts in which war can be carried on, the congress recommends a larger extension of the rule of neutralization, and expresses the wish, (1) that all treaties which at present assure to certain states the benefit of neutrality remain in force, or if necessary be amended in a manner to render the neutrality more effective, either by extending neutralization to the whole of the state or by ordering the demolition of fortresses, which constitute rather a peril than a guarantee for neutrality; (2) that new treaties in harmony with the wishes of the populations concerned be concluded for establishing the neutralization of other states.

"18. The sub-committee proposes, (1) that the annual Peace Congress should be held either immediately before the meeting of the annual Sub-parliamentary Conference, or immediately after it in the same town; (2) that the question of an international peace emblem be postponed *sine die*; (3) that the following resolutions be adopted:

"*a.* To express satisfaction at the official overtures of the Presbyterian Church in the United States addressed to the highest representatives of each church organization in Christendom to unite in a general conference to promote the substitution of international arbitration for war.

"*b.* To express in the name of the congress its profound reverence for the memory of Aurelio Saffi, the great Italian jurist, a member of the committee of the International League of Peace and Liberty.

"(4) That the memorial adopted by this congress and signed by the president to the heads of the civilized states should, as far as practicable, be presented to each power by influential deputations.

"(5) That the following resolutions be adopted:

"*a.* A resolution of thanks to the presidents of the various sittings of the congress.

"*b.* A resolution of thanks to the chairman, the secretaries, and the members of the bureau of the congress.

"*c.* A resolution of thanks to the conveners and members of the sectional committees.

"*d.* A resolution of thanks to Rev. Canon Scott Holland, Rev. Dr. Reuen Thomas, and Rev. J. Morgan Gibbon for their pulpit addresses before the congress, and also to the authorities of St. Paul's Cathedral, the City Temple, and Stamford Hill Congregational Church for the use of those buildings for public services.

"*e.* A letter of thanks to her Majesty for permission to visit Windsor Castle.

"*f.* And also a resolution of thanks to the Lord Mayor and Lady Mayoress, to Mr. Passmore Edwards, and other friends who have extended their hospitality to the members of the congress.

"19. The congress places on record a heartfelt expression of gratitude to Almighty God for the remarkable harmony and concord which have characterized the meetings of the assembly, in which so many men and women of varied nations, creeds, tongues, and races have gathered in closest co-operation, and for the conclusion of the labors of the congress; and expresses its firm and unshaken belief in the ultimate triumph of the cause of peace and of the principles advocated at these meetings."

The fundamental idea of the congress is the necessity (1) of diffusing among all people by all means the conviction of the disadvantages of war and the great blessing of peace, and (2) of rousing governments to the sense of the superiority of international arbitration over war and of the consequent advisability and necessity of disarmament. To attain the first aim the congress has recourse to teachers of history, to women, and to the clergy, with the advice to the latter to preach on the evil of war and the blessing of peace every third Sunday in December. To attain the second object the congress appeals to governments with the suggestion that they should disband their armies and replace war by arbitration.

To preach to men of the evil of war and the blessing of peace! But the blessing of peace is so well known to men that, ever since there have been men at all, their best wish has been expressed in the greeting, "Peace be with you." So why preach about it?

Not only Christians, but pagans, thousands of years ago, all recognized the evil of war and the blessing of peace. So that the recommendation to ministers of the Gospel to preach on the evil of war and the blessing of peace every third Sunday in December is quite superfluous.

The Christian cannot but preach on that subject every day of his life. If Christians and preachers of Christianity do not do so, there must be reasons for it. And until these have been removed no recommendations will be effective. Still less effective will be the recommendations to governments to disband their armies and replace them by international boards of arbitration. Governments, too, know very well the difficulty and the burdensomeness of raising and maintaining forces, and if in spite of that knowledge they do, at the cost of terrible strain and effort, raise and maintain forces, it is evident that they cannot do otherwise, and the recommendation of the congress can never change it. But the learned gentlemen are unwilling to see that, and keep hoping to find a political combination, through which governments shall be induced to limit their powers themselves.

"Can we get rid of war"? asks a learned writer in the *Revue des Revues*. "All are agreed that if it were to break out in Europe, its consequences would be like those of the great inroads of barbarians. The existence of whole nationalities would be at stake, and therefore the war would be desperate, bloody, atrocious.

"This consideration, together with the terrible engines of destruction invented by modern science, retards the moment of declaring war, and maintains the present temporary situation, which might continue for an indefinite period, except for the fearful cost of maintaining armaments which are exhausting the European states and threatening to reduce nations to a state of misery hardly less than that of war itself.

"Struck by this reflection, men of various countries have tried to find means for preventing, or at least for softening, the results of the terrible slaughter with which we are threatened.

"Such are the questions brought forward by the Peace Congress shortly to be held in Rome, and the publication of a pamphlet, 'Sur le Désarmement'.

"It is unhappily beyond doubt that with the present organization of the majority of European states, isolated from one another and guided by distinct interests, the absolute suppression of war is an illusion with which it would be dangerous to cheat ourselves. Wiser rules and regulations imposed on these duels between nations might, however, at least limit its horrors.

"It is equally chimerical to reckon on projects of disarmament, the execution of which is rendered almost impossible by considerations of a popular character present to the mind of all our readers. [This probably means that France cannot disband its army before taking its revenge.] Public opinion is not prepared to accept them, and moreover, the international relations between different peoples are not such as to make their acceptance possible. Disarmament imposed on one nation by another in circumstances threatening its security would be equivalent to a declaration of war.

"However, one may admit that an exchange of ideas between the nations interested could aid, to a certain degree, in bringing about the good understanding indispensable to any negotiations, and would render possible a considerable reduction of the military expenditure which is crushing the nations of Europe and greatly hindering the solution of the social question, which each individually must solve on pain of having internal war as the price for escaping it externally.

"We might at least demand the reduction of the enormous expenses of war organized as it is at present with a view to the power of invasion within twenty-four hours and a decisive battle within a week of the declaration of war.

"We ought to manage so that states could not make the attack suddenly and invade each other's territories within twenty-four hours."

This practical notion has been put forth by Maxime du Camp, and his article concludes with it.

The propositions of M. du Camp are as follows:

1. A diplomatic congress to be held every year.

2. No war to be declared till two months after the incident which provoked it. (The difficulty here would be to decide precisely what incident did provoke the war, since whenever war is declared there are very many such incidents, and one would have to decide from which to reckon the two months' interval.)

3. No war to be declared before it has been submitted to a plebiscitum of the nations preparing to take part in it.

4. No hostilities to be commenced till a month after the official declaration of war.

"No war to be declared. No hostilities to be commenced," etc. But who is to arrange that no war is to be declared? Who is to compel people to do this and that? Who is to force states to delay their operations for a certain fixed time? All the other states. But all these others are also states which want holding in check and keeping within limits, and forcing, too. Who is to force them, and how? Public opinion. But if there is a public opinion which can force governments to delay their operations for a fixed period, the same public opinion can force governments not to declare war at all.

But, it will be replied, there may be such a balance of power, such a *pondération de forces*, as would lead states to hold back of their own accord. Well, that has been tried and is being tried even now. The Holy Alliance was nothing but that, the League of Peace was another attempt at the same thing, and so on.

But, it will be answered, suppose all were agreed. If all were agreed there would be no more war certainly, and no need for arbitration either.

"A court of arbitration! Arbitration shall replace war. Questions shall be decided by a court of arbitration. The Alabama question was decided by a court of arbitration, and the question of the Caroline Islands was submitted to the decision of the Pope. Switzerland, Belgium, Denmark, and Holland have all declared that they prefer arbitration to war."

I dare say Monaco has expressed the same preference. The only unfortunate thing is that Germany, Russia, Austria, and France have not so far shown the same inclination. It is amazing how men can deceive themselves when they find it necessary! Governments consent to decide their disagreements by arbitration and to disband their armies! The differences between Russia and Poland, between England and Ireland, between Austria and Bohemia, between Turkey and the Slavonic states, between France and Germany, to be soothed away by amiable conciliation!

One might as well suggest to merchants and bankers that they should sell nothing for a greater price than they gave for it, should undertake the distribution of wealth for no profit, and should abolish money, as it would thus be rendered unnecessary.

But since commercial and banking operations consist in nothing but selling for more than the cost price, this would be equivalent to an invitation to suppress themselves. It is the same in regard to governments. To suggest to governments that they should not have recourse to violence, but should decide their misunderstandings in accordance with equity, is inviting them to abolish themselves as rulers, and that no government can ever consent to do.

The learned men form societies (there are more than a hundred such societies), assemble in congresses (such as those recently held in London and Paris, and shortly to be held in Rome), deliver addresses, eat public dinners and make speeches, publish journals, and prove by every means possible that the nations forced to support millions of troops are strained to the furthest limits of their endurance, that the maintenance of these huge armed forces is in opposition to all the aims, the interests, and the wishes of the people, and that it is possible, moreover, by writing numerous papers, and uttering a great many words, to bring all men into agreement and to arrange so that they shall have no antagonistic interests, and then there will be no more war.

When I was a little boy they told me if I wanted to catch a bird I must put salt on its tail. I ran after the birds with the salt in my hand, but I soon convinced myself that if I could put salt on a bird's tail, I could catch it, and realized that I had been hoaxed.

People ought to realize the same fact when they read books and articles on arbitration and disarmament.

If one could put salt on a bird's tail, it would be because it could not fly and there would be no difficulty in catching it. If the bird had wings and did not want to be caught, it would not let one put salt on its tail, because the specialty of a bird is to fly. In precisely the same way the specialty of government is not to obey, but to enforce obedience. And a government is only a government so long as it can make itself obeyed, and therefore it always strives for that and will never willingly abandon its power. But since it is on the army that the power of government rests, it will never give up the army, and the use of the army in war.

The error arises from the learned jurists deceiving themselves and others, by asserting that government is not what it really is, one set of men banded together to oppress another set of men, but, as shown by science, is the representation of the citizens in their collective capacity. They have so long been persuading other people of this that at last they have persuaded themselves of it; and thus they often seriously suppose that government can be bound by considerations of justice. But history shows that from Cæsar to Napoleon, and from Napoleon to Bismarck, government is in its essence always a force acting in violation of justice, and that it cannot be otherwise. Justice can have no binding force on a ruler or rulers who keep men, deluded and drilled in readiness for acts of violence—soldiers, and by means of them control others. And so governments can never be brought to consent to diminish the number of these drilled slaves, who constitute their whole power and importance.

Such is the attitude of certain learned men to the contradiction under which our society is being crushed, and such are their methods of solving it. Tell these people that the whole matter rests on the personal attitude of each man to the moral and religious question put nowadays to everyone, the question, that is, whether it is lawful or unlawful for him to take his share of military service, and these learned gentlemen will shrug their shoulders and not condescend to listen or to answer you. The solution of the question in their idea is to be found in reading addresses, writing books, electing presidents, vice-presidents, and secretaries, and meeting and speaking first in one town and then in another. From all this speechifying and writing it will come to pass, according to their notions, that governments will cease to levy the soldiers, on whom their whole strength depends, will listen to their discourses, and will disband their forces, leaving themselves without any defense, not only against their neighbors, but also against their own subjects. As though a band of brigands, who have some unarmed travelers bound and ready to be plundered, should be so touched by their complaints of the pain caused by the cords they are fastened with as to let them go again.

Still there are people who believe in this, busy themselves over peace congresses, read addresses, and write books. And governments, we may be quite sure, express their sympathy and make a show of encouraging them. In the same way they pretend to support temperance societies, while they are living principally on the drunkenness of the people; and pretend to encourage education, when their whole strength is based on ignorance; and to support constitutional freedom, when their strength rests on the absence of freedom; and to be anxious for the improvement of the condition of the working classes, when their very existence depends on their oppression; and to support Christianity, when Christianity destroys all government.

To be able to do this they have long ago elaborated methods encouraging temperance, which cannot suppress drunkenness; methods of supporting education, which not only fail to prevent ignorance, but even increase it; methods of aiming at freedom and constitutionalism, which are no hindrance to despotism; methods of protecting the working classes, which will not free them from slavery; and a Christianity, too, they have elaborated, which does not destroy, but supports governments.

Now there is something more for the government to encourage—peace. The sovereigns, who nowadays take counsel with their ministers, decide by their will alone whether the butchery of millions is to be begun this year or next. They know very well that all these discourses upon peace will not hinder them from sending millions of men to butchery when it seems good to them. They listen even with satisfaction to these discourses, encourage them, and take part in them.

All this, far from being detrimental, is even of service to governments, by turning people's attention from the most important and pressing question: Ought or ought not each man called upon for military service to submit to serve in the army?

"Peace will soon be arranged, thanks to alliances and congresses, to books and pamphlets; meantime go and put on your uniform, and prepare to cause suffering and to endure it for our benefit," is the government's line of argument. And the learned gentlemen who get up congresses and write articles are in perfect agreement with it.

This is the attitude of one set of thinkers. And since it is that most beneficial to governments, it is also the most encouraged by all intelligent governments.

Another attitude to war has something tragical in it. There are men who maintain that the love for peace and the inevitability of war form a hideous contradiction, and that such is the fate of man. These are mostly gifted and sensitive men, who see and realize all the horror and imbecility and cruelty of war, but through some strange perversion of mind neither see nor seek to find any way out of this position, and seem to take pleasure in teasing the wound by dwelling on the desperate position of humanity. A notable example of such an attitude to war is to be found in the celebrated French writer Guy de Maupassant. Looking from his yacht at the drill and firing practice of the French soldiers the following reflections occur to him:

"When I think only of this word war, a kind of terror seizes upon me, as though I were listening to some tale of sorcery, of the Inquisition, some long past, remote abomination, monstrous, unnatural.

"When cannibalism is spoken of, we smile with pride, proclaiming our superiority to these savages. Which are the savages, the real savages? Those who fight to eat the conquered, or those who fight to kill, for nothing but to kill?

"The young recruits, moving about in lines yonder, are destined to death like the flocks of sheep driven by the butcher along the road. They will fall in some plain with a saber cut in the head, or a bullet through the breast. And these are young men who might work, be productive and useful. Their fathers are old and poor. Their mothers, who have loved them for twenty years, worshiped them as none but mothers can, will learn in six months' time, or a year perhaps, that their son, their boy, the big boy reared with so much labor, so much expense, so much love, has been thrown in a hole like some dead dog, after being disemboweled by a bullet, and trampled, crushed, to a mass of pulp by the charges of cavalry. Why have they killed her boy, her handsome boy, her one hope, her pride, her life? She does not know. Ah, why?

"War! fighting! slaughter! massacres of men! And we have now, in our century, with our civilization, with the spread of science, and the degree of philosophy which the genius of man is supposed to have attained, schools for training to kill, to kill very far off, to perfection, great numbers at once, to kill poor devils of innocent men with families and without any kind of trial.

LEO TOLSTOY

"*And what is most bewildering is that the people do not rise against their governments. For what difference is there between monarchies and republics? The most bewildering thing is that the whole of society is not in revolt at the word war.*"

"Ah! we shall always live under the burden of the ancient and odious customs, the criminal prejudices, the ferocious ideas of our barbarous ancestors, for we are beasts, and beasts we shall remain, dominated by instinct and changed by nothing. Would not any other man than Victor Hugo have been exiled for that mighty cry of deliverance and truth? 'To-day force is called violence, and is being brought to judgment; war has been put on its trial. At the plea of the human race, civilization arraigns warfare, and draws up the great list of crimes laid at the charge of conquerors and generals. The nations are coming to understand that the magnitude of a crime cannot be its extenuation; that if killing is a crime, killing many can be no extenuating circumstance; that if robbery is disgraceful, invasion cannot be glorious. Ah! let us proclaim these absolute truths; let us dishonor war!'

"Vain wrath," continues Maupassant, "a poet's indignation. War is held in more veneration than ever.

"A skilled proficient in that line, a slaughterer of genius, Von Moltke, in reply to the peace delegates, once uttered these strange words:

"'War is holy, war is ordained of God. It is one of the most sacred laws of the world. It maintains among men all the great and noble sentiments—honor, devotion, virtue, and courage, and saves them in short from falling into the most hideous materialism.'

"So, then, bringing millions of men together into herds, marching by day and by night without rest, thinking of nothing, studying nothing, learning nothing, reading nothing, being useful to no one, wallowing in filth, sleeping in mud, living like brutes in a continual state of stupefaction, sacking towns, burning villages, ruining whole populations, then meeting another mass of human flesh, falling upon them, making pools of blood, and plains of flesh mixed with trodden mire and red with heaps of corpses, having your arms or legs carried off, your brains blown out for no advantage to anyone, and dying in some corner of a field while your old parents, your wife and children are perishing of hunger—that is what is meant by not falling into the most hideous materialism!

"Warriors are the scourge of the world. We struggle against nature and ignorance and obstacles of all kinds to make our wretched life less hard. Learned men—benefactors of all—spend their lives in working, in seeking what can aid, what be of use, what can alleviate the lot of their fellows. They devote themselves unsparingly to their task of usefulness, making one discovery after another, enlarging the sphere of human intelligence, extending the bounds of science, adding each day some new store to the sum of knowledge, gaining each day prosperity, ease, strength for their country.

"War breaks out. In six months the generals have destroyed the work of twenty years of effort, of patience, and of genius.

"That is what is meant by not falling into the most hideous materialism.

"We have seen it, war. We have seen men turned to brutes, frenzied, killing for fun, for terror, for bravado, for ostentation. Then when right is no more, law is dead, every notion of justice has disappeared. We have seen men shoot innocent creatures found on the road, and suspected because they were afraid. We have seen them kill dogs chained at their masters' doors to try their new revolvers. We have seen them fire on cows lying in a field for no reason whatever, simply for the sake of shooting, for a joke.

"That is what is meant by not falling into the most hideous materialism.

"Going into a country, cutting the man's throat who defends his house because he wears a blouse and has not a military cap on his head, burning the dwellings of wretched beings who have nothing to eat, breaking furniture and stealing goods, drinking the wine found in the cellars, violating the women in the streets, burning thousands of francs' worth of powder, and leaving misery and cholera in one's track—

"That is what is meant by not falling into the most hideous materialism.

"What have they done, those warriors, that proves the least intelligence? Nothing. What have they invented? Cannons and muskets. That is all.

"What remains to us from Greece? Books and statues. Is Greece great from her conquests or her creations?

"Was it the invasions of the Persians which saved Greece from falling into the most hideous materialism?

"Were the invasions of the barbarians what saved and regenerated Rome?

"Was it Napoleon I. who carried forward the great intellectual movement started by the philosophers of the end of last century?

"Yes, indeed, since government assumes the right of annihilating peoples thus, there is nothing surprising in the fact that the peoples assume the right of annihilating governments.

"They defend themselves. They are right. No one has an absolute right to govern others. It ought only to be done for the benefit of those who are governed. And it is as much the duty of anyone who governs to avoid war as it is the duty of a captain of a ship to avoid shipwreck.

"When a captain has let his ship come to ruin, he is judged and condemned, if he is found guilty of negligence or even incapacity.

"Why should not the government be put on its trial after every declaration of war? *If the people understood that, if they themselves passed judgment on murderous governments, if they refused to let themselves be killed for nothing, if they would only turn their arms against those who have given them to them for massacre, on that day war would be no more. But that day will never come.*"

The author sees all the horror of war. He sees that it is caused by governments forcing men by deception to go out to slaughter and be slain without any advantage to themselves. And he sees, too, that the men who make up the armies could turn their arms against the governments and bring them to judgment. But he thinks that that will never come to pass, and that there is, therefore, no escape from the present position. "I think war is terrible, but that it is inevitable; that compulsory military service is as inevitable as death, and that since government will always desire it, war will always exist."

So writes this talented and sincere writer, who is endowed with that power of penetrating to the innermost core of the subjects which is the essence of the poetic faculty. He brings before us all the cruelty of the inconsistency between men's moral sense and their actions, but without trying to remove it; seems to admit that this inconsistency must exist and that it is the poetic tragedy of life.

Another no less gifted writer, Edouard Rod, paints in still more vivid colors the cruelty and madness of the present state of things. He too only aims at presenting its tragic features, without suggesting or forseeing any issue from the position.

"What is the good of doing anything? What is the good of undertaking any enterprise? And how are we to love men in these troubled times when every fresh day is a menace of danger?... All we have begun, the plans we are developing, our schemes of work, the little good we may have been able to do, will it not all be swept away by the tempest that is in preparation?... Every where the earth is shaking under our feet and storm-clouds are gathering on our horizon which will have no pity on us.

"Ah! if all we had to dread were the revolution which is held up as a specter to terrify us! Since I cannot imagine a society more detestable than ours, I feel more skeptical than alarmed in regard to that which will replace it. If I should have to suffer from the change, I should be consoled by thinking that the executioners of that day were the victims of the previous time, and the hope of something better would help us to endure the worst. But it is not that remote peril which frightens me. I see another danger, nearer and far more cruel; more cruel because there is no excuse for it, because it is absurd, because it can lead to no good. Every day one balances the chances of war on the morrow, every day they become more merciless.

"The imagination revolts before the catastrophe which is coming at the end of our century as the goal of the progress of our era, and yet we must get used to facing it. For twenty years past every resource of science has been exhausted in the invention of engines of destruction, and soon a few charges of cannon will suffice to annihilate a whole army. No longer a few thousands of poor devils, who were paid a price for their blood, are kept under arms, but whole nations are under arms to cut each other's throats. They are robbed of their time now (by compulsory service) that they may be robbed of their lives later. To prepare them for the work of massacre, their hatred is kindled by persuading them that they are hated. And peaceable men let themselves be played on thus and go and fall on one another with the ferocity of wild beasts; furious troops of peaceful citizens taking up arms at an empty word of command, for some ridiculous question of frontiers or colonial trade interests—Heaven only knows what.... They will go like sheep to the slaughter, knowing all the while where they are going, knowing that they are leaving their wives, knowing that their children will want for food, full of misgivings, yet intoxicated by the fine-sounding lies that are dinned into their ears. *They will march without revolt, passive, resigned—though the numbers and the strength are theirs, and they might, if they knew how to co-operate together, establish the reign of good sense and fraternity*, instead of the barbarous trickery of diplomacy. They will march to battle so deluded, so duped, that they will believe slaughter to be a duty, and will ask the benediction of God on their lust for blood. They will march to battle trampling underfoot the harvests they have sown, burning the towns they have built—with songs of triumph, festive music, and cries of jubilation. And their sons will raise statues to those who have done most in their slaughter.

"The destiny of a whole generation depends on the hour in which some ill-fated politician may give the signal that will be followed. We know that the best of us will be cut down and our work will be destroyed in embryo. *We know it and tremble with rage, but we can do nothing.* We are held fast in the toils of officialdom and red tape, and too rude a shock would be needed to set us free. We are enslaved by the laws we set up for our protection, which have become our oppression. *We are but the tools of that autocratic abstraction the state, which enslaves each individual in the name of the will of all, who would all, taken individually, desire exactly the opposite of what they will be made to do.*

"And if it were only a generation that must be sacrificed! But there are graver interests at stake.

"The paid politicians, the ambitious statesmen, who exploit the evil passions of the populace, and the imbeciles who are deluded by fine-sounding phrases, have so embittered national feuds that the existence of a whole race will be at stake in the war of the morrow. One of the elements that constitute the modern world is threatened, the conquered people will be wiped out of existence, and whichever it may be, we shall see a moral force annihilated, as if there were too many forces to work for good—we shall have a new Europe formed on foundations so unjust, so brutal, so sanguinary, stained with so monstrous a crime, that it cannot but be worse than the Europe of to-day—more iniquitous, more barbarous, more violent.

"Thus one feels crushed under the weight of an immense discouragement. We are struggling in a *cul de sac* with muskets aimed at us from the housetops. Our labor is like that of sailors executing their last task as the ship begins to sink. Our pleasures are those of the condemned victim, who is offered his choice of dainties a quarter of an hour before his execution. Thought is paralyzed by anguish, and the most it is capable of is to calculate—interpreting the vague phrases of ministers, spelling out the sense of the speeches of sovereigns, and ruminating on the words attributed to diplomatists reported on the uncertain authority of the newspapers—whether it is to be to-morrow or the day after, this year or the next, that we are to be murdered.

So that one might seek in vain in history an epoch more insecure, more crushed under the weight of suffering."

Here it is pointed out that the force is in the hands of those who work their own destruction, in the hands of the individual men who make up the masses; it is pointed out that the source of the evil is the government. It would seem evident that the contradiction between life and conscience had reached the limit beyond which it cannot go, and after reaching this limit some solution of it must be found.

But the author does not think so. He sees in this the tragedy of human life, and after depicting all the horror of the position he concludes that human life must be spent in the midst of this horror.

So much for the attitude to war of those who regard it as something tragic and fated by destiny.

The third category consists of men who have lost all conscience and, consequently, all common sense and feeling of humanity.

To this category belongs Moltke, whose opinion has been quoted above by Maupassant, and the majority of military men, who have been educated in this cruel superstition, live by it, and consequently are often in all simplicity convinced that war is not only an inevitable, but even a necessary and beneficial thing. This is also the view of some civilians, so-called educated and cultivated people.

Here is what the celebrated academician Camille Doucet writes in reply to the editor of the *Revue des Revues*, where several letters on war were published together:

"DEAR SIR: When you ask the least warlike of academicians whether he is a partisan of war, his answer is known beforehand.

"Alas! sir, you yourself speak of the pacific ideal inspiring your generous compatriots as a dream.

"During my life I have heard a great many good people protest against this frightful custom of international butchery, which all admit and deplore; but how is it to be remedied?

"Often, too, there have been attempts to suppress dueling; one would fancy that seemed an easy task: but not at all! All that has been done hitherto with that noble object has never been and never will be of use.

"All the congresses of both hemispheres may vote against war, and against dueling too, but above all arbitrations, conventions, and legislations there will always be the *personal honor of individual men*, which has always demanded dueling, and *the interests of nations*, which will always demand war.

"I wish none the less from the depths of my heart that the Congress of Universal Peace may succeed at last in its very honorable and difficult enterprise.

"I am, dear sir, etc.,

"CAMILLE DOUCET."

The upshot of this is that personal honor requires men to fight, and the interests of nations require them to ruin and exterminate each other. As for the efforts to abolish war, they call for nothing but a smile.

The opinion of another well-known academician, Jules Claretie, is of the same kind.

"DEAR SIR [he writes]: For a man of sense there can be but one opinion on the subject of peace and war.

"Humanity is created to live, to live free, to perfect and ameliorate its fate by peaceful labor. The general harmony preached by the Universal Peace Congress is but a dream perhaps, but at least it is the fairest of all dreams. Man is always looking toward the Promised Land, and there the harvests are to ripen with no fear of their being torn up by shells or crushed by cannon wheels.... But! Ah! but—since philosophers and philanthropists are not the controlling powers, it is well for our soldiers to guard our frontier and homes, and their arms, skillfully used, are perhaps the surest guarantee of the peace we all love.

"Peace is a gift only granted to the strong and the resolute.

"I am, dear sir, etc.,

"Jules Claretie."

The upshot of this letter is that there is no harm in talking about what no one intends or feels obliged to do. But when it comes to practice, we must fight.

And here now is the view lately expressed by the most popular novelist in Europe, Émile Zola:

"I regard war as a fatal necessity, which appears inevitable for us from its close connection with human nature and the whole constitution of the world. I should wish that war could be put off for the longest possible time. Nevertheless, the moment will come when we shall be forced to go to war. I am considering it at this moment from the standpoint of universal humanity, and making no reference to our misunderstanding with Germany—a most trivial incident in the history of mankind. I say that war is necessary and beneficial, since it seems one of the conditions of existence for humanity. War confronts us everywhere, not only war between different races and peoples, but war too, in private and family life. It seems one of the principal elements of progress, and every step in advance that humanity has taken hitherto has been attended by bloodshed.

"Men have talked, and still talk, of disarmament, while disarmament is something impossible, to which, even if it were possible, we ought not to consent. I am convinced that a general disarmament throughout the world would involve something like a moral decadence, which would show itself in general feebleness, and would hinder the progressive advancement of humanity. A warlike nation has always been strong and flourishing. The art of war has led to the development of all the other arts. History bears witness to it. So in Athens and in Rome, commerce, manufactures, and literature never attained so high a point of development as when those cities were masters of the whole world by force of arms. To take an example from times nearer our own, we may recall the age of Louis XIV. The wars of the Grand Monarque were not only no hindrance to the progress of the arts and sciences, but even, on the contrary, seem to have promoted and favored their development."

So war is a beneficial thing!

But the best expression of this attitude is the view of the most gifted of the writers of this school, the academician de Vogüé. This is what he writes in an article on the Military Section of the Exhibition of 1889:

"On the Esplanade des Invalides, among the exotic and colonial encampments, a building in a more severe style overawes the picturesque bazaar; all these fragments of the globe have come to gather round the Palace of War, and in turn our guests mount guard submissively before the mother building, but for whom they would not be here. Fine subject for the antithesis of rhetoric, of humanitarians who could not fail to whimper over this juxtaposition, and to say that '*ceci tuera cela*,' that the union of the nations through science and labor will overcome the instinct of war. Let us leave them to cherish the chimera of a golden age, which would soon become, if it could be realized, an age of mud. All history teaches us that the one is created for the other, that blood is needed to hasten and cement the union of the nations. Natural science has ratified in our day the mysterious law revealed to Joseph de Maistre by the intuition of his genius and by meditation on fundamental truths; he saw the world redeeming itself from hereditary degenerations by sacrifice; science shows it advancing to perfection through struggle and violent selection; there is the statement of the same law in both, expressed in different formulas. The statement is disagreeable, no doubt; but the laws of the world are not made for our pleasure, they are made for our progress. Let us enter this inevitable, necessary palace of war; we shall be able to observe there how the most tenacious of our instincts, without losing any of its vigor, is transformed and adapted to the varying exigencies of historical epochs."

M. de Vogüé finds the necessity for war, according to his views, well expressed by the two great writers, Joseph de Maistre and

Darwin, whose statements he likes so much that he quotes them again.

"DEAR SIR [he writes to the editor of the *Revue des Revues*]: You ask me my view as to the possible success of the Universal Congress of Peace. I hold with Darwin that violent struggle is a law of nature which overrules all other laws; I hold with Joseph de Maistre that it is a divine law; two different ways of describing the same thing. If by some impossible chance a fraction of human society—all the civilized West, let us suppose—were to succeed in suspending the action of this law, some races of stronger instincts would undertake the task of putting it into action against us: those races would vindicate nature's reasoning against human reason; they would be successful, because the certainty of peace—I do not say *peace*, I say *the certainty of peace*—would, in half a century, engender a corruption and a decadence more destructive for mankind than the worst of wars. I believe that we must do with war—the criminal law of humanity—as with all our criminal laws, that is, soften them, put them in force as rarely as possible; use every effort to make their application unnecessary. But all the experience of history teaches us that they cannot be altogether suppressed so long as two men are left on earth, with bread, money, and a woman between them.

"I should be very happy if the Congress would prove me in error. But I doubt if it can prove history, nature, and God in error also.

"I am, dear sir, etc.,

"E. M. DE VOGÜÉ."

This amounts to saying that history, human nature, and God show us that so long as there are two men, and bread, money and a woman—there will be war. That is to say that no progress will lead men to rise above the savage conception of life, which regards no participation of bread, money (money is good in this context) and woman possible without fighting.

They are strange people, these men who assemble in Congresses, and make speeches to show us how to catch birds by putting salt on their tails, though they must know it is impossible to do it.

And amazing are they too, who, like Maupassant, Rod, and many others, see clearly all the horror of war, all the inconsistency of men not doing what is needful, right, and beneficial for them to do; who lament over the tragedy of life, and do not see that the whole tragedy is at an end directly men, ceasing to take account of any unnecessary considerations, refuse to do what is hateful and disastrous to them. They are amazing people truly, but those who, like De Vogüé and others, who, professing the doctrine of evolution, regard war as not only inevitable, but beneficial, and therefore desirable—they are terrible, hideous, in their moral perversion. The others, at least, say that they hate evil, and love good, but these openly declare that good and evil do not exist.

All discussion of the possibility of re-establishing peace instead of everlasting war—is the pernicious sentimentality of phrasemongers. There is a law of evolution by which it follows that I must live and act in an evil way; what is to be done? I am an educated man, I know the law of evolution, and therefore I will act in an evil way. "*Entrons au palais de la guerre.*" There is the law of evolution, and therefore there is neither good nor evil, and one must live for the sake of one's personal existence, leaving the rest to the action of the law of evolution. This is the last word of refined culture, and with it, of that overshadowing of conscience which has come upon the educated classes of our times. The desire of the educated classes to support the ideas they prefer, and the order of existence based on them, has attained its furthest limits. They lie, and delude themselves, and one another, with the subtlest forms of deception, simply to obscure, to deaden conscience.

Instead of transforming their life into harmony with their conscience, they try by every means to stifle its voice. But it is in darkness that the light begins to shine, and so the light is rising upon our epoch.

CHAPTER VII: SIGNIFICANCE OF COMPULSORY SERVICE

Universal Compulsory Service is not a Political Accident, but the Furthest Limit of the Contradiction Inherent in the Social Conception of Life—Origin of Authority in Society—Basis of Authority is Physical Violence—To be Able to Perform its Acts of Violence Authority Needs a Special Organization—The Army—Authority, that is, Violence, is the Principle which is Destroying the Social Conception of Life—Attitude of Authority to the Masses, that is, Attitude of Government to Working Oppressed Classes—Governments Try to Foster in Working Classes the Idea that State Force is Necessary to Defend Them from External Enemies—But the Army is Principally Needed to Preserve Government from its own Subjects—The Working Classes—Speech of M. de Caprivi—All Privileges of Ruling Classes Based on Violence—The Increase of Armies up to Point of Universal Service—Universal Compulsory Service Destroys all the Advantages of Social Life, which Government is Intended to Preserve—Compulsory Service is the Furthest Limit of Submission, since in Name of the State it Requires Sacrifice of all that can be Precious to a Man—Is Government Necessary?—The Sacrifices Demanded by Government in Compulsory Service have No Longer any Reasonable Basis—And there is More Advantage to be Gained by not Submitting to the Demands of the State than by Submitting to Them.

Educated people of the upper classes are trying to stifle the ever-growing sense of the necessity of transforming the existing social order. But life, which goes on growing more complex, and developing in the same direction, and increases the inconsistencies and the sufferings of men, brings them to the limit beyond which they cannot go. This furthest limit of inconsistency is universal compulsory military service.

It is usually supposed that universal military service and the increased armaments connected with it, as well as the resulting increase of taxes and national debts, are a passing phenomenon, produced by the particular political situation of Europe, and that it may be removed by certain political combinations without any modification of the inner order of life.

This is absolutely incorrect. Universal military service is only the internal inconsistency inherent in the social conception of life, carried to its furthest limits, and becoming evident when a certain stage of material development is reached.

The social conception of life, we have seen, consists in the transfer of the aim of life from the individual to groups and their maintenance—to the tribe, family, race, or state.

In the social conception of life it is supposed that since the aim of life is found in groups of individuals, individuals will voluntarily sacrifice their own interests for the interests of the group. And so it has been, and still is, in fact, in certain groups, the distinction being that they are the most primitive forms of association in the family or tribe or race, or even in the patriarchal state. Through tradition handed down by education and supported by religious sentiment, individuals without compulsion merged their interests in the interest of the group and sacrificed their own good for the general welfare.

But the more complex and the larger societies become, and especially the more often conquest becomes the cause of the amalgamation of people into a state, the more often individuals strive to attain their own aims at the public expense, and the more often it becomes necessary to restrain these insubordinate individuals by recourse to authority, that is, to violence. The champions of the social conception of life usually try to connect the idea of authority, that is, of violence, with the idea of moral influence, but this connection is quite impossible.

The effect of moral influence on a man is to change his desires and to bend them in the direction of the duty required of him. The man who is controlled by moral influence acts in accordance with his own desires. Authority, in the sense in which the word is ordinarily understood, is a means of forcing a man to act in opposition to his desires. The man who submits to authority does not do as he chooses but as he is obliged by authority. Nothing can oblige a man to do what he does not choose except physical force, or the threat of it, that is—deprivation of freedom, blows, imprisonment, or threats—easily carried out—of such punishments. This is what authority consists of and always has consisted of.

In spite of the unceasing efforts of those who happen to be in authority to conceal this and attribute some other significance to it, authority has always meant for man the cord, the chain with which he is bound and fettered, or the knout with which he is to be flogged, or the ax with which he is to have hands, ears, nose, or head cut off, or at the very least, the threat of these terrors. So it was under Nero and Ghenghis Khan, and so it is to-day, even under the most liberal government in the Republics of the United States or of France. If men submit to authority, it is only because they are liable to these punishments in case of non-submission. All state obligations, payment of taxes, fulfillment of state duties, and submission to punishments, exile, fines, etc., to which people appear to submit voluntarily, are always based on bodily violence or the threat of it.

The basis of authority is bodily violence. The possibility of applying bodily violence to people is provided above all by an organization of armed men, trained to act in unison in submission to one will. These bands of armed men, submissive to a single will, are what constitute the army. The army has always been and still is the basis of power. Power is always in the hands of those who control the army, and all men in power—from the Roman Cæsars to the Russian and German Emperors—take more interest in their army than in anything, and court popularity in the army, knowing that if that is on their side their power is secure.

The formation and aggrandizement of the army, indispensable to the maintenance of authority, is what has introduced into the social conception of life the principle that is destroying it.

The object of authority and the justification for its existence lie in the restraint of those who aim at attaining their personal interests to the detriment of the interests of society.

But however power has been gained, those who possess it are in no way different from other men, and therefore no more disposed than others to subordinate their own interests to those of the society. On the contrary, having the power to do so at their disposal, they are more disposed than others to subordinate the public interests to their own. Whatever means men have devised for preventing those in authority from over-riding public interests for their own benefit, or for intrusting power only to the most faultless people, they have not so far succeeded in either of those aims.

All the methods of appointing authorities that have been tried, divine right, and election, and heredity, and balloting, and assemblies and parliaments and senate—have all proved ineffectual. Everyone knows that not one of these methods attains the aim either of intrusting power only to the incorruptible, or of preventing power from being abused. Everyone knows on the contrary that men in authority—be they emperors, ministers, governors, or police officers—are always, simply from the possession of power, more liable to be demoralized, that is, to subordinate public interests to their personal aims than those who have not the power to do so. Indeed, it could not be otherwise.

The state conception of life could be justified only so long as all men voluntarily sacrificed their personal interests to the public welfare. But so soon as there were individuals who would not voluntarily sacrifice their own interests, and authority, that is, violence, was needed to restrain them, then the disintegrating principle of the coercion of one set of people by another set entered into the social conception of the organization based on it.

For the authority of one set of men over another to attain its object of restraining those who override public interests for their personal ends, power ought only to be put into the hands of the impeccable, as it is supposed to be among the Chinese, and as it was supposed to be in the Middle Ages, and is even now supposed to be by those who believe in the consecration by anointing. Only under those conditions could the social organization be justified.

But since this is not the case, and on the contrary men in power are always far from being saints, through the very fact of their possession of power, the social organization based on power has no justification.

Even if there was once a time when, owing to the low standard of morals, and the disposition of men to violence, the existence of an authority to restrain such violence was an advantage, because the violence of government was less than the violence of individuals, one cannot but see that this advantage could not be lasting. As the disposition of individuals to violence diminished, and as the habits of the people became more civilized, and as power grew more demoralized through lack of restraint, this advantage disappeared.

The whole history of the last two thousand years is nothing but the history of this gradual change of relation between the moral development of the masses on the one hand and the demoralization of governments on the other.

This, put simply, is how it has come to pass.

Men lived in families, tribes, and races, at feud with one another, plundering, outraging, and killing one another. These violent hostilities were carried on on a large and on a small scale: man against man, family against family, tribe against tribe, race against race, and people against people. The larger and stronger groups conquered and absorbed the weaker, and the larger and stronger they became, the more internal feuds disappeared and the more the continuity of the group seemed assured.

The members of a family or tribe, united into one community, are less hostile among themselves, and families and tribes do not die like one man, but have a continuity of existence. Between the members of one state, subject to a single authority, the strife between individuals seems still less and the life of the state seems even more secure.

Their association into larger and larger groups was not the result of the conscious recognition of the benefits of such associations, as it is said to be in the story of the Varyagi. It was produced, on one hand, by the natural growth of population, and, on the other, by struggle and conquest.

After conquest the power of the emperor puts an end to internal dissensions, and so the state conception of life justifies itself. But this justification is never more than temporary. Internal dissensions disappear only in proportion to the degree of oppression exerted by the authority over the dissentient individuals. The violence of internal feud crushed by authority reappears in authority itself, which falls into the hands of men who, like the rest, are frequently or always ready to sacrifice the public welfare to their personal interest, with the difference that their subjects cannot resist them, and thus they are exposed to all the demoralizing influence of authority. And thus the evil of violence, when it passes into the hands of authority, is always growing and growing, and in time becomes greater than the evil it is supposed to suppress, while, at the same time, the tendency to violence in the members of the society becomes weaker and weaker, so that the violence of authority is less and less needed.

Government authority, even if it does suppress private violence, always introduces into the life of men fresh forms of violence, which tend to become greater and greater in proportion to the duration and strength of the government.

So that though the violence of power is less noticeable in government than when it is employed by members of society against one another, because it finds expression in submission, and not in strife, it nevertheless exists, and often to a greater degree than in former days.

And it could not be otherwise, since, apart from the demoralizing influence of power, the policy or even the unconscious tendency of those in power will always be to reduce their subjects to the extreme of weakness, for the weaker the oppressed, the less effort need be made to keep him in subjection.

And therefore the oppression of the oppressed always goes on growing up to the furthest limit, beyond which it cannot go without killing the goose with the golden eggs. And if the goose lays no more eggs, like the American Indians, negroes, and Fijians, then it is killed in spite of the sincere protests of philanthropists.

The most convincing example of this is to be found in the condition of the working classes of our epoch, who are in reality no better than the slaves of ancient times subdued by conquest.

In spite of the pretended efforts of the higher classes to ameliorate the position of the workers, all the working classes of the present day are kept down by the inflexible iron law by which they only get just what is barely necessary, so that they are forced to work without ceasing while still retaining strength enough to labor for their employers, who are really those who have conquered and enslaved them.

So it has always been. In ratio to the duration and increasing strength of authority its advantages for its subjects disappear and its disadvantages increase.

And this has been so, independently of the forms of government under which nations have lived. The only difference is that under a despotic form of government the authority is concentrated in a small number of oppressors and violence takes a cruder form; under constitutional monarchies and republics as in France and America authority is divided among a great number of oppressors and the forms assumed by violence is less crude, but its effect of making the disadvantages of authority greater than its advantages, and of enfeebling the oppressed to the furthest extreme to which they can be reduced with advantage to the oppressors, remains always the same.

Such has been and still is the condition of all the oppressed, but hitherto they have not recognized the fact. In the majority of instances they have believed in all simplicity that governments exist for their benefit; that they would be lost without a government; that the very idea of living without a government is a blasphemy which one hardly dare put into words; that this is the—for some reason terrible—doctrine of anarchism, with which a mental picture of all kinds of horrors is associated.

People have believed, as though it were something fully proved, and so needing no proof, that since all nations have hitherto developed in the form of states, that form of organization is an indispensable condition of the development of humanity.

And in that way it has lasted for hundreds and thousands of years, and governments—those who happened to be in power—have tried it, and are now trying more zealously than ever to keep their subjects in this error.

So it was under the Roman emperors and so it is now. In spite of the fact that the sense of the uselessness and even injurious effects of state violence is more and more penetrating into men's consciousness, things might have gone on in the same way forever if governments were not under the necessity of constantly increasing their armies in order to maintain their power.

It is generally supposed that governments strengthen their forces only to defend the state from other states, in oblivion of the fact that armies are necessary, before all things, for the defense of governments from their own oppressed and enslaved subjects.

That has always been necessary, and has become more and more necessary with the increased diffusion of education among the masses, with the improved communication between people of the same and of different nationalities. It has become particularly indispensable now in the face of communism, socialism, anarchism, and the labor movement generally. Governments feel that it is so, and strengthen the force of their disciplined armies.

In the German Reichstag not long ago, in reply to a question why funds were needed for raising the salaries of the under-officers, the German Chancellor openly declared that trustworthy under-officers were necessary to contend against socialism. Caprivi only said aloud what every statesman knows and assiduously conceals from the people. The reason to which he gave expression is essentially the same as that which made the French kings and the popes engage Swiss and Scotch guards, and makes the Russian authorities of to-day so carefully distribute the recruits, so that the regiments from the frontiers are stationed in central districts, and the regiments from the center are stationed on the frontiers. The meaning of Caprivi's speech, put into plain language, is that funds are needed, not to resist foreign foes, but to *buy under-officers* to be ready to act against the enslaved toiling masses.

Caprivi incautiously gave utterance to what everyone knows perfectly well, or at least feels vaguely if he does not recognize it, that is, that the existing order of life is as it is, not, as would be natural and right, because the people wish it to be so, but because it is so maintained by state violence, by the army with its *bought under-officers* and generals.

If the laborer has no land, if he cannot use the natural right of every man to derive subsistence for himself and his family out of the land, that is not because the people wish it to be so, but because a certain set of men, the land-owners, have appropriated the right of giving or refusing admittance to the land to the laborers. And this abnormal order of things is maintained by the army. If the immense wealth produced by the labor of the working classes is not regarded as the property of all, but as the property of a few exceptional persons; if labor is taxed by authority and the taxes spent by a few on what they think fit; if strikes on the part of laborers are repressed, while on the part of capitalists they are encouraged; if certain persons appropriate the right of choosing the form of the education, religious and secular, of children, and certain persons monopolize the right of making the laws all must obey, and so dispose of the lives and properties of other people—all this is not done because the people wish it and because it is what is natural and right, but because the government and ruling classes wish this to be so for their own benefit, and insist on its being so even by physical violence.

Everyone, if he does not recognize this now, will know that it is so at the first attempt at insubordination or at a revolution of the existing order.

Armies, then, are needed by governments and by the ruling classes above all to support the present order, which, far from being the result of the people's needs, is often in direct antagonism to them, and is only beneficial to the government and ruling classes.

To keep their subjects in oppression and to be able to enjoy the fruits of their labor the government must have armed forces.

But there is not only one government. There are other governments, exploiting their subjects by violence in the same way, and always ready to pounce down on any other government and carry off the fruits of the toil of its enslaved subjects. And so every government needs an army also to protect its booty from its neighbor brigands. Every government is thus involuntarily reduced to the necessity of emulating one another in the increase of their armies. This increase is contagious, as Montesquieu pointed out 150 years ago.

Every increase in the army of one state, with the aim of self-defense against its subjects, becomes a source of danger for neighboring states and calls for a similar increase in their armies.

The armed forces have reached their present number of millions not only through the menace of danger from neighboring states, but principally through the necessity of subduing every effort at revolt on the part of the subjects.

Both causes, mutually dependent, contribute to the same result at once; troops are required against internal forces and also to keep up a position with other states. One is the result of the other. The despotism of a government always increases with the strength of the army and its external successes, and the aggressiveness of a government increases with its internal despotism.

The rivalry of the European states in constantly increasing their forces has reduced them to the necessity of having recourse to universal military service, since by that means the greatest possible number of soldiers is obtained at the least possible expense. Germany first hit on this device. And directly one state adopted it the others were obliged to do the same. And by this means all citizens are under arms to support the iniquities practiced upon them; all citizens have become their own oppressors.

Universal military service was an inevitable logical necessity, to which we were bound to come. But it is also the last expression of the inconsistency inherent in the social conception of life, when violence is needed to maintain it. This inconsistency has become obvious in universal military service. In fact, the whole significance of the social conception of life consists in man's recognition of the barbarity of strife between individuals, and the transitoriness of personal life itself, and the transference of the aim of life to groups of persons. But with universal military service it comes to pass that men, after making every sacrifice to get rid of the cruelty of strife and the insecurity of existence, are called upon to face all the perils they had meant to avoid. And in addition to this the state, for whose sake individuals renounced their personal advantages, is exposed again to the same risks of insecurity and lack of permanence as the individual himself was in previous times.

Governments were to give men freedom from the cruelty of personal strife and security in the permanence of the state order of existence. But instead of doing that they expose the individuals to the same necessity of strife, substituting strife with individuals of other states for strife with neighbors. And the danger of destruction for the individual, and the state too, they leave just as it was.

Universal military service may be compared to the efforts of a man to prop up his falling house who so surrounds it and fills it with props and buttresses and planks and scaffolding that he manages to keep the house standing only by making it impossible to live in it.

In the same way universal military service destroys all the benefits of the social order of life which it is employed to maintain.

The advantages of social organization are security of property and labor and associated action for the improvement of existence—universal military service destroys all this.

The taxes raised from the people for war preparations absorb the greater part of the produce of labor which the army ought to defend.

The withdrawing of all men from the ordinary course of life destroys the possibility of labor itself. The danger of war, ever ready to break out, renders all reforms of social life vain and fruitless.

In former days if a man were told that if he did not acknowledge the authority of the state, he would be exposed to attack from enemies domestic and foreign, that he would have to resist them alone, and would be liable to be killed, and that therefore it would be to his advantage to put up with some hardships to secure himself from these calamities, he might well believe it, seeing that the sacrifices he made to the state were only partial and gave him the hope of a tranquil existence in a permanent state. But now, when the sacrifices have been increased tenfold and the promised advantages are disappearing, it would be a natural reflection that submission to authority is absolutely useless.

But the fatal significance of universal military service, as the manifestation of the contradiction inherent in the social conception of life, is not only apparent in that. The greatest manifestation of this contradiction consists in the fact that every citizen in being made a soldier becomes a prop of the government organization, and shares the responsibility of everything the government does, even though he may not admit its legitimacy.

Governments assert that armies are needed above all for external defense, but that is not true. They are needed principally against their subjects, and every man, under universal military service, becomes an accomplice in all the acts of violence of the government against the citizens without any choice of his own.

To convince oneself of this one need only remember what things are done in every state, in the name of order and the public welfare, of which the execution always falls to the army. All civil outbreaks for dynastic or other party reasons, all the executions that follow on such disturbances, all repression of insurrections, and military intervention to break up meetings and to suppress strikes, all forced extortion of taxes, all the iniquitous distributions of land, all the restrictions on labor—are either carried out directly by the military or by the police with the army at their back. Anyone who serves his time in the army shares the responsibility of all these things, about which he is, in some cases, dubious, while very often they are directly opposed to his conscience. People are unwilling to be turned out of the land they have cultivated for generations, or they are unwilling to disperse when the government authority orders them, or they are unwilling to pay the taxes required of them, or to recognize laws as binding on them when they have had no hand in making them, or to be deprived of their nationality—and I, in the fulfillment of my military duty, must go and shoot them for it. How can I help asking myself when I take part in such punishments, whether they are just, and whether I ought to assist in carrying them out?

Universal service is the extreme limit of violence necessary for the support of the whole state organization, and it is the extreme limit to which submission on the part of the subjects can go. It is the keystone of the whole edifice, and its fall will bring it all down.

The time has come when the ever-growing abuse of power by governments and their struggles with one another has led to their demanding such material and even moral sacrifices from their subjects that everyone is forced to reflect and ask himself, "Can I make these sacrifices? And for the sake of what am I making them? I am expected for the sake of the state to make these sacrifices, to renounce everything that can be precious to man— peace, family, security, and human dignity." What is this state, for whose sake such terrible sacrifices have to be made? And why is it so indispensably necessary? "The state," they tell us, "is indispensably needed, in the first place, because without it we should not be protected against the attacks of evil-disposed persons; and secondly, except for the state we should be savages and should have neither religion, culture, education, nor commerce, nor means of communication, nor other social institutions; and thirdly, without the state to defend us we should be liable to be conquered and enslaved by neighboring peoples."

"Except for the state," they say, "we should be exposed to the attacks of evil-disposed persons in our own country."

But who are these evil-disposed persons in our midst from whose attacks we are preserved by the state and its army? Even if, three or four centuries ago, when men prided themselves on their warlike prowess, when killing men was considered an heroic achievement, there were such persons; we know very well that there are no such persons now, that we do not nowadays carry or use firearms, but everyone professes humane principles and feels sympathy for his fellows, and wants nothing more than we all do—that is, to be left in peace to enjoy his existence undisturbed. So that nowadays there are no special malefactors from whom the state could defend us. If by these evil-disposed persons is meant the men who are punished as criminals, we know very well that they are not a different kind of being like wild beasts among sheep, but are men just like ourselves, and no more naturally inclined to crimes than those against whom they commit them. We know now that threats and punishments cannot diminish their number; that that can only be done by change of environment and moral influence. So that the justification of state violence on the ground of the protection it gives us from evil-disposed persons, even if it had some foundation three or four centuries ago, has none whatever now. At present one would rather say on the contrary that the action of the state with its cruel methods of punishment, behind the general moral standard of the age, such as prisons, galleys, gibbets, and guillotines, tends rather to brutalize the people than to civilize them, and consequently rather to increase than diminish the number of malefactors.

"Except for the state," they tell us, "we should not have any religion, education, culture, means of communication, and so on. Without the state men would not have been able to form the social institutions needed for doing anything." This argument too was well founded only some centuries ago.

LEO TOLSTOY

If there was a time when people were so disunited, when they had so little means of communication and interchange of ideas, that they could not co-operate and agree together in any common action in commerce, economics, or education without the state as a center, this want of common action exists no longer. The great extension of means of communication and interchange of ideas has made men completely able to dispense with state aid in forming societies, associations, corporations, and congresses for scientific, economic, and political objects. Indeed government is more often an obstacle than an assistance in attaining these aims.

From the end of last century there has hardly been a single progressive movement of humanity which has not been retarded by the government. So it has been with abolition of corporal punishment, of trial by torture, and of slavery, as well as with the establishment of the liberty of the press and the right of public meeting. In our day governments not only fail to encourage, but directly hinder every movement by which people try to work out new forms of life for themselves. Every attempt at the solution of the problems of labor, land, politics, and religion meets with direct opposition on the part of government.

"Without governments nations would be enslaved by their neighbors." It is scarcely necessary to refute this last argument. It carries its refutation on the face of it. The government, they tell us, with its army, is necessary to defend us from neighboring states who might enslave us. But we know this is what all governments say of one another, and yet we know that all the European nations profess the same principles of liberty and fraternity, and therefore stand in no need of protection against one another. And if defense against barbarous nations is meant, one-thousandth part of the troops now under arms would be amply sufficient for that purpose. We see that it is really the very opposite of what we have been told. The power of the state, far from being a security against the attacks of our neighbors, exposes us, on the contrary, to much greater danger of such attacks. So that every man who is led, through his compulsory service in the army, to reflect on the value of the state for whose sake he is expected to be ready to sacrifice his peace, security, and life, cannot fail to perceive that there is no kind of justification in modern times for such a sacrifice.

And it is not only from the theoretical standpoint that every man must see that the sacrifices demanded by the state have no justification. Even looking at it practically, weighing, that is to say, all the burdens laid on him by the state, no man can fail to see that for him personally to comply with state demands and serve in the army, would, in the majority of cases, be more disadvantageous than to refuse to do so.

If the majority of men choose to submit rather than to refuse, it is not the result of sober balancing of advantages and disadvantages, but because they are induced by a kind of hypnotizing process practiced upon them. In submitting they simply yield to the suggestions given them as orders, without thought or effort of will. To resist would need independent thought and effort of which every man is not capable. Even apart from the moral significance of compliance or non-compliance, considering material advantage only, non-compliance will be more advantageous in general.

Whoever I may be, whether I belong to the well-to-do class of the oppressors, or the working class of the oppressed, in either case the disadvantages of non-compliance are less and its advantages greater than those of compliance. If I belong to the minority of oppressors the disadvantages of non-compliance will consist in my being brought to judgment for refusing to perform my duties to the state, and if I am lucky, being acquitted or, as is done in the case of the Mennonites in Russia, being set to work out my military service at some civil occupation for the state; while if I am unlucky, I may be condemned to exile or imprisonment for two or three years (I judge by the cases that have occurred in Russia), possibly to even longer imprisonment, or possibly to death, though the probability of that latter is very remote.

So much for the disadvantages of non-compliance. The disadvantages of compliance will be as follows: if I am lucky I shall not be sent to murder my fellow-creatures, and shall not be exposed to great danger of being maimed and killed, but shall only be enrolled into military slavery. I shall be dressed up like a clown, I shall be at the beck and call of every man of a higher grade than my own from corporal to field-marshal, shall be put through any bodily contortions at their pleasure, and after being kept from one to five years I shall have for ten years afterward to be in readiness to undertake all of it again at any minute. If I am unlucky I may, in addition, be sent to war, where I shall be forced to kill men of foreign nations who have done me no harm, where I may be maimed or killed, or sent to certain destruction as in the case of the garrison of Sevastopol, and other cases in every war, or what would be most terrible of all, I may be sent against my own compatriots and have to kill my own brothers for some dynastic or other state interests which have absolutely nothing to do with me. So much for the comparative disadvantages.

The comparative advantages of compliance and non-compliance are as follows:

For the man who submits, the advantages will be that, after exposing himself to all the humiliation and performing all the barbarities required of him, he may, if he escapes being killed, get a decoration of red or gold tinsel to stick on his clown's dress; he may, if he is very lucky, be put in command of hundreds of thousands of others as brutalized as himself; be called a field-marshal, and get a lot of money.

The advantages of the man who refuses to obey will consist in preserving his dignity as a man, gaining the approbation of good men, and above all knowing that he is doing the work of God, and so undoubtedly doing good to his fellow-men.

So much for the advantages and disadvantages of both lines of conduct for a man of the wealthy classes, an oppressor. For a man of the poor working class the advantages and disadvantages will be the same, but with a great increase of disadvantages. The disadvantages for the poor man who submits will be aggravated by the fact that he will by taking part in it, and, as it were, assenting to it strengthen the state of subjection in which he is held himself.

But no considerations as to how far the state is useful or beneficial to the men who help to support it by serving in the army, nor of the advantages or disadvantages for the individual of compliance or non-compliance with state demands, will decide the question of the continued existence or the abolition of government. This question will be finally decided beyond appeal by the religious consciousness or conscience of every man who is forced, whether he will or no, through universal conscription, to face the question whether the state is to continue to exist or not.

CHAPTER VIII: DOCTRINE OF NON-RESISTANCE TO EVIL BY FORCE MUST INEVITABLY BE ACCEPTED BY MEN OF THE PRESENT DAY

Christianity is Not a System of Rules, but a New Conception of Life, and therefore it was Not Obligatory and was Not Accepted in its True Significance by All, but only by a Few—Christianity is, Moreover, Prophetic of the Destruction of the Pagan Life, and therefore of Necessity of the Acceptance of the Christian Doctrines—Non-resistance of Evil by Force is One Aspect of the Christian Doctrine, which must Inevitably in Our Times be Accepted by Men—Two Methods of Deciding Every Quarrel—First Method is to Find a Universal Definition of Evil, which All Must Accept, and to Resist this Evil by Force—Second Method is the Christian One of Complete Non-resistance by Force—Though the Failure of the First Method was Recognized since the Early Days of Christianity, it was Still Proposed, and only as Mankind has Progressed it has Become More and More Evident that there Cannot be any Universal Definition of Evil—This is Recognized by All at the Present Day, and if Force is Still Used to Resist Evil, it is Not Because it is Now Regarded as Right, but Because People Don't Know How to Avoid It—The Difficulty of Avoiding It is the Result of the Subtle and Complex Character of the Government Use of Force—Force is Used in Four Ways:

Intimidation, Bribery, Hypnotism, and Coercion by Force of Arms—State Violence Can Never be Suppressed by the Forcible Overthrow of the Government—Men are Led by the Sufferings of the Pagan Mode of Life to the Necessity of Accepting Christ's Teaching with its Doctrine of Non-resistance by Force—The Consciousness of its Truth which is Diffused Throughout Our Society, Will also Bring About its Acceptance—This Consciousness is in Complete Contradiction with Our Life—This is Specially Obvious in Compulsory Military Service, but Through Habit and the Application of the Four Methods of Violence by the State, Men do not See this Inconsistency of Christianity with Life of a Soldier—They do Not even See It, though the Authorities Themselves Show all the Immorality of a Soldier's Duties with Perfect Clearness—The Call to Military Service is the Supreme Test for Every Man, when the Choice is Offered Him, between Adopting the Christian Doctrine of Non-resistance, or Slavishly Submitting to the Existing State Organization—Men Usually Renounce All They Hold Sacred, and Submit to the Demands of Government, Seeming to See No Other Course Open to Them—For Men of the Pagan Conception of Life there is No Other Course Open, and Never Will Be, in Spite of the Growing Horrors of War—Society, Made Up of Such Men, Must Perish, and No Social Reorganization Can Save It—Pagan Life Has Reached Its Extreme Limit, and Will Annihilate Itself.

It is often said that if Christianity is a truth, it ought to have been accepted by everyone directly it appeared, and ought to have transformed men's lives for the better. But this is like saying that if the seed were ripe it ought at once to bring forth stalk, flower, and fruit.

The Christian religion is not a legal system which, being imposed by violence, may transform men's lives. Christianity is a new and higher conception of life. A new conception of life cannot be imposed on men; it can only be freely assimilated. And it can only be freely assimilated in two ways: one spiritual and internal, the other experimental and external.

Some people—a minority—by a kind of prophetic instinct divine the truth of the doctrine, surrender themselves to it and adopt it. Others—the majority—only through a long course of mistakes, experiments, and suffering are brought to recognize the truth of the doctrine and the necessity of adopting it.

And by this experimental external method the majority of Christian men have now been brought to this necessity of assimilating the doctrine. One sometimes wonders what necessitated the corruption of Christianity which is now the greatest obstacle to its acceptance in its true significance.

If Christianity had been presented to men in its true, uncorrupted form, it would not have been accepted by the majority, who would have been as untouched by it as the nations of Asia are now. The peoples who accepted it in its corrupt form were subjected to its slow but certain influence, and by a long course of errors and experiments and their resultant sufferings have now been brought to the necessity of assimilating it in its true significance.

The corruption of Christianity and its acceptance in its corrupt form by the majority of men was as necessary as it is that the seed should remain hidden for a certain time in the earth in order to germinate.

Christianity is at once a doctrine of truth and a prophecy. Eighteen centuries ago Christianity revealed to men the truth in which they ought to live, and at the same time foretold what human life would become if men would not live by it but continued to live by their previous principles, and what it would become if they accepted the Christian doctrine and carried it out in their lives.

Laying down in the Sermon on the Mount the principles by which to guide men's lives, Christ said: "Whosoever heareth these sayings of mine, and doeth them, I will liken him unto a wise man, who built his house upon a rock; and the rain descended, and the floods came, and the winds blew, and beat upon that house; and it fell not, for it was founded upon a rock. And everyone that heareth these sayings, and doeth them not, shall be likened unto a foolish man, who built his house upon the sand; and the rain descended, and the floods came, and the winds blew, and beat upon that house; and it fell: and great was the fall of it" (Matt. vii. 24-27).

And now after eighteen centuries the prophecy has been fulfilled. Not having followed Christ's teaching generally and its application to social life in non-resistance to evil, men have been brought in spite of themselves to the inevitable destruction foretold by Christ for those who do not fulfill his teaching.

People often think the question of non-resistance to evil by force is a theoretical one, which can be neglected. Yet this question is presented by life itself to all men, and calls for some answer from every thinking man. Ever since Christianity has been outwardly professed, this question is for men in their social life like the question which presents itself to a traveler when the road on which he has been journeying divides into two branches. He must go on and he cannot say: I will not think about it, but will go on just as I did before. There was one road, now there are two, and he must make his choice.

In the same way since Christ's teaching has been known by men they cannot say: I will live as before and will not decide the question of resistance or non-resistance to evil by force. At every new struggle that arises one must inevitably decide; am I, or am I not, to resist by force what I regard as evil.

The question of resistance or non-resistance to evil arose when the first conflict between men took place, since every conflict is nothing else than resistance by force to what each of the combatants regards as evil. But before Christ, men did not see that resistance by force to what each regards as evil, simply because one thinks evil what the other thinks good, is only one of the methods of settling the dispute, and that there is another method, that of not resisting evil by force at all.

Before Christ's teaching, it seemed to men that the one only means of settling a dispute was by resistance to evil by force. And they acted accordingly, each of the combatants trying to convince himself and others that what each respectively regards as evil, is actually, absolutely evil.

And to do this from the earliest time men have devised definitions of evil and tried to make them binding on everyone. And such definitions of evil sometimes took the form of laws, supposed to have been received by supernatural means, sometimes of the commands of rulers or assemblies to whom infallibility was attributed. Men resorted to violence against others, and convinced themselves and others that they were directing their violence against evil recognized as such by all.

This means was employed from the earliest times, especially by those who had gained possession of authority, and for a long while its irrationality was not detected.

But the longer men lived in the world and the more complex their relations became, the more evident it was that to resist by force what each regarded as evil was irrational, that conflict was in no way lessened thereby, and that no human definitions can succeed in making what some regard as evil be accepted as such by others.

Already at the time Christianity arose, it was evident to a great number of people in the Roman Empire where it arose, that what was regarded as evil by Nero and Caligula could not be regarded as evil by others. Even at that time men had begun to understand that human laws, though given out for divine laws, were compiled by men, and cannot be infallible, whatever the external majesty with which they are invested, and that erring men are not rendered infallible by assembling together and calling themselves a senate or any other name. Even at that time this was felt and understood by many. And it was then that Christ preached his doctrine, which consisted not only of the prohibition of resistance to evil by force, but gave a new conception of life and a means of putting an end to conflict between all men, not by making it the duty of one section only of mankind to submit without conflict to what is prescribed to them by certain authorities, but by making it the duty of all—and consequently of those in authority—not to resort to force against anyone in any circumstances.

This doctrine was accepted at the time by only a very small number of disciples. The majority of men, especially all who were in power, even after the nominal acceptance of Christianity, continued to maintain for themselves the principle of resistance by force to what they regarded as evil. So it was under the Roman and Byzantine emperors, and so it continued to be later.

The insufficiency of the principle of the authoritative definition of evil and resistance to it by force, evident as it was in the early ages of Christianity, becomes still more obvious through the division of the Roman Empire into many states of equal authority, through their hostilities and the internal conflicts that broke out within them.

But men were not ready to accept the solution given by Christ, and the old definitions of evil, which ought to be resisted, continued to be laid down by means of making laws binding on all and enforced by forcible means. The authority who decided what ought to be regarded as evil and resisted by force was at one time the Pope, at another an emperor or king, an elective assembly or a whole nation. But both within and without the state there were always men to be found who did not accept as binding on themselves the laws given out as the decrees of a god, or made by men invested with a sacred character, or the institutions supposed to represent the will of the nation; and there were men who thought good what the existing authorities regarded as bad, and who struggled against the authorities with the same violence as was employed against them.

The men invested with religious authority regarded as evil what the men and institutions invested with temporal authority regarded as good and *vice versa*, and the struggle grew more and more intense. And the longer men used violence as the means of settling their disputes, the more obvious it became that it was an unsuitable means, since there could be no external authority able to define evil recognized by all.

Things went on like this for eighteen centuries, and at last reached the present position in which it is absolutely obvious that there is, and can be, no external definition of evil binding upon all. Men have come to the point of ceasing to believe in the possibility or even desirability of finding and establishing such a general definition. It has come to men in power ceasing to attempt to prove that what they regard as evil is evil, and simply declaring that they regard as evil what they don't like, while their subjects no longer obey them because they accept the definition of evil laid down by them, but simply obey because they cannot help themselves. It was not because it was a good thing, necessary and beneficial to men, and the contrary course would have been an evil, but simply because it was the will of those in power that Nice was incorporated into France, and Lorraine into Germany, and Bohemia into Austria, and that Poland was divided, and Ireland and India ruled by the English government, and that the Chinese are attacked and the Africans slaughtered, and the Chinese prevented from immigrating by the Americans, and the Jews persecuted by the Russians, and that landowners appropriate lands they do not cultivate and capitalists enjoy the fruits of the labor of others. It has come to the present state of things; one set of men commit acts of violence no longer on the pretext of resistance to evil, but simply for their profit or their caprice, and another set submit to violence, not because they suppose, as was supposed in former times, that this violence was practised upon them for the sake of securing them from evil, but simply because they cannot avoid it.

If the Roman, or the man of mediæval times, or the average Russian of fifty years ago, as I remember him, was convinced without a shade of doubt that the violence of authority was indispensable to preserve him from evil; that taxes, dues, serfage, prisons, scourging, knouts, executions, the army and war were what ought to be—we know now that one can seldom find a man who believes that all these means of violence preserve anyone from any evil whatever, and indeed does not clearly perceive that most of these acts of violence to which he is exposed, and in which he has some share, are in themselves a great and useless evil.

There is no one to-day who does not see the uselessness and injustice of collecting taxes from the toiling masses to enrich idle officials; or the senselessness of inflicting punishments on weak or depraved persons in the shape of transportation from one place to another, or of imprisonment in a fortress where, living in security and indolence, they only become weaker and more depraved; or the worse than uselessness and injustice, the positive insanity and barbarity of preparations for war and of wars, causing devastation and ruin, and having no kind of justification. Yet these forms of violence continue and are supported by the very people who see their uselessness, injustice, and cruelty, and suffer from them. If fifty years ago the idle rich man and the illiterate laborer were both alike convinced that their state of everlasting holiday for one and everlasting toil for the other was ordained by God himself, we know very well that nowadays, thanks to the growth of population and the diffusion of books and education, it would be hard to find in Europe or even in Russia, either among rich or poor, a man to whom in one shape or another a doubt as to the justice of this state of things had never presented itself. The rich know that they are guilty in the very fact of being rich, and try to expiate their guilt by sacrifices to art and science, as of old they expiated their sins by sacrifices to the Church. And even the larger half of the working people openly declare that the existing order is iniquitous and bound to be destroyed or reformed. One set of religious people of whom there are millions in Russia, the so-called sectaries, consider the existing social order as unjust and to be destroyed on the ground of the Gospel teaching taken in its true sense. Others regard it as unjust on the ground of the socialistic, communistic, or anarchistic theories, which are springing up in the lower strata of the working people. Violence no longer rests on the belief in its utility, but only on the fact of its having existed so long, and being organized by the ruling classes who profit by it, so that those who are under their authority cannot extricate themselves from it. The governments of our day—all of them, the most despotic and the liberal alike—have become what Herzen so well called "Ghenghis Khan with the telegraph;" that is to say, organizations of violence based on no principle but the grossest tyranny, and at the same time taking advantage of all the means invented by science for the peaceful collective social activity of free and equal men, used by them to enslave and oppress their fellows.

Governments and the ruling classes no longer take their stand on right or even on the semblance of justice, but on a skillful organization carried to such a point of perfection by the aid of science that everyone is caught in the circle of violence and has no chance of escaping from it. This circle is made up now of four methods of working upon men, joined together like the links of a chain ring.

The first and oldest method is intimidation. This consists in representing the existing state organization—whatever it may be, free republic or the most savage despotism—as something sacred and immutable, and therefore following any efforts to alter it with the cruellest punishments. This method is in use now—as it has been from olden times—wherever there is a government: in Russia against the so-called Nihilists, in America against Anarchists, in France against Imperialists, Legitimists, Communards, and Anarchists.

Railways, telegraphs, telephones, photographs, and the great perfection of the means of getting rid of men for years, without killing them, by solitary confinement, where, hidden from the world, they perish and are forgotten, and the many other modern inventions employed by government, give such power that when once authority has come into certain hands, the police, open and secret, the administration and prosecutors, jailers and executioners of all kinds, do their work so zealously that there is no chance of overturning the government, however cruel and senseless it may be.

The second method is corruption. It consists in plundering the industrious working people of their wealth by means of taxes and distributing it in satisfying the greed of officials, who are bound in return to support and keep up the oppression of the people. These bought officials, from the highest ministers to the poorest copying clerks, make up an unbroken network of men bound together by the same interest—that of living at the expense of the people. They become the richer the more submissively they carry out the will of the government; and at all times and places, sticking at nothing, in all departments support by word and deed the violence of government, on which their own prosperity also rests.

The third method is what I can only describe as hypnotizing the people. This consists in checking the moral development of men, and by various suggestions keeping them back in the ideal of life, outgrown by mankind at large, on which the power of government rests. This hypnotizing process is organized at the present in the most complex manner, and starting from their earliest childhood, continues to act on men till the day of their death. It begins in their earliest years in the compulsory schools, created for this purpose, in which the children have instilled into them the ideas of life of their ancestors, which are in direct antagonism with the conscience of the modern world. In countries where there is a state religion, they teach the children the senseless blasphemies of the Church catechisms, together with the duty of obedience to their superiors. In republican states they teach them the savage superstition of patriotism and the same pretended obedience to the governing authorities.

The process is kept up during later years by the encouragement of religious and patriotic superstitions.

The religious superstition is encouraged by establishing, with money taken from the people, temples, processions, memorials, and festivals, which, aided by painting, architecture, music, and incense, intoxicate the people, and above all by the support of the clergy, whose duty consists in brutalizing the people and keeping them in a permanent state of stupefaction by their teaching, the solemnity of their services, their sermons, and their interference in private life—at births, deaths, and marriages. The patriotic superstition is encouraged by the creation, with money taken from the people, of national fêtes, spectacles, monuments, and festivals to dispose men to attach importance to their own nation, and to the aggrandizement of the state and its rulers, and to feel antagonism and even hatred for other nations. With these objects under despotic governments there is direct prohibition against printing and disseminating books to enlighten the people, and everyone who might rouse the people from their lethargy is exiled or imprisoned. Moreover, under every government without exception everything is kept back that might emancipate and everything encouraged that tends to corrupt the people, such as literary works tending to keep them in the barbarism of religious and patriotic superstition, all kinds of sensual amusements, spectacles, circuses, theaters, and even the physical means of inducing stupefaction, as tobacco and alcohol, which form the principal source of revenue of states. Even prostitution is encouraged, and not only recognized, but even organized by the government in the majority of states. So much for the third method.

The fourth method consists in selecting from all the men who have been stupefied and enslaved by the three former methods a certain number, exposing them to special and intensified means of stupefaction and brutalization, and so making them into a passive instrument for carrying out all the cruelties and brutalities needed by the government. This result is attained by taking them at the youthful age when men have not had time to form clear and definite principles of morals, and removing them from all natural and human conditions of life, home, family and kindred, and useful labor. They are shut up together in barracks, dressed in special clothes, and worked upon by cries, drums, music, and shining objects to go through certain daily actions invented for this purpose, and by this means are brought into an hypnotic condition in which they cease to be men and become mere senseless machines, submissive to the hypnotizer. These physically vigorous young men (in these days of universal conscription, all young men), hypnotized, armed with murderous weapons, always obedient to the governing authorities and ready for any act of violence at their command, constitute the fourth and principal method of enslaving men.

By this method the circle of violence is completed.

Intimidation, corruption, and hypnotizing bring people into a condition in which they are willing to be soldiers; the soldiers give the power of punishing and plundering them (and purchasing officials with the spoils), and hypnotizing them and converting them in time into these same soldiers again.

The circle is complete, and there is no chance of breaking through it by force.

Some persons maintain that freedom from violence, or at least a great diminution of it, may be gained by the oppressed forcibly overturning the oppressive government and replacing it by a new one under which such violence and oppression will be unnecessary, but they deceive themselves and others, and their efforts do not better the position of the oppressed, but only make it worse. Their conduct only tends to increase the despotism of government. Their efforts only afford a plausible pretext for government to strengthen their power.

Even if we admit that under a combination of circumstances specially unfavorable for the government, as in France in 1870, any government might be forcibly overturned and the power transferred to other hands, the new authority would rarely be less oppressive than the old one; on the contrary, always having to defend itself against its dispossessed and exasperated enemies, it would be more despotic and cruel, as has always been the rule in all revolutions.

While socialists and communists regard the individualistic, capitalistic organization of society as an evil, and the anarchists regard as an evil all government whatever, there are royalists, conservatives, and capitalists who consider any socialistic or communistic organization or anarchy as an evil, and all these parties have no means other than violence to bring men to agreement. Whichever of these parties were successful in bringing their schemes to pass, must resort to support its authority to all the existing methods of violence, and even invent new ones.

The oppressed would be another set of people, and coercion would take some new form; but the violence and oppression would be unchanged or even more cruel, since hatred would be intensified by the struggle, and new forms of oppression would have been devised. So it has always been after all revolutions and all attempts at revolution, all conspiracies, and all violent changes of government. Every conflict only strengthens the means of oppression in the hands of those who happen at a given moment to be in power.

The position of our Christian society, and especially the ideals most current in it, prove this in a strikingly convincing way.

There remains now only one sphere of human life not encroached upon by government authority—that is the domestic, economic sphere, the sphere of private life and labor. And even this is now—thanks to the efforts of communists and socialists—being gradually encroached upon by government, so that labor and recreation, dwellings, dress, and food will gradually, if the hopes of the reformers are successful, be prescribed and regulated by government.

The slow progress of eighteen centuries has brought the Christian nations again to the necessity of deciding the question they have evaded—the question of the acceptance or non-acceptance of Christ's teaching, and the question following upon it in social life of resistance or non-resistance to evil by force. But there is this difference, that whereas formerly men could accept or refuse to accept the solution given by Christ, now that solution cannot be avoided, since it alone can save men from the slavery in which they are caught like a net.

But it is not only the misery of the position which makes this inevitable.

While the pagan organization has been proved more and more false, the truth of the Christian religion has been growing more and more evident.

Not in vain have the best men of Christian humanity, who apprehended the truth by spiritual intuition, for eighteen centuries testified to it in spite of every menace, every privation, and every suffering. By their martyrdom they passed on the truth to the masses, and impressed it on their hearts.

Christianity has penetrated into the consciousness of humanity, not only negatively by the demonstration of the impossibility of continuing in the pagan life, but also through its simplification, its increased clearness and freedom from the superstitions intermingled with it, and its diffusion through all classes of the population.

Eighteen centuries of Christianity have not passed without an effect even on those who accepted it only externally. These eighteen centuries have brought men so far that even while they continue to live the pagan life which is no longer consistent with the development of humanity, they not only see clearly all the wretchedness of their position, but in the depths of their souls they believe (they can only live through this belief) that the only salvation from this position is to be found in fulfilling the Christian doctrine in its true significance. As to the time and manner of salvation, opinions are divided according to the intellectual development and the prejudices of each society. But every man of the modern world recognizes that our salvation lies in fulfilling the law of Christ. Some believers in the supernatural character of Christianity hold that salvation will come when all men are brought to believe in Christ, whose second coming is at hand. Other believers in supernatural Christianity hold that salvation will come through the Church, which will draw all men into its fold, train them in the Christian virtues, and transform their life. A third section, who do not admit the divinity of Christ, hold that the salvation of mankind will be brought about by slow and gradual progress, through which the pagan principles of our existence will be replaced by the principles of liberty, equality, and fraternity—that is, by Christian principles. A fourth section, who believe in the social revolution, hold that salvation will come when through a violent revolution men are forced into community of property, abolition of government, and collective instead of individual industry—that is to say, the realization of one side of the Christian doctrine. In one way or another all men of our day in their inner consciousness condemn the existing effete pagan order, and admit, often unconsciously and while regarding themselves as hostile to Christianity, that our salvation is only to be found in the application of the Christian doctrine, or parts of it, in its true significance to our daily life.

Christianity cannot, as its Founder said, be realized by the majority of men all at once; it must grow like a huge tree from a tiny seed. And so it has grown, and now has reached its full development, not yet in actual life, but in the conscience of men of to-day.

Now not only the minority, who have always comprehended Christianity by spiritual intuition, but all the vast majority who seem so far from it in their social existence recognize its true significance.

Look at individual men in their private life, listen to their standards of conduct in their judgment of one another; hear not only their public utterances, but the counsels given by parents and guardians to the young in their charge; and you will see that, far as their social life based on violence may be from realizing Christian truth, in their private life what is considered good by all without exception is nothing but the Christian virtues; what is considered as bad is nothing but the antichristian vices. Those who consecrate their lives self-sacrificingly to the service of humanity are regarded as the best men. The selfish, who make use of the misfortunes of others for their own advantage, are regarded as the worst of men.

Though some non-Christian ideals, such as strength, courage, and wealth, are still worshiped by a few who have not been penetrated by the Christian spirit, these ideals are out of date and are abandoned, if not by all, at least by all those regarded as the best people. There are no ideals, other than the Christian ideals, which are accepted by all and regarded as binding on all.

The position of our Christian humanity, if you look at it from the outside with all its cruelty and degradation of men, is terrible indeed. But if one looks at it within, in its inner consciousness, the spectacle it presents is absolutely different.

All the evil of our life seems to exist only because it has been so for so long; those who do the evil have not had time yet to learn how to act otherwise, though they do not want to act as they do.

All the evil seems to exist through some cause independent of the conscience of men.

Strange and contradictory as it seems, all men of the present day hate the very social order they are themselves supporting.

LEO TOLSTOY

I think it is Max Müller who describes the amazement of an Indian convert to Christianity, who after absorbing the essence of the Christian doctrine came to Europe and saw the actual life of Christians. He could not recover from his astonishment at the complete contrast between the reality and what he had expected to find among Christian nations. If we feel no astonishment at the contrast between our convictions and our conduct, that is because the influences, tending to obscure the contrast, produce an effect upon us too. We need only look at our life from the point of view of that Indian, who understood Christianity in its true significance, without any compromises or concessions, we need but look at the savage brutalities of which our life is full, to be appalled at the contradictions in the midst of which we live often without observing them.

We need only recall the preparations for war, the mitrailleuses, the silver-gilt bullets, the torpedoes, and—the Red Cross; the solitary prison cells, the experiments of execution by electricity—and the care of the hygienic welfare of prisoners; the philanthropy of the rich, and their life, which produces the poor they are benefiting.

And these inconsistencies are not, as it might seem, because men pretend to be Christians while they are really pagans, but because of something lacking in men, or some kind of force hindering them from being what they already feel themselves to be in their consciousness, and what they genuinely wish to be. Men of the present day do not merely pretend to hate oppression, inequality, class distinction, and every kind of cruelty to animals as well as human beings. They genuinely detest all this, but they do not know how to put a stop to it, or perhaps cannot decide to give up what preserves it all, and seems to them necessary.

Indeed, ask every man separately whether he thinks it laudable and worthy of a man of this age to hold a position from which he receives a salary disproportionate to his work; to take from the people—often in poverty—taxes to be spent on constructing cannon, torpedoes, and other instruments of butchery, so as to make war on people with whom we wish to be at peace, and who feel the same wish in regard to us; or to receive a salary for devoting one's whole life to constructing these instruments of butchery, or to preparing oneself and others for the work of murder. And ask him whether it is laudable and worthy of a man, and suitable for a Christian, to employ himself, for a salary, in seizing wretched, misguided, often illiterate and drunken, creatures because they appropriate the property of others—on a much smaller scale than we do—or because they kill men in a different fashion from that in which we undertake to do it—and shutting them in prison for it, ill treating them and killing them; and whether it is laudable and worthy of a man and a Christian to preach for a salary to the people not Christianity, but superstitions which one knows to be stupid and pernicious; and whether it is laudable and worthy of a man to rob his neighbor for his gratification of what he wants to satisfy his simplest needs, as the great landowners do; or to force him to exhausting labor beyond his strength to augment one's wealth, as do factory owners and manufacturers; or to profit by the poverty of men to increase one's gains, as merchants do. And everyone taken separately, especially if one's remarks are directed at someone else, not himself, will answer, No! And yet the very man who sees all the baseness of those actions, of his own free will, uncoerced by anyone, often even for no pecuniary profit, but only from childish vanity, for a china cross, a scrap of ribbon, a bit of fringe he is allowed to wear, will enter military service, become a magistrate or justice of the peace, commissioner, archbishop, or beadle, though in fulfilling these offices he must commit acts the baseness and shamefulness of which he cannot fail to recognize.

I know that many of these men will confidently try to prove that they have reasons for regarding their position as legitimate and quite indispensable. They will say in their defense that authority is given by God, that the functions of the state are indispensable for the welfare of humanity, that property is not opposed to Christianity, that the rich young man was only commanded to sell all he had and give to the poor if he wished to be perfect, that the existing distribution of property and our commercial system must always remain as they are, and are to the advantage of all, and so on. But, however much they try to deceive themselves and others, they all know that what they are doing is opposed to all the beliefs which they profess, and in the depths of their souls, when they are left alone with their conscience, they are ashamed and miserable at the recollection of it, especially if the baseness of their action has been pointed out to them. A man of the present day, whether he believes in the divinity of Christ or not, cannot fail to see that to assist in the capacity of tzar, minister, governor, or commissioner in taking from a poor family its last cow for taxes to be spent on cannons, or on the pay and pensions of idle officials, who live in luxury and are worse than useless; or in putting into prison some man we have ourselves corrupted, and throwing his family on the streets; or in plundering and butchering in war; or in inculcating savage and idolatrous superstitions in the place of the law of Christ; or in impounding the cow found on one's land, though it belongs to a man who has no land; or to cheat the workman in a factory, by imposing fines for accidentally spoiled articles; or making a poor man pay double the value for anything simply because he is in the direst poverty;—not a man of the present day can fail to know that all these actions are base and disgraceful, and that they need not do them. They all know it. They know that what they are doing is wrong, and would not do it for anything in the world if they had the power of resisting the forces which shut their eyes to the criminality of their actions and impel them to commit them.

In nothing is the pitch of inconsistency modern life has attained to so evident as in universal conscription, which is the last resource and the final expression of violence.

Indeed, it is only because this state of universal armament has been brought about gradually and imperceptibly, and because governments have exerted, in maintaining it, every resource of intimidation, corruption, brutalization, and violence, that we do not see its flagrant inconsistency with the Christian ideas and sentiments by which the modern world is permeated.

We are so accustomed to the inconsistency that we do not see all the hideous folly and immorality of men voluntarily choosing the profession of butchery as though it were an honorable career, of poor wretches submitting to conscription, or in countries where compulsory service has not been introduced, of people voluntarily abandoning a life of industry to recruit soldiers and train them as murderers. We know that all of these men are either Christians, or profess humane and liberal principles, and they know that they thus become partly responsible—through universal conscription, personally responsible—for the most insane, aimless, and brutal murders. And yet they all do it.

More than that, in Germany, where compulsory service first originated, Caprivi has given expression to what had been hitherto so assiduously concealed—that is, that the men that the soldiers will have to kill are not foreigners alone, but their own countrymen, the very working people from whom they themselves are taken. And this admission has not opened people's eyes, has not horrified them! They still go like sheep to the slaughter, and submit to everything required of them.

And that is not all: the Emperor of Germany has lately shown still more clearly the duties of the army, by thanking and rewarding a soldier for killing a defenseless citizen who made his approach incautiously. By rewarding an action always regarded as base and cowardly even by men on the lowest level of morality, William has shown that a soldier's chief duty—the one most appreciated by the authorities—is that of executioner; and not a professional executioner who kills only condemned criminals, but one ready to butcher any innocent man at the word of command.

And even that is not all. In 1892, the same William, the *enfant terrible* of state authority, who says plainly what other people only think, in addressing some soldiers gave public utterance to the following speech, which was reported next day in thousands of newspapers: "Conscripts!" he said, "you have sworn fidelity to *me* before the altar and the minister of God! You are still too young to understand all the importance of what has been said here; let your care before all things be to obey the orders and instructions given you. You have sworn fidelity *to me*, lads of my guard; *that means that you are now my soldiers*, that *you have given yourselves to me body and soul*. For you there is now but one enemy, *my* enemy. *In these days of socialistic sedition it may come to pass that I command you to fire on your own kindred, your brothers, even your own fathers and mothers—which God forbid!*—even then you are bound to obey my orders without hesitation."

This man expresses what all sensible rulers think, but studiously conceal. He says openly that the soldiers are in *his* service, at *his* disposal, and must be ready for *his* advantage to murder even their brothers and fathers.

In the most brutal words he frankly exposes all the horrors and criminality for which men prepare themselves in entering the army, and the depths of ignominy to which they fall in promising obedience. Like a bold hypnotizer, he tests the degree of insensibility of the hypnotized subject. He touches his skin with a red-hot iron; the skin smokes and scorches, but the sleeper does not awake.

This miserable man, imbecile and drunk with power, outrages in this utterance everything that can be sacred for a man of the modern world. And yet all the Christians, liberals, and cultivated people, far from resenting this outrage, did not even observe it.

The last, the most extreme test is put before men in its coarsest form. And they do not seem even to notice that it is a test, that there is any choice about it. They seem to think there is no course open but slavish submission. One would have thought these insane words, which outrage everything a man of the present day holds sacred, must rouse indignation. But there has been nothing of the kind.

All the young men through the whole of Europe are exposed year after year to this test, and with very few exceptions they renounce all that a man can hold sacred, all express their readiness to kill their brothers, even their fathers, at the bidding of the first crazy creature dressed up in a livery with red and gold trimming, and only wait to be told where and when they are to kill. And they actually are ready.

Every savage has something he holds sacred, something for which he is ready to suffer, something he will not consent to do. But what is it that is sacred to the civilized man of to-day? They say to him: "You must become my slave, and this slavery may force you to kill even your own father;" and he, often very well educated, trained in all the sciences at the university, quietly puts his head under the yoke. They dress him up in a clown's costume, and order him to cut capers, turn and twist and bow, and kill—he does it all submissively. And when they let him go, he seems to shake himself and go back to his former life, and he continues to discourse upon the dignity of man, liberty, equality, and fraternity as before.

"Yes, but what is one to do?" people often ask in genuine perplexity. "If everyone would stand out it would be something, but by myself, I shall only suffer without doing any good to anyone."

And that is true. A man with the social conception of life cannot resist. The aim of his life is his personal welfare. It is better for his personal welfare for him to submit, and he submits.

Whatever they do to him, however they torture or humiliate him, he will submit, for, alone, he can do nothing; he has no principle for the sake of which he could resist violence alone. And those who control them never allow them to unite together. It is often said that the invention of terrible weapons of destruction will put an end to war. That is an error. As the means of extermination are improved, the means of reducing men who hold the state conception of life to submission can be improved to correspond. They may slaughter them by thousands, by millions, they may tear them to pieces, still they will march to war like senseless cattle. Some will want beating to make them move, others will be proud to go if they are allowed to wear a scrap of ribbon or gold lace.

And of this mass of men so brutalized as to be ready to promise to kill their own parents, the social reformers—conservatives, liberals, socialists, and anarchists—propose to form a rational and moral society. What sort of moral and rational society can be formed out of such elements? With warped and rotten planks you cannot build a house, however you put them together. And to form a rational moral society of such men is just as impossible a task. They can be formed into nothing but a herd of cattle, driven by the shouts and whips of the herdsmen. As indeed they are.

So, then, we have on one side men calling themselves Christians, and professing the principles of liberty, equality, and fraternity, and along with that ready, in the name of liberty, to submit to the most slavish degradation; in the name of equality, to accept the crudest, most senseless division of men by externals merely into higher and lower classes, allies and enemies; and, in the name of fraternity, ready to murder their brothers.

The contradiction between life and conscience and the misery resulting from it have reached the extreme limit and can go no further. The state organization of life based on violence, the aim of which was the security of personal, family, and social welfare, has come to the point of renouncing the very objects for which it was founded—it has reduced men to absolute renunciation and loss of the welfare it was to secure.

The first half of the prophecy has been fulfilled in the generation of men who have not accepted Christ's teaching. Their descendants have been brought now to the absolute necessity of putting the truth of the second half to the test of experience.

CHAPTER IX: THE ACCEPTANCE OF THE CHRISTIAN CONCEPTION OF LIFE WILL EMANCIPATE MEN FROM THE MISERIES OF OUR PAGAN LIFE.

The External Life of Christian Peoples Remains Pagan Though they are Penetrated by Christian Consciousness—The Way Out of this Contradiction is by the Acceptance of the Christian Theory of Life—Only Through Christianity is Every Man Free, and Emancipated of All Human Authority—This Emancipation can be Effected by no Change in External Conditions of Life, but

Only by a Change in the Conception of Life—The Christian Ideal of Life Requires Renunciation of all Violence, and in Emancipating the Man who Accepts it, Emancipates the Whole World from All External Authorities—The Way Out of the Present Apparently Hopeless Position is for Every Man who is Capable of Assimilating the Christian Conception of Life, to Accept it and Live in Accordance with it—But Men Consider this Way too Slow, and Look for Deliverance Through Changes in Material Conditions of Life Aided by Government—That Will Lead to No Improvement, as it is simply Increasing the Evil under which Men are Suffering—A Striking Instance of this is the Submission to Compulsory Military Service, which it would be More Advantageous for Every Man to Refuse than to Submit to—The Emancipation of Men Can Only be Brought About by each Individual Emancipating Himself, and the Examples of this Self-emancipation which are already Appearing Threaten the Destruction of Governmental Authority—Refusal to Comply with the Unchristian Demands of Government Undermines the Authority of the State and Emancipates Men—And therefore Cases of such Non-compliance are Regarded with more Dread by State Authorities than any Conspiracies or Acts of Violence— Examples of Non-compliance in Russia, in Regard to Oath of Allegiance, Payment of Taxes, Passports, Police Duties, and Military Service—Examples of such Non-compliance in other States—Governments do not Know how to Treat Men who Refuse to Comply with their Demands on Christian Grounds— Such People, without Striking a Blow, Undermine the very Basis of Government from Within—To Punish them is Equivalent to Openly Renouncing Christianity, and Assisting in Diffusing the Very Principle by which these Men Justify their Non-compliance—So Governments are in a Helpless Position—Men who Maintain the Uselessness of Personal Independence, only Retard the Dissolution of the Present State Organization Based on Force.

The position of the Christian peoples in our days has remained just as cruel as it was in the times of paganism. In many respects, especially in the oppression of the masses, it has become even more cruel than it was in the days of paganism.

But between the condition of men in ancient times and their condition in our days there is just the difference that we see in the world of vegetation between the last days of autumn and the first days of spring. In the autumn the external lifelessness in nature corresponds with its inward condition of death, while in the spring the external lifelessness is in sharp contrast with the internal state of reviving and passing into new forms of life.

In the same way the similarity between the ancient heathen life and the life of to-day is merely external: the inward condition of men in the times of heathenism was absolutely different from their inward condition at the present time.

Then the outward condition of cruelty and of slavery was in complete harmony with the inner conscience of men, and every step in advance intensified this harmony; now the outward condition of cruelty and of slavery is completely contradictory to the Christian consciousness of men, and every step in advance only intensifies this contradiction.

Humanity is passing through seemingly unnecessary, fruitless agonies. It is passing through something like the throes of birth. Everything is ready for the new life, but still the new life does not come.

There seems no way out of the position. And there would be none, except that a man (and thereby all men) is gifted with the power of forming a different, higher theory of life, which at once frees him from all the bonds by which he seems indissolubly fettered.

And such a theory is the Christian view of life made known to mankind eighteen hundred years ago.

A man need only make this theory of life his own, for the fetters which seemed so indissolubly forged upon him to drop off of themselves, and for him to feel himself absolutely free, just as a bird would feel itself free in a fenced-in place directly it took to its wings.

People talk about the liberty of the Christian Church, about giving or not giving freedom to Christians. Underlying all these ideas and expressions there is some strange misconception. Freedom cannot be bestowed on or taken from a Christian or Christians. Freedom is an inalienable possession of the Christian.

If we talk of bestowing freedom on Christians or withholding it from them, we are obviously talking not of real Christians but of people who only call themselves Christians. A Christian cannot fail to be free, because the attainment of the aim he sets before himself cannot be prevented or even hindered by anyone or anything.

Let a man only understand his life as Christianity teaches him to understand it, let him understand, that is, that his life belongs not to him—not to his own individuality, nor to his family, nor to the state—but to him who has sent him into the world, and let him once understand that he must therefore fulfill not the law of his own individuality, nor his family, nor of the state, but the infinite law of him from whom he has come; and he will not only feel himself absolutely free from every human power, but will even cease to regard such power as at all able to hamper anyone.

Let a man but realize that the aim of his life is the fulfillment of God's law, and that law will replace all other laws for him, and he will give it his sole allegiance, so that by that very allegiance every human law will lose all binding and controlling power in his eyes.

The Christian is independent of every human authority by the fact that he regards the divine law of love, implanted in the soul of every man, and brought before his consciousness by Christ, as the sole guide of his life and other men's also.

The Christian may be subjected to external violence, he may be deprived of bodily freedom, he may be in bondage to his passions (he who commits sin is the slave of sin), but he cannot be in bondage in the sense of being forced by any danger or by any threat of external harm to perform an act which is against his conscience.

He cannot be compelled to do this, because the deprivations and sufferings which form such a powerful weapon against men of the state conception of life, have not the least power to compel him.

Deprivations and sufferings take from them the happiness for which they live; but far from disturbing the happiness of the Christian, which consists in the consciousness of fulfilling the will of God, they may even intensify it, when they are inflicted on him for fulfilling his will.

And therefore the Christian, who is subject only to the inner divine law, not only cannot carry out the enactments of the external law, when they are not in agreement with the divine law of love which he acknowledges (as is usually the case with state obligations), he cannot even recognize the duty of obedience to anyone or anything whatever, he cannot recognize the duty of what is called allegiance.

For a Christian the oath of allegiance to any government whatever—the very act which is regarded as the foundation of the existence of a state—is a direct renunciation of Christianity. For the man who promises unconditional obedience in the future to laws, made or to be made, by that very promise is in the most positive manner renouncing Christianity, which means obeying in every circumstance of life only the divine law of love he recognizes within him.

Under the pagan conception of life it was possible to carry out the will of the temporal authorities, without infringing the law of God expressed in circumcisions, Sabbaths, fixed times of prayer, abstention from certain kinds of food, and so on. The one law was not opposed to the other. But that is just the distinction between the Christian religion and heathen religion. Christianity does not require of a man certain definite negative acts, but puts him in a new, different relation to men, from which may result the most diverse acts, which cannot be defined beforehand. And therefore the Christian not only cannot promise to obey the will of any other man, without knowing what will be required by that will; he not only cannot obey the changing laws of man, but he cannot even promise to do anything definite at a certain time, or to abstain from doing anything for a certain time. For he cannot know what at any time will be required of him by that Christian law of love, obedience to which constitutes the meaning of life for him. The Christian, in promising unconditional fulfillment of the laws of men in the future, would show plainly by that promise that the inner law of God does not constitute for him the sole law of his life.

For a Christian to promise obedience to men, or the laws of men, is just as though a workman bound to one employer should also promise to carry out every order that might be given him by outsiders. One cannot serve two masters.

The Christian is independent of human authority, because he acknowledges God's authority alone. His law, revealed by Christ, he recognizes in himself, and voluntarily obeys it.

And this independence is gained, not by means of strife, not by the destruction of existing forms of life, but only by a change in the interpretation of life. This independence results first from the Christian recognizing the law of love, revealed to him by his teacher, as perfectly sufficient for all human relations, and therefore he regards every use of force as unnecessary and unlawful; and secondly, from the fact that those deprivations and sufferings, or threats of deprivations and sufferings (which reduce the man of the social conception of life to the necessity of obeying) to the Christian from his different conception of life, present themselves merely as the inevitable conditions of existence. And these conditions, without striving against them by force, he patiently endures, like sickness, hunger, and every other hardship, but they cannot serve him as a guide for his actions. The only guide for the Christian's actions is to be found in the divine principle living within him, which cannot be checked or governed by anything.

The Christian acts according to the words of the prophecy applied to his teacher: "He shall not strive, nor cry; neither shall any man hear his voice in the streets. A bruised reed shall he not break, and smoking flax shall he not quench, till he send forth judgment unto victory." (Matt. xii. 19, 20.)

The Christian will not dispute with anyone, nor attack anyone, nor use violence against anyone. On the contrary, he will bear violence without opposing it. But by this very attitude to violence, he will not only himself be free, but will free the whole world from all external power.

"Ye shall know the truth, and the truth shall make you free." If there were any doubt of Christianity being the truth, the perfect liberty, that nothing can curtail, which a man experiences directly he makes the Christian theory of life his own, would be an unmistakable proof of its truth.

Men in their present condition are like a swarm of bees hanging in a cluster to a branch. The position of the bees on the branch is temporary, and must inevitably be changed. They must start off and find themselves a habitation. Each of the bees knows this, and desires to change her own and the others' position, but no one of them can do it till the rest of them do it. They cannot all start off at once, because one hangs on to another and hinders her from separating from the swarm, and therefore they all continue to hang there. It would seem that the bees could never escape from their position, just as it seems that worldly men, caught in the toils of the state conception of life, can never escape. And there would be no escape for the bees, if each of them were not a living, separate creature, endowed with wings of its own. Similarly there would be no escape for men, if each were not a living being endowed with the faculty of entering into the Christian conception of life.

If every bee who could fly, did not try to fly, the others, too, would never be stirred, and the swarm would never change its position. And if the man who has mastered the Christian conception of life would not, without waiting for other people, begin to live in accordance with this conception, mankind would never change its position. But only let one bee spread her wings, start off, and fly away, and after her another, and another, and the clinging, inert cluster would become a freely flying swarm of bees. Just in the same way, only let one man look at life as Christianity teaches him to look at it, and after him let another and another do the same, and the enchanted circle of existence in the state conception of life, from which there seemed no escape, will be broken through.

But men think that to set all men free by this means is too slow a process, that they must find some other means by which they could set all men free at once. It is just as though the bees who want to start and fly away should consider it too long a process to wait for all the swarm to start one by one; and should think they ought to find some means by which it would not be necessary for every separate bee to spread her wings and fly off, but by which the whole swarm could fly at once where it wanted to. But that is not possible; till a first, a second, a third, a hundredth bee spreads her wings and flies off of her own accord, the swarm will not fly off and will not begin its new life. Till every individual man makes the Christian conception of life his own, and begins to live in accord with it, there can be no solution of the problem of human life, and no establishment of a new form of life.

One of the most striking phenomena of our times is precisely this advocacy of slavery, which is promulgated among the masses, not by governments, in whom it is inevitable, but by men who, in advocating socialistic theories, regard themselves as the champions of freedom.

These people advance the opinion that the amelioration of life, the bringing of the facts of life into harmony with the conscience, will come, not as the result of the personal efforts of individual men, but of itself as the result of a certain possible reconstruction of society effected in some way or other. The idea is promulgated that men ought not to walk on their own legs where they want and ought to go, but that a kind of floor under their feet will be moved somehow, so that on it they can reach where they ought to go without moving their own legs. And, therefore, all their efforts ought to be directed, not to going so far as their strength allows in the direction they ought to go, but to standing still and constructing such a floor.

In the sphere of political economy a theory is propounded which amounts to saying that the worse things are the better they are; that the greater the accumulation of capital, and therefore the oppression of the workman, the nearer the day of emancipation, and, therefore, every personal effort on the part of a man to free himself from the oppression of capital is useless. In the sphere of government it is maintained that the greater the power of the government, which, according to this theory, ought to intervene in every department of private life in which it has not yet intervened, the better it will be, and that therefore we ought to invoke the interference of government in private life. In politics and international questions it is maintained that the improvement of the means of destruction, the multiplication of armaments, will lead to the necessity of making war by means of congresses, arbitration, and so on. And, marvelous to say, so great is the dullness of men, that they believe in these theories, in spite of the fact that the whole course of life, every step they take, shows how unworthy they are of belief.

The people are suffering from oppression, and to deliver them from this oppression they are advised to frame general measures for the improvement of their position, which measures are to be intrusted to the authorities, and themselves to continue to yield obedience to the authorities. And obviously all that results from this is only greater power in the hands of the authorities, and greater oppression resulting from it.

Not one of the errors of men carries them so far away from the aim toward which they are struggling as this very one. They do all kinds of different things for the attainment of their aim, but not the one simple obvious thing which is within reach of everyone. They devise the subtlest means for changing the position which is irksome to them, but not that simplest means, that everyone should refrain from doing what leads to that position.

I have been told a story of a gallant police officer, who came to a village where the peasants were in insurrection and the military had been called out, and he undertook to pacify the insurrection in the spirit of Nicholas I., by his personal influence alone. He ordered some loads of rods to be brought, and collecting all the peasants together into a barn, he went in with them, locking the door after him. To begin with, he so terrified the peasants by his loud threats that, reduced to submission by him, they set to work to flog one another at his command. And so they flogged one another until a simpleton was found who would not allow himself to be flogged, and shouted to his companions not to flog one another. Only then the flogging ceased, and the police officer made his escape. Well, this simpleton's advice would never be followed by men of the state conception of life, who continue to flog one another, and teach people that this very act of self-castigation is the last word of human wisdom.

Indeed, can one imagine a more striking instance of men flogging themselves than the submissiveness with which men of our times will perform the very duties required of them to keep them in slavery, especially the duty of military service? We see people enslaving themselves, suffering from this slavery, and believing that it must be so, that it does not matter, and will not hinder the emancipation of men, which is being prepared somewhere, somehow, in spite of the ever-increasing growth of slavery.

In fact, take any man of the present time whatever (I don't mean a true Christian, but an average man of the present day), educated or uneducated, believing or unbelieving, rich or poor, married or unmarried. Such a man lives working at his work, or enjoying his amusements, spending the fruits of his labors on himself or on those near to him, and, like everyone, hating every kind of restriction and deprivation, dissension and suffering. Such a man is going his way peaceably, when suddenly people come and say to him: First, promise and swear to us that you will slavishly obey us in everything we dictate to you, and will consider absolutely good and authoritative everything we plan, decide, and call law. Secondly, hand over a part of the fruits of your labors for us to dispose of—we will use the money to keep you in slavery, and to hinder you from forcibly opposing our orders. Thirdly, elect others, or be yourself elected, to take a pretended share in the government, knowing all the while that the government will proceed quite without regard to the foolish speeches you, and those like you, may utter, and knowing that its proceedings will be according to our will, the will of those who have the army in their hands. Fourthly, come at a certain time to the law courts and take your share in those senseless cruelties which we perpetrate on sinners, and those whom we have corrupted, in the shape of penal servitude, exile, solitary confinement, and death. And fifthly and lastly, more than all this, in spite of the fact that you may be on the friendliest terms with people of other nations, be ready, directly we order you to do so, to regard those whom we indicate to you as your enemies; and be ready to assist, either in person or by proxy, in devastation, plunder, and murder of their men, women, children, and aged alike—possibly your own kinsmen or relations—if that is necessary to us.

One would expect that every man of the present day who has a grain of sense left, might reply to such requirements, "But why should I do all this?" One would think every right-minded man must say in amazement: Why should I promise to yield obedience to everything that has been decreed first by Salisbury, then by Gladstone; one day by Boulanger, and another by Parliament; one day by Peter III., the next by Catherine, and the day after by Pougachef; one day by a mad king of Bavaria, another by William? Why should I promise to obey them, knowing them to be wicked or foolish people, or else not knowing them at all? Why am I to hand over the fruits of my labors to them in the shape of taxes, knowing that the money will be spent on the support of officials, prisons, churches, armies, on things that are harmful, and on my own enslavement? Why should I punish myself? Why should I go wasting my time and hoodwinking myself, giving to miscreant evildoers a semblance of legality, by taking part in elections, and pretending that I am taking part in the government, when I know very well that the real control of the government is in the hands of those who have got hold of the army? Why should I go to the law courts to take part in the trial and punishment of men because they have sinned, knowing, if I am a Christian, that the law of vengence is replaced by the law of love, and, if I am an educated man, that punishments do not reform, but only deprave those on whom they are inflicted? And why, most of all, am I to consider as enemies the people of a neighboring nation, with whom I have hitherto lived and with whom I wish to live in love and harmony, and to kill and rob them, or to bring them to misery, simply in order that the keys of the temple at Jerusalem may be in the hands of one archbishop and not another, that one German and not another may be prince in Bulgaria, or that the English rather than the American merchants may capture seals?

And why, most of all, should I take part in person or hire others to murder my own brothers and kinsmen? Why should I flog myself? It is altogether unnecessary for me; it is hurtful to me, and from every point of view it is immoral, base, and vile. So why should I do this? If you tell me that if I do it not I shall receive some injury from someone, then, in the first place, I cannot anticipate from anyone an injury so great as the injury you bring on me if I obey you; and secondly, it is perfectly clear to me that if we our own selves do not flog ourselves, no one will flog us.

As for the government—that means the tzars, ministers, and officials with pens in their hands, who cannot force us into doing anything, as that officer of police compelled the peasants; the men who will drag us to the law court, to prison, and to execution, are not tzars or officials with pens in their hands, but the very people who are in the same position as we are. And it is just as unprofitable and harmful and unpleasant to them to be flogged as to me, and therefore there is every likelihood that if I open their eyes they not only would not treat me with violence, but would do just as I am doing.

Thirdly, even if it should come to pass that I had to suffer for it, even then it would be better for me to be exiled or sent to prison for standing up for common sense and right—which, if not to-day, at least within a very short time, must be triumphant—than to suffer for folly and wrong which must come to an end directly. And therefore, even in that case, it is better to run the risk of their banishing me, shutting me up in prison, or executing me, than of my living all my life in bondage, through my own fault, to wicked men. Better is this than the possibility of being destroyed by victorious enemies, and being stupidly tortured and killed by them, in fighting for a cannon, or a piece of land of no use to anyone, or for a senseless rag called a banner.

I don't want to flog myself and I won't do it. I have no reason to do it. Do it yourselves, if you want it done; but I won't do it.

One would have thought that not religious or moral feeling alone, but the simplest common sense and foresight should impel every man of the present day to answer and to act in that way. But not so. Men of the state conception of life are of the opinion that to act in that way is not necessary, and is even prejudicial to the attainment of their object, the emancipation of men from slavery. They hold that we must continue, like the police officer's peasants, to flog one another, consoling ourselves with the reflection that we are talking away in the assemblies and meetings, founding trades unions, marching through the streets on the 1st of May, getting up conspiracies, and stealthily teasing the government that is flogging us, and that through all this it will be brought to pass that, by enslaving ourselves in closer and closer bondage, we shall very soon be free.

Nothing hinders the emancipation of men from slavery so much as this amazing error. Instead of every man directing his energies to freeing himself, to transforming his conception of life, people seek for an external united method of gaining freedom, and continue to rivet their chains faster and faster.

It is much as if men were to maintain that to make up a fire there was no need to kindle any of the coals, but that all that was necessary was to arrange the coals in a certain order. Yet the fact that the freedom of all men will be brought about only through the freedom of individual persons, becomes more and more clear as time goes on. The freedom of individual men, in the name of the Christian conception of life, from state domination, which was formerly an exceptional and unnoticed phenomenon, has of late acquired threatening significance for state authorities.

If in a former age, in the Roman times, it happened that a Christian confessed his religion and refused to take part in sacrifices, and to worship the emperors or the gods; or in the Middle Ages a Christian refused to worship images, or to acknowledge the authority of the Pope—these cases were in the first place a matter of chance. A man might be placed under the necessity of confessing his faith, or he might live all his life without being placed under this necessity. But now all men, without exception, are subjected to this trial of their faith. Every man of the present day is under the necessity of taking part in the cruelties of pagan life, or of refusing all participation in them. And secondly, in those days cases of refusal to worship the gods or the images or the Pope were not incidents that had any material bearing on the state. Whether men worshiped or did not worship the gods or the images or the Pope, the state remained just as powerful. But now cases of refusing to comply with the unchristian demands of the government are striking at the very root of state authority, because the whole authority of the state is based on the compliance with these unchristian demands.

The sovereign powers of the world have in the course of time been brought into a position in which, for their own preservation, they must require from all men actions which cannot be performed by men who profess true Christianity.

And therefore in our days every profession of true Christianity, by any individual man, strikes at the most essential power of the state, and inevitably leads the way for the emancipation of all.

What importance, one might think, can one attach to such an incident as some dozens of crazy fellows, as people will call them, refusing to take the oath of allegiance to the government, refusing to pay taxes, to take part in law proceedings or in military service?

These people are punished and exiled to a distance, and life goes on in its old way. One might think there was no importance in such incidents; but yet, it is just those incidents, more than anything else, that will undermine the power of the state and prepare the way for the freedom of men. These are the individual bees, who are beginning to separate from the swarm, and are flying near it, waiting till the whole swarm can no longer be prevented from starting off after them. And the governments know this, and fear such incidents more than all the socialists, communists, and anarchists, and their plots and dynamite bombs.

A new reign is beginning. According to the universal rule and established order it is required that all the subjects should take the oath of allegiance to the new government. There is a general decree to that effect, and all are summoned to the council-houses to take the oath. All at once one man in Perm, another in Tula, a third in Moscow, and a fourth in Kalouga declare that they will not take the oath, and though there is no communication between them, they all explain their refusal on the same grounds— namely, that swearing is forbidden by the law of Christ, and that even if swearing had not been forbidden, they could not, in the spirit of the law of Christ, promise to perform the evil actions required of them in the oath, such as informing against all such as may act against the interests of the government, or defending their government with firearms or attacking its enemies. They are brought before rural police officers, district police captains, priests, and governors. They are admonished, questioned, threatened, and punished; but they adhere to their resolution, and do not take the oath. And among the millions of those who did take the oath, those dozens go on living who did not take the oath. And they are questioned:

"What, didn't you take the oath?"

"No, I didn't take the oath."

"And what happened—nothing?"

"Nothing."

The subjects of a state are all bound to pay taxes. And everyone pays taxes, till suddenly one man in Kharkov, another in Tver, and a third in Samara refuse to pay taxes—all, as though in collusion, saying the same thing. One says he will only pay when they tell him what object the money taken from him will be spent on. "If it is for good deeds," he says, "he will give it of his own accord, and more even than is required of him. If for evil deeds, then he will give nothing voluntarily, because by the law of Christ, whose follower he is, he cannot take part in evil deeds." The others, too, say the same in other words, and will not voluntarily pay the taxes.

Those who have anything to be taken have their property taken from them by force; as for those who have nothing, they are left alone.

"What, didn't you pay the tax?"

"No, I didn't pay it."

"And what happened—nothing?"

"Nothing."

There is the institution of passports. Everyone moving from his place of residence is bound to carry one, and to pay a duty on it. Suddenly people are to be found in various places declaring that to carry a passport is not necessary, that one ought not to recognize one's dependence on a state which exists by means of force; and these people do not carry passports, or pay the duty on them. And again, it's impossible to force those people by any means to do what is required. They send them to jail, and let them out again, and these people live without passports.

All peasants are bound to fill certain police offices—that of village constable, and of watchman, and so on. Suddenly in Kharkov a peasant refuses to perform this duty, justifying his refusal on the ground that by the law of Christ, of which he is a follower, he cannot put any man in fetters, lock him up, or drag him from place to place. The same declaration is made by a peasant in Tver, another in Tambov. These peasants are abused, beaten, shut up in prison, but they stick to their resolution and don't fill these offices against their convictions. And at last they cease to appoint them as constables. And again nothing happens.

All citizens are obliged to take a share in law proceedings in the character of jurymen. Suddenly the most different people— mechanics, professors, tradesmen, peasants, servants, as though by agreement refuse to fill this office, and not on the grounds allowed as sufficient by law, but because any process at law is, according to their views, unchristian. They fine these people, trying not to let them have an opportunity of explaining their motives in public, and replace them by others. And again nothing can be done.

All young men of twenty-one years of age are obliged to draw lots for service in the army. All at once one young man in Moscow, another in Tver, a third in Kharkov, and a fourth in Kiev present themselves before the authorities, and, as though by previous agreement, declare that they will not take the oath, they will not serve because they are Christians. I will give the details of one of the first cases, since they have become more frequent, which I happen to know about. The same treatment has been repeated in every other case. A young man of fair education refuses in the Moscow Townhall to take the oath. No attention is paid to what he says, and it is requested that he should pronounce the words of the oath like the rest. He declines, quoting a particular passage of the Gospel in which swearing is forbidden. No attention is paid to his arguments, and he is again requested to comply with the order, but he does not comply with it. Then it is supposed that he is a sectary and therefore does not understand Christianity in the right sense, that is to say, not in the sense in which the priests in the pay of the government understand it. And the young man is conducted under escort to the priests, that they may bring him to reason. The priests begin to reason with him, but their efforts in Christ's name to persuade him to renounce Christ obviously have no influence on him; he is pronounced incorrigible and sent back again to the army. He persists in not taking the oath and openly refuses to perform any military duties. It is a case that has not been provided for by the laws. To overlook such a refusal to comply with the demands of the authorities is out of the question, but to put such a case on a par with simple breach of discipline is also out of the question.

After deliberation among themselves, the military authorities decide to get rid of the troublesome young man, to consider him as a revolutionist, and they dispatch him under escort to the committee of the secret police. The police authorities and gendarmes cross-question him, but nothing that he says can be brought under the head of any of the misdemeanors which come under their jurisdiction. And there is no possibility of accusing him either of revolutionary acts or revolutionary plotting, since he declares that he does not wish to attack anything, but, on the contrary, is opposed to any use of force, and, far from plotting in secret, he seeks every opportunity of saying and doing all that he says and does in the most open manner. And the gendarmes, though they are bound by no hard-and-fast rules, still find no ground for a criminal charge in the young man, and, like the clergy, they send him back to the army. Again the authorities deliberate together, and decide to accept him though he has not taken the oath, and to enrol him among the soldiers. They put him into the uniform, enrol him, and send him under guard to the place where the army is quartered. There the chief officer of the division which he enters again expects the young man to perform his military duties, and again he refuses to obey, and in the presence of other soldiers explains the reason of his refusal, saying that he as a Christian cannot voluntarily prepare himself to commit murder, which is forbidden by the law of Moses.

This incident occurs in a provincial town. The case awakens the interest, and even the sympathy, not only of outsiders, but even of the officers. And the chief officers consequently do not decide to punish this refusal of obedience with disciplinary measures. To save appearances, though, they shut the young man up in prison, and write to the highest military authorities to inquire what they are to do. To refuse to serve in the army, in which the Tzar himself serves, and which enjoys the blessing of the Church, seems insanity from the official point of view. Consequently they write from Petersburg that, since the young man must be out of his mind, they must not use any severe treatment with him, but must send him to a lunatic asylum, that his mental condition may be inquired into and be scientifically treated. They send him to the asylum in the hope that he will remain there, like another young man, who refused ten years ago at Tver to serve in the army, and who was tortured in the asylum till he submitted. But even this step does not rid the military authorities of the inconvenient man. The doctors examine him, interest themselves warmly in his case, and naturally finding in him no symptoms of mental disease, send him back to the army. There they receive him, and making believe to have forgotten his refusal, and his motives for it, they again request him to go to drill, and again in the presence of the other soldiers he refuses and explains the reason of his refusal. The affair continues to attract more and more attention, both among the soldiers and the inhabitants of the town. Again they write to Petersburg, and thence comes the decree to transfer the young man to some division of the army stationed on the frontier, in some place where the army is under martial law, where he can be shot for refusing to obey, and where the matter can proceed without attracting observation, seeing that there are few Russians and Christians in such a distant part, but the majority are foreigners and Mohammedans. This is accordingly done. They transfer him to a division stationed on the Zacaspian border, and in company with convicts send him to a chief officer who is notorious for his harshness and severity.

All this time, through all these changes from place to place, the young man is roughly treated, kept in cold, hunger, and filth, and life is made burdensome to him generally. But all these sufferings do not compel him to change his resolution. On the Zacaspian border, where he is again requested to go on guard fully armed, he again declines to obey. He does not refuse to go and stand near the haystacks where they place him, but refuses to take his arms, declaring that he will not use violence in any case against anyone. All this takes place in the presence of the other soldiers. To let such a refusal pass unpunished is impossible, and the young man is put on his trial for breach of discipline. The trial takes place, and he is sentenced to confinement in the military prison for two years. He is again transferred, in company with convicts, by étape, to Caucasus, and there he is shut up in prison and falls under the irresponsible power of the jailer. There he is persecuted for a year and a half, but he does not for all that alter his decision not to bear arms, and he explains why he will not do this to everyone with whom he is brought in contact. At the end of the second year they set him free, before the end of his term of imprisonment, reckoning it contrary to law to keep him in prison after his time of military service was over, and only too glad to get rid of him as soon as possible.

Other men in various parts of Russia behave, as though by agreement, precisely in the same way as this young man, and in all these cases the government has adopted the same timorous, undecided, and secretive course of action. Some of these men are sent to the lunatic asylum, some are enrolled as clerks and transferred to Siberia, some are sent to work in the forests, some are sent to prison, some are fined. And at this very time some men of this kind are in prison, not charged with their real offense—that is, denying the lawfulness of the action of the government, but for non-fulfillment of special obligations imposed by government. Thus an officer of reserve, who did not report his change of residence, and justified this on the ground that he would not serve in the army any longer, was fined thirty rubles for non-compliance with the orders of the superior authority. This fine he also declined voluntarily to pay. In the same way some peasants and soldiers who have refused to be drilled and to bear arms have been placed under arrest on a charge of breach of discipline and insolence.

And cases of refusing to comply with the demands of government when they are opposed to Christianity, and especially cases of refusing to serve in the army, are occurring of late not in Russia only, but everywhere. Thus I happen to know that in Servia men of the so-called sect of Nazarenes steadily refuse to serve in the army, and the Austrian Government has been carrying on a fruitless contest with them for years, punishing them with imprisonment. In the year 1885 there were 130 such cases. I know that in Switzerland in the year 1890 there were men in prison in the castle of Chillon for declining to serve in the army, whose resolution was not shaken by their punishment. There have been such cases in Sweden, and the men who refused obedience were sent to prison in exactly the same way, and the government studiously concealed these cases from the people. There have been similar cases also in Prussia. I know of the case of a sub-lieutenant of the Guards, who in 1891 declared to the authorities in Berlin that he would not, as a Christian, continue to serve, and in spite of all admonitions, threats, and punishments he stuck to his resolution. In the south of France a society has arisen of late bearing the name of the Hinschists (these facts are taken from the *Peace Herald*, July, 1891), the members of which refuse to enter military service on the grounds of their Christian principles. At first they were enrolled in the ambulance corps, but now, as their numbers increase, they are subjected to punishment for non-compliance, but they still refuse to bear arms just the same.

The socialists, the communists, the anarchists, with their bombs and riots and revolutions, are not nearly so much dreaded by governments as these disconnected individuals coming from different parts, and all justifying their non-compliance on the grounds of the same religion, which is known to all the world.

Every government knows by what means and in what manner to defend itself from revolutionists, and has resources for doing so, and therefore does not dread these external foes. But what are governments to do against men who show the uselessness, superfluousness, and perniciousness of all governments, and who do not contend against them, but simply do not need them and do without them, and therefore are unwilling to take any part in them?

The revolutionists say: The form of government is bad in this respect and that respect; we must overturn it and substitute this or that form of government. The Christian says: I know nothing about the form of government, I don't know whether it is good or bad, and I don't want to overturn it precisely because I don't know whether it's good or bad, but for the very same reason I don't want to support it either. And I not only don't want to, but I can't, because what it demands of me is against my conscience.

All state obligations are against the conscience of a Christian— the oath of allegiance, taxes, law proceedings, and military service. And the whole power of the government rests on these very obligations.

Revolutionary enemies attack the government from without. Christianity does not attack it at all, but, from within, it destroys all the foundations on which government rests.

Among the Russian people, especially since the age of Peter I., the protest of Christianity against the government has never ceased, and the social organization has been such that men emigrate in communes to Turkey, to China, and to uninhabited lands, and not only feel no need of state aid, but always regard the state as a useless burden, only to be endured as a misfortune, whether it happens to be Turkish, Russian, or Chinese. And so, too, among the Russian people more and more frequent examples have of late appeared of conscious Christian freedom from subjection to the state. And these examples are the more alarming for the government from the fact that these non-compliant persons often belong not to the so-called lower uneducated classes, but are men of fair or good education; and also from the fact that they do not in these days justify their position by any mystic and exceptional views, as in former times, do not associate themselves with any superstitious or fanatic rites, like the sects who practice self-immolation by fire, or the wandering pilgrims, but put their refusal on the very simplest and clearest grounds, comprehensible to all, and recognized as true by all.

Thus they refuse the voluntary payment of taxes, because taxes are spent on deeds of violence—on the pay of men of violence—soldiers, on the construction of prisons, fortresses, and cannons. They as Christians regard it as sinful and immoral to have any hand in such deeds.

Those who refuse to take the oath of allegiance refuse because to promise obedience to authorities, that is, to men who are given to deeds of violence, is contrary to the sense of Christ's teaching. They refuse to take the oath in the law courts, because oaths are directly forbidden by the Gospel. They refuse to perform police duties, because in the performance of these duties they must use force against their brothers and ill treat them, and a Christian cannot do that. They refuse to take part in trials at law, because they consider every appeal to law is fulfilling the law of vengeance, which is inconsistent with the Christian law of forgiveness and love. They refuse to take any part in military preparations and in the army, because they cannot be executioners, and they are unwilling to prepare themselves to be so.

The motives in all these cases are so excellent that, however despotic governments may be, they could hardly punish them openly. To punish men for refusing to act against their conscience the government must renounce all claim to good sense and benevolence. And they assure people that they only rule in the name of good sense and benevolence.

What are governments to do against such people?

Governments can of course flog to death or execute or keep in perpetual imprisonment all enemies who want to overturn them by violence, they can lavish gold on that section of the people who are ready to destroy their enemies. But what can they do against men who, without wishing to overturn or destroy anything, desire simply for their part to do nothing against the law of Christ, and who, therefore, refuse to perform the commonest state requirements, which are, therefore, the most indispensable to the maintenance of the state?

If they had been revolutionists, advocating and practicing violence and murder, their suppression would have been an easy matter; some of them could have been bought over, some could have been duped, some could have been overawed, and these who could not be bought over, duped, or overawed would have been treated as criminals, enemies of society, would have been executed or imprisoned, and the crowd would have approved of the action of the government. If they had been fanatics, professing some peculiar belief, it might have been possible, in disproving the superstitious errors mixed in with their religion, to attack also the truth they advocate. But what is to be done with men who profess no revolutionary ideas nor any peculiar religious dogmas, but merely because they are unwilling to do evil to any man, refuse to take the oath, to pay taxes, to take part in law proceedings, to serve in the army, to fulfill, in fact, any of the obligations upon which the whole fabric of a state rests? What is to done with such people? To buy them over with bribes is impossible; the very risks to which they voluntarily expose themselves show that they are incorruptible. To dupe them into believing that this is their duty to God is also impossible, since their refusal is based on the clear, unmistakable law of God, recognized even by those who are trying to compel men to act against it. To terrify them by threats is still less possible, because the deprivations and sufferings to which they are subjected only strengthen their desire to follow the faith by which they are commanded: to obey God rather than men, and not to fear those who can destroy the body, but to fear him who can destroy body and soul. To kill them or keep them in perpetual imprisonment is also impossible. These men have friends, and a past; their way of thinking and acting is well known; they are known by everyone for good, gentle, peaceable people, and they cannot be regarded as criminals who must be removed for the safety of society. And to put men to death who are regarded as good men is to provoke others to champion them and justify their refusal. And it is only necessary to explain the reasons of their refusal to make clear to everyone that these reasons have the same force for all other men, and that they all ought to have done the same long ago. These cases put the ruling powers into a desperate position. They see that the prophecy of Christianity is coming to pass, that it is loosening the fetters of those in chains, and setting free them that are in bondage, and that this must inevitably be the end of all oppressors. The ruling authorities see this, they know that their hours are numbered, and they can do nothing. All that they can do to save themselves is only deferring the hour of their downfall. And this they do, but their position is none the less desperate.

It is like the position of a conqueror who is trying to save a town which has been been set on fire by its own inhabitants. Directly he puts out the conflagration in one place, it is alight in two other places; directly he gives in to the fire and cuts off what is on fire from a large building, the building itself is alight at both ends. These separate fires may be few, but they are burning with a flame which, however small a spark it starts from, never ceases till it has set the whole ablaze.

Thus it is that the ruling authorities are in such a defenseless position before men who advocate Christianity, that but little is necessary to overthrow this sovereign power which seems so powerful, and has held such an exalted position for so many centuries. And yet social reformers are busy promulgating the idea that it is not necessary and is even pernicious and immoral for every man separately to work out his own freedom. As though, while one set of men have been at work a long while turning a river into a new channel, and had dug out a complete water-course and had only to open the floodgates for the water to rush in and do the rest, another set of men should come along and begin to advise them that it would be much better, instead of letting the water out, to construct a machine which would ladle the water up from one side and pour it over the other side.

But the thing has gone too far. Already ruling governments feel their weak and defenseless position, and men of Christian principles are awakening from their apathy, and already begin to feel their power.

"I am come to send a fire on the earth," said Christ, "and what will I, if it be already kindled?"

And this fire is beginning to burn.

CHAPTER X: EVIL CANNOT BE SUPPRESSED BY THE PHYSICAL FORCE OF THE GOVERNMENT— THE MORAL PROGRESS OF HUMANITY IS BROUGHT ABOUT NOT ONLY BY INDIVIDUAL RECOGNITION OF TRUTH, BUT ALSO THROUGH THE ESTABLISHMENT OF A PUBLIC OPINION

Christianity Destroys the State—But Which is Most Necessary: Christianity or the State?—There are Some who Assert the Necessity of a State Organization, and Others who Deny it, both Arguing from same First Principles—Neither Contention can be Proved by Abstract Argument—The Question must be Decided by the Stage in the Development of Conscience of Each Man, which will either Prevent or Allow him to Support a Government Organization—Recognition of the Futility and Immorality of Supporting a State Organization Contrary to Christian Principles will Decide the Question for Every Man, in Spite of any Action on Part of the State—Argument of those who Defend the Government, that it is a Form of Social Life, Needed to Protect the Good from the Wicked, till all Nations and all Members of each Nation have Become Christians—The Most Wicked are Always those in Power—The whole History of Humanity is the

History of the Forcible Appropriation of Power by the Wicked and their Oppression of the Good—The Recognition by Governments of the Necessity of Opposing Evil by Force is Equivalent to Suicide on their Part—The Abolition of State-violence cannot Increase the Sum Total of Acts of Violence—The Suppression of the Use of Force is not only Possible, but is even Taking Place before Our Eyes—But it will Never be Suppressed by the Violence of Government, but through Men who have Attained Power by Evidence Recognizing its Emptiness and Becoming Better and Less Capable of Using Force—Individual Men and also Whole Nations Pass Through this Process—By this Means Christianity is Diffused Through Consciousness of Men, not only in Spite of Use of Violence by Government, but even Through its Action, and therefore the Suppression is not to be Dreaded, but is Brought About by the National Progress of Life—Objection of those who Defend State Organization that Universal Adoption of Christianity is hardly Likely to be Realized at any Time—The General Adoption of the Truths of Christianity is being Brought About not only by the Gradual and Inward Means, that is, by Knowledge of the Truth, Prophetic Insight, and Recognition of the Emptiness of Power, and Renunciation of it by Individuals, but also by Another External Means, the Acceptance of a New Truth by Whole Masses of Men on a Lower Level of Development Through Simple Confidence in their Leaders—When a Certain Stage in the Diffusion of a Truth has been Reached, a Public Opinion is Created which Impels a Whole Mass of Men, formerly Antagonistic to the New Truth, to Accept it—And therefore all Men may Quickly be Brought to Renounce the use of Violence when once a Christian Public Opinion is Established—The Conviction of Force being Necessary Hinders the Establishment of a Christian Public Opinion—The Use of Violence Leads Men to Distrust the Spiritual Force which is the Only Force by which they Advance—Neither Nations nor Individuals have been really Subjugated by Force, but only by Public Opinion, which no Force can Resist—Savage Nations and Savage Men can only be Subdued by the Diffusion of a Christian Standard among them, while actually Christian Nations in order to Subdue them do all they can to Destroy a Christian Standard—These Fruitless

Attempts to Civilize Savages Cannot be Adduced as Proofs that Men Cannot be Subdued by Christianity—Violence by Corrupting Public Opinion, only Hinders the Social Organization from being What it Ought to Be—And by the Use of Violence being Suppressed, a Christian Public Opinion would be Established—Whatever might be the Result of the Suppression of Use of Force, this Unknown Future could not be Worse than the Present Condition, and so there is no Need to Dread it—To Attain Knowledge of the Unknown, and to Move Toward it, is the Essence of Life.

Christianity in its true sense puts an end to government. So it was understood at its very commencement; it was for that cause that Christ was crucified. So it has always been understood by people who were not under the necessity of justifying a Christian government. Only from the time that the heads of government assumed an external and nominal Christianity, men began to invent all the impossible, cunningly devised theories by means of which Christianity can be reconciled with government. But no honest and serious-minded man of our day can help seeing the incompatibility of true Christianity—the doctrine of meekness, forgiveness of injuries, and love—with government, with its pomp, acts of violence, executions, and wars. The profession of true Christianity not only excludes the possibility of recognizing government, but even destroys its very foundations.

But if it is so, and we are right in saying that Christianity is incompatible with government, then the question naturally presents itself: which is more necessary to the good of humanity, in which way is men's happiness best to be secured, by maintaining the organization of government or by destroying it and replacing it by Christianity?

Some people maintain that government is more necessary for humanity, that the destruction of the state organization would involve the destruction of all that humanity has gained, that the state has been and still is the only form in which humanity can develop. The evil which we see among peoples living under a government organization they attribute not to that type of society, but to its abuses, which, they say, can be corrected without destroying it, and thus humanity, without discarding the state organization, can develop and attain a high degree of happiness. And men of this way of thinking bring forward in support of their views arguments which they think irrefutable drawn from history, philosophy, and even religion. But there are men who hold on the contrary that, as there was a time when humanity lived without government, such an organization is temporary, and that a time must come when men need a new organization, and that that time has come now. And men of this way of thinking also bring forward in support of their views arguments which they think irrefutable from philosophy, history, and religion.

Volumes may be written in defense of the former view (and volumes indeed have long ago been written and more will still be written on that side), but much also can be written against it (and much also, and most briliantly, has been written—though more recently—on this side).

And it cannot be proved, as the champions of the state maintain, that the destruction of government involves a social chaos, mutual spoliation and murder, the destruction of all social institutions, and the return of mankind to barbarism. Nor can it be proved as the opponents of government maintain that men have already become so wise and good that they will not spoil or murder one another, but will prefer peaceful associations to hostilities; that of their own accord, unaided by the state, they will make all the arrangements that they need, and that therefore government, far from being any aid, under show of guarding men exerts a pernicious and brutalizing influence over them. It is impossible to prove either of these contentions by abstract reasoning. Still less possible is it to prove them by experiment, since the whole matter turns on the question, ought we to try the experiment? The question whether or not the time has come to make an end of government would be unanswerable, except that there exists another living means of settling it beyond dispute.

We may dispute upon the question whether the nestlings are ready to do without the mother-hen and to come out of the eggs, or whether they are not yet advanced enough. But the young birds will decide the question without any regard for our arguments when they find themselves cramped for space in the eggs. Then they will begin to try them with their beaks and come out of them of their own accord.

It is the same with the question whether the time has come to do away with the governmental type of society and to replace it by a new type. If a man, through the growth of a higher conscience, can no longer comply with the demands of government, he finds himself cramped by it and at the same time no longer needs its protection. When this comes to pass, the question whether men are ready to discard the governmental type is solved. And the conclusion will be as final for them as for the young birds hatched out of the eggs. Just as no power in the world can put them back into the shells, so can no power in the world bring men again under the governmental type of society when once they have outgrown it.

"It may well be that government was necessary and is still necessary for all the advantages which you attribute to it," says the man who has mastered the Christian theory of life. "I only know that on the one hand, government is no longer necessary for *me*, and on the other hand, *I* can no longer carry out the measures that are necessary to the existence of a government. Settle for yourselves what you need for your life. I cannot prove the need or the harm of governments in general. I know only what I need and do not need, what I can do and what I cannot. I know that I do not need to divide myself off from other nations, and therefore I cannot admit that I belong exclusively to any state or nation, or that I owe allegiance to any government. I know that I do not need all the government institutions organized within the state, and therefore I cannot deprive people who need my labor to give it in the form of taxes to institutions which I do not need, which for all I know may be pernicious. I know that I have no need of the administration or of courts of justice founded upon force, and therefore I can take no part in either. I know that I do not need to attack and slaughter other nations or to defend myself from them with arms, and therefore I can take no part in wars or preparations for wars. It may well be that there are people who cannot help regarding all this as necessary and indispensable. I cannot dispute the question with them, I can only speak for myself; but I can say with absolute certainty that I do not need it, and that I cannot do it. And I do not need this and I cannot do it, not because such is my own, my personal will, but because such is the will of him who sent me into life, and gave me an indubitable law for my conduct through life."

Whatever arguments may be advanced in support of the contention that the suppression of government authority would be injurious and would lead to great calamities, men who have once outgrown the governmental form of society cannot go back to it again. And all the reasoning in the world cannot make the man who has outgrown the governmental form of society take part in actions disallowed by his conscience, any more than the full-grown bird can be made to return into the egg-shell.

"But even it be so," say the champions of the existing order of things, "still the suppression of government violence can only be possible and desirable when all men have become Christians. So long as among people nominally Christians there are unchristian wicked men, who for the gratification of their own lusts are ready to do harm to others, the suppression of government authority, far from being a blessing to others, would only increase their miseries. The suppression of the governmental type of society is not only undesirable so long as there is only a minority of true Christians; it would not even be desirable if the whole of a nation were Christians, but among and around them were still unchristian men of other nations. For these unchristian men would rob, outrage, and kill the Christians with impunity and would make their lives miserable. All that would result, would be that the bad would oppress and outrage the good with impunity. And therefore the authority of government must not be suppressed till all the wicked and rapacious people in the world are extinct. And since this will either never be, or at least cannot be for a long time to come, in spite of the efforts of individual Christians to be independent of government authority, it ought to be maintained in the interests of the majority. The champions of government assert that without it the wicked will oppress and outrage the good, and that the power of the government enables the good to resist the wicked."

But in this assertion the champions of the existing order of things take for granted the proposition they want to prove. When they say that except for the government the bad would oppress the good, they take it for granted that the good are those who at the present time are in possession of power, and the bad are those who are in subjection to it. But this is just what wants proving. It would only be true if the custom of our society were what is, or rather is supposed to be, the custom in China; that is, that the good always rule, and that directly those at the head of government cease to be better than those they rule over, the citizens are bound to remove them. This is supposed to be the custom in China. In reality it is not so and can never be so. For to remove the heads of a government ruling by force, it is not the right alone, but the power to do so that is needed. So that even in China this is only an imaginary custom. And in our Christian world we do not even suppose such a custom, and we have nothing on which to build up the supposition that it is the good or the superior who are in power; in reality it is those who have seized power and who keep it for their own and their retainers' benefit.

The good cannot seize power, nor retain it; to do this men must love power. And love of power is inconsistent with goodness; but quite consistent with the very opposite qualities—pride, cunning, cruelty.

Without the aggrandizement of self and the abasement of others, without hypocrisies and deceptions, without prisons, fortresses, executions, and murders, no power can come into existence or be maintained.

"If the power of government is suppressed the more wicked will oppress the less wicked," say the champions of state authority. But when the Egyptians conquered the Jews, the Romans conquered the Greeks, and the Barbarians conquered the Romans, is it possible that all the conquerors were always better than those they conquered? And the same with the transitions of power within a state from one personage to another: has the power always passed from a worse person to a better one? When Louis XVI. was removed and Robespierre came to power, and afterward Napoleon—who ruled then, a better man or a worse? And when were better men in power, when the Versaillist party or when the Commune was in power? When Charles I. was ruler, or when Cromwell? And when Peter III. was Tzar, or when he was killed and Catherine was Tzaritsa in one-half of Russia and Pougachef ruled the other? Which was bad then, and which was good? All men who happen to be in authority assert that their authority is necessary to keep the bad from oppressing the good, assuming that they themselves are the good *par excellence*, who protect other good people from the bad.

But ruling means using force, and using force means doing to him to whom force is used, what he does not like and what he who uses the force would certainly not like done to himself. Consequently ruling means doing to others what we would not they should do unto us, that is, doing wrong.

To submit means to prefer suffering to using force. And to prefer suffering to using force means to be good, or at least less wicked than those who do unto others what they would not like themselves.

And therefore, in all probability, not the better but the worse have always ruled and are ruling now. There may be bad men among those who are ruled, but it cannot be that those who are better have generally ruled those who are worse.

It might be possible to suppose this with the inexact heathen definition of good; but with the clear Christian definition of good and evil, it is impossible to imagine it.

If the more or less good, and the more or less bad cannot be distinguished in the heathen world, the Christian conception of good and evil has so clearly defined the characteristics of the good and the wicked, that it is impossible to confound them. According to Christ's teaching the good are those who are meek and long-suffering, do not resist evil by force, forgive injuries, and love their enemies; those are wicked who exalt themselves, oppress, strive, and use force. Therefore by Christ's teaching there can be no doubt whether the good are to be found among rulers or ruled, and whether the wicked are among the ruled or the rulers. Indeed it is absurd even to speak of Christians ruling.

Non-Christians, that is those who find the aim of their lives in earthly happiness, must always rule Christians, the aim of whose lives is the renunciation of such earthly happiness.

This difference has always existed and has become more and more defined as the Christian religion has been more widely diffused and more correctly understood.

The more widely true Christianity was diffused and the more it penetrated men's conscience, the more impossible it was for Christians to be rulers, and the easier it became for non-Christians to rule them.

"To get rid of governmental violence in a society in which all are not true Christians, will only result in the wicked dominating the good and oppressing them with impunity," say the champions of the existing order of things. But it has never been, and cannot be otherwise. So it has always been from the beginning of the world, and so it is still. *The wicked will always dominate the good, and will always oppress them.* Cain overpowered Abel, the cunning Jacob oppressed the guileless Esau and was in his turn deceived by Laban, Caiaphas and Pilate oppressed Christ, the Roman emperors oppressed Seneca, Epictetus, and the good Romans who lived in their times. John IV. with his favorites, the syphilitic drunken Peter with his buffoons, the vicious Catherine with her paramours, ruled and oppressed the industrious religious Russians of their times.

William is ruling over the Germans, Stambouloff over the Bulgarians, the Russian officials over the Russian people. The Germans have dominated the Italians, now they dominate the Hungarians and Slavonians; the Turks have dominated and still dominate the Slavonians and Greeks; the English dominate the Hindoos, the Mongolians dominate the Chinese.

So that whether governmental violence is suppressed or not, the position of good men, in being oppressed by the wicked, will be unchanged.

To terrify men with the prospect of the wicked dominating the good is impossible, for that is just what has always been, and is now, and cannot but be.

The whole history of pagan times is nothing but a recital of the incidents and means by which the more wicked gained possession of power over the less wicked, and retained it by cruelties and deceptions, ruling over the good under the pretense of guarding the right and protecting the good from the wicked. All the revolutions in history are only examples of the more wicked seizing power and oppressing the good. In declaring that if their authority did not exist the more wicked would oppress the good, the ruling authorities only show their disinclination to let other oppressors come to power who would like to snatch it from them.

But in asserting this they only accuse themselves. They say that their power, *i. e.*, violence, is needed to defend men from other possible oppressors in the present or the future.

The weakness of the use of violence lies in the fact that all the arguments brought forward by oppressors in their own defense can with even better reason be advanced against them. They plead the danger of violence—most often imagined in the future—but they are all the while continuing to practice actual violence themselves. "You say that men used to pillage and murder in the past, and that you are afraid that they will pillage and murder one another if your power were no more. That may happen—or it may not happen. But the fact that you ruin thousands of men in prisons, fortresses, galleys, and exile, break up millions of families and ruin millions of men, physically as well as morally, in the army, that fact is not an imaginary but a real act of violence, which, according to your own argument, one ought to oppose by violence. And so you are yourselves these wicked men against whom, according to your own argument, it is absolutely necessary to use violence," the oppressed are sure to say to their oppressors. And non-Christian men always do say, and think and act on this reasoning. If the oppressed are more wicked than their oppressors, they attack them and try to overthrow them; and in favorable circumstances they succeed in overthrowing them, or what is more common, they rise into the ranks of the oppressors and assist in their acts of violence.

So that the very violence which the champions of government hold up as a terror—pretending that except for its oppressive power the wicked would oppress the good—has really always existed and will exist in human society. And therefore the suppression of state violence cannot in any case be the cause of increased oppression of the good by the wicked.

If state violence ceased, there would be acts of violence perhaps on the part of different people, other than those who had done deeds of violence before. But the total amount of violence could not in any case be increased by the mere fact of power passing from one set of men to another.

"State violence can only cease when there are no more wicked men in society," say the champions of the existing order of things, assuming in this of course that since there will always be wicked men, it can never cease. And that would be right enough if it were the case, as they assume, that the oppressors are always the best of men, and that the sole means of saving men from evil is by violence. Then, indeed, violence could never cease. But since this is not the case, but quite the contrary, that it is not the better oppress the worse, but the worse oppress the better, and since violence will never put an end to evil, and there is, moreover, another means of putting an end to it, the assertion that violence will never cease is incorrect. The use of violence grows less and less and evidently must disappear. But this will not come to pass, as some champions of the existing order imagine, through the oppressed becoming better and better under the influence of government (on the contrary, its influence causes their continual degradation), but through the fact that all men are constantly growing better and better of themselves, so that even the most wicked, who are in power, will become less and less wicked, till at last they are so good as to be incapable of using violence.

The progressive movement of humanity does not proceed from the better elements in society seizing power and making those who are subject to them better, by forcible means, as both conservatives and revolutionists imagine. It proceeds first and principally from the fact that all men in general are advancing steadily and undeviatingly toward a more and more conscious assimilation of the Christian theory of life; and secondly, from the fact that, even apart from conscious spiritual life, men are unconsciously brought into a more Christian attitude to life by the very process of one set of men grasping the power, and again being replaced by others.

The worse elements of society, gaining possession of power, under the sobering influence which always accompanies power, grow less and less cruel, and become incapable of using cruel forms of violence. Consequently others are able to seize their place, and the same process of softening and, so to say, unconscious Christianizing goes on with them. It is something like the process of ebullition. The majority of men, having the non-Christian view of life, always strive for power and struggle to obtain it. In this struggle the most cruel, the coarsest, the least Christian elements of society overpower the most gentle, well-disposed, and Christian, and rise by means of their violence to the upper ranks of society. And in them is Christ's prophecy fulfilled: "Woe to you that are rich! woe unto you that are full! woe unto you when all men shall speak well of you!" For the men who are in possession of power and all that results from it—glory and wealth—and have attained the various aims they set before themselves, recognize the vanity of it all and return to the position from which they came. Charles V., John IV., Alexander I., recognizing the emptiness and the evil of power, renounced it because they were incapable of using violence for their own benefit as they had done.

But they are not the solitary examples of this recognition of the emptiness and evil of power. Everyone who gains a position of power he has striven for, every general, every minister, every millionaire, every petty official who has gained the place he has coveted for ten years, every rich peasant who has laid by some hundred rubles, passes through this unconscious process of softening.

And not only individual men, but societies of men, whole nations, pass through this process.

The seductions of power, and all the wealth, honor, and luxury it gives, seem a sufficient aim for men's efforts only so long as they are unattained. Directly a man reaches them he sees all their vanity, and they gradually lose all their power of attraction. They are like clouds which have form and beauty only from the distance; directly one ascends into them, all their splendor vanishes.

Men who are in possession of power and wealth, sometimes even those who have gained for themselves their power and wealth, but more often their heirs, cease to be so eager for power, and so cruel in their efforts to obtain it.

Having learnt by experience, under the operation of Christian influence, the vanity of all that is gained by violence, men sometimes in one, sometimes in several generations lose the vices which are generated by the passion for power and wealth. They become less cruel and so cannot maintain their position, and are expelled from power by others less Christian and more wicked. Thus they return to a rank of society lower in position, but higher in morality, raising thereby the average level of Christian consciousness in men. But directly after them again the worst, coarsest, least Christian elements of society rise to the top, and are subjected to the same process as their predecessors, and again in a generation or so, seeing the vanity of what is gained by violence, and having imbibed Christianity, they come down again among the oppressed, and their place is again filled by new oppressors, less brutal than former oppressors, though more so than those they oppress. So that, although power remains externally the same as it was, with every change of the men in power there is a constant increase of the number of men who have been brought by experience to the necessity of assimilating the Christian conception of life, and with every change—though it is the coarsest, cruelest, and least Christian who come into possession of power, they are less coarse and cruel and more Christian than their predecessors when they gained possession of power.

Power selects and attracts the worst elements of society, transforms them, improves and softens them, and returns them to society.

Such is the process by means of which Christianity, in spite of the hindrances to human progress resulting from the violence of power, gains more and more hold of men. Christianity penetrates to the consciousness of men, not only in spite of the violence of power, but also by means of it.

And therefore the assertion of the champions of the state, that if the power of government were suppressed the wicked would oppress the good, not only fails to show that that is to be dreaded, since it is just what happens now, but proves, on the contrary, that it is governmental power which enables the wicked to oppress the good, and is the evil most desirable to suppress, and that it is being gradually suppressed in the natural course of things.

"But if it be true that governmental power will disappear when those in power become so Christian that they renounce power of their own accord, and there are no men found willing to take their place, and even if this process is already going on," say the champions of the existing order, "when will that come to pass? If, after eighteen hundred years, there are still so many eager for power, and so few anxious to obey, there seems no likelihood of its happening very soon—or indeed of its ever happening at all.

"Even if there are, as there have always been, some men who prefer renouncing power to enjoying it, the mass of men in reserve, who prefer dominion to subjection, is so great that it is difficult to imagine a time when the number will be exhausted.

"Before this Christianizing process could so affect all men one after another that they would pass from the heathen to the Christian conception of life, and would voluntarily abandon power and wealth, it would be necessary that all the coarse, half-savage men, completely incapable of appreciating Christianity or acting upon it, of whom there are always a great many in every Christian society, should be converted to Christianity. More than this, all the savage and absolutely non-Christian peoples, who are so numerous outside the Christian world, must also be converted. And therefore, even if we admit that this Christianizing process will some day affect everyone, still, judging by the amount of progress it has made in eighteen hundred years, it will be many times eighteen centuries before it will do so. And it is therefore impossible and unprofitable to think at present of anything so impracticable as the suppression of authority. We ought only to try to put authority into the best hands."

And this criticism would be perfectly just, if the transition from one conception of life to another were only accomplished by the single process of all men, separately and successively, realizing, each for himself, the emptiness of power, and reaching Christian truth by the inner spiritual path. That process goes on unceasingly, and men are passing over to Christianity one after another by this inner way.

But there is also another external means by which men reach Christianity and by which the transition is less gradual.

This transition from one organization of life to another is not accomplished by degrees like the sand running through the hourglass grain after grain. It is more like the water filling a vessel floating on water. At first the water only runs in slowly on one side, but as the vessel grows heavier it suddenly begins to sink, and almost instantaneously fills with water.

It is just the same with the transitions of mankind from one conception—and so from one organization of life—to another. At first only gradually and slowly, one after another, men attain to the new truth by the inner spiritual way, and follow it out in life. But when a certain point in the diffusion of the truth has been reached, it is suddenly assimilated by everyone, not by the inner way, but, as it were, involuntarily.

That is why the champions of the existing order are wrong in arguing that, since only a small section of mankind has passed over to Christianity in eighteen centuries, it must be many times eighteen centuries before all the remainder do the same. For in that argument they do not take into account any other means, besides the inward spiritual one, by which men assimilate a new truth and pass from one order of life to another.

Men do not only assimilate a truth through recognizing it by prophetic insight, or by experience of life. When the truth has become sufficiently widely diffused, men at a lower stage of development accept it all at once simply through confidence in those who have reached it by the inner spiritual way, and are applying it to life.

Every new truth, by which the order of human life is changed and humanity is advanced, is at first accepted by only a very small number of men who understand it through inner spiritual intuition. The remainder of mankind who accepted on trust the preceding truth on which the existing order is based, are always opposed to the diffusion of the new truth.

But seeing that, to begin with, men do not stand still, but are steadily advancing to a greater recognition of the truth and a closer adaptation of their life to it, and secondly, all men in varying degrees according to their age, their education, and their race are capable of understanding the new truths, at first those who are nearest to the men who have attained the new truth by spiritual intuition, slowly and one by one, but afterward more and more quickly, pass over to the new truth. Thus the number of men who accept the new truth becomes greater and greater, and the truth becomes more and more comprehensible.

And thus more confidence is aroused in the remainder, who are at a less advanced stage of capacity for understanding the truth. And it becomes easier for them to grasp it, and an increasing number accept it.

And so the movement goes on more and more quickly, and on an ever-increasing scale, like a snowball, till at last a public opinion in harmony with the new truth is created, and then the whole mass of men is carried over all at once by its momentum to the new truth and establishes a new social order in accordance with it.

Those men who accept a new truth when it has gained a certain degree of acceptance, always pass over all at once in masses.

They are like the ballast with which every ship is always loaded, at once to keep it upright and enable it to sail properly. If there were no ballast, the ship would not be low enough in the water, and would shift its position at the slightest change in its conditions. This ballast, which strikes one at first as superfluous and even as hindering the progress of the vessel, is really indispensable to its good navigation.

It is the same with the mass of mankind, who not individually, but always in a mass, under the influence of a new social idea pass all at once from one organization of life to another. This mass always hinders, by its inertia, frequent and rapid revolutions in the social order which have not been sufficiently proved by human experience. And it delays every truth a long while till it has stood the test of prolonged struggles, and has thoroughly permeated the consciousness of humanity.

And that is why it is a mistake to say that because only a very small minority of men has assimilated Christianity in eighteen centuries, it must take many times as many centuries for all mankind to assimilate it, and that since that time is so far off, we who live in the present need not even think about it. It is a mistake, because the men at a lower stage of culture, the men and the nations who are represented as the obstacle to the realization of the Christian order of life, are the very people who always pass over in masses all at once to any truth that has once been recognized by public opinion.

And therefore the transformation of human life, through which men in power will renounce it, and there will be none anxious to take their place, will not come only by all men consciously and separately assimilating the Christian conception of life. It will come when a Christian public opinion has arisen, so definite and easily comprehensible as to reach the whole of the inert mass, which is not able to attain truth by its own intuition, and therefore is always under the sway of public opinion.

Public opinion arises spontaneously and spreads for hundreds and thousands of years, but it has the power of working on men by infection, and with great rapidity gains a hold on great numbers of men.

"But," say the champions of the existing order, "even if it is true that public opinion, when it has attained a certain degree of definiteness and precision, can convert the inert mass of men outside the Christian world—the non-Christian races—as well as the coarse and depraved who are living in its midst, what proofs have we that this Christian public opinion has arisen and is able to replace force and render it unnecessary.

"We must not give up force, by which the existing order is maintained, and by relying on the vague and impalpable influence of public opinion expose Christians to the risk of being pillaged, murdered, and outraged in every way by the savages inside and outside of civilized society.

"Since, even supported by the use of force, we can hardly control the non-Christian elements which are always ready to pour down on us and to destroy all that has been gained by civilization, is it likely that public opinion could take the place of force and render us secure? And besides, how are we to find the moment when public opinion has become strong enough to be able to replace the use of force? To reject the use of force and trust to public opinion to defend us would be as insane as to remove all weapons of defense in a menagerie, and then to let loose all the lions and tigers, relying on the fact that the animals seemed peaceable when kept in their cages and held in check by red-hot irons. And therefore people in power, who have been put in positions of authority by fate or by God, have not the right to run the risk, ruining all that has been gained by civilization, just because they want to try an experiment to see whether public opinion is or is not able to replace the protection given by authority."

A French writer, forgotten now, Alphonse Karr, said somewhere, trying to show the impossibility of doing away with the death penalty: "Que messieurs les assassins commencent par nous donner l'exemple." Often have I heard this *bon mot* repeated by men who thought that these words were a witty and convincing argument against the abolition of capital punishment. And yet all the erroneousness of the argument of those who consider that governments cannot give up the use of force till all people are capable of doing the same, could not be more clearly expressed than it is in that epigram.

"Let the murderers," say the champions of state violence, "set us the example by giving up murder and then we will give it up." But the murderers say just the same, only with much more right. They say: "Let those who have undertaken to teach us and guide us set us the example of giving up legal murder, and then we will imitate them." And they say this, not as a jest, but seriously, because it is the actual state of the case.

"We cannot give up the use of violence, because we are surrounded by violent ruffians." Nothing in our days hinders the progress of humanity and the establishment of the organization corresponding to its present development more than this false reasoning. Those in authority are convinced that men are only guided and only progress through the use of force, and therefore they confidently make use of it to support the existing organization. The existing order is maintained, not by force, but by public opinion, the action of which is disturbed by the use of force. So that the effect of using force is to disturb and to weaken the very thing it tries to maintain.

Violence, even in the most favorable case, when it is not used simply for some personal aims of those in power, always punishes under the one inelastic formula of the law what has long before been condemned by public opinion. But there is this difference, that while public opinion censures and condemns all the acts opposed to the moral law, including the most varied cases in its reprobation, the law which rests on violence only condemns and punishes a certain very limited range of acts, and by so doing seems to justify all other acts of the same kind which do not come under its scope.

Public opinion ever since the time of Moses has regarded covetousness, profligacy, and cruelty as wrong, and censured them accordingly. And it condemns every kind of manifestation of covetousness, not only the appropriation of the property of others by force or fraud or trickery, but even the cruel abuse of wealth; it condemns every form of profligacy, whether with concubine, slave, divorced woman, or even one's own wife; it condemns every kind of cruelty, whether shown in blows, in ill-treatment, or in murder, not only of men, but even of animals. The law resting on force only punishes certain forms of covetousness, such as robbery and swindling, certain forms of profligacy and cruelty, such as conjugal infidelity, murder, and wounding. And in this way it seems to countenance all the manifestations of covetousness, profligacy, and cruelty which do not come under its narrow definition.

But besides corrupting public opinion, the use of force leads men to the fatal conviction that they progress, not through the spiritual impulse which impels them to the attainment of truth and its realization in life, and which constitutes the only source of every progressive movement of humanity, but by means of violence, the very force which, far from leading men to truth, always carries them further away from it. This is a fatal error, because it leads men to neglect the chief force underlying their life—their spiritual activity—and to turn all their attention and energy to the use of violence, which is superficial, sluggish, and most generally pernicious in its action.

They make the same mistake as men who, trying to set a steam engine in motion, should turn its wheels round with their hands, not suspecting that the underlying cause of its movement was the expansion of the steam, and not the motion of the wheels. By turning the wheels by hand and by levers they could only produce a semblance of movement, and meantime they would be wrenching the wheels and so preventing their being fit for real movement.

That is just what people are doing who think to make men advance by means of external force.

They say that the Christian life cannot be established without the use of violence, because there are savage races outside the pale of Christian societies in Africa and in Asia (there are some who even represent the Chinese as a danger to civilization), and that in the midst of Christian societies there are savage, corrupt, and, according to the new theory of heredity, congenital criminals. And violence, they say, is necessary to keep savages and criminals from annihilating our civilization.

But these savages within and without Christian society, who are such a terror to us, have never been subjugated by violence, and are not subjugated by it now. Nations have never subjugated other nations by violence alone. If a nation which subjugated another was on a lower level of civilization, it has never happened that it succeeded in introducing its organization of life by violence. On the contrary, it was always forced to adopt the organization of life existing in the conquered nation. If ever any of the nations conquered by force have been really subjugated, or even nearly so, it has always been by the action of public opinion, and never by violence, which only tends to drive a people to further rebellion.

When whole nations have been subjugated by a new religion, and have become Christian or Mohammedan, such a conversion has never been brought about because the authorities made it obligatory (on the contrary, violence has much oftener acted in the opposite direction), but because public opinion made such a change inevitable. Nations, on the contrary, who have been driven by force to accept the faith of their conquerors have always remained antagonistic to it.

It is just the same with the savage elements existing in the midst of our civilized societies. Neither the increased nor the diminished severity of punishment, nor the modifications of prisons, nor the increase of police will increase or diminish the number of criminals. Their number will only be diminished by the change of the moral standard of society. No severities could put an end to duels and vendettas in certain districts. In spite of the number of Tcherkesses executed for robbery, they continue to be robbers from their youth up, for no maiden will marry a Tcherkess youth till he has given proof of his bravery by carrying off a horse, or at least a sheep. If men cease to fight duels, and the Tcherkesses cease to be robbers, it will not be from fear of punishment (indeed, that invests the crime with additional charm for youth), but through a change in the moral standard of public opinion. It is the same with all other crimes. Force can never suppress what is sanctioned by public opinion. On the contrary, public opinion need only be in direct opposition to force to neutralize the whole effect of the use of force. It has always been so and always will be in every case of martyrdom.

What would happen if force were not used against hostile nations and the criminal elements of society we do not know. But we do know by prolonged experience that neither enemies nor criminals have been successfully suppressed by force.

And indeed how could nations be subjugated by violence who are led by their whole education, their traditions, and even their religion to see the loftiest virtue in warring with their oppressors and fighting for freedom? And how are we to suppress by force acts committed in the midst of our society which are regarded as crimes by the government and as daring exploits by the people?

To exterminate such nations and such criminals by violence is possible, and indeed is done, but to subdue them is impossible.

The sole guide which directs men and nations has always been and is the unseen, intangible, underlying force, the resultant of all the spiritual forces of a certain people, or of all humanity, which finds its outward expression in public opinion.

The use of violence only weakens this force, hinders it and corrupts it, and tries to replace it by another which, far from being conducive to the progress of humanity, is detrimental to it.

To bring under the sway of Christianity all the savage nations outside the pale of the Christian world—all the Zulus, Mandchoos, and Chinese, whom many regard as savages—and the savages who live in our midst, there is only *one means*. That means is the propagation among these nations of the Christian ideal of society, which can only be realized by a Christian life, Christian actions, and Christian examples. And meanwhile, though this is the *one only means* of gaining a hold over the people who have remained non-Christian, the men of our day set to work in the directly opposite fashion to attain this result.

To bring under the sway of Christianity savage nations who do not attack us and whom we have therefore no excuse for oppressing, we ought before all things to leave them in peace, and in case we need or wish to enter into closer relations with them, we ought only to influence them by Christian manners and Christian teaching, setting them the example of the Christian virtues of patience, meekness, endurance, purity, brotherhood, and love. Instead of that we begin by establishing among them new markets for our commerce, with the sole aim of our own profit; then we appropriate their lands, *i. e.*, rob them; then we sell them spirits, tobacco, and opium, *i. e.*, corrupt them; then we establish our morals among them, teach them the use of violence and new methods of destruction, *i. e.*, we teach them nothing but the animal law of strife, below which man cannot sink, and we do all we can to conceal from them all that is Christian in us. After this we send some dozens of missionaries prating to them of the hypocritical absurdities of the Church, and then quote the failure of our efforts to turn the heathen to Christianity as an incontrovertible proof of the impossibility of applying the truths of Christianity in practical life.

It is just the same with the so-called criminals living in our midst. To bring these people under the sway of Christianity there is *one only means*, that is, the Christian social ideal, which can only be realized among them by true Christian teaching and supported by a true example of the Christian life. And to preach this Christian truth and to support it by Christian example we set up among them prisons, guillotines, gallows, preparations for murder; we diffuse among the common herd idolatrous superstitions to stupefy them; we sell them spirits, tobacco, and opium to brutalize them; we even organize legalized prostitution; we give land to those who do not need it; we make a display of senseless luxury in the midst of suffering poverty; we destroy the possibility of anything like a Christian public opinion, and studiously try to suppress what Christian public opinion is existing. And then, after having ourselves assiduously corrupted men, we shut them up like wild beasts in places from which they cannot escape, and where they become still more brutalized, or else we kill them. And these very men whom we have corrupted and brutalized by every means, we bring forward as a proof that one cannot deal with criminals except by brute force.

We are just like ignorant doctors who put a man, recovering from illness by the force of nature, into the most unfavorable conditions of hygiene, and dose him with the most deleterious drugs, and then assert triumphantly that their hygiene and their drugs saved his life, when the patient would have been well long before if they had left him alone.

Violence, which is held up as the means of supporting the Christian organization of life, not only fails to produce that effect, it even hinders the social organization of life from being what it might and ought to be. The social organization is as good as it is not as a result of force, but in spite of it.

And therefore the champions of the existing order are mistaken in arguing that since, even with the aid of force, the bad and non-Christian elements of humanity can hardly be kept from attacking us, the abolition of the use of force and the substitution of public opinion for it would leave humanity quite unprotected.

They are mistaken, because force does not protect humanity, but, on the contrary, deprives it of the only possible means of really protecting itself, that is, the establishment and diffusion of a Christian public opinion. Only by the suppression of violence will a Christian public opinion cease to be corrupted, and be enabled to be diffused without hindrance, and men will then turn their efforts in the spiritual direction by which alone they can advance.

"But how are we to cast off the visible tangible protection of an armed policeman, and trust to something so intangible as public opinion? Does it yet exist? Moreover, the condition of things in which we are living now, we know, good or bad; we know its shortcomings and are used to it, we know what to do, and how to behave under present conditions. But what will happen when we give it up and trust ourselves to something invisible and intangible, and altogether unknown?"

The unknown world on which they are entering in renouncing their habitual ways of life appears itself as dreadful to them. It is all very well to dread the unknown when our habitual position is sound and secure. But our position is so far from being secure that we know, beyond all doubt, that we are standing on the brink of a precipice.

If we must be afraid let us be afraid of what is really alarming, and not what we imagine as alarming.

Fearing to make the effort to detach ourselves from our perilous position because the future is not fully clear to us, we are like passengers in a foundering ship who, through being afraid to trust themselves to the boat which would carry them to the shore, shut themselves up in the cabin and refuse to come out of it; or like sheep, who, terrified by their barn being on fire, huddle in a corner and do not go out of the wide-open door.

We are standing on the threshold of the murderous war of social revolution, terrific in its miseries, beside which, as those who are preparing it tell us, the horrors of 1793 will be child's play. And can we talk of the danger threatening us from the warriors of Dahomey, the Zulus, and such, who live so far away and are not dreaming of attacking us, and from some thousands of swindlers, thieves, and murderers, brutalized and corrupted by ourselves, whose number is in no way lessened by all our sentences, prisons, and executions?

Moreover this dread of the suppression of the visible protection of the policeman is essentially a sentiment of townspeople, that is, of people who are living in abnormal and artificial conditions. People living in natural conditions of life, not in towns, but in the midst of nature, and carrying on the struggle with nature, live without this protection and know how little force can protect us from the real dangers with which we are surrounded. There is something sickly in this dread, which is essentially dependent on the artificial conditions in which many of us live and have been brought up.

A doctor, a specialist in insanity, told a story that one summer day when he was leaving the asylum, the lunatics accompanied him to the street door. "Come for a walk in the town with me?" the doctor suggested to them. The lunatics agreed, and a small band followed the doctor. But the further they proceeded along the street where healthy people were freely moving about, the more timid they became, and they pressed closer and closer to the doctor, hindering him from walking. At last they all began to beg him to take them back to the asylum, to their meaningless but customary way of life, to their keepers, to blows, strait waistcoats, and solitary cells.

This is just how men of to-day huddle in terror and draw back to their irrational manner of life, their factories, law courts, prisons, executions, and wars, when Christianity calls them to liberty, to the free, rational life of the future coming age.

People ask, "How will our security be guaranteed when the existing organization is suppressed? What precisely will the new organization be that is to replace it? So long as we do not know precisely how our life will be organized, we will not stir a step forward."

An explorer going to an unknown country might as well ask for a detailed map of the country before he would start.

If a man, before he passed from one stage to another, could know his future life in full detail, he would have nothing to live for. It is the same with the life of humanity. If it had a programme of the life which awaited it before entering a new stage, it would be the surest sign that it was not living, nor advancing, but simply rotating in the same place.

The conditions of the new order of life cannot be known by us because we have to create them by our own labors. That is all that life is, to learn the unknown, and to adapt our actions to this new knowledge.

That is the life of each individual man, and that is the life of human societies and of humanity.

CHAPTER XI: THE CHRISTIAN CONCEPTION OF LIFE HAS ALREADY ARISEN IN OUR SOCIETY, AND WILL INFALLIBLY PUT AN END TO THE PRESENT ORGANIZATION OF OUR LIFE BASED ON FORCE— WHEN THAT WILL BE

The Condition and Organization of our Society are Terrible, but they Rest only on Public Opinion, and can be Destroyed by it— Already Violence is Regarded from a Different Point of View; the Number of those who are Ready to Serve the Government is Diminishing; and even the Servants of Government are Ashamed of their Position, and so often Do Not Perform their Duties— These Facts are all Signs of the Rise of a Public Opinion, which Continually Growing will Lead to No One being Willing to Enter Government Service—Moreover, it Becomes More and More Evident that those Offices are of No Practical Use—Men already Begin to Understand the Futility of all Institutions Based on Violence, and if a Few already Understand it, All will One Day Understand it—The Day of Deliverance is Unknown, but it Depends on Men Themselves, on how far Each Man Lives According to the Light that is in Him.

The position of Christian humanity with its prisons, galleys, gibbets, its factories and accumulation of capital, its taxes, churches, gin-palaces, licensed brothels, its ever-increasing armament and its millions of brutalized men, ready, like chained dogs, to attack anyone against whom their master incites them, would be terrible indeed if it were the product of violence, but it is pre-eminently the product of public opinion. And what has been established by public opinion can be destroyed by public opinion—and, indeed, is being destroyed by public opinion.

Money lavished by hundreds of millions, tens of millions of disciplined troops, weapons of astounding destructive power, all organizations carried to the highest point of perfection, a whole army of men charged with the task of deluding and hypnotizing the people, and all this, by means of electricity which annihilates distance, under the direct control of men who regard such an organization of society not only as necessary for profit, but even for self-preservation, and therefore exert every effort of their ingenuity to preserve it—what an invincible power it would seem! And yet we need only imagine for a moment what will really inevitably come to pass, that is, the Christian social standard replacing the heathen social standard and established with the same power and universality, and the majority of men as much ashamed of taking any part in violence or in profiting by it, as they are to-day of thieving, swindling, begging, and cowardice; and at once we see the whole of this complex, and seemingly powerful organization of society falls into ruins of itself without a struggle.

And to bring this to pass, nothing new need be brought before men's minds. Only let the mist, which veils from men's eyes the true meaning of certain acts of violence, pass away, and the Christian public opinion which is springing up would overpower the extinct public opinion which permitted and justified acts of violence. People need only come to be as much ashamed to do deeds of violence, to assist in them or to profit by them, as they now are of being, or being reputed a swindler, a thief, a coward, or a beggar. And already this change is beginning to take place. We do not notice it just as we do not notice the movement of the earth, because we are moved together with everything around us.

It is true that the organization of society remains in its principal features just as much an organization based on violence as it was one thousand years ago, and even in some respects, especially in the preparation for war and in war itself, it appears still more brutal. But the rising Christian ideal, which must at a certain stage of development replace the heathen ideal of life, already makes its influence felt. A dead tree stands apparently as firmly as ever—it may even seem firmer because it is harder—but it is rotten at the core, and soon must fall. It is just so with the present order of society, based on force. The external aspect is unchanged. There is the same division of oppressors and oppressed, but their view of the significance and dignity of their respective positions is no longer what it once was.

The oppressors, that is, those who take part in government, and those who profit by oppression, that is, the rich, no longer imagine, as they once did, that they are the elect of the world, and that they constitute the ideal of human happiness and greatness, to attain which was once the highest aim of the oppressed.

Very often now it is not the oppressed who strive to attain the position of the oppressors, and try to imitate them, but on the contrary the oppressors who voluntarily abandon the advantages of their position, prefer the condition of the oppressed, and try to resemble them in the simplicity of their life.

Not to speak of the duties and occupations now openly despised, such as that of spy, agent of secret police, money-lender, and publican, there are a great number of professions formerly regarded as honorable, such as those of police officials, courtiers, judges, and administrative functionaries, clergymen, military officers, speculators, and bankers, which are no longer considered desirable positions by everyone, and are even despised by a special circle of the most respected people. There are already men who voluntarily abandon these professions which were once reckoned irreproachable, and prefer less lucrative callings which are in no way connected with the use of force.

And there are even rich men who, not through religious sentiment, but simply through special sensitiveness to the social standard that is springing up, relinquish their inherited property, believing that a man can only justly consume what he has gained by his own labor.

The position of a government official or of a rich man is no longer, as it once was, and still is among non-Christian peoples, regarded as necessarily honorable and deserving of respect, and under the special blessing of God. The most delicate and moral people (they are generally also the most cultivated) avoid such positions and prefer more humble callings that are not dependent on the use of force.

The best of our young people, at the age when they are still uncorrupted by life and are choosing a career, prefer the calling of doctor, engineer, teacher, artist, writer, or even that of simple farmer living on his own labor, to legal, administrative, clerical, and military positions in the pay of government, or to an idle existence living on their incomes.

Monuments and memorials in these days are mostly not erected in honor of government dignitaries, or generals, or still less of rich men, but rather of artists, men of science, and inventors, persons who have nothing in common with the government, and often have even been in conflict with it. They are the men whose praises are celebrated in poetry, who are honored by sculpture and received with triumphant jubilations.

The best men of our day are all striving for such places of honor. Consequently the class from which the wealthy and the government officials are drawn grows less in number and lower in intelligence and education, and still more in moral qualities. So that nowadays the wealthy class and men at the head of government do not constitute, as they did in former days, the *élite* of society; on the contrary, they are inferior to the middle class.

In Russia and Turkey as in America and France, however often the government change its officials, the majority of them are self-seeking and corrupt, of so low a moral standard that they do not even come up the elementary requirements of common honesty expected by the government. One may often nowadays hear from persons in authority the naïve complaint that the best people are always, by some strange—as it seems to them—fatality, to be found in the camp of the opposition. As though men were to complain that those who accepted the office of hangman were— by some strange fatality—all persons of very little refinement or beauty of character.

The most cultivated and refined people of our society are not nowadays to be found among the very rich, as used formerly to be the rule. The rich are mostly coarse money grubbers, absorbed only, in increasing their hoard, generally by dishonest means, or else the degenerate heirs of such money grubbers, who, far from playing any prominent part in society, are mostly treated with general contempt.

And besides the fact that the class from which the servants of government and the wealthy are drawn grows less in number and lower in caliber, they no longer themselves attach the same importance to their positions as they once did; often they are ashamed of the ignominy of their calling and do not perform the duties they are bound to perform in their position. Kings and emperors scarcely govern at all; they scarcely ever decide upon an internal reform or a new departure in foreign politics. They mostly leave the decision of such questions to government institutions or to public opinion. All their duties are reduced to representing the unity and majesty of government. And even this duty they perform less and less successfully. The majority of them do not keep up their old unapproachable majesty, but become more and more democratized and even vulgarized, casting aside the external prestige that remained to them, and thereby destroying the very thing it was their function to maintain.

It is just the same with the army. Military officers of the highest rank, instead of encouraging in their soldiers the brutality and ferocity necessary for their work, diffuse education among the soldiers, inculcate humanity, and often even themselves share the socialistic ideas of the masses and denounce war. In the last plots against the Russian Government many of the conspirators were in the army. And the number of the disaffected in the army is always increasing. And it often happens (there was a case, indeed, within the last few days) that when called upon to quell disturbances they refuse to fire upon the people. Military exploits are openly reprobated by the military themselves, and are often the subject of jests among them.

It is the same with judges and public prosecutors. The judges, whose duty it is to judge and condemn criminals, conduct the proceedings so as to whitewash them as far as possible. So that the Russian Government, to procure the condemnation of those whom they want to punish, never intrust them to the ordinary tribunals, but have them tried before a court martial, which is only a parody of justice. The prosecutors themselves often refuse to proceed, and even when they do proceed, often in spite of the law, really defend those they ought to be accusing. The learned jurists whose business it is to justify the violence of authority, are more and more disposed to deny the right of punishment and to replace it by theories of irresponsibility and even of moral insanity, proposing to deal with those they call criminals by medical treatment only.

Jailers and overseers of galleys generally become the champions of those whom they ought to torture. Police officers and detectives are continually assisting the escape of those they ought to arrest. The clergy preach tolerance, and even sometimes condemn the use of force, and the more educated among them try in their sermons to avoid the very deception which is the basis of their position and which it is their duty to support. Executioners refuse to perform their functions, so that in Russia the death penalty cannot be carried out for want of executioners. And in spite of all the advantages bestowed on these men, who are selected from convicts, there is a constantly diminishing number of volunteers for the post. Governors, police officials, tax collectors often have compassion on the people and try to find pretexts for not collecting the tax from them. The rich are not at ease in spending their wealth only on themselves, and lavish it on works of public utility. Landowners build schools and hospitals on their property, and some even give up the ownership of their land and transfer it to the cultivators, or establish communities upon it. Millowners and manufacturers build hospitals, schools, savings banks, asylums, and dwellings for their workpeople. Some of them form co-operative associations in which they have shares on the same terms as the others. Capitalists expend a part of their capital on educational, artistic, philanthropic, and other public institutions. And many, who are not equal to parting with their wealth in their lifetime, leave it in their wills to public institutions.

All these phenomena might seem to be mere exceptions, except that they can all be referred to one common cause. Just as one might fancy the first leaves on the budding trees in April were exceptional if we did not know that they all have a common cause, the spring, and that if we see the branches on some trees shooting and turning green, it is certain that it will soon be so with all.

So it is with the manifestation of the Christian standard of opinion on force and all that is based on force. If this standard already influences some, the most impressionable, and impels each in his own sphere to abandon advantages based on the use of force, then its influence will extend further and further till it transforms the whole order of men's actions and puts it into accord with the Christian ideal which is already a living force in the vanguard of humanity.

And if there are now rulers, who do not decide on any step on their own authority, who try to be as unlike monarchs, and as like plain mortals as possible, who state their readiness to give up their prerogatives and become simply the first citizens of a republic; if there are already soldiers who realize all the sin and harm of war, and are not willing to fire on men either of their own or a foreign country; judges and prosecutors who do not like to try and to condemn criminals; priests, who abjure deception; tax-gatherers who try to perform as little as they can of their duties, and rich men renouncing their wealth—then the same thing will inevitably happen to other rulers, other soldiers, other judges, priests, tax-gatherers, and rich men. And when there are no longer men willing to fill these offices, these offices themselves will disappear too.

But this is not the only way in which public opinion is leading men to the abolition of the prevailing order and the substitution of a new order. As the positions based on the rule of force become less attractive and fewer men are found willing to fill them, the more will their uselessness be apparent.

Everywhere throughout the Christian world the same rulers, and the same governments, the same armies, the same law courts, the same tax-gatherers, the same priests, the same rich men, landowners, manufacturers, and capitalists, as ever, but the attitude of the world to them, and their attitude to themselves is altogether changed.

The same sovereigns have still the same audiences and interviews, hunts and banquets, and balls and uniforms; there are the same diplomats and the same deliberations on alliances and wars; there are still the same parliaments, with the same debates on the Eastern question and Africa, on treaties and violations of treaties, and Home Rule and the eight-hour day; and one set of ministers replacing another in the same way, and the same speeches and the same incidents. But for men who observe how one newspaper article has more effect on the position of affairs than dozens of royal audiences or parliamentary sessions, it becomes more and more evident that these audiences and interviews and debates in parliaments do not direct the course of affairs, but something independent of all that, which cannot be concentrated in one place.

The same generals and officers and soldiers, and cannons and fortresses, and reviews and maneuvers, but no war breaks out. One year, ten, twenty years pass by. And it becomes less and less possible to rely on the army for the pacification of riots, and more and more evident, consequently, that generals, and officers, and soldiers are only figures in solemn processions—objects of amusement for governments—a sort of immense—and far too expensive—*corps de ballet*.

The same lawyers and judges, and the same assizes, but it becomes more and more evident that the civil courts decide cases on the most diverse grounds, but regardless of justice, and that criminal trials are quite senseless, because the punishments do not attain the objects aimed at by the judges themselves. These institutions therefore serve no other purpose than to provide a means of livelihood for men who are not capable of doing anything more useful.

The same priests and archbishops and churches and synods, but it becomes more and more evident that they have long ago ceased to believe in what they preach, and therefore they can convince no one of the necessity of believing what they don't believe themselves.

The same tax collectors, but they are less and less capable of taking men's property from them by force, and it becomes more and more evident that people can collect all that is necessary by voluntary subscription without their aid.

The same rich men, but it becomes more and more evident that they can only be of use by ceasing to administer their property in person and giving up to society the whole or at least a part of their wealth.

And when all this has become absolutely evident to everyone, it will be natural for men to ask themselves: "But why should we keep and maintain all these kings, emperors, presidents, and members of all sorts of senates and ministries, since nothing comes of all their debates and audiences? Wouldn't it be better, as some humorist suggested, to make a queen of india-rubber?"

And what good to us are these armies with their generals and bands and horses and drums? And what need is there of them when there is no war, and no one wants to make war? and if there were a war, other nations would not let us gain any advantage from it; while the soldiers refuse to fire on their fellow-countrymen.

And what is the use of these lawyers and judges who don't decide civil cases with justice and recognize themselves the uselessness of punishments in criminal cases?

And what is the use of tax collectors who collect the taxes unwillingly, when it is easy to raise all that is wanted without them?

What is the use of the clergy, who don't believe in what they preach?

And what is the use of capital in the hands of private persons, when it can only be of use as the property of all?

And when once people have asked themselves these questions they cannot help coming to some decision and ceasing to support all these institutions which are no longer of use.

But even before those who support these institutions decide to abolish them, the men who occupy these positions will be reduced to the necessity of throwing them up.

Public opinion more and more condemns the use of force, and therefore men are less and less willing to fill positions which rest on the use of force, and if they do occupy them, are less and less able to make use of force in them. And hence they must become more and more superfluous.

I once took part in Moscow in a religious meeting which used to take place generally in the week after Easter near the church in the Ohotny Row. A little knot of some twenty men were collected together on the pavement, engaged in serious religious discussion. At the same time there was a kind of concert going on in the buildings of the Court Club in the same street, and a police officer noticing the little group collected near the church sent a mounted policeman to disperse it. It was absolutely unnecessary for the officer to disperse it. A group of twenty men was no obstruction to anyone, but he had been standing there the whole morning, and he wanted to do something. The policeman, a young fellow, with a resolute flourish of his right arm and a clink of his saber, came up to us and commanded us severely: "Move on! what's this meeting about?" Everyone looked at the policeman, and one of the speakers, a quiet man in a peasant's dress, answered with a calm and gracious air, "We are speaking of serious matters, and there is no need for us to move on; you would do better, young man, to get off your horse and listen. It might do you good"; and turning round he continued his discourse. The policeman turned his horse and went off without a word.

That is just what should be done in all cases of violence.

The officer was bored, he had nothing to do. He had been put, poor fellow, in a position in which he had no choice but to give orders. He was shut off from all human existence; he could do nothing but superintend and give orders, and give orders and superintend, though his superintendence and his orders served no useful purpose whatever. And this is the position in which all these unlucky rulers, ministers, members of parliament, governors, generals, officers, archbishops, priests, and even rich men find themselves to some extent already, and will find themselves altogether as time goes on. They can do nothing but give orders, and they give orders and send their messengers, as the officer sent the policeman, to interfere with people. And because the people they hinder turn to them and request them not to interfere, they fancy they are very useful indeed.

But the time will come and is coming when it will be perfectly evident to everyone that they are not of any use at all, and only a hindrance, and those whom they interfere with will say gently and quietly to them, like my friend in the street meeting, "Pray don't interfere with us." And all the messengers and those who send them too will be obliged to follow this good advice, that is to say, will leave off galloping about, with their arms akimbo, interfering with people, and getting off their horses and removing their spurs, will listen to what is being said, and mixing with others, will take their place with them in some real human work.

The time will come and is inevitably coming when all institutions based on force will disappear through their uselessness, stupidity, and even inconvenience becoming obvious to all.

The time must come when the men of our modern world who fill offices based upon violence will find themselves in the position of the emperor in Andersen's tale of "The Emperor's New Clothes," when the child seeing the emperor undressed, cried in all simplicity, "Look, he is naked!" And then all the rest, who had seen him and said nothing, could not help recognizing it too.

The story is that there was once an emperor, very fond of new clothes. And to him came two tailors, who promised to make him some extraordinary clothes. The emperor engages them and they begin to sew at them, but they explain that the clothes have the extraordinary property of remaining invisible to anyone who is unfit for his position. The courtiers come to look at the tailors' work and see nothing, for the men are plying their needles in empty space. But remembering the extraordinary property of the clothes, they all declare they see them and are loud in their admiration. The emperor does the same himself. The day of the procession comes in which the emperor is to go out in his new clothes. The emperor undresses and puts on his new clothes, that is to say, remains naked, and naked he walks through the town. But remembering the magic property of the clothes, no one ventures to say that he has nothing on till a little child cries out: "Look, he is naked!"

This will be exactly the situation of all who continue through inertia to fill offices which have long become useless directly someone who has no interest in concealing their uselessness exclaims in all simplicity: "But these people have been of no use to anyone for a long time past!"

The condition of Christian humanity with its fortresses, cannons, dynamite, guns, torpedoes, prisons, gallows, churches, factories, customs offices, and palaces is really terrible. But still cannons and guns will not fire themselves, prisons will not shut men up of themselves, gallows will not hang them, churches will not delude them, nor customs offices hinder them, and palaces and factories are not built nor kept up of themselves. All those things are the work of men. If men come to understand that they ought not to do these things, then they will cease to be. And already they are beginning to understand it. Though all do not understand it yet, the advanced guard understand and the rest will follow them. And the advanced guard cannot cease to understand what they have once understood; and what they understand the rest not only can but must inevitably understand hereafter.

So that the prophecy that the time will come when men will be taught of God, will learn war no more, will beat their swords into plowshares and their spears into reaping-hooks, which means, translating it into our language, the fortresses, prisons, barracks, palaces, and churches will remain empty, and all the gibbets and guns and cannons will be left unused, is no longer a dream, but the definite new form of life to which mankind is approaching with ever-increasing rapidity.

But when will it be?

Eighteen hundred years ago to this question Christ answered that the end of the world (that is, of the pagan organization of life) shall come when the tribulation of men is greater than it has ever been, and when the Gospel of the kingdom of God, that is, the possibility of a new organization of life, shall be preached in the world unto all nations. (Matt. xxiv. 3-28.) But of that day and hour knoweth no man but the Father only (Matt. xxiv. 3-6), said Christ. For it may come any time, in such an hour as ye think not.

To the question when this hour cometh Christ answers that we cannot know, but just because we cannot know when that hour is coming we ought to be always ready to meet it, just as the master ought to watch who guards his house from thieves, as the virgins ought to watch with lamps alight for the bridegroom; and further, we ought to work with all the powers given us to bring that hour to pass, as the servants ought to work with the talents intrusted to them. (Matt. xxiv. 43, and xxvi. 13, 14-30.)

And there could be no answer but this one. Men cannot know when the day and the hour of the kingdom of God will come, because its coming depends on themselves alone.

The answer is like that of the wise man who, when asked whether it was far to the town, answered, "Walk!"

How can we tell whether it is far to the goal which humanity is approaching, when we do not know how men are going toward it, while it depends on them whether they go or do not go, stand still, slacken their pace or hasten it?

All we can know is what we who make up mankind ought to do, and not to do, to bring about the coming of the kingdom of God. And that we all know. And we need only each begin to do what we ought to do, we need only each live with all the light that is in us, to bring about at once the promised kingdom of God to which every man's heart is yearning.

CHAPTER XII: CONCLUSION—REPENT YE, FOR THE KINGDOM OF HEAVEN IS AT HAND

1. Chance Meeting with a Train Carrying Soldiers to Restore Order Among the Famishing Peasants—Reason of the Expedition—How the Decisions of the Higher Authorities are Enforced in Cases of Insubordination on Part of the Peasants—What Happened at Orel, as an Example of How the Rights of the Propertied Classes are Maintained by Murder and Torture—All the Privileges of the Wealthy are Based on Similar Acts of Violence.

2. The Elements that Made up the Force Sent to Toula, and the Conduct of the Men Composing it—How these Men Could Carry Out such Acts—The Explanation is Not to be Found in Ignorance, Conviction, Cruelty, Heartlessness, or Want of Moral Sense—They do these Things Because they are Necessary to Support the Existing Order, which they Consider it Every Man's Duty to Support—The Basis of this Conviction that the Existing Order is Necessary and Inevitable—In the Upper Classes this Conviction is Based on the Advantages of the Existing Order for Themselves—But what Forces Men of the Lower Classes to Believe in the Immutability of the Existing Order, from which they Derive no Advantage, and which they Aid in Maintaining, Facts Contrary to their Conscience?—This is the Result of the Lower Classes being Deluded by the Upper, Both as to the Inevitability of the Existing Order and the Lawfulness of the Acts of Violence Needed to Maintain it—Deception in General—Special Form of Deception in Regard to Military Service—Conscription.

3. How can Men Allow that Murder is Permissible while they Preach Principles of Morality, and How can they Allow of the Existence in their Midst of a Military Organization of Physical Force which is a Constant Menace to Public Security?—It is only Allowed by the Upper Classes, who Profit by this Organization, Because their Privileges are Maintained by it—The Upper Classes Allow it, and the Lower Classes Carry it into Effect in Spite of their Consciousness of the Immorality of the Deeds of Violence, the More Readily Because Through the Arrangements

of the Government the Moral Responsibility for such Deeds is Divided among a Great Number of Participants in it, and Everyone Throws the Responsibility on Someone Else—Moreover, the Sense of Moral Responsibility is Lost through the Delusion of Inequality, and the Consequent Intoxication of Power on the Part of Superiors, and Servility on the Part of Inferiors—The Condition of these Men, Acting against the Dictates of their Conscience, is Like that of Hypnotized Subjects Acting by Suggestion—The Difference between this Obedience to Government Suggestion, and Obedience to Public Opinion, and to the Guidance of Men of a Higher Moral Sense—The Existing Order of Society, which is the Result of an Extinct Public Opinion and is Inconsistent with the Already Existing Public Opinion of the Future, is only Maintained by the Stupefaction of the Conscience, Produced Spontaneously by Self-interest in the Upper Classes and Through Hypnotizing in the Lower Classes—The Conscience or the Common Sense of such Men may Awaken, and there are Examples of its Sudden Awakening, so that one can Never be Sure of the Deeds of Violence they are Prepared for—It Depends Entirely on the Point which the Sense of the Unlawfulness of Acts of Violence has Reached, and this Sense may Spontaneously Awaken in Men, or may be Reawakened by the Influence of Men of more Conscience.

4. Everything Depends on the Strength of the Consciousness of Christian Truths in Each Individual Man—The Leading Men of Modern Times, however, do not Think it Necessary to Preach or Practice the Truths of Christianity, but Regard the Modification of the External Conditions of Existence within the Limit Imposed by Governments as Sufficient to Reform the Life of Humanity—On this Scientific Theory of Hypocrisy, which has Replaced the Hypocrisy of Religion, Men of the Wealthy Classes Base their Justification of their Position—Through this Hypocrisy they can Enjoy the Exclusive Privileges of their Position by Force and Fraud, and Still Pretend to be Christians to One Another and be Easy in their Minds—This Hypocrisy Allows Men who Preach Christianity to Take Part in Institutions Based on Violence—No External Reformation of Life will

Render it Less Miserable—Its Misery the Result of Disunion Caused by Following Lies, not the Truth—Union only Possible in Truth—Hypocrisy Hinders this Union, since Hypocrites Conceal from themselves and Others the Truth they Know—Hypocrisy Turns all Reforms of Life to Evil—Hypocrisy Distorts the Idea of Good and Evil, and so Stands in the Way of the Progress of Men toward Perfection—Undisguised Criminals and Malefactors do Less Harm than those who Live by Legalized Violence, Disguised by Hypocrisy—All Men Feel the Iniquity of our Life, and would Long Ago have Transformed it if it had not been Dissimulated by Hypocrisy—But Seem to have Reached the Extreme Limits of Hypocrisy, and we Need only Make an Effort of Conscience to Awaken as from a Nightmare to a Different Reality.

5. Can Man Make this Effort?—According to the Hypocritical Theory of the Day, Man is not Free to Transform his Life—Man is not Free in his Actions, but he is Free to Admit or to Deny the Truth he Knows—When Truth is Once Admitted, it Becomes the Basis of Action—Man's Threefold Relation to Truth—The Reason of the Apparent Insolubility of the Problem of Free Will—Man's Freedom Consists in the Recognition of the Truth Revealed to him. There is no Other Freedom—Recognition of Truth Gives Freedom, and Shows the Path Along which, Willingly or Unwillingly by Mankind, Man Must Advance—The Recognition of Truth and Real Freedom Enables Man to Share in the Work of God, not as the Slave, but as the Creator of Life—Men Need only Make the Effort to Renounce all Thought of Bettering the External Conditions of Life and Bend all their Efforts to Recognizing and Preaching the Truth they Know, to put an End to the Existing Miserable State of Things, and to Enter upon the Kingdom of God so far as it is yet Accessible to Man—All that is Needed is to Make an End of Lying and Hypocrisy—But then what Awaits us in the Future?—What will Happen to Humanity if Men Follow the Dictates of their Conscience, and how can Life go on with the Conditions of Civilized Life to which we are Accustomed?—All Uneasiness on these Points may be Removed by the Reflection that Nothing

True and Good can be Destroyed by the Realization of Truth, but will only be Freed from the Alloy of Falsehood.

6. Our Life has Reached the Extreme Limit of Misery and Cannot be Improved by any Systems of Organization—All our Life and all our Institutions are Quite Meaningless—Are we Doing what God Wills of us by Preserving our Privileges and Duties to Government?—We are put in this Position not Because the World is so Made and it is Inevitable, but Because we Wish it to be so, Because it is to the Advantage of Some of us—Our Conscience is in Opposition to our Position and all our Conduct, and the Way Out of the Contradiction is to be Found in the Recognition of the Christian Truth: Do Not unto Others what you Would Not they should Do unto You—As our Duties to Self Must be Subordinated to our Duties to Others, so Must our Duties to Others be Subordinated to our Duties to God—The Only Way Out of our Position Lies, if not in Renouncing our Position and our Privileges, at Least in Recognizing our Sin and not Justifying it nor Disguising it—The Only Object of Life is to Learn the Truth and to Act on it—Acceptance of the Position and of State Action Deprives Life of all Object—It is God's Will that we should Serve Him in our Life, that is, that we should Bring About the Greatest Unity of all that has Life, a Unity only Possible in Truth.

I was finishing this book, which I had been working at for two years, when I happened on the 9th of September to be traveling by rail through the governments of Toula and Riazan, where the peasants were starving last year and where the famine is even more severe now. At one of the railway stations my train passed an extra train which was taking a troop of soldiers under the conduct of the governor of the province, together with muskets, cartridges, and rods, to flog and murder these same famishing peasants.

The punishment of flogging by way of carrying the decrees of the authorities into effect has been more and more frequently adopted of late in Russia, in spite of the fact that corporal punishment was abolished by law thirty years ago.

I had heard of this, I had even read in the newspapers of the fearful floggings which had been inflicted in Tchernigov, Tambov, Saratov, Astrakhan, and Orel, and of those of which the governor of Nijni-Novgorod, General Baranov, had boasted. But I had never before happened to see men in the process of carrying out these punishments.

And here I saw the spectacle of good Russians full of the Christian spirit traveling with guns and rods to torture and kill their starving brethren. The reason for their expedition was as follows:

On one of the estates of a rich landowner the peasants had common rights on the forest, and having always enjoyed these rights, regarded the forest as their own, or at least as theirs in common with the owner. The landowner wished to keep the forest entirely to himself and began to fell the trees. The peasants lodged a complaint. The judges in the first instance gave an unjust decision (I say unjust on the authority of the lawyer and governor, who ought to understand the matter), and decided the case in favor of the landowner. All the later decisions, even that of the senate, though they could see that the matter had been unjustly decided, confirmed the judgment and adjudged the forest to the landowner. He began to cut down the trees, but the peasants, unable to believe that such obvious injustice could be done them by the higher authorities, did not submit to the decision and drove away the men sent to cut down the trees, declaring that the forest belonged to them and they would go to the Tzar before they would let them cut it down.

The matter was referred to Petersburg, and the order was transmitted to the governor to carry the decision of the court into effect. The governor asked for a troop of soldiers. And here were the soldiers with bayonets and cartridges, and moreover, a supply of rods, expressly prepared for the purpose and heaped up in one of the trucks, going to carry the decision of the higher authorities into effect.

The decisions of the higher authorities are carried into effect by means of murder or torture, or threats of one or the other, according to whether they offer resistance or not.

In the first case if the peasants offer resistance the practice is in Russia, and it is the same everywhere where a state organization and private property exist, as follows:

The governor delivers an address in which he demands submission. The excited crowd, generally deluded by their leaders, don't understand a word of what the representative of authority is saying in the pompous official language, and their excitement continues. Then the governor announces that if they do not submit and disperse, he will be obliged to have recourse to force. If the crowd does not disperse even on this, the governor gives the order to fire over the heads of the crowd. If the crowd does not even then disperse, the governor gives the order to fire straight into the crowd; the soldiers fire and the killed and wounded fall about the street. Then the crowd usually runs away in all directions, and the troops at the governor's command take those who are supposed to be the ringleaders and lead them off under escort. Then they pick up the dying, the wounded, and the dead, covered with blood, sometimes women and children among them. The dead they bury and the wounded they carry to the hospital. Those whom they regard as the ringleaders they take to the town hall and have them tried by a special court-martial. And if they have had recourse to violence on their side, they are condemned to be hanged. And then the gallows is erected. And they solemnly strangle a few defenseless creatures. This is what has often been done in Russia, and is and must always be done where the social order is based on force.

But in the second case, when the peasants do submit, something quite special, peculiar to Russia, takes place. The governor arrives on the scene of action and delivers an harangue to the people, reproaching them for their insubordination, and either stations troops in the houses of the villages, where sometimes for a whole month the soldiers drain the resources of the peasants, or contenting himself with threats, he mercifully takes leave of the people, or what is the most frequent course, he announces that the ringleaders must be punished, and quite arbitrarily without any trial selects a certain number of men, regarded as ringleaders, and commands them to be flogged in his presence.

In order to give an idea of how such things are done I will describe a proceeding of the kind which took place in Orel, and received the full approval of the highest authorities.

This is what took place in Orel. Just as here in the Toula province, a landlord wanted to appropriate the property of the peasants and just in the same way the peasants opposed it. The matter in dispute was a fall of water, which irrigated the peasants' fields, and which the landowner wanted to cut off and divert to turn his mill. The peasants rebelled against this being done. The landowner laid a complaint before the district commander, who illegally (as was recognized later even by a legal decision) decided the matter in favor of the landowner, and allowed him to divert the water course. The landowner sent workmen to dig the conduit by which the water was to be let off to turn the mill. The peasants were indignant at this unjust decision, and sent their women to prevent the landowner's men from digging this conduit. The women went to the dykes, overturned the carts, and drove away the men. The landowner made a complaint against the women for thus taking the law into their own hands. The district commander made out an order that from every house throughout the village one woman was to be taken and put in prison. The order was not easily executed. For in every household there were several women, and it was impossible to know which one was to be arrested. Consequently the police did not carry out the order. The landowner complained to the governor of the neglect on the part of the police, and the latter, without examining into the affair, gave the chief official of the police strict orders to carry out the instructions of the district commander without delay. The police official, in obedience to his superior, went to the village and with the insolence peculiar to Russian officials ordered his policemen to take one woman out of each house. But since there were more than one woman in each house, and there was no knowing which one was sentenced to imprisonment, disputes and opposition arose. In spite of these disputes and opposition, however, the officer of police gave orders that some woman, whichever came first, should be taken from each household and led away to prison. The peasants began to defend their wives and mothers, would not let them go, and beat the police and their officer. This was a fresh and terrible crime: resistance was offered to the authorities. A report of this new offense was sent to the town. And so this governor—precisely as the governor of Toula was doing on that day—with a battalion of soldiers with guns and rods, hastily brought together by means of telegraphs and telephones and railways, proceeded by a special train to the scene of action, with a learned doctor whose duty it was to insure the flogging being of an hygienic character. Herzen's prophecy of the modern Ghenghis Khan with his telegrams is completely realized by this governor.

Before the town hall of the district were the soldiery, a battalion of police with their revolvers slung round them with red cords, the persons of most importance among the peasants, and the culprits. A crowd of one thousand or more people were standing round. The governor, on arriving, stepped out of his carriage, delivered a prepared harangue, and asked for the culprits and a bench. The latter demand was at first not understood. But a police constable whom the governor always took about with him, and who undertook to organize such executions—by no means exceptional in that province—explained that what was meant was a bench for flogging. A bench was brought as well as the rods, and then the executioners were summoned (the latter had been selected beforehand from some horsestealers of the same village, as the soldiers refused the office). When everything was ready, the governor ordered the first of the twelve culprits pointed out by the landowner as the most guilty to come forward. The first to come forward was the head of a family, a man of forty who had always stood up manfully for the rights of his class, and therefore was held in the greatest esteem by all the villagers. He was led to the bench and stripped, and then ordered to lie down.

The peasant attempted to supplicate for mercy, but seeing it was useless, he crossed himself and lay down. Two police constables hastened to hold him down. The learned doctor stood by, in readiness to give his aid and his medical science when they should be needed. The convicts spit into their hands, brandished the rods, and began to flog. It seemed, however, that the bench was too narrow, and it was difficult to keep the victim writhing in torture upon it. Then the governor ordered them to bring another bench and to put a plank across them. Soldiers, with their hands raised to their caps, and respectful murmurs of "Yes, your Excellency," hasten obediently to carry out this order. Meanwhile the tortured man, half naked, pale and scowling, stood waiting, his eyes fixed on the ground and his teeth chattering. When another bench had been brought they again made him lie down, and the convicted thieves again began to flog him.

The victim's back and thighs and legs, and even his sides, became more and more covered with scars and wheals, and at every blow there came the sound of the deep groans which he could no longer restrain. In the crowd standing round were heard the sobs of wives, mothers, children, the families of the tortured man and of all the others picked out for punishment.

The miserable governor, intoxicated with power, was counting the strokes on his fingers, and never left off smoking cigarettes, while several officious persons hastened on every opportunity to offer him a burning match to light them. When more than fifty strokes had been given, the peasant ceased to shriek and writhe, and the doctor, who had been educated in a government institution to serve his sovereign and his country with his scientific attainments, went up to the victim, felt his pulse, listened to his heart, and announced to the representative of authority that the man undergoing punishment had lost consciousness, and that, in accordance with the conclusions of science, to continue the punishment would endanger the victim's life. But the miserable governor, now completely intoxicated by the sight of blood, gave orders that the punishment should go on, and the flogging was continued up to seventy strokes, the number which the governor had for some reason fixed upon as necessary. When the seventieth stroke had been reached, the governor said "Enough! Next one!" And the mutilated victim, his back covered with blood, was lifted up and carried away unconscious, and another was led up. The sobs and groans of the crowd grew louder. But the representative of the state continued the torture.

Thus they flogged each of them up to the twelfth, and each of them received seventy strokes. They all implored mercy, shrieked and groaned. The sobs and cries of the crowd of women grew louder and more heart-rending, and the men's faces grew darker and darker. But they were surrounded by troops, and the torture did not cease till it had reached the limit which had been fixed by the caprice of the miserable half-drunken and insane creature they called the governor.

The officials, and officers, and soldiers not only assisted in it, but were even partly responsible for the affair, since by their presence they prevented any interference on the part of the crowd.

When I inquired of one of the governors why they made use of this kind of torture when people had already submitted and soldiers were stationed in the village, he replied with the important air of a man who thoroughly understands all the subtleties of statecraft, that if the peasants were not thoroughly subdued by flogging, they would begin offering opposition to the decisions of authorities again. When some of them had been thoroughly tortured, the authority of the state would be secured forever among them.

And so that was why the Governor of Toula was going in his turn with his subordinate officials, officers, and soldiers to carry out a similar measure. By precisely the same means, *i. e.*, by murder and torture, obedience to the decision of the higher authorities was to be secured. And this decision was to enable a young landowner, who had an income of one hundred thousand, to gain three thousand rubles more by stealing a forest from a whole community of cold and famished peasants, to spend it, in two or three weeks in the saloons of Moscow, Petersburg, or Paris. That was what those people whom I met were going to do.

After my thoughts had for two years been turned in the same direction, fate seemed expressly to have brought me face to face for the first time in my life with a fact which showed me absolutely unmistakably in practice what had long been clear to me in theory, that the organization of our society rests, not as people interested in maintaining the present order of things like to imagine, on certain principles of jurisprudence, but on simple brute force, on the murder and torture of men.

People who own great estates or fortunes, or who receive great revenues drawn from the class who are in want even of necessities, the working class, as well as all those who like merchants, doctors, artists, clerks, learned professors, coachmen, cooks, writers, valets, and barristers, make their living about these rich people, like to believe that the privileges they enjoy are not the result of force, but of absolutely free and just interchange of services, and that their advantages, far from being gained by such punishments and murders as took place in Orel and several parts of Russia this year, and are always taking place all over Europe and America, have no kind of connection with these acts of violence. They like to believe that their privileges exist apart and are the result of free contract among people; and that the violent cruelties perpetrated on the people also exist apart and are the result of some general judicial, political, or economical laws. They try not to see that they all enjoy their privileges as a result of the same fact which forces the peasants who have tended the forest, and who are in the direct need of it for fuel, to give it up to a rich landowner who has taken no part in caring for its growth and has no need of it whatever—the fact, that is, that if they don't give it up they will be flogged or killed.

And yet if it is clear that it was only by means of menaces, blows, or murder, that the mill in Orel was enabled to yield a larger income, or that the forest which the peasants had planted became the property of a landowner, it should be equally clear that all the other exclusive rights enjoyed by the rich, by robbing the poor of their necessities, rest on the same basis of violence. If the peasants, who need land to maintain their families, may not cultivate the land about their houses, but one man, a Russian, English, Austrian, or any other great landowner, possesses land enough to maintain a thousand families, though he does not cultivate it himself, and if a merchant profiting by the misery of the cultivators, taking corn from them at a third of its value, can keep this corn in his granaries with perfect security while men are starving all around him, and sell it again for three times its value to the very cultivators he bought it from, it is evident that all this too comes from the same cause. And if one man may not buy of another a commodity from the other side of a certain fixed line, called the frontier, without paying certain duties on it to men who have taken no part whatever in its production—and if men are driven to sell their last cow to pay taxes which the government distributes among its functionaries, and spends on maintaining soldiers to murder these very taxpayers—it would appear self-evident that all this does not come about as the result of any abstract laws, but is based on just what was done in Orel, and which may be done in Toula, and is done periodically in one form or another throughout the whole world wherever there is a government, and where there are rich and poor.

Simply because torture and murder are not employed in every instance of oppression by force, those who enjoy the exclusive privileges of the ruling classes persuade themselves and others that their privileges are not based on torture and murder, but on some mysterious general causes, abstract laws, and so on. Yet one would think it was perfectly clear that if men, who consider it unjust (and all the working classes do consider it so nowadays), still pay the principal part of the produce of their labor away to the capitalist and the landowner, and pay taxes, though they know to what a bad use these taxes are put, they do so not from recognition of abstract laws of which they have never heard, but only because they know they will be beaten and killed if they don't do so.

And if there is no need to imprison, beat, and kill men every time the landlord collects his rents, every time those who are in want of bread have to pay a swindling merchant three times its value, every time the factory hand has to be content with a wage less than half of the profit made by the employer, and every time a poor man pays his last ruble in taxes, it is because so many men have been beaten and killed for trying to resist these demands, that the lesson has now been learnt very thoroughly.

Just as a trained tiger, who does not eat meat put under his nose, and jumps over a stick at the word of command, does not act thus because he likes it, but because he remembers the red-hot irons or the fast with which he was punished every time he did not obey; so men submitting to what is disadvantageous or even ruinous to them, and considered by them as unjust, act thus because they remember what they suffered for resisting it.

As for those who profit by the privileges gained by previous acts of violence, they often forget and like to forget how these privileges were obtained. But one need only recall the facts of history, not the history of the exploits of different dynasties of rulers, but real history, the history of the oppression of the majority by a small number of men, to see that all the advantages the rich have over the poor are based on nothing but flogging, imprisonment, and murder.

One need but reflect on the unceasing, persistent struggle of all to better their material position, which is the guiding motive of men of the present day, to be convinced that the advantages of the rich over the poor could never and can never be maintained by anything but force.

There may be cases of oppression, of violence, and of punishments, though they are rare, the aim of which is not to secure the privileges of the propertied classes. But one may confidently assert that in any society where, for every man living in ease, there are ten exhausted by labor, envious, covetous, and often suffering with their families from direct privation, all the privileges of the rich, all their luxuries and superfluities, are obtained and maintained only by tortures, imprisonment, and murder.

The train I met on the 9th of September going with soldiers, guns, cartridges, and rods, to confirm the rich landowner in the possession of a small forest which he had taken from the starving peasants, which they were in the direst need of, and he was in no need of at all, was a striking proof of how men are capable of doing deeds directly opposed to their principles and their conscience without perceiving it.

The special train consisted of one first-class carriage for the governor, the officials, and officers, and several luggage vans crammed full of soldiers. The latter, smart young fellows in their clean new uniforms, were standing about in groups or sitting swinging their legs in the wide open doorways of the luggage vans. Some were smoking, nudging each other, joking, grinning, and laughing, others were munching sunflower seeds and spitting out the husks with an air of dignity. Some of them ran along the platform to drink some water from a tub there, and when they met the officers they slackened their pace, made their stupid gesture of salutation, raising their hands to their heads with serious faces as though they were doing something of the greatest importance. They kept their eyes on them till they had passed by them, and then set off running still more merrily, stamping their heels on the platform, laughing and chattering after the manner of healthy, good-natured young fellows, traveling in lively company.

They were going to assist at the murder of their fathers or grandfathers just as if they were going on a party of pleasure, or at any rate on some quite ordinary business.

The same impression was produced by the well-dressed functionaries and officers who were scattered about the platform and in the first-class carriage. At a table covered with bottles was sitting the governor, who was responsible for the whole expedition, dressed in his half-military uniform and eating something while he chatted tranquilly about the weather with some acquaintances he had met, as though the business he was upon was of so simple and ordinary a character that it could not disturb his serenity and his interest in the change of weather.

At a little distance from the table sat the general of the police. He was not taking any refreshment, and had an impenetrable bored expression, as though he were weary of the formalities to be gone through. On all sides officers were bustling noisily about in their red uniforms trimmed with gold; one sat at a table finishing his bottle of beer, another stood at the buffet eating a cake, and brushing the crumbs off his uniform, threw down his money with a self-confident air; another was sauntering before the carriages of our train, staring at the faces of the women.

All these men who were going to murder or to torture the famishing and defenseless creatures who provide them their sustenance had the air of men who knew very well that they were doing their duty, and some were even proud, were "glorying" in what they were doing.

What is the meaning of it?

All these people are within half an hour of reaching the place where, in order to provide a wealthy young man with three thousand rubles stolen from a whole community of famishing peasants, they may be forced to commit the most horrible acts one can conceive, to murder or torture, as was done in Orel, innocent beings, their brothers. And they see the place and time approaching with untroubled serenity.

To say that all these government officials, officers, and soldiers do not know what is before them is impossible, for they are prepared for it. The governor must have given directions about the rods, the officials must have sent an order for them, purchased them, and entered the item in their accounts. The military officers have given and received orders about cartridges. They all know that they are going to torture, perhaps to kill, their famishing fellow-creatures, and that they must set to work within an hour.

To say, as is usually said, and as they would themselves repeat, that they are acting from conviction of the necessity for supporting the state organization, would be a mistake. For in the first place, these men have probably never even thought about state organization and the necessity of it; in the second place, they cannot possibly be convinced that the act in which they are taking part will tend to support rather than to ruin the state; and thirdly, in reality the majority, if not all, of these men, far from ever sacrificing their own pleasure or tranquillity to support the state, never let slip an opportunity of profiting at the expense of the state in every way they can increase their own pleasure and ease. So that they are not acting thus for the sake of the abstract principle of the state.

What is the meaning of it?

Yet I know all these men. If I don't know all of them personally, I know their characters pretty nearly, their past, and their way of thinking. They certainly all have mothers, some of them wives and children. They are certainly for the most part good, kind, even tender-hearted fellows, who hate every sort of cruelty, not to speak of murder; many of them would not kill or hurt an animal. Moreover, they are all professed Christians and regard all violence directed against the defenseless as base and disgraceful.

Certainly not one of them would be capable in everyday life, for his own personal profit, of doing a hundredth part of what the Governor of Orel did. Every one of them would be insulted at the supposition that he was capable of doing anything of the kind in private life.

And yet they are within half an hour of reaching the place where they may be reduced to the inevitable necessity of committing this crime.

What is the meaning of it?

But it is not only these men who are going by train prepared for murder and torture. How could the men who began the whole business, the landowner, the commissioner, the judges, and those who gave the order and are responsible for it, the ministers, the Tzar, who are also good men, professed Christians, how could they elaborate such a plan and assent to it, knowing its consequences? The spectators even, who took no part in the affair, how could they, who are indignant at the sight of any cruelty in private life, even the overtaxing of a horse, allow such a horrible deed to be perpetrated? How was it they did not rise in indignation and bar the roads, shouting, "No; flog and kill starving men because they won't let their last possession be stolen from them without resistance, that we won't allow!" But far from anyone doing this, the majority, even of those who were the cause of the affair, such as the commissioner, the landowner, the judge, and those who took part in it and arranged it, as the governor, the ministers, and the Tzar, are perfectly tranquil and do not even feel a prick of conscience. And apparently all the men who are going to carry out this crime are equally undisturbed.

The spectators, who one would suppose could have no personal interest in the affair, looked rather with sympathy than with disapproval at all these people preparing to carry out this infamous action. In the same compartment with me was a wood merchant, who had risen from a peasant. He openly expressed aloud his sympathy with such punishments. "They can't disobey the authorities," he said; "that's what the authorities are for. Let them have a lesson; send their fleas flying! They'll give over making commotions, I warrant you. That's what they want."

What is the meaning of it?

It is not possible to say that all these people who have provoked or aided or allowed this deed are such worthless creatures that, knowing all the infamy of what they are doing, they do it against their principles, some for pay and for profit, others through fear of punishment. All of them in certain circumstances know how to stand up for their principles. Not one of these officials would steal a purse, read another man's letter, or put up with an affront without demanding satisfaction. Not one of these officers would consent to cheat at cards, would refuse to pay a debt of honor, would betray a comrade, run away on the field of battle, or desert the flag. Not one of these soldiers would spit out the holy sacrament or eat meat on Good Friday. All these men are ready to face any kind of privation, suffering, or danger rather than consent to do what they regard as wrong. They have therefore the strength to resist doing what is against their principles.

It is even less possible to assert that all these men are such brutes that it is natural and not distasteful to them to do such deeds. One need only talk to these people a little to see that all of them, the landowner even, and the judge, and the minister and the Tzar and the government, the officers and the soldiers, not only disapprove of such things in the depth of their soul, but suffer from the consciousness of their participation in them when they recollect what they imply. But they try not to think about it.

One need only talk to any of these who are taking part in the affair from the landowner to the lowest policeman or soldier to see that in the depth of their soul they all know it is a wicked thing, that it would be better to have nothing to do with it, and are suffering from the knowledge.

A lady of liberal views, who was traveling in the same train with us, seeing the governor and the officers in the first-class saloon and learning the object of the expedition, began, intentionally raising her voice so that they should hear, to abuse the existing order of things and to cry shame on men who would take part in such proceedings. Everyone felt awkward, none knew where to look, but no one contradicted her. They tried to look as though such remarks were not worth answering. But one could see by their faces and their averted eyes that they were ashamed. I noticed the same thing in the soldiers. They too knew that what they were sent to do was a shameful thing, but they did not want to think about what was before them.

When the wood merchant, as I suspect insincerely only to show that he was a man of education, began to speak of the necessity of such measures, the soldiers who heard him all turned away from him, scowling and pretending not to hear.

All the men who, like the landowner, the commissioner, the minister, and the Tzar, were responsible for the perpetration of this act, as well as those who were now going to execute it, and even those who were mere spectators of it, knew that it was a wickedness, and were ashamed of taking any share in it, and even of being present at it.

Then why did they do it, or allow it to be done?

Ask them the question. And the landowner who started the affair, and the judge who pronounced a clearly unjust even though formally legal decision, and those who commanded[298] the execution of the decision, and those who, like the policemen, soldiers, and peasants, will execute the deed with their own hands, flogging and killing their brothers, all who have devised, abetted, decreed, executed, or allowed such crimes, will make substantially the same reply.

The authorities, those who have started, devised, and decreed the matter, will say that such acts are necessary for the maintenance of the existing order; the maintenance of the existing order is necessary for the welfare of the country and of humanity, for the possibility of social existence and human progress.

Men of the poorer class, peasants and soldiers, who will have to execute the deed of violence with their own hands, say that they do so because it is the command of their superior authority, and the superior authority knows what he is about. That those are in authority who ought to be in authority, and that they know what they are doing appears to them a truth of which there can be no doubt. If they could admit the possibility of mistake or error, it would only be in functionaries of a lower grade; the highest authority on which all the rest depends seems to them immaculate beyond suspicion.

Though expressing the motives of their conduct differently, both those in command and their subordinates are agreed in saying that they act thus because the existing order is the order which must and ought to exist at the present time, and that therefore to support it is the sacred duty of every man.

On this acceptance of the necessity and therefore immutability of the existing order, all who take part in acts of violence on the part of government base the argument always advanced in their justification. "Since the existing order is immutable," they say, "the refusal of a single individual to perform the duties laid upon him will effect no change in things, and will only mean that some other man will be put in his place who may do the work worse, that is to say, more cruelly, to the still greater injury of the victims of the act of violence."

This conviction that the existing order is the necessary and therefore immutable order, which it is a sacred duty for every man to support, enables good men, of high principles in private life, to take part with conscience more or less untroubled in crimes such as that perpetrated in Orel, and that which the men in the Toula train were going to perpetrate.

But what is this conviction based on? It is easy to understand that the landowner prefers to believe that the existing order is inevitable and immutable, because this existing order secures him an income from his hundreds and thousands of acres, by means of which he can lead his habitual indolent and luxurious life.

It is easy to understand that the judge readily believes in the necessity of an order of things through which he receives a wage fifty times as great as the most industrious laborer can earn, and the same applies to all the higher officials. It is only under the existing *régime* that as governor, prosecutor, senator, members of the various councils, they can receive their several thousands of rubles a year, without which they and their families would at once sink into ruin, since if it were not for the position they occupy they would never by their own abilities, industry, or acquirements get a thousandth part of their salaries. The minister, the Tzar, and all the higher authorities are in the same position. The only distinction is that the higher and the more exceptional their position, the more necessary it is for them to believe that the existing order is the only possible order of things. For without it they would not only be unable to gain an equal position, but would be found to fall lower than all other people. A man who has of his own free will entered the police force at a wage of ten rubles, which he could easily earn in any other position, is hardly dependent on the preservation of the existing *régime*, and so he may not believe in its immutability. But a king or an emperor, who receives millions for his post, and knows that there are thousands of people round him who would like to dethrone him and take his place, who knows that he will never receive such a revenue or so much honor in any other position, who knows, in most cases through his more or less despotic rule, that if he were dethroned he would have to answer for all his abuse of power—he cannot but believe in the necessity and even sacredness of the existing order. The higher and the more profitable a man's position, the more unstable it becomes, and the more terrible and dangerous a fall from it for him, the more firmly the man believes in the existing order, and therefore with the more ease of conscience can such a man perpetrate cruel and wicked acts, as though they were not in his own interest, but for the maintenance of that order.

This is the case with all men in authority, who occupy positions more profitable than they could occupy except for the present *régime*, from the lowest police officer to the Tzar. All of them are more or less convinced that the existing order is immutable, because—the chief consideration—it is to their advantage. But the peasants, the soldiers, who are at the bottom of the social scale, who have no kind of advantage from the existing order, who are in the very lowest position of subjection and humiliation, what forces them to believe that the existing order in which they are in their humble and disadvantageous position is the order which ought to exist, and which they ought to support even at the cost of evil actions contrary to their conscience?

What forces these men to the false reasoning that the existing order is unchanging, and that therefore they ought to support it, when it is so obvious, on the contrary, that it is only unchanging because they themselves support it?

What forces these peasants, taken only yesterday from the plow and dressed in ugly and unseemly costumes with blue collars and gilt buttons, to go with guns and sabers and murder their famishing fathers and brothers? They gain no kind of advantage and can be in no fear of losing the position they occupy, because it is worse than that from which they have been taken.

The persons in authority of the higher orders—landowners, merchants, judges, senators, governors, ministers, tzars, and officers—take part in such doings because the existing order is to their advantage. In other respects they are often good and kind-hearted men, and they are more able to take part in such doings because their share in them is limited to suggestions, decisions, and orders. These persons in authority never do themselves what they suggest, decide, or command to be done. For the most part they do not even see how all the atrocious deeds they have suggested and authorized are carried out. But the unfortunate men of the lower orders, who gain no kind of advantage from the existing *régime*, but, on the contrary, are treated with the utmost contempt, support it even by dragging people with their own hands from their families, handcuffing them, throwing them in prison, guarding them, shooting them.

Why do they do it? What forces them to believe that the existing order is unchanging and they must support it?

All violence rests, we know, on those who do the beating, the handcuffing, the imprisoning, and the killing with their own hands. If there were no soldiers or armed policemen, ready to kill or outrage anyone as they are ordered, not one of those people who sign sentences of death, imprisonment, or galley-slavery for life would make up his mind to hang, imprison, or torture a thousandth part of those whom, quietly sitting in his study, he now orders to be tortured in all kinds of ways, simply because he does not see it nor do it himself, but only gets it done at a distance by these servile tools.

All the acts of injustice and cruelty which are committed in the ordinary course of daily life have only become habitual because there are these men always ready to carry out such acts of injustice and cruelty. If it were not for them, far from anyone using violence against the immense masses who are now ill-treated, those who now command their punishment would not venture to sentence them, would not even dare to dream of the sentences they decree with such easy confidence at present. And if it were not for these men, ready to kill or torture anyone at their commander's will, no one would dare to claim, as all the idle landowners claim with such assurance, that a piece of land, surrounded by peasants, who are in wretchedness from want of land, is the property of a man who does not cultivate it, or that stores of corn taken by swindling from the peasants ought to remain untouched in the midst of a population dying of hunger because the merchants must make their profit. If it were not for these servile instruments at the disposal of the authorities, it could never have entered the head of the landowner to rob the peasants of the forest they had tended, nor of the officials to think they are entitled to their salaries, taken from the famishing people, the price of their oppression; least of all could anyone dream of killing or exiling men for exposing falsehood and telling the truth. All this can only be done because the authorities are confidently assured that they have always these servile tools at hand, ready to carry all their demands into effect by means of torture and murder.

LEO TOLSTOY

All the deeds of violence of tyrants from Napoleon to the lowest commander of a company who fires upon a crowd, can only be explained by the intoxicating effect of their absolute power over these slaves. All force, therefore, rests on these men, who carry out the deeds of violence with their own hands, the men who serve in the police or the army, especially the army, for the police only venture to do their work because the army is at their back.

What, then, has brought these masses of honest men, on whom the whole thing depends, who gain nothing by it, and who have to do these atrocious deeds with their own hands, what has brought them to accept the amazing delusion that the existing order, unprofitable, ruinous, and fatal as it is for them, is the order which ought to exist?

Who has led them into this amazing delusion?

They can never have persuaded themselves that they ought to do what is against their conscience, and also the source of misery and ruin for themselves, and all their class, who make up nine-tenths of the population.

"How can you kill people, when it is written in God's commandment: 'Thou shalt not kill'?" I have often inquired of different soldiers. And I always drove them to embarrassment and confusion by reminding them of what they did not want to think about. They knew they were bound by the law of God, "Thou shalt not kill," and knew too that they were bound by their duty as soldiers, but had never reflected on the contradiction between these duties. The drift of the timid answers I received to this question was always approximately this: that killing in war and executing criminals by command of the government are not included in the general prohibition of murder. But when I said this distinction was not made in the law of God, and reminded them of the Christian duty of fraternity, forgiveness of injuries, and love, which could not be reconciled with murder, the peasants usually agreed, but in their turn began to ask me questions. "How does it happen," they inquired, "that the government [which according to their ideas cannot do wrong] sends the army to war and orders criminals to be executed." When I answered that the government does wrong in giving such orders, the peasants fell into still greater confusion, and either broke off the conversation or else got angry with me.

"They must have found a law for it. The archbishops know as much about it as we do, I should hope," a Russian soldier once observed to me. And in saying this the soldier obviously set his mind at rest, in the full conviction that his spiritual guides had found a law which authorized his ancestors, and the tzars and their descendants, and millions of men, to serve as he was doing himself, and that the question I had put him was a kind of hoax or conundrum on my part.

Everyone in our Christian society knows, either by tradition or by revelation or by the voice of conscience, that murder is one of the most fearful crimes a man can commit, as the Gospel tells us, and that the sin of murder cannot be limited to certain persons, that is, murder cannot be a sin for some and not a sin for others. Everyone knows that if murder is a sin, it is always a sin, whoever are the victims murdered, just like the sin of adultery, theft, or any other. At the same time from their childhood up men see that murder is not only permitted, but even sanctioned by the blessing of those whom they are accustomed to regard as their divinely appointed spiritual guides, and see their secular leaders with calm assurance organizing murder, proud to wear murderous arms, and demanding of others in the name of the laws of the country, and even of God, that they should take part in murder. Men see that there is some inconsistency here, but not being able to analyze it, involuntarily assume that this apparent inconsistency is only the result of their ignorance. The very grossness and obviousness of the inconsistency confirms them in this conviction.

They cannot imagine that the leaders of civilization, the educated classes, could so confidently preach two such opposed principles as the law of Christ and murder. A simple uncorrupted youth cannot imagine that those who stand so high in his opinion, whom he regards as holy or learned men, could for any object whatever mislead him so shamefully. But this is just what has always been and always is done to him. It is done (1) by instilling, by example and direct instruction, from childhood up, into the working people, who have not time to study moral and religious questions for themselves, the idea that torture and murder are compatible with Christianity, and that for certain objects of state, torture and murder are not only admissible, but ought to be employed; and (2) by instilling into certain of the people, who have either voluntarily enlisted or been taken by compulsion into the army, the idea that the perpetration of murder and torture with their own hands is a sacred duty, and even a glorious exploit, worthy of praise and reward.

The general delusion is diffused among all people by means of the catechisms or books, which nowadays replace them, in use for the compulsory education of children. In them it is stated that violence, that is, imprisonment and execution, as well as murder in civil or foreign war in the defense and maintenance of the existing state organization (whatever that may be, absolute or limited monarchy, convention, consulate, empire of this or that Napoleon or Boulanger, constitutional monarchy, commune or republic) is absolutely lawful and not opposed to morality and Christianity.

This is stated in all catechisms or books used in schools. And men are so thoroughly persuaded of it that they grow up, live and die in that conviction without once entertaining a doubt about it.

This is one form of deception, the general deception instilled into everyone, but there is another special deception practiced upon the soldiers or police who are picked out by one means or another to do the torturing and murdering necessary to defend and maintain the existing *régime*.

In all military instructions there appears in one form or another what is expressed in the Russian military code in the following words:

Article 87. To carry out exactly and without comment the orders of a superior officer means: to carry out an order received from a superior officer exactly without considering whether it is good or not, and whether it is possible to carry it out. The superior officer is responsible for the consequences of the order he gives.

Article 88. The subordinate ought never to refuse to carry out the orders of a superior officer except when he sees clearly that in carrying out his superior officer's command, he breaks [the law of God, one involuntarily expects; not at all] *his oath of fidelity and allegiance to the Tzar.*

It is here said that the man who is a soldier can and ought to carry out all the orders of his superior without exception. And as these orders for the most part involve murder, it follows that he ought to break all the laws of God and man. The one law he may not break is that of fidelity and allegiance to the man who happens at a given moment to be in power.

Precisely the same thing is said in other words in all codes of military instruction. And it could not be otherwise, since the whole power of the army and the state is based in reality on this delusive emancipation of men from their duty to God and their conscience, and the substitution of duty to their superior officer for all other duties.

This, then, is the foundation of the belief of the lower classes that the existing *régime* so fatal for them is the *régime* which ought to exist, and which they ought therefore to support even by torture and murder.

This belief is founded on a conscious deception practiced on them by the higher classes.

And it cannot be otherwise. To compel the lower classes, which are more numerous, to oppress and ill treat themselves, even at the cost of actions opposed to their conscience, it was necessary to deceive them. And it has been done accordingly.

Not many days ago I saw once more this shameless deception being openly practiced, and once more I marveled that it could be practiced so easily and impudently.

At the beginning of November, as I was passing through Toula, I saw once again at the gates of the Zemsky Court-house the crowd of peasants I had so often seen before, and heard the drunken shouts of the men mingled with the pitiful lamentations of their wives and mothers. It was the recruiting session.

I can never pass by the spectacle. It attracts me by a kind of fascination of repulsion. I again went into the crowd, took my stand among the peasants, looked about and asked questions. And once again I was amazed that this hideous crime can be perpetrated so easily in broad daylight and in the midst of a large town.

As the custom is every year, in all the villages and hamlets of the one hundred millions of Russians, on the 1st of November, the village elders had assembled the young men inscribed on the lists, often their own sons among them, and had brought them to the town.

On the road the recruits have been drinking without intermission, unchecked by the elders, who feel that going on such an insane errand, abandoning their wives and mothers and renouncing all they hold sacred in order to become a senseless instrument of destruction, would be too agonizing if they were not stupefied with spirits.

And so they have come, drinking, swearing, singing, fighting and scuffling with one another. They have spent the night in taverns. In the morning they have slept off their drunkenness and have gathered together at the Zemsky Court-house.

Some of them, in new sheepskin pelisses, with knitted scarves round their necks, their eyes swollen from drinking, are shouting wildly to one another to show their courage; others, crowded near the door, are quietly and mournfully waiting their turn, between their weeping wives and mothers (I had chanced upon the day of the actual enrolling, that is, the examination of those whose names are on the list); others meantime were crowding into the hall of the recruiting office.

Inside the office the work was going on rapidly. The door is opened and the guard calls Piotr Sidorov. Piotr Sidorov starts, crosses himself, and goes into a little room with a glass door, where the conscripts undress. A comrade of Piotr Sidorov's, who has just been passed for service, and come naked out of the revision office, is dressing hurriedly, his teeth chattering. Sidorov has already heard the news, and can see from his face too that he has been taken. He wants to ask him questions, but they hurry him and tell him to make haste and undress. He throws off his pelisse, slips his boots off his feet, takes off his waistcoat and draws his shirt over his head, and naked, trembling all over, and exhaling an odor of tobacco, spirits, and sweat, goes into the revision office, not knowing what to do with his brawny bare arms.

Directly facing him in the revision office hangs in a great gold frame a portrait of the Tzar in full uniform with decorations, and in the corner a little portrait of Christ in a shirt and a crown of thorns. In the middle of the room is a table covered with green cloth, on which there are papers lying and a three-cornered ornament surmounted by an eagle—the zertzal. Round the table are sitting the revising officers, looking collected and indifferent. One is smoking a cigarette; another is looking through some papers. Directly Sidorov comes in, a guard goes up to him, places him under the measuring frame, raising him under his chin, and straightening his legs.

The man with the cigarette—he is the doctor—comes up, and without looking at the recruit's face, but somewhere beyond it, feels his body over with an air of disgust, measures him, tests him, tells the guard to open his mouth, tells him to breathe, to speak. Someone notes something down. At last without having once looked him in the face the doctor says, "Right. Next one!" and with a weary air sits down again at the table. The soldiers again hustle and hurry the lad. He somehow gets into his trousers, wraps his feet in rags, puts on his boots, looks for his scarf and cap, and bundles his pelisse under his arm. Then they lead him into the main hall, shutting him off apart from the rest by a bench, behind which all the conscripts who have been passed for service are waiting. Another village lad like himself, but from a distant province, now a soldier armed with a gun with a sharp-pointed bayonet at the end, keeps watch over him, ready to run him through the body if he should think of trying to escape.

Meantime the crowd of fathers, mothers, and wives, hustled by the police, are pressing round the doors to hear whose lad has been taken, whose is let off. One of the rejected comes out and announces that Piotr is taken, and at once a shrill cry is heard from Piotr's young wife, for whom this word "taken" means separation for four or five years, the life of a soldier's wife as a servant, often a prostitute.

But here comes a man along the street with flowing hair and in a peculiar dress, who gets out of his droshky and goes into the Zemsky Court-house. The police clear a way for him through the crowd. It is the "reverend father" come to administer the oath, And this "father," who has been persuaded that he is specially and exclusively devoted to the service of Christ, and who, for the most part, does not himself see the deception in which he lives, goes into the hall where the conscripts are waiting. He throws round him a kind of curtain of brocade, pulls his long hair out over it, opens the very Gospel in which swearing is forbidden, takes the cross, the very cross on which Christ was crucified because he would not do what this false servant of his is telling men to do, and puts them on the lectern. And all these unhappy, defenseless, and deluded lads repeat after him the lie, which he utters with the assurance of familiarity.

He reads and they repeat after him:

"I promise and swear by Almighty God upon his holy Gospel," etc., "to defend," etc., and that is, to murder anyone I am told to, and to do everything I am told by men I know nothing of, and who care nothing for me except as an instrument for perpetrating the crimes by which they are kept in their position of power, and my brothers in their condition of misery. All the conscripts repeat these ferocious words without thinking. And then the so-called "father" goes away with a sense of having correctly and conscientiously done his duty. And all these poor deluded lads believe that these nonsensical and incomprehensible words which they have just uttered set them free for the whole time of their service from their duties as men, and lay upon them fresh and more binding duties as soldiers.

And this crime is perpetrated publicly and no one cries out to the deceiving and the deceived: "Think what you are doing; this is the basest, falsest lie, by which not bodies only, but souls too, are destroyed."

No one does this. On the contrary, when all have been enrolled, and they are to be let out again, the military officer goes with a confident and majestic air into the hall where the drunken, cheated lads are shut up, and cries in a bold, military voice: "Your health, my lads! I congratulate you on 'serving the Tzar!'" And they, poor fellows (someone has given them a hint beforehand), mutter awkwardly, their voices thick with drink, something to the effect that they are glad.

Meantime the crowd of fathers, mothers, and wives is standing at the doors waiting. The women keep their tearful eyes fixed on the doors. They open at last, and out come the conscripts, unsteady, but trying to put a good face on it. Here are Piotr and Vania and Makar trying not to look their dear ones in the face. Nothing is heard but the wailing of the wives and mothers. Some of the lads embrace them and weep with them, others make a show of courage, and others try to comfort them.

The wives and mothers, knowing that they will be left for three, four, or five years without their breadwinners, weep and rehearse their woes aloud. The fathers say little. They only utter a clucking sound with their tongues and sigh mournfully, knowing that they will see no more of the steady lads they have reared and trained to help them, that they will come back not the same quiet hard-working laborers, but for the most part conceited and demoralized, unfitted for their simple life.

And then all the crowd get into their sledges again and move away down the street to the taverns and pot-houses, and louder than ever sounds the medley of singing and sobbing, drunken shouts, and the wailing of the wives and mothers, the sounds of the accordeon and oaths. They all turn into the taverns, whose revenues go to the government, and the drinking bout begins, which stifles their sense of the wrong which is being done them.

For two or three weeks they go on living at home, and most of that time they are "jaunting," that is, drinking.

On a fixed day they collect them, drive them together like a flock of sheep, and begin to train them in the military exercises and drill. Their teachers are fellows like themselves, only deceived and brutalized two or three years sooner. The means of instruction are: deception, stupefaction, blows, and vodka. And before a year has passed these good, intelligent, healthy-minded lads will be as brutal beings as their instructors.

"Come, now, suppose your father were arrested and tried to make his escape?" I asked a young soldier.

"I should run him through with my bayonet," he answered with the foolish intonation peculiar to soldiers; "and if he made off, I ought to shoot him," he added, obviously proud of knowing what he must do if his father were escaping.

And when a good-hearted lad has been brought to a state lower than that of a brute, he is just what is wanted by those who use him as an instrument of violence. He is ready; the man has been destroyed and a new instrument of violence has been created. And all this is done every year, every autumn, everywhere, through all Russia in broad daylight in the midst of large towns, where all may see it, and the deception is so clever, so skillful, that though all men know the infamy of it in their hearts, and see all its horrible results, they cannot throw it off and be free.

When one's eyes are opened to this awful deception practiced upon us, one marvels that the teachers of the Christian religion and of morals, the instructors of youth, or even the good-hearted and intelligent parents who are to be found in every society, can teach any kind of morality in a society in which it is openly admitted (it is so admitted, under all governments and all churches) that murder and torture form an indispensable element in the life of all, and that there must always be special men trained to kill their fellows, and that any one of us may have to become such a trained assassin.

How can children, youths, and people generally be taught any kind of morality—not to speak of teaching in the spirit of Christianity—side by side with the doctrine that murder is necessary for the public weal, and therefore legitimate, and that there are men, of whom each of us may have to be one, whose duty is to murder and torture and commit all sorts of crimes at the will of those who are in possession of authority. If this is so, and one can and ought to murder and torture, there is not, and cannot be, any kind of moral law, but only the law that might is right. And this is just how it is. In reality that is the doctrine—justified to some by the theory of the struggle for existence—which reigns in our society.

And, indeed, what sort of ethical doctrine could admit the legitimacy of murder for any object whatever? It is as impossible as a theory of mathematics admitting that two is equal to three.

There may be a semblance of mathematics admitting that two is equal to three, but there can be no real science of mathematics. And there can only be a semblance of ethics in which murder in the shape of war and the execution of criminals is allowed, but no true ethics. The recognition of the life of every man as sacred is the first and only basis of all ethics.

The doctrine of an eye for an eye and a tooth for a tooth has been abrogated by Christianity, because it is the justification of immorality, and a mere semblance of equity, and has no real meaning. Life is a value which has no weight nor size, and cannot be compared to any other, and so there is no sense in destroying a life for a life. Besides, every social law aims at the amelioration of man's life. What way, then, can the annihilation of the life of some men ameliorate men's life? Annihilation of life cannot be a means of the amelioration of life; it is a suicidal act.

To destroy another life for the sake of justice is as though a man, to repair the misfortune of losing one arm, should cut off the other arm for the sake of equity.

But putting aside the sin of deluding men into regarding the most awful crime as a duty, putting aside the revolting sin of using the name and authority of Christ to sanction what he most condemned, not to speak of the curse on those who cause these "little ones" to offend—how can people who cherish their own way of life, their progress, even from the point of view of their personal security, allow the formation in their midst of an overwhelming force as senseless, cruel, and destructive as every government is organized on the basis of an army? Even the most cruel band of brigands is not so much to be dreaded as such a government.

The power of every brigand chief is at least so far limited that the men of his band preserve at least some human liberty, and can refuse to commit acts opposed to their conscience. But, owing to the perfection to which the discipline of the army has been brought, there is no limit to check men who form part of a regularly organized government. There are no crimes so revolting that they would not readily be committed by men who form part of a government or army, at the will of anyone (such as Boulanger, Napoleon, or Pougachef) who may chance to be at their head.

Often when one sees conscription levies, military drills and maneuvers, police officers with loaded revolvers, and sentinels at their posts with bayonets on their rifles; when one hears for whole days at a time (as I hear it in Hamovniky where I live) the whistle of balls and the dull thud as they fall in the sand; when one sees in the midst of a town where any effort at violence in self-defense is forbidden, where the sale of powder and of chemicals, where furious driving and practicing as a doctor without a diploma, and so on, are not allowed, thousands of disciplined troops, trained to murder, and subject to one man's will; one asks oneself how can people who prize their security quietly allow it, and put up with it? Apart from the immorality and evil effects of it, nothing can possibly be more unsafe. What are people thinking about? I don't mean now Christians, ministers of religion, philanthropists, and moralists, but simply people who value their life, their security, and their comfort. This organization, we know, will work just as well in one man's hands as another's. To-day, let us assume, power is in the hands of a ruler who can be endured, but to-morrow it may be seized by a Biron, an Elizabeth, a Catherine, a Pougachef, a Napoleon I., or a Napoleon III.

And the man in authority, endurable to-day, may become a brute to-morrow, or may be succeeded by a mad or imbecile heir, like the King of Bavaria or our Paul I.

And not only the highest authorities, but all little satraps scattered over everywhere, like so many General Baranovs, governors, police officers even, and commanders of companies, can perpetrate the most awful crimes before there is time for them to be removed from office. And this is what is constantly happening.

One involuntarily asks how can men let it go on, not from higher considerations only, but from regard to their own safety?

The answer to this question is that it is not all people who do tolerate it (some—the greater proportion—deluded and submissive, have no choice and have to tolerate anything). It is tolerated by those who only under such an organization can occupy a position of profit. They tolerate it, because for them the risks of suffering from a foolish or cruel man being at the head of the government or the army are always less than the disadvantages to which they would be exposed by the destruction of the organization itself.

A judge, a commander of police, a governor, or an officer will keep his position just the same under Boulanger or the republic, under Pougachef or Catherine. He will lose his profitable position for certain, if the existing order of things which secured it to him is destroyed. And so all these people feel no uneasiness as to who is at the head of the organization, they will adapt themselves to anyone; they only dread the downfall of the organization itself, and that is the reason—though often an unconscious one—that they support it.

One often wonders why independent people, who are not forced to do so in any way, the so-called *élite* of society, should go into the army in Russia, England, Germany, Austria, and even France, and seek opportunities of becoming murderers. Why do even high-principled parents send their boys to military schools? Why do mothers buy their children toy helmets, guns, and swords as playthings? (The peasant's children never play at soldiers, by the way). Why do good men and even women, who have certainly no interest in war, go into raptures over the various exploits of Skobeloff and others, and vie with one another in glorifying them? Why do men, who are not obliged to do so, and get no fee for it, devote, like the marshals of nobility in Russia, whole months of toil to a business physically disagreeable and morally painful—the enrolling of conscripts? Why do all kings and emperors wear the military uniform? Why do they all hold military reviews, why do they organize maneuvers, distribute rewards to the military, and raise monuments to generals and successful commanders? Why do rich men of independent position consider it an honor to perform a valet's duties in attendance on crowned personages, flattering them and cringing to them and pretending to believe in their peculiar superiority? Why do men who have ceased to believe in the superstitions of the mediæval Church, and who could not possibly believe in them seriously and consistently, pretend to believe in and give their support to the demoralizing and blasphemous institution of the church? Why is it that not only governments but private persons of the higher classes, try so jealously to maintain the ignorance of the people? Why do they fall with such fury on any effort at breaking down religious superstitions or really enlightening the people? Why do historians, novelists, and poets, who have no hope of gaining anything by their flatteries, make heroes of kings, emperors, and conquerors of past times? Why do men, who call themselves learned, dedicate whole lifetimes to making theories to prove that violence employed by authority against the people is not violence at all, but a special right? One often wonders why a fashionable lady or an artist, who, one would think, would take no interest in political or military questions, should always condemn strikes of working people, and defend war; and should always be found without hesitation opposed to the one, favorable to the other.

But one no longer wonders when one realizes that in the higher classes there is an unerring instinct of what tends to maintain and of what tends to destroy the organization by virtue of which they enjoy their privileges. The fashionable lady had certainly not reasoned out that if there were no capitalists and no army to defend them, her husband would have no fortune, and she could not have her entertainments and her ball-dresses. And the artist certainly does not argue that he needs the capitalists and the troops to defend them, so that they may buy his pictures. But instinct, replacing reason in this instance, guides them unerringly. And it is precisely this instinct which leads all men, with few exceptions, to support all the religious, political, and economic institutions which are to their advantage.

But is it possible that the higher classes support the existing order of things simply because it is to their advantage? Cannot they see that this order of things is essentially irrational, that it is no longer consistent with the stage of moral development attained by people, and with public opinion, and that it is fraught with perils? The governing classes, or at least the good, honest, and intelligent people of them, cannot but suffer from these fundamental inconsistencies, and see the dangers with which they are threatened. And is it possible that all the millions of the lower classes can feel easy in conscience when they commit such obviously evil deeds as torture and murder from fear of punishment? Indeed, it could not be so, neither the former nor the latter could fail to see the irrationality of their conduct, if the complexity of government organization did not obscure the unnatural senselessness of their actions.

So many instigate, assist, or sanction the commission of every one of these actions that no one who has a hand in them feels himself morally responsible for it.

It is the custom among assassins to oblige all the witnesses of a murder to strike the murdered victim, that the responsibility may be divided among as large a number of people as possible. The same principle in different forms is applied under the government organization in the perpetration of the crimes, without which no government organization could exist. Rulers always try to implicate as many citizens as possible in all the crimes committed in their support.

Of late this tendency has been expressed in a very obvious manner by the obligation of all citizens to take part in legal processes as jurors, in the army as soldiers, in the local government, or legislative assembly, as electors or members.

Just as in a wicker basket all the ends are so hidden away that it is hard to find them, in the state organization the responsibility for the crimes committed is so hidden away that men will commit the most atrocious acts without seeing their responsibility for them.

In ancient times tyrants got credit for the crimes they committed, but in our day the most atrocious infamies, inconceivable under the Neros, are perpetrated and no one gets blamed for them.

One set of people have suggested, another set have proposed, a third have reported, a fourth have decided, a fifth have confirmed, a sixth have given the order, and a seventh set of men have carried it out. They hang, they flog to death women, old men, and innocent people, as was done recently among us in Russia at the Yuzovsky factory, and is always being done everywhere in Europe and America in the struggle with the anarchists and all other rebels against the existing order; they shoot and hang men by hundreds and thousands, or massacre millions in war, or break men's hearts in solitary confinement, and ruin their souls in the corruption of a soldier's life, and no one is responsible.

At the bottom of the social scale soldiers, armed with guns, pistols, and sabers, injure and murder people, and compel men through these means to enter the army, and are absolutely convinced that the responsibility for the actions rests solely on the officers who command them.

At the top of the scale—the Tzars, presidents, ministers, and parliaments decree these tortures and murders and military conscription, and are fully convinced that since they are either placed in authority by the grace of God or by the society they govern, which demands such decrees from them, they cannot be held responsible. Between these two extremes are the intermediary personages who superintend the murders and other acts of violence, and are fully convinced that the responsibility is taken off their shoulders partly by their superiors who have given the order, partly by the fact that such orders are expected from them by all who are at the bottom of the scale.

The authority who gives the orders and the authority who executes them at the two extreme ends of the state organization, meet together like the two ends of a ring; they support and rest on one another and inclose all that lies within the ring.

Without the conviction that there is a person or persons who will take the whole responsibility of his acts, not one soldier would ever lift a hand to commit a murder or other deed of violence.

Without the conviction that it is expected by the whole people not a single king, emperor, president, or parliament would order murders or acts of violence.

Without the conviction that there are persons of a higher grade who will take the responsibility, and people of a lower grade who require such acts for their welfare, not one of the intermediate class would superintend such deeds.

The state is so organized that wherever a man is placed in the social scale, his irresponsibility is the same. The higher his grade the more he is under the influence of demands from below, and the less he is controlled by orders from above, and *vice versa.*

All men, then, bound together by state organization, throw the responsibility of their acts on one another, the peasant soldier on the nobleman or merchant who is his officer, and the officer on the nobleman who has been appointed governor, the governor on the nobleman or son of an official who is minister, the minister on the member of the royal family who occupies the post of Tzar, and the Tzar again on all these officials, noblemen, merchants, and peasants. But that is not all. Besides the fact that men get rid of the sense of responsibility for their actions in this way, they lose their moral sense of responsibility also, by the fact that in forming themselves into a state organization they persuade themselves and each other so continually, and so indefatigably, that they are not all equal, but "as the stars apart," that they come to believe it genuinely themselves. Thus some are persuaded that they are not simple people like everyone else, but special people who are to be specially honored. It is instilled into another set of men by every possible means that they are inferior to others, and therefore must submit without a murmur to every order given them by their superiors.

On this inequality, above all, on the elevation of some and the degradation of others, rests the capacity men have of being blind to the insanity of the existing order of life, and all the cruelty and criminality of the deception practiced by one set of men on another.

Those in whom the idea has been instilled that they are invested with a special supernatural grandeur and consequence, are so intoxicated with a sense of their own imaginary dignity that they cease to feel their responsibility for what they do.

While those, on the other hand, in whom the idea is fostered that they are inferior animals, bound to obey their superiors in everything, fall, through this perpetual humiliation, into a strange condition of stupefied servility, and in this stupefied state do not see the significance of their actions and lose all consciousness of responsibility for what they do.

The intermediate class, who obey the orders of their superiors on the one hand and regard themselves as superior beings on the other, are intoxicated by power and stupefied by servility at the same time and so lose the sense of their responsibility.

One need only glance during a review at the commander-in-chief, intoxicated with self-importance, followed by his retinue, all on magnificent and gayly appareled horses, in splendid uniforms and wearing decorations, and see how they ride to the harmonious and solemn strains of music before the ranks of soldiers, all presenting arms and petrified with servility. One need only glance at this spectacle to understand that at such moments, when they are in a state of the most complete intoxication, commander-in-chief, soldiers, and intermediate officers alike, would be capable of committing crimes of which they would never dream under other conditions.

The intoxication produced by such stimulants as parades, reviews, religious solemnities, and coronations, is, however, an acute and temporary condition; but there are other forms of chronic, permanent intoxication, to which those are liable who have any kind of authority, from that of the Tzar to that of the lowest police officer at the street corner, and also those who are in subjection to authority and in a state of stupefied servility. The latter, like all slaves, always find a justification for their own servility, in ascribing the greatest possible dignity and importance to those they serve.

It is principally through this false idea of inequality, and the intoxication of power and of servility resulting from it, that men associated in a state organization are enabled to commit acts opposed to their conscience without the least scruple or remorse.

Under the influence of this intoxication, men imagine themselves no longer simply men as they are, but some special beings—noblemen, merchants, governors, judges, officers, tzars, ministers, or soldiers—no longer bound by ordinary human duties, but by other duties far more weighty—the peculiar duties of a nobleman, merchant, governor, judge, officer, tzar, minister, or soldier.

Thus the landowner, who claimed the forest, acted as he did only because he fancied himself not a simple man, having the same rights to life as the peasants living beside him and everyone else, but a great landowner, a member of the nobility, and under the influence of the intoxication of power he felt his dignity offended by the peasants' claims. It was only through this feeling that, without considering the consequences that might follow, he sent in a claim to be reinstated in his pretended rights.

In the same way the judges, who wrongfully adjudged the forest to the proprietor, did so simply because they fancied themselves not simply men like everyone else, and so bound to be guided in everything only by what they consider right, but, under the intoxicating influence of power, imagined themselves the representatives of the justice which cannot err; while under the intoxicating influence of servility they imagined themselves bound to carry out to the letter the instructions inscribed in a certain book, the so-called law. In the same way all who take part in such an affair, from the highest representative of authority who signs his assent to the report, from the superintendent presiding at the recruiting sessions, and the priest who deludes the recruits, to the lowest soldier who is ready now to fire on his own brothers, imagine, in the intoxication of power or of servility, that they are some conventional characters. They do not face the question that is presented to them, whether or not they ought to take part in what their conscience judges an evil act, but fancy themselves various conventional personages—one as the Tzar, God's anointed, an exceptional being, called to watch over the happiness of one hundred millions of men; another as the representative of nobility; another as a priest, who has received special grace by his ordination; another as a soldier, bound by his military oath to carry out all he is commanded without reflection.

Only under the intoxication of the power or the servility of their imagined positions could all these people act as they do.

Were not they all firmly convinced that their respective vocations of tzar, minister, governor, judge, nobleman, landowner, superintendent, officer, and soldier are something real and important, not one of them would even think without horror and aversion of taking part in what they do now.

The conventional positions, established hundreds of years, recognized for centuries and by everyone, distinguished by special names and dresses, and, moreover, confirmed by every kind of solemnity, have so penetrated into men's minds through their senses, that, forgetting the ordinary conditions of life common to all, they look at themselves and everyone only from this conventional point of view, and are guided in their estimation of their own actions and those of others by this conventional standard.

Thus we see a man of perfect sanity and ripe age, simply because he is decked out with some fringe, or embroidered keys on his coat tails, or a colored ribbon only fit for some gayly dressed girl, and is told that he is a general, a chamberlain, a knight of the order of St. Andrew, or some similar nonsense, suddenly become self-important, proud, and even happy, or, on the contrary, grow melancholy and unhappy to the point of falling ill, because he has failed to obtain the expected decoration or title. Or what is still more striking, a young man, perfectly sane in every other matter, independent and beyond the fear of want, simply because he has been appointed judicial prosecutor or district commander, separates a poor widow from her little children, and shuts her up in prison, leaving her children uncared for, all because the unhappy woman carried on a secret trade in spirits, and so deprived the revenue of twenty-five rubles, and he does not feel the least pang of remorse. Or what is still more amazing; a man, otherwise sensible and good-hearted, simply because he is given a badge or a uniform to wear, and told that he is a guard or customs officer, is ready to fire on people, and neither he nor those around him regard him as to blame for it, but, on the contrary, would regard him as to blame if he did not fire. To say nothing of judges and juries who condemn men to death, and soldiers who kill men by thousands without the slightest scruple merely because it has been instilled into them that they are not simply men, but jurors, judges, generals, and soldiers.

This strange and abnormal condition of men under state organization is usually expressed in the following words: "As a man, I pity him; but as guard, judge, general, governor, tzar, or soldier, it is my duty to kill or torture him." Just as though there were some positions conferred and recognized, which would exonerate us from the obligations laid on each of us by the fact of our common humanity.

So, for example, in the case before us, men are going to murder and torture the famishing, and they admit that in the dispute between the peasants and the landowner the peasants are right (all those in command said as much to me). They know that the peasants are wretched, poor, and hungry, and the landowner is rich and inspires no sympathy. Yet they are all going to kill the peasants to secure three thousand rubles for the landowner, only because at that moment they fancy themselves not men but governor, official, general of police, officer, and soldier, respectively, and consider themselves bound to obey, not the eternal demands of the conscience of man, but the casual, temporary demands of their positions as officers or soldiers.

Strange as it may seem, the sole explanation of this astonishing phenomenon is that they are in the condition of the hypnotized, who, they say, feel and act like the creatures they are commanded by the hypnotizer to represent. When, for instance, it is suggested to the hypnotized subject that he is lame, he begins to walk lame, that he is blind, and he cannot see, that he is a wild beast, and he begins to bite. This is the state, not only of those who were going on this expedition, but of all men who fulfill their state and social duties in preference to and in detriment of their human duties.

The essence of this state is that under the influence of one suggestion they lose the power of criticising their actions, and therefore do, without thinking, everything consistent with the suggestion to which they are led by example, precept, or insinuation.

The difference between those hypnotized by scientific men and those under the influence of the state hypnotism, is that an imaginary position is suggested to the former suddenly by one person in a very brief space of time, and so the hypnotized state appears to us in a striking and surprising form, while the imaginary position suggested by state influence is induced slowly, little by little, imperceptibly from childhood, sometimes during years, or even generations, and not in one person alone but in a whole society.

"But," it will be said, "at all times, in all societies, the majority of persons—all the children, all the women absorbed in the bearing and rearing of the young, all the great mass of the laboring population, who are under the necessity of incessant and fatiguing physical labor, all those of weak character by nature, all those who are abnormally enfeebled intellectually by the effects of nicotine, alcohol, opium, or other intoxicants—are always in a condition of incapacity for independent thought, and are either in subjection to those who are on a higher intellectual level, or else under the influence of family or social traditions, of what is called public opinion, and there is nothing unnatural or incongruous in their subjection."

And truly there is nothing unnatural in it, and the tendency of men of small intellectual power to follow the lead of those on a higher level of intelligence is a constant law, and it is owing to it that men can live in societies and on the same principles at all. The minority consciously adopt certain rational principles through their correspondence with reason, while the majority act on the same principles unconsciously because it is required by public opinion.

Such subjection to public opinion on the part of the unintellectual does not assume an unnatural character till the public opinion is split into two.

But there are times when a higher truth, revealed at first to a few persons, gradually gains ground till it has taken hold of such a number of persons that the old public opinion, founded on a lower order of truths, begins to totter and the new is ready to take its place, but has not yet been firmly established. It is like the spring, this time of transition, when the old order of ideas has not quite broken up and the new has not quite gained a footing. Men begin to criticise their actions in the light of the new truth, but in the meantime in practice, through inertia and tradition, they continue to follow the principles which once represented the highest point of rational consciousness, but are now in flagrant contradiction with it.

Then men are in an abnormal, wavering condition, feeling the necessity of following the new ideal, and yet not bold enough to break with the old-established traditions.

Such is the attitude in regard to the truth of Christianity not only of the men in the Toula train, but of the majority of men of our times, alike of the higher and the lower orders.

Those of the ruling classes, having no longer any reasonable justification for the profitable positions they occupy, are forced, in order to keep them, to stifle their higher rational faculty of loving, and to persuade themselves that their positions are indispensable. And those of the lower classes, exhausted by toil and brutalized of set purpose, are kept in a permanent deception, practiced deliberately and continuously by the higher classes upon them.

Only in this way can one explain the amazing contradictions with which our life is full, and of which a striking example was presented to me by the expedition I met on the 9th of September; good, peaceful men, known to me personally, going with untroubled tranquillity to perpetrate the most beastly, senseless, and vile of crimes. Had not they some means of stifling their conscience, not one of them would be capable of committing a hundredth part of such a villainy.

It is not that they have not a conscience which forbids them from acting thus, just as, even three or four hundred years ago, when people burnt men at the stake and put them to the rack they had a conscience which prohibited it; the conscience is there, but it has been put to sleep—in those in command by what the psychologists call auto-suggestion; in the soldiers, by the direct conscious hypnotizing exerted by the higher classes.

Though asleep, the conscience is there, and in spite of the hypnotism it is already speaking in them, and it may awake.

All these men are in a position like that of a man under hypnotism, commanded to do something opposed to everything he regards as good and rational, such as to kill his mother or his child. The hypnotized subject feels himself bound to carry out the suggestion—he thinks he cannot stop—but the nearer he gets to the time and the place of the action, the more the benumbed conscience begins to stir, to resist, and to try to awake. And no one can say beforehand whether he will carry out the suggestion or not; which will gain the upper hand, the rational conscience or the irrational suggestion. It all depends on their relative strength.

That is just the case with the men in the Toula train and in general with everyone carrying out acts of state violence in our day.

There was a time when men who set out with the object of murder and violence, to make an example, did not return till they had carried out their object, and then, untroubled by doubts or scruples, having calmly flogged men to death, they returned home and caressed their children, laughed, amused themselves, and enjoyed the peaceful pleasures of family life. In those days it never struck the landowners and wealthy men who profited by these crimes, that the privileges they enjoyed had any direct connection with these atrocities. But now it is no longer so. Men know now, or are not far from knowing, what they are doing and for what object they do it. They can shut their eyes and force their conscience to be still, but so long as their eyes are opened and their conscience undulled, they must all—those who carry out and those who profit by these crimes alike—see the import of them. Sometimes they realize it only after the crime has been perpetrated, sometimes they realize it just before its perpetration. Thus those who commanded the recent acts of violence in Nijni-Novgorod, Saratov, Orel, and the Yuzovsky factory realized their significance only after their perpetration, and now those who commanded and those who carried out these crimes are ashamed before public opinion and their conscience. I have talked to soldiers who had taken part in these crimes, and they always studiously turned the conversation off the subject, and when they spoke of it it was with horror and bewilderment. There are cases, too, when men come to themselves just before the perpetration of the crime. Thus I know the case of a sergeant-major who had been beaten by two peasants during the repression of disorder and had made a complaint. The next day, after seeing the atrocities perpetrated on the other peasants, he entreated the commander of his company to tear up his complaint and let off the two peasants. I know cases when soldiers, commanded to fire, have refused to obey, and I know many cases of officers who have refused to command expeditions for torture and murder. So that men sometimes come to their senses long before perpetrating the suggested crime, sometimes at the very moment before perpetrating it, sometimes only afterward.

The men traveling in the Toula train were going with the object of killing and injuring their fellow-creatures, but none could tell whether they would carry out their object or not. However obscure his responsibility for the affair is to each, and however strong the idea instilled into all of them that they are not men, but governors, officials, officers, and soldiers, and as such beings can violate every human duty, the nearer they approach the place of the execution, the stronger their doubts as to its being right, and this doubt will reach its highest point when the very moment for carrying it out has come.

The governor, in spite of all the stupefying effect of his surroundings, cannot help hesitating when the moment comes to give final decisive command. He knows that the action of the Governor of Orel has called down upon him the disapproval of the best people, and he himself, influenced by the public opinion of the circles in which he moves, has more than once expressed his disapprobation of him. He knows that the prosecutor, who ought to have come, flatly refused to have anything to do with it, because he regarded it as disgraceful. He knows, too, that there may be changes any day in the government, and that what was a ground for advancement yesterday may be the cause of disgrace to-morrow. And he knows that there is a press, if not in Russia, at least abroad, which may report the affair and cover him with ignominy forever. He is already conscious of a change in public opinion which condemns what was formerly a duty. Moreover, he cannot feel fully assured that his soldiers will at the last moment obey him. He is wavering, and none can say beforehand what he will do.

All the officers and functionaries who accompany him experience in greater or less degree the same emotions. In the depths of their hearts they all know that what they are doing is shameful, that to take part in it is a discredit and blemish in the eyes of some people whose opinion they value. They know that after murdering and torturing the defenseless, each of them will be ashamed to face his betrothed or the woman he is courting. And besides, they too, like the governor, are doubtful whether the soldiers' obedience to orders can be reckoned on. What a contrast with the confident air they all put on as they sauntered about the station and platform! Inwardly they were not only in a state of suffering but even of suspense. Indeed they only assumed this bold and composed manner to conceal the wavering within. And this feeling increased as they drew near the scene of action.

And imperceptible as it was, and strange as it seems to say so, all that mass of lads, the soldiers, who seemed so submissive, were in precisely the same condition.

These are not the soldiers of former days, who gave up the natural life of industry and devoted their whole existence to debauchery, plunder, and murder, like the Roman legionaries or the warriors of the Thirty Years' War, or even the soldiers of more recent times who served for twenty-five years in the army. They have mostly been only lately taken from their families, and are full of the recollections of the good, rational, natural life they have left behind them.

All these lads, peasants for the most part, know what is the business they have come about; they know that the landowners always oppress their brothers the peasants, and that therefore it is most likely the same thing here. Moreover, a majority of them can now read, and the books they read are not all such as exalt a military life; there are some which point out its immorality. Among them are often free-thinking comrades—who have enlisted voluntarily—or young officers of liberal ideas, and already the first germ of doubt has been sown in regard to the unconditional legitimacy and glory of their occupation.

It is true that they have all passed through that terrible, skillful education, elaborated through centuries, which kills all initiative in a man, and that they are so trained to mechanical obedience that at the word of command: "Fire!—All the line!—Fire!" and so on, their guns will rise of themselves and the habitual movements will be performed. But "Fire!" now does not mean shooting into the sand for amusement, it means firing on their broken-down, exploited fathers and brothers whom they see there in the crowd, with women and children shouting and waving their arms. Here they are—one with his scanty beard and patched coat and plaited shoes of reed, just like the father left at home in Kazan or Riazan province; one with gray beard and bent back, leaning on a staff like the old grand-father; one, a young fellow in boots and a red shirt, just as he was himself a year ago—he, the soldier who must fire upon him. There, too, a woman in reed shoes and *panyova*, just like the mother left at home.

Is it possible they must fire on them? And no one knows what each soldier will do at the last minute. The least word, the slightest allusion would be enough to stop them.

At the last moment they will all find themselves in the position of a hypnotized man to whom it has been suggested to chop a log, who coming up to what has been indicated to him as a log, with the ax already lifted to strike, sees that it is not a log but his sleeping brother. He may perform the act that has been suggested to him, and he may come to his senses at the moment of performing it. In the same way all these men may come to themselves in time or they may go on to the end.

If they do not come to themselves, the most fearful crime will be committed, as in Orel, and then the hypnotic suggestion under which they act will be strengthened in all other men. If they do come to themselves, not only this terrible crime will not be perpetrated, but many also who hear of the turn the affair has taken will be emancipated from the hypnotic influence in which they were held, or at least will be nearer being emancipated from it.

Even if a few only come to themselves, and boldly explain to the others all the wickedness of such a crime, the influence of these few may rouse the others to shake off the controlling suggestion, and the atrocity will not be perpetrated.

More than that, if a few men, even of those who are not taking part in the affair but are only present at the preparations for it, or have heard of such things being done in the past, do not remain indifferent but boldly and plainly express their detestation of such crimes to those who have to execute them, and point out to them all the senselessness, cruelty, and wickedness of such acts, that alone will be productive of good.

That was what took place in the instance before us. It was enough for a few men, some personally concerned in the affair and others simply outsiders, to express their disapproval of floggings that had taken place elsewhere, and their contempt and loathing for those who had taken part in inflicting them, for a few persons in the Toula case to express their repugnance to having any share in it; for a lady traveling by the train, and a few other bystanders at the station, to express to those who formed the expedition their disgust at what they were doing; for one of the commanders of a company, who was asked for troops for the restoration of order, to reply that soldiers ought not to be butchers—and thanks to these and a few other seemingly insignificant influences brought to bear on these hypnotized men, the affair took a completely different turn, and the troops, when they reached the place, did not inflict any punishment, but contented themselves with cutting down the forest and giving it to the landowner.

Had not a few persons had a clear consciousness that what they were doing was wrong, and consequently influenced one another in that direction, what was done at Orel would have taken place at Toula. Had this consciousness been still stronger, and had the influence exerted been therefore greater than it was, it might well have been that the governor with his troops would not even have ventured to cut down the forest and give it to the landowner. Had that consciousness been stronger still, it might well have been that the governor would not have ventured to go to the scene of action at all; even that the minister would not have ventured to form this decision or the Tzar to ratify it.

All depends, therefore, on the strength of the consciousness of Christian truth on the part of each individual man.

And, therefore, one would have thought that the efforts of all men of the present day who profess to wish to work for the welfare of humanity would have been directed to strengthening this consciousness of Christian truth in themselves and others.

But, strange to say, it is precisely those people who profess most anxiety for the amelioration of human life, and are regarded as the leaders of public opinion, who assert that there is no need to do that, and that there are other more effective means for the amelioration of men's condition. They affirm that the amelioration of human life is effected not by the efforts of individual men, to recognize and propagate the truth, but by the gradual modification of the general conditions of life, and that therefore the efforts of individuals should be directed to the gradual modification of external conditions for the better. For every advocacy of a truth inconsistent with the existing order by an individual is, they maintain, not only useless but injurious, since it provokes coercive measures on the part of the authorities, restricting these individuals from continuing any action useful to society. According to this doctrine all modifications in human life are brought about by precisely the same laws as in the life of the animals.

So that, according to this doctrine, all the founders of religions, such as Moses and the prophets, Confucius, Lao-Tse, Buddha, Christ, and others, preached their doctrines and their followers accepted them, not because they loved the truth, but because the political, social, and above all economic conditions of the peoples among whom these religions arose were favorable for their origination and development.

And therefore the chief efforts of the man who wishes to serve society and improve the condition of humanity ought, according to this doctrine, to be directed not to the elucidation and propagation of truth, but to the improvement of the external political, social, and above all economic conditions. And the modification of these conditions is partly effected by serving the government and introducing liberal and progressive principles into it, partly in promoting the development of industry and the propagation of socialistic ideas, and most of all by the diffusion of science. According to this theory it is of no consequence whether you profess the truth revealed to you, and therefore realize it in your life, or at least refrain from committing actions opposed to the truth, such as serving the government and strengthening its authority when you regard it as injurious, profiting by the capitalistic system when you regard it as wrong, showing veneration for various ceremonies which you believe to be degrading superstitions, giving support to the law when you believe it to be founded on error, serving as a soldier, taking oaths, and lying, and lowering yourself generally. It is useless to refrain from all that; what is of use is not altering the existing forms of life, but submitting to them against your own convictions, introducing liberalism into the existing institutions, promoting commerce, the propaganda of socialism, and the triumphs of what is called science, and the diffusion of education. According to this theory one can remain a landowner, merchant, manufacturer, judge, official in government pay, officer or soldier, and still be not only a humane man, but even a socialist and revolutionist.

Hypocrisy, which had formerly only a religious basis in the doctrine of original sin, the redemption, and the Church, has in our day gained a new scientific basis and has consequently caught in its nets all those who had reached too high a stage of development to be able to find support in religious hypocrisy. So that while in former days a man who professed the religion of the Church could take part in all the crimes of the state, and profit by them, and still regard himself as free from any taint of sin, so long as he fulfilled the external observances of his creed, nowadays all who do not believe in the Christianity of the Church, find similar well-founded irrefutable reasons in science for regarding themselves as blameless and even highly moral in spite of their participation in the misdeeds of government and the advantages they gain from them.

A rich landowner—not only in Russia, but in France, England, Germany, or America—lives on the rents exacted from the people living on his land, and robs these generally poverty-stricken people of all he can get from them. This man's right of property in the land rests on the fact that at every effort on the part of the oppressed people, without his consent, to make use of the land he considers his, troops are called out to subject them to punishment and murder. One would have thought that it was obvious that a man living in this way was an evil, egoistic creature and could not possibly consider himself a Christian or a liberal. One would have supposed it evident that the first thing such a man must do, if he wishes to approximate to Christianity or liberalism, would be to cease to plunder and ruin men by means of acts of state violence in support of his claim to the land. And so it would be if it were not for the logic of hypocrisy, which reasons that from a religious point of view possession or non-possession of land is of no consequence for salvation, and from the scientific point of view, giving up the ownership of land is a useless individual renunciation, and that the welfare of mankind is not promoted in that way, but by a gradual modification of external forms. And so we see this man, without the least trouble of mind or doubt that people will believe in his sincerity, organizing an agricultural exhibition, or a temperance society, or sending some soup and stockings by his wife or children to three old women, and boldly in his family, in drawing rooms, in committees, and in the press, advocating the Gospel or humanitarian doctrine of love for one's neighbor in general and the agricultural laboring population in particular whom he is continually exploiting and oppressing. And other people who are in the same position as he believe him, commend him, and solemnly discuss with him measures for ameliorating the condition of the working-class, on whose exploitation their whole life rests, devising all kinds of possible methods for this, except the one without which all improvement of their condition is impossible, *i. e.*, refraining from taking from them the land necessary for their subsistence. (A striking example of this hypocrisy was the solicitude displayed by the Russian landowners last year, their efforts to combat the famine which they had caused, and by which they profited, selling not only bread at the highest price, but even potato haulm at five rubles the dessiatine (about $2\frac{4}{5}$ acres) for fuel to the freezing peasants.)

Or take a merchant whose whole trade—like all trade indeed—is founded on a series of trickery, by means of which, profiting by the ignorance or need of others, he buys goods below their value and sells them again above their value. One would have fancied it obvious that a man whose whole occupation was based on what in his own language is called swindling, if it is done under other conditions, ought to be ashamed of his position, and could not any way, while he continues a merchant, profess himself a Christian or a liberal.

But the sophistry of hypocrisy reasons that the merchant can pass for a virtuous man without giving up his pernicious course of action; a religious man need only have faith and a liberal man need only promote the modification of external conditions—the progress of industry. And so we see the merchant (who often goes further and commits acts of direct dishonesty, selling adulterated goods, using false weights and measures, and trading in products injurious to health, such as alcohol and opium) boldly regarding himself and being regarded by others, so long as he does not directly deceive his colleagues in business, as a pattern of probity and virtue. And if he spends a thousandth part of his stolen wealth on some public institution, a hospital or museum or school, then he is even regarded as the benefactor of the people on the exploitation and corruption of whom his whole prosperity has been founded: if he sacrifices, too, a portion of his ill-gotten gains on a Church and the poor, then he is an exemplary Christian.

A manufacturer is a man whose whole income consists of value squeezed out of the workmen, and whose whole occupation is based on forced, unnatural labor, exhausting whole generations of men. It would seem obvious that if this man professes any Christian or liberal principles, he must first of all give up ruining human lives for his own profit. But by the existing theory he is promoting industry, and he ought not to abandon his pursuit. It would even be injuring society for him to do so. And so we see this man, the harsh slave-driver of thousands of men, building almshouses with little gardens two yards square for the workmen broken down in toiling for him, and a bank, and a poorhouse, and a hospital—fully persuaded that he has amply expiated in this way for all the human lives morally and physically ruined by him—and calmly going on with his business, taking pride in it.

Any civil, religious, or military official in government employ, who serves the state from vanity, or, as is most often the case, simply for the sake of the pay wrung from the harassed and toilworn working classes (all taxes, however raised, always fall on labor), if he, as is very seldom the case, does not directly rob the government in the usual way, considers himself, and is considered by his fellows, as a most useful and virtuous member of society.

A judge or a public prosecutor knows that through his sentence or his prosecution hundreds or thousands of poor wretches are at once torn from their families and thrown into prison, where they may go out of their minds, kill themselves with pieces of broken glass, or starve themselves; he knows that they have wives and mothers and children, disgraced and made miserable by separation from them, vainly begging for pardon for them or some alleviation of their sentence, and this judge or this prosecutor is so hardened in his hypocrisy that he and his fellows and his wife and his household are all fully convinced that he may be a most exemplary man. According to the metaphysics of hypocrisy it is held that he is doing a work of public utility. And this man who has ruined hundreds, thousands of men, who curse him and are driven to desperation by his action, goes to mass, a smile of shining benevolence on his smooth face, in perfect faith in good and in God, listens to the Gospel, caresses his children, preaches moral principles to them, and is moved by imaginary sufferings.

All these men and those who depend on them, their wives, tutors, children, cooks, actors, jockeys, and so on, are living on the blood which by one means or another, through one set of bloodsuckers or another, is drawn out of the working class, and every day their pleasures cost hundreds or thousands of days of labor. They see the sufferings and privations of these laborers and their children, their aged, their wives, and their sick, they know the punishments inflicted on those who resist this organized plunder, and far from decreasing, far from concealing their luxury, they insolently display it before these oppressed laborers who hate them, as though intentionally provoking them with the pomp of their parks and palaces, their theaters, hunts, and races. At the same time they continue to persuade themselves and others that they are all much concerned about the welfare of these working classes, whom they have always trampled under their feet, and on Sundays, richly dressed, they drive in sumptuous carriages to the houses of God built in very mockery of Christianity, and there listen to men, trained to this work of deception, who in white neckties or in brocaded vestments, according to their denomination, preach the love for their neighbor which they all gainsay in their lives. And these people have so entered into their part that they seriously believe that they really are what they pretend to be.

The universal hypocrisy has so entered into the flesh and blood of all classes of our modern society, it has reached such a pitch that nothing in that way can rouse indignation. Hypocrisy in the Greek means "acting," and acting—playing a part—is always possible. The representatives of Christ give their blessing to the ranks of murderers holding their guns loaded against their brothers; "for prayer" priests, ministers of various Christian sects are always present, as indispensably as the hangman, at executions, and sanction by their presence the compatibility of murder with Christianity (a clergyman assisted at the attempt at murder by electricity in America)—but such facts cause no one any surprise.

There was recently held at Petersburg an international exhibition of instruments of torture, handcuffs, models of solitary cells, that is to say instruments of torture worse than knouts or rods, and sensitive ladies and gentlemen went and amused themselves by looking at them.

No one is surprised that together with its recognition of liberty, equality, and fraternity, liberal science should prove the necessity of war, punishment, customs, the censure, the regulation of prostitution, the exclusion of cheap foreign laborers, the hindrance of emigration, the justifiableness of colonization, based on poisoning and destroying whole races of men called savages, and so on.

People talk of the time when all men shall profess what is called Christianity (that is, various professions of faith hostile to one another), when all shall be well-fed and clothed, when all shall be united from one end of the world to the other by telegraphs and telephones, and be able to communicate by balloons, when all the working classes are permeated by socialistic doctrines, when the Trades Unions possess so many millions of members and so many millions of rubles, when everyone is educated and all can read newspapers and learn all the sciences.

But what good or useful thing can come of all these improvements, if men do not speak and act in accordance with what they believe to be the truth?

The condition of men is the result of their disunion. Their disunion results from their not following the truth which is one, but falsehoods which are many. The sole means of uniting men is their union in the truth. And therefore the more sincerely men strive toward the truth, the nearer they get to unity.

But how can men be united in the truth or even approximate to it, if they do not even express the truth they know, but hold that there is no need to do so, and pretend to regard as truth what they believe to be false?

And therefore no improvement is possible so long as men are hypocritical and hide the truth from themselves, so long as they do not recognize that their union and therefore their welfare is only possible in the truth, and do not put the recognition and profession of the truth revealed to them higher than everything else.

All the material improvements that religious and scientific men can dream of may be accomplished; all men may accept Christianity, and all the reforms desired by the Bellamys may be brought about with every possible addition and improvement, but if the hypocrisy which rules nowadays still exists, if men do not profess the truth they know, but continue to feign belief in what they do not believe and veneration for what they do not respect, their condition will remain the same, or even grow worse and worse. The more men are freed from privation; the more telegraphs, telephones, books, papers, and journals there are; the more means there will be of diffusing inconsistent lies and hypocrisies, and the more disunited and consequently miserable will men become, which indeed is what we see actually taking place.

All these material reforms may be realized, but the position of humanity will not be improved. But only let each man, according to his powers, at once realize in his life the truth he knows, or at least cease to support the falsehoods he is supporting in the place of the truth, and at once, in this year 1893, we should see such reforms as we do not dare to hope for within a century—the emancipation of men and the reign of truth upon earth.

Not without good reason was Christ's only harsh and threatening reproof directed against hypocrites and hypocrisy. It is not theft nor robbery nor murder nor fornication, but falsehood, the special falsehood of hypocrisy, which corrupts men, brutalizes them and makes them vindictive, destroys all distinction between right and wrong in their conscience, deprives them of what is the true meaning of all real human life, and debars them from all progress toward perfection.

LEO TOLSTOY

Those who do evil through ignorance of the truth provoke sympathy with their victims and repugnance for their actions, they do harm only to those they attack; but those who know the truth and do evil masked by hypocrisy, injure themselves and their victims, and thousands of other men as well who are led astray by the falsehood with which the wrongdoing is disguised.

Thieves, robbers, murderers, and cheats, who commit crimes recognized by themselves and everyone else as evil, serve as an example of what ought not to be done, and deter others from similar crimes. But those who commit the same thefts, robberies, murders, and other crimes, disguising them under all kinds of religious or scientific or humanitarian justifications, as all landowners, merchants, manufacturers, and government officials do, provoke others to imitation, and so do harm not only to those who are directly the victims of their crimes, but to thousands and millions of men whom they corrupt by obliterating their sense of the distinction between right and wrong.

A single fortune gained by trading in goods necessary to the people or in goods pernicious in their effects, or by financial speculations, or by acquiring land at a low price the value of which is increased by the needs of the population, or by an industry ruinous to the health and life of those employed in it, or by military or civil service of the state, or by any employment which trades on men's evil instincts—a single fortune acquired in any of these ways, not only with the sanction, but even with the approbation of the leading men in society, and masked with an ostentation of philanthropy, corrupts men incomparably more than millions of thefts and robberies committed against the recognized forms of law and punishable as crimes.

A single execution carried out by prosperous educated men uninfluenced by passion, with the approbation and assistance of Christian ministers, and represented as something necessary and even just, is infinitely more corrupting and brutalizing to men than thousands of murders committed by uneducated working people under the influence of passion. An execution such as was proposed by Joukovsky, which would produce even a sentiment of religious emotion in the spectators, would be one of the most perverting actions imaginable. (*See* vol. iv. of the works of Joukovsky.)

Every war, even the most humanely conducted, with all its ordinary consequences, the destruction of harvests, robberies, the license and debauchery, and the murder with the justifications of its necessity and justice, the exaltation and glorification of military exploits, the worship of the flag, the patriotic sentiments, the feigned solicitude for the wounded, and so on, does more in one year to pervert men's minds than thousands of robberies, murders, and arsons perpetrated during hundreds of years by individual men under the influence of passion.

The luxurious expenditure of a single respectable and so-called honorable family, even within the conventional limits, consuming as it does the produce of as many days of labor as would suffice to provide for thousands living in privation near, does more to pervert men's minds than thousands of the violent orgies of coarse tradespeople, officers, and workmen of drunken and debauched habits, who smash up glasses and crockery for amusement.

One solemn religious procession, one service, one sermon from the altar-steps or the pulpit, in which the preacher does not believe, produces incomparably more evil than thousands of swindling tricks, adulteration of food, and so on.

We talk of the hypocrisy of the Pharisees. But the hypocrisy of our society far surpasses the comparatively innocent hypocrisy of the Pharisees. They had at least an external religious law, the fulfillment of which hindered them from seeing their obligations to their neighbors. Moreover, these obligations were not nearly so clearly defined in their day. Nowadays we have no such religious law to exonerate us from our duties to our neighbors (I am not speaking now of the coarse and ignorant persons who still fancy their sins can be absolved by confession to a priest or by the absolution of the Pope). On the contrary, the law of the Gospel which we all profess in one form or another directly defines these duties. Besides, the duties which had then been only vaguely and mystically expressed by a few prophets have now been so clearly formulated, have become such truisms, that they are repeated even by schoolboys and journalists. And so it would seem that men of to-day cannot pretend that they do not know these duties.

A man of the modern world who profits by the order of things based on violence, and at the same time protests that he loves his neighbor and does not observe what he is doing in his daily life to his neighbor, is like a brigand who has spent his life in robbing men, and who, caught at last, knife in hand, in the very act of striking his shrieking victim, should declare that he had no idea that what he was doing was disagreeable to the man he had robbed and was prepared to murder. Just as this robber and murderer could not deny what was evident to everyone, so it would seem that a man living upon the privations of the oppressed classes cannot persuade himself and others that he desires the welfare of those he plunders, and that he does not know how the advantages he enjoys are obtained.

It is impossible to convince ourselves that we do not know that there are a hundred thousand men in prison in Russia alone to guarantee the security of our property and tranquillity, and that we do not know of the law tribunals in which we take part, and which, at our initiative, condemn those who have attacked our property or our security to prison, exile, or forced labor, whereby men no worse than those who condemn them are ruined and corrupted; or that we do not know that we only possess all that we do possess because it has been acquired and is defended for us by murder and violence.

We cannot pretend that we do not see the armed policeman who marches up and down beneath our windows to guarantee our security while we eat our luxurious dinner, or look at the new piece at the theater, or that we are unaware of the existence of the soldiers who will make their appearance with guns and cartridges directly our property is attacked.

We know very well that we are only allowed to go on eating our dinner, to finish seeing the new play, or to enjoy to the end the ball, the Christmas fête, the promenade, the races or the hunt, thanks to the policeman's revolver or the soldier's rifle, which will shoot down the famished outcast who has been robbed of his share, and who looks round the corner with covetous eyes at our pleasures, ready to interrupt them instantly, were not the policeman and the soldier there prepared to run up at our first call for help.

And therefore just as a brigand caught in broad daylight in the act cannot persuade us that he did not lift his knife in order to rob his victim of his purse, and had no thought of killing him, we too, it would seem, cannot persuade ourselves or others that the soldiers and policemen around us are not to guard us, but only for defense against foreign foes, and to regulate traffic and fêtes and reviews; we cannot persuade ourselves and others that we do not know that men do not like dying of hunger, bereft of the right to gain their subsistence from the earth on which they live; that they do not like working underground, in the water, or in stifling heat, for ten to fourteen hours a day, at night in factories to manufacture objects for our pleasure. One would imagine it impossible to deny what is so obvious. Yet it is denied.

Still, there are, among the rich, especially among the young, and among women, persons whom I am glad to meet more and more frequently, who, when they are shown in what way and at what cost their pleasures are purchased, do not try to conceal the truth, but hiding their heads in their hands, cry: "Ah! don't speak of that. If it is so, life is impossible." But though there are such sincere people who even though they cannot renounce their fault, at least see it, the vast majority of the men of the modern world have so entered into the parts they play in their hypocrisy that they boldly deny what is staring everyone in the face.

"All that is unjust," they say; "no one forces the people to work for the landowners and manufacturers. That is an affair of free contract. Great properties and fortunes are necessary, because they provide and organize work for the working classes. And labor in the factories and workshops is not at all the terrible thing you make it out to be. Even if there are some abuses in factories, the government and the public are taking steps to obviate them and to make the labor of the factory workers much easier, and even agreeable. The working classes are accustomed to physical labor, and are, so far, fit for nothing else. The poverty of the people is not the result of private property in land, nor of capitalistic oppression, but of other causes: it is the result of the ignorance, brutality, and intemperance of the people. And we men in authority who are striving against this impoverishment of the people by wise legislation, we capitalists who are combating it by the extension of useful inventions, we clergymen by religious instruction, and we liberals by the formation of trades unions, and the diffusion of education, are in this way increasing the prosperity of the people without changing our own positions. We do not want all to be as poor as the poor; we want all to be as rich as the rich. As for the assertion that men are ill treated and murdered to force them to work for the profit of the rich, that is a sophism. The army is only called out against the mob, when the people, in ignorance of their own interests, make disturbances and destroy the tranquillity necessary for the public welfare. In the same way, too, it is necessary to keep in restraint the malefactors for whom the prisons and gallows are established. We ourselves wish to suppress these forms of punishment and are working in that direction."

Hypocrisy in our day is supported on two sides: by false religion and by false science. And it has reached such proportions that if we were not living in its midst, we could not believe that men could attain such a pitch of self-deception. Men of the present day have come into such an extraordinary condition, their hearts are so hardened, that seeing they see not, hearing they do not hear, and understand not.

Men have long been living in antagonism to their conscience. If it were not for hypocrisy they could not go on living such a life. This social organization in opposition to their conscience only continues to exist because it is disguised by hypocrisy.

And the greater the divergence between actual life and men's conscience, the greater the extension of hypocrisy. But even hypocrisy has its limits. And it seems to me that we have reached those limits in the present day.

Every man of the present day with the Christian principles assimilated involuntarily in his conscience, finds himself in precisely the position of a man asleep who dreams that he is obliged to do something which even in his dream he knows he ought not to do. He knows this in the depths of his conscience, and all the same he seems unable to change his position; he cannot stop and cease doing what he ought not to do. And just as in a dream, his position becoming more and more painful, at last reaches such a pitch of intensity that he begins sometimes to doubt the reality of what is passing and makes a moral effort to shake off the nightmare which is oppressing him.

This is just the condition of the average man of our Christian society. He feels that all that he does himself and that is done around him is something absurd, hideous, impossible, and opposed to his conscience; he feels that his position is becoming more and more unendurable and reaching a crisis of intensity.

It is not possible that we modern men, with the Christian sense of human dignity and equality permeating us soul and body, with our need for peaceful association and unity between nations, should really go on living in such a way that every joy, every gratification we have is bought by the sufferings, by the lives of our brother men, and moreover, that we should be every instant within a hair's-breadth of falling on one another, nation against nation, like wild beasts, mercilessly destroying men's lives and labor, only because some benighted diplomatist or ruler says or writes some stupidity to another equally benighted diplomatist or ruler.

It is impossible. Yet every man of our day sees that this is so and awaits the calamity. And the situation becomes more and more insupportable.

And as the man who is dreaming does not believe that what appears to him can be truly the reality and tries to wake up to the actual real world again, so the average man of modern days cannot in the bottom of his heart believe that the awful position in which he is placed and which is growing worse and worse can be the reality, and tries to wake up to a true, real life, as it exists in his conscience.

And just as the dreamer need only make a moral effort and ask himself, "Isn't it a dream?" and the situation which seemed to him so hopeless will instantly disappear, and he will wake up to peaceful and happy reality, so the man of the modern world need only make a moral effort to doubt the reality presented to him by his own hypocrisy and the general hypocrisy around him, and to ask himself, "Isn't it all a delusion?" and he will at once, like the dreamer awakened, feel himself transported from an imaginary and dreadful world to the true, calm, and happy reality.

And to do this a man need accomplish no great feats or exploits. He need only make a moral effort.

But can a man make this effort?

According to the existing theory so essential to support hypocrisy, man is not free and cannot change his life.

"Man cannot change his life, because he is not free. He is not free, because all his actions are conditioned by previously existing causes. And whatever the man may do there are always some causes or other through which he does these or those acts, and therefore man cannot be free and change his life," say the champions of the metaphysics of hypocrisy. And they would be perfectly right if man were a creature without conscience and incapable of moving toward the truth; that is to say, if after recognizing a new truth, man always remained at the same stage of moral development. But man is a creature with a conscience and capable of attaining a higher and higher degree of truth. And therefore even if man is not free as regards performing these or those acts because there exists a previous cause for every act, the very causes of his acts, consisting as they do for the man of conscience of the recognition of this or that truth, are within his own control.

So that though man may not be free as regards the performance of his actions, he is free as regards the foundation on which they are performed. Just as the mechanician who is not free to modify the movement of his locomotive when it is in motion, is free to regulate the machine beforehand so as to determine what the movement is to be.

Whatever the conscious man does, he acts just as he does, and not otherwise, only because he recognizes that to act as he is acting is in accord with the truth, or because he has recognized it at some previous time, and is now only through inertia, through habit, acting in accordance with his previous recognition of truth.

In any case, the cause of his action is not to be found in any given previous fact, but in the consciousness of a given relation to truth, and the consequent recognition of this or that fact as a sufficient basis for action.

Whether a man eats or does not eat, works or rests, runs risks or avoids them, if he has a conscience he acts thus only because he considers it right and rational, because he considers that to act thus is in harmony with truth, or else because he has made this reflection in the past.

The recognition or non-recognition of a certain truth depends not on external causes, but on certain other causes within the man himself. So that at times under external conditions apparently very favorable for the recognition of truth, one man will not recognize it, and another, on the contrary, under the most unfavorable conditions will, without apparent cause, recognize it. As it is said in the Gospel, "No man can come unto me, except the Father which hath sent me draw him." That is to say, the recognition of truth, which is the cause of all the manifestations of human life, does not depend on external phenomena, but on certain inner spiritual characteristics of the man which escape our observation.

And therefore man, though not free in his acts, always feels himself free in what is the motive of his acts—the recognition or non-recognition of truth. And he feels himself independent not only of facts external to his own personality, but even of his own actions.

Thus a man who under the influence of passion has committed an act contrary to the truth he recognizes, remains none the less free to recognize it or not to recognize it; that is, he can by refusing to recognize the truth regard his action as necessary and justifiable, or he may recognize the truth and regard his act as wrong and censure himself for it.

Thus a gambler or a drunkard who does not resist temptation and yields to his passion is still free to recognize gambling and drunkenness as wrong or to regard them as a harmless pastime. In the first case even if he does not at once get over his passion, he gets the more free from it the more sincerely he recognizes the truth about it; in the second case he will be strengthened in his vice and will deprive himself of every possibility of shaking it off.

In the same way a man who has made his escape alone from a house on fire, not having had the courage to save his friend, remains free, recognizing the truth that a man ought to save the life of another even at the risk of his own, to regard his action as bad and to censure himself for it, or, not recognizing this truth, to regard his action as natural and necessary and to justify it to himself. In the first case, if he recognizes the truth in spite of his departure from it, he prepares for himself in the future a whole series of acts of self-sacrifice necessarily flowing from this recognition of the truth; in the second case, a whole series of egoistic acts.

Not that a man is always free to recognize or to refuse to recognize every truth. There are truths which he has recognized long before or which have been handed down to him by education and tradition and accepted by him on faith, and to follow these truths has become a habit, a second nature with him; and there are truths, only vaguely, as it were distantly, apprehended by him. The man is not free to refuse to recognize the first, nor to recognize the second class of truths. But there are truths of a third kind, which have not yet become an unconscious motive of action, but yet have been revealed so clearly to him that he cannot pass them by, and is inevitably obliged to do one thing or the other, to recognize or not to recognize them. And it is in regard to these truths that the man's freedom manifests itself.

Every man during his life finds himself in regard to truth in the position of a man walking in the darkness with light thrown before him by the lantern he carries. He does not see what is not yet lighted up by the lantern; he does not see what he has passed which is hidden in the darkness; but at every stage of his journey he sees what is lighted up by the lantern, and he can always choose one side or the other of the road.

There are always unseen truths not yet revealed to the man's intellectual vision, and there are other truths outlived, forgotten, and assimilated by him, and there are also certain truths that rise up before the light of his reason and require his recognition. And it is in the recognition or non-recognition of these truths that what we call his freedom is manifested.

All the difficulty and seeming insolubility of the question of the freedom of man results from those who tried to solve the question imagining man as stationary in his relation to the truth.

Man is certainly not free if we imagine him stationary, and if we forget that the life of a man and of humanity is nothing but a continual movement from darkness into light, from a lower stage of truth to a higher, from a truth more alloyed with errors to a truth more purified from them.

Man would not be free if he knew no truth at all, and in the same way he would not be free and would not even have any idea of freedom if the whole truth which was to guide him in life had been revealed once for all to him in all its purity without any admixture of error.

But man is not stationary in regard to truth, but every individual man as he passes through life, and humanity as a whole in the same way, is continually learning to know a greater and greater degree of truth, and growing more and more free from error.

And therefore men are in a threefold relation to truth. Some truths have been so assimilated by them that they have become the unconscious basis of action, others are only just on the point of being revealed to him, and a third class, though not yet assimilated by him, have been revealed to him with sufficient clearness to force him to decide either to recognize them or to refuse to recognize them.

These, then, are the truths which man is free to recognize or to refuse to recognize.

The liberty of man does not consist in the power of acting independently of the progress of life and the influences arising from it, but in the capacity for recognizing and acknowledging the truth revealed to him, and becoming the free and joyful participator in the eternal and infinite work of God, the life of the world; or on the other hand for refusing to recognize the truth, and so being a miserable and reluctant slave dragged whither he has no desire to go.

Truth not only points out the way along which human life ought to move, but reveals also the only way along which it can move. And therefore all men must willingly or unwillingly move along the way of truth, some spontaneously accomplishing the task set them in life, others submitting involuntarily to the law of life. Man's freedom lies in the power of this choice.

This freedom within these narrow limits seems so insignificant to men that they do not notice it. Some—the determinists—consider this amount of freedom so trifling that they do not recognize it at all. Others—the champions of complete free will—keep their eyes fixed on their hypothetical free will and neglect this which seemed to them such a trivial degree of freedom.

This freedom, confined between the limits of complete ignorance of the truth and a recognition of a part of the truth, seems hardly freedom at all, especially since, whether a man is willing or unwilling to recognize the truth revealed to him, he will be inevitably forced to carry it out in life.

A horse harnessed with others to a cart is not free to refrain from moving the cart. If he does not move forward the cart will knock him down and go on dragging him with it, whether he will or not. But the horse is free to drag the cart himself or to be dragged with it. And so it is with man.

Whether this is a great or small degree of freedom in comparison with the fantastic liberty we should like to have, it is the only freedom that really exists, and in it consists the only happiness attainable by man.

And more than that, this freedom is the sole means of accomplishing the divine work of the life of the world.

According to Christ's doctrine, the man who sees the significance of life in the domain in which it is not free, in the domain of effects, that is, of acts, has not the true life. According to the Christian doctrine, that man is living in the truth who has transported his life to the domain in which it is free—the domain of causes, that is, the knowledge and recognition, the profession and realization in life of revealed truth.

Devoting his life to works of the flesh, a man busies himself with actions depending on temporary causes outside himself. He himself does nothing really, he merely seems to be doing something. In reality all the acts which seem to be his are the work of a higher power, and he is not the creator of his own life, but the slave of it. Devoting his life to the recognition and fulfillment of the truth revealed to him, he identifies himself with the source of universal life and accomplishes acts not personal, and dependent on conditions of space and time, but acts unconditioned by previous causes, acts which constitute the causes of everything else, and have an infinite, unlimited significance.

"The kingdom of heaven suffereth violence, and the violent take it by force." (Matt. xi. 12.)

It is this violent effort to rise above external conditions to the recognition and realization of truth by which the kingdom of heaven is taken, and it is this effort of violence which must and can be made in our times.

Men need only understand this, they need only cease to trouble themselves about the general external conditions in which they are not free, and devote one-hundredth part of the energy they waste on those material things to that in which they are free, to the recognition and realization of the truth which is before them, and to the liberation of themselves and others from deception and hypocrisy, and, without effort or conflict, there would be an end at once of the false organization of life which makes men miserable, and threatens them with worse calamities in the future. And then the kingdom of God would be realized, or at least that first stage of it for which men are ready now by the degree of development of their conscience.

Just as a single shock may be sufficient, when a liquid is saturated with some salt, to precipitate it at once in crystals, a slight effort may be perhaps all that is needed now that the truth already revealed to men may gain a mastery over hundreds, thousands, millions of men, that a public opinion consistent with conscience may be established, and through this change of public opinion the whole order of life may be transformed. And it depends upon us to make this effort.

Let each of us only try to understand and accept the Christian truth which in the most varied forms surrounds us on all sides and forces itself upon us; let us only cease from lying and pretending that we do not see this truth or wish to realize it, at least in what it demands from us above all else; only let us accept and boldly profess the truth to which we are called, and we should find at once that hundreds, thousands, millions of men are in the same position as we, that they see the truth as we do, and dread as we do to stand alone in recognizing it, and like us are only waiting for others to recognize it also.

Only let men cease to be hypocrites, and they would at once see that this cruel social organization, which holds them in bondage, and is represented to them as something stable, necessary, and ordained of God, is already tottering and is only propped up by the falsehood of hypocrisy, with which we, and others like us, support it.

But if this is so, if it is true that it depends on us to break down the existing organization of life, have we the right to destroy it, without knowing clearly what we shall set up in its place? What will become of human society when the existing order of things is at an end?

"What shall we find the other side of the walls of the world we are abandoning?

LEO TOLSTOY

"Fear will come upon us—a void, a vast emptiness, freedom—how are we to go forward not knowing whither, how face loss, not seeing hope of gain?... If Columbus had reasoned thus he would never have weighed anchor. It was madness to set off upon the ocean, not knowing the route, on the ocean on which no one had sailed, to sail toward a land whose existence was doubtful. By this madness he discovered a new world. Doubtless if the peoples of the world could simply transfer themselves from one furnished mansion to another and better one—it would make it much easier; but unluckily there is no one to get humanity's new dwelling ready for it. The future is even worse than the ocean—there is nothing there—it will be what men and circumstances make it.

"If you are content with the old world, try to preserve it, it is very sick and cannot hold out much longer. But if you cannot bear to live in everlasting dissonance between your beliefs and your life, thinking one thing and doing another, get out of the mediæval whited sepulchers, and face your fears. I know very well it is not easy.

"It is not a little thing to cut one's self off from all to which a man has been accustomed from his birth, with which he has grown up to maturity. Men are ready for tremendous sacrifices, but not for those which life demands of them. Are they ready to sacrifice modern civilization, their manner of life, their religion, the received conventional morality?

"Are we ready to give up all the results we have attained with such effort, results of which we have been boasting for three centuries; to give up every convenience and charm of our existence, to prefer savage youth to the senile decay of civilization, to pull down the palace raised for us by our ancestors only for the pleasure of having a hand in the founding of a new house, which will doubtless be built long after we are gone?" (Herzen, vol. v. p. 55.)

Thus wrote almost half a century ago the Russian writer, who with prophetic insight saw clearly then, what even the most unreflecting man sees to-day, the impossibility, that is, of life continuing on its old basis, and the necessity of establishing new forms of life.

It is clear now from the very simplest, most commonplace point of view, that it is madness to remain under the roof of a building which cannot support its weight, and that we must leave it. And indeed it is difficult to imagine a position more wretched than that of the Christian world to-day, with its nations armed against one another, with its constantly increasing taxation to maintain its armies, with the hatred of the working class for the rich ever growing more intense, with the Damocles sword of war forever hanging over the heads of all, ready every instant to fall, certain to fall sooner or later.

Hardly could any revolution be more disastrous for the great mass of the population than the present order or rather disorder of our life, with its daily sacrifices to exhausting and unnatural toil, to poverty, drunkenness, and profligacy, with all the horrors of the war that is at hand, which will swallow up in one year more victims than all the revolutions of the century.

What will become of humanity if each of us performs the duty God demands of us through the conscience implanted within us? Will not harm come if, being wholly in the power of a master, I carry out, in the workshop erected and directed by him, the orders he gives me, strange though they may seem to me who do not know the Master's final aims?

But it is not even this question "What will happen?" that agitates men when they hesitate to fulfill the Master's will. They are troubled by the question how to live without those habitual conditions of life which we call civilization, culture, art, and science. We feel ourselves all the burdensomeness of life as it is; we see also that this organization of life must inevitably be our ruin, if it continues. At the same time we want the conditions of our life which arise out of this organization—our civilization, culture, art, and science—to remain intact. It is as though a man, living in an old house and suffering from cold and all sorts of inconvenience in it, knowing, too, that it is on the point of falling to pieces, should consent to its being rebuilt, but only on the condition that he should not be required to leave it: a condition which is equivalent to refusing to have it rebuilt at all.

"But what if I leave the house and give up every convenience for a time, and the new house is not built, or is built on a different plan so that I do not find in it the comforts to which I am accustomed?" But seeing that the materials and the builders are here, there is every likelihood that the new house will on the contrary be better built than the old one. And at the same time, there is not only the likelihood but the certainty that the old house will fall down and crush those who remain within it. Whether the old habitual conditions of life are supported, or whether they are abolished and altogether new and better conditions arise; in any case, there is no doubt we shall be forced to leave the old forms of life which have become impossible and fatal, and must go forward to meet the future.

"Civilization, art, science, culture, will disappear!"

Yes, but all these we know are only various manifestations of truth, and the change that is before us is only to be made for the sake of a closer attainment and realization of truth. How then can the manifestations of truth disappear through our realizing it? These manifestations will be different, higher, better, but they will not cease to be. Only what is false in them will be destroyed; all the truth there was in them will only be stronger and more flourishing.

Take thought, oh, men, and have faith in the Gospel, in whose teaching is your happiness. If you do not take thought, you will perish just as the men perished, slain by Pilate, or crushed by the tower of Siloam; as millions of men have perished, slayers and slain, executing and executed, torturers and tortured alike, and as the man foolishly perished, who filled his granaries full and made ready for a long life and died the very night that he planned to begin his life. Take thought and have faith in the Gospel, Christ said eighteen hundred years ago, and he says it with even greater force now that the calamities foretold by him have come to pass, and the senselessness of our life has reached the furthest point of suffering and madness.

Nowadays, after so many centuries of fruitless efforts to make our life secure by the pagan organization of life, it must be evident to everyone that all efforts in that direction only introduce fresh dangers into personal and social life, and do not render it more secure in any way.

Whatever names we dignify ourselves with, whatever uniforms we wear, whatever priests we anoint ourselves before, however many millions we possess, however many guards are stationed along our road, however many policemen guard our wealth, however many so-called criminals, revolutionists, and anarchists we punish, whatever exploits we have performed, whatever states we may have founded, fortresses and towers we may have erected—from Babel to the Eiffel Tower—there are two inevitable conditions of life, confronting all of us, which destroy its whole meaning; (1) death, which may at any moment pounce upon each of us; and (2) the transitoriness of all our works, which so soon pass away and leave no trace. Whatever we may do—found companies, build palaces and monuments, write songs and poems—it is all not for long time. Soon it passes away, leaving no trace. And therefore, however we may conceal it from ourselves, we cannot help seeing that the significance of our life cannot lie in our personal fleshly existence, the prey of incurable suffering and inevitable death, nor in any social institution or organization. Whoever you may be who are reading these lines, think of your position and of your duties—not of your position as landowner, merchant, judge, emperor, president, minister, priest, soldier, which has been temporarily allotted you by men, and not of the imaginary duties laid on you by those positions, but of your real positions in eternity as a creature who at the will of Someone has been called out of unconsciousness after an eternity of non-existence to which you may return at any moment at his will. Think of your duties—not your supposed duties as a landowner to your estate, as a merchant to your business, as emperor, minister, or official to the state, but of your real duties, the duties that follow from your real position as a being called into life and endowed with reason and love.

Are you doing what he demands of you who has sent you into the world, and to whom you will soon return? Are you doing what he wills? Are you doing his will, when as landowner or manufacturer you rob the poor of the fruits of their toil, basing your life on this plunder of the workers, or when, as judge or governor, you ill treat men, sentence them to execution, or when as soldiers you prepare for war, kill and plunder?

You will say that the world is so made that this is inevitable, and that you do not do this of your own free will, but because you are forced to do so. But can it be that you have such a strong aversion to men's sufferings, ill treatment, and murder, that you have such an intense need of love and co-operation with your fellows that you see clearly that only by the recognition of the equality of all, and by mutual services, can the greatest possible happiness be realized; that your head and your heart, the faith you profess, and even science itself tell you the same thing, and yet that in spite of it all you can be forced by some confused and complicated reasoning to act in direct opposition to all this; that as landowner or capitalist you are bound to base your whole life on the oppression of the people; that as emperor or president you are to command armies, that is, to be the head and commander of murderers; or that as government official you are forced to take from the poor their last pence for rich men to profit and share them among themselves; or that as judge or juryman you could be forced to sentence erring men to ill treatment and death because the truth was not revealed to them, or above all, for that is the basis of all the evil, that you could be forced to become a soldier, and renouncing your free will and your human sentiments, could undertake to kill anyone at the command of other men?

It cannot be.

Even if you are told that all this is necessary for the maintenance of the existing order of things, and that this social order with its pauperism, famines, prisons, gallows, armies, and wars is necessary to society; that still greater disasters would ensue if this organization were destroyed; all that is said only by those who profit by this organization, while those who suffer from it—and they are ten times as numerous—think and say quite the contrary. And at the bottom of your heart you know yourself that it is not true, that the existing organization has outlived its time, and must inevitably be reconstructed on new principles, and that consequently there is no obligation upon you to sacrifice your sentiments of humanity to support it.

Above all, even if you allow that this organization is necessary, why do you believe it to be your duty to maintain it at the cost of your best feelings? Who has made you the nurse in charge of this sick and moribund organization? Not society nor the state nor anyone; no one has asked you to undertake this; you who fill your position of landowner, merchant, tzar, priest, or soldier know very well that you occupy that position by no means with the unselfish aim of maintaining the organization of life necessary to men's happiness, but simply in your own interests, to satisfy your own covetousness or vanity or ambition or indolence or cowardice. If you did not desire that position, you would not be doing your utmost to retain it. Try the experiment of ceasing to commit the cruel, treacherous, and base actions that you are constantly committing in order to retain your position, and you will lose it at once. Try the simple experiment, as a government official, of giving up lying, and refusing to take a part in executions and acts of violence; as a priest, of giving up deception; as a soldier, of giving up murder; as landowner or manufacturer, of giving up defending your property by fraud and force; and you will at once lose the position which you pretend is forced upon you, and which seems burdensome to you.

A man cannot be placed against his will in a situation opposed to his conscience.

If you find yourself in such a position it is not because it is necessary to anyone whatever, but simply because you wish it. And therefore knowing that your position is repugnant to your heart and your head, and to your faith, and even to the science in which you believe, you cannot help reflecting upon the question whether in retaining it, and above all trying to justify it, you are doing what you ought to do.

You might risk making a mistake if you had time to see and retrieve your fault, and if you ran the risk for something of some value. But when you know beyond all doubt that you may disappear any minute, without the least possibility either for yourself or those you draw after you into your error, of retrieving the mistake, when you know that whatever you may do in the external organization of life it will all disappear as quickly and surely as you will yourself, and will leave no trace behind, it is clear that you have no reasonable ground for running the risk of such a fearful mistake.

It would be perfectly simple and clear if you did not by your hypocrisy disguise the truth which has so unmistakably been revealed to us.

Share all that you have with others, do not heap up riches, do not steal, do not cause suffering, do not kill, do not unto others what you would not they should do unto you, all that has been said not eighteen hundred, but five thousand years ago, and there could be no doubt of the truth of this law if it were not for hypocrisy. Except for hypocrisy men could not have failed, if not to put the law in practice, at least to recognize it, and admit that it is wrong not to put it in practice.

But you will say that there is the public good to be considered, and that on that account one must not and ought not to conform to these principles; for the public good one may commit acts of violence and murder. It is better for one man to die than that the whole people perish, you will say like Caiaphas, and you sign the sentence of death of one man, of a second, and a third; you load your gun against this man who is to perish for the public good, you imprison him, you take his possessions. You say that you commit these acts of cruelty because you are a part of the society and of the state; that it is your duty to serve them, and as landowner, judge, emperor, or soldier to conform to their laws. But besides belonging to the state and having duties created by that position, you belong also to eternity and to God, who also lays duties upon you. And just as your duties to your family and to society are subordinate to your superior duties to the state, in the same way the latter must necessarily be subordinated to the duties dictated to you by the eternal life and by God. And just as it would be senseless to pull up the telegraph posts for fuel for a family or society and thus to increase its welfare at the expense of public interests, in the same way it is senseless to do violence, to execute, and to murder to increase the welfare of the nation, because that is at the expense of the interests of humanity.

Your duties as a citizen cannot but be subordinated to the superior obligations of the eternal life of God, and cannot be in opposition to them. As Christ's disciples said eighteen centuries ago: "Whether it be right in the sight of God to hearken unto you more than unto God, judge ye" (Acts iv. 19); and, "We ought to obey God rather than men" (Acts v. 29).

It is asserted that, in order that the unstable order of things, established in one corner of the world for a few men, may not be destroyed, you ought to commit acts of violence which destroy the eternal and immutable order established by God and by reason. Can that possibly be?

And therefore you cannot but reflect on your position as landowner, manufacturer, judge, emperor, president, minister, priest, and soldier, which is bound up with violence, deception, and murder, and recognize its unlawfulness.

I do not say that if you are a landowner you are bound to give up your lands immediately to the poor; if a capitalist or manufacturer, your money to your workpeople; or that if you are Tzar, minister, official, judge, or general, you are bound to renounce immediately the advantages of your position; or if a soldier, on whom all the system of violence is based, to refuse immediately to obey in spite of all the dangers of insubordination.

If you do so, you will be doing the best thing possible. But it may happen, and it is most likely, that you will not have the strength to do so. You have relations, a family, subordinates and superiors; you are under an influence so powerful that you cannot shake it off; but you can always recognize the truth and refuse to tell a lie about it. You need not declare that you are remaining a landowner, manufacturer, merchant, artist, or writer because it is useful to mankind; that you are governor, prosecutor, or tzar, not because it is agreeable to you, because you are used to it, but for the public good; that you continue to be a soldier, not from fear of punishment, but because you consider the army necessary to society. You can always avoid lying in this way to yourself and to others, and you ought to do so; because the one aim of your life ought to be to purify yourself from falsehood and to confess the truth. And you need only do that and your situation will change directly of itself.

There is one thing, and only one thing, in which it is granted to you to be free in life, all else being beyond your power: that is to recognize and profess the truth.

And yet simply from the fact that other men as misguided and as pitiful creatures as yourself have made you soldier, tzar, landowner, capitalist, priest, or general, you undertake to commit acts of violence obviously opposed to your reason and your heart, to base your existence on the misfortunes of others, and above all, instead of filling the one duty of your life, recognizing and professing the truth, you feign not to recognize it and disguise it from yourself and others.

And what are the conditions in which you are doing this? You who may die any instant, you sign sentences of death, you declare war, you take part in it, you judge, you punish, you plunder the working people, you live luxuriously in the midst of the poor, and teach weak men who have confidence in you that this must be so, that the duty of men is to do this, and yet it may happen at the moment when you are acting thus that a bacterium or a bull may attack you and you will fall and die, losing forever the chance of repairing the harm you have done to others, and above all to yourself, in uselessly wasting a life which has been given you only once in eternity, without having accomplished the only thing you ought to have done.

However commonplace and out of date it may seem to us, however confused we may be by hypocrisy and by the hypnotic suggestion which results from it, nothing can destroy the certainty of this simple and clearly defined truth. No external conditions can guarantee our life, which is attended with inevitable sufferings and infallibly terminated by death, and which consequently can have no significance except in the constant accomplishment of what is demanded by the Power which has placed us in life with a sole certain guide—the rational conscience.

That is why that Power cannot require of us what is irrational and impossible: the organization of our temporary external life, the life of society or of the state. That Power demands of us only what is reasonable, certain, and possible: to serve the kingdom of God, that is, to contribute to the establishment of the greatest possible union between all living beings—a union possible only in the truth; and to recognize and to profess the revealed truth, which is always in our power.

"But seek ye first the kingdom of God, and his righteousness, and all these things shall be added unto you." (Matt. vi. 33.)

The sole meaning of life is to serve humanity by contributing to the establishment of the kingdom of God, which can only be done by the recognition and profession of the truth by every man.

"The kingdom of God cometh not with outward show; neither shall they say, Lo here! or, Lo there! for behold, the kingdom of God is within you." (Luke xvii. 20, 21.)

6. FATHER SERGIUS

CHAPTER I

In Petersburg in the eighteen-forties a surprising event occurred. An officer of the Cuirassier Life Guards, a handsome prince who everyone predicted would become aide-de-camp to the Emperor Nicholas I. and have a brilliant career, left the service, broke off his engagement to a beautiful maid of honour, a favourite of the Empress's, gave his small estate to his sister, and retired to a monastery to become a monk.

This event appeared extraordinary and inexplicable to those who did not know his inner motives, but for Prince Stepan Kasatsky himself it all occurred so naturally that he could not imagine how he could have acted otherwise.

His father, a retired colonel of the Guards, had died when Stepan was twelve, and sorry as his mother was to part from her son, she entered him at the Military College as her deceased husband had intended.

The widow herself, with her daughter, Varvara, moved to Petersburg to be near her son and have him with her for the holidays.

The boy was distinguished both by his brilliant ability and by his immense self-esteem. He was first both in his studies— especially in mathematics, of which he was particularly fond— and also in drill and in riding. Though of more than average height, he was handsome and agile, and he would have been an altogether exemplary cadet had it not been for his quick temper. He was remarkably truthful, and was neither dissipated nor addicted to drink. The only faults that marred his conduct were fits of fury to which he was subject and during which he lost control of himself and became like a wild animal. He once nearly threw out of the window another cadet who had begun to tease him about his collection of minerals. On another occasion he came almost completely to grief by flinging a whole dish of cutlets at an officer who was acting as steward, attacking him and, it was said, striking him for having broken his word and told a barefaced lie. He would certainly have been reduced to the ranks had not the Director of the College hushed up the whole matter and dismissed the steward.

By the time he was eighteen he had finished his College course and received a commission as lieutenant in an aristocratic regiment of the Guards.

The Emperor Nicholas Pavlovich (Nicholas I) had noticed him while he was still at the College, and continued to take notice of him in the regiment, and it was on this account that people predicted for him an appointment as aide-de-camp to the Emperor. Kasatsky himself strongly desired it, not from ambition only but chiefly because since his cadet days he had been passionately devoted to Nicholas Pavlovich. The Emperor had often visited the Military College and every time Kasatsky saw that tall erect figure, with breast expanded in its military overcoat, entering with brisk step, saw the cropped side-whiskers, the moustache, the aquiline nose, and heard the sonorous voice exchanging greetings with the cadets, he was seized by the same rapture that he experienced later on when he met the woman he loved. Indeed, his passionate adoration of the Emperor was even stronger: he wished to sacrifice something—everything, even himself—to prove his complete devotion. And the Emperor Nicholas was conscious of evoking this rapture and deliberately aroused it. He played with the cadets, surrounded himself with them, treating them sometimes with childish simplicity, sometimes as a friend, and then again with majestic solemnity. After that affair with the officer, Nicholas Pavlovich said nothing to Kasatsky, but when the latter approached he waved him away theatrically, frowned, shook his finger at him, and afterwards when leaving, said: 'Remember that I know everything. There are some things I would rather not know, but they remain here,' and he pointed to his heart.

When on leaving College the cadets were received by the Emperor, he did not again refer to Kasatsky's offence, but told them all, as was his custom, that they should serve him and the fatherland loyally, that he would always be their best friend, and that when necessary they might approach him direct. All the cadets were as usual greatly moved, and Kasatsky even shed tears, remembering the past, and vowed that he would serve his beloved Tsar with all his soul.

When Kasatsky took up his commission his mother moved with her daughter first to Moscow and then to their country estate. Kasatsky gave half his property to his sister and kept only enough to maintain himself in the expensive regiment he had joined.

To all appearance he was just an ordinary, brilliant young officer of the Guards making a career for himself; but intense and complex strivings went on within him. From early childhood his efforts had seemed to be very varied, but essentially they were all one and the same. He tried in everything he took up to attain such success and perfection as would evoke praise and surprise. Whether it was his studies or his military exercises, he took them up and worked at them till he was praised and held up as an example to others. Mastering one subject he took up another, and obtained first place in his studies. For example, while still at College he noticed in himself an awkwardness in French conversation, and contrived to master French till he spoke it as well as Russian, and then he took up chess and became an excellent player.

Apart from his main vocation, which was the service of his Tsar and the fatherland, he always set himself some particular aim, and however unimportant it was, devoted himself completely to it and lived for it until it was accomplished. And as soon as it was attained another aim would immediately present itself, replacing its predecessor. This passion for distinguishing himself, or for accomplishing something in order to distinguish himself, filled his life. On taking up his commission he set himself to acquire the utmost perfection in knowledge of the service, and very soon became a model officer, though still with the same fault of ungovernable irascibility, which here in the service again led him to commit actions inimical to his success. Then he took to reading, having once in conversation in society felt himself deficient in general education—and again achieved his purpose. Then, wishing to secure a brilliant position in high society, he learnt to dance excellently and very soon was invited to all the balls in the best circles, and to some of their evening gatherings. But this did not satisfy him: he was accustomed to being first, and in this society was far from being so.

The highest society then consisted, and I think always consist, of four sorts of people: rich people who are received at Court, people not wealthy but born and brought up in Court circles, rich people who ingratiate themselves into the Court set, and people neither rich nor belonging to the Court but who ingratiate themselves into the first and second sets.

Kasatsky did not belong to the first two sets, but was readily welcomed in the others. On entering society he determined to have relations with some society lady, and to his own surprise quickly accomplished this purpose. He soon realized, however, that the circles in which he moved were not the highest, and that though he was received in the highest spheres he did not belong to them. They were polite to him, but showed by their whole manner that they had their own set and that he was not of it. And Kasatsky wished to belong to that inner circle. To attain that end it would be necessary to be an aide-de-camp to the Emperor—which he expected to become—or to marry into that exclusive set, which he resolved to do. And his choice fell on a beauty belonging to the Court, who not merely belonged to the circle into which he wished to be accepted, but whose friendship was coveted by the very highest people and those most firmly established in that highest circle. This was Countess Korotkova. Kasatsky began to pay court to her, and not merely for the sake of his career. She was extremely attractive and he soon fell in love with her. At first she was noticeably cool towards him, but then suddenly changed and became gracious, and her mother gave him pressing invitations to visit them. Kasatsky proposed and was accepted. He was surprised at the facility with which he attained such happiness. But though he noticed something strange and unusual in the behaviour towards him of both mother and daughter, he was blinded by being so deeply in love, and did not realize what almost the whole town knew—namely, that his fiancee had been the Emperor Nicholas's mistress the previous year.

Two weeks before the day arranged for the wedding, Kasatsky was at Tsarskoe Selo at his fiancee's country place. It was a hot day in May. He and his betrothed had walked about the garden and were sitting on a bench in a shady linden alley. Mary's white muslin dress suited her particularly well, and she seemed the personification of innocence and love as she sat, now bending her head, now gazing up at the very tall and handsome man who was speaking to her with particular tenderness and self-restraint, as if he feared by word or gesture to offend or sully her angelic purity.

Kasatsky belonged to those men of the eighteen-forties (they are now no longer to be found) who while deliberately and without any conscientious scruples condoning impurity in themselves, required ideal and angelic purity in their women, regarded all unmarried women of their circle as possessed of such purity, and treated them accordingly. There was much that was false and harmful in this outlook, as concerning the laxity the men permitted themselves, but in regard to the women that old-fashioned view (sharply differing from that held by young people to-day who see in every girl merely a female seeking a mate) was, I think, of value. The girls, perceiving such adoration, endeavoured with more or less success to be goddesses.

Such was the view Kasatsky held of women, and that was how he regarded his fiancee. He was particularly in love that day, but did not experience any sensual desire for her. On the contrary he regarded her with tender adoration as something unattainable.

He rose to his full height, standing before her with both hands on his sabre.

'I have only now realized what happiness a man can experience! And it is you, my darling, who have given me this happiness,' he said with a timid smile.

Endearments had not yet become usual between them, and feeling himself morally inferior he felt terrified at this stage to use them to such an angel.

'It is thanks to you that I have come to know myself. I have learnt that I am better than I thought.'

'I have known that for a long time. That was why I began to love you.'

Nightingales trilled near by and the fresh leafage rustled, moved by a passing breeze.

He took her hand and kissed it, and tears came into his eyes.

She understood that he was thanking her for having said she loved him. He silently took a few steps up and down, and then approached her again and sat down.

'You know... I have to tell you... I was not disinterested when I began to make love to you. I wanted to get into society; but later... how unimportant that became in comparison with you—when I got to know you. You are not angry with me for that?'

She did not reply but merely touched his hand. He understood that this meant: 'No, I am not angry.'

'You said...' He hesitated. It seemed too bold to say. 'You said that you began to love me. I believe it—but there is something that troubles you and checks your feeling. What is it?'

'Yes—now or never!' thought she. 'He is bound to know of it anyway. But now he will not forsake me. Ah, if he should, it would be terrible!' And she threw a loving glance at his tall, noble, powerful figure. She loved him now more than she had loved the Tsar, and apart from the Imperial dignity would not have preferred the Emperor to him.

'Listen! I cannot deceive you. I have to tell you. You ask what it is? It is that I have loved before.'

She again laid her hand on his with an imploring gesture. He was silent.

'You want to know who it was? It was—the Emperor.'

'We all love him. I can imagine you, a schoolgirl at the Institute...'

'No, it was later. I was infatuated, but it passed... I must tell you...'

'Well, what of it?'

'No, it was not simply—' She covered her face with her hands.

'What? You gave yourself to him?'

She was silent.

'His mistress?'

She did not answer.

He sprang up and stood before her with trembling jaws, pale as death. He now remembered how the Emperor, meeting him on the Nevsky, had amiably congratulated him.

'O God, what have I done! Stiva!'

'Don't touch me! Don't touch me! Oh, how it pains!'

He turned away and went to the house. There he met her mother.

'What is the matter, Prince? I...' She became silent on seeing his face. The blood had suddenly rushed to his head.

'You knew it, and used me to shield them! If you weren't a woman...!' he cried, lifting his enormous fist, and turning aside he ran away.

Had his fiancee's lover been a private person he would have killed him, but it was his beloved Tsar.

Next day he applied both for furlough and his discharge, and professing to be ill, so as to see no one, he went away to the country.

He spent the summer at his village arranging his affairs. When summer was over he did not return to Petersburg, but entered a monastery and there became a monk.

His mother wrote to try to dissuade him from this decisive step, but he replied that he felt God's call which transcended all other considerations. Only his sister, who was as proud and ambitious as he, understood him.

She understood that he had become a monk in order to be above those who considered themselves his superiors. And she understood him correctly. By becoming a monk he showed contempt for all that seemed most important to others and had seemed so to him while he was in the service, and he now ascended a height from which he could look down on those he had formerly envied.... But it was not this alone, as his sister Varvara supposed, that influenced him. There was also in him something else—a sincere religious feeling which Varvara did not know, which intertwined itself with the feeling of pride and the desire for pre-eminence, and guided him. His disillusionment with Mary, whom he had thought of angelic purity, and his sense of injury, were so strong that they brought him to despair, and the despair led him—to what? To God, to his childhood's faith which had never been destroyed in him.

CHAPTER II

Kasatsky entered the monastery on the feast of the Intercession of the Blessed Virgin. The Abbot of that monastery was a gentleman by birth, a learned writer and a starets, that is, he belonged to that succession of monks originating in Walachia who each choose a director and teacher whom they implicitly obey. This Superior had been a disciple of the starets Ambrose, who was a disciple of Makarius, who was a disciple of the starets Leonid, who was a disciple of Paussy Velichkovsky.

To this Abbot Kasatsky submitted himself as to his chosen director. Here in the monastery, besides the feeling of ascendency over others that such a life gave him, he felt much as he had done in the world: he found satisfaction in attaining the greatest possible perfection outwardly as well as inwardly. As in the regiment he had been not merely an irreproachable officer but had even exceeded his duties and widened the borders of perfection, so also as a monk he tried to be perfect, and was always industrious, abstemious, submissive, and meek, as well as pure both in deed and in thought, and obedient. This last quality in particular made life far easier for him. If many of the demands of life in the monastery, which was near the capital and much frequented, did not please him and were temptations to him, they were all nullified by obedience: 'It is not for me to reason; my business is to do the task set me, whether it be standing beside the relics, singing in the choir, or making up accounts in the monastery guest-house.' All possibility of doubt about anything was silenced by obedience to the starets. Had it not been for this, he would have been oppressed by the length and monotony of the church services, the bustle of the many visitors, and the bad qualities of the other monks. As it was, he not only bore it all joyfully but found in it solace and support. 'I don't know why it is necessary to hear the same prayers several times a day, but I know that it is necessary; and knowing this I find joy in them.' His director told him that as material food is necessary for the maintenance of the life of the body, so spiritual food—the church prayers—is necessary for the maintenance of the spiritual life. He believed this, and though the church services, for which he had to get up early in the morning, were a difficulty, they certainly calmed him and gave him joy. This was the result of his consciousness of humility, and the certainty that whatever he had to do, being fixed by the starets, was right.

The interest of his life consisted not only in an ever greater and greater subjugation of his will, but in the attainment of all the Christian virtues, which at first seemed to him easily attainable. He had given his whole estate to his sister and did not regret it, he had no personal claims, humility towards his inferiors was not merely easy for him but afforded him pleasure. Even victory over the sins of the flesh, greed and lust, was easily attained. His director had specially warned him against the latter sin, but Kasatsky felt free from it and was glad.

One thing only tormented him—the remembrance of his fiancee; and not merely the remembrance but the vivid image of what might have been. Involuntarily he recalled a lady he knew who had been a favourite of the Emperor's, but had afterwards married and become an admirable wife and mother. The husband had a high position, influence and honour, and a good and penitent wife.

In his better hours Kasatsky was not disturbed by such thoughts, and when he recalled them at such times he was merely glad to feel that the temptation was past. But there were moments when all that made up his present life suddenly grew dim before him, moments when, if he did not cease to believe in the aims he had set himself, he ceased to see them and could evoke no confidence in them but was seized by a remembrance of, and—terrible to say—a regret for, the change of life he had made.

The only thing that saved him in that state of mind was obedience and work, and the fact that the whole day was occupied by prayer. He went through the usual forms of prayer, he bowed in prayer, he even prayed more than usual, but it was lip-service only and his soul was not in it. This condition would continue for a day, or sometimes for two days, and would then pass of itself. But those days were dreadful. Kasatsky felt that he was neither in his own hands nor in God's, but was subject to something else. All he could do then was to obey the starets, to restrain himself, to undertake nothing, and simply to wait. In general all this time he lived not by his own will but by that of the starets, and in this obedience he found a special tranquillity.

So he lived in his first monastery for seven years. At the end of the third year he received the tonsure and was ordained to the priesthood by the name of Sergius. The profession was an important event in his inner life. He had previously experienced a great consolation and spiritual exaltation when receiving communion, and now when he himself officiated, the performance of the preparation filled him with ecstatic and deep emotion. But subsequently that feeling became more and more deadened, and once when he was officiating in a depressed state of mind he felt that the influence produced on him by the service would not endure. And it did in fact weaken till only the habit remained.

In general in the seventh year of his life in the monastery Sergius grew weary. He had learnt all there was to learn and had attained all there was to attain, there was nothing more to do and his spiritual drowsiness increased. During this time he heard of his mother's death and his sister Varvara's marriage, but both events were matters of indifference to him. His whole attention and his whole interest were concentrated on his inner life.

In the fourth year of his priesthood, during which the Bishop had been particularly kind to him, the starets told him that he ought not to decline it if he were offered an appointment to higher duties. Then monastic ambition, the very thing he had found so repulsive in other monks, arose within him. He was assigned to a monastery near the metropolis. He wished to refuse but the starets ordered him to accept the appointment. He did so, and took leave of the starets and moved to the other monastery.

The exchange into the metropolitan monastery was an important event in Sergius's life. There he encountered many temptations, and his whole will-power was concentrated on meeting them.

In the first monastery, women had not been a temptation to him, but here that temptation arose with terrible strength and even took definite shape. There was a lady known for her frivolous behaviour who began to seek his favour. She talked to him and asked him to visit her. Sergius sternly declined, but was horrified by the definiteness of his desire. He was so alarmed that he wrote about it to the starets. And in addition, to keep himself in hand, he spoke to a young novice and, conquering his sense of shame, confessed his weakness to him, asking him to keep watch on him and not let him go anywhere except to service and to fulfil his duties.

Besides this, a great pitfall for Sergius lay in the fact of his extreme antipathy to his new Abbot, a cunning worldly man who was making a career for himself in the Church. Struggle with himself as he might, he could not master that feeling. He was submissive to the Abbot, but in the depths of his soul he never ceased to condemn him. And in the second year of his residence at the new monastery that ill-feeling broke out.

The Vigil service was being performed in the large church on the eve of the feast of the Intercession of the Blessed Virgin, and there were many visitors. The Abbot himself was conducting the service. Father Sergius was standing in his usual place and praying: that is, he was in that condition of struggle which always occupied him during the service, especially in the large church when he was not himself conducting the service. This conflict was occasioned by his irritation at the presence of fine folk, especially ladies. He tried not to see them or to notice all that went on: how a soldier conducted them, pushing the common people aside, how the ladies pointed out the monks to one another—especially himself and a monk noted for his good looks. He tried as it were to keep his mind in blinkers, to see nothing but the light of the candles on the altar-screen, the icons, and those conducting the service. He tried to hear nothing but the prayers that were being chanted or read, to feel nothing but self-oblivion in consciousness of the fulfilment of duty—a feeling he always experienced when hearing or reciting in advance the prayers he had so often heard.

So he stood, crossing and prostrating himself when necessary, and struggled with himself, now giving way to cold condemnation and now to a consciously evoked obliteration of thought and feeling. Then the sacristan, Father Nicodemus—also a great stumbling-block to Sergius who involuntarily reproached him for flattering and fawning on the Abbot—approached him and, bowing low, requested his presence behind the holy gates. Father Sergius straightened his mantle, put on his biretta, and went circumspectly through the crowd.

'Lise, regarde a droite, c'est lui!' he heard a woman's voice say.

'Ou, ou? Il n'est pas tellement beau.'

He knew that they were speaking of him. He heard them and, as always at moments of temptation, he repeated the words, 'Lead us not into temptation,' and bowing his head and lowering his eyes went past the ambo and in by the north door, avoiding the canons in their cassocks who were just then passing the altar-screen. On entering the sanctuary he bowed, crossing himself as usual and bending double before the icons. Then, raising his head but without turning, he glanced out of the corner of his eye at the Abbot, whom he saw standing beside another glittering figure.

The Abbot was standing by the wall in his vestments. Having freed his short plump hands from beneath his chasuble he had folded them over his fat body and protruding stomach, and fingering the cords of his vestments was smilingly saying something to a military man in the uniform of a general of the Imperial suite, with its insignia and shoulder-knots which Father Sergius's experienced eye at once recognized. This general had been the commander of the regiment in which Sergius had served. He now evidently occupied an important position, and Father Sergius at once noticed that the Abbot was aware of this and that his red face and bald head beamed with satisfaction and pleasure. This vexed and disgusted Father Sergius, the more so when he heard that the Abbot had only sent for him to satisfy the general's curiosity to see a man who had formerly served with him, as he expressed it.

'Very pleased to see you in your angelic guise,' said the general, holding out his hand. 'I hope you have not forgotten an old comrade.'

The whole thing—the Abbot's red, smiling face amid its fringe of grey, the general's words, his well-cared-for face with its self-satisfied smile and the smell of wine from his breath and of cigars from his whiskers—revolted Father Sergius. He bowed again to the Abbot and said:

'Your reverence deigned to send for me?'—and stopped, the whole expression of his face and eyes asking why.

'Yes, to meet the General,' replied the Abbot.

'Your reverence, I left the world to save myself from temptation,' said Father Sergius, turning pale and with quivering lips. 'Why do you expose me to it during prayers and in God's house?'

'You may go! Go!' said the Abbot, flaring up and frowning.

Next day Father Sergius asked pardon of the Abbot and of the brethren for his pride, but at the same time, after a night spent in prayer, he decided that he must leave this monastery, and he wrote to the starets begging permission to return to him. He wrote that he felt his weakness and incapacity to struggle against temptation without his help and penitently confessed his sin of pride. By return of post came a letter from the starets, who wrote that Sergius's pride was the cause of all that had happened. The old man pointed out that his fits of anger were due to the fact that in refusing all clerical honours he humiliated himself not for the sake of God but for the sake of his pride. 'There now, am I not a splendid man not to want anything?' That was why he could not tolerate the Abbot's action. 'I have renounced everything for the glory of God, and here I am exhibited like a wild beast!' 'Had you renounced vanity for God's sake you would have borne it. Worldly pride is not yet dead in you. I have thought about you,

Sergius my son, and prayed also, and this is what God has suggested to me. At the Tambov hermitage the anchorite Hilary, a man of saintly life, has died. He had lived there eighteen years. The Tambov Abbot is asking whether there is not a brother who would take his place. And here comes your letter. Go to Father Paissy of the Tambov Monastery. I will write to him about you, and you must ask for Hilary's cell. Not that you can replace Hilary, but you need solitude to quell your pride. May God bless you!'

Sergius obeyed the starets, showed his letter to the Abbot, and having obtained his permission, gave up his cell, handed all his possessions over to the monastery, and set out for the Tambov hermitage.

There the Abbot, an excellent manager of merchant origin, received Sergius simply and quietly and placed him in Hilary's cell, at first assigning to him a lay brother but afterwards leaving him alone, at Sergius's own request. The cell was a dual cave, dug into the hillside, and in it Hilary had been buried. In the back part was Hilary's grave, while in the front was a niche for sleeping, with a straw mattress, a small table, and a shelf with icons and books. Outside the outer door, which fastened with a hook, was another shelf on which, once a day, a monk placed food from the monastery.

And so Sergius became a hermit.

CHAPTER III

At Carnival time, in the sixth year of Sergius's life at the hermitage, a merry company of rich people, men and women from a neighbouring town, made up a troyka-party, after a meal of carnival-pancakes and wine. The company consisted of two lawyers, a wealthy landowner, an officer, and four ladies. One lady was the officer's wife, another the wife of the landowner, the third his sister—a young girl—and the fourth a divorcee, beautiful, rich, and eccentric, who amazed and shocked the town by her escapades.

The weather was excellent and the snow-covered road smooth as a floor. They drove some seven miles out of town, and then stopped and consulted as to whether they should turn back or drive farther.

'But where does this road lead to?' asked Makovkina, the beautiful divorcee.

'To Tambov, eight miles from here,' replied one of the lawyers, who was having a flirtation with her.

'And then where?'

'Then on to L——, past the Monastery.'

'Where that Father Sergius lives?'

'Yes.'

'Kasatsky, the handsome hermit?'

'Yes.'

'Mesdames et messieurs, let us drive on and see Kasatsky! We can stop at Tambov and have something to eat.'

'But we shouldn't get home to-night!'

'Never mind, we will stay at Kasatsky's.'

'Well, there is a very good hostelry at the Monastery. I stayed there when I was defending Makhin.'

'No, I shall spend the night at Kasatsky's!'

'Impossible! Even your omnipotence could not accomplish that!'

'Impossible? Will you bet?'

'All right! If you spend the night with him, the stake shall be whatever you like.'

'A DISCRETION!'

'But on your side too!'

'Yes, of course. Let us drive on.'

Vodka was handed to the drivers, and the party got out a box of pies, wine, and sweets for themselves. The ladies wrapped up in their white dogskins. The drivers disputed as to whose troyka should go ahead, and the youngest, seating himself sideways with a dashing air, swung his long knout and shouted to the horses. The troyka-bells tinkled and the sledge-runners squeaked over the snow.

The sledge swayed hardly at all. The shaft-horse, with his tightly bound tail under his decorated breechband, galloped smoothly and briskly; the smooth road seemed to run rapidly backwards, while the driver dashingly shook the reins. One of the lawyers and the officer sitting opposite talked nonsense to Makovkina's neighbour, but Makovkina herself sat motionless and in thought, tightly wrapped in her fur. 'Always the same and always nasty! The same red shiny faces smelling of wine and cigars! The same talk, the same thoughts, and always about the same things! And they are all satisfied and confident that it should be so, and will go on living like that till they die. But I can't. It bores me. I want something that would upset it all and turn it upside down. Suppose it happened to us as to those people—at Saratov was it?—who kept on driving and froze to death.... What would our people do? How would they behave? Basely, for certain. Each for himself. And I too should act badly. But I at any rate have beauty. They all know it. And how about that monk? Is it possible that he has become indifferent to it? No! That is the one thing they all care for—like that cadet last autumn. What a fool he was!'

'Ivan Nikolaevich!' she said aloud.

'What are your commands?'

'How old is he?'

'Who?'

'Kasatsky.'

'Over forty, I should think.'

'And does he receive all visitors?'

'Yes, everybody, but not always.'

'Cover up my feet. Not like that—how clumsy you are! No! More, more—like that! But you need not squeeze them!'

So they came to the forest where the cell was.

Makovkina got out of the sledge, and told them to drive on. They tried to dissuade her, but she grew irritable and ordered them to go on.

When the sledges had gone she went up the path in her white dogskin coat. The lawyer got out and stopped to watch her.

It was Father Sergius's sixth year as a recluse, and he was now forty-nine. His life in solitude was hard—not on account of the fasts and the prayers (they were no hardship to him) but on account of an inner conflict he had not at all anticipated. The sources of that conflict were two: doubts, and the lust of the flesh. And these two enemies always appeared together. It seemed to him that they were two foes, but in reality they were one and the same. As soon as doubt was gone so was the lustful desire. But thinking them to be two different fiends he fought them separately.

'O my God, my God!' thought he. 'Why dost thou not grant me faith? There is lust, of course: even the saints had to fight that—Saint Anthony and others. But they had faith, while I have moments, hours, and days, when it is absent. Why does the whole world, with all its delights, exist if it is sinful and must be renounced? Why hast Thou created this temptation? Temptation? Is it not rather a temptation that I wish to abandon all the joys of earth and prepare something for myself there where perhaps there is nothing?' And he became horrified and filled with disgust at himself. 'Vile creature! And it is you who wish to become a saint!' he upbraided himself, and he began to pray. But as soon as he started to pray he saw himself vividly as he had been at the Monastery, in a majestic post in biretta and mantle, and he shook his head. 'No, that is not right. It is deception. I may deceive others, but not myself or God. I am not a majestic man, but a pitiable and ridiculous one!' And he threw back the folds of his cassock and smiled as he looked at his thin legs in their underclothing.

Then he dropped the folds of the cassock again and began reading the prayers, making the sign of the cross and prostrating himself. 'Can it be that this couch will be my bier?' he read. And it seemed as if a devil whispered to him: 'A solitary couch is itself a bier. Falsehood!' And in imagination he saw the shoulders of a widow with whom he had lived. He shook himself, and went on reading. Having read the precepts he took up the Gospels, opened the book, and happened on a passage he often repeated and knew by heart: 'Lord, I believe. Help thou my unbelief!'—and he put away all the doubts that had arisen. As one replaces an object of insecure equilibrium, so he carefully replaced his belief on its shaky pedestal and carefully stepped back from it so as not to shake or upset it. The blinkers were adjusted again and he felt tranquillized, and repeating his childhood's prayer: 'Lord, receive me, receive me!' he felt not merely at ease, but thrilled and joyful. He crossed himself and lay down on the bedding on his narrow bench, tucking his summer cassock under his head. He fell asleep at once, and in his light slumber he seemed to hear the tinkling of sledge bells. He did not know whether he was dreaming or awake, but a knock at the door aroused him. He sat up, distrusting his senses, but the knock was repeated. Yes, it was a knock close at hand, at his door, and with it the sound of a woman's voice.

'My God! Can it be true, as I have read in the Lives of the Saints, that the devil takes on the form of a woman? Yes—it is a woman's voice. And a tender, timid, pleasant voice. Phui!' And he spat to exorcise the devil. 'No, it was only my imagination,' he assured himself, and he went to the corner where his lectern stood, falling on his knees in the regular and habitual manner which of itself gave him consolation and satisfaction. He sank down, his hair hanging over his face, and pressed his head, already going bald in front, to the cold damp strip of drugget on the draughty floor. He read the psalm old Father Pimon had told him warded off temptation. He easily raised his light and emaciated body on his strong sinewy legs and tried to continue saying his prayers, but instead of doing so he involuntarily strained his hearing. He wished to hear more. All was quiet. From the corner of the roof regular drops continued to fall into the tub below. Outside was a mist and fog eating into the snow that lay on the ground. It was still, very still. And suddenly there was a rustling at the window and a voice—that same tender, timid voice, which could only belong to an attractive woman— said:

'Let me in, for Christ's sake!'

It seemed as though his blood had all rushed to his heart and settled there. He could hardly breathe. 'Let God arise and let his enemies be scattered...'

'But I am not a devil!' It was obvious that the lips that uttered this were smiling. 'I am not a devil, but only a sinful woman who has lost her way, not figuratively but literally!' She laughed. 'I am frozen and beg for shelter.'

He pressed his face to the window, but the little icon-lamp was reflected by it and shone on the whole pane. He put his hands to both sides of his face and peered between them. Fog, mist, a tree, and—just opposite him—she herself. Yes, there, a few inches from him, was the sweet, kindly frightened face of a woman in a cap and a coat of long white fur, leaning towards him. Their eyes met with instant recognition: not that they had ever known one another, they had never met before, but by the look they exchanged they—and he particularly—felt that they knew and understood one another. After that glance to imagine her to be a devil and not a simple, kindly, sweet, timid woman, was impossible.

'Who are you? Why have you come?' he asked.

'Do please open the door!' she replied, with capricious authority. 'I am frozen. I tell you I have lost my way.'

'But I am a monk—a hermit.'

'Oh, do please open the door—or do you wish me to freeze under your window while you say your prayers?'

'But how have you...'

'I shan't eat you. For God's sake let me in! I am quite frozen.'

She really did feel afraid, and said this in an almost tearful voice.

He stepped back from the window and looked at an icon of the Saviour in His crown of thorns. 'Lord, help me! Lord, help me!' he exclaimed, crossing himself and bowing low. Then he went to the door, and opening it into the tiny porch, felt for the hook that fastened the outer door and began to lift it. He heard steps outside. She was coming from the window to the door. 'Ah!' she suddenly exclaimed, and he understood that she had stepped into the puddle that the dripping from the roof had formed at the threshold. His hands trembled, and he could not raise the hook of the tightly closed door.

'Oh, what are you doing? Let me in! I am all wet. I am frozen! You are thinking about saving your soul and are letting me freeze to death...'

He jerked the door towards him, raised the hook, and without considering what he was doing, pushed it open with such force that it struck her.

'Oh—PARDON!' he suddenly exclaimed, reverting completely to his old manner with ladies.

She smiled on hearing that PARDON. 'He is not quite so terrible, after all,' she thought. 'It's all right. It is you who must pardon me,' she said, stepping past him. 'I should never have ventured, but such an extraordinary circumstance...'

'If you please!' he uttered, and stood aside to let her pass him. A strong smell of fine scent, which he had long not encountered, struck him. She went through the little porch into the cell where he lived. He closed the outer door without fastening the hook, and stepped in after her.

'Lord Jesus Christ, Son of God, have mercy on me a sinner! Lord, have mercy on me a sinner!' he prayed unceasingly, not merely to himself but involuntarily moving his lips. 'If you please!' he said to her again. She stood in the middle of the room, moisture dripping from her to the floor as she looked him over. Her eyes were laughing.

'Forgive me for having disturbed your solitude. But you see what a position I am in. It all came about from our starting from town for a sledge-drive, and my making a bet that I would walk back by myself from the Vorobevka to the town. But then I lost my way, and if I had not happened to come upon your cell...' She began lying, but his face confused her so that she could not continue, but became silent. She had not expected him to be at all such as he was. He was not as handsome as she had imagined, but was nevertheless beautiful in her eyes: his greyish hair and beard, slightly curling, his fine, regular nose, and his eyes like glowing coal when he looked at her, made a strong impression on her.

He saw that she was lying.

'Yes... so,' said he, looking at her and again lowering his eyes. 'I will go in there, and this place is at your disposal.'

And taking down the little lamp, he lit a candle, and bowing low to her went into the small cell beyond the partition, and she heard him begin to move something about there. 'Probably he is barricading himself in from me!' she thought with a smile, and throwing off her white dogskin cloak she tried to take off her cap, which had become entangled in her hair and in the woven kerchief she was wearing under it. She had not got at all wet when standing under the window, and had said so only as a pretext to get him to let her in. But she really had stepped into the puddle at the door, and her left foot was wet up to the ankle and her overshoe full of water. She sat down on his bed—a bench only covered by a bit of carpet—and began to take off her boots. The little cell seemed to her charming. The narrow little room, some seven feet by nine, was as clean as glass. There was nothing in it but the bench on which she was sitting, the book-shelf above it, and a lectern in the corner. A sheepskin coat and a cassock hung on nails by the door. Above the lectern was the little lamp and an icon of Christ in His crown of thorns. The room smelt strangely of perspiration and of earth. It all pleased her— even that smell. Her wet feet, especially one of them, were uncomfortable, and she quickly began to take off her boots and stockings without ceasing to smile, pleased not so much at having achieved her object as because she perceived that she had abashed that charming, strange, striking, and attractive man. 'He did not respond, but what of that?' she said to herself.

'Father Sergius! Father Sergius! Or how does one call you?'

'What do you want?' replied a quiet voice.

'Please forgive me for disturbing your solitude, but really I could not help it. I should simply have fallen ill. And I don't know that I shan't now. I am all wet and my feet are like ice.'

'Pardon me,' replied the quiet voice. 'I cannot be of any assistance to you.'

'I would not have disturbed you if I could have helped it. I am only here till daybreak.'

He did not reply and she heard him muttering something, probably his prayers.

'You will not be coming in here?' she asked, smiling. 'For I must undress to dry myself.'

He did not reply, but continued to read his prayers.

'Yes, that is a man!' thought she, getting her dripping boot off with difficulty. She tugged at it, but could not get it off. The absurdity of it struck her and she began to laugh almost inaudibly. But knowing that he would hear her laughter and would be moved by it just as she wished him to be, she laughed louder, and her laughter—gay, natural, and kindly—really acted on him just in the way she wished.

'Yes, I could love a man like that—such eyes and such a simple noble face, and passionate too despite all the prayers he mutters!' thought she. 'You can't deceive a woman in these things. As soon as he put his face to the window and saw me, he understood and knew. The glimmer of it was in his eyes and remained there. He began to love me and desired me. Yes—desired!' said she, getting her overshoe and her boot off at last and starting to take off her stockings. To remove those long stockings fastened with elastic it was necessary to raise her skirts. She felt embarrassed and said:

'Don't come in!'

But there was no reply from the other side of the wall. The steady muttering continued and also a sound of moving.

'He is prostrating himself to the ground, no doubt,' thought she. 'But he won't bow himself out of it. He is thinking of me just as I am thinking of him. He is thinking of these feet of mine with the same feeling that I have!' And she pulled off her wet stockings and put her feet up on the bench, pressing them under her. She sat a while like that with her arms round her knees and looking pensively before her. 'But it is a desert, here in this silence. No one would ever know....'

She rose, took her stockings over to the stove, and hung them on the damper. It was a queer damper, and she turned it about, and then, stepping lightly on her bare feet, returned to the bench and sat down there again with her feet up.

There was complete silence on the other side of the partition. She looked at the tiny watch that hung round her neck. It was two o'clock. 'Our party should return about three!' She had not more than an hour before her. 'Well, am I to sit like this all alone? What nonsense! I don't want to. I will call him at once.'

'Father Sergius, Father Sergius! Sergey Dmitrich! Prince Kasatsky!'

Beyond the partition all was silent.

'Listen! This is cruel. I would not call you if it were not necessary. I am ill. I don't know what is the matter with me!' she exclaimed in a tone of suffering. 'Oh! Oh!' she groaned, falling back on the bench. And strange to say she really felt that her strength was failing, that she was becoming faint, that everything in her ached, and that she was shivering with fever.

'Listen! Help me! I don't know what is the matter with me. Oh! Oh!' She unfastened her dress, exposing her breast, and lifted her arms, bare to the elbow. 'Oh! Oh!'

All this time he stood on the other side of the partition and prayed. Having finished all the evening prayers, he now stood motionless, his eyes looking at the end of his nose, and mentally repeated with all his soul: 'Lord Jesus Christ, Son of God, have mercy upon me!'

But he had heard everything. He had heard how the silk rustled when she took off her dress, how she stepped with bare feet on the floor, and had heard how she rubbed her feet with her hand. He felt his own weakness, and that he might be lost at any moment. That was why he prayed unceasingly. He felt rather as the hero in the fairy-tale must have felt when he had to go on and on without looking round. So Sergius heard and felt that danger and destruction were there, hovering above and around him, and that he could only save himself by not looking in that direction for an instant. But suddenly the desire to look seized him. At the same instant she said:

'This is inhuman. I may die....'

'Yes, I will go to her, but like the Saint who laid one hand on the adulteress and thrust his other into the brazier. But there is no brazier here.' He looked round. The lamp! He put his finger over the flame and frowned, preparing himself to suffer. And for a rather long time, as it seemed to him, there was no sensation, but suddenly—he had not yet decided whether it was painful enough—he writhed all over, jerked his hand away, and waved it in the air. 'No, I can't stand that!'

'For God's sake come to me! I am dying! Oh!'

'Well—shall I perish? No, not so!'

'I will come to you directly,' he said, and having opened his door, he went without looking at her through the cell into the porch where he used to chop wood. There he felt for the block and for an axe which leant against the wall.

'Immediately!' he said, and taking up the axe with his right hand he laid the forefinger of his left hand on the block, swung the axe, and struck with it below the second joint. The finger flew off more lightly than a stick of similar thickness, and bounding up, turned over on the edge of the block and then fell to the floor.

He heard it fall before he felt any pain, but before he had time to be surprised he felt a burning pain and the warmth of flowing blood. He hastily wrapped the stump in the skirt of his cassock, and pressing it to his hip went back into the room, and standing in front of the woman, lowered his eyes and asked in a low voice: 'What do you want?'

She looked at his pale face and his quivering left cheek, and suddenly felt ashamed. She jumped up, seized her fur cloak, and throwing it round her shoulders, wrapped herself up in it.

'I was in pain... I have caught cold... I... Father Sergius... I...'

He let his eyes, shining with a quiet light of joy, rest upon her, and said:

'Dear sister, why did you wish to ruin your immortal soul? Temptations must come into the world, but woe to him by whom temptation comes. Pray that God may forgive us!'

She listened and looked at him. Suddenly she heard the sound of something dripping. She looked down and saw that blood was flowing from his hand and down his cassock.

'What have you done to your hand?' She remembered the sound she had heard, and seizing the little lamp ran out into the porch. There on the floor she saw the bloody finger. She returned with her face paler than his and was about to speak to him, but he silently passed into the back cell and fastened the door.

'Forgive me!' she said. 'How can I atone for my sin?'

'Go away.'

'Let me tie up your hand.'

'Go away from here.'

She dressed hurriedly and silently, and when ready sat waiting in her furs. The sledge-bells were heard outside.

'Father Sergius, forgive me!'

'Go away. God will forgive.'

'Father Sergius! I will change my life. Do not forsake me!'

'Go away.'

'Forgive me—and give me your blessing!'

'In the name of the Father and of the Son and of the Holy Ghost!'—she heard his voice from behind the partition. 'Go!'

She burst into sobs and left the cell. The lawyer came forward to meet her.

'Well, I see I have lost the bet. It can't be helped. Where will you sit?'

'It is all the same to me.'

She took a seat in the sledge, and did not utter a word all the way home.

A year later she entered a convent as a novice, and lived a strict life under the direction of the hermit Arseny, who wrote letters to her at long intervals.

CHAPTER IV

Father Sergius lived as a recluse for another seven years. At first he accepted much of what people brought him—tea, sugar, white bread, milk, clothing, and fire-wood. But as time went on he led a more and more austere life, refusing everything superfluous, and finally he accepted nothing but rye-bread once a week. Everything else that was brought to him he gave to the poor who came to him. He spent his entire time in his cell, in prayer or in conversation with callers, who became more and more numerous as time went on. Only three times a year did he go out to church, and when necessary he went out to fetch water and wood.

The episode with Makovkina had occurred after five years of his hermit life. That occurrence soon became generally known—her nocturnal visit, the change she underwent, and her entry into a convent. From that time Father Sergius's fame increased. More and more visitors came to see him, other monks settled down near his cell, and a church was erected there and also a hostelry. His fame, as usual exaggerating his feats, spread ever more and more widely. People began to come to him from a distance, and began bringing invalids to him whom they declared he cured.

His first cure occurred in the eighth year of his life as a hermit. It was the healing of a fourteen-year-old boy, whose mother brought him to Father Sergius insisting that he should lay his hand on the child's head. It had never occurred to Father Sergius that he could cure the sick. He would have regarded such a thought as a great sin of pride; but the mother who brought the boy implored him insistently, falling at his feet and saying: 'Why do you, who heal others, refuse to help my son?' She besought him in Christ's name. When Father Sergius assured her that only God could heal the sick, she replied that she only wanted him to lay his hands on the boy and pray for him. Father Sergius refused and returned to his cell. But next day (it was in autumn and the nights were already cold) on going out for water he saw the same mother with her son, a pale boy of fourteen, and was met by the same petition.

He remembered the parable of the unjust judge, and though he had previously felt sure that he ought to refuse, he now began to hesitate and, having hesitated, took to prayer and prayed until a decision formed itself in his soul. This decision was, that he ought to accede to the woman's request and that her faith might save her son. As for himself, he would in this case be but an insignificant instrument chosen by God.

And going out to the mother he did what she asked—laid his hand on the boy's head and prayed.

The mother left with her son, and a month later the boy recovered, and the fame of the holy healing power of the starets Sergius (as they now called him) spread throughout the whole district. After that, not a week passed without sick people coming, riding or on foot, to Father Sergius; and having acceded to one petition he could not refuse others, and he laid his hands on many and prayed. Many recovered, and his fame spread more and more.

So seven years passed in the Monastery and thirteen in his hermit's cell. He now had the appearance of an old man: his beard was long and grey, but his hair, though thin, was still black and curly.

CHAPTER V

For some weeks Father Sergius had been living with one persistent thought: whether he was right in accepting the position in which he had not so much placed himself as been placed by the Archimandrite and the Abbot. That position had begun after the recovery of the fourteen-year-old boy. From that time, with each month, week, and day that passed, Sergius felt his own inner life wasting away and being replaced by external life. It was as if he had been turned inside out.

Sergius saw that he was a means of attracting visitors and contributions to the monastery, and that therefore the authorities arranged matters in such a way as to make as much use of him as possible. For instance, they rendered it impossible for him to do any manual work. He was supplied with everything he could want, and they only demanded of him that he should not refuse his blessing to those who came to seek it. For his convenience they appointed days when he would receive. They arranged a reception-room for men, and a place was railed in so that he should not be pushed over by the crowds of women visitors, and so that he could conveniently bless those who came.

They told him that people needed him, and that fulfilling Christ's law of love he could not refuse their demand to see him, and that to avoid them would be cruel. He could not but agree with this, but the more he gave himself up to such a life the more he felt that what was internal became external, and that the fount of living water within him dried up, and that what he did now was done more and more for men and less and less for God.

Whether he admonished people, or simply blessed them, or prayed for the sick, or advised people about their lives, or listened to expressions of gratitude from those he had helped by precepts, or alms, or healing (as they assured him)—he could not help being pleased at it, and could not be indifferent to the results of his activity and to the influence he exerted. He thought himself a shining light, and the more he felt this the more was he conscious of a weakening, a dying down of the divine light of truth that shone within him.

'In how far is what I do for God and in how far is it for men?' That was the question that insistently tormented him and to which he was not so much unable to give himself an answer as unable to face the answer.

In the depth of his soul he felt that the devil had substituted an activity for men in place of his former activity for God. He felt this because, just as it had formerly been hard for him to be torn from his solitude so now that solitude itself was hard for him. He was oppressed and wearied by visitors, but at the bottom of his heart he was glad of their presence and glad of the praise they heaped upon him.

There was a time when he decided to go away and hide. He even planned all that was necessary for that purpose. He prepared for himself a peasant's shirt, trousers, coat, and cap. He explained that he wanted these to give to those who asked. And he kept these clothes in his cell, planning how he would put them on, cut his hair short, and go away. First he would go some three hundred versts by train, then he would leave the train and walk from village to village. He asked an old man who had been a soldier how he tramped: what people gave him, and what shelter they allowed him. The soldier told him where people were most charitable, and where they would take a wanderer in for the night, and Father Sergius intended to avail himself of this information. He even put on those clothes one night in his desire to go, but he could not decide what was best—to remain or to escape. At first he was in doubt, but afterwards this indecision passed. He submitted to custom and yielded to the devil, and only the peasant garb reminded him of the thought and feeling he had had.

Every day more and more people flocked to him and less and less time was left him for prayer and for renewing his spiritual strength. Sometimes in lucid moments he thought he was like a place where there had once been a spring. 'There used to be a feeble spring of living water which flowed quietly from me and through me. That was true life, the time when she tempted me!' (He always thought with ecstasy of that night and of her who was now Mother Agnes.) She had tasted of that pure water, but since then there had not been time for it to collect before thirsty people came crowding in and pushing one another aside. And they had trampled everything down and nothing was left but mud.

So he thought in rare moments of lucidity, but his usual state of mind was one of weariness and a tender pity for himself because of that weariness.

It was in spring, on the eve of the mid-Pentecostal feast. Father Sergius was officiating at the Vigil Service in his hermitage church, where the congregation was as large as the little church could hold—about twenty people. They were all well-to-do proprietors or merchants. Father Sergius admitted anyone, but a selection was made by the monk in attendance and by an assistant who was sent to the hermitage every day from the monastery. A crowd of some eighty people—pilgrims and peasants, and especially peasant-women—stood outside waiting for Father Sergius to come out and bless them. Meanwhile he conducted the service, but at the point at which he went out to the tomb of his predecessor, he staggered and would have fallen had he not been caught by a merchant standing behind him and by the monk acting as deacon.

'What is the matter, Father Sergius? Dear man! O Lord!' exclaimed the women. 'He is as white as a sheet!'

But Father Sergius recovered immediately, and though very pale, he waved the merchant and the deacon aside and continued to chant the service.

Father Seraphim, the deacon, the acolytes, and Sofya Ivanovna, a lady who always lived near the hermitage and tended Father Sergius, begged him to bring the service to an end.

'No, there's nothing the matter,' said Father Sergius, slightly smiling from beneath his moustache and continuing the service. 'Yes, that is the way the Saints behave!' thought he.

'A holy man—an angel of God!' he heard just then the voice of Sofya Ivanovna behind him, and also of the merchant who had supported him. He did not heed their entreaties, but went on with the service. Again crowding together they all made their way by the narrow passages back into the little church, and there, though abbreviating it slightly, Father Sergius completed vespers.

Immediately after the service Father Sergius, having pronounced the benediction on those present, went over to the bench under the elm tree at the entrance to the cave. He wished to rest and breathe the fresh air—he felt in need of it. But as soon as he left the church the crowd of people rushed to him soliciting his blessing, his advice, and his help. There were pilgrims who constantly tramped from one holy place to another and from one starets to another, and were always entranced by every shrine and every starets. Father Sergius knew this common, cold, conventional, and most irreligious type. There were pilgrims, for the most part discharged soldiers, unaccustomed to a settled life, poverty-stricken, and many of them drunken old men, who tramped from monastery to monastery merely to be fed. And there were rough peasants and peasant-women who had come with their selfish requirements, seeking cures or to have doubts about quite practical affairs solved for them: about marrying off a daughter, or hiring a shop, or buying a bit of land, or how to atone for having overlaid a child or having an illegitimate one.

All this was an old story and not in the least interesting to him. He knew he would hear nothing new from these folk, that they would arouse no religious emotion in him; but he liked to see the crowd to which his blessing and advice was necessary and precious, so while that crowd oppressed him it also pleased him. Father Seraphim began to drive them away, saying that Father Sergius was tired.

But Father Sergius, remembering the words of the Gospel: 'Forbid them' (children) 'not to come unto me,' and feeling tenderly towards himself at this recollection, said they should be allowed to approach.

He rose, went to the railing beyond which the crowd had gathered, and began blessing them and answering their questions, but in a voice so weak that he was touched with pity for himself. Yet despite his wish to receive them all he could not do it. Things again grew dark before his eyes, and he staggered and grasped the railings. He felt a rush of blood to his head and first went pale and then suddenly flushed.

'I must leave the rest till to-morrow. I cannot do more to-day,' and, pronouncing a general benediction, he returned to the bench. The merchant again supported him, and leading him by the arm helped him to be seated.

'Father!' came voices from the crowd. 'Dear Father! Do not forsake us. Without you we are lost!'

The merchant, having seated Father Sergius on the bench under the elm, took on himself police duties and drove the people off very resolutely. It is true that he spoke in a low voice so that Father Sergius might not hear him, but his words were incisive and angry.

'Be off, be off! He has blessed you, and what more do you want? Get along with you, or I'll wring your necks! Move on there! Get along, you old woman with your dirty leg-bands! Go, go! Where are you shoving to? You've been told that it is finished. To-morrow will be as God wills, but for to-day he has finished!'

'Father! Only let my eyes have a glimpse of his dear face!' said an old woman.

'I'll glimpse you! Where are you shoving to?'

Father Sergius noticed that the merchant seemed to be acting roughly, and in a feeble voice told the attendant that the people should not be driven away. He knew that they would be driven away all the same, and he much desired to be left alone and to rest, but he sent the attendant with that message to produce an impression.

'All right, all right! I am not driving them away. I am only remonstrating with them,' replied the merchant. 'You know they wouldn't hesitate to drive a man to death. They have no pity, they only consider themselves.... You've been told you cannot see him. Go away! To-morrow!' And he got rid of them all.

He took all these pains because he liked order and liked to domineer and drive the people away, but chiefly because he wanted to have Father Sergius to himself. He was a widower with an only daughter who was an invalid and unmarried, and whom he had brought fourteen hundred versts to Father Sergius to be healed. For two years past he had been taking her to different places to be cured: first to the university clinic in the chief town of the province, but that did no good; then to a peasant in the province of Samara, where she got a little better; then to a doctor in Moscow to whom he paid much money, but this did no good at all. Now he had been told that Father Sergius wrought cures, and had brought her to him. So when all the people had been driven away he approached Father Sergius, and suddenly falling on his knees loudly exclaimed:

'Holy Father! Bless my afflicted offspring that she may be healed of her malady. I venture to prostrate myself at your holy feet.'

And he placed one hand on the other, cup-wise. He said and did all this as if he were doing something clearly and firmly appointed by law and usage—as if one must and should ask for a daughter to be cured in just this way and no other. He did it with such conviction that it seemed even to Father Sergius that it should be said and done in just that way, but nevertheless he bade him rise and tell him what the trouble was. The merchant said that his daughter, a girl of twenty-two, had fallen ill two years ago, after her mother's sudden death. She had moaned (as he expressed it) and since then had not been herself. And now he had brought her fourteen hundred versts and she was waiting in the hostelry till Father Sergius should give orders to bring her. She did not go out during the day, being afraid of the light, and could only come after sunset.

'Is she very weak?' asked Father Sergius.

'No, she has no particular weakness. She is quite plump, and is only "nerastenic" the doctors say. If you will only let me bring her this evening, Father Sergius, I'll fly like a spirit to fetch her. Holy Father! Revive a parent's heart, restore his line, save his afflicted daughter by your prayers!' And the merchant again threw himself on his knees and bending sideways, with his head resting on his clenched fists, remained stock still. Father Sergius again told him to get up, and thinking how heavy his activities were and how he went through with them patiently notwithstanding, he sighed heavily and after a few seconds of silence, said:

'Well, bring her this evening. I will pray for her, but now I am tired....' and he closed his eyes. 'I will send for you.'

The merchant went away, stepping on tiptoe, which only made his boots creak the louder, and Father Sergius remained alone.

His whole life was filled by Church services and by people who came to see him, but to-day had been a particularly difficult one. In the morning an important official had arrived and had had a long conversation with him; after that a lady had come with her son. This son was a sceptical young professor whom the mother, an ardent believer and devoted to Father Sergius, had brought that he might talk to him. The conversation had been very trying. The young man, evidently not wishing to have a controversy with a monk, had agreed with him in everything as with someone who was mentally inferior. Father Sergius saw that the young man did not believe but yet was satisfied, tranquil, and at ease, and the memory of that conversation now disquieted him.

'Have something to eat, Father,' said the attendant.

'All right, bring me something.'

The attendant went to a hut that had been arranged some ten paces from the cave, and Father Sergius remained alone.

The time was long past when he had lived alone doing everything for himself and eating only rye-bread, or rolls prepared for the Church. He had been advised long since that he had no right to neglect his health, and he was given wholesome, though Lenten, food. He ate sparingly, though much more than he had done, and often he ate with much pleasure, and not as formerly with aversion and a sense of guilt. So it was now. He had some gruel, drank a cup of tea, and ate half a white roll.

The attendant went away, and Father Sergius remained alone under the elm tree.

It was a wonderful May evening, when the birches, aspens, elms, wild cherries, and oaks, had just burst into foliage.

The bush of wild cherries behind the elm tree was in full bloom and had not yet begun to shed its blossoms, and the nightingales—one quite near at hand and two or three others in the bushes down by the river—burst into full song after some preliminary twitters. From the river came the far-off songs of peasants returning, no doubt, from their work. The sun was setting behind the forest, its last rays glowing through the leaves. All that side was brilliant green, the other side with the elm tree was dark. The cockchafers flew clumsily about, falling to the ground when they collided with anything.

After supper Father Sergius began to repeat a silent prayer: 'O Lord Jesus Christ, Son of God, have mercy upon us!' and then he read a psalm, and suddenly in the middle of the psalm a sparrow flew out from the bush, alighted on the ground, and hopped towards him chirping as it came, but then it took fright at something and flew away. He said a prayer which referred to his abandonment of the world, and hastened to finish it in order to send for the merchant with the sick daughter. She interested him in that she presented a distraction, and because both she and her father considered him a saint whose prayers were efficacious. Outwardly he disavowed that idea, but in the depths of his soul he considered it to be true.

He was often amazed that this had happened, that he, Stepan Kasatsky, had come to be such an extraordinary saint and even a worker of miracles, but of the fact that he was such there could not be the least doubt. He could not fail to believe in the miracles he himself witnessed, beginning with the sick boy and ending with the old woman who had recovered her sight when he had prayed for her.

Strange as it might be, it was so. Accordingly the merchant's daughter interested him as a new individual who had faith in him, and also as a fresh opportunity to confirm his healing powers and enhance his fame. 'They bring people a thousand versts and write about it in the papers. The Emperor knows of it, and they know of it in Europe, in unbelieving Europe'—thought he. And suddenly he felt ashamed of his vanity and again began to pray. 'Lord, King of Heaven, Comforter, Soul of Truth! Come and enter into me and cleanse me from all sin and save and bless my soul. Cleanse me from the sin of worldly vanity that troubles me!' he repeated, and he remembered how often he had prayed about this and how vain till now his prayers had been in that respect. His prayers worked miracles for others, but in his own case God had not granted him liberation from this petty passion.

He remembered his prayers at the commencement of his life at the hermitage, when he prayed for purity, humility, and love, and how it seemed to him then that God heard his prayers. He had retained his purity and had chopped off his finger. And he lifted the shrivelled stump of that finger to his lips and kissed it. It seemed to him now that he had been humble then when he had always seemed loathsome to himself on account of his sinfulness; and when he remembered the tender feelings with which he had then met an old man who was bringing a drunken soldier to him to ask alms; and how he had received HER, it seemed to him that he had then possessed love also. But now? And he asked himself whether he loved anyone, whether he loved Sofya Ivanovna, or Father Seraphim, whether he had any feeling of love for all who had come to him that day—for that learned young man with whom he had had that instructive discussion in which he was concerned only to show off his own intelligence and that he had not lagged behind the times in knowledge. He wanted and needed their love, but felt none towards them. He now had neither love nor humility nor purity.

He was pleased to know that the merchant's daughter was twenty-two, and he wondered whether she was good-looking. When he inquired whether she was weak, he really wanted to know if she had feminine charm.

'Can I have fallen so low?' he thought. 'Lord, help me! Restore me, my Lord and God!' And he clasped his hands and began to pray.

The nightingales burst into song, a cockchafer knocked against him and crept up the back of his neck. He brushed it off. 'But does He exist? What if I am knocking at a door fastened from outside? The bar is on the door for all to see. Nature—the nightingales and the cockchafers—is that bar. Perhaps the young man was right.' And he began to pray aloud. He prayed for a long time till these thoughts vanished and he again felt calm and confident. He rang the bell and told the attendant to say that the merchant might bring his daughter to him now.

The merchant came, leading his daughter by the arm. He led her into the cell and immediately left her.

She was a very fair girl, plump and very short, with a pale, frightened, childish face and a much developed feminine figure. Father Sergius remained seated on the bench at the entrance and when she was passing and stopped beside him for his blessing he was aghast at himself for the way he looked at her figure. As she passed by him he was acutely conscious of her femininity, though he saw by her face that she was sensual and feeble-minded. He rose and went into the cell. She was sitting on a stool waiting for him, and when he entered she rose.

'I want to go back to Papa,' she said.

'Don't be afraid,' he replied. 'What are you suffering from?'

'I am in pain all over,' she said, and suddenly her face lit up with a smile.

'You will be well,' said he. 'Pray!'

'What is the use of praying? I have prayed and it does no good'—and she continued to smile. 'I want you to pray for me and lay your hands on me. I saw you in a dream.'

'How did you see me?'

'I saw you put your hands on my breast like that.' She took his hand and pressed it to her breast. 'Just here.'

He yielded his right hand to her.

'What is your name?' he asked, trembling all over and feeling that he was overcome and that his desire had already passed beyond control.

'Marie. Why?'

She took his hand and kissed it, and then put her arm round his waist and pressed him to herself.

'What are you doing?' he said. 'Marie, you are a devil!'

'Oh, perhaps. What does it matter?'

And embracing him she sat down with him on the bed.

At dawn he went out into the porch.

'Can this all have happened? Her father will come and she will tell him everything. She is a devil! What am I to do? Here is the axe with which I chopped off my finger.' He snatched up the axe and moved back towards the cell.

The attendant came up.

'Do you want some wood chopped? Let me have the axe.'

Sergius yielded up the axe and entered the cell. She was lying there asleep. He looked at her with horror, and passed on beyond the partition, where he took down the peasant clothes and put them on. Then he seized a pair of scissors, cut off his long hair, and went out along the path down the hill to the river, where he had not been for more than three years.

A road ran beside the river and he went along it and walked till noon. Then he went into a field of rye and lay down there. Towards evening he approached a village, but without entering it went towards the cliff that overhung the river. There he again lay down to rest.

It was early morning, half an hour before sunrise. All was damp and gloomy and a cold early wind was blowing from the west. 'Yes, I must end it all. There is no God. But how am I to end it? Throw myself into the river? I can swim and should not drown. Hang myself? Yes, just throw this sash over a branch.' This seemed so feasible and so easy that he felt horrified. As usual at moments of despair he felt the need of prayer. But there was no one to pray to. There was no God. He lay down resting on his arm, and suddenly such a longing for sleep overcame him that he could no longer support his head on his hand, but stretched out his arm, laid his head upon it, and fell asleep. But that sleep lasted only for a moment. He woke up immediately and began not to dream but to remember.

He saw himself as a child in his mother's home in the country. A carriage drives up, and out of it steps Uncle Nicholas Sergeevich, with his long, spade-shaped, black beard, and with him Pashenka, a thin little girl with large mild eyes and a timid pathetic face. And into their company of boys Pashenka is brought and they have to play with her, but it is dull. She is silly, and it ends by their making fun of her and forcing her to show how she can swim. She lies down on the floor and shows them, and they all laugh and make a fool of her. She sees this and blushes red in patches and becomes more pitiable than before, so pitiable that he feels ashamed and can never forget that crooked, kindly, submissive smile. And Sergius remembered having seen her since then. Long after, just before he became a monk, she had married a landowner who squandered all her fortune and was in the habit of beating her. She had had two children, a son and a daughter, but the son had died while still young. And Sergius remembered having seen her very wretched. Then again he had seen her in the monastery when she was a widow. She had been still the same, not exactly stupid, but insipid, insignificant, and pitiable. She had come with her daughter and her daughter's fiancé. They were already poor at that time and later on he had heard that she was living in a small provincial town and was very poor.

'Why am I thinking about her?' he asked himself, but he could not cease doing so. 'Where is she? How is she getting on? Is she still as unhappy as she was then when she had to show us how to swim on the floor? But why should I think about her? What am I doing? I must put an end to myself.'

And again he felt afraid, and again, to escape from that thought, he went on thinking about Pashenka.

So he lay for a long time, thinking now of his unavoidable end and now of Pashenka. She presented herself to him as a means of salvation. At last he fell asleep, and in his sleep he saw an angel who came to him and said: 'Go to Pashenka and learn from her what you have to do, what your sin is, and wherein lies your salvation.'

He awoke, and having decided that this was a vision sent by God, he felt glad, and resolved to do what had been told him in the vision. He knew the town where she lived. It was some three hundred versts (two hundred miles) away, and he set out to walk there.

CHAPTER VI

Pashenka had already long ceased to be Pashenka and had become old, withered, wrinkled Praskovya Mikhaylovna, mother-in-law of that failure, the drunken official Mavrikyev. She was living in the country town where he had had his last appointment, and there she was supporting the family: her daughter, her ailing neurasthenic son-in-law, and her five grandchildren. She did this by giving music lessons to tradesmen's daughters, giving four and sometimes five lessons a day of an hour each, and earning in this way some sixty rubles (6 pounds) a month. So they lived for the present, in expectation of another appointment. She had sent letters to all her relations and acquaintances asking them to obtain a post for her son-in-law, and among the rest she had written to Sergius, but that letter had not reached him.

It was a Saturday, and Praskovya Mikhaylovna was herself mixing dough for currant bread such as the serf-cook on her father's estate used to make so well. She wished to give her grandchildren a treat on the Sunday.

Masha, her daughter, was nursing her youngest child, the eldest boy and girl were at school, and her son-in-law was asleep, not having slept during the night. Praskovya Mikhaylovna had remained awake too for a great part of the night, trying to soften her daughter's anger against her husband.

She saw that it was impossible for her son-in-law, a weak creature, to be other than he was, and realized that his wife's reproaches could do no good—so she used all her efforts to soften those reproaches and to avoid recrimination and anger. Unkindly relations between people caused her actual physical suffering. It was so clear to her that bitter feelings do not make anything better, but only make everything worse. She did not in fact think about this: she simply suffered at the sight of anger as she would from a bad smell, a harsh noise, or from blows on her body.

She had—with a feeling of self-satisfaction—just taught Lukerya how to mix the dough, when her six-year-old grandson Misha, wearing an apron and with darned stockings on his crooked little legs, ran into the kitchen with a frightened face.

'Grandma, a dreadful old man wants to see you.'

Lukerya looked out at the door.

'There is a pilgrim of some kind, a man...'

Praskovya Mikhaylovna rubbed her thin elbows against one another, wiped her hands on her apron and went upstairs to get a five-kopek piece [about a penny] out of her purse for him, but remembering that she had nothing less than a ten-kopek piece she decided to give him some bread instead. She returned to the cupboard, but suddenly blushed at the thought of having grudged the ten-kopek piece, and telling Lukerya to cut a slice of bread, went upstairs again to fetch it. 'It serves you right,' she said to herself. 'You must now give twice over.'

She gave both the bread and the money to the pilgrim, and when doing so—far from being proud of her generosity—she excused herself for giving so little. The man had such an imposing appearance.

Though he had tramped two hundred versts as a beggar, though he was tattered and had grown thin and weatherbeaten, though he had cropped his long hair and was wearing a peasant's cap and boots, and though he bowed very humbly, Sergius still had the impressive appearance that made him so attractive. But Praskovya Mikhaylovna did not recognize him. She could hardly do so, not having seen him for almost twenty years.

'Don't think ill of me, Father. Perhaps you want something to eat?'

He took the bread and the money, and Praskovya Mikhaylovna was surprised that he did not go, but stood looking at her.

'Pashenka, I have come to you! Take me in...'

His beautiful black eyes, shining with the tears that started in them, were fixed on her with imploring insistence. And under his greyish moustache his lips quivered piteously.

Praskovya Mikhaylovna pressed her hands to her withered breast, opened her mouth, and stood petrified, staring at the pilgrim with dilated eyes.

'It can't be! Stepa! Sergey! Father Sergius!'

'Yes, it is I,' said Sergius in a low voice. 'Only not Sergius, or Father Sergius, but a great sinner, Stepan Kasatsky—a great and lost sinner. Take me in and help me!'

'It's impossible! How have you so humbled yourself? But come in.'

She reached out her hand, but he did not take it and only followed her in.

But where was she to take him? The lodging was a small one. Formerly she had had a tiny room, almost a closet, for herself, but later she had given it up to her daughter, and Masha was now sitting there rocking the baby.

'Sit here for the present,' she said to Sergius, pointing to a bench in the kitchen.

He sat down at once, and with an evidently accustomed movement slipped the straps of his wallet first off one shoulder and then off the other.

'My God, my God! How you have humbled yourself, Father! Such great fame, and now like this...'

Sergius did not reply, but only smiled meekly, placing his wallet under the bench on which he sat.

'Masha, do you know who this is?'—And in a whisper Praskovya Mikhaylovna told her daughter who he was, and together they then carried the bed and the cradle out of the tiny room and cleared it for Sergius.

Praskovya Mikhaylovna led him into it.

'Here you can rest. Don't take offence... but I must go out.'

'Where to?'

'I have to go to a lesson. I am ashamed to tell you, but I teach music!'

'Music? But that is good. Only just one thing, Praskovya Mikhaylovna, I have come to you with a definite object. When can I have a talk with you?'

'I shall be very glad. Will this evening do?'

'Yes. But one thing more. Don't speak about me, or say who I am. I have revealed myself only to you. No one knows where I have gone to. It must be so.'

'Oh, but I have told my daughter.'

'Well, ask her not to mention it.'

And Sergius took off his boots, lay down, and at once fell asleep after a sleepless night and a walk of nearly thirty miles.

When Praskovya Mikhaylovna returned, Sergius was sitting in the little room waiting for her. He did not come out for dinner, but had some soup and gruel which Lukerya brought him.

'How is it that you have come back earlier than you said?' asked Sergius. 'Can I speak to you now?'

'How is it that I have the happiness to receive such a guest? I have missed one of my lessons. That can wait... I had always been planning to go to see you. I wrote to you, and now this good fortune has come.'

'Pashenka, please listen to what I am going to tell you as to a confession made to God at my last hour. Pashenka, I am not a holy man, I am not even as good as a simple ordinary man; I am a loathsome, vile, and proud sinner who has gone astray, and who, if not worse than everyone else, is at least worse than most very bad people.'

Pashenka looked at him at first with staring eyes. But she believed what he said, and when she had quite grasped it she touched his hand, smiling pityingly, and said:

'Perhaps you exaggerate, Stiva?'

'No, Pashenka. I am an adulterer, a murderer, a blasphemer, and a deceiver.'

'My God! How is that?' exclaimed Praskovya Mikhaylovna.

'But I must go on living. And I, who thought I knew everything, who taught others how to live—I know nothing and ask you to teach me.'

'What are you saying, Stiva? You are laughing at me. Why do you always make fun of me?'

'Well, if you think I am jesting you must have it as you please. But tell me all the same how you live, and how you have lived your life.'

'I? I have lived a very nasty, horrible life, and now God is punishing me as I deserve. I live so wretchedly, so wretchedly...'

'How was it with your marriage? How did you live with your husband?'

'It was all bad. I married because I fell in love in the nastiest way. Papa did not approve. But I would not listen to anything and just got married. Then instead of helping my husband I tormented him by my jealousy, which I could not restrain.'

'I heard that he drank...'

'Yes, but I did not give him any peace. I always reproached him, though you know it is a disease! He could not refrain from it. I now remember how I tried to prevent his having it, and the frightful scenes we had!'

And she looked at Kasatsky with beautiful eyes, suffering from the remembrance.

Kasatsky remembered how he had been told that Pashenka's husband used to beat her, and now, looking at her thin withered neck with prominent veins behind her ears, and her scanty coil of hair, half grey half auburn, he seemed to see just how it had occurred.

'Then I was left with two children and no means at all.'

'But you had an estate!'

'Oh, we sold that while Vasya was still alive, and the money was all spent. We had to live, and like all our young ladies I did not know how to earn anything. I was particularly useless and helpless. So we spent all we had. I taught the children and improved my own education a little. And then Mitya fell ill when he was already in the fourth form, and God took him. Masha fell in love with Vanya, my son-in-law. And—well, he is well-meaning but unfortunate. He is ill.'

'Mamma!'—her daughter's voice interrupted her—'Take Mitya! I can't be in two places at once.'

Praskovya Mikhaylovna shuddered, but rose and went out of the room, stepping quickly in her patched shoes. She soon came back with a boy of two in her arms, who threw himself backwards and grabbed at her shawl with his little hands.

'Where was I? Oh yes, he had a good appointment here, and his chief was a kind man too. But Vanya could not go on, and had to give up his position.'

'What is the matter with him?'

'Neurasthenia—it is a dreadful complaint. We consulted a doctor, who told us he ought to go away, but we had no means.... I always hope it will pass of itself. He has no particular pain, but...'

'Lukerya!' cried an angry and feeble voice. 'She is always sent away when I want her. Mamma...'

'I'm coming!' Praskovya Mikhaylovna again interrupted herself. 'He has not had his dinner yet. He can't eat with us.'

She went out and arranged something, and came back wiping her thin dark hands.

'So that is how I live. I always complain and am always dissatisfied, but thank God the grandchildren are all nice and healthy, and we can still live. But why talk about me?'

'But what do you live on?'

'Well, I earn a little. How I used to dislike music, but how useful it is to me now!' Her small hand lay on the chest of drawers beside which she was sitting, and she drummed an exercise with her thin fingers.

'How much do you get for a lesson?'

'Sometimes a ruble, sometimes fifty kopeks, or sometimes thirty. They are all so kind to me.'

'And do your pupils get on well?' asked Kasatsky with a slight smile.

Praskovya Mikhaylovna did not at first believe that he was asking seriously, and looked inquiringly into his eyes.

'Some of them do. One of them is a splendid girl—the butcher's daughter—such a good kind girl! If I were a clever woman I ought, of course, with the connexions Papa had, to be able to get an appointment for my son-in-law. But as it is I have not been able to do anything, and have brought them all to this—as you see.'

'Yes, yes,' said Kasatsky, lowering his head. 'And how is it, Pashenka—do you take part in Church life?'

'Oh, don't speak of it. I am so bad that way, and have neglected it so! I keep the fasts with the children and sometimes go to church, and then again sometimes I don't go for months. I only send the children.'

'But why don't you go yourself?'

'To tell the truth' (she blushed) 'I am ashamed, for my daughter's sake and the children's, to go there in tattered clothes, and I haven't anything else. Besides, I am just lazy.'

'And do you pray at home?'

'I do. But what sort of prayer is it? Only mechanical. I know it should not be like that, but I lack real religious feeling. The only thing is that I know how bad I am...'

'Yes, yes, that's right!' said Kasatsky, as if approvingly.

'I'm coming! I'm coming!' she replied to a call from her son-in-law, and tidying her scanty plait she left the room.

But this time it was long before she returned. When she came back, Kasatsky was sitting in the same position, his elbows resting on his knees and his head bowed. But his wallet was strapped on his back.

When she came in, carrying a small tin lamp without a shade, he raised his fine weary eyes and sighed very deeply.

'I did not tell them who you are,' she began timidly. 'I only said that you are a pilgrim, a nobleman, and that I used to know you. Come into the dining-room for tea.'

'No...'

'Well then, I'll bring some to you here.'

'No, I don't want anything. God bless you, Pashenka! I am going now. If you pity me, don't tell anyone that you have seen me. For the love of God don't tell anyone. Thank you. I would bow to your feet but I know it would make you feel awkward. Thank you, and forgive me for Christ's sake!'

'Give me your blessing.'

'God bless you! Forgive me for Christ's sake!'

He rose, but she would not let him go until she had given him bread and butter and rusks. He took it all and went away.

It was dark, and before he had passed the second house he was lost to sight. She only knew he was there because the dog at the priest's house was barking.

'So that is what my dream meant! Pashenka is what I ought to have been but failed to be. I lived for men on the pretext of living for God, while she lived for God imagining that she lives for men. Yes, one good deed—a cup of water given without thought of reward—is worth more than any benefit I imagined I was bestowing on people. But after all was there not some share of sincere desire to serve God?' he asked himself, and the answer was: 'Yes, there was, but it was all soiled and overgrown by desire for human praise. Yes, there is no God for the man who lives, as I did, for human praise. I will now seek Him!'

And he walked from village to village as he had done on his way to Pashenka, meeting and parting from other pilgrims, men and women, and asking for bread and a night's rest in Christ's name. Occasionally some angry housewife scolded him, or a drunken peasant reviled him, but for the most part he was given food and drink and even something to take with him. His noble bearing disposed some people in his favour, while others on the contrary seemed pleased at the sight of a gentleman who had come to beggary.

But his gentleness prevailed with everyone.

Often, finding a copy of the Gospels in a hut he would read it aloud, and when they heard him the people were always touched and surprised, as at something new yet familiar.

When he succeeded in helping people, either by advice, or by his knowledge of reading and writing, or by settling some quarrel, he did not wait to see their gratitude but went away directly afterwards. And little by little God began to reveal Himself within him.

Once he was walking along with two old women and a soldier. They were stopped by a party consisting of a lady and gentleman in a gig and another lady and gentleman on horseback. The husband was on horseback with his daughter, while in the gig his wife was driving with a Frenchman, evidently a traveller.

The party stopped to let the Frenchman see the pilgrims who, in accord with a popular Russian superstition, tramped about from place to place instead of working.

They spoke French, thinking that the others would not understand them.

'Demandez-leur,' said the Frenchman, 's'ils sont bien sur de ce que leur pelerinage est agreable a Dieu.'

The question was asked, and one old woman replied:

'As God takes it. Our feet have reached the holy places, but our hearts may not have done so.'

They asked the soldier. He said that he was alone in the world and had nowhere else to go.

They asked Kasatsky who he was.

'A servant of God.'

'Qu'est-ce qu'il dit? Il ne repond pas.'

'Il dit qu'il est un serviteur de Dieu. Cela doit etre un fils de preetre. Il a de la race. Avez-vous de la petite monnaie?'

The Frenchman found some small change and gave twenty kopeks to each of the pilgrims.

'Mais dites-leur que ce n'est pas pour les cierges que je leur donne, mais pour qu'ils se regalent de the. Chay, chay pour vous, mon vieux!' he said with a smile. And he patted Kasatsky on the shoulder with his gloved hand.

'May Christ bless you,' replied Kasatsky without replacing his cap and bowing his bald head.

He rejoiced particularly at this meeting, because he had disregarded the opinion of men and had done the simplest, easiest thing—humbly accepted twenty kopeks and given them to his comrade, a blind beggar. The less importance he attached to the opinion of men the more did he feel the presence of God within him.

For eight months Kasatsky tramped on in this manner, and in the ninth month he was arrested for not having a passport. This happened at a night-refuge in a provincial town where he had passed the night with some pilgrims. He was taken to the police-station, and when asked who he was and where was his passport, he replied that he had no passport and that he was a servant of God. He was classed as a tramp, sentenced, and sent to live in Siberia.

In Siberia he has settled down as the hired man of a well-to-do peasant, in which capacity he works in the kitchen-garden, teaches children, and attends to the sick.

7. ALYOSHA THE POT

ALYOSHA was the younger brother. He was called the Pot, because his mother had once sent him with a pot of milk to the deacon's wife, and he had stumbled against something and broken it. His mother had beaten him, and the children had teased him. Since then he was nicknamed the Pot. Alyosha was a tiny, thin little fellow, with ears like wings, and a huge nose. "Alyosha has a nose that looks like a dog on a hill!" the children used to call after him. Alyosha went to the village school, but was not good at lessons; besides, there was so little time to learn. His elder brother was in town, working for a merchant, so Alyosha had to help his father from a very early age. When he was no more than six he used to go out with the girls to watch the cows and sheep in the pasture, and a little later he looked after the horses by day and by night. And at twelve years of age he had already begun to plough and to drive the cart. The skill was there though the strength was not. He was always cheerful. Whenever the children made fun of him, he would either laugh or be silent. When his father scolded him he would stand mute and listen attentively, and as soon as the scolding was over would smile and go on with his work. Alyosha was nineteen when his brother was taken as a soldier. So his father placed him with the merchant as a yard-porter. He was given his brother's old boots, his father's old coat and cap, and was taken to town. Alyosha was delighted with his clothes, but the merchant was not impressed by his appearance.

"I thought you would bring me a man in Simeon's place," he said, scanning Alyosha; "and you've brought me THIS! What's the good of him?"

"He can do everything; look after horses and drive. He's a good one to work. He looks rather thin, but he's tough enough. And he's very willing."

"He looks it. All right; we'll see what we can do with him."

So Alyosha remained at the merchant's.

The family was not a large one. It consisted of the merchant's wife: her old mother: a married son poorly educated who was in his father's business: another son, a learned one who had finished school and entered the University, but having been expelled, was living at home: and a daughter who still went to school.

They did not take to Alyosha at first. He was uncouth, badly dressed, and had no manner, but they soon got used to him. Alyosha worked even better than his brother had done; he was really very willing. They sent him on all sorts of errands, but he did everything quickly and readily, going from one task to another without stopping. And so here, just as at home, all the work was put upon his shoulders. The more he did, the more he was given to do. His mistress, her old mother, the son, the daughter, the clerk, and the cook—all ordered him about, and sent him from one place to another.

"Alyosha, do this! Alyosha, do that! What! have you forgotten, Alyosha? Mind you don't forget, Alyosha!" was heard from morning till night. And Alyosha ran here, looked after this and that, forgot nothing, found time for everything, and was always cheerful.

His brother's old boots were soon worn out, and his master scolded him for going about in tatters with his toes sticking out. He ordered another pair to be bought for him in the market. Alyosha was delighted with his new boots, but was angry with his feet when they ached at the end of the day after so much running about. And then he was afraid that his father would be annoyed when he came to town for his wages, to find that his master had deducted the cost of the boots.

In the winter Alyosha used to get up before daybreak. He would chop the wood, sweep the yard, feed the cows and horses, light the stoves, clean the boots, prepare the samovars and polish them afterwards; or the clerk would get him to bring up the goods; or the cook would set him to knead the bread and clean the saucepans. Then he was sent to town on various errands, to bring the daughter home from school, or to get some olive oil for the old mother. "Why the devil have you been so long?" first one, then another, would say to him. Why should they go?

Alyosha can go. "Alyosha! Alyosha!" And Alyosha ran here and there. He breakfasted in snatches while he was working, and rarely managed to get his dinner at the proper hour. The cook used to scold him for being late, but she was sorry for him all the same, and would keep something hot for his dinner and supper.

At holiday times there was more work than ever, but Alyosha liked holidays because everybody gave him a tip. Not much certainly, but it would amount up to about sixty kopeks [1s 2d]—his very own money. For Alyosha never set eyes on his wages. His father used to come and take them from the merchant, and only scold Alyosha for wearing out his boots.

When he had saved up two roubles [4s], by the advice of the cook he bought himself a red knitted jacket, and was so happy when he put it on, that he couldn't close his mouth for joy. Alyosha was not talkative; when he spoke at all, he spoke abruptly, with his head turned away. When told to do anything, or asked if he could do it, he would say yes without the smallest hesitation, and set to work at once.

Alyosha did not know any prayer; and had forgotten what his mother had taught him. But he prayed just the same, every morning and every evening, prayed with his hands, crossing himself.

He lived like this for about a year and a half, and towards the end of the second year a most startling thing happened to him. He discovered one day, to his great surprise, that, in addition to the relation of usefulness existing between people, there was also another, a peculiar relation of quite a different character. Instead of a man being wanted to clean boots, and go on errands and harness horses, he is not wanted to be of any service at all, but another human being wants to serve him and pet him. Suddenly Alyosha felt he was such a man.

He made this discovery through the cook Ustinia. She was young, had no parents, and worked as hard as Alyosha. He felt for the first time in his life that he—not his services, but he himself—was necessary to another human being. When his mother used to be sorry for him, he had taken no notice of her. It had seemed to him quite natural, as though he were feeling sorry for himself. But here was Ustinia, a perfect stranger, and sorry for him. She would save him some hot porridge, and sit watching him, her chin propped on her bare arm, with the sleeve rolled up, while he was eating it. When he looked at her she would begin to laugh, and he would laugh too.

This was such a new, strange thing to him that it frightened Alyosha. He feared that it might interfere with his work. But he was pleased, nevertheless, and when he glanced at the trousers that Ustinia had mended for him, he would shake his head and smile. He would often think of her while at work, or when running on errands. "A fine girl, Ustinia!" he sometimes exclaimed.

Ustinia used to help him whenever she could, and he helped her. She told him all about her life; how she had lost her parents; how her aunt had taken her in and found a place for her in the town; how the merchant's son had tried to take liberties with her, and how she had rebuffed him. She liked to talk, and Alyosha liked to listen to her. He had heard that peasants who came up to work in the towns frequently got married to servant girls. On one occasion she asked him if his parents intended marrying him soon. He said that he did not know; that he did not want to marry any of the village girls.

"Have you taken a fancy to some one, then?"

"I would marry you, if you'd be willing."

"Get along with you, Alyosha the Pot; but you've found your tongue, haven't you?" she exclaimed, slapping him on the back with a towel she held in her hand. "Why shouldn't I?"

At Shrovetide Alyosha's father came to town for his wages. It had come to the ears of the merchant's wife that Alyosha wanted to marry Ustinia, and she disapproved of it. "What will be the use of her with a baby?" she thought, and informed her husband.

The merchant gave the old man Alyosha's wages.

"How is my lad getting on?" he asked. "I told you he was willing."

"That's all right, as far as it goes, but he's taken some sort of nonsense into his head. He wants to marry our cook. Now I don't approve of married servants. We won't have them in the house."

"Well, now, who would have thought the fool would think of such a thing?" the old man exclaimed. "But don't you worry. I'll soon settle that."

He went into the kitchen, and sat down at the table waiting for his son. Alyosha was out on an errand, and came back breathless.

"I thought you had some sense in you; but what's this you've taken into your head?" his father began.

"I? Nothing."

"How, nothing? They tell me you want to get married. You shall get married when the time comes. I'll find you a decent wife, not some town hussy."

His father talked and talked, while Alyosha stood still and sighed. When his father had quite finished, Alyosha smiled.

"All right. I'll drop it."

"Now that's what I call sense."

When he was left alone with Ustinia he told her what his father had said. (She had listened at the door.)

"It's no good; it can't come off. Did you hear? He was angry—won't have it at any price."

Ustinia cried into her apron.

Alyosha shook his head.

"What's to be done? We must do as we're told."

"Well, are you going to give up that nonsense, as your father told you?" his mistress asked, as he was putting up the shutters in the evening.

"To be sure we are," Alyosha replied with a smile, and then burst into tears.

From that day Alyosha went about his work as usual, and no longer talked to Ustinia about their getting married. One day in Lent the clerk told him to clear the snow from the roof. Alyosha climbed on to the roof and swept away all the snow; and, while he was still raking out some frozen lumps from the gutter, his foot slipped and he fell over. Unfortunately he did not fall on the snow, but on a piece of iron over the door. Ustinia came running up, together with the merchant's daughter.

"Have you hurt yourself, Alyosha?"

"Ah! no, it's nothing."

But he could not raise himself when he tried to, and began to smile.

He was taken into the lodge. The doctor arrived, examined him, and asked where he felt the pain.

"I feel it all over," he said. "But it doesn't matter. I'm only afraid master will be annoyed. Father ought to be told."

Alyosha lay in bed for two days, and on the third day they sent for the priest.

"Are you really going to die?" Ustinia asked.

"Of course I am. You can't go on living for ever. You must go when the time comes." Alyosha spoke rapidly as usual. "Thank you, Ustinia. You've been very good to me. What a lucky thing they didn't let us marry! Where should we have been now? It's much better as it is."

When the priest came, he prayed with his bands and with his heart. "As it is good here when you obey and do no harm to others, so it will be there," was the thought within it.

He spoke very little; he only said he was thirsty, and he seemed full of wonder at something.

He lay in wonderment, then stretched himself, and died.

8. THERE ARE NO GUILTY PEOPLE

MINE is a strange and wonderful lot! The chances are that there is not a single wretched beggar suffering under the luxury and oppression of the rich who feels anything like as keenly as I do either the injustice, the cruelty, and the horror of their oppression of and contempt for the poor; or the grinding humiliation and misery which befall the great majority of the workers, the real producers of all that makes life possible. I have felt this for a long time, and as the years have passed by the feeling has grown and grown, until recently it reached its climax. Although I feel all this so vividly, I still live on amid the depravity and sins of rich society; and I cannot leave it, because I have neither the knowledge nor the strength to do so. I cannot. I do not know how to change my life so that my physical needs—food, sleep, clothing, my going to and fro—may be satisfied without a sense of shame and wrongdoing in the position which I fill.

There was a time when I tried to change my position, which was not in harmony with my conscience; but the conditions created by the past, by my family and its claims upon me, were so complicated that they would not let me out of their grasp, or rather, I did not know how to free myself. I had not the strength. Now that I am over eighty and have become feeble, I have given up trying to free myself; and, strange to say, as my feebleness increases I realise more and more strongly the wrongfulness of my position, and it grows more and more intolerable to me.

It has occurred to me that I do not occupy this position for nothing: that Providence intended that I should lay bare the truth of my feelings, so that I might atone for all that causes my suffering, and might perhaps open the eyes of those—or at least of some of those—who are still blind to what I see so clearly, and thus might lighten the burden of that vast majority who, under existing conditions, are subjected to bodily and spiritual suffering by those who deceive them and also deceive themselves. Indeed, it may be that the position which I occupy gives me special facilities for revealing the artificial and criminal relations which exist between men—for telling the whole truth in regard to that position without confusing the issue by attempting to vindicate myself, and without rousing the envy of the rich and feelings of oppression in the hearts of the poor and downtrodden. I am so placed that I not only have no desire to vindicate myself; but, on the contrary, I find it necessary to make an effort lest I should exaggerate the wickedness of the great among whom I live, of whose society I am ashamed, whose attitude towards their fellow-men I detest with my whole soul, though I find it impossible to separate my lot from theirs. But I must also avoid the error of those democrats and others who, in defending the oppressed and the enslaved, do not see their failings and mistakes, and who do not make sufficient allowance for the difficulties created, the mistakes inherited from the past, which in a degree lessens the responsibility of the upper classes.

Free from desire for self-vindication, free from fear of an emancipated people, free from that envy and hatred which the oppressed feel for their oppressors, I am in the best possible position to see the truth and to tell it. Perhaps that is why Providence placed me in such a position. I will do my best to turn it to account.

Alexander Ivanovich Volgin, a bachelor and a clerk in a Moscow bank at a salary of eight thousand roubles a year, a man much respected in his own set, was staying in a country-house. His host was a wealthy landowner, owning some twenty-five hundred acres, and had married his guest's cousin. Volgin, tired after an evening spent in playing vint* for small stakes with [* A game of cards similar to auction bridge.] members of the family, went to his room and placed his watch, silver cigarette-case, pocket-book, big leather purse, and pocket-brush and comb on a small table covered with a white cloth, and then, taking off his coat, waistcoat, shirt, trousers, and underclothes, his silk socks and English boots, put on his nightshirt and dressing-gown. His watch pointed to midnight. Volgin smoked a cigarette, lay on his face for about five minutes reviewing the day's impressions; then, blowing out his candle, he turned over on his side and fell asleep about one o'clock, in spite of a good deal of restlessness. Awaking next morning at eight he put on his slippers and dressing-gown, and rang the bell.

The old butler, Stephen, the father of a family and the grandfather of six grandchildren, who had served in that house for thirty years, entered the room hurriedly, with bent legs, carrying in the newly blackened boots which Volgin had taken off the night before, a well-brushed suit, and a clean shirt. The guest thanked him, and then asked what the weather was like (the blinds were drawn so that the sun should not prevent any one from sleeping till eleven o'clock if he were so inclined), and whether his hosts had slept well. He glanced at his watch—it was still early—and began to wash and dress. His water was ready, and everything on the washing-stand and dressing-table was ready for use and properly laid out—his soap, his tooth and hair brushes, his nail scissors and files. He washed his hands and face in a leisurely fashion, cleaned and manicured his nails, pushed back the skin with the towel, and sponged his stout white body from head to foot. Then he began to brush his hair. Standing in front of the mirror, he first brushed his curly beard, which was beginning to turn grey, with two English brushes, parting it down the middle. Then he combed his hair, which was already showing signs of getting thin, with a large tortoise-shell comb. Putting on his underlinen, his socks, his boots, his trousers—which were held up by elegant braces—and his waistcoat, he sat down coatless in an easy chair to rest after dressing, lit a cigarette, and began to think where he should go for a walk that morning—to the park or to Littleports (what a funny name for a wood!). He thought he would go to Littleports. Then he must answer Simon Nicholaevich's letter; but there was time enough for that. Getting up with an air of resolution, he took out his watch. It was already five minutes to nine. He put his watch into his waistcoat pocket, and his purse—with all that was left of the hundred and eighty roubles he had taken for his journey, and for the incidental expenses of his fortnight's stay with his cousin—and then he placed into his trouser pocket his cigarette-case and electric cigarette-lighter, and two clean handkerchiefs into his coat pockets, and went out of the room, leaving as usual the mess and confusion which he had made to be cleared up by Stephen, an old man of over fifty. Stephen expected Volgin to "remunerate" him, as he said, being so accustomed to the work that he did not feel the slightest repugnance for it. Glancing at a mirror, and feeling satisfied with his appearance, Volgin went into the dining-room.

There, thanks to the efforts of the housekeeper, the footman, and under-butler—the latter had risen at dawn in order to run home to sharpen his son's scythe—breakfast was ready. On a spotless white cloth stood a boiling, shiny, silver samovar (at least it looked like silver), a coffee-pot, hot milk, cream, butter, and all sorts of fancy white bread and biscuits. The only persons at table were the second son of the house, his tutor (a student), and the secretary. The host, who was an active member of the Zemstvo and a great farmer, had already left the house, having gone at eight o'clock to attend to his work. Volgin, while drinking his coffee, talked to the student and the secretary about the weather, and yesterday's vint, and discussed Theodorite's peculiar behaviour the night before, as he had been very rude to his father without the slightest cause. Theodorite was the grown-up son of the house, and a ne'er-do-well. His name was Theodore, but some one had once called him Theodorite either as a joke or to tease him; and, as it seemed funny, the name stuck to him, although his doings were no longer in the least amusing. So it was now. He had been to the university, but left it in his second year, and joined a regiment of horse guards; but he gave that up also, and was now living in the country, doing nothing, finding fault, and feeling discontented with everything. Theodorite was still in bed: so were the other members of the household—Anna Mikhailovna, its mistress; her sister, the widow of a general; and a landscape painter who lived with the family.

Volgin took his panama hat from the hall table (it had cost twenty roubles) and his cane with its carved ivory handle, and went out. Crossing the veranda, gay with flowers, he walked through the flower garden, in the centre of which was a raised round bed, with rings of red, white, and blue flowers, and the initials of the mistress of the house done in carpet bedding in the centre. Leaving the flower garden Volgin entered the avenue of lime trees, hundreds of years old, which peasant girls were tidying and sweeping with spades and brooms. The gardener was busy measuring, and a boy was bringing something in a cart. Passing these Volgin went into the park of at least a hundred and twenty-five acres, filled with fine old trees, and intersected by a network of well-kept walks. Smoking as he strolled Volgin took his favourite path past the summer-house into the fields beyond. It was pleasant in the park, but it was still nicer in the fields. On the right some women who were digging potatoes formed a mass of bright red and white colour; on the left were wheat fields, meadows, and grazing cattle; and in the foreground, slightly to the right, were the dark, dark oaks of Littleports. Volgin took a deep breath, and felt glad that he was alive, especially here in his cousin's home, where he was so thoroughly enjoying the rest from his work at the bank.

"Lucky people to live in the country," he thought. "True, what with his farming and his Zemstvo, the owner of the estate has very little peace even in the country, but that is his own lookout." Volgin shook his head, lit another cigarette, and, stepping out firmly with his powerful feet clad in his thick English boots, began to think of the heavy winter's work in the bank that was in front of him. "I shall be there every day from ten to two, sometimes even till five. And the board meetings . . . And private interviews with clients. . . . Then the Duma. Whereas here. . . . It is delightful. It may be a little dull, but it is not for long." He smiled. After a stroll in Littleports he turned back, going straight across a fallow field which was being ploughed. A herd of cows, calves, sheep, and pigs, which belonged to the village community, was grazing there. The shortest way to the park was to pass through the herd. He frightened the sheep, which ran away one after another, and were followed by the pigs, of which two little ones stared solemnly at him. The shepherd boy called to the sheep and cracked his whip. "How far behind Europe we are," thought Volgin, recalling his frequent holidays abroad. "You would not find a single cow like that anywhere in Europe." Then, wanting to find out where the path which branched off from the one he was on led to and who was the owner of the herd, he called to the boy.

"Whose herd is it?"

The boy was so filled with wonder, verging on terror, when he gazed at the hat, the well-brushed beard, and above all the gold-rimmed eyeglasses, that he could not reply at once. When Volgin repeated his question the boy pulled himself together, and said, "Ours." "But whose is 'ours'?" said Volgin, shaking his head and smiling. The boy was wearing shoes of plaited birch bark, bands of linen round his legs, a dirty, unbleached shirt ragged at the shoulder, and a cap the peak of which had been torn.

"Whose is 'ours'?"

"The Pirogov village herd."

"How old are you?

"I don't know."

"Can you read?"

"No, I can't."

"Didn't you go to school?"

"Yes, I did."

"Couldn't you learn to read?"

"No."

"Where does that path lead?"

The boy told him, and Volgin went on towards the house, thinking how he would chaff Nicholas Petrovich about the deplorable condition of the village schools in spite of all his efforts.

On approaching the house Volgin looked at his watch, and saw that it was already past eleven. He remembered that Nicholas Petrovich was going to drive to the nearest town, and that he had meant to give him a letter to post to Moscow; but the letter was not written. The letter was a very important one to a friend, asking him to bid for him for a picture of the Madonna which was to be offered for sale at an auction. As he reached the house he saw at the door four big, well-fed, well-groomed, thoroughbred horses harnessed to a carriage, the black lacquer of which glistened in the sun. The coachman was seated on the box in a kaftan, with a silver belt, and the horses were jingling their silver bells from time to time.

A bare-headed, barefooted peasant in a ragged kaftan stood at the front door. He bowed. Volgin asked what he wanted.

"I have come to see Nicholas Petrovich."

"What about?"

"Because I am in distress—my horse has died."

Volgin began to question him. The peasant told him how he was situated. He had five children, and this had been his only horse. Now it was gone. He wept.

"What are you going to do?"

"To beg." And he knelt down, and remained kneeling in spite of Volgin's expostulations.

"What is your name?"

"Mitri Sudarikov," answered the peasant, still kneeling.

Volgin took three roubles from his purse and gave them to the peasant, who showed his gratitude by touching the ground with his forehead, and then went into the house. His host was standing in the hall.

"Where is your letter?" he asked, approaching Volgin; "I am just off."

"I'm awfully sorry, I'll write it this minute, if you will let me. I forgot all about it. It's so pleasant here that one can forget anything."

"All right, but do be quick. The horses have already been standing a quarter of an hour, and the flies are biting viciously. Can you wait, Arsenty?" he asked the coachman.

"Why not?" said the coachman, thinking to himself, "why do they order the horses when they aren't ready? The rush the grooms and I had—just to stand here and feed the flies."

"Directly, directly," Volgin went towards his room, but turned back to ask Nicholas Petrovich about the begging peasant.

"Did you see him?—He's a drunkard, but still he is to be pitied. Do be quick!"

Volgin got out his case, with all the requisites for writing, wrote the letter, made out a cheque for a hundred and eighty roubles, and, sealing down the envelope, took it to Nicholas Petrovich.

"Good-bye."

Volgin read the newspapers till luncheon. He only read the Liberal papers: The Russian Gazette, Speech, sometimes The Russian Word—but he would not touch The New Times, to which his host subscribed.

While he was scanning at his ease the political news, the Tsar's doings, the doings of President, and ministers and decisions in the Duma, and was just about to pass on to the general news, theatres, science, murders and cholera, he heard the luncheon bell ring.

Thanks to the efforts of upwards of ten human beings—counting laundresses, gardeners, cooks, kitchen-maids, butlers and footmen—the table was sumptuously laid for eight, with silver waterjugs, decanters, kvass, wine, mineral waters, cut glass, and fine table linen, while two men-servants were continually hurrying to and fro, bringing in and serving, and then clearing away the hors d'oeuvre and the various hot and cold courses.

The hostess talked incessantly about everything that she had been doing, thinking, and saying; and she evidently considered that everything that she thought, said, or did was perfect, and that it would please every one except those who were fools. Volgin felt and knew that everything she said was stupid, but it would never do to let it be seen, and so he kept up the conversation. Theodorite was glum and silent; the student occasionally exchanged a few words with the widow. Now and again there was a pause in the conversation, and then Theodorite interposed, and every one became miserably depressed. At such moments the hostess ordered some dish that had not been served, and the footman hurried off to the kitchen, or to the housekeeper, and hurried back again. Nobody felt inclined either to talk or to eat. But they all forced themselves to eat and to talk, and so luncheon went on.

The peasant who had been begging because his horse had died was named Mitri Sudarikov. He had spent the whole day before he went to the squire over his dead horse. First of all he went to the knacker, Sanin, who lived in a village near. The knacker was out, but he waited for him, and it was dinner-time when he had finished bargaining over the price of the skin. Then he borrowed a neighbour's horse to take his own to a field to be buried, as it is forbidden to bury dead animals near a village. Adrian would not lend his horse because he was getting in his potatoes, but Stephen took pity on Mitri and gave way to his persuasion. He even lent a hand in lifting the dead horse into the cart. Mitri tore off the shoes from the forelegs and gave them to his wife. One was broken, but the other one was whole. While he was digging the grave with a spade which was very blunt, the knacker appeared and took off the skin; and the carcass was then thrown into the hole and covered up. Mitri felt tired, and went into Matrena's hut, where he drank half a bottle of vodka with Sanin to console himself. Then he went home, quarrelled with his wife, and lay down to sleep on the hay. He did not undress, but slept just as he was, with a ragged coat for a coverlet. His wife was in the hut with the girls—there were four of them, and the youngest was only five weeks old. Mitri woke up before dawn as usual. He groaned as the memory of the day before broke in upon him—how the horse had struggled and struggled, and then fallen down. Now there was no horse, and all he had was the price of the skin, four roubles and eighty kopeks. Getting up he arranged the linen bands on his legs, and went through the yard into the hut. His wife was putting straw into the stove with one hand, with the other she was holding a baby girl to her breast, which was hanging out of her dirty chemise.

Mitri crossed himself three times, turning towards the corner in which the ikons hung, and repeated some utterly meaningless words, which he called prayers, to the Trinity and the Virgin, the Creed and our Father.

"Isn't there any water?"

"The girl's gone for it. I've got some tea. Will you go up to the squire?"

"Yes, I'd better." The smoke from the stove made him cough. He took a rag off the wooden bench and went into the porch. The girl had just come back with the water. Mitri filled his mouth with water from the pail and squirted it out on his hands, took some more in his mouth to wash his face, dried himself with the rag, then parted and smoothed his curly hair with his fingers and went out. A little girl of about ten, with nothing on but a dirty shirt, came towards him. "Good-morning, Uncle Mitri," she said; "you are to come and thrash." "All right, I'll come," replied Mitri. He understood that he was expected to return the help given the week before by Kumushkir, a man as poor as he was himself, when he was thrashing his own corn with a horse-driven machine.

"Tell them I'll come—I'll come at lunch time. I've got to go to Ugrumi." Mitri went back to the hut, and changing his birch-bark shoes and the linen bands on his legs, started off to see the squire. After he had got three roubles from Volgin, and the same sum from Nicholas Petrovich, he returned to his house, gave the money to his wife, and went to his neighbour's. The thrashing machine was humming, and the driver was shouting. The lean horses were going slowly round him, straining at their traces. The driver was shouting to them in a monotone, "Now, there, my dears." Some women were unbinding sheaves, others were raking up the scattered straw and ears, and others again were gathering great armfuls of corn and handing them to the men to feed the machine. The work was in full swing. In the kitchen garden, which Mitri had to pass, a girl, clad only in a long shirt, was digging potatoes which she put into a basket.

"Where's your grandfather?" asked Mitri. "He's in the barn." Mitri went to the barn and set to work at once. The old man of eighty knew of Mitri's trouble. After greeting him, he gave him his place to feed the machine.

Mitri took off his ragged coat, laid it out of the way near the fence, and then began to work vigorously, raking the corn together and throwing it into the machine. The work went on without interruption until the dinner-hour. The cocks had crowed two or three times, but no one paid any attention to them; not because the workers did not believe them, but because they were scarcely heard for the noise of the work and the talk about it. At last the whistle of the squire's steam thrasher sounded three miles away, and then the owner came into the barn. He was a straight old man of eighty. "It's time to stop," he said; "it's dinner-time." Those at work seemed to redouble their efforts. In a moment the straw was cleared away; the grain that had been thrashed was separated from the chaff and brought in, and then the workers went into the hut.

The hut was smoke-begrimed, as its stove had no chimney, but it had been tidied up, and benches stood round the table, making room for all those who had been working, of whom there were nine, not counting the owners. Bread, soup, boiled potatoes, and kvass were placed on the table.

An old one-armed beggar, with a bag slung over his shoulder, came in with a crutch during the meal.

"Peace be to this house. A good appetite to you. For Christ's sake give me something."

"God will give it to you," said the mistress, already an old woman, and the daughter-in-law of the master. "Don't be angry with us." An old man, who was still standing near the door, said, "Give him some bread, Martha. How can you?"

"I am only wondering whether we shall have enough." "Oh, it is wrong, Martha. God tells us to help the poor. Cut him a slice."

Martha obeyed. The beggar went away. The man in charge of the thrashing-machine got up, said grace, thanked his hosts, and went away to rest.

Mitri did not lie down, but ran to the shop to buy some tobacco. He was longing for a smoke. While he smoked he chatted to a man from Demensk, asking the price of cattle, as he saw that he would not be able to manage without selling a cow. When he returned to the others, they were already back at work again; and so it went on till the evening.

Among these downtrodden, duped, and defrauded men, who are becoming demoralised by overwork, and being gradually done to death by underfeeding, there are men living who consider themselves Christians; and others so enlightened that they feel no further need for Christianity or for any religion, so superior do they appear in their own esteem. And yet their hideous, lazy lives are supported by the degrading, excessive labour of these slaves, not to mention the labour of millions of other slaves, toiling in factories to produce samovars, silver, carriages, machines, and the like for their use. They live among these horrors, seeing them and yet not seeing them, although often kind at heart—old men and women, young men and maidens, mothers and children—poor children who are being vitiated and trained into moral blindness.

Here is a bachelor grown old, the owner of thousands of acres, who has lived a life of idleness, greed, and over-indulgence, who reads The New Times, and is astonished that the government can be so unwise as to permit Jews to enter the university. There is his guest, formerly the governor of a province, now a senator with a big salary, who reads with satisfaction that a congress of lawyers has passed a resolution in favor of capital punishment. Their political enemy, N. P., reads a liberal paper, and cannot understand the blindness of the government in allowing the union of Russian men to exist.

Here is a kind, gentle mother of a little girl reading a story to her about Fox, a dog that lamed some rabbits. And here is this little girl. During her walks she sees other children, barefooted, hungry, hunting for green apples that have fallen from the trees; and, so accustomed is she to the sight, that these children do not seem to her to be children such as she is, but only part of the usual surroundings—the familiar landscape.

Why is this?

9. THREE QUESTIONS

It once occurred to a certain king, that if he always knew the right time to begin everything; if he knew who were the right people to listen to, and whom to avoid; and, above all, if he always knew what was the most important thing to do, he would never fail in anything he might undertake.

And this thought having occurred to him, he had it proclaimed throughout his kingdom that he would give a great reward to any one who would teach him what was the right time for every action, and who were the most necessary people, and how he might know what was the most important thing to do.

And learned men came to the King, but they all answered his questions differently.

In reply to the first question, some said that to know the right time for every action, one must draw up in advance, a table of days, months and years, and must live strictly according to it. Only thus, said they, could everything be done at its proper time. Others declared that it was impossible to decide beforehand the right time for every action; but that, not letting oneself be absorbed in idle pastimes, one should always attend to all that was going on, and then do what was most needful. Others, again, said that however attentive the King might be to what was going on, it was impossible for one man to decide correctly the right time for every action, but that he should have a Council of wise men, who would help him to fix the proper time for everything.

But then again others said there were some things which could not wait to be laid before a Council, but about which one had at once to decide whether to undertake them or not. But in order to decide that, one must know beforehand what was going to happen. It is only magicians who know that; and, therefore, in order to know the right time for every action, one must consult magicians.

Equally various were the answers to the second question. Some said, the people the King most needed were his councillors; others, the priests; others, the doctors; while some said the warriors were the most necessary.

To the third question, as to what was the most important occupation: some replied that the most important thing in the world was science. Others said it was skill in warfare; and others, again, that it was religious worship.

All the answers being different, the King agreed with none of them, and gave the reward to none. But still wishing to find the right answers to his questions, he decided to consult a hermit, widely renowned for his wisdom.

The hermit lived in a wood which he never quitted, and he received none but common folk. So the King put on simple clothes, and before reaching the hermit's cell dismounted from his horse, and, leaving his body-guard behind, went on alone.

When the King approached, the hermit was digging the ground in front of his hut. Seeing the King, he greeted him and went on digging. The hermit was frail and weak, and each time he stuck his spade into the ground and turned a little earth, he breathed heavily.

The King went up to him and said: "I have come to you, wise hermit, to ask you to answer three questions: How can I learn to do the right thing at the right time? Who are the people I most need, and to whom should I, therefore, pay more attention than to the rest? And, what affairs are the most important, and need my first attention?"

The hermit listened to the King, but answered nothing. He just spat on his hand and recommenced digging.

"You are tired," said the King, "let me take the spade and work awhile for you."

"Thanks!" said the hermit, and, giving the spade to the King, he sat down on the ground.

When he had dug two beds, the King stopped and repeated his questions. The hermit again gave no answer, but rose, stretched out his hand for the spade, and said:

"Now rest awhile-and let me work a bit."

But the King did not give him the spade, and continued to dig. One hour passed, and another. The sun began to sink behind the trees, and the King at last stuck the spade into the ground, and said:

"I came to you, wise man, for an answer to my questions. If you can give me none, tell me so, and I will return home."

"Here comes some one running," said the hermit, "let us see who it is."

The King turned round, and saw a bearded man come running out of the wood. The man held his hands pressed against his stomach, and blood was flowing from under them. When he reached the King, he fell fainting on the ground moaning feebly. The King and the hermit unfastened the man's clothing. There was a large wound in his stomach. The King washed it as best he could, and bandaged it with his handkerchief and with a towel the hermit had. But the blood would not stop flowing, and the King again and again removed the bandage soaked with warm blood, and washed and rebandaged the wound. When at last the blood ceased flowing, the man revived and asked for something to drink. The King brought fresh water and gave it to him. Meanwhile the sun had set, and it had become cool. So the King, with the hermit's help, carried the wounded man into the hut and laid him on the bed. Lying on the bed the man closed his eyes and was quiet; but the King was so tired with his walk and with the work he had done, that he crouched down on the threshold, and also fell asleep—so soundly that he slept all through the short summer night. When he awoke in the morning, it was long before he could remember where he was, or who was the strange bearded man lying on the bed and gazing intently at him with shining eyes.

"Forgive me!" said the bearded man in a weak voice, when he saw that the King was awake and was looking at him.

"I do not know you, and have nothing to forgive you for," said the King.

"You do not know me, but I know you. I am that enemy of yours who swore to revenge himself on you, because you executed his brother and seized his property. I knew you had gone alone to see the hermit, and I resolved to kill you on your way back. But the day passed and you did not return. So I came out from my ambush to find you, and I came upon your bodyguard, and they recognized me, and wounded me. I escaped from them, but should have bled to death had you not dressed my wound. I wished to kill you, and you have saved my life. Now, if I live, and if you wish it, I will serve you as your most faithful slave, and will bid my sons do the same. Forgive me!"

The King was very glad to have made peace with his enemy so easily, and to have gained him for a friend, and he not only forgave him, but said he would send his servants and his own physician to attend him, and promised to restore his property.

Having taken leave of the wounded man, the King went out into the porch and looked around for the hermit. Before going away he wished once more to beg an answer to the questions he had put. The hermit was outside, on his knees, sowing seeds in the beds that had been dug the day before.

The King approached him, and said:

"For the last time, I pray you to answer my questions, wise man."

"You have already been answered!" said the hermit, still crouching on his thin legs, and looking up at the King, who stood before him.

"How answered? What do you mean?" asked the King.

"Do you not see," replied the hermit. "If you had not pitied my weakness yesterday, and had not dug those beds for me, but had gone your way, that man would have attacked you, and you would have repented of not having stayed with me. So the most important time was when you were digging the beds; and I was the most important man; and to do me good was your most important business. Afterwards when that man ran to us, the most important time was when you were attending to him, for if you had not bound up his wounds he would have died without having made peace with you. So he was the most important man, and what you did for him was your most important business. Remember then: there is only one time that is important—Now! It is the most important time because it is the only time when we have any power. The most necessary man is he with whom you are, for no man knows whether he will ever have dealings with any one else: and the most important affair is, to do him good, because for that purpose alone was man sent into this life!"

10. THE COFFEE HOUSE OF SURAT

In the town of Surat, in India, was a coffee-house where many travellers and foreigners from all parts of the world met and conversed.

One day a learned Persian theologian visited this coffee-house. He was a man who had spent his life studying the nature of the Deity, and reading and writing books upon the subject. He had thought, read, and written so much about God, that eventually he lost his wits, became quite confused, and ceased even to believe in the existence of a God. The Shah, hearing of this, had banished him from Persia.

After having argued all his life about the First Cause, this unfortunate theologian had ended by quite perplexing himself, and instead of understanding that he had lost his own reason, he began to think that there was no higher Reason controlling the universe.

This man had an African slave who followed him everywhere. When the theologian entered the coffee-house, the slave remained outside, near the door, sitting on a stone in the glare of the sun, and driving away the flies that buzzed around him. The Persian having settled down on a divan in the coffee-house, ordered himself a cup of opium. When he had drunk it and the opium had begun to quicken the workings of his brain, he addressed his slave through the open door:

"Tell me, wretched slave," said he, "do you think there is a God, or not?"

"Of course there is," said the slave, and immediately drew from under his girdle a small idol of wood.

"There," said he, "that is the God who has guarded me from the day of my birth. Every one in our country worships the fetish tree, from the wood of which this God was made."

This conversation between the theologian and his slave was listened to with surprise by the other guests in the coffee-house.

They were astonished at the master's question, and yet more so at the slave's reply.

One of them, a Brahmin, on hearing the words spoken by the slave, turned to him and said:

"Miserable fool! Is it possible you believe that God can be carried under a man's girdle? There is one God—Brahma, and he is greater than the whole world, for he created it. Brahma is the One, the mighty God, and in His honour are built the temples on the Ganges' banks, where his true priests, the Brahmins, worship him. They know the true God, and none but they. A thousand score of years have passed, and yet through revolution after revolution these priests have held their sway, because Brahma, the one true God, has protected them."

So spoke the Brahmin, thinking to convince every one; but a Jewish broker who was present replied to him, and said:

"No! the temple of the true God is not in India. Neither does God protect the Brahmin caste. The true God is not the God of the Brahmins, but of Abraham, Isaac, and Jacob. None does He protect but His chosen people, the Israelites. From the commencement of the world, our nation has been beloved of Him, and ours alone. If we are now scattered over the whole earth, it is but to try us; for God has promised that He will one day gather His people together in Jerusalem. Then, with the Temple of Jerusalem—the wonder of the ancient world—restored to its splendor, shall Israel be established a ruler over all nations."

So spoke the Jew, and burst into tears. He wished to say more, but an Italian missionary who was there interrupted him.

"What you are saying is untrue," said he to the Jew. "You attribute injustice to God. He cannot love your nation above the rest. Nay rather, even if it be true that of old He favored the Israelites, it is now nineteen hundred years since they angered Him, and caused Him to destroy their nation and scatter them over the earth, so that their faith makes no converts and has died out except here and there. God shows preference to no nation, but calls all who wish to be saved to the bosom of the Catholic

Church of Rome, the one outside whose borders no salvation can be found."

So spoke the Italian. But a Protestant minister, who happened to be present, growing pale, turned to the Catholic missionary and exclaimed:

"How can you say that salvation belongs to your religion? Those only will be saved, who serve God according to the Gospel, in spirit and in truth, as bidden by the word of Christ."

Then a Turk, an office-holder in the custom-house at Surat, who was sitting in the coffee-house smoking a pipe, turned with an air of superiority to both the Christians.

"Your belief in your Roman religion is vain," said he. "It was superseded twelve hundred years ago by the true faith: that of Mohammed! You cannot but observe how the true Mohammed faith continues to spread both in Europe and Asia, and even in the enlightened country of China. You say yourselves that God has rejected the Jews; and, as a proof, you quote the fact that the Jews are humiliated and their faith does not spread. Confess then the truth of Mohammedanism, for it is triumphant and spreads far and wide. None will be saved but the followers of Mohammed, God's latest prophet; and of them, only the followers of Omar, and not of Ali, for the latter are false to the faith."

To this the Persian theologian, who was of the sect of Ali, wished to reply; but by this time a great dispute had arisen among all the strangers of different faiths and creeds present. There were Abyssinian Christians, Llamas from Thibet, Ismailians and Fireworshippers. They all argued about the nature of God, and how He should be worshipped. Each of them asserted that in his country alone was the true God known and rightly worshipped.

Every one argued and shouted, except a Chinaman, a student of Confucius, who sat quietly in one corner of the coffee-house, not joining in the dispute. He sat there drinking tea and listening to what the others said, but did not speak himself.

The Turk noticed him sitting there, and appealed to him, saying:

"You can confirm what I say, my good Chinaman. You hold your peace, but if you spoke I know you would uphold my opinion. Traders from your country, who come to me for assistance, tell me that though many religions have been introduced into China, you Chinese consider Mohammedanism the best of all, and adopt it willingly. Confirm, then, my words, and tell us your opinion of the true God and of His prophet."

"Yes, yes," said the rest, turning to the Chinaman, "let us hear what you think on the subject."

The Chinaman, the student of Confucius, closed his eyes, and thought a while. Then he opened them again, and drawing his hands out of the wide sleeves of his garment, and folding them on his breast, he spoke as follows, in a calm and quiet voice.

Sirs, it seems to me that it is chiefly pride that prevents men agreeing with one another on matters of faith. If you care to listen to me, I will tell you a story which will explain this by an example.

I came here from China on an English steamer which had been round the world. We stopped for fresh water, and landed on the east coast of the island of Sumatra. It was midday, and some of us, having landed, sat in the shade of some cocoanut palms by the seashore, not far from a native village. We were a party of men of different nationalities.

As we sat there, a blind man approached us. We learned afterwards that he had gone blind from gazing too long and too persistently at the sun, trying to find out what it is, in order to seize its light.

He strove a long time to accomplish this, constantly looking at the sun; but the only result was that his eyes were injured by its brightness, and he became blind.

Then he said to himself:

"The light of the sun is not a liquid; for if it were a liquid it would be possible to pour it from one vessel into another, and it would be moved, like water, by the wind. Neither is it fire; for if it were fire, water would extinguish it. Neither is light a spirit, for it is seen by the eye; nor is it matter, for it cannot be moved.

Therefore, as the light of the sun is neither liquid, nor fire, nor spirit, nor matter, it is—nothing!"

So he argued, and, as a result of always looking at the sun and always thinking about it, he lost both his sight and his reason. And when he went quite blind, he became fully convinced that the sun did not exist.

With this blind man came a slave, who after placing his master in the shade of a cocoanut tree, picked up a cocoanut from the ground, and began making it into a night-light. He twisted a wick from the fibre of the cocoanut: squeezed oil from the nut in the shell, and soaked the wick in it.

As the slave sat doing this, the blind man sighed and said to him:

"Well, slave, was I not right when I told you there is no sun? Do you not see how dark it is? Yet people say there is a sun.... But if so, what is it?"

"I do not know what the sun is," said the slave. "That is no business of mine. But I know what light is. Here I have made a night-light, by the help of which I can serve you and find anything I want in the hut."

And the slave picked up the cocoanut shell, saying:

"This is my sun."

A lame man with crutches, who was sitting near by, heard these words, and laughed:

"You have evidently been blind all your life," said he to the blind man, "not to know what the sun is. I will tell you what it is. The sun is a ball of fire, which rises every morning out of the sea and goes down again among the mountains of our island each evening. We have all seen this, and if you had had your eyesight you too would have seen it."

A fisherman, who had been listening to the conversation said:

"It is plain enough that you have never been beyond your own island. If you were not lame, and if you had been out as I have in a fishing-boat, you would know that the sun does not set among the mountains of our island, but as it rises from the ocean every morning so it sets again in the sea every night. What I am telling you is true, for I see it every day with my own eyes."

Then an Indian who was of our party, interrupted him by saying:

"I am astonished that a reasonable man should talk such nonsense. How can a ball of fire possibly descend into the water and not be extinguished? The sun is not a ball of fire at all, it is the Deity named Deva, who rides for ever in a chariot round the golden mountain, Meru. Sometimes the evil serpents Ragu and Ketu attack Deva and swallow him: and then the earth is dark. But our priests pray that the Deity may be released, and then he is set free. Only such ignorant men as you, who have never been beyond their own island, can imagine that the sun shines for their country alone."

Then the master of an Egyptian vessel, who was present, spoke in his turn.

"No," said he, "you also are wrong. The sun is not a Deity, and does not move only round India and its golden mountain. I have sailed much on the Black Sea, and along the coasts of Arabia, and have been to Madagascar and to the Philippines. The sun lights the whole earth, and not India alone. It does not circle round one mountain, but rises far in the East, beyond the Isles of Japan, and sets far, far away in the West, beyond the islands of England. That is why the Japanese call their country 'Nippon,' that is, 'the birth of the sun.' I know this well, for I have myself seen much, and heard more from my grandfather, who sailed to the very ends of the sea."

He would have gone on, but an English sailor from our ship interrupted him.

"There is no country," he said "where people know so much about the sun's movements as in England. The sun, as every one in England knows, rises nowhere and sets nowhere. It is always moving round the earth. We can be sure of this for we have just been round the world ourselves, and nowhere knocked up against the sun. Wherever we went, the sun showed itself in the morning and hid itself at night, just as it does here."

And the Englishman took a stick and, drawing circles on the sand, tried to explain how the sun moves in the heavens and goes round the world. But he was unable to explain it clearly, and pointing to the ship's pilot said:

"This man knows more about it than I do. He can explain it properly."

The pilot, who was an intelligent man, had listened in silence to the talk till he was asked to speak. Now every one turned to him, and he said:

"You are all misleading one another, and are yourselves deceived. The sun does not go round the earth, but the earth goes round the sun, revolving as it goes, and turning towards the sun in the course of each twenty-four hours, not only Japan, and the Philippines, and Sumatra where we now are, but Africa, and Europe, and America, and many lands besides. The sun does not shine for some one mountain, or for some one island, or for some one sea, nor even for one earth alone, but for other planets as well as our earth. If you would only look up at the heavens, instead of at the ground beneath your own feet, you might all understand this, and would then no longer suppose that the sun shines for you, or for your country alone."

Thus spoke the wise pilot, who had voyaged much about the world, and had gazed much upon the heavens above.

"So on matters of faith," continued the Chinaman, the student of Confucius, "it is pride that causes error and discord among men. As with the sun, so it is with God. Each man wants to have a special God of his own, or at least a special God for his native land. Each nation wishes to confine in its own temples Him, whom the world cannot contain.

"Can any temple compare with that which God Himself has built to unite all men in one faith and one religion?

"All human temples are built on the model of this temple, which is God's own world. Every temple has its fonts, its vaulted roof, its lamps, its pictures or sculptures, its inscriptions, its books of the law, its offerings, its altars and its priests. But in what temple is there such a font as the ocean; such a vault as that of the heavens; such lamps as the sun, moon, and stars; or any figures to be compared with living, loving, mutually-helpful men? Where are there any records of God's goodness so easy to understand as the blessings which God has strewn abroad for man's happiness? Where is there any book of the law so clear to each man as that written in his heart? What sacrifices equal the self-denials which loving men and women make for one another? And what altar can be compared with the heart of a good man, on which God Himself accepts the sacrifice?

"The higher a man's conception of God, the better will he know Him. And the better he knows God, the nearer will he draw to Him, imitating His goodness, His mercy, and His love of man.

"Therefore, let him who sees the sun's whole light filling the world, refrain from blaming or despising the superstitious man, who in his own idol sees one ray of that same light. Let him not despise even the unbeliever who is blind and cannot see the sun at all."

So spoke the Chinaman, the student of Confucius; and all who were present in the coffee-house were silent, and disputed no more as to whose faith was the best.

LEO TOLSTOY

ABOUT THE AUTHOR

Leo Tolstoy (1828-1910) stands as one of the towering literary figures of the 19th century, renowned for his epic novels such as "War and Peace" and "Anna Karenina." However, in the later years of his life, Tolstoy underwent a profound spiritual metamorphosis that would shape the trajectory of his philosophical and literary contributions.

In a journey of self-discovery, Tolstoy turned to the teachings of Christianity, seeking solace in a deeply personal interpretation of the Gospels. His exploration led him to embrace Christian anarchism and to articulate a vision of faith that transcended institutional boundaries.

This collection gathers Tolstoy's poignant and introspective religious writings, showcasing a side of the author often overshadowed by his monumental novels. From moral parables to reflections on the nature of love and the pursuit of a meaningful life, these works reveal Tolstoy's profound engagement with spirituality and his quest for a genuine connection with God.

As you delve into this anthology, you will encounter Tolstoy not only as a literary giant but also as a seeker of truth and a spiritual guide. His writings, though rooted in a specific time and context, continue to resonate with readers, offering timeless insights into the human condition and the enduring quest for meaning.

Join us on a journey into the heart and soul of Leo Tolstoy, where the power of his words transcends fiction to illuminate the spiritual dimensions of existence.

Printed in Great Britain
by Amazon